AFGHANISTAN

JAMES WILLCOX
WITH DANA FACAROS

www.bradtguides.com

Bradt Guides Ltd, UK
The Globe Pequot Press Inc, USA

Bradt GUIDES
TRAVEL TAKEN SERIOUSLY

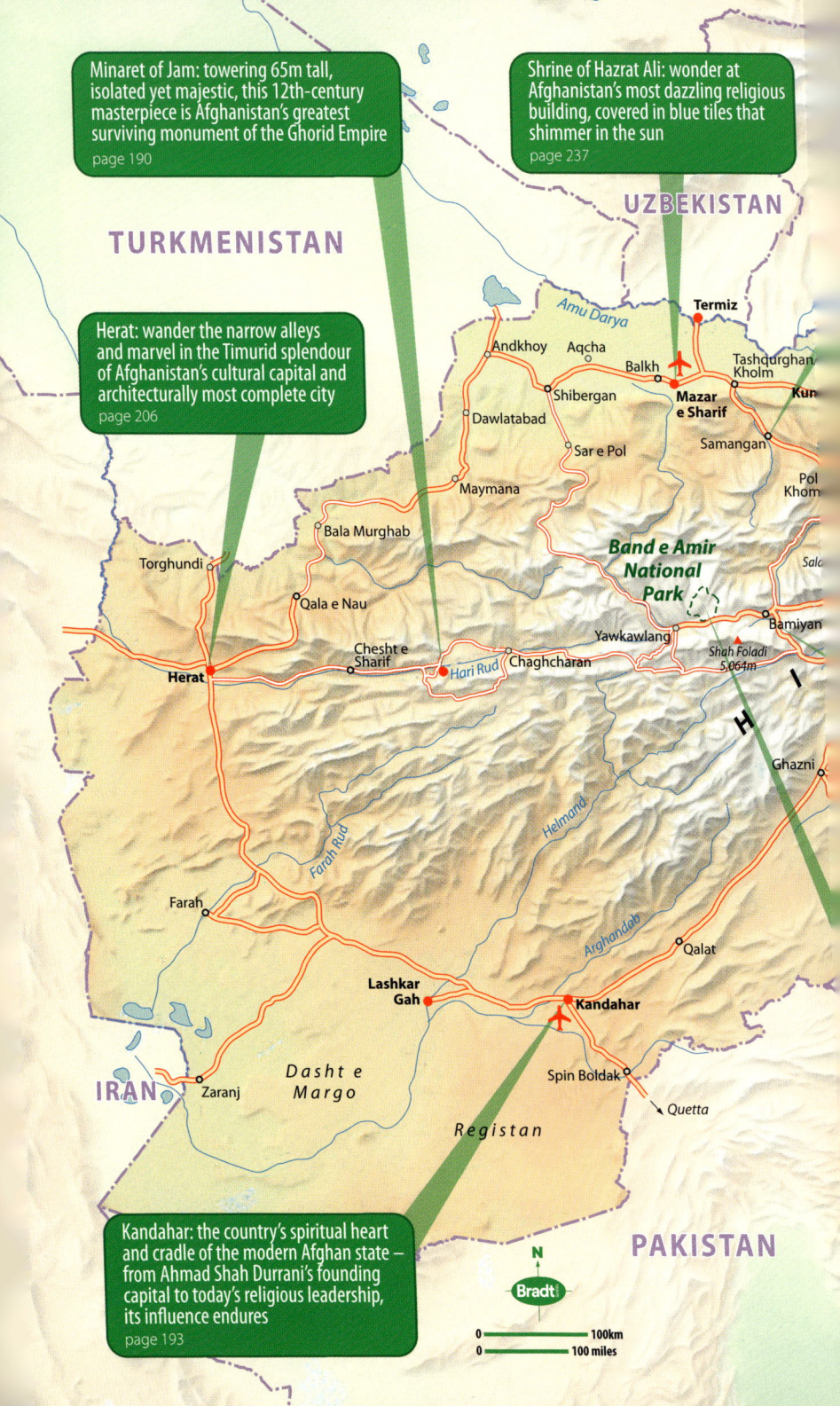

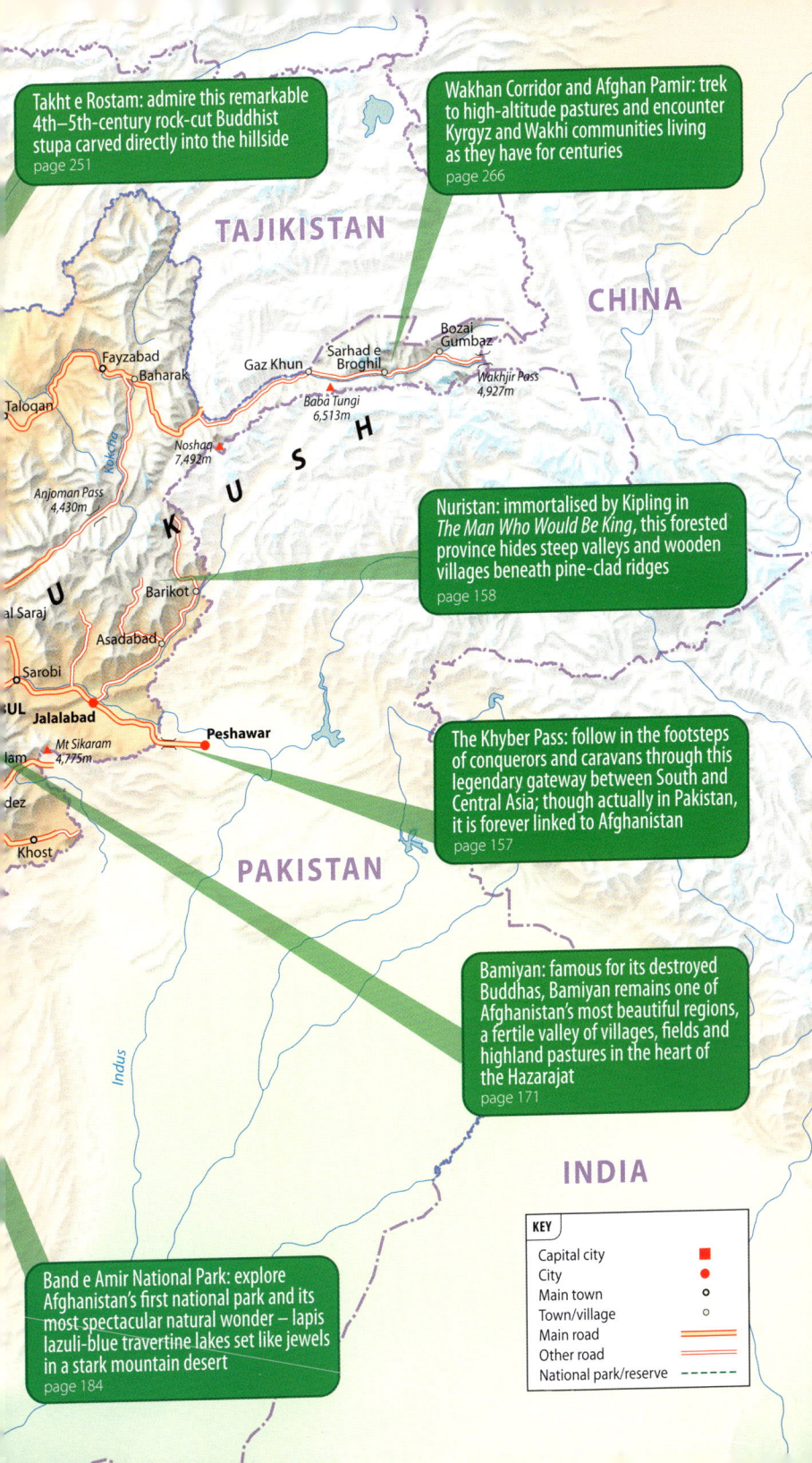

AFGHANISTAN
DON'T MISS...

BUZKASHI
Afghanistan's national sport requires incredible courage, skill and horsemanship PAGE 63
(SS)

THE SHRINE OF HAZRAT ALI
As the light changes over the course of the day, so do the shimmering blue tiles that adorn the Shrine of Hazrat Ali in Mazar e Sharif PAGE 237
(UB)

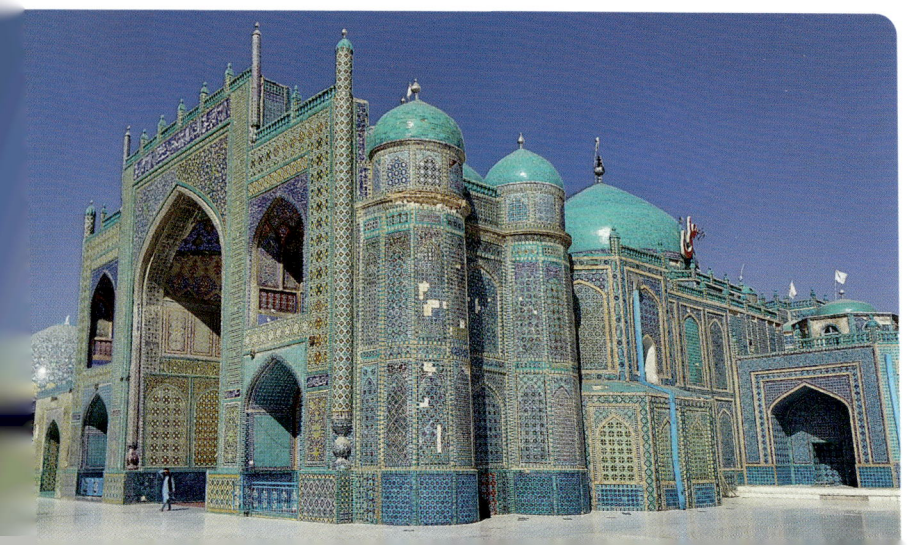

BAND E AMIR NATIONAL PARK
The park's lapis-lazuli-blue lakes appear utterly surreal in the arid country west of Bamiyan PAGE 184
(P73/S)

BAMIYAN'S BUDDHA NICHES
The enormous, empty niches of Bamiyan are a powerful testimony to the spread of Buddhism in ancient Afghanistan PAGE 179
(MB/S)

NURISTAN
With its rushing rivers, forests and fascinating traditional culture, Nuristan is unlike anywhere else in Afghanistan PAGE 158
(UB)

AFGHANISTAN
IN COLOUR

above (IW/D) The Friday Mosque in Herat boasts some of the most intricately designed tilework in Afghanistan **PAGE 217**

below (WC/S) The Shah e Do Shamshira Mosque adds a touch of fin de siècle charm to central Kabul **PAGE 130**

Sakhi Shrine is one of the busiest religious buildings in the capital PAGE 134 — above (MB/D)

The Shrine of Mirwais Hotak in Kandahar honours the first Afghan leader to revolt against the Persian Empire PAGE 200 — below left (T/S)

Paghman, not far from Kabul, is the 'Garden Capital of Afghanistan' PAGE 140 — below right (MB/S)

JOIN
THE TRAVEL CLUB

THE MEMBERSHIP CLUB FOR SERIOUS TRAVELLERS FROM BRADT GUIDES

Be inspired
Free books and exclusive insider travel tips and inspiration

Save money
Special offers and discounts from our favourite travel brands

Plan the trip of a lifetime
Access our exclusive concierge service and have a bespoke itinerary created for you by a Bradt author

Join here:
bradtguides.com/travelclub

Membership levels to suit all budgets

Bradt GUIDES

TRAVEL TAKEN SERIOUSLY

AUTHORS

James Willcox founded the travel company Untamed Borders in 2008 and has been arranging travel services and logistics across central Asia, the Middle East and North Africa ever since. He has visited Afghanistan 35 times and was awarded a letter of commendation for developing ski tourism in Afghanistan and a medal from the Afghan Olympic Committee for his part in organising Afghanistan's first international marathon. He has visited 30 of Afghanistan's 34 provinces. Outside of Afghanistan, he is a fellow of the Royal Geographical Society, has guided Michael Palin in Iraq and once was a wedding planner for a couple who got married on the edge of an active volcano in the Democratic Republic of the Congo.

Dana Facaros wrote her first travel guide to the Greek Islands in 1977, and has since written or co-authored dozens more on Greece, Spain, Italy and France.

EXPLORE Afghanistan
with Bradt author James Willcox
& Untamed Borders

Group & Private trips to Afghanistan – Cultural | Trekking | Skiing | Marathons

Untamed borders
info@untamedborders.com | www.untamedborders.com | +44 (0)1304 262002

First edition published February 2026
Bradt Travel Guides Ltd
31a High Street, Chesham, Buckinghamshire, HP5 1BW, England
www.bradtguides.com
Print edition published in the USA by The Globe Pequot Press Inc,
PO Box 480, Guilford, Connecticut 06437-0480

Text copyright © Bradt Travel Guides Ltd, 2026
Maps copyright © Bradt Travel Guides Ltd, 2026; includes map data © MapTiler © OpenStreetMap contributors
Photographs copyright © Individual photographers, 2026 (see below)
Project Manager: Susannah Lord
Cover research: Pepi Bluck, Perfect Picture

Thank you for buying an authorised edition of this book published by Bradt Travel Guides. For over 50 years, Bradt Travel Guides has encouraged adventurous, immersive and responsible travel, and this is only possible because of the support of our readers. By purchasing our books, you are enabling us to continue to commission expert authors who genuinely know and love the places they write about, and who write their books after thorough, on-the-ground research.

The author(s) and publisher have made every effort to ensure the accuracy of the information in this book at the time of going to press. However, they cannot accept any responsibility for loss, injury or inconvenience resulting from the use of information contained in this guide. All rights reserved. No part of this book may be reproduced, scanned or distributed by any means without the written permission of Bradt Travel Guides, nor used or reproduced in any way to train artificial intelligence technologies/models. Bradt Travel Guides and the author(s) unequivocally reserve this work from the text and data mining exception, as per Article 4(3) of the Digital Single Market Directive 2019/790.

ISBN: 9781804692905

British Library Cataloguing in Publication Data
A catalogue record for this book is available from the British Library

Importer to the EU: Freytag-Berndt u. Artaria KG, Ölzeltgasse 3/10, 1030 Wien, Österreich

Photographs Dreamstime.com: Jonathan Wilson (JW/D), Maurice Brand (MB/D); James Willcox (JW); Shutterstock.com: Jon Duncan (JD/S), Jono Photography (JP/S), Mushtaq B (MB/S), Pvince73 (P73/S), Torsten Pursche (TP/S), tuzla (T/S), Wirestock Creators (WC/S); Simon Urwin (SU); SuperStock (SS); Untamed Borders (UB)
Front cover The Buddha Niches, Bamiyan town (SU)
Back cover, clockwise from top left Band e Amir National Park (UB); the Minaret of Jam (JW); detail of ancient tilework inside Herat's Great Mosque (JW/D)
Title page, left to right Herat Citadel (T/S); a woman walking beside the Shrine of Hazrat Ali, Mazar e Sharif (SU)

Maps David McCutcheon FBCart.S. FRGS, assisted by Simonetta Giori, Daniella Levin and Pearl Geo Solutions; colour map relief base by TipTopMap/Alamy Stock Photo

Typeset by Ian Spick, Bradt Guides
Printed in India by Imprint Press
Digital conversion by www.dataworks.co.in

AUTHOR'S STORY — James Willcox

I first visited Afghanistan in 2008, and that trip changed the course of my life. What began as a personal journey soon became something bigger: it led me to establish Untamed Borders, a travel company dedicated to journeys in less obvious places. Afghanistan has remained close to my heart ever since. That first visit became the starting point for a lifetime of returns and, in some small way, a role in shaping modern tourism in the country.

Back then, there was almost no tourism infrastructure. I was involved in introducing ski tourism to Afghanistan and was one of the founders of the Marathon of Afghanistan. Along the way, I helped arrange trips for documentary crews, kayakers, photographers and researchers. We collected rugs for the British Museum, organised a concert for singer Joss Stone in Kabul and opened doors for people who wanted to see the country beyond the headlines. To have played even a minor role in Afghanistan's tourism story has been a rare honour.

I never set out to be a guidebook writer, but Afghanistan was the exception. For years, I pestered Hilary Bradt to let me take it on, and eventually she relented. Writing this book gave me the perfect excuse to explore places I had never previously reached, and even provided a credible reason to explain to the Taliban why I wanted to visit the ancient lapis mines of Sar e Sang or to travel to Khost. Researching Afghanistan is unlike anywhere else: in an age when every travel detail seems available online, information here is still hard-won – pieced together through long journeys, conversations in teahouses, and contradictory reports that sometimes only make sense after you've seen them with your own eyes.

And still, after more than 30 visits, Afghanistan finds ways to surprise me. While researching this book, I found myself in Nuristan, talking with villagers about a local festival.

'After the cow fighting,' explained one man, 'we play Ludo.'
'Ludo?' I asked, bemused.
'Yes, like the app – but for real,' he laughed, flipping a spoon to mimic rolling dice.

That a British parlour game from the 1980s featured in a Nuristani festival left me astonished. But then I learned that ludo is a British version of pachisi, once played on vast boards by the Mughal emperors – whose ancestors, of course, came from Afghanistan. Another reminder that this so-called 'graveyard of empires' is in fact a crossroads of histories and cultures, a place entirely its own.

HOW TO USE THIS GUIDE

AUTHOR'S FAVOURITES Finding genuinely charactertful accommodation or that unmissable off-the-beaten-track café can be difficult, so the author has chosen a few of his favourite places throughout the country to point you in the right direction. These 'author's favourites' are marked with a ✻.

PRICE CODES Throughout this guide we have used price codes to indicate the cost of those places to stay and eat listed in the guide. For a key to these price codes, see page 95 for accommodation and page 100 for restaurants.

MAPS
Keys and symbols Maps include alphabetical keys covering the locations of those places to stay, eat or drink that are featured in the book. Note that regional maps may not show all hotels and restaurants in the area: other establishments may be located in towns shown on the map.

Grids and grid references Several maps use gridlines to allow easy location of sites. Map grid references are listed in square brackets after the name of the place or site of interest in the text, with page number followed by grid number, eg: [125 C3].

KEY TO SYMBOLS

—··—	International boundary	♣	Buddhist site
═══	Main road	⌂	Cemetery
═══	Minor road	╲	City walls
═══	Other road	∴	Historic (archaeological) site
----------	Footpath	✿	Gardens
✈	Airport	☼	Viewpoint
🚌	Buses	▶	Golf course
🚖	Taxis	✕	Restaurant/food stalls
🛈	Registration office/information	火	Sports facility
🏺	Museum/art gallery	⚐	Featured trek
♜	Fort	⤛⤜	Border crossing
▲	Historic tower	⏝	Mountain pass
⌂	Imortant/historic building	▲	Summit (height in metres)
$	Bank/moneychangers	●	Other point of interest
❺	Embassy/consulate	⌒	Cave
✉	Post office		Glacier
✚	Hospital		Dry/salt lake
✚	Pharmacy		Urban market/bazaar
♀	Mosque		Urban park
🕌	Tomb/shrine		National park

Acknowledgements

All the people mentioned below gave me inspiration and granted me patience over the last 18 years to help me gather the information and experience to complete this book. Some names do not appear because they have asked not to be mentioned; I appreciate their help nonetheless. Others are missing because I have forgotten to mention them; for that I apologise.

I thank: Mohamed Jan Wafa, Kausar Hussein, Gul Hussein Baizada, Ali Shah Farhang, Sajjad Husseini, Rahimullah, Ferdinando Rollando, Nancy Hatch Dupree, Richard Willcox, Gay Willcox, Felix Willcox, Turquoise Mountain NGO, Jan Bakker, John Mock, Jan Chipchase, Charlie Gammell, Omid (for the mines), the Aga Khan Foundation, Azim Ziyahee, Malang Jan Dario, Ian McWilliam, Keith MacIntosh, James Bingham, Fatima Haideri, Susannah Walden, all at Free to Run, the Bamiyan Ski Club, the Bamiyan Alpine Ski Club, Stacey Bare, Ben Sturgulewski, Katie Stjernholm, the Italian government, Amir Foladi, Ana Tasic, Adrian Summers, Madelene Madsen, Kate Archer, David Harrison, Elise Wortley, Rajjan Parmer, Matthew Traver, Taria Dawson, Lisa Helmanis, Mamnoon Ahmad Afzali, Sayed Mokhtar Hasanyar, Rahmatullah Elch, Haji Alabirdi Shahi, Turyalai Weesa, Geoff Hann, Mujtaba, Eazatullah, Stephane Ostrowski, Ayub Alavi and Susannah Lord.

Any errors made in this book are mine and any success is only possible through a huge collaborative effort.

James Willcox

DEDICATION

This book is dedicated to Sayed Hussain Shah (Sangin) and Mubarak Shah, who were sadly taken from us too soon.

Contents

	Introduction	viii
PART ONE	**GENERAL INFORMATION**	**1**
Chapter 1	**Background Information**	**3**
	Geography and geology 3, Climate 6, Natural history and conservation 6, Archaeology 14, History 16, Government and politics 39, Economy 40, People 43, Language 52, Religion and beliefs 53, Education 55, Culture 55	
Chapter 2	**Practical Information**	**66**
	When to visit 66, Highlights 67, Suggested itineraries 68, Tour operators 70, Red tape 70, Getting there and away 73, Health 75, Safety 82, Women travellers 85, Travelling with a disability 86, LGBTQIA+ travellers 87, Travelling with kids 87, What to take 88, Money and budgeting 89, Getting around 90, Accommodation 93, Eating and drinking 95, Public holidays and festivals 101, Shopping 102, Arts and entertainment 104, Activities 105, Opening times 106, Media and communications 106, Cultural etiquette 109, Travelling positively 111	
PART TWO	**THE GUIDE**	**113**
Chapter 3	**Kabul and around**	**114**
	History 114, Getting there and away 118, Getting around 120, Tourist information and registration 122, Orientation 122, Where to stay 122, Where to eat and drink 124, Entertainment and nightlife 127, Shopping 127, Sports and activities 129, Other practicalities 129, What to see and do 130, Around Kabul 139, Panjshir Valley 144	
Chapter 4	**The East: Jalalabad, Nuristan and Loya Paktia**	**149**
	Jalalabad 149, Nuristan 158, Kunar Province 164, Southeast Afghanistan: Loya Paktia 164	

Chapter 5	**Bamiyan and Central Afghanistan**	171
	Bamiyan town 171, Band e Amir National Park 184, The central route from Bamiyan to Herat 187	
Chapter 6	**Kandahar and Southern Afghanistan**	191
	Kandahar 193, Helmand Province 201, Ghazni 203	
Chapter 7	**Herat and Western Afghanistan**	206
	Herat 206, Southwest Afghanistan 222, Zaranj 227	
Chapter 8	**Mazar e Sharif and Northern Afghanistan**	231
	Mazar e Sharif 231, Balkh 239, The drive from Mazar e Sharif to Herat 246, East of Mazar e Sharif 250, Kunduz 252	
Chapter 9	**Badakhshan and the Wakhan Corridor**	257
	Fayzabad 258, Southern Badakhshan to the Anjoman Pass 263, The Wakhan Corridor and the Afghan Pamir 266	
Appendix 1	**Language**	276
Appendix 2	**Glossary**	281
Appendix 3	**Further Information**	284
Index		289
Index of Advertisers		293

LIST OF MAPS

Afghanistan	1st colour section	Kabul and around	115
Balkh	241	Kandahar: centre	197
Bamiyan, Around	183	Kandahar: overview	194
Bamiyan town	177	Khost	167
Band e Amir National Park	185	Kunduz	252
Central Afghanistan	172	Mazar e Sharif	234
Eastern Afghanistan	150	Northeast Afghanistan	257
Fayzabad	260	Northern Afghanistan	230
Herat: centre	214	Southern Afghanistan	192
Herat: overview	209	Wakhan Corridor and	
Jalalabad	153	Afghan Pamir: trekking	271
Kabul: Old City	125	Western Afghanistan	207
Kabul: overview	121	Zaranj	227
Kabul: Shahre Nau	128		

Introduction

To the first-time visitor, Afghanistan feels at once familiar and utterly alien. It is a place many people think they know, thanks to the nightly news or the headlines of the last four decades. Names like Kabul, the Hindu Kush, the Khyber Pass, Kandahar, Bagram, the Taliban, the mujahideen – these words echo with recognition. Yet to trace them on to real places, lived-in streets and ordinary people going about their day is disorienting and thrilling in equal measure. The country that looms so large in the imagination becomes something tangible, textured, and unexpectedly human.

My own fascination with central Asia began with this very sense of uncertainty. Before I first travelled there, I felt I had some kind of picture of its neighbours – the Middle East, Russia, China, the subcontinent. Each was new when I visited, yet they came with identities I could imagine. Central Asia, however, was an experiential blank. To set foot there was exhilarating: familiar fragments appeared in strange and unexpected forms. Green tea poured beside kebabs, men in *shalwar kameez* driving battered Russian trucks while eating dumplings that seemed straight out of a central Europe kitchen. These collisions of the recognisable and the unfamiliar were intoxicating.

The former Soviet republics had their own allure, but Afghanistan, sitting at the heart of the region, contained all of it at once. Its tragic recent history, though devastating, has left much of the country in spirit as it has always been: traditions intact, ways of life preserved, landscapes and monuments left raw and unvarnished. The land itself is hard, rocky and arid, yet threaded with pristine rivers that feed orchards heavy with fruit. It is a landscape that mirrors its people – resilient, unyielding, yet with a surprising softness at the core. Afghanistan's legendary warriors, living with little more than the basics of life, often have flowers tucked behind their ears and kohl lining their eyes.

This apparent lack of modernity conceals a deeper truth – that for centuries, Afghanistan was anything but a backwater. It stood at the crossroads of empires, the meeting place of great civilisations, and it is still littered with reminders of that layered history. A heady mix of the familiar, the unexpected, and the monumental are what hooked me. My first journey to Afghanistan in 2008 led to many return visits, and to wanting others to come and see it too.

A visit to Afghanistan today reveals a country suspended between tradition and modernity. After decades of conflict and outside influence, it is now more independent than at any point in recent history. Yet that independence brings challenges. The Taliban's strict interpretation of Islam shapes daily life and limits Afghanistan's engagement with the wider world, while economic hardship and the pressures of climate change loom large. Modernity knocks at the door, but in many ways the old rhythms of life continue much as they always have. For travellers, this means Afghanistan offers a rare chance to encounter traditions, landscapes and ways of life that feel both timeless and fragile. This book is not intended to argue for or against visiting, but to provide insight for those who wish to see Afghanistan first-hand, and for those who are simply curious about the country as it is today.

James Willcox

A NOTE ON SPELLING

Transliterating places and names from Dari and Pashto into English is a tricky business. Bamiyan, for instance, could be spelled 'Bamyan' or 'Bamian'; Hamun could just as easily be 'Hamoun'. We have tried to use the most common spelling across the board, nearly always choosing the spelling on Google maps, to make it easier for visitors. In Afghanistan spellings are quite relaxed, and often different spellings will be found on the same signage or document and no-one in Afghanistan outside of academic circles seems overly sensitive to the issue, but we do apologise for any confusion or errors.

FEEDBACK REQUEST

At Bradt Guides we're aware that guidebooks start to go out of date on the day they're published – and that you, our readers, are out there in the field doing research of your own. You'll find out before us when a fine new family-run hotel opens or a favourite restaurant changes hands and goes downhill. So why not tell us about your experiences? Contact us on 01753 893444 or e info@bradtguides.com. We will forward emails to the author who may post updates on the Bradt website at w bradtguides.com/updates. Alternatively, you can add a review of the book to Amazon, or share your adventures with us on Facebook, X or Instagram (@BradtGuides).

JOURNEY BOOKS

CONTRACT PUBLISHING FROM BRADT GUIDES

DO YOU HAVE A STORY TO TELL?

- Publish your book with a leading trade publisher
- Expert management of your book by our experienced editors
- Professional layout, cover design and printing
- **Unique** access to trade distribution for print books and ebooks
- Competitive pricing and a range of tailor-made packages
- Aimed at both first-timers and previously published authors

"Unfailingly pleasant"... "Undoubtedly one of the best publishers I have worked with"... "Excellent and incredibly prompt communication"... "Unfailingly courteous"... "Superb"...

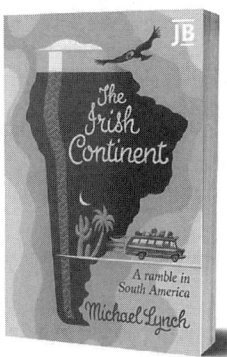

For more information – and many more endorsements from our delighted authors – please visit: **bradtguides.com/journeybooks**.

Journey Books is the contract publishing imprint of award-winning travel publisher, Bradt Guides. All subjects are considered for Journey Books, not just travel. Our contract publishing is a complement to our traditional publishing, not a replacement, and we welcome traditional submissions from new and established travel writers. Please visit bradtguides.com/write-for-us to find out more.

Part One

GENERAL INFORMATION

AFGHANISTAN AT A GLANCE

Location Central Asia, bordered by Iran to the west, Turkmenistan, Uzbekistan and Tajikistan to the north, Pakistan to the east and south, and China at the east end of the Wakhan Corridor – the narrow finger of Afghanistan between Tajikistan and Pakistan.
Size 652,869km^2
GDP per capita US$347
Population 43,372,950
Life expectancy 63 years
Climate Subtropical semi-arid
Capital Kabul
Other main towns Herat, Kandahar, Mazar e Sharif
Main airports Kabul, Herat, Kandahar, Mazar e Sharif
Languages Officially Pashto and Dari; also Uzbeki, Turkmeni, Balochi, Pashai, Nuristani and many others
Religion Sunni Islam (85–90%), Shi'a Islam (10–15%), Sikhism (>0.1%), Hinduism (>0.1%)
Currency Afghani
Exchange rate £1=87AFN; US$1=66AFN; €1=77AFN (November 2025)
International telephone code +93
Time GMT +4 hours 30 minutes
Electrical voltage 220V supply voltage and 50Hz
Public holidays 15 February (Liberation Day), 28 April (birthday of Mullah Omar), 1 May (International Workers' Day), 15 August (Afghan Jihad Victory Day), 19 August (Afghan Independence), 31 August (American Withdrawal Day). Religious holidays are variable (page 101).

1

Background Information

GEOGRAPHY AND GEOLOGY

It was created by nature in a rumbustious mood. A set of blow-ups of the soaring mountain ranges that ring the country places us at a momentous Euro-Asian crossroads...This isn't just a collection of mountain descents and important trade routes in waiting. It is a rocky approximation of the earth's navel.

Waldemar Januszczak

At 652,869km^2, Afghanistan is larger than France and smaller than Texas. Set on the Iranian plateau, with around half the country at 2,000m or above, it is landlocked and mountainous, fringed in the east by some of the highest peaks in the world. In satellite images, much of the land is arid and khaki coloured (from the Persian word for soil), but is often lush green in the river valleys.

AFGHANISTAN'S FIVE GEOGRAPHICAL ZONES

Hindu Kush Eastern Afghanistan is dominated by this relatively young 966km range that forms a mighty rampart north of Kabul. In antiquity, these mountains were named the Caucasus Indicus, which Greeks believed marked the end of the earth, where Prometheus, for the crime of giving humankind fire, had been bound by Zeus and had his liver devoured by an eagle every day. The current name, 'Hindu Killer', comes from the days when enslaved people captured in India often perished when transported through the icy mountains.

Up in the eastern Hindu Kush, **Noshaq** (7,492m), Afghanistan's highest mountain, is the world's westernmost peak over 7,000m. The prominent pyramid of **Mir Samir** (5,809m), the mountain that Eric Newby and Hugh Carless almost climbed in Newby's *A Short Walk in the Hindu Kush*, stands between the **Panjshir Valley** and **Nuristan**. In spite of locals saying it was impossible, on 24 July 1959, Harald Biller, his wife and two companions reached the summit.

The Hindu Kush receives around 700mm of rain a year, mainly in the form of snow; its glaciers are concentrated in the north, while a small section of Khost Province in the southeast is watered by monsoon rains. There are some 16 passes over the Hindu Kush: the **Khawak Pass** at the head of the **Panjshir** was favoured by conquerors from Alexander (page 146) to Genghis Khan and Timur, while the **Salang Pass** is now accessed via a Soviet-built tunnel.

Central Highlands The Hindu Kush declines into the smaller mountain ranges of central Afghanistan. The **Koh-i-Baba** (highest peak: Shah Foladi, 5,142m) stretches southwest into central Afghanistan, extending west towards Herat as the **Feroz Koh**. The **Safed Koh** (or Spin Ghar, the 'White Mountains', culminating at 4,755m) run southeast from Kabul to the Khyber Pass and the one-time bin Laden hideout of Tora Bora. Between Herat and Chaghcharan, the **Paropamisus Mountains**, or **Selseleh-ye Safid Kuh** (highest peak: 3,592m), frame the north bank of the Hari River. Along the east edge of the Iranian plateau, the north–south **Koh-e-Sulayman** mountains peak at 3,383m and extend into the empty quarters of Balochistan.

Between the mountains lie steep, generally V-shaped valleys where people live and farm along the rivers or wherever they can irrigate. The rain that falls on the strikingly barren mountain slopes penetrates deep into aquifers that can be accessed by wells.

Steppe The rolling country of northern Afghanistan is a continuation of the semi-desert, treeless steppe of central Asia, bisected by the mighty Amu Darya River. The northern hills act as a barrier to the silt blown off the steppes, leaving the area covered in a layer of fertile, mineral-rich loess (notably around Maymana), which, however, is subject to mudslides. The alpine grasslands of the **Wakhan Corridor** are part of the Karakoram-West Tibetan Plateau.

The Registan Desert One of the driest parts of the world, stretching across southeast Iran and southwest Afghanistan, the Registan is perhaps better known by its Iranian name, Sistan (from Sakastan, the land of the Saka nomads). Here blows the infamous Sadobist Roozeh, the hot abrasive 'Wind of 120 days' ('the most vile and abominable in the universe', according to Lord Curzon). Laden with dust and salt, it blows from late May to September from north to south across the Helmand basin. The wind can form sand dunes up to 15m high that occasionally block the roads.

The Helmand River feeds (or rather fed) the ephemeral **Lake Hamun e Helmand**, formerly an important wildlife oasis, one of the very few wetlands in the region. The amount of water flowing from the river into the lake has been a bone of contention ever since the 1940s, when the US financed construction of dams along the Helmand and its tributaries. In 1973, Afghanistan signed an agreement with Iran to allow a minimum of 26m^3 of water per second to flow into the lake. In the six-year drought that began in 1999, the Taliban turned off the taps, pointing out that the treaty allows them to send less water when water levels are below a certain point. Iran is not happy that Afghanistan has built more dams on the Helmand, including the Kamal Khan Dam finished in 2021, just before the return of the Taliban.

For five millennia, hundreds of thousands of Afghans and Iranians lived along the lake's shores, fishing and farming; Hamun e Helmand was even once nicknamed the 'breadbasket of Iran'. Now some 100 villages lie buried in sand. The wetlands have been reduced to three small lakes, the largest of which is in Iran. In parts, it now resembles the Aral Sea, a dustbowl, creating massive sand and dust storms visible from outer space, encroaching on former farmland and blocking irrigation canals. With drought increasingly an issue, the situation may not improve; many nomads formerly living here have been forced to move on.

Eastern Afghanistan The Himalayas are so high they block the Indian summer monsoons of south Asia from reaching Afghanistan. The exception is the far east, from Khost Province in the southeast up to Nuristan, which catch the fringe of the monsoon; Khost, for instance, receives an average of 500–1,000mm of rain per year.

RIVERS Afghanistan is dependent on the fresh water flowing out of its mountains, especially the Hindu Kush. Permanent settlements have always sprung up in the valleys or in places where the rivers lose their force and spread into alluvial fans; Balkh, at the outlet of the **Balkh River**, is a prime example.

GEOGRAPHY AND GEOLOGY

The 2,400km **Amu Darya**, antiquity's River Oxus, begins at the confluence of the **Panj** and the **Wakhsch** (Pamir or Surkhab) rivers on the Tajikistan border. One of the key rivers of central Asia, it gave rise to an early, if relatively unknown, civilisation (page 16). In former times, the Oxus divided Greater Persia and Turan (central Asia); today the Amu Darya divides Afghanistan from former Soviet republics Tajikistan, Uzbekistan and Turkmenistan. A formal agreement sharing the waters fell into disuse with the collapse of the USSR. A lot of the Amu Darya's water diverted for irrigation goes to waste through leakage in badly built canals in Uzbekistan, before ever reaching the sad remnants of the Aral Sea, once the third largest lake in the world (now renamed the Aralkum Desert). In March 2022, the Taliban government began their own canal: the 285km Qosh Tepa Canal (page 248).

The great watershed of the Koh-i-Baba range is the source of three of Afghanistan's biggest rivers: the **Kabul/Kunar**, which flows east into the Indus; the **Hari Rud/Herat**, which flows into Turkmenistan; and the 400km **Arghandab**, which rises near Ghazni and flows into the 1,300km **Helmand River**. Dammed north of Kandahar, the Helmand provides water for farmers through the Helmand and Arghandab Valley Authority; curiously the Helmand's very name comes from the ancient Iranian Haetumant, meaning 'dammed'. Other rivers flowing out of the Koh-i-Baba are the Farah, Murghab, Balkh and Kunduz.

LAKES Afghanistan has a handful of beautiful high-altitude lakes, especially the six lakes of **Band e Amir** in the Hazarajat, now part of a national park (page 184). They are among the world's very few natural travertine lakes; carbon-dioxide-rich water oozing out of the faults in the mountains formed the steep limestone walls that naturally dammed the lakes.

Glacial **Lake Zorkul** (also known as Big Pamir Lake), at 4,200m above sea level on the border with Tajikistan, is one of the largest high-altitude lakes in the world, stretching for 25km amid magnificent mountain peaks. The other lakes in the Wakhan Corridor are equally striking, including **Chaqmaqtin** (4,024m), and **Lake Shewa**, which has kept its pre-Islamic name (Shiva). All three lakes are sources of the mighty Oxus (page 264).

GEOLOGY Afghanistan's landforms are very old and very complicated, with rocks from the Archaeon (4,000–2,500 million years ago) to far more recent times; it has been called a 'jigsaw puzzle' of crustal blocks or terranes, each with its own geological history and mineral potential. Sixty-five million years ago, Afghanistan was covered by the marshy Tethys Ocean, dotted with volcanic islands. Ten million years later, the Arabian-Eurasian tectonic plate, once part of the great southern continent of Gowanda, broke away and collided with the Indo-Australian plate, forming the Himalaya, Altai, Kunlun, Karakoram and Hindu Kush mountains, with the Pamir Knot, a lofty plateau nicknamed the 'Roof of the World' in the centre, just over the border in Tajikistan.

Earthquakes trouble Afghanistan along two major faults: the Chaman Fault from Kandahar to Kabul on the edge of the Indo-Australian plate, and the 1,200km Herat or Hari Rud Fault on the edge of the Eurasian plate, running from Herat and the Hari Rud River, through the Bamiyan and Ghorband valleys.

Afghanistan's geology bequeathed the country its remarkable mineral wealth. Badakhshan's 9,000-year-old lapis lazuli mine is the oldest active mine in the world. Recent surveys suggest the country sits on US$1–3 trillion worth of minerals (page 42).

1 | BACKGROUND INFORMATION

CLIMATE

Much of Afghanistan has a continental climate which can run to extremes, from 50°C below zero to 50°C above. Winters are cold and dry but have deep snowfalls in the mountains, where temperatures can remain well below zero for days on end. Spring is the wettest season. Summers in low-lying regions and in Herat and Kandahar can see very high temperatures, even into the 40s (although the thermometer drops noticeably when the sun goes down); while in the Central Highlands and Hindu Kush temperatures tend to stay in the 20s. In summer it almost never rains, except in the eastern monsoon forest strip. Autumn is generally dry and comfortable. Rainfall varies widely. In the southwest, a region increasingly prone to heatwaves and drought, the average rainfall is only 150mm per year, while in the Hindu Kush it can be over 1,000mm.

Afghanistan is responsible for only 0.06% of the world's greenhouse gas emissions but ranks in the top ten of countries most at risk from the climate crisis. Higher temperatures, hard sun-baked soil, deforestation and extreme rainfall have led to flash floods and mudslides. These have in turn led to the loss of arable land, as has the salinisation caused by improper irrigation from the 20th-century Helmand and Nangarhar projects.

The glaciers that feed the country's rivers are in retreat (estimates suggest their flows will peak in 2050). Before the Soviet invasion in 1979, an estimated 70% of Afghanistan was at risk of desertification. A severe drought between 1998 and 2001 was exacerbated by low snowfall in the Himalayas. In 2024, half a million Afghans, mainly in Herat and Farah provinces in the west, were internally displaced because of climate change. Decreasing ground water is a concern in cities, most acutely in rapidly growing Kabul, as pollution and waste from decrepit infrastructure take their toll; UNICEF reports that the capital may run out of water as soon as 2030.

The UN has estimated that Afghanistan would need US$20 billion between 2020 and 2030 to prepare for climate change, but as with historic preservation, donors hesitate to contribute as long as the Taliban excludes women from public life.

NATURAL HISTORY AND CONSERVATION

Most of Afghanistan's fauna is Palaearctic and Indo-Malayan. Most species are Palaearctic, part of the enormous zone stretching from Europe to the Himalayas, while many Indo-Malayan species have dispersed into Afghanistan. The country's mountains, including the Hindu Kush, provide numerous (and diverse) habitats, with varying degrees of temperature and precipitation, to which various species have adapted. According to Afghanistan's National Biodiversity Strategy and Actions Plan (2024), species in major taxa (fauna) include 140 mammals, 448 birds, 107 reptiles and 85 fish.

MAMMALS Climate change, 4x4s, poaching, wildlife smuggling and decades of war have not done Afghanistan's 140 mammal species any favours. Although the Taliban has completely banned hunting (except in cases where it issues licences for particular species at certain periods as in the case of the houbara; page 11), illegal hunting remains an ongoing issue, sometimes for trophies or revenge after a carnivore savages a domestic flock, but far more often for smuggling. Each year Afghanistan's National Environmental Protection Agency (NEPA) rescues over 10,000 birds and animals from traffickers and releases them back into the wild.

The current status of many rarer creatures is not known; the best source of information is the Wildlife Conservation Society (w wcs.org), which is the last international conservation group still active to some degree in Afghanistan.

Wild sheep and goats Named after the man who first described them, **Marco Polo sheep** (or Pamir Argali; *Ovis ammon polii*) are the largest sheep in the world, coifed with magnificent coiling headwear (the longest horns ever recorded measured 1.9m and weighed 27kg). In Afghanistan, they live in the Pamirs of Wakhan, in the most extreme habitat of any sheep.

Argalis are fast, have excellent eyesight and are preyed on by wolves and occasionally by snow leopards. Kyrgyz nomads and Wakhi herders traditionally hunted them for meat. Foreign trophy hunters in Tajikistan and Kyrgyzstan pay tens of thousands of dollars for a chance to kill one; the sheep recently made the headlines when a breeder in Texas was caught importing body parts, hoping to clone argalis for hunting. They were the first animal to be included on the list of protected species issued by NEPA in June 2009, and are considered Near Threatened on the International Union for the Conservation of Nature (IUCN) Red List.

Living above altitudes of 2,000m, in the Pamirs, Hindu Kush and Hazarajat, **urials** (*Ovis vignei*) are rather smaller but nearly as impressive-looking. The rams have winter ruffs and large, curling horns; the horns are sometimes used to decorate graves and cairns. Related to the European mouflon, urials are the ancestors of domestic sheep and there are several subspecies. The IUCN rates them Vulnerable.

If the Marco Polo is the king of sheep, the mighty, spiral-horned **markhor** (*Capra falconeri*) is the king of goats. There are four subspecies, distinguished by the shape of their horns, three of which are found or used to be found in Afghanistan, notably the straight-horned Kabul markhor (*C. f. megaceros*). The national animal of Pakistan, markhors are found up to 3,200m in forested areas in northern Badakhshan and in Nuristan. A prized trophy and frequently poached, it is classified as Near Threatened.

Afghanistan forms the westernmost habitat of the **Siberian ibex** (*Capra sibirica*), mountain goats that are nearly as big as markhors, with long, sweeping, curved horns. They live above the treeline, on craggy mountains and cliff faces, in Bamiyan, Badakhshan and Nuristan where they are well camouflaged.

Deer and antelope Native to Afghanistan, Pakistan, India and Nepal, the little **Kashmir musk deer** (*Moschus cupreus*) is only 60cm tall and can be found on steep slopes in Nuristan, Kunar and Laghman provinces. Males have small 'vampire-esque' tusks. These deer have preputial scent glands under their skin which, unfortunately, are in great demand for the perfume industry – the animals are often poached and are now highly endangered. The graceful **goitered gazelle** (*Gazella subgutturosa*) is named after a neck enlargement, or 'goitre', that occurs in males during the rut. This gazelle was once abundant from Saudi Arabia to Mongolia, where it was hunted by tazis (page 9). Today poachers use motorbikes and 4x4s, and the gazelles, designated Vulnerable by the IUCN throughout their range, are rarely sighted.

Cats Habitat destruction and hunting have led to the extinction of the Asiatic cheetah and Caspian tiger in Afghanistan, but two species of leopard are believed still to be present. Listed as Endangered by the IUCN, the **Persian** or **Anatolian leopard** (*Panthera pardus tulliana*), with its beautiful plush coat grown to face the

NOTABLE DOMESTIC ANIMALS

Named after the ancient region of Bactria, the **Bactrian camel** was, as far as we know, first described in the written record by Aristotle. The shaggy two-humped symbol of Silk Road caravans is a truly remarkable creature, able to tolerate extreme temperatures, both cold and hot, to carry loads of 170–250kg over 47km per day, and go for a week without water and a month without food. It is one of the few animals that can eat snow. Although the caravans have been replaced by trucks these days, you may still spot camels as well as yaks working as pack animals with nomads in the mountains. These camels have been domesticated for so long that the wild Bactrian camel, which still exists in China and Mongolia, is a different species.

Like camels, Afghanistan's eight kinds of **fat-tailed sheep** store fat in one part of their body – in this case in their rumps or long tails – which can supply energy in lean times. Although the meat of fat-tailed sheep is leaner than that of other sheep, the fat is used as a preservative and is much valued as a cooking fat. Herodotus in the 5th century BCE wrote that some sheep had tails so long and fat that shepherds would build little carts for the sheep to drag along to support the weight – which Afghan shepherds really did in the 19th and 20th centuries, when exporting fat as ghee to India was an important source of income. The shaggy karakul, prized for its exceptional wool, is a very hardy breed of fat-tailed sheep which can survive in temperatures between -30°C and 48°C.

Although Islam regards dogs as impure, Muslims are permitted to keep guard and hunting dogs. The large **Afghan shepherd**, or **Kuchi dog** (named after the harsh winters, may still live in Badakhshan, Paktika, the Paropamisus Mountains, Bamiyan Plateau and Nuristan, where wild sheep and goats are its main prey. Camera trap photos by the Wildlife Conservation Society report of human–wildlife conflicts, and pelts offered for sale in Kabul are the best evidence of their presence. **Snow leopards** (*Panthera uncia*) live in Badakhshan and appear in Nuristan, the western edge of their alpine and sub-alpine habitat (3,000–4,500m). A solitary creature, the snow leopard has a thick, spotted coat, fur between its toes and a long, thick tail that helps it balance on icy slopes and keeps the leopard's face warm when wrapped around at night like a blanket. They mainly hunt mountain sheep and marmots but have also attacked domestic flocks, which is why many are killed by angry shepherds. They are listed as Vulnerable.

Smaller wild cats are rated Less Concern by the IUCN. The grey or sandy-coloured **jungle cat** (*Felis chaus*) is a day hunter found in Khost and the wetlands and along the tributaries of the Amu Darya. It has short legs, a short tail and little black ear tufts and mainly hunts rodents, but will also plunge into water to catch a fish. The bigger, slender, long-legged **caracal** (*Caracal caracal*) resembles a lynx, with its tufted ears; its name comes from the Turkish for 'black eyes' because of the markings around its eyes. Secretive and nocturnal, it can leap high and catch birds on the fly. Little round ears, a long, thick grey coat and a big bushy tail characterise the **Pallas's cat** or **manul** (*Otocolobus manul*), which resembles a chunky version of the domestic cat. It is well adapted to the cold where it lives in grasslands and the Hindu Kush and preys on rodents. The little **leopard cat** (*Prionailurus bengalensis*), named after its beautiful tawny and brown spotted coat, inhabits the wooded areas of the Kunar Valley. Bengal cats are descended from leopard cats bred with domestic cats, which are about the same size.

nomads who keep them; page 47), guards flocks from wolves, bears, hyenas and leopards, as well as human thieves. There are two kinds: the lion type, with heavy build, thick coat and bear-shaped head; and the lighter, nimbler tiger type with shorter coat. Both are fast, tenacious and ferocious when attacking and will defend their territory against intruders. Peter Levi wrote that they were blamed for killing (and eating) two American tourists whose car broke down in the 1960s (see page 85 for safety advice).

Tazis or **Afghan hounds**, which hunt rabbits (these days, secretly) by sight, are mostly found in remote villages. Famous for their 'Eastern gaze', which 'looks at and through one' according to the UK Afghan Hound Association, they are faithful, intelligent animals and are especially popular in the Hazarajat. These dogs are prized possessions, allowed to sleep inside by the fire. There are a dozen different kinds of tazi; the long-haired ones are *bakhmali* (velvet) or tiger tazis. The first ones were brought to Britain in the 19th century, but it was an exceptional velvet tazi named Zardin who won the best foreign dog prize in a kennel show in 1907 and started a craze for the breed, so much so that when Zardin died he was stuffed and put in the British Museum. Another, named Sirdar of Ghazni from the royal kennels of King Amanullah, became the ancestor of some 30% of Afghan hounds in the UK, selectively bred for their long, silky coats. Their numbers have declined because of all the expense, time and work involved in their care.

Dogs Afghanistan's apex predator, the **grey wolf** (*Canis lupus*) lives in all regions of the country, except in the southern deserts, and preys on wild goats and sheep, and domestic ones at lower altitudes in the winter. Another, far more abundant canine native, the **golden jackal** (*Canis aureus*) resembles the wolf but is smaller, and buff to grey to golden in colour. A cunning omnivore, it often lives outside villages and can be heard at twilight. These animals tend to hunt alone and can be a nuisance, preying on domestic stock and eating crops, including melons. The golden jackal dominates, and is three times bigger than, the equally cunning **Eurasian red fox** (*Vulpes vulpes*), which is sometimes hunted for its beautiful winter coat but mainly because it attacks poultry.

A resident of the steppe and lower altitudes, the **striped hyena** (*Hyaena hyaena*) is a nocturnal scavenger, crushing bones of carrion with its powerful teeth, but will occasionally prey on foxes and jackals.

Other mammals The **Asiatic black bear** or **moon bear** (*Ursus thibetanus*) has a distinctive white moon-shaped mark on its chest. One of the largest tree-dwelling mammals, feeding on berries, roots, insects and carrion, the bear lives in the forests of Nuristan, where it has been known to raid crops. It is designated Vulnerable on the IUCN Red List. The more common **Himalayan brown bear** (*Ursus actos isabellinus*), typically bigger than the Asiatic black bear, is occasionally sighted in Badakhshan.

Since 2010, the **Eurasian otter** (*Lutra lutra*) lives in the Panj/Amu Darya river system. The thick-skinned, black-and-white **honey badger** (*Mellivora capensis*), also known as ratel, lives in the northeast, Paktika and Khost, and is legendary for its ferocity when cornered, able to repel hyenas and even wolves. It will eat almost anything, but especially likes honey and honeybee larva. Bee stings can hardly

1 | BACKGROUND INFORMATION

penetrate its hide, a trait it shares with the **Indian crested porcupine** (*Hystrix indica*), a nocturnal herbivorous rodent that lives in burrows in rocky hillsides and defends itself by charging backwards to stab an attacker with its thickest quills, which can kill leopards and hyenas, if not immediately then by infection from the bacteria on its quills.

Afghanistan also shares other mammals with the Indian subcontinent. The range of the **rhesus macaque** (*Macaca mulatta*) extends from Thailand to southeast Afghanistan, where they live in groups mainly in Nuristan. These primates are very adaptable and survive at altitudes of up to 3,000m, and often pose a nuisance to farmers. The **small Indian mongoose** (*Urva auropunctata*) lives near villages, in thickets and hedges, and feeds on rats and insects; and, like the larger grey Indian mongoose, can kill venomous reptiles. The larger, omnivorous, robust **yellow-throated marten** (*Martes flavigula*), with a dark head, tail and legs and lighter body, lives in northern Afghanistan and hunts during the day on lizards, ground-nesting birds and even young deer and musk deer.

Numerous specials of jerboa (the mini-kangaroo or 'hopping rat') have been reported in Afghanistan, including **small five-toed jerboa** (*Allactaga elater*), **Euphrates jerboa** (*Scarturus euphraticus*), **Hotson's five-toed jerboa** (*Allactaga hotsoni*), **greater three-toed jerboa** (*Jaculus blanfordi*) and **Thomas's pygmy jerboa** (*Salpingotus thomasi*). The tail-less relative of the rabbit, the **large-eared pika** (*Ochotona macrotis*) lives up to 6,000m in mountain crevices.

Afghanistan is also home to more familiar mammals: the **Eurasian badger** (*Meles meles*), **least weasel** (*Mustela nivalis*), **beech marten** (*Martes foina*), **stoat** (*Mustela erminea*) and **wild boar** (*Sus scrofa*). The latter lives along the river basins, and is hunted in response to the damage it does to crops.

BIRDS Afghanistan's National Biodiversity Strategy and Action Plan 2024 counted some 448 native species (including extinct and endemic species) and 45 uncertain species of bird. Commonly sighted birds include crows, starlings, magpies, ravens, hoopoes, pigeons, cuckoos, chukar partridges, pheasants, quails, choughs, sparrows, swifts, swallows and kestrels. The current status of waterfowl catalogued in the early 1970s is hard to pin down. The half a million birds that once visited Lake Hamun e Helmand are a distant memory. The brackish, high-altitude lakes of Ab e Istada and Dasht e Nawur west of Ghazni are famous for hosting the loftiest-known breeding colonies of pink flamingos, although their current status is uncertain.

The country's only endemic bird is the little grey-brown **Afghan snowfinch** (*Pyrgilauda theresae*), a seed-eating cousin of the sparrow and resident of the north Hindu Kush and Central Highlands. The bowling ball-sized **Himalayan snowcock** (*Tetraogallus himalayensis*) lives in the highest peaks in the Wakhan and Central Highlands, dining on seeds, forbs and grasses and using its thick bill to dig for roots and tubers. Perhaps the best-loved bird is the sociable, sweet singing bulbul; the **white-eared bulbul** (*Pycnonotus leucotis*) is common in the dry regions of the south.

The prize prey for falconers is the **Asian houbara** or **MacQueen's bustard** (*Chlamydotis macqueenii*), which lives in scrubby desert regions and in October migrates from the steppe to western Afghanistan's Farah Province. Well camouflaged, the houbara is able to fly in high spirals, making it a sporting challenge for falconers. The meat is considered a delicacy and an aphrodisiac. This bird is listed as Vulnerable.

Raptors Peregrine falcons (*Falco peregrinus*), are the world's fastest animal reaching speeds of 389km/h, which enables it to catch birds, mainly pigeons and

NATURAL HISTORY AND CONSERVATION

FALCONRY IN AFGHANISTAN

Nomads in central Asia have practised falconry for the last three millennia if not longer. Few Afghans do these days, but some earn considerable sums by illegally netting saker and peregrine falcons as the birds migrate, and selling them via middlemen to wealthy Gulf fanciers for eye-watering amounts. The falconers' favourite prey is the houbara (see opposite), but as the birds have become scarce, the Qatari Al Gharrafa Foundation (w algharrafa.org. af) has stepped in to finance houbara breeding programmes in Afghanistan. Wealthy Arabs pay for licences to bring their falcons to Farah Province every winter, and hire local guides and guards, contributing to the local economy in one of the poorest corners of the country.

doves on the fly. It nests on cliffs over river valleys; others migrate south from central Asia and Russia in the autumn. The **saker falcon** (*Falco cherrug*) is a relatively large falcon that breeds in central Asia and can attain speeds of 300km/h. It hunts horizontally rather than by swooping like a peregrine, and has been prized for millennia by falconers (see above) in the Middle East, Hungary and Mongolia; it is the national bird for many countries. So many sakers have been captured worldwide that it's now on the IUCN Red List as endangered in the wild.

One of the world's largest raptors, the **golden eagle** (*Aquila chrysaetos*) with a wingspan of up to 2.3m is Afghanistan's national bird, living on cliffs and feeding on ground squirrels, marmots and hares; it's nearly as fast as the peregrine, reaching speeds of 320km/h. The **Lammergeier** or **bearded vulture** (*Gypaetus barbatus*) in the Koh-i-Baba mountains is easy to recognise by its immense yet narrow wingspan stretching to 2.8m; it is the only vertebrate whose diet derives mainly from bones, picking them up and dropping them on the rocks if they are too big to eat, and splitting them open for their nutritious marrow.

SNAKES There are, at last count, around 30 snake species and subspecies in Afghanistan, six of which are venomous. Two of these live in eastern Afghanistan: the little **Halys pit viper** (*Gloydius halys*) is less than 60cm long, can be any colour from grey to yellow and has a black stripe behind its eye; and the big 1.5m **Lebetine** or **blunt-nosed viper** (*Macrovipera lebetinus*) and a subspecies (or two) is characterised by its distinct triangular head. Deserts, tall grasses and rocky limestone hills are the habitats of the mainly nocturnal, slow-moving **Persian horned viper** (*Pseudocerastes persicus*), 45–116cm long, with a very broad head sprouting little 'horns'.

Sochurek's saw-scaled viper (*Echis carinatus sochureki*) grows to 38–80cm long, and has a flat, broad head marked with a cross, and patterns and colours to match its habitat in the desert, rocky areas or scrublands of southern Afghanistan; it hides during the day, often in bushes and trees. Most dangerous of all is the **Caspian cobra** (*Naja oxiana*), a heavy-bodied snake 100–140cm long, with an elongated hood. Found in the north and east, usually near water or hiding in tree hollows, the cobras are most active in early evening and early morning. They are shy but very aggressive if cornered; if untreated its bite is usually fatal.

FLORA Vegetation in Afghanistan is incredibly diverse. The authority is S W Breckle and M D Rafiqpoor's *Field Guide Afghanistan: Flora and Vegetation*, published in 2010 and distributed to schools in Afghanistan, although now rare and hard to find.

1 | BACKGROUND INFORMATION

Breckle and Rafiqpoor recorded some 4,500 species and subspecies of flowering plants, nearly a third of which are endemic; the country's ancient geology, wide variety of habitats and steep isolated valleys saw hundreds of plants evolve to fit their unique environments. Many plants in arid landscapes bloom only briefly, but spectacularly, after the first spring rains; most famous are the wild red tulips in the hills above Mazar e Sharif (page 231).

Botanists believe Afghanistan was one of several places in the world where essential crops such as wheat, peas, lentils, sesame, onion, garlic, spinach, carrot, pistachio, pear, almond and grape were first domesticated, and where wild versions still exist that may be useful in the future for creating crops resilient to climate change.

Kabul used to be a city of trees until the Soviets chopped them down, fearing mujahideen snipers (many have since been replanted). The best-preserved forests in the country are in Nuristan and Kunar, which under the Islamic Republic (page 36) were two of the most dangerous parts of the country. The native **Chalghoza pine** (*Pinus gerardiana*) grows naturally at altitudes of 1,800–3,000m in the Hindu Kush, and is valued for its pine nuts, an important cash crop. Here too you might spot an **Afghan pine** (*Pinus brutia* ssp. *eldarica*), the national tree, a hardy specimen that can grow in marginal soil with an extraordinary ability to tolerate cold or hot climates. The pine's hardiness and pretty pyramidal shape makes it a popular species for Christmas tree growers in the American southwest. Here too is the best-loved tree, the majestic **deodar** or **Himalayan cedar** (*Cedrus deodara*), the 'wood of the gods' in Sanskrit, the tallest standing 60m, with its level branches emerging from a slender trunk.

THREATS TO BIODIVERSITY IN AFGHANISTAN

Members of the Wildlife Conservation Society

Afghanistan's rich natural environment is increasingly threatened by the degradation and loss of natural ecosystems, as well as the over-exploitation of natural resources, resulting from 45 years of instability and rapid population growth. Climate change also poses a major threat that could lead to a reduction in biodiversity due to habitat shrinkage. Other, less significant, threats include environmental pollution, invasive species, water diversion and unsustainable use, and the loss of genetic diversity in both wild and domestic species.

As population pressures on the environment mount, ever-larger areas of Afghanistan's natural landscapes are being converted to human use or are damaged. Overgrazing, plant harvest and *lalmi* (rain-fed agriculture) are reducing vegetation cover, leading to soil erosion, weed invasion, nutrient loss and soil carbon depletion. Deforestation leads to soil erosion, landslides and avalanches, also depriving people of a vital resource for building, heating and cooking. With the loss of vegetation, the habitats of many plant and animal species are being destroyed. The diversion or construction of dams for irrigation and the over-exploitation of aquifers are drying up species-rich wetlands, leading to the extinction of many species and the disappearance of Afghanistan's few but vital stopover sites along the Central Asian Bird Flyway.

Over-exploitation of biodiversity refers to humans harvesting plants and animals at a greater rate than these species can reproduce. Overgrazing by livestock, uncontrolled timber harvest, hunting of rare species and excessive commercial collection of wild plants for traditional medicine, are all serious

CONSERVATION Preserving nature has not been a priority in impoverished, war-battered Afghanistan. However, after the fall of the first Taliban regime, the Asian Development Bank (ADB) decided one way to generate revenue for the country was to promote tourism, and identified the Band e Amir and Wakhan areas as potential national parks. Technical studies in the two areas included land-use plans and their ecotourism potential (hotels were banned within 5km of the Band e Amir lakes, local residents were trained to house tourists to generate revenue and to give them incentives to protect the area). A mini-hydropower (100kW) project was considered to generate electricity to local communities; instead ADB provided solar power to homes and installed a micro hydropower project. Today the World Conservation Society continues ADB's work.

In 2009 Band e Amir became Afghanistan's first national park. In 2014, Wakhan National Park was established, again with the aid of the WCS who have made snow leopards one of their special causes; as wildlife knows no borders, hopes are that the park may someday be expanded into an international park with Tajikistan, China and Pakistan.

The Nuristan National Park was designated in 2020 to preserve some of Afghanistan's last deciduous and high conifer forests. When the park was first proposed in 1981, the nearby Kunar and Laghman valleys had lush monsoon forests, although they have since lost 60% of their trees. The Taliban, who perhaps surprisingly regard themselves as environmental stewards, have continued the ban on logging from the previous government, but in remote forests on the Pakistan border the law is next to impossible to enforce when for many it's the only way to feed their families.

problems in Afghanistan. Loss of species through over-exploitation has effects that ripple through the ecosystem, not only from direct loss of the exploited species but also from those that depend on them. For example, overgrazing leaves less forage for wild ungulates which in turn affects populations of large predators such as snow leopards and Persian leopards. Over-exploitation of natural resources leads inevitably to increased poverty among land users.

Afghanistan is one of the countries in the world most likely to be severely affected by the climate crisis. Climate changes observed to date in the country include an increase in the frequency and duration of droughts, a rise in the average annual temperature, an increase in the frequency of hot days and nights, a decrease in spring rainfall, a slight increase in winter rainfall, and more extreme rainfall events. These changes have far-reaching effects on nature, often leading to ecosystem transitions and significant changes in local biodiversity. Some species disappear and new ones appear in a given area, mobile species move, while others adapt to new conditions. Unfortunately, in Afghanistan, land degradation, over-exploitation of natural resources and climate change almost always act in concert, tripling the risk of irreversible loss of biodiversity and associated ecosystems.

Protecting biodiversity is essential to maintaining the capability of the land to support human livelihoods and sustain ecosystem integrity. Since 2006, the Wildlife Conservation Society (w wcs.org) is the only international non-governmental organisation active in the field of wildlife conservation in Afghanistan. By making a gift to the WCS-Afghanistan, you'll join an enthusiastic team of Afghan conservationists in their commitment to work with Afghan people to save wildlife and wild places of Afghanistan.

1 | BACKGROUND INFORMATION

In November 2019, the Bamiyan Plateau Protected Area was established, covering some 5,500km² across Bamiyan, Sar e Pol and Samangan provinces in the heart of the inaccessible Hindu Kush, north of Band e Amir National Park. Here rolling hills, remote valleys (including the beautiful Ajar River valley, a former royal hunting reserve for Siberian ibex) and spectacular steep-sided canyons (1,888–4,203m) host an abundant array of globally important fauna and flora and diverse local cultures. Proposals are to make the area Afghanistan's first Natural Landscape, with the hopes of someday seeking UNESCO World Heritage Site designation.

Today 98% of Afghanistan has no trees at all. Mullahs have been directed to offer prayers for environmental protection. In 2025, the Afghanistan National Environmental Protection Agency plans to plant 2 million trees across the country and 400,000 saplings along the Qosh Tepa Canal.

During the Islamic Republic, several areas in Afghanistan were designated as future wildlife reserves, including the Imam Sahib on the Amu Darya north of Kunduz, which is known for its waterfowl as well as its rice paddies, a designation confirmed in 2025. In 2024, a Taliban delegation was accepted for the first time as observers at COP29, in spite of opposition because of their human rights record. Others have pointed out that most Afghan women work in agriculture and any restoration of funds to help mitigate the country's increasingly sharp drought flood cycles will help them perhaps most of all.

ARCHAEOLOGY

In spite of Genghis Khan's best efforts to turn the entire country into grasslands for nomads (page 24), Afghanistan is rich in archaeological sites. In 1919, King Amanullah invited foreign archaeologists – first French, then Italian, Russian, Japanese, American and eventually British and Indian – to lead campaigns and to train Afghan archaeologists, with agreements on distributing the finds (which is why the Musée Guimet in Paris has such a superb Graeco-Buddhist collection). Some of the artefacts were rare and dazzling and opened up a whole new chapter in the history of art. First displayed in Kabul's Bagh e Bala palace, finds were moved in 1931 to the city's National Museum of Afghanistan.

Things began to go seriously wrong after the Soviet withdrawal. In 1993, a rocket aimed at the Ministry of Defence hit the museum, leaving it wide open to looters. Then, under Taliban rule, some statues were beheaded or destroyed to fit in with the Taliban's strict interpretation of Islam that allows no representation of the human figure. Outside of Kabul, treasure hunters converged on unguarded archaeological sites.

In 1998, the Taliban and the Northern Alliance jointly requested that the museum's surviving displays be removed from the country for safe keeping. A container full of artefacts was prepared, but then the container was destroyed in the war. Afterwards, Afghans and foreigners smuggled items out to preserve them and stored them in the Afghan Museum in Exile, run by the Swiss Foundation Bibliotheca Afghanica (w phototheca-afghanica.ch/afghanistanmuseum/index.html).

In 2007, reckoning it was safe, the museum in exile sent 1,423 ethnographic and archaeological items back to the National Museum. When the museum was reopened in 2021 under the Taliban, artefacts showing human imagery such as Gandharan statues or Kafiristani idols were removed from display, their condition unknown.

Although the Taliban has promised to safeguard the country's cultural heritage, there is a lack of funds (in 2022 they applied for World Heritage funds to preserve

Babur's Gardens in Kabul but have had no reply, and it's unlikely they will get one until they address UNESCO's concerns over women's rights).

The lack of security has meant some archaeological sites have been lost forever. One is **Diberjin**, a 16ha walled city with a large round citadel and a Greek temple 40km northwest of Balkh, at the northern end of its irrigated oasis. Probably founded by the Achaemenids in the 5th century BCE, it flourished under the Greeks and Kushans and was abandoned in the 5th century CE; it had colourful wall paintings and coins and Kushan inscriptions in the Bactrian language. Satellite images show that since 2019 it has been looted on the same industrial scale that Isis looted sites in Syria.

Balkh, the 'Mother of Cities' where Alexander spent time, has a remarkable 2,300-year-old 12km ring of walls and Bala Hissar (page 245), but as much as archaeologists or looters have dug, no-one has pinpointed much in the way of Hellenistic remains. The most intact of the ancient Greek cities was **Ai Khanoum** (page 255), excavated over a 15-year period by a French team led by Paul Bernard until the Saur Revolution in 1978 put an end to the work. Peter Levi left a vivid description of its appearance just before then. It was striking how Greek the city was, with its Hellenistic art, temples, agora, gymnasium, theatre, acropolis, mint and large palace – so very far from Greece. Among the coins found there are some depicting Hindu deities and inscribed with both Greek and Brahmi scripts. One rare item was a large glass phallus embedded in the city's foundation stone which is believed to be one of the few surviving objects that might have been touched by Alexander the Great. In 2007 it was returned to the National Museum, though its current location is unknown. Today, although the site of Ai Khanoum is beautiful, there is little to see.

On the whole, Buddhist archaeological sites, first explored by Charles Masson for the East India Company in the 1830s (page 143), have survived better than Greek ones, despite the loss of the Bamiyan Buddhas. Perhaps the most impressive is **Takht e Rostam** (page 251) and the Buddhist monasteries and stupas around Kabul. The earliest known Buddhist manuscripts, from the 1st century CE (now in the British Library), were discovered at the monasteries and stupas at **Hadda**, 10km south of Jalalabad. Excavated by the French in the 1930s and again in the 1970s, it yielded 23,000 stunning and still very Greek-looking clay and plaster sculptures. Hadda was tragically ransacked and destroyed by Hekmatyar's Hezb e Islami, but some of the works survive in Paris's Musée Guimet and in photographs.

In Bagram, once the summer capital of the Kushan Empire, French archaeologists in 1936–40 uncovered two ancient storerooms, filled with over 1,000 decorative pieces from the 1st and 2nd centuries CE. Known as the **Bagram Ivories** (page 141), the storerooms also contained bronzes, Roman and Greek enamels and glass. Small and portable, the items are believed to be have been the stock of traders on the Silk Road: a splendid Bagram ivory of Lakshmi was even discovered in the ruins of Pompeii, destroyed in 79CE.

Mes Aynak (35km south of Kabul) means 'little source of copper', which it turns out is not so little (page 43). Excavations revealed a wealthy settlement with more than 400 Buddha statues, stupas, markets and residences covering 40ha that thrived between the 1st century and 7th century CE at the time of the Kushans and Alchon Huns. Underneath the monasteries, archaeologists discovered a Bronze Age settlement dating back 5,000 years.

Threatened by a contract with the Chinese State mining company, rescue digs took place at various times between 2010 and 2013 in the face of Taliban threats (they claimed that the archaeologists were promoting Buddhism), but estimates are that 90% of the site has yet to be explored. In 2014, Brent E Huffman released his documentary, *Saving Mes Aynak*, on Afghan archaeologist Qadir Temori's efforts to save the site. The Swiss foundation Aliph sent a US$1 million grant to the Aga Khan Trust for Culture to protect it. Aliph also funded the Aga Khan Trust's restoration of the stupa at Shewaki south of Kabul (page 142), and works at Kabul's Bala Hissar and the fifth minaret in Herat's Musalla Complex.

HISTORY

We will not be a pawn in someone else's game, we will always be Afghanistan!
Ahmad Shah Massoud

Sitting at one of the world's great crossroads, Afghanistan has been called the 'cockpit of Asia'. Surrounded by tremendous civilisations – Persian to the west, Indian to the east, and south and central Asian to the north – it has been influenced by all three over the millennia, but also by cultures further afield, headlined by conquerors sweeping through, from Alexander the Great to Genghis Khan and Timur (Tamerlane).

Not as well known, perhaps, is that Afghanistan – often viewed as a 'graveyard of empires' – was just as often an incubator of empires. The Ghaznavid and Ghorid empires (founded when Baghdad was the most enlightened city in the world), as well as several Indian dynasties including the mighty Mughal empire, all had their origins in what is now Afghanistan.

Afghanistan as an independent country only dates to the 18th century, when the indigenous Pashtun tribes of the south (long known as the Afghans) were able to take advantage of their neighbours' decline; though forming a state free of foreign influences has always been a challenge.

PREHISTORY AND PERSIA Prehistoric Afghanistan was a precocious place, where the first signs of human habitation go back to 50,000BCE. By 4000BCE, they had domesticated animals and farmed the Hindu Kush foothills, and a millennia later they were living in villages and cities. Early irrigation methods on the Oxus River (later the Amu Darya) allowed northern Afghanistan to bloom, and in Turkmenistan, Tajikistan and Uzbekistan in what is known today as the **Bactria-Margiana Archaeological Complex (BMAC)** or Oxus Civilisation.

Contemporary with the Bronze Age in Europe, BMAC flourished for a thousand years, characterised by monumental architecture and social complexity (the largest city found so far, Gonur Tepe, is now isolated in a desert in Turkmenistan). It left behind extremely distinctive, sophisticated works of art, notably figures known as Bactrian idols and other works made of luxury materials sourced from the hills of northern Afghanistan – gold, copper, garnet, carnelian and lapis lazuli, the blue 'stone of heaven'. Pictographs on BMAC seals may represent a very early writing system.

Trade was already important – BMAC artefacts have been found from the Persian Gulf to the Indus Valley. A lapis- and tin-trading colony of the **Indus Valley (or Harappan) Civilisation** established around 2000BCE was located at Shortugai on the Amu Darya north of the lapis mines. Some of its blue stone went to Egypt to adorn the mask of Tutankhamun (c1323BCE).

Mundigak (north of Kandahar) was the centre of another Bronze Age civilisation: the **Helmand Culture**, leaving behind a 9m-tall mound, excavated in the 1950s by French archaeologists. The oldest layer, dated to c4000BCE, revealed a palace, temple and urban centre with features similar to sites from the same period in Iran.

HISTORY

Climate change bringing bitterly cold winters saw **Proto-Indo-European-speakers** from eastern Europe migrate eastwards across the central Asian steppe and over the Oxus River into what is now Afghanistan in waves from c2000BCE to 1500BCE. Noted for the domestication of the horse and the invention of the chariot, they were called Aryans (the 'noble ones') in the Sanskrit *Rigveda*, and hence 'Ariana', the ancient Greek and Roman name for Afghanistan. These Iranic-speaking tribes settled around Balkh in northern Afghanistan and became part of the ancient nation of Bakhdhi, or **Bactria**. Others spent time in the Hari Rud valley, then moved west to the Iranian plateau, while others, the Indo-Aryans, went east into the Indus Valley.

Thanks to the Greek historian Herodotus, we start having names and dates by the 6th century BCE. After Cyrus the Great of the **Achaemenid dynasty** conquered much of central Asia in his 545–540BCE campaign, his successors Darius the Great and Xerxes divided Afghanistan into satrapies: Bactria (Balkh), Ariana (Herat), Gandhara (Kabul and its valley), Arachosia (Kandahar), Drangiana (Registan) and Sattagydai (central Afghanistan). The satraps that governed them were responsible for supplying the kings with money and soldiers. Many were followers of **Zarathustra** (page 239).

ALEXANDER IN AFGHANISTAN After inheriting his father's dream of leading a combined Greek army to conquer Persia (page 18), Alexander was unstoppable. He never lost a battle. The tactics he invented in 331BCE to defeat the army of Persian King Darius III at Gaugamela (modern Iraqi Kurdistan), despite being vastly outnumbered, would be copied by Napoleon at Austerlitz. After Gaugamela, he captured, pillaged and burned Persepolis, the holy city and capital of the Achaemenids.

It should have been job done then, and many Greeks of the Panhellenic League of Corinth returned home. But when Alexander learned that Darius had fled east to raise an army among his satraps, he raised what was in effect a private, mostly Macedonian, army fiercely loyal to him and went into pursuit. He found Darius dead or dying, having been stabbed by Bessus, the satrap of Bactria, who claimed the Persian crown. Alexander was furious at his treason and, after sending Darius's body back to Persepolis for a royal burial, went after Bessus in the satrapies of Afghanistan.

Three years (330–327BCE) of tough guerrilla warfare followed. Along the way Alexander founded garrison towns at Alexandria Areion (Herat), Alexandria Arachoisa (most likely Kandahar) and Alexandria ad Caucasum (Bagram), so named because the Macedonians mistook the Hindu Kush for the Caucasus. When Bessus, holed up safely in Balkh, was shocked to hear that Alexander had done the impossible – led his army over the Hindu Kush's Khawak Pass in the middle of winter (page 148) – he fled over the Amu Darya, believing Alexander could never get his army over the river when there was no wood nearby to build a bridge or boats. But Alexander had his troops stuff their tents (which were made of skins) with straw and float across, and Bessus, minus nose and ears, was sent back to Persia for execution. Back in Balkh, Alexander went on to marry Roxana, the most beautiful woman in Asia (page 242).

After that the Achaemenid lands in the Indus Valley lured Alexander further east: he wanted to go to the end of the world, or what the ancient Greeks called Ocean. His main army crossed the Khyber Pass, while Alexander led a much smaller force over the mountains through Nuristan. Along the way, much to the Greeks' delight they came across Nysa (identified as Nagara Ghundi or Dionysopolis, 4km west of

1 | BACKGROUND INFORMATION

ALEXANDER THE GREAT AND HIS LEGACY

Although Alexander (356–323BCE) liked to fancy himself the son of the god Zeus, he inherited his military chops from his mortal father. Philip II of Macedon made himself the master of Greece as a prelude to his plans for leading a Panhellenic invasion of Persia – revenge for Persia's subjugating of Greek cities in Asia Minor and two 5th-century BCE invasions of Greece.

Philip carefully prepared his son to take over his throne while he was away at war; he even hired Aristotle to tutor the teenage Alexander in natural sciences, medicine, ethics, logic, politics, maths, philosophy and poetry. Aristotle taught him to observe everything around him carefully with clear eyes (one of the traits that would make him one of history's great field commanders). Aristotle also gave him an annotated copy of the *Iliad*, which Alexander would always keep under his pillow. He wanted to be a new Achilles who, when given the choice between peaceful old age or glory, chose the latter.

He combined ambition with an iron will, personal courage and ruthlessness. When Philip was assassinated in 336BCE, Alexander first executed all rivals to the throne. When Thebes rebelled against the Macedonian yoke, he massacred 6,000 and burned the city to the ground, *pour encourager les autres*. No-one argued when the League of Corinth, the union of Greek city states formed by Philip, proclaimed Alexander the leader of the invasion of Asia. Even the Delphic oracle proclaimed him 'invincible'.

The army he assembled included surveyors, architects, engineers, scientists, historians and artists; from the start, it was clear that what he envisioned was far more than mere revenge. He was the lord of all Greece. He was made pharaoh of Egypt. After defeating the Persian king Darius, Alexander wanted to be acclaimed king of Asia by the Magi, as the chosen one of Ahura Mazda (page 239). But after lingering in Persepolis, and seeing that the Zoroastrian priests weren't going to do it (the Persians took their religion seriously), he burned Xerxes' magnificent palace,

Jalalabad), a city Alexander spared because the inhabitants told him it had been founded by Dionysos the wine god, surprising but not surprising: long before Alexander, there were Greek in Bactria, as Persian kings Darius I and Xerxes often resettled their troublesome Asia Minor Greeks here. Here the army saw ivy for the first time in years, the occasion for Dionysiac celebrations.

Alexander won his last major battle on the banks of the Hydaspes (Beas) in 326BCE against King Porus on the eastern edge of Darius's empire, before his exhausted officers revolted and forced him to turn back towards Greece. As punishment, he made them return the hard way, putting half on ships (the lucky ones) while the others endured a 60-day march at his side, along the coast through the deserts of Balochistan. At least 12,000 men and camp followers perished along the way. Alexander himself made it as far as Babylon, where he died, aged 32, probably from malaria. His faithful troops mourned him; the rest of the world probably heaved a sigh of relief.

HELLENISTIC AFGHANISTAN (312–10BCE) One of history's great oddities were these easternmost outposts of Hellenism in Afghanistan, Pakistan and India, a year's journey from Greece. After Alexander's death, his generals spent over a decade fighting over the spoils of his conquests. **Seleucus**, commander of Alexander's Companion Cavalry, took Babylon in 312BCE and spent the next nine years taking but not before removing the equivalent of £6,362,000,000 of treasure in today's money, enough to fund his adventures further east.

Armies love a winner, especially one who rewarded them so well, but as they moved east into Persia's Afghan satrapies, Alexander's Macedonian officers were dismayed when he adopted Persian dress (except for 'effeminate' trousers… that was a step too far for a Greek). He incorporated Persians into his army and administration, nearly causing a mutiny. He married the Persian princess Roxana of Balkh (when his officers complained, he pointed out that Achilles also married an Asian princess), then found Persian wives for 80 of his officers, and gave generous dowries to all soldiers who married Persian women, hoping to found a new Greek Persian race and civilisation.

When his army halted, Alexander proved he was Aristotle's pupil, always sending out explorers, keen to learn more about the local geography and nature. By the time of his death in Babylon at age 32 (after a two-week fever, perhaps West Nile virus encephalitis), he had founded some 70 cities, many of which have survived to this day. He created a standard coinage based on the silver coin of Athens which greatly facilitated trade, which would bring the first pepper and silk to the west. He laid the foundations of a cosmopolitan, Hellenistic world – continued by his Seleucid successors – that stretched from the eastern Mediterranean to India, in which people, goods and ideas circulated as never before. Greek was the common language in the east for centuries, laying the groundwork for Roman and Byzantine empires and the spread of Christianity.

In all his voluminous writings, however, Aristotle never once mentioned Alexander. It may have been personal (Alexander had Aristotle's nephew, the historian Callisthenes, put to death on suspicion of treason), but it may also have been Alexander's total disregard for one of Aristotle's dearest precepts: that non-Greek 'barbarians' should be treated as slaves.

the rest of the former Persian empire including Afghanistan, before moving into Western Anatolia.

Meanwhile, **Chandragupta Maurya** (aka Sandrocottus, 322–297BCE) was busy conquering the northern Indian kingdoms, founding the Mauryan Empire and threatening Seleucus' eastern frontier. But rather than try to defend it, Seleucus signed a peace treaty with Chandragupta in 305BCE, giving him a daughter in marriage and ceding the territory south of the Hindu Kush, including the Indus Valley, in exchange for pots of gold and 500 war elephants.

Seleucus was assassinated while trying to extend his empire into Europe. Although his heirs were too busy fighting rivals in the Mediterranean to pay much attention to the east, a strong Hellenistic presence remained through their strategy of luring Greek colonists to the east with offers of land and privileged positions in the government and military. Temples to the Greek gods went up, but it seems that the Greeks and local tribes kept to themselves, not indulging in the kind of intermarriage promoted by Alexander.

In c256BCE, the Seleucid satrap of Bactria, **Diodotus**, declared himself ruler of an independent Graeco-Bactrian Kingdom, which at its peak would include northern Afghanistan, Pakistan, Uzbekistan, Tajikistan, Turkmenistan, and parts of Kazakhstan and Iran. Nicknamed the 'land of a thousand cities', it was legendary for its wealth, its copper and lapis lazuli, profiting as east–west trade accelerated

1 | BACKGROUND INFORMATION

along the Silk Road, once China's Han dynasty (206BCE–220CE) secured it against threats from nomadic tribes.

Yet unlike the PR-savvy Alexander, who had the forethought to take chroniclers on his expedition, little was written about the Graeco-Bactrians. No-one is even certain of the original name of the city excavated at Ai Khanoum (page 255); the best guess it was Eucratideia, the capital of the warrior-king **Eucratides I** in the 2nd century BCE, who conquered and pillaged much of northern India. We do know, however, the names of more than 40 rulers (historical records only mentioned seven), thanks to 600 coins in the Kunduz Hoard, discovered in 1946.

In 200BCE the Graeco-Bactrian king **Demetrius** invaded the subcontinent, getting as far as modern Patna on the Ganges, and founding there Indo-Greek kingdoms that included regions west of the Kabul River and Helmand Province. The Indo-Greek kingdoms thrived as the Mauryan Empire slowly collapsed after the death of Ashoka (see below). Their greatest king, **Menander** (reigned c165–130BCE), born in Bagram of Greek parents, converted to Buddhism. He is famous in Buddhist literature as Milinda, in the *Milinda Panha* ('The Questions of King Milinda').

Isolated from the rest of the Hellenistic world, the Graeco-Bactrian state disintegrated through civil strife by 145BCE, yielding to the pressure of the nomadic tribes pushing in waves westward across central Asia. The Indo-Greek kingdoms survived until 10BCE. They are remembered, most strikingly in the fusion of Graeco-Buddhist art (page 55).

ASHOKA THE GREAT (269–233BCE) The life of the greatest Mauryan emperor, grandson of Chandragupta and who was quite possibly also the great grandson of Alexander the Great's general Seleucus, was so unique for his time that for centuries it was believed he was a figure of legend – until the Brahmi script that told of his deeds was deciphered.

Ashoka started his reign in the same vein as his ancestors, ruthlessly conquering his neighbour Kalinga. His realm would eventually include nearly all of India, Pakistan, Bangladesh and southern Afghanistan. Around 250BCE, however, he became horrified by the suffering he had caused and most likely converted to Buddhism, at the time a small Indian sect. Thanks in no small part to Ashoka, who spent the rest of his reign spreading the word far and wide, it became a world religion.

Ashoka sent out missionaries (*Dhamma-mahamattas*) and left inscriptions in several languages, known as Major Rock Edicts and Major Pillar Edicts, on Dhamma (promoting piety, humility, social responsibility, ethics and tolerance of other sects, and ending war and the killing of animals), placed where people could read them. Among the most famous are the ones in Greek and Aramaic discovered in Old Kandahar (page 199). Many edicts were marked with a spoked wheel, the Ashoka Chakra, a symbol showing that there is life in movement and death in stagnation. It still holds pride of place on the flag of India.

THE KUSHAN EMPIRE (CIRCA 30BCE–C300CE) When Yuezhi nomads in what is now the western Chinese province of Gansu were defeated in battle by another tribe in 176BCE, they started a wave of migration into central Asia, first pushing the **Saka** (Scythian) nomads into Bactria, and then out again as the **Yuezhi** moved in. The Saka (or the Yuezhi) left behind royal tombs at Tillya Tepe in northwest Afghanistan, filled with the country's greatest treasures: the Bactrian Gold (page 138). Heraois (1–30CE), chief of one of the five aristocratic Yuezhi tribes, was the first Kushan emperor, followed by Kujula Kadphises, who united the Yuezhi nomads.

The Kushans adopted the Greek alphabet and coin style, and used Greek for administration and trade, but spoke in Bactrian (a now-extinct eastern Iranian language that has survived in 4th–8th-century CE documents discovered in Balkh and Bamiyan). The great middlemen of the Silk Road, the Kushans seem to have been an exceptionally tolerant syncretising people, following Graeco-Buddhist cultural traditions and styles while patronising a mix of Buddhism, Greek religion, Zoroastrianism and Hinduism.

Under **Kanishka the Great** (c127–150CE), the Kushan Empire reached its greatest extent, stretching from the Indus Valley and the Indian Ocean to the oasis city of Turpan (Xinjiang) and Samarkand. Kanishka built the massive (if now much-looted and -eroded) Zoroastrian fire temple at Surkh Kotal (page 251). The Rabatak Inscription, discovered in 1993 by mujahideen digging a trench on an artificial hill at Rabatak near Surkh Kotal records how Kanishka discarded Greek as the language of administration and adopted Bactrian.

As the Roman Empire now had cash to splash, the Silk Road became a busy highway, and the Kushans, who also traded by sea, became fabulously wealthy. Kanishka had his capital at Peshawar in Gandhara and a summer capital at Kapisa (Bagram), where archaeologists found a stunning hoard of ivories (page 141) from his time. But as Rome and the Han dynasty in China slowly collapsed, trade on the Silk Road slowed, and the Kushans split into smaller principalities that were easily gobbled up by others.

BUDDHISM IN AFGHANISTAN Kanishka may have patronised Zoroastrianism, but Buddhism was his favourite religion. Although like Ashoka (see opposite) he may never have officially converted, Kanishka played a fundamental role in the spread of Buddhism east along the Silk Road into China. The Kushans promoted Graeco-Buddhist art (page 55) which created the first anthropomorphic depictions of the Buddha as a human (around 30BCE), with Hercules as his protector. The Kushan monk, Lokaksema, was the first to translate Buddhist scriptures from Gandhari Prakrit into Chinese in c178CE.

Under the Tang emperors, Chinese Buddhist monks settled in scores of monasteries along the Silk Road and beyond, joined by Indian monks. Among the most important monasteries were Nava Vihara south of Balkh (page 243), Mes Aynak (page 142), Hadda (page 155) and Bamiyan (page 179). Tepe Sardar overlooking Ghazni was built in the 3rd century CE when it was known as the Temple of Great King Kanishka; destroyed by fire in the mid 7th century, it was rebuilt much larger and stronger and survived into the early 9th century. Fondukistan monastery was built in c700CE high on one of the foothills of the Hindu Kush in the Ghorband Valley in Parwan Province, where the art represents the tail end of the Gandhara style.

ALCHONS AND HEPHTHALITES, MOSTLY (4TH–7TH CENTURIES CE) The Persian **Sassanian emperors** asserted their rule over the small principalities of the Kushans. But not for long, as a wave of nomadic invaders – pushed out of their Altay homelands by drought – arrived on the scene, starting with the **Kidarites** or Red Huns (335CE), with the **Alchon Huns** (370CE) on their heels, who would follow with the invasion of Kabul and India a century later. The Alchons stood out for their artificially deformed skulls which made them look as if they were always wearing crowns, as seen on the coins of their most notable king, Khingila (c430–90CE).

1 | BACKGROUND INFORMATION

The **Hephthalites** (or White Huns), whose origins have been debated for centuries, appeared around 450CE, and took Khorasan (the name given to Bactria and beyond by the Sassanians). They were stopped from taking the rest of Sassanian Persia by Shah Bahram Gur. The Hephthalite capital was probably Kunduz. Like the Kushans they adopted the Bactrian language, and grew rich from ransoms paid by the Sassanians. They sent embassies to China, and asked the Church of the East (or Nestorian) to send them a bishop in c550CE (he did; both Herat and Balkh would have Christian churches into the 10th century).

Although the Hephthalites had once destroyed Buddhist monasteries (in 630CE the traveller Xuanzang (page 182) wrote of the Kabul Valley: 'There are a million Buddhist monasteries that are in ruins and deserted. They are overgrown with weeds and constitute a mournful solitude'), later Hephthalite princes converted to Buddhism and appear in the murals as the donors of the two giant Buddhas of Bamiyan; carbon dating showed they were sculpted in c544CE and 644CE (the larger one).

Around 560CE the **Western Turks** and Sassanians joined forces to conquer the Hephthalite Empire. Bactria became better known as Tokharistan and came under the control of the Western Turks, while Kabul and regions south of Hindu Kush were ruled by a Buddhist dynasty known as the Turkishahi.

ISLAMIC DYNASTIES (7TH CENTURY–1219)

Weakened by the incessant wars with the Byzantine Empire, the Persian Sassanians were in decline, while the Arab tribes, fired up by their new religion, were in ascendancy. They took Persia a decade after the Prophet Muhammad's death (642CE), although Afghanistan would prove a much harder nut to crack, and only gradually converted. Locals often revolted, especially in Balkh, leading to the razing of its Zoroastrian shrine, while conflicts between the Umayyad and Abbasid caliphates slowed progress. Turkishahi Kabul wasn't fully Islamised until 988CE. Isolated Nuristan wouldn't convert until the 19th century.

Far from the centre of power in Baghdad, Afghanistan, or rather parts of it would be ruled by Islamic dynasties, often in quick succession. Ghazni (ancient Alexandria in Opiana) became the regional power centre. The **Saffarids**, whose base was in Registan, ruled much of the country for a few decades, but were defeated by another powerful family, the **Samanids**, who in the 10th century made Bukhara (Uzbekistan) their capital and ruled much of Afghanistan from there. As the Saffarids continued to cause trouble in the southeast, the Samanids brought in *mamluks* (Turkic enslaved soldiers) to help control them; only in 960CE, the mamluks revolted under their leader Sabuktigin and took over Ghazni, founding yet another dynasty, the **Ghaznavids**.

Sabuktigin's son **Mahmud the Great** was a great military strategist, who by 998CE controlled most of Afghanistan. After his rule was legitimised by the Caliph, he invaded northern India 17 times, encouraging conversions to Sunni Islam (one of his nicknames was 'Idol-breaker') wherever he went, and picking up immense plunder along the way. By the time he was done, he ruled a domain stretching from Varanasi to the Caspian Sea. With his fortune he built lavishly in Ghazni, brought over whole libraries from Persia and hosted the great poet Ferdowsi, author of the Persian national epic, the *Shahnameh*. His winter capital was in Lashkargah (ancient Bost) in southeast Afghanistan, where ruins of his palaces remain.

After Mahmud's death in 1030, his twin sons and their sons fought for control while a new wave of invaders, the **Seljuk Turks**, arrived on the scene and defeated the Ghaznavids, taking Balkh and making them pay tribute.

In the 1140s, Ala al-Din Husayn, chieftain of an ancient people from the mountains of Ghor (near Herat), took advantage of the rivalries between the Ghaznavids and the Seljuks to take power in 1149 and destroy the fabulous city of Ghazni in revenge for the deaths of his two brothers (earning himself the nickname 'World-burner'). Actually, he didn't destroy it; he made the inhabitants carry all the mud bricks of their city to the mountains, then slaughtered them to mix their blood with the mud to build a remote capital called the Turquoise Mountain. The **Ghorids** briefly became an extraordinarily powerful dynasty, conquering nearly everything between Baghdad and India, making Herat their more accessible capital, and taking Delhi, where their successors would rule the Delhi sultanate for centuries. Their brief day in the sun in Afghanistan saw the construction of the domes of Chist, the Minaret of Jam (all that survives of the Turquoise Mountain) and the Masjid-i-Juma (Friday Mosque) in Herat.

They were replaced by the **Khwarazmians**, another Sunni Turkic group, who defeated the Seljuks and the Ghorids and briefly ruled most of central Asia, Afghanistan and Iran, until along came the man that archaeologist Louis Dupree called 'the atom bomb of his day': Genghis Khan.

GENGHIS KHAN, AND THE AFTERMATH (1219–1363)

Central Asian history is full of nomadic tribes thundering westwards through the Eurasian steppes. Sedentary cultures provided them with food, manufactured goods, slaves and booty. Most would eventually settle, often adopting local customs, language, etc, then grow weak, self-destructing in dynastic quarrels over the throne, until the next tribe arrived to take over.

The great exception was Genghis Khan, who began life as an orphan named Temüjin and ended up reigning over the largest contiguous state in world history, stretching from the Pacific coast to Hungary. A charismatic and shrewd administrator, he united the Mongol tribes, changed his name and was proclaimed their emperor in 1206, consolidating his power by erasing age-old tribal loyalties, and replacing them with loyalty only to him and his family. He maintained their allegiance by equally dividing the spoils and the fruits of economic growth. He ran his military as a meritocracy, and made recruitment easy to understand in a decimal system. Ten thousand were recruited as bodyguards and administrators of the institutions he created.

Genghis Khan encouraged trade, building roads and providing capital for merchants. After defeating the Jin dynasty in northern China, he controlled the eastern Silk Road and sent envoys to the Persian Khwarazmian Shah Muhammad II to re-establish trade with the west. Muhammad didn't want to know. In 1218, Genghis sent a caravan of 500 camels weighed down with gold, silver, silks and furs and a message: 'I am the lord of the sunrise, and you the lord of the sunset. Let there be a firm treaty of friendship and peace between us, and let our caravans and traders come and go…'

It was too tempting a prize; the local governor at the Persian border confiscated the goods and massacred all the merchants, thinking no-one would ever know; only he missed a young camel boy who had been in the hammam and escaped to tell the tale. Genghis then sent envoys to Muhammad II, wanting to avoid war but demanding that the governor be punished. In what must be history's most consequential stupid acts, Muhammad mocked them and sent them back to Genghis with singed beards.

In 1219, the Mongols invaded and left utter devastation in their wake, massacring entire populations of the cities they sacked and razed, including central Asia's most illustrious cultural centres – Samarkand, Bukhara, Balkh, Ghazni and Herat. History says it took the Mongols a week to massacre all but 40 of the 1.6 million people in Herat with arrows, clubs and swords. When Genghis's favourite grandson Mutugen was killed in battle in 1221, Genghis ordered the annihilation of every man, woman, child, animal and plant in the valley of Bamiyan, leaving only the ruins of Shahr e Zohak, the red city, and Shahr e Gholghola, the city of sighs, to tell the tale.

And they did it all on grass power – which fed their horses (each warrior had six or seven) and enormous herds of cattle, yaks and camels that travelled with them, transporting their tents, temples and other necessaries. Extensive irrigation systems were destroyed; Genghis hated farms because they robbed his 'roaring ocean' army of grazing lands. As they travelled, the Mongols lived off mare's milk (preferably fermented), meat tenderised under their saddles (marinated marmot was a favourite) and blood from their horses when they had nothing else to eat. Marco Polo wrote they ate a lot of hamsters. They made themselves as ugly as possible by shaving their heads, leaving long strands at the side. They never washed their clothes. They stank.

When he died in 1227, Genghis's empire was divided between his four sons. Destroyed and depopulated, there was little news from Afghanistan for decades. Herat, surrounded by fertile land and located on a main trade route, was the first city to revive – in 1245, the Mongols granted it to the Kurt Maliks, cousins of the Ghorids.

In the Pax Mongolica, Genghis's descendants ruled what was left of Afghanistan from Kabul. The Silk Road was safer than ever to travel. One of the Italian families who did business with the Mongols were the Polos of Venice, who left in 1271 and returned to Venice in 1295, with golden tablets bearing letters of passage from Genghis's grandson, Kublai Khan. Catholic priests went east and won numerous converts: from the time of Genghis (himself a Shamanist), the Mongols were curious about and tolerant of all religions. And the mail service was legendary for its speed.

It all began to fall apart with the devastation of the Black Death in the mid 14th century. Perhaps Genghis's most lasting legacy is his DNA; he fathered more modern descendants than anyone in history (with 500 wives and concubines, he had a head start) – one in every 200 people on earth is a descendant.

TIMUR AND THE TIMURIDS (1364–1530) After decades of disorder, a Turkic-Mongol son of a minor noble born near Samarkand saw his chance. While employed by a warlord in Registan, he was shot in the knee with an arrow and lost two fingers while trying to steal a sheep and has gone down in history as Timur-Lenk (Timur the Lame, or Tamerlane). His rise to power was slow and complicated, but after executing his main rival, his brother-in-law and former companion in Balkh, princes rallied around him, and for the next 35 years, at the head of a Mongol-Turkic army, Timur destroyed cities from Delhi to Anatolia (where he captured the Ottoman Sultan Bayezid I, much to the delight of the Christian kings of Europe). Only his death in 1404 prevented an attack on China.

Timur was a Sunni Muslim, a renowned chess player, and a great patron of the arts and poetry, sparking the Timurid Renaissance. He was also a brilliant but psychopathic general who liked to build mountains out of human heads. Historians credit him for single-handedly eliminating the Christian Church of the East. Often the only people he spared were the artisans, whom he sent to embellish his capital, Samarkand – in Uzbekistan he is a national hero.

Although Timur modelled his empire on Genghis Khan's, the western part soon broke away, but his youngest son, **Shah Rukh** (1405–47), who ruled from Herat, spent his reign, after the usual dynastic struggles, repairing the damage wrought by his father. Shah Rukh has been compared to Lorenzo de' Medici; his time was a golden age. Profits from the Silk Road made him immensely wealthy, allowing him to fill the city with new buildings, poets, calligraphers, miniature painters and scientists. His empress, **Gowhar Shad** (nicknamed the 'Queen of Sheba' of her day), built Herat's famous Musallah complex. His nephew, Ulugh Beg, Viceroy of Samarkand, built an astronomical observatory.

After several years of the usual dynastic squabbles, **Husayn Bayqara** (1468–1506), a descendant of Timur and Genghis Khan, became ruler. He was another renowned Timurid patron of the arts, of the greatest Persian miniaturist Bihzad, of the mystic Jami, and of Mirkhwand, the greatest Persian historian of the age. His sons, however, were more interested in drunken parties than defending Herat. It was captured by the Uzbeks in 1507, and then by the rising dynasty in Persia, the **Safavids** in 1510, who held on to Herat but neglected it. The Uzbeks would hold on to northern Afghanistan into the 18th century, and the Safavids would similarly rule the west.

One last descendant of both Timur and Genghis Khan would become the emperor of eastern Afghanistan and of India: Zahir-ud-Din Muhammad, better known as **Babur** 'Tiger' (1483–1530), founder of the Mughal Empire. He especially loved Kabul, where he asked to be buried in the famous gardens he planted there (page 135).

THE CREATION OF AFGHANISTAN (1531–1808)

Into the 18th century, what is now Afghanistan remained divided into three blocks: a Sunni Mughal-ruled east (Kabul was one the *subahs*, or provincial capitals), a Shia Persian Safavid west, while the Uzbek Khanate of Bukhara ruled the north. Kandahar acted as a kind of buffer zone that sometimes went from side to side. Occasionally, the Pashtun tribes rebelled.

Things began to change when the Persians sent a brutal Georgian governor, Gurgin Khan, to Kandahar, home of one of the chief Pashtun tribes, the Ghilzai. Suspecting the Pashtuns of conspiring with the Mughals, Gurgin Khan started stomping on all dissent, trying to force them to convert to Shiism. He sent the Ghilzai chief, **Mirwais Hotak**, to be tried by the shah in Persia, but the charismatic Mirwais convinced the shah it was all a mistake, and to Gurgin Khan's surprise the shah sent Mirwais back to Kandahar in robes of honour.

But Mirwais had seen how decadent the Persians were and in 1709 led the Ghilzai takeover of Kandahar, executing Gurgin Khan. Around the same time, another powerful Pashtun tribe, the Abdali, rivals of the Ghilzai, took Herat. After the death of Mirwais in 1715, his son, **Mir Mahmud Hotak**, eventually took over as tribal leader, made the Abdali submit and defeated the Persian army and besieged the Persian capital Isfahan, eventually sacking and massacring the population, before inviting a large group of Safavid nobles to a banquet only to massacre them too. In 1725, Mir Mahmud, by then a homicidal maniac, was killed by his cousin Ashraf. Ashraf defeated the Ottomans who were trying to take advantage of the Persian weakness.

Meanwhile, the Persians, under a bold Turkmen adventurer and former camel driver from the Afshar tribe named Nader Qali Beg, defeated Ashraf, took Kandahar and drove the Ghilzai back to Herat. He became allies with the Abdali, some of whom became his personal bodyguard, declared himself **Nader Shah Ashfar**, ruler of Persia in 1736. In 1738 he invaded the still wealthy but militarily weak Mughal

Empire, destroyed Kandahar, captured Kabul and Ghazni, and sacked Delhi (and made off with the Koh-i-Noor diamond and the solid gold and jewel-encrusted Mughal Peacock Throne), forming what became known as the **Afsharid Empire**, at that time arguably the richest and most powerful in the world. After leading armies against Samarkand and Bukhara, Nader Shah too degenerated into a homicidal maniac, leaving, like his idol Timur, towers of skulls in his wake until he was beheaded by his own officers on 19 June 1747.

His Abdali bodyguard returned to Kandahar, where a 25-year-old officer and Nader's former treasurer, Ahmad Khan, proposed holding a *loya jirga* ('great council') to select a new leader, reckoning that if they could unite, they could take advantage of current circumstances: both the Persians and Mughals were very weak. Some say the Abdalis chose Ahmad Khan because he was young and would be easy to control, although that turned out to be hardly the case. Crowned with a garland of wheat, he became known as Ahmad Shah Dur-i-Durrani, 'pearl of pearls'; from then on, the Abdali clan would become the Durrani (or Saddozai) that would rule Afghanistan with intermissions until 1818, and through a subtribe, until 1978.

Initially **Ahmad Shah Durrani** ruled only the Pashtun south. He managed to capture the caravan bringing Nader's massive treasure from India, including the Koh-i-Noor diamond, which gave him the funds to pay an army to conquer all of present-day Afghanistan and more to found what became known as the Durrani Empire. He took Herat and a big chunk of Iran from the Persians. He agreed that the Amu Darya and its tributary, the Panj, would be the country's northern border, confirmed when the Emir of Bukhara gave him the Prophet Muhammad's cloak (although in Kandahar they tell a different story; page 199). Then Ahmad Shah went east and seized all of modern-day Pakistan and Kashmir, decimating a massive Maratha army at Panipat (1761), which created a power vacuum that the Sikhs and British would fill. He died peacefully aged 50 in 1772 and is buried in Kandahar.

Although a brilliant military leader, poet, and an excellent diplomat who managed to keep all the Pashtun tribes on board, Ahmad Shah was not an administrator, and he failed to set up lasting institutions to govern Afghanistan. His second-eldest son and heir, **Timur Shah Durrani**, made Kabul his capital, relying on mercenaries to defend his throne. He had at least 30 children with various wives, including 20 sons – and no designated heir, initiating a merry-go-round of vicious infighting, blindings and executions, and in the meantime losing much of the territory Ahmad Shah had conquered.

Of his sons, the three main contenders to the kingship, **Shuja Shah** ruled the longest, taking the throne from his brother Zaman Shah, who was blinded by the third brother Mahmud in 1803. Mahmud then started a blood feud with the powerful **Barakzai** branch of the Durrani tribe. Even without the Durrani–Barakzai feud, any chance of a peaceful reign was upended as Afghanistan was on the verge of becoming a pawn in the Great Game.

PLAYING THE GREAT GAME (1809–38) Coined in 1840 by British intelligence officer Captain Arthur Conolly and popularised by Rudyard Kipling in his novel *Kim*, the 'Great Game' described the Russian and British competition over Afghanistan, Persia and Tibet; the Russians knew it as the 'Tournament of Shadows'. Each power hoped to redraw borders and protect its interests through a mix of military intervention, espionage, tribal alliances and diplomacy. While the Tsar's armies were busy conquering central Asia, Britain, still the greatest sea power of the age, began to fear Russian ambitions in India. Britain hoped to make Afghanistan a protectorate, one that would, along with the Ottoman Empire and Persia, serve as a buffer between the Russian Empire and the Persian Gulf and Indian Ocean. Neither power ever considered that the Afghans had any right to self-determination.

It began with Napoleon, who encouraged Tsar Paul of Russia and then his son Alexander I to join him in an invasion of British India; when that fell through, Napoleon sent military agents into Persia to stir the pot. Alarmed, Shuja Shah, a weak and cruel man who liked to chop off bits of courtiers who displeased him, allied Afghanistan with British India in 1809, initiating the first contact between Afghanistan and Britain.

In the meantime, Ranjit Singh, the Maharaja of Punjab, was creating a Sikh powerhouse in northern India, taking Kashmir and then Peshawar from the Afghans in 1834 – an act that rankles to this day. In that same year, Shuja Shah was overthrown by Durrani rival **Dost Mohammad Barakzai** who declared himself amir in his place. Shuja Shah went to live in exile, as a guest of the British in Ludhiana, where he continued cutting off bits of his courtiers.

This set off a series of miscalculations that would lead to disaster. Britain mistrusted Dost Mohammad and feared he would collude with the Russians, who would move into India; some feared he would collude with the Persians to lead a Muslim invasion of India. What Dost Mohammad did in fact do was invite a Russian envoy, Count Witkiewicz, to Kabul in 1837, hoping to frighten Britain into allying with him against his arch enemy Ranjit Singh and force Singh to relinquish Peshawar.

Lord Auckland, the imperious Governor-General of India, sent a letter ordering Dost Mohammad to stop all contact with Russia. It was so offensive that the famous traveller, writer and diplomat Alexander Burnes, then serving as the East India Company's chief political officer in Kabul, didn't want to give it to Dost Mohammad. Dost Mohammad, wanting to prevent war, sent his special advisor, the American adventurer Josiah Harlan (page 146), to negotiate with Burnes, but Burnes had no power to negotiate. In April 1838, Dost Mohammad expelled the British Mission.

FIRST ANGLO–AFGHAN WAR (1838–42)

Britain's fears intensified when the Russians helped the Persian Qajar dynasty besiege Herat, the 'breadbasket of central Asia'. In October 1838, Lord Auckland issued a deceitful piece of propaganda called the Simla Manifesto, declaring Dost Mohammad was plotting with the Russians to attack India, and that the Afghans would, after 30 years, welcome the return of their 'rightful' king, the spiteful Shuja Shah. Shortly afterwards, the Russians and Persians lifted their eight-month siege of Herat, and Tsar Nicholas I recalled Count Witkiewicz from Kabul.

The Russian threat, if there ever was one, was over, but Auckland still wanted to invade. Back in London, the Duke of Wellington said it was 'stupid' and rightly predicted that while the invasion would be easy, holding Afghanistan would be nothing but trouble.

The First Anglo–Afghan War began in March 1839, when the East India Company's 'Army of the Indus' (21,000 British and Indian troops, 38,000 Indian camp followers, huge herds of cattle and 30,000 supply-carrying camels; one British officer required two camels just to carry his cigarettes, another took along 40 personal servants) invaded and had little trouble moving into Afghanistan. Dost Mohammad fled north, where he was put under house arrest in Bukhara, after the emir there refused to help him.

It was obvious from the start there was little enthusiasm among the Afghans for the return of the Shuja Shah. Some 4,500 British and Indian troops and around 12,000 camp followers had to stay in Kabul to protect their sadistic puppet, who nevertheless prevented them from staying in Kabul's citadel, the Bala Hissar; instead, they built an ill-defended camp on the outskirts of town. Meanwhile Dost Mohammad escaped from Bukhara and organised the resistance. Although he defeated the British in a battle, he surrendered and was sent to live in exile in the house in Ludhiana where Shuja Shah had stayed.

In November 1841, a crowd of locals in Kabul, fed up with Shuja Shah and enraged by the dissolute behaviour of the foreigners, killed Alexander Burnes and his family. In the face of the uprising, loss of treasure and supplies, the British led by the elderly, gouty **Major General William Elphinstone** were forced to retreat from Kabul, in freezing weather in January 1842. All were massacred on Gandamak Hill (page 155) by troops led by Dost Mohammad's wazir, Akbar Khan. The only survivor, assistant surgeon William Brydon, reached the besieged garrison at Jalalabad on 13 January 1842.

Britain replied with an 'Army of Retribution' that succeeded in rescuing some 2,100 captives, wrecking Kabul's famous bazaar and raping and murdering nearly everyone they met while razing one of Afghanistan's most beautiful and historic villages, Istalif. Dost Mohammad was released from house arrest. He had come to admire the British during his captivity, and reportedly said: 'I have been struck with the magnitude of your resources, your ships, your arsenals, but what I cannot understand is why the rulers of so vast and flourishing an empire should have gone cross the Indus to deprive me of my poor and barren country.'

DOST MOHAMMAD TO THE SECOND ANGLO–AFGHAN WAR (1842–80)

After more dynastic squabbling and the assassination of Shuja Shah, Dost Mohammad returned to Afghanistan and spent the rest of his reign consolidating his rule over Kandahar, Balkh, Afghan Turkestan and Herat. He signed a treaty with the British to stay out of each other's affairs, and kept his word even during the India Mutiny of 1857, when he could have easily seized Peshawar. But the frontier issue remained unsettled. Local Pashtun tribes looted and kidnapped and the British retaliated and tried to play the tribes off each other.

Dost Mohammad died in 1863, two weeks after capturing Herat, and was buried in the Gazargah shrine outside the city. He was succeeded by his son, **Sher Ali Khan**, then governor of Ghazni; although for the next six years he had to fight his brothers and nephew Abdur Rahman for the title. Sher Ali was a reformer who introduced a postal service and public schools; he created a minister of finance and instituted monetary reforms. He refrained from appointing his sons as provincial governors, and he modernised the army with the aid of British arms.

Meanwhile, the Russians were gobbling up central Asia, confirming some of Britain's greatest fears. Sher Ali tried to remain neutral while hawks on the British side were urging a 'forward policy' of occupying southern Afghanistan and bringing in a British mission to handle the country's foreign affairs. When Sher Ali received a Russian delegation in 1878, Britain decided to act, invaded Kabul, and the **Second Anglo-Afghan War** was underway. Sher Ali fled north to Mazar e Sharif, hoping to find help from the Russians, found none and died there in February 1879.

His son **Yakub Khan**, the new amir, met the British and ended hostilities by ceding more land and allowing a permanent mission in Kabul, which would direct Afghanistan's foreign policy. There were riots in the city after a delay in army pay, then another massacre of the British in Kabul, followed by another army of revenge. **General Frederick Roberts** marched on Kabul, sowed terror, and destroyed the Bala Hissar; Yakub Khan abdicated, went into exile in India and Roberts declared himself ruler.

This provoked fierce resistance, and it wasn't long before the British were looking for a way out of a costly war and occupation. Help came from an unexpected quarter in the form of Dost Mohammed's grandson, **Abdur Rahman**, who had left Afghanistan in 1868 and was living in Samarkand with a Russian pension – and who appeared in the north with money and rifles, gathering support from the tribes as he went. In spite of British misgivings about Russian influence, Abdur Rahman was recognised as amir, with the agreement that the British would withdraw from Afghanistan, and the new amir would only have foreign relations with Britain. After Roberts led a famous forced march to rescue the British garrison in Kandahar when it was besieged by Yakub Khan's brother Ayub, another pretender to the throne, British forces finally withdrew in April 1881.

AFGHANISTAN MODERNISES, AND MORE WAR (1880–1933)

Abdur Rahman consolidated his rule relatively quickly, defeating Ayub Khan in Kandahar and fiercely putting down any tribal dissent. He was the first Afghan ruler to declare his authority came from God, and not from the Pashtun tribal leaders (which allowed him to ignore and defy the mullahs, writing in his autobiography 'the tyranny and cruelty of these men were unbelievable'). He shrewdly kept both Britain and Russia out of Afghanistan. He officially let Britain conduct his foreign policy, in exchange for an annual subvention, because he knew Russia's policy was to dismember and weaken Afghanistan.

In 1893, as tribal problems persisted along India's eastern frontier, the British government sent Mortimer Durand to fix the border between British India and Afghanistan; when Abdur Rahman hesitated to accept, as the proposed **Durand Line** (page 165) divides the Pashtun homeland in two, Britain upped his subvention and promised to continue sending arms. Even so, the Durand Line has never been accepted by many Afghans; soon after its creation, Britain had to put down a major Pashtun uprising on their side of the line, only the first of the many troubles. As a buffer between the British and Russian empires, the British gave Afghanistan the Wakhan Corridor as a bonus.

Inspired by Peter the Great, Abdur Rahman established a conscript army, funded and armed by the British, that was able to put down any dissent to his authority, earning himself the nickname the 'Iron Amir'. He put down some 40 revolts during his reign, and forced his troublesome Pashtun rivals to migrate north into Tajik and Uzbek areas, where his spies could keep an eye on them. In the early 1890s, when the Hazara revolted against his rule, he launched a genocidal campaign and killed and enslaved an estimated 60% of that population. In 1895 he invaded Kafiristan, the last pagan valley in the Hindu Kush, to forcibly convert the indigenous people, which he renamed Nuristan, the 'land of light'. He was proud of mending all the clocks in Kabul.

One of Abdur Rahman's accomplishments was to leave the throne to his eldest son, **Habidullah**, when he died in 1901, without any dynastic disputes. While continuing to let Britain dictate Afghanistan's foreign policy, Habidullah was as good natured as his father was stern, and he began to modernise the country, building factories, roads and hydro-electric plants, introducing modern medicine at the first hospital; he founded a high school based on the French lycée model (attended by Ahmad Shah Massoud) and a military academy to prepare Afghans to govern themselves in the 20th century. It would be the beginning of a critical social division between the urban elite of Kabul and the countryside.

Habidullah invited families his father had sent into exile to return; one was **Mahmud Beg Tarzi**, who was inspired by the Young Turks movement and started the country's first newspaper, which promoted pan-Islamist and anti-Imperialist sentiment, calling for keeping the country neutral during World War I. But there was dissent. In 1915 a Turkish and German delegation arrived, encouraging jihad against British India; others demanded a constitutional government. Feeling the pressure and seeing opportunity in the 1917 Bolshevik Revolution, Habidullah wrote to London, requesting full independence in external affairs as a reward for his support; he never received a reply and in February 1919 he was assassinated in his sleep during a hunting party.

Although initially Habidullah's brother Nasrullah was proclaimed amir by the local tribes, his favourite son, **Amanullah**, who had remained in Kabul, soon took over in a coup and declared himself king. Amanullah had been tutored by Mahmud Beg Tarzi and married one of his daughters, Soraya. With Tarzi as his foreign minister, he declared Afghanistan an independent country. In May 1919 he launched an unprovoked attack on British India through the Khyber Pass, starting the **Third Anglo–Afghan War**, which soon turned into a stalemate. Britain was weary of war by then, and a peace treaty recognising the independence of Afghanistan was signed in August 1919.

The 1920s would be a decade of upheaval. Thousands of Turkmens, Uzbeks and Tajiks moved into Afghanistan to escape the Soviet occupation of their lands; so many Muslims moved in to escape 'infidel' India that Amanullah had to stop any more from coming. With Tarzi's advice, Amanullah drafted Afghanistan's first constitution in 1922, giving equal rights and freedoms to all citizens, creating a government with a role for religion that managed to upset both the progressives who wanted a Turkish-style secular state and the mullahs who believed the state should only be an expression of divine will. Amanullah formally abolished slavery in 1923, encouraged the education of girls in 320 new schools across Afghanistan, and created an independent judiciary, a government budget and tax reforms. Pashto was made an official language alongside Dari.

During their Grand Tour of the Middle East and Europe in 1927–28, Amanullah became even more enthused about modernising. He returned from Tehran driving a new Rolls-Royce and convened a loya jirga, this time ordering participants to cut their beards and hair and dress in suits. He ordered the people of Kabul to wear Western clothing. His wife Soraya was the first queen to appear in public with her husband, and even joined his hunting parties on horseback. The two publicly campaigned against the veil and polygamy, and promoted a minimum age for marriage and more education for women.

Little of this sat well with the tribal leaders and mullahs, who were losing their former influence and income. Many Afghans believed his reforms were un-Islamic, and were appalled that Queen Soraya had been photographed unveiled in the West. Revolts broke out in the Pashtun tribes, and a Tajik 'Robin Hood' **Habibullah Kalakani** known as Bacha e Saqaw, 'son of the water-carrier', led his party, the Saqqawists, on an assault on Kabul and took over as amir. Amanullah abdicated and drove off in his Rolls-Royce, and lived in Italy until he died in 1960.

Although initially supported by many Pashtun tribes and religious authorities, Habibullah Kalakani's rule only lasted into October 1929 before they turned against him, unwilling to be ruled by a Tajik. **Nadir Shah**, a great nephew of Dost Mohammad and Amanullah's minister of war and ambassador to France, arrived with his brothers to take control, and executed Kalakani and his inner circle in Kabul. Nadir Shah cancelled most of Amanullah's social reforms, revoked women's rights and appeased the mullahs by putting the religious courts in charge.

But he also kept the constitution, though gave all the important government posts to his brothers. He did much for the economy, reforming the currency, making cotton an important export, reopening the schools, establishing Kabul University and building the first road through the Hindu Kush before he was assassinated in 1933, while visiting a high school. Nadir's Musahiban brothers immediately rallied around his 19-year-old son **Mohammed Zahir Shah**.

ZAHIR SHAH (1933–73) With his uncles acting as regents for the first two decades of his reign, Afghanistan's longest-serving ruler, the shy and modest Zahir Shah, fond of chess, photography and cigars, ruled one of the country's most peaceful interludes. The country joined the League of Nations in 1934, was recognised the following year by the United States, and in World War II, managed to stay neutral.

In 1946, the youngest and most liberal Musahiban brother, Shah Mahmud, became prime minister. He released political prisoners and promoted economic growth; his special project was building a hydro-electric dam and irrigating the Helmand Valley and settling the country's many nomads.

British withdrawal from India in 1947 brought about hopes for a 'Pashtunistan' uniting all Pashtun tribes, or at least giving the Afghans some say in the matter, but the UK insisted that what happened east of the Durand Line was none of their business. The West had decided Pakistan was to be part of the United States' anti-communist coalition. No-one wanted to rock the boat. Afghanistan was the only country to vote against its admission to the UN. Feelings remained high on both sides; the Afghans repudiated all treaties made with the British. There were tribal incursions; in 1950, when Pakistan blockaded Afghanistan's oil imports, the USSR stepped in and offered to barter oil for cotton and wool on preferential terms.

Zahir Shah's government, pragmatically noting that Afghanistan had a vast border with the Soviet Union, pursued a policy of friendship with both Moscow and the West, although the Americans, whom the Afghans had hoped would replace the British in acting as a counterweight to the Russians, weren't offering much help. In 1953, Zahir Shah appointed his cousin and brother-in-law, **Daoud Khan**, as prime minister, who turned to the Soviets for assistance. Khrushchev visited in 1955 and agreed to a five-year plan for Afghanistan; the Soviets trained Afghan officers and supplied military aid, built paved roads and the Salang Tunnel (page 147). In 1959, President Dwight Eisenhower visited Kabul, and the United States too started to play catch up, funding projects, mainly in the south. Afghanistan would be the only country to receive aid from both Cold War powers. Daoud was quoted saying he was happiest when he could 'light his American cigarettes with Soviet matches'.

In 1960, Daoud took up the lost cause of Pashtunistan and made a few incursions over the Durand Line which were firmly repulsed, leading to a breakdown of diplomatic relations with Pakistan. Afghanistan closed the border, which left the country increasingly dependent on the Soviet Union. The economy went into decline, inflation soared, development projects faltered without supplies and Daoud, who had urged the king to adopt an authoritarian one-party system, was asked to resign in 1963.

The next decade brought a whole series of reforms to Afghanistan. In 1964, a new liberal constitution was agreed in a loya jirga. Afghans enjoyed freedom of the press, political parties (including the communist **People's Democratic Party of Afghanistan, PDPA**, secretly founded in 1965 by **Babrak Karmal** and **Nur Mohammad Taraki**), elections and a bicameral parliament, the Shura. Burqas became optional, as many young women adopted the latest Western fashions, including high heels and miniskirts while their brothers dressed in jeans; boys and girls went to school together and learned French, German and English; women attended university. Hotels and restaurants catering to tourists opened, as

1 | BACKGROUND INFORMATION

Afghanistan was firmly on the **hippie trail** (page 116) from London to Kathmandu. As Kabul loosened old restrictions and allowed more freedom of speech, the capital saw chronic student unrest, both political and personal – job prospects for graduates in Afghanistan paid very little.

But it was a small elite bubble of young Afghans dancing to the Rolling Stones in Kabul; 90% of Afghans, especially in rural areas, remained very conservative, and many thought the changes were happening too fast.

TWO COUPS (1973–79) In 1973, the new prime minister **Moosa Safiq** was making great progress on tackling the budget and corruption, but when Zahir Shah was out of the country seeking medical treatment, Daoud with his military and communist supporters staged a bloodless coup, abolished the monarchy, disbanded parliament, nationalised the banks and made himself president of the Republic of Afghanistan. He clamped down on Islamists, including a student named **Gulbuddin Hekmatyar**, who went into exile in Pakistan and founded his **Hezb e Islami** (Islamic Party). Once in power, however, Daoud upset many of his supporters and the Soviets by looking instead towards India, Egypt, Iran and the United States for development aid.

The USSR thought Daoud was too hasty in his changes: rural, impoverished Afghanistan was decades away from being ripe for communism. The local PDPA thought otherwise, and after Daoud started arresting party leaders, on 27 April 1978 one of them, Hafizullah Amin, launched a military coup known as the **Saur Revolution** (after the Dari name of the month). Daoud and most of his family were assassinated in the Presidential Palace, along with an estimated 200 of his supporters.

Almost from the beginning, the PDPA was split between the hard-line Marxist Lenin ideologues of the **Khalq** faction and the moderate, more nationalistic **Parcham**. Khalqist Nur Mohammad Taraki, who had been educated as a teacher at the University of Wisconsin, became the first General Secretary of the now renamed Democratic Republic of Afghanistan, taking on the title of 'Great Teacher' in the regime's propaganda. The Soviet Communist party tried to reconcile the two sides, but it wasn't long before the Khalqists began to purge the Parchami, locking up and slaughtering dissidents in a brutal reign of terror. There was a major uprising in Herat that saw government officials and Russians massacred before the army with Russian aid took the city back, costing the lives of as many as 25,000, although many soldiers went on to join the mujahideen under a former officer, **Ismail Khan** (page 210).

But resistance and protests were growing everywhere as the government managed to antagonise rural areas as well, with its programme of land distribution and social reforms, abolishing dowries, adding Russian and Marxism lessons to the education. The USSR sent military advisors and weaponry and economic assistance, but were dismayed that they had little influence over policy. The US Ambassador Adolph Dubs was kidnapped on his way to the American embassy in Kabul, then killed under suspicious circumstances when Afghan forces attempted a rescue (February 1979).

Hafizullah Amin started as Taraki's right-hand man, until they fell out; Taraki, on orders from Moscow, tried to assassinate him, but Amin murdered Taraki instead (September 1979) and took over. The Soviets and the Afghans, who considered him brutal and treacherous, were less than impressed. Large numbers of soldiers deserted. Fearing that the revolution would fail and lead to copycat revolts against communism elsewhere, the Soviets sought to get rid of him. After an attempt to poison Amin failed, they invaded the country on 26 December, killed Amin and all the males in his family, and installed **Babrak Kamal**, a Parchami who had been living in exile in Czechoslovakia, as Afghanistan's puppet president.

SOVIET–AFGHAN WAR (1979–89) The Russian invasion was immediately condemned around the world. In Afghanistan, the Russians were soon met with resistance from guerrilla fighters, the mujahideen and large elements of the Afghan army who rebelled. **Sibghatullah Mojaddedi**, a religious moderate and Sufi shaikh, called for jihad to repel the invaders. His **Jebh-e-Nejat-e Melli** (National Liberation Front) united anti-communist and pro-Islamists and ethnic groups across Afghanistan. In Pakistan, Akhtar Abdur Rahman, director of the **ISI** (Inter-Services Intelligence), declared 'Kabul must burn!' and came up with the idea of using religious extremists to fight a proxy war against the communists.

The war soon became the Soviet Union's Vietnam. The mountains of Pakistan were the base for mujahideen training camps. Rahman's ISI joined with the CIA in its Operation Cyclone, along with Saudi Arabia, Iran and China. They provided somewhere between US$6–12 billion (facts are impossible to pin down) in funds for training and weapons for tens of thousands of mujahideen, nearly all channelled through the ISI, which had its own agenda.

Corruption was rife. While united in the desire to rid Afghanistan of the Soviet invaders, the various parties had rival leaders and ethnicities and hardly ever co-ordinated. The bulk of the CIA funds went to the ISI favourite, hard-liner Hekmatyar (page 254) and his Hezb e Islami, which was best known for attacking rival mujahideen rather than the Soviets (Ahmad Shah Massoud compared them to cancer). A more moderate breakaway group with the same name, run by mullah **Yunis Khalis** (Hezb e Islami-Khalis), had as its military commander **Abdul Haq**, a well-connected Pashtun; he became an important contact between the mujahideen and the CIA and successfully led guerrilla activities around Kabul.

Another big beneficiary was fundamentalist **Jalaluddin Haqqani**, founder of the Haqqani Network. Funded by independent Saudi donors, Haqqani recruited foreign Muslim fighters in the name of global jihad and developed a close relationship with **Osama bin Laden** (page 35). The CIA never suspected that when the communists were stopped, Islamic extremists would turn all their weapons and training back on the West.

Then there was the more moderate Burhanuddin Rabbani's **Jamiat-i-Islami**, commanded by ex-student, **Ahmad Shah Massoud**, whose superior guerrilla tactics and PR skills brought him international recognition; another skilful Tajik commander, Ismail Khan from Herat, was in charge of the western section. Also in the west were Shi'a mujahideen, mainly Hazara, financed and armed by Iran, but handicapped by factionalism even more than the others.

Faced with fierce fighting, the Soviets tried to divide and conquer and actively stirred up the pot of ethnic rivalries. They formed false bands of mujahideen to sow confusion and distrust. Hoping to win hearts and minds, they granted the Tajiks, Uzbeks and Hazaras a good amount of autonomy for the first time in history. Some of these minorities were recruited into the army, but turned out to be too prone to collaborating with the locals.

As the Soviets were ill equipped to fight the mujahideen in mountains and narrow valleys, the Red Army only really controlled the urban centres. From there they went out only in convoys; they bulldozed villages and ran a scorched earth reign of terror not unlike Genghis Khan's, leaving booby traps and landmines (page 83) behind. As Steve Coll wrote in *Ghost Wars*: 'Soviet soldiers besieged by CIA-supplied Afghan rebels called them *dukhi*, or ghosts. The Soviets could never quite grasp and hold their enemy… From its first days before the Soviet invasion until its last hours in the late summer of 2001, this was a struggle among ghosts.'

Faced with an expensive, unpopular and unwinnable war – made more unwinnable once President Ronald Reagan gave portable, shoulder-held heat-seeking Stinger missiles to the mujahideen capable of bringing down Soviet helicopters – the new President Mikhail Gorbachev began to look for a way out of the USSR's 'bleeding wound'. In 1986, Babrak Kamal was exiled to the Soviet Union and was replaced by **Mohammad Najibullah** (aka Dr Najib – he once studied medicine), former head of the KhAD, the Afghan State Intelligence Agency, who had impressed the Soviets with his efficiency at the head of an organisation of 30,000, but who was known among Afghans for spying, imprisoning, torturing and killing political enemies.

In 1989, the United States, USSR, Pakistan and Afghanistan signed the Geneva Accords that guaranteed Afghan independence and the withdrawal of 100,000 Soviet troops. An estimated 26,000 Soviet and 58,000 Afghan troops had been killed; the economic hit and loss of prestige would lead directly to the break-up of the Soviet Union. The war left 3.5 million Afghan refugees in Pakistan, 1.5 million in Iran, and in Afghanistan an estimated 90,000 mujahideen and 2 million to 3 million Afghan civilians dead. No-one really knows.

The Russians left Dr Najib's Parcham-dominated government in place, supported by massive quantities of arms, equipment and SCUD missiles. As the US continued to support the resistance, Najibullah pleaded for National Reconciliation, for all the mujahideen and secular leaders to come together, but no-one trusted him and his words were disregarded. Instead, the mujahideen with Pakistan's support attacked Jalalabad – and lost badly.

AFGHAN CIVIL WAR (1992–96) In January 1992, the United States, Russia and Pakistan agreed to cease financial and military support for both the Afghan government and mujahideen. As Najibullah's government slowly collapsed, the Afghan army's fickle **General Abdul Rashid Dostum** (page 232), who controlled northern Afghanistan, saw how the wind was blowing and joined up with Massoud to capture the country's main military airport at Bagram 70km north of Kabul.

The Najibullah administration invited Massoud to enter Kabul and take over, but he refused, instead asking other mujahideen leaders, then mostly in exile in Peshawar, to come up with a power-sharing agreement: 'All the parties had participated in the war, in jihad in Afghanistan, so they had to have their share in the government, and in the formation of the government.' The Peshawar Accords to create an interim government of an Islamic Republic with Sibghatullah Mojaddedi serving as president for three months were agreed on by the mujahideen leaders – unfortunately except for Gulbuddin Hekmatyar, who saw his chance to take power and told Massoud he would enter Kabul 'with our naked sword. No-one can stop us.'

Massoud moved into Kabul to do precisely that, saying he had to defend the people from Hekmatyar's forces. Repulsed, Hekmatyar launched rocket attacks on Kabul. Dostum captured Dr Najib after he resigned and was making his way to Kabul Airport; he took refuge in the UN office.

Elegant Kabul, with its gardens and broad streets, had mostly been spared under the Soviets. In the four years and five months of civil war that followed, the city was reduced to ruins. The mujahideen became war lords; all sides committed atrocities. An estimated 60,000 Kabulis died. Thousands in rural areas died too, unable to access food or medical care. Meanwhile, Pakistan, Iran, Saudi Arabia and Uzbekistan supported their proxies in the fight. Sides changed frequently.

In the confusion, Afghanistan's minority groups managed to keep much of the autonomy they had enjoyed under the Soviets, notably the Uzbeks in Mazar e Sharif under Dostum.

As the war dragged on, Pakistan, which had hoped for a friendly Islamic Pashtun-ruled Afghanistan that would reopen the old central Asian trade routes and take back the millions of Afghan refugees, gave up on Hekmatyar and began to favour the Taliban.

THE TALIBAN (1996–2001) The Taliban hit the world's consciousness in their pick-up trucks, turbans and mascara (modern version of *kohl*, believed to be *Sunnah* or 'the way of the Prophet Muhammad' – as Muhammad is said to have used kohl around his eyes for medicinal reasons).

The Taliban had been founded in Kandahar in 1994 by **Mullah Omar** (page 195), with financing and logistical support from Pakistan's intelligence and especially Benazir Bhutto's Interior Minister General **Naseerullah Babar**, who called the Taliban 'my boys'. Promising to free Afghanistan from the warlords and form a true Islamic state, they were by then well trained and well armed, complete with an air force financed by the Saudis.

In 1996, the warring mujahideen parties finally implemented a power-sharing agreement in Kabul – prompting the Pakistanis and the Saudis to supply reinforcements and money for the Taliban's all-out assault on the city. When Hekmatyar's troops abandoned the east, the Taliban poured through in September. One of the first things on the new rulers' agenda was to drag Najibullah out of his UN sanctuary and hang him.

Dostum held out in Mazar e Sharif until 1998, leaving only the northeast (the Panjshir valley, Takhar, parts of Parwan and Badakhshan) under Massoud, where his men would fight the Taliban as part of the **Northern Alliance United Front**. The Taliban offered to make Massoud prime minister if he would stop fighting, but he refused when they refused to make any transition to democracy.

The Taliban renamed the country the **Islamic Emirate of Afghanistan**, and imposed their extreme form of Sharia law, forbidding female education and employment, and banning television, shaving and kite flying. Human representation also being banned, they covered up beauty salon and clothing ads and even beheaded some of the antiquities in the Kabul Archaeology Museum, before later dynamiting the giant Buddhas of Bamiyan. Earthquakes in 1998 caused destruction, and then famine as aid agencies were forbidden to enter the country.

But bin Laden and other extremists, including Chechen separatists who caused two wars in Russia in the 1990s, were allowed to train their acolytes in Afghanistan in the name of global jihad. After bomb attacks on US embassies in Africa, also in 1998, President Bill Clinton ordered a cruise missile attack on al-Qaeda bases in Afghanistan without any effect. In the meantime, Massoud and his Pashtun ally, Abdul Haq 'the Lion of Kabul', defended their northern enclave from Taliban attacks and created democratic institutions, including police, education and health systems. He invited leaders from all of Afghanistan's ethnic groups to his northern Afghanistan headquarters for a loya jirga to plan a post-Taliban government.

In early 2001, Massoud went to address the European Parliament to request humanitarian aid for Afghanistan, saying that the Taliban and al-Qaeda were not representative of Islam, and that without the support of Pakistan, Saudi Arabia and al-Qaeda, the Taliban would collapse. And he warned that bin Laden was planning a major terrorist attack – and that Afghanistan's problems would become American problems.

1 | BACKGROUND INFORMATION

On 9 September 2001, Afghans, and the rest of the world, were shocked when Ahmad Shah Massoud was assassinated by two suicide bombers pretending to be journalists, sent by Osama bin Laden who wanted to appease the Taliban, knowing the attack on the World Trade Center in New York and the Pentagon two days later would cause trouble. After the Taliban ignored Washington's request to turn bin Laden over, the United States led the invasion of Afghanistan. With the help of the Northern Alliance, they routed the Taliban in early December. The US sent a band of mujahideen into Tora Bora to find bin Laden, but he escaped on horseback at the last minute.

THE ISLAMIC REPUBLIC (2001–21) Although many Afghans were hoping that the elderly, mild-mannered King Zahir would regain the throne, their hopes were nixed by the US; the Americans feared the king, who never acknowledged the Durand Line, would upset Pakistan which they were trying to keep onside. Instead, moderate **Hamid Karzai**, chief of the Popalzai Durrani Pashtuns in Kandahar, was appointed interim leader, confirmed by a loya jirga in 2002. NATO, acting for the first time outside of Europe, took over the security mission in 2003 at the request of the UN. Forty-two countries contributed 65,000 troops.

The new constitution of 2004 gave all Afghans aged 18 and over the right vote. In the first election, Karzai was elected with 55% of the vote. A parliament was elected later in the year. The UN established the **International Security Assistance Force (ISAF)**, with the goal of re-establishing an Afghan government and training the **Afghan National Security Forces (ANSF).** One of Massoud's most effective followers, **Amrullah Saleh**, was made head of the National Directorate of Security and successfully infiltrated Pakistan's ISI and the Taliban (he tracked down Osama bin Laden to Abbottabad back in 2006, only to meet Pakistani denials). Most of his warnings were ignored.

There was a notable effort to include women in power: by the end of the Islamic Republic, Afghanistan would have 352 female parliamentarians, 800 attorneys, 300 judges, 242 prosecutors, 13 women ministers, and eight deputy governors and 4,000 policewomen. However, because of the difficulty in organising the rural vote, many of the old warlords, guilty of corruption and human rights violations, regained power, along with drug lords: the opium and heroin trade was booming. Corruption everywhere was rife. American employment of the exceptionally brutal warlord Amir Dado, who hanged anyone who disagreed with him as the intelligence chief in Helmand province, was hardly a good advertisement for Western-style democracy.

Although President George W Bush promised a new Marshall Plan to rebuild Afghanistan, nothing approaching the necessary reconstruction funds ever materialised. The world's attention had moved on to the war in Iraq.

Meanwhile the Taliban and their allies, the Haqqani Network, regrouped with impunity over the Pakistan border, and waged guerrilla warfare and suicide bombings, while ISAF's killing of civilians bred much resentment. In his second term Karzai adopted a policy of appeasement towards Pakistan that led to the resignation of Amrullah Saleh, who founded the anti-Taliban **Basej e Milli** party (National Movement) in 2010.

Security for Westerners working in the country plummeted in 2011, especially after American pastor Terry Jones publicly burned Qurans, leading to riots and deaths in Afghanistan. Taliban insurgency, and suicide and roadside bombings against the ISAF and ANSF increased. In that same year, US forces killed Osama bin Laden (2 May 2011) in Pakistan and dumped his body at sea.

In 2014, **Ashraf Ghani**, the finance minister in Karzai's cabinet, won a disputed election against **Abdullah Abdullah** (who initially, like many Afghans had just one name, and adopted his second name after journalists kept pestering him for a surname), resulting in both sharing power. NATO ended its combat mission, although the security situation continued to deteriorate. The emergence of **Islamic State Khorasan (IS-K)** attracted militants who considered the Taliban's aims too nationalistic for global jihad. President Barack Obama abandoned plans to withdraw all US forces by the end of his presidency in 2017, and left 5,500 US troops and military advisors.

In 2016, the Taliban chose a new leader, **Hibatullah Akhundzada**. In Kabul, Ghani was re-elected in a second contested election in 2019, and attempted to run a technocratic government, but it was doomed. America's top brass had already decided the war was unwinnable on 29 February 2020; President Donald Trump's envoys, after negotiating with the Taliban, signed the **Doha Agreement** leading to the withdrawal of US troops by August 2021 in exchange for the Taliban's promise to not harbour terrorists. The Americans judged that the Afghan government (which was notably not consulted) and ANSF could hold out for six months, but because part of the agreement was to limit ANSF's air support, the Taliban were able to make rapid gains across Afghanistan. By May 2021, they controlled most of the provinces in the country.

When he came into office, President Joe Biden stuck with the Trump team's schedule, but as the withdrawal deadline approached, ANSF's ability to hold out for six months turned into less than a week, leaving the US, UK and other coalition members caught woefully unprepared to evacuate their personnel, citizens and the many Afghans who had worked with them over the previous two decades, especially once President Ghani fled in a helicopter on 15 August 2021, 'to avoid bloodshed'. Many Afghans consider him a traitor. Vice President Amrullah Saleh briefly took over the government before escaping into the Panjshir Valley.

The world witnessed heart-wrenching images of desperate Afghans swarming Kabul Airport, scaling the fence and even clinging hopelessly to planes as they took off. On 26 August, while the evacuation was taking place, an IS-K suicide bomber killed 180 people, including 13 US service members who became the final casualties in America's longest-ever war. In the end, more than 123,000 people were evacuated by the coalition. The Doha Agreement's provisions for intra-Afghan negotiations and agreement on a political road map for the future never happened.

As Luke Harding wrote in *The Guardian* (2 June 2024), 'The US-led campaign in Afghanistan – a 20-year saga of wishful thinking and blunders – [ended] in ignominy and farce.' The details that emerged from the Afghanistan papers, published by the *Washington Post* in 2019, showed that America's top brass had little idea what they were doing all along, had no idea what Afghanistan was really like but had continued to mislead the public and spend a trillion dollars, costing the lives of 3,621 coalition soldiers, and 176,000 Afghan civilians, soldiers and opposition fighters.

THE TALIBAN AGAIN (2021–PRESENT) The Taliban quickly reinstated the Islamic Emirate of Afghanistan. Their victory happened so quickly that much of Afghanistan's infrastructure was intact – along with billions of dollars' worth of US military equipment.

Among the few international humanitarian organisations that remain in the country are the United Nations High Commissioner for Refugees (UNHCR), the World Health Organisation (WHO) and Médecins Sans Frontières (MSF), who fortunately were on hand when three 6.3 magnitude earthquakes struck western Afghanistan around Herat in October 2023, killing more than 2,000 people; and when a severe drought was followed by flash floods in May and June 2024, costing the lives of over 300 people and destroying crops, livestock and over 10,000 mudbrick-built homes. In August and September 2025, three powerful earthquakes struck mountainous Kunar, killing more than 2,200 people, burying villages and livestock in rockslides, and damaging some 6,700 homes in the province.

At the time of writing, the **National Resistance Front** (NRF) is run by Ahmad Shah Massoud's son, **Ahmad Massoud**, who attended King's College, London and Sandhurst in the UK and claims to have 5,000 fighters. Once a base for the Northern Alliance, Tajikistan (Afghanistan's most anti-Taliban neighbour) is now headquarters of **Amrullah Saleh**; as the last vice president, he has declared himself the real president of the country according to the Afghan constitution. The two men work with the **Afghanistan Freedom Front** (AFF), a mobile resistance force headed by Hazara leader **Daoud Naji**, allied with the National Resistance Council for the Salvation of Afghanistan. Members include former mujahideen leaders in exile such as Rashid Dostum, Atta Mohammad Nur, Mohammad Mohaqiq, Abdulrab Rasul Sayyaf and Ismail Khan. They claim to have fighters in about a third of the provinces.

After the ISI allowed the Taliban to build sanctuaries in Pakistani tribal areas, betting that they would take control of Afghanistan as soon as the US left, their meddling has come back to bite them as they also incubated a radical Taliban offshoot, **Tehreek-e-Taliban Pakistan** (TTP), dedicated to overthrowing the Pakistani government and expanding the Islamic emirate. Since 2021, thousands of Pakistani civilians and members of the security forces have been killed in TTP terrorist attacks. It was the strategy of Ayman al-Zawahiri, Osama bin Laden's number two and mastermind, to merge the local branch of al-Qaeda with the TTP – before he was killed by a US drone strike in August 2022 while staying at a Kabul 'safe house' hosted by Sirajuddin Haqqani, who has family ties with the TTP.

In October 2025, the long-running war of words and accusations by Islamabad that the Taliban government has been supporting the TTP in Afghanistan flared into a brief shooting war along the border, including a bombing of Kabul and the Taliban base in Kandahar.

Within Afghanistan today, ISIS Khorasan Province (IS-K) is the most serious threat to security. Although decimated by coalition forces and the Taliban, their numbers are estimated to be over 5,000. They regard the Taliban as a nationalist entity in the way of IS-K's goals of transnational jihad that would establish a new caliphate. Within Afghanistan they have perpetuated suicide bombings targeting ethnic and religious minorities, Sufis and Taliban, as well as the killing of three Spanish tourists at Bamiyan in 2024, while waging spectacular terrorist attacks abroad, in Iran at the memorial for General Suleyman that killed more than 100 and at the Crocus City Hall concert in Russia in March 2024 which left 133 dead.

Afghanistan continues to search for its place in the modern world – both internationally and at home. Efforts to strengthen ties with countries such as India and Russia have contrasted with a sharp deterioration in relations with Pakistan. Domestically, the regime remains torn between control and progress. The decision to switch off the entire country's internet for 48 hours in October 2025 may have curtailed what authorities called the 'moral corruption' of young men and the online voices of women seeking education, but it also brought the nation to a standstill – an apt metaphor for a country caught between isolation and the desire to move forward.

AFGHANISTAN TODAY It's safer to live and travel in Afghanistan now than any time in the past few decades. The Taliban have begun actively to court visitors, claiming in December 2024, that 14,500 tourists have come to Afghanistan since they've been in power, bringing along some much-needed cash (and at least half have uploaded their videos of the country to social media). Among the 6 million plus Afghan refugees who have returned (or were forcibly returned from Pakistan and Iran) since 2021 are some who are very well off, along with diaspora Afghans and foreigners who want to get in on the ground floor of rebuilding the country; property prices in the smarter quarters of Kabul have soared. Most, however, were forced to leave with little more than the clothes on their backs, especially after the 12-day Israel–Iran conflict in June 2025.

At the same time, Afghanistan continues to face international sanctions over the Taliban's human rights record and gender apartheid. International financial transactions are blocked and the banking system barely functions. However, the Taliban has done some positive things for Afghan economy. Since taking power, they have centralised revenues from taxes, cutting out corrupt local warlords. They have forbidden officials and members of the security forces from owning mineral rights (the biggest potential source of revenue for the country; page 42). They have re-evaluated previous contracts, hiked mining royalties and pressed companies to pay up front. Neighbouring countries are happy that drugs are no longer pouring out of Afghanistan.

Things are changing, and by the time you read this, the country may have moved on in ways we can't imagine. Read up on reports in the local media before you visit (page 107).

GOVERNMENT AND POLITICS

The Islamic Emirate of Afghanistan (IEA) currently has no elections, no constitution and no civil code of laws. The Supreme Leader Hibatullah Akhundzada issues edicts and decrees reinforced in varying degrees across the country; other directives (*hukm*) are considered weaker and 'advisory' and left to local Taliban officials to interpret as they will. At the time of writing, the IEA has been officially recognised only by Russia, although as of 2023 a Taliban ambassador was accredited in Beijing and an increasing number of embassies have opened in Kabul.

The government has become more exclusionary, favouring Pashtuns, especially southern Pashtuns who are Akhundzada's main supporters. Even within the Taliban non-Pashtun leaders have been dismissed. While initially many civil servants, many with key managerial skills and knowledge, have kept their jobs, Akhundzada ruled that by 2026 they should have trained Taliban fighters to take their jobs. Ten loyal Quran-memorising clerics have been put in charge of the mining process. An ally of Akhundzada said Herat University should issue university degrees to Taliban fighters based on how many landmines they planted in the last 20 years.

There are growing signs of an internal split in the movement, as some Taliban have even said out loud (before leaving the country) that Afghanistan should reopen higher education and other opportunities to women, seek international recognition and investment; but Akhundzada, secluded among his supporters in Kandahar, remains obdurate in believing no sacrifice is too great when it comes to maintaining his version of Sharia law. Some Afghans wonder if he even exists (there only seems to be one photo of him) or if he's a front for the Pakistan Inter-Service Intelligence who invented the Taliban. Others say he is purposefully staying mysterious and elusive to increase his power to instil fear.

1 | BACKGROUND INFORMATION

On 9 July 2025, the International Criminal Court issued arrest warrants for the Taliban supreme leader, Akhundzada, and Afghanistan's chief justice, Abdul Hakim Haqqani, accusing them of crimes against humanity for depriving women and girls of 'education, privacy and family life and the freedoms of movement, expression, thought, conscience and religion.'

ECONOMY

Afghanistan is a poor country. Its GDP fell by more than 20% in 2021 and remains nearly a quarter smaller than it was in 2020, although there was a bit of improvement in 2024. Growth is severely limited by the Taliban's pariah status. The Save the Children charity found children as young as four working the brick factory kilns north of Kabul to help support their families.

As the Taliban returned to power, the United States froze the US$9.5 billion of assets of the Da Afghanistan Central Bank (DAB) with dire economic consequences. In September 2022, a special Afghan fund (w afghanfund.ch) of US$3.5 billion was sent to the Bank of International Settlements (BIS) in Basel, intended to be used for the benefit of the people of Afghanistan, administered by two Afghan economists, and representatives of the American and Swiss governments. All four have to agree to send any money to Afghanistan. So far none has been sent, even though the two Afghan economists have pleaded for a US$15 million monthly payment to the DAB to stabilise the economy.

International sanctions have kept Afghanistan out of the global banking system, turning simple transactions into conundrums. Payments often go through Dubai and Pakistan to be converted into bags of cash before crossing the border.

Since withdrawing in 2021, the US, more than any other country, supplied humanitarian aid, donating US$3.71 billion in support of health, education, agriculture and food security, most of which was administered through UN programmes and the World Bank – that is, until January 2025, when President Trump ordered a halt to US foreign aid programmes.

Unable to find jobs at home, many Afghan men have gone abroad to work, especially in Iran and the Gulf states. Because of the banking restrictions, they send money home using the centuries-old *hawala* system – informal money transfers based on trust and personal relationships of the *hawaladars* (dealers), with fees paid by the sender. Four large networks dominate the scene, trading in 30 currencies, and are generally regarded by Afghans as more reliable than banks (especially in a country where only 10% or so of the people have been able to establish formal financial accounts). There are moves to regulate the hawala system, to prevent it from being used for criminal activities and funding terrorism. Some are used by Afghans abroad to distribute money for charity at home, trusting hawaladars to give it to the neediest.

MEGA-PROJECTS In spite of political friction, Afghanistan's neighbours are co-operating on a number of economic projects, such as the Central Asia–South Asia Electricity Transmission and Trade Project (CASA-1000), with components in Pakistan, Kyrgyzstan and Tajikistan. Other mega-projects include the restoration of the 2,092km AO1 (the world's longest ring road) linking 16 of the 34 provinces, begun by the Soviets, ruined in subsequent wars, and partially rebuilt with US and Saudi money.

In October 2024, a freight railway between the Chinese city of Nantong and the port of Hayratan on the Amu Darya River in Balkh Province opened, going by way of Kyrgyzstan and Uzbekistan, as part of China's 'Belt and Road Initiative'.

Numerous other projects have been touted, including trans-Afghan rail corridors from Uzbekistan and Turkmenistan to the borders of Pakistan and another linking Iran to China, as well as a Mazar e Sharif–Herat–Kandahar line.

The most urgent mega-projects, however, involve supplying water to Kabul, where the population has grown from 2 million in 2000 to over 6 million in 2025 and there are dire warnings that the city may completely run out by 2030. Much of the available groundwater is contaminated and unsuitable for drinking, forcing people to send family members on long walks to fetch water from the remaining free supply points or spend a good portion of their income on water from tankers. There are solutions if the funds can be found: US$236 million needed for completing the Shahtoot dam and reservoir, 30km southwest of Kabul, and building the US$170 million 200km Panjshir River Pipeline to Kabul. The UN Office for the

POPPIES

Afghanistan was the world's leading producer of opium for decades. Helmand Province alone, with a perfect climate for growing three crops a year, produced over half of the world's opium between 2002 and 2022; as it was also one of the most insecure provinces during that period, poppies also helped farmers survive. Many purchased or leased solar panels to pump water to irrigate the fields.

Poppy was the perfect crop in a dangerous, corrupt time: it required no bribes, and properly dried and stored as a paste, it lasted indefinitely. With the porous frontier of Pakistan's Balochistan to the south, it was also easy to smuggle out. In 2021, it added US$2.7 billion to the economy, the equivalent of over 10% of the country's legal GDP.

This came to an abrupt halt in 2022, when the Taliban banned poppy growing without any plan to make up what was a devastating economic blow to small farmers, especially in Helmand (in other places, enforcement was erratic, and production in remote areas of Badakhshan, Nangarhar and Kandahar actually increased). Nationwide, output plummeted 95%. Because of the scarcity, the lucky ones who had stores of opium paste and heroin were able to sell it at a handsome profit. In 2024, the price of opium in Afghanistan reached US$750 per kilo, a tenfold increase from 2022, when it stood at US$75 per kilo. International organised crime syndicates have stepped in (some allegedly linked to the Taliban), stockpiling supply and waiting for the price to rise even further.

In 2021 Myanmar became the world's top opium supplier, producing 995 tonnes in 2024 compared with Afghanistan's 433 tonnes. To support their families, former poppy farmers in Helmand and Kandahar have gone over the Durand Line into Balochistan and Khyber Pakhtunkhwa, renting land or sharecropping poppies there.

Driven by poverty and despair, Afghans themselves are heavy users (according to the UN, 10% of the population are addicts). Many have turned to cheap crystal meth or methamphetamine-based Tablet K pills. With the ready availability of the ephedra plant, which remains legal in Afghanistan, small producers in Farah, Nimroz and Herat provinces on the border of Iran, produce quality meth for a tenth of the price of labs in southeast Asia. The Taliban periodically rounds up addicts and takes them to centres where they spend 45 days. The only treatment is withdrawal.

1 | BACKGROUND INFORMATION

Coordination of Humanitarian Affairs has also asked donors for US$264 million required to repair Kabul's water treatment and sanitation system, but so far has received only a fraction of that amount.

AGRICULTURE Some 70–80% of Afghans depend on agriculture – in a country where only 12% of its territory has arable soil. In the past many farmers supplemented subsistence incomes by growing poppies, although this has now been banned (page 41). Many grow wheat (an NGO supplied seed and fertilizer), maize and rice instead, though often it is just enough to feed their own families. Some farmers hope to plant more valuable crops such as pomegranate, almond, pistachio and *hing* (asafoetida), although they take longer to mature. Many goods are imported from Iran and Pakistan. To aid farmers in the north, the government is digging the 295km Qosh Tepa Canal (page 248), 'Asia's longest artificial river', designed to transform 550,000ha of desert into irrigated farmland. It's in the face of opposition from Uzbekistan, one of the world's largest cotton producers. There are also concerns about the quality of the construction, especially after a major leak in 2023.

MINERALS From lapis lazuli to iron, minerals have been important to Afghanistan's economy since antiquity. The Taliban are pinning their hopes for the country's economic future on its vast deposits of lithium, chromite, rare earths, nephrite, copper, marble, salt, talc, lead, coal, cobalt, gold, silver, mica and gemstones. Although the United States poured half a billion dollars into extraction industries before withdrawing from Afghanistan, most of this mineral wealth is still in the ground. Today the Chinese (mostly), Russians, Iranians and others are more than ready to sign contracts. Yet serious problems remain: lack of infrastructure (notably railways), electricity, water sources, a lack of explosives due to the Taliban's pariah status, and sketchy security in remote areas.

Studies by the US Geological Survey and Afghan Ministry of Mines and Industry suggest the Hajigak Pass south of Bamiyan holds an estimated 110 million tonnes of iron ore. There are 3.6 billion barrels of oil and 4.5 trillion cubic metres of natural gas in the Amu Darya basin. The Chinese Xinjiang Central Asia Petroleum and Gas Company signed a contract in 2023 to extract the gas over 25 years. The TAPI (Turkmenistan–Afghanistan–Pakistan–India) gas pipeline project, initiated by the Taliban during their first rule, was revived in September 2024, although whether all parties can get along to make it work remains in doubt.

PRECIOUS AND SEMI-PRECIOUS STONES

Afghanistan is renowned for its precious and semi-precious gemstones, many of which are considered some of the finest in the world, including lapis lazuli, emeralds, rubies, red spinels (balas rubies) and turquoise. These stones are mined in various regions, but especially in Badakhshan, and are often used to create intricate jewellery and ornaments.

Perhaps Afghanistan's most famous export is lapis lazuli, a deep blue stone with gold specks that has been mined for thousands of years in Badakhshan Province (page 266). Lapis is used to make beautiful jewellery pieces, small carvings and other decorative items. Some of the highest-quality emeralds in the world are sourced from the Kunar and Panjsher valleys, highly prized for their rich colour and clarity. In addition, you can also find semi-precious stones such as garnets and agates in markets across Afghanistan.

Discovered by Afghan and Russian geologists in 1973, Mes Aynak in Logar Province is believed to be the world's largest untapped copper deposit, with an estimated 4.4 billion metric tonnes of copper ore – estimates that could yield 2.5 million tonnes of copper per year that could annually bring in US$300–400 million.

In 2007, the Afghan government signed a US$3 billion 30-year contract with the Chinese state-owned Metallurgical Group Corp (MCC) to exploit Mes Aynak, but arguments over the contract (a railway, a 400MW power plant and a coal mine were promised to generate the necessary power and transport but have yet to materialise) have led to delays. There are concerns about preserving the archaeological site (page 15); the Chinese have promised they would, but there are no plans for an independent monitor. Locals are concerned about water (very scarce there) and pollution (processing a single tonne of copper generates 200 tonnes of waste). There are also fears that the Taliban's lack of technical expertise may lead to the rampant exploitation of the site. For all that, work on the project began in 2024 with a road to the mine.

WOMEN There are few chances for half the population to earn a living, outside of farming, where in many cases they are the only breadwinner in the family. Government restrictions hit city dwellers hardest, and deprived Afghanistan of hundreds of doctors, scientists, engineers, journalists and more. Although it was rare in traditional Afghan society for women to work outside the home – only some 14% did before all of the country's wars and troubles – the Afghanistan Women's Chamber of Commerce in March 2021 counted more than 50,000 women-owned businesses, creating more than 129,000 jobs, over three-quarters of which were held by women. Today all businesses, even if all the work is done by women, must be owned by men.

Jobs that women have been able to do include teaching girls in primary schools, tailoring, producing food, carpet-making and other handicrafts and cleaning. Women wanting to pursue medical careers attended nursing and midwife courses until Akhundzada banned them in February 2024. He then banned any NGO that employed women from working in Afghanistan.

Poverty and lack of educational opportunities has seen impoverished families force their daughters, often still children themselves, into marriages in order to have one less mouth to feed – an increase of 25% since the Taliban take over. Some parents in the poorest villages have sold a child to be able to feed another.

PEOPLE

As might be expected in a nation divided by and set upon a great mountain range, Afghanistan's culture is influenced by those of its neighbours. Even as a fairly recent independent country, it has its own unique culture, even if its patterns are as complex and intricate as one of its rugs.

Located at the crossroads of Asia, with people coming and going and then often staying throughout history, Afghanistan not surprisingly has an extremely diverse multi-ethnic population, counting no fewer than 54 according to the National Statistics and Information Authority in 2021. But Afghanistan is hardly a melting pot. Ethnicity remains a very sensitive subject, especially as the civil war was fought along ethnic lines. Because even the name 'Afghan' is most closely associated with the Pashtuns (page 44), the issuing of national identity cards (*tazkira* and *e-tazkira*) has been fraught. It was decided to include both 'Afghan' and the ethnicity or tribe for each person, although others believe that will only heighten divisions.

1 | BACKGROUND INFORMATION

Described on the following pages are the main ethnic groups in the country by size, although all population figures are rough estimates: Afghanistan's most recent census, in 1979, was never finished, and there hasn't been one since.

PASHTUNS (Also known as Pathans, Pashtoons or Paktuns) Making up around 45% of the Afghan population, some 19 million Pashtuns are divided into 350–400 tribes and live mostly in southern and eastern Afghanistan, as well as over a broad geographical area of northwest Pakistan (home to over 46 million). Other sizeable minorities live in India, the UK and the US. The Durand Line between Afghanistan and Pakistan drawn in 1893 and ratified in 1919 was never accepted by the Afghan

PASHTUNWALI: THE WAY OF THE PASHTUNS

The Pashtunwali is a code of conduct and ethics pre-dating Islam and passed down over the generations in Pashtun tribal areas in Afghanistan and Pakistan, long before there was a central government. Decisions and judgements over disputes are made in a *jirga*, an assembly of leaders; a *loya jirga* is a great council called by a king or head of state.

The Pashtunwali has eight directives for personal conduct:

ASYLUM (NANAWATEY) Pashtuns must offer asylum to anyone who seeks their help, even if they are their enemies.

BRAVERY (TUREH) Pashtuns must defend their property and family.

COMMITMENT (QARAR) Pashtuns are expected to honour commitments and promises, even at the expense of sacrificing their own interests.

HONESTY (IMANDARI) Pashtuns should be honest and truthful in their dealings with others.

HONOUR (NANG) Honour is paramount, and it's essential to protect one's honour, and that of the family, especially the women (*namus*).

HOSPITALITY (MILMASTIA) Guests are sacred: a Pashtun must provide food, shelter and protection for anyone who requests it.

REVENGE (BADAL) Pashtuns are expected to take revenge for any wrongdoing against themselves, their family, or their tribe to restore lost honour.

SELF-RESPECT (GHAYRAT) Pashtuns are expected to have self-respect and dignity and not engage in any activity that brings shame to themselves or their family.

In 1809 an East India Company official with the excellent name of Mountstuart Elphinstone compared the Pashtun tribes to the Highland clans of Scotland: 'Their vices are revenge, envy, avarice, rapacity and obstinacy; on the other hand, they are fond of liberty, faithful to their friends, kind to their dependents, hospitable, brave, hardy, frugal, laborious, and prudent.' He became quite fond of them.

government, as it was imposed by Britain and divides what many Pashtuns believe should have been 'Pashtunistan'.

Originally a nomadic, pastoral people like many in the country, the Pashtuns were first mentioned around 1500 BCE in the *Rigveda*. Herodotus in c430 BCE called them Pactyans, 'the most warlike of all the Indians'. Pashtuns have also been called 'Afghans' since antiquity, from Aśvakan, the Sanskrit name used for the inhabitants of the Hindu Kush, first recorded in a 4th-century CE Greek document in Bactria.

According to Pashtun tradition, they are descended from Qais, a companion of the Prophet, and their various tribes were founded by his descendants. Theories that they descended from a lost tribe of Israel or the ancient Greeks are not supported by DNA, which has found that they are most closely related to other central Asians.

Traditionally, to be a Pashtun one must be a Sunni Muslim, speak Pashto, and follow the Pashtunwali, part code of honour and part tribal interpretation of Sharia law (page 85). While male Pashtuns have a good deal of individual freedom and participate democratically in *jirgas*, purdah has always been part of their culture for women, who are secluded in the home and expected to be covered from head to toe if they go out, in order to protect their family honour.

While Pashtuns have traditionally dominated politics in Afghanistan, they have never formed a homogeneous group. Rivalries for power and leadership have historically divided the two main tribes, the Durranis (who founded the Afghan royal house) and the Ghalzai. The 'Iron Amir' Abdur Rahman (page 29) forcibly relocated many Pashtun families to northern Afghanistan in an attempt to solidify and mix the country's population. Many would suffer reprisals from the Uzbeks and Tajiks after the collapse of the Taliban in 2001, even if they had nothing to do with the movement.

After the Soviet invasion in 1979, some 85% of the 4 million plus Afghan refugees in Pakistan were Pashtuns. Many have since then considered it home. Another 800,000 fled in 2021 when the Taliban took power. Beginning in 2023, citing security reasons, an upsurge in attacks around the border and the belief that the Taliban has been offering safe havens to the TTP (page 38), Pakistan has ordered Afghans to leave, even though many were born in Pakistan and owned businesses.

TAJIKS The second largest ethnic group, Tajiks are descended from the ancient Bactrians and Sogdians (the ancient region north of the Amu Darya). Today they make up around 25–37% of Afghanistan's population and are concentrated in the northeast, Kabul, and Herat Province in the west. Relatively wealthy and educated, Tajiks have traditionally formed Afghanistan's elite, with close links to the Pashtun Durrani royal family. Many Tajiks are fair, with blue or green eyes, and although tribal ties have largely broken down, they maintain ancient traditions of hospitality.

Pashtuns sometimes refer to Tajiks as Farsiwan, speakers of Farsi. Most Tajiks are Sunni Muslims, but a few around Herat are Twelver Shi'a. Badakhshan in the far northeast of Afghanistan is the only place in the world where the majority of the population, mostly Tajiks, are Shi'a Ismailis, followers of the Aga Khan, whose cultural foundation is still very active across Afghanistan. But the Taliban have increasingly pressured 'these infidels and non-Muslims' to convert to their Hanafi school of Islam, forcing many Ismailis to seek refuge in Pakistan.

Under Commander Ahmad Shah Massoud of Panjshir, Tajiks were key to the Northern Alliance opposing the Soviets and put up a fierce fight against the Taliban. They were well represented in the Karzai and Ghani governments, and reportedly have been targeted by the Taliban in the Panjshir, Kabul and northeast provinces in reprisals for their presumed support of the National Resistance Front (NRF), now headed by Massoud's son.

1 | BACKGROUND INFORMATION

HAZARA Some 6 million, or roughly 19% of Afghanistan's population, are Hazara, believed by some to be descended from the Mongols of Genghis Khan (the name Hazara comes from the word for a 'thousand' as if they were a great horde). Others say they are the heirs of the Kushans (page 20) and have lived in the central Afghanistan highlands ever since antiquity, as their features resemble the figures in the paintings around the long-lost Buddhas in Bamiyan.

Most Hazara are Twelver Shi'a (page 53), although some 5% (the Chahar Aimaq subtribe) are Sunni; a few Hazara are Ismaili. Hazara Sayyeds claim descent from Muhammad through his daughter Fatima. Many Hazara clergy have gone to study in the madrasas in Iran.

The Hazara speak a dialect of Persian called Hazaragi, and a majority still live in the Hazarajat homeland (Bamiyan and Daykundi and parts of Ghor, Uruzgan, Wardak and Ghazni provinces); other large communities are located in Kabul, Herat, Mazar e Sharif and Puli Khumri.

Men wear the *perahan tunban* (a loose, mid-thigh-length collarless shirt) made of *barak*, the special soft wool of lambs raised in the Hazarajat. Young boys and girls often wear pompoms on their caps. Hazara women have striking traditional costumes – long silk or velvet dresses in vibrant colours, often embroidered with gold or silver thread (*zari*), and enormous necklaces that cover their chests with silver coins, and often elaborate silver headpieces.

The Hazara have distinctive music and literary traditions, and a relatively high rate of literacy. The men are famous for playing the lute-like *dambura*; during the years of the Islamic Republic, many women worked as teachers and nurses. Marriage between cousins is frequent, but because wealthier Hazaras have more than one wife, there is a shortage of available women. Women often have seven or eight children, although because infant mortality is so high, they tend not to celebrate a birth until a child loses a first tooth.

Because of their Shi'a faith and distinctive appearance, the Hazara have long faced discrimination and poverty. They are estimated to have formed 67% of Afghanistan's population until 1890–93, when after meeting resistance to his rule in the Hazarajat, King Abdur Rahman Khan waged a genocidal jihad against them, massacring 60% of all Hazara, selling men and women into slavery and taking over their lands. Many fled to Mashad, Iran or Quetta, Pakistan; today the Hazara diaspora is estimated at 4 million. Even in the 1970s, there were firebrand Sunni mullahs who promised their followers that killing Hazaras was the key to paradise.

Since the 1960s, Hazaras have campaigned for equal rights as citizens, which under the Soviets many felt they had finally achieved. Others, notably the Hazara resistance group, Hezb e Wahdat led by nationalist Abdul Ali Mazari, fought against the Soviet occupation. In 1995, Mazari was captured and killed by the Taliban as Hezb e Wahdat withdrew from Kabul. In August 1998, the Taliban massacred thousands of prominent Hazaras in Mazar e Sharif (page 200) then in the following month they killed another 500 in Bamiyan.

In 2004, Shi'a Islam was recognised in Afghanistan's constitution for the first time. But little development aid reached the Hazarajat under the Islamic Republic, forcing many Hazaris to move to Kabul's Dasht e Barchi neighbourhood in search of work. So many were attacked by the Taliban and IS-K terrorists that the Bamiyan–Kabul route became known as 'Death Road'. With the return of the Taliban, government employees even in the Hazarajat have been replaced by Pashtuns, although recently, as the Taliban have developed closer ties with Shi'a Iran, they have softened their stance.

UZBEKS Most of Afghanistan's 2.5 million Uzbeks live in the far northwest district of Afghan Turkistan in and around Mazar e Sharif and Fariab Province. The most populous of several Turkic communities in Afghanistan, descended from the waves of Turkic Mongoloid nomads who swept through central Asia, they make up around 9% of the population of Afghanistan. Uzbeks are Sunni Muslims and have long been grain and cotton farmers and raisers of livestock, who like their Turkmen cousins raise karakul sheep and Qatgani, a Turkmen breed of horse that General Dostum famously rode in his cavalry charge liberating Mazar e Sharif (page 233). They are credited with introducing the sport of buzkashi (page 63) to Afghanistan. They are also business and craftspeople.

'Uzbek' comes from *uz* (independent) and *bek* (master). Because they settled in the northwest so far from Kabul (many arrived in the 1920s to escape Soviet persecution), the Uzbek community long enjoyed a great deal of independence. After officially granting them autonomy, the Soviets then tried to recruit many into the Afghan army – which backfired when leading General Dostum defected from the Najibullah regime and set up his own fief, and even his own airline, in Mazar e Sharif (page 232).

Uzbeki men often wear Western-style clothing but may sport an embroidered skullcap (*do'ppi*) and a chapon, with a shirt (*yaktak*) and loose trousers as part of their traditional dress. Women wear long colourful dresses and sometimes wear the do'ppi, and especially ornate ones with long dangling chains around their faces when they marry. Uzbeks, like all Afghans, love poetry and have their unique music and instruments. Women make rugs, and unusually for Afghanistan, pasta, which may have been introduced centuries ago along the Silk Road. Today there are occasional tensions with the Pashtuns who over the decades were relocated north and who today form the majority in former Uzbek areas.

KUCHIS (or Pawindas) In the Dari language, Kuchi simply means 'nomad'. Most Kuchi people are Pashtuns belonging to a dozen Ghilzai tribes and who have traditionally roamed the southern and eastern provinces of Afghanistan and the Registan Desert, herding their sheep and goats to wherever they can find pastures.

Their culture has strict gender roles. Men are the leaders, the khans of the clan (each clan consists of around 11 families, with 400–600 heads of livestock), ruling through jirgas. Men also do the herding and trading. Women take care of the children, milk the sheep or goats, and produce the wool or cashmere. They make their own clothing, three-piece dresses in dazzling bright colours, heavily embroidered, with sequins and mirrors sewn into the fabric; they also make silver plate jewellery, decorated with coins, beads and lapis lazuli, designed to be worn daily and which are meant to bring the wearer good luck. Some older women have geometric face tattoos.

The Kuchis' hard lives were brightened with festivities with shooting and riding competitions, music, and dancing, but now most have been banned.

For many, the term Kuchi evokes a romantic image, although today less than half of the estimated 2.5 million Kuchis in Afghanistan – who historically managed about half of the country's flocks for meat – follow this traditional nomadic way of life; those who still do, transport their austere brown goat's-wool tents and gear on pick-up trucks instead of camels. Over a million Kuchis are now settled or semi-settled, constituting the largest internally displaced community in Afghanistan. Many find themselves living in slums on the outskirts of cities, and lack the essential paperwork needed to access jobs and aid.

Up until the mid 20th century, Kuchi traders and their camel caravans supplied products such as sugar, tea, kerosine and matches to remote villages, and helped harvest crops in season. Since then, the nomads have faced the loss of that trade, in addition to wars, landmines, far more strictly controlled borders between Pakistan and Iran and serious clashes with sedentary communities, especially the Hazara. Kuchi people are seen as intruders now that farms and houses occupy their former grazing lands. Because they are Pashtuns, they were considered Taliban supporters during the republic and even more marginalised by others.

AIMAQ Not an ethnically distinct group, the estimated 1.8 million Aimaq are a traditional nomadic people living on the high plateaus of Ghor, Herat and Badghis; Chaghcharan in Ghor Province is their 'capital'. The Aimaq speak various dialects of Farsi mixed with Western Turkic/Mongolian. Some claim descent from the armies of Genghis Khan, though two of the six main tribes consider themselves Pashtuns and have adopted Pashto. In the past, the tribes would unite to defend themselves from invaders.

Aimaq men are known as great warriors and fought with the mujahideen against the Soviets. As with other nomads, faced with conflict and drought, most Aimaq (those who still have flocks) are now semi-nomadic or sedentary, living in mudbrick villages as subsistence farmers. They also weave valuable carpets, flat-woven rugs known as *kilims*.

Unusually in Afghanistan, Aimaq women have considerable status and can participate in councils, and are not afraid of voicing their opinions to men. They wear white or brightly coloured trousers (*tumbons*) covered with sequins (although they wear burqas in the towns). Marriages are arranged between young teenagers,

TURKMEN CARPETS

Although they represent a small minority of the population, Turkmen bat well over their weight in the Afghan economy. They aren't the only Afghans who make carpets (page 102), but theirs have a reputation few can match. They are pricey, but that's no surprise – each carpet can take nine months to a year to complete. Among the 24 Turkmen tribes, weavers from the little Esari clan are considered the best of the best.

Most Turkmen carpets are made exclusively of karakul wool. The fat-tailed karakul sheep have a dual fleece: an outer one of long fibres, and a very soft, curly inner one. They are sheared in the spring and often in September; the best carpets use the spring wool. The wool has to be carefully sorted and hand-carded, a task generally done by older members of the extended family, until all the fibres face in the same direction.

Then the wool is hand spun by specialist women and the yarn is dyed. Although market pressures have forced some makers to turn to synthetic dyes, many Turkmen still use the same high-quality natural dyes that have been used for centuries, time-consuming though they are to produce. Roots of the madder bush are used to create the famous Turkmen red; yellow comes from a wild flower called *zard-i-chub*; tannin-rich walnut hulls are used for dark brown; while pomegranate rinds and straw are for lighter tones. Esari carpets may use indigo for blue backgrounds. Older Turkmen carpets sometimes feature a rare natural green, much prized by collectors.

Once the yarn is ready, girls and women stretch the warp threads lengthwise, usually over horizontal looms as they are the easiest to pack up and transport. The ends of the threads are packed with a mud paste that hardens to keep the but girls in the Pashtun Aimaq only marry at 18 and can refuse husbands chosen for them by their fathers.

TURKMENS Living in northern Afghanistan, mostly along the Turkmenistan border, Turkmens (1.2 million) make up about 3% of the total population. Semi-nomadic, they speak Turkmeni, a language close to Turkish. Most follow the Sunni Hanafi tradition, although some, the Qizilbash who arrived in the 18th century during the reign of Nader Shah, are Twelver Shi'a and live mainly in Kabul; they now number around 30,000.

Formerly feared for their lightning raids on caravans, Turkmen tribes came from east of the Caspian Sea into Afghanistan at various periods, especially after the failure of the Basmachi revolts against the Bolsheviks in the 1920s. They settled between Balkh and Herat provinces, where they are now concentrated.

Turkmens in Afghanistan are farmer-herders and important contributors to the economy. They introduced karakul sheep to Afghanistan, whose pelts are significant export commodities. Turkmen women always receive a high dowry as they make valuable carpets (page 48), although sums have fallen under the Taliban. At the time of writing, a Turkmen bride's dowry is down to US$10,000 – although that is still high compared to US$800 for a Hazara bride. Unusually, the bride's family may compensate the groom's family with a small sum for raising him.

Both men and women wear red woollen robes called *chyrpies*, often covered with embroidery. Men wear *chapans* in the winter, while Turkmen women wear long, loose-fitted silk or cotton dresses called *koyneks* with embroidery on the neck and

---

threads from slipping, and then the weaving can begin. The number of women working simultaneously on a single carpet depends on the size. Often a beginner works next to an experienced weaver. Large carpets are usually made outside in the summer because few Turkmen homes have rooms big enough for the looms, while rugs woven on smaller looms are made in winter.

The weavers create patterns nearly always from memory. A common design features a single large octagonal medallion (known as an elephant's foot, *fil-pai gul* or Bukhara) surrounded by smaller motifs. Others have multiple small medallions or all-over patterns of geometric, abstract or floral designs (the intricate *bastani* pattern is a favourite); others concentrate on elaborate border designs. The more knots per square inch, the higher the quality of carpet – the average is between 50 and 200 knots per square inch, while some carpets have up to 1,000. When a piece is completed, the makers may burn a tiny bit of wool on the fringe, an old Turkmen superstition believed to make the carpet sell quickly. Carpets made for export are then shipped to Pakistan where they are washed, their knots expertly trimmed and the carpets then sold to dealers.

Some Turkmen carpets are special. Khal Mohammadi carpets from Andkhoy in Faryab Province are named after Khan Muhammad, a famous yarn dyer who invented their characteristic deep, intense reds. Then there are kilims from Maymana, which often use the natural, undyed browns, greys, beige and off-whites of the wool for a minimalist look. Other Turkmen carpet-making centres are Dowlatabad (hence 'Daulatabads', as Afghan carpets are sometimes called) and Shindbad, where the designs, almost unique among carpets made in Muslim-majority countries, can feature animals and stylised humans.

bodice and turban-like headdresses, often beautifully decorated, even with jewels. Both men and women also wear patterned *kalpak* caps and ornate leather boots; in winter men wear the big, fluffy white, black or brown *telpek* hats made of karakul wool with soft leather on the inside which take specialist families weeks to make; other Afghan men wear them as well.

BALOCH The Baloch people, traditionally pastoral nomads who speak a Western Iranic language called Balochi, are believed to have arrived in the Middle Ages from the Caspian Sea region. Originally Zoroastrians, some say they are the descendants of the ancient Medes. Just over a million live across a vast, mainly desert area in Kandahar, Helmand and in the Registan. Another 4.8 million live in Iran but the majority, some 14 million live in Pakistan's vast impoverished Balochistan Province, where Baloch militants have fought for independence intermittently since 1948 despite Pakistan's long-running and bloody crackdown. Other Baloch separatist groups are active in Iran, causing frequent border conflicts.

The Baloch are reputed for their colourful geometric embroidery on dresses and most other textiles, often encompassing tiny mirrors and coins. They hold poetry in high esteem, and have numerous heroic epics, often the subject of their songs. Dances often involve rhythmic clapping. In Nimruz, camel riding is a popular sport, as is riding Balochi horses, which have distinctive curved, turned-in ears – these horses are related to Indian Kathiawari horses, bred for desert conditions. A traditional Balochi dish is *tabaheg*, made of salted meat dried with sour pomegranate then cooked with rice.

PASHAYI (Also Pashai, Safi, Kohistani, formerly Alina) One of the most ancient peoples of Afghanistan, the approximately 400,000 Pashayi are an Indo-Aryan people related to the Kashmiri. Some say they are indigenous to the Kunar Valley and Laghman Province; others say they were pushed out of the more fertile northeast plains by the Pashtuns. Today they also live in the Dara-i-Nur Valley in Nangarhar Province, and in scattered communities in the Jaghori district.

Pashayi are considered Pashayi because of their Dardic language, although the dialects they speak are so local that Pashayi in different districts cannot understand each other. Many Pashayi consider themselves Pashtun who also speak Pashayi. Some in the Panjshir Valley are also known as Panjshiri, but are often lumped together with the Tajiks. Others identify with the Nuristani.

The Pashayi were first mentioned in the West by Strabo in the 1st century CE. Marco Polo described them as 'practitioners of sorcery and witchcraft' whose men wore gem-encrusted brooches and earrings. Today they take pride in being warriors; most Pashayi men carry knives and are said to be prone to feuds. They attend village councils similar to Pashtun jirgas. Agriculture (rice, wheat, maize, walnuts and mulberries) is their main source of income. Pashayi living at higher altitudes primarily raise goats but also sheep and cattle. Before converting to Islam in the 16th century, the Pashayi were animists, Buddhists and Hindus. Like the Nuristani they have a special regard for goats stemming from their animist days (their founding myth involves a goat who rescued and raised their ancestor when he was exposed as a newborn). Celebrations feature a circle dance, where young men and women hold each other by their shoulders and sing traditional songs.

NURISTANIS The Nuristanis inhabit the south slopes of the Hindu Kush, the second-most remote corner of Afghanistan after the Wakhan Corridor. Each of Nuristan's four beautiful wooded valleys has its own distinct Indo-Iranian language: Kati, Waigali, Ashkun and Parsun. Even the Nuristani say the languages are so complex that even the devil can't understand them, and even they struggle to understand people in the next valley. Unlike most Afghans, many Nuristani people, whose population is estimated at 167,000, are blond or red-haired and blue- or green-eyed, which has led to theories that they are descendants of Alexander's Greeks, or (more likely) the indigenous Indo-Aryan people of Afghanistan (page 17). Some have noted that Nuristani sports (shot put, javelin and discus throwing) are distinctly Greek.

The region of Nuristan, the 'Land of Light', was once known as Kafiristan. Eric Newby wrote in *A Short Walk in the Hindu Kush*:

> In 1895 the happy existence of the Kafirs as robbers, murderers of Muslims, drinkers of prodigious quantities of wine, keepers of slaves, worshippers of…the whole Kafir pantheon with its sixteen principal deities, came to an end when Abdur Rahman sent his armies under the command of his gigantic Commander-in-Chief, Ghulam Haider Khan, on a jehad against the infidel and converted them to Islam by the sword; probably the last time in history that such a conversion has taken place.
>
> According to his own admission, Abdur Rahman was thoroughly fed up with the Kafirs. He had invited their chiefs to visit him in Kabul and sent them back to their country loaded with rupees. With the money they immediately bought rifles from the Russians which they used to slaughter more Afghans.

Before their conversion to Islam, the Nuristani's Vedic religion, with one chief god, Yama Râja, and many local gods, resembled a primitive version of Hinduism. They carved large wooden, often equestrian, statues of their ancestors wearing funnel-shaped hats; Abdur Rahman brought 14 back to Kabul, which are in the National Museum (page 138). The ceremonies held by the shamans and priests frequently involved the sacrifice of goats, which held an important place in their culture.

The Nuristani were tough customers. It took Alexander a long time to conquer them; Genghis Khan avoided them (but then again, the Mongols tended to avoid the mountains). Timur, according to his autobiography *Tuzak-i-Timuri*, defeated some, and was defeated by others. They were the first in Afghanistan to fight against the Saur Revolution (page 32), and it was General Issa Nuristani, second in command after King Zahir in 1979, who declared a jihad against the Soviets. Many indigenous Nuristani were killed in the subsequent wars, starting in 1979 when there was intense guerrilla fighting, and later when the valley became a main entrance for the Taliban coming into Afghanistan from Pakistan.

Nuristani men are excellent wood carvers and make their own furniture. They herd goats and cattle which supply milk, meat, yoghurt and cheese, log the forests mostly to the profit of Pakistani timber dealers and dig (illegally) for rubies, emeralds and tourmalines. The women farm small terraced plots (*pattis*) on the mountainsides, growing potatoes, red beans, corn, barley, spinach, okra, onions and wheat. Although the community is Sunni Muslim, Nuristani women have never been required to wear the veil and don't marry until they are at least 20. They dress in reds, pinks and purples, with head coverings of black or blue sometimes decorated with sequins. If a strange man unexpectedly appears while they are working in the fields, they cover their faces with their scarves and turn their backs; most of the day, men stay away so women can get on with their hard, essential work.

The Nuristani used to have festivals with music including choral singing and dancing, although most of these have been supressed by Islam and the Taliban. Still, they won't eat poultry, as they believe birds represent dead souls.

1 | BACKGROUND INFORMATION

TATARS Most Tatars are Sunni and in Afghanistan have lived for centuries under the radar, while some migrated in the 1920s from Tatarstan (around the Volga River in Russia) to escape communism. It was European writers in the 13th century who added an 'r' to make Tatars into Tartars, because when they came west with Genghis Khan it seemed like they came straight out of Tartarus, or hell.

An estimated 100,000 Tatars live in Afghanistan today, mostly in rural areas of Balkh and Samangan in Afghan Turkestan, who work in agriculture. Others are traders. Most speak Dari or Pashto although a few still speak Afghan Tatar, an endangered language that the Afghan Tatar Cultural Foundation is struggling to preserve. They were only recognised as a community in March 2021 so they could have their ethnicity inscribed on their ID cards.

SHUGHNI First mentioned in Chinese texts in the 6th century CE, an estimated 40,000 Shughni today live in the far northeastern province of Badakhshan (most today live over the border in Tajikistan, where they once ruled a micro kingdom called Darvaz). An important Pamiri tribe, they speak an Eastern Iranic language called Shunghi-Rushani; most are Ismaili and scratch a subsistence living from high-altitude agriculture. They live in the same region and share characteristics such as clothing and lifestyle with the Wakhis (see below), and are often mistaken as such by visitors, but their languages are distinct, derived from very different linguistic roots.

WAKHIS (Also Guhjali or Khik) The estimated 23,000 'Mountain Tajiks' in Afghanistan live in 64 remote villages in the lower Wakhan Corridor on the left bank of the Panj River; their 'capital' is Khandud. Wakhis speak an Indo-Iranian language called Wakhi and most are Ismaili (page 262). Some live semi-nomadically, with herds of horses and yaks. Others are farmers. Wakhi communities also live in China, Pakistan and Tajikistan.

KYRGYZ A Turkic people, the Kyrgyz pastoral nomads of the Afghan Pamir and high Wakhan (estimated population of 1,400) comprise the most remote high-altitude community on earth. Originally from Siberia and northeast China, they fled the Mongols and settled in the high mountains between Russia and China in the 15th century, moving their white felt yurts with their camels, horses, sheep, goats and yaks twice a year to richer pastures, trading their dairy products and meat with the Wakhis for grains and vegetables. The Kyrgyz are Sunni, but hold some pre-Islamic shamanistic beliefs, especially in healing. Women and girls wear beautiful red dresses and tall hats with long white or red veils trailing behind like medieval princesses. They are very respected in their society, although the men, the khans, are always the leaders of their clans. Many dream of moving to Türkiye where some of their cousins have settled and nomad life is easier than on the roof of the world.

LANGUAGE

Many Afghans are bilingual. Most speak Dari, the country's lingua franca, which is similar to Farsi, or Persian. It's one of Afghanistan's official languages, along with Pashto, which is spoken by roughly half the population (for some useful phrases in Dari and Pashto, see page 276). Both languages belong to the Iranic family. Uzbek, Turkmen, Balochi, Pashayi and Nuristani are also considered official in the regions where they are spoken. Many Afghans also speak English or Urdu (especially around Kabul).

In addition, some 31 other distinct languages are spoken in Afghanistan, including 23 endangered ones, many on the eastern frontier belonging to the Nuristani, Dravidian and Indo-Aryan linguist families. Most Afghans do not speak Arabic, although the Taliban have started changing place names into Arabic, usually to erase remnants of former regimes and heroes; for instance, Charikar, the provincial capital of Parwan, an ancient city with Buddhist roots, is now officially Imam Azam.

RELIGION AND BELIEFS

ISLAM Nearly all Afghans are Muslim. The majority belong to the **Hanafi School**, one of the four main branches of Sunni Islam, based on the teachings of the jurist and theologian Abu Hanafa (c699–767CE). Hanafi Islam relies on the study of law and the reasoning of the worshippers. Mullahs (clergy or scholars) influence juridical, ritual, educational and cultural life.

Some 10–15% of Afghans, mainly the Hazara, are **Twelver Shi'a Muslims**, who believe that 12 imams followed the death of the Prophet Muhammad, beginning with his son-in-law Ali and Ali's sons Hasan and Hussein. The Shi'a (the name comes from the Arabic meaning 'followers of Ali') believe the Quran contains hidden layers of meaning that have been revealed by the imams. The 12th imam is the hidden imam, the Mahdi or 'the divinely guided one'. He disappeared in 874CE but Twelver Shi'a Muslims believe that he has been kept alive by God, hidden somewhere on earth, and will make himself known at the end of times and bring justice and equality to all.

Other branches of Shiism follow different imams. In Afghanistan these are mainly **Ismailis**, who considered the seventh and last imam to be Isma'il, whose son is the hidden imam and will be the Mahdi. They have been compared to Neoplatonists. Throughout history, hard-line Sunnis have considered both Shi'a and Ismailis apostates and have often persecuted them.

While fighting the Soviets, Saudi jihadis ran a programme to convert mujahideen to **Salafism**, a fundamentalist movement that seeks to revive Sunni Islam to its purest origins. Today there are several hundred thousand in Afghanistan, mainly in Kunar, Nangarhar and Nuristan. Their madrasas and mosques were closed under the first Taliban regime as the Taliban associate them with IS-K, although lately they have allowed them to reopen.

Afghanistan has an esoteric **Sufi** tradition going back to the earliest days of Islam, producing dozens of much-loved poets and spiritual teachers (*pirs*), who are honoured with *ziyarats*, shrines often containing the holy man's tomb, where many Afghans go to pray when in need of help (health, money, etc). The most famous of the Persian Sufi poets was Molana Jalal ad-Din Muhammad, born in Balkh in 1207 and who became known to the world as Rumi ('Roman'); in 2016, when Iran and Türkiye submitted a proposal to UNESCO, claiming Rumi as their joint cultural heritage, Afghanistan protested loudly. Once Kabul became the country's capital, the city attracted Sufi teachers and their followers who opened lodges, called *khanaqahs*; one of the oldest surviving lodges is Kabul's 18th-century Pahlawan khanaqah. Most Sufis are Hanafi Sunnis, and they used to teach poetry in Afghanistan's religious schools.

Under the communist PDPA, between 1978 and 1989, when religious teaching was suppressed, the Afghan faithful attended an estimated 94,000 'hidden mosques'. Sufi leaders were imprisoned, and many took refuge abroad. Because Sufism promotes spiritual reflection, co-existence and tolerance, the movement had to go underground again when the Taliban took over in the 1990s, but it enjoyed a revival under the Islamic Republic. Since the Taliban's return, Sufism is again being stifled, with the closing down of khanaqahs and the banning of Sufi clerics and university professors from broadcasting and debating.

OTHER RELIGIONS AND BELIEFS For centuries, **Hindus** and **Sikhs** formed Afghanistan's largest non-Muslim minority. In the 1970s, there were an estimated 500,000 Hindus and 200,000 Sikhs, living mainly in Kabul and Jalalabad. Hindus have lived there for as long as anyone can remember (a 5th-century CE sculpture of Ganesha was found in Gardez), while in 921CE the geographer Istakhri wrote: 'Kabul has a castle celebrated for its strength, accessible only by one road. In it there are Musulmans, and it has a town, in which are infidels from Hind.' The founder of Sikhism, Guru Nanak, came to Kabul in the 16th century and converted both Pashto and Dari-speaking Afghans; their community would later include Sikhs who arrived from India as merchants.

Today, after decades of war, terrorist attacks, religious persecution and severe limitations on education and jobs, only a handful of Hindus and Sikhs remain, nearly all men who have sent their families abroad (to India, Europe and North America) and remain to care for the last Hindu temples and gurdwaras in Afghanistan.

THE LAST JEW IN AFGHANISTAN

Jews lived in Afghanistan since ancient times. In the late 19th century, the country had an estimated Jewish population of 40,000, including many who had fled forced conversion in Iran. Large communities in Herat and Kabul spoke Judeo-Persian and were involved in the fur, cotton, wool and precious gem trades, with dealers in London. Numbers dropped dramatically after 1948, when many of the remaining 5,000 Jews living in Afghanistan emigrated to Israel or the USA – King Zahir Shah was the only ruler who allowed the Jews to emigrate without losing their citizenship. Others left after the 1979 Soviet invasion, except for two men who lived in Kabul's shabby Flower Street Synagogue: Ishaq Levin and Zablon Simintov, who happened to hate each other's guts.

Their falling out occurred in 1998, when Simintov, who ran a carpet shop, was asked to bring the elderly Levin to Israel; only Levin refused to go, thinking Simintov wanted to sell the synagogue for his own profit. After that the feud was relentless: if they spoke to each other, it was to utter curses. Under the first Taliban regime, Simintov accused Levin of renting rooms to prostitutes, and Levin accused Simintov of being a thief; the Taliban beat both of them. In 1999, Simintov's wife and daughters left for Israel, and when Levin died aged 80 in 2005 (of natural causes; the police had to make sure Simintov hadn't murdered him), Simintov lobbied Israel to pay to repair the synagogue; but as he was the last Jew in Afghanistan, no-one could see the point.

Simintov became a celebrity, giving up his carpets for a kebab shop and charging hefty sums for interviews to pay for his whisky and food for his pet partridge. Although he said he wasn't afraid of the Taliban, he was finally convinced to leave Afghanistan because of the threat of being kidnapped by IS-K. It turns out, however, a Jewish woman named Tova Moradi, a distant cousin of Simintov, left months later with her grandchildren, in November 2021. And now, as far as anyone knows, there are no Jews in Afghanistan.

EDUCATION

Before the reinstatement of Taliban rule in 2021, millions of Afghan women and girls were enrolled in education. Schools and universities employed nearly 80,000 female instructors, many of whom taught boys as well. Now there is a serious lack of teachers, especially in the girls' schools in rural and mountainous areas, where lack of security, poor infrastructure and distances to schools also combine to keep enrolment low. Family disapproval of schooling also plays a factor: 40% of girls, compared with just 3% of boys, never started school even before the Taliban's return to power.

Girls are allowed to attend public school up to age 12, although they can continue in madrasas, which, while emphasising religion, also do teach some maths, science and languages for families who can afford the tuition. In many provinces, the Taliban has linked madrasa attendance by daughters to a family's ability to access aid or jobs. Girls with internet access or who live in various cities can continue their studies with international or Afghan diaspora-run programmes such as Solax (w solax.org), the Parry Sound International School (w parrysoundinternationalschool.com), LEARN (w learnafghan.org) and Brac International (w bracinternational.org). Some women have gone abroad to further their education: some 60,000 were enrolled in universities in Iran, although after the 12-day Israel–Iran conflict in June 2025, most have been forced to return to Afghanistan.

While boys are free to go to school and university, those living in rural areas suffer from the same problems as girls, including a lack of teachers as women are no longer allowed to teach boys. If there is a male teacher, they are often unqualified, books are rare and corporal punishments are severe. Poverty is often another factor, forcing boys to work to help support the family instead of going to school.

Unless parents can afford the US$90–200 annual tuition to send their sons to private schools, their education is controlled by the Taliban, who insist on a militant religious curriculum similar to the one used in the madrasas where they themselves were taught. Wealthy donors keen on currying favour with the government have gone on a madrasa-building spree (currently there are around 22,000, with more under construction), where the teaching may include military training.

CULTURE

Afghanistan's cultural life has long been shaped by its deep-rooted traditions in architecture, music, poetry and visual art. While it may not offer the range of arts and entertainment found in more open societies, the creative spirit has not vanished. It simply finds new forms and quieter venues. Poetry, calligraphy, textiles and craftsmanship all continue to serve as means of expression and cultural continuity. In a time of uncertainty, these quieter forms of art remain essential to the Afghan identity.

ART AND ARCHITECTURE Today Afghanistan may have only hints of the great art and architecture described by travellers of yore, but they are well worth seeking out.

Graeco-Buddhist art Besides the remarkable Bronze Age finds from the Bactria–Margiana Archaeological Complex (page 16), Afghanistan's earliest distinctive art is the syncretic Graeco-Buddhist or Gandhara, named after the ancient Indo-Aryan region in northwest Pakistan and eastern Afghanistan. It's the most tangible legacy of Alexander the Great in this part of the world, combining the sensuous poses and elaborate drapery of Hellenistic art with serene, contemplative Buddhist facial expressions.

Local artists, initially Greeks who converted to Buddhism, left some of their finest works first at Hadda (page 15) before producing the earliest known human representation of Gautama Buddha. Lively, sensuous and full of imagination, the style reached its peak in the 3rd to 6th centuries CE under the Kushans (Bagram Ivories; page 141). You can see examples at the National Museum in Kabul, as well as in the fragments of frescoes in the caves at Bamiyan (page 171) and in the caves near the stupa at Samangan.

Early Islamic architecture The remains, especially the ornate stucco work of Balkh's 9th-century No Gombad Mosque (page 245) hint at what was lost to Genghis Khan. Other examples include the intricate geometric brick and tile work in the two Ghazni minarets from the 12th century (page 205) and the remote 62m Minaret of Jam (page 190), which integrates lapis lazuli in the design, along with verses from the Quran in Kufic calligraphy. It was built by the Ghorids, who also left the colourful Friday Mosque in Herat.

Timurids (1390–1507) Timur (Tamerlane) may have been a brutal conqueror, but he also loved art, and his heirs, especially Shah Rukh, his wife Gowhar Shad and Husayn Bayqara, made Herat the Muslim Florence of the 15th century. Examples of Timurid architecture, featuring brilliant-coloured tilework, are: the glorious 15th-century Friday or Green Mosque of Herat (1421), partially built around its Ghorid predecessor by Husayn Bayqara; the Gowhar Shad Mausoleum; the Ali-Shir Nava'i Mausoleum; the Gazar Gah; the sadly damaged Musalla Complex with its five surviving (out of an original 20) minarets, and madrasa and mosque complex; and the shrine of Khoja Parsa in Balkh. Herat's metal workers produced stunning vessels and lamps in bronze, brass and steel.

Manuscripts, often on Sufi themes, were written by master calligraphers and adorned with exquisite colourful miniatures, notably by Bihzad and his followers, reaching the very summit of Persian figurative art (scholars questioned whether the portrayal of the human form was proper, but the caliph ruled it was fine as long as no-one tried to portray Allah or his prophet). Many manuscripts were taken to Persia after 1510, where they survived, unlike the ones that went up in flames in a library north of Kabul in 1996.

The same century saw the construction in Mazar e Sharif of the Shrine of Hazrat Ali, better known as Blue Mosque, completely covered in glistening tilework in various hues of blue and turquoise, in a lavish neo-Timurid style.

Mughals After the decline of the Timurids, their art and architecture would influence Islamic styles from Istanbul to the east. After visiting his cousins in Herat, Babur, the future founder of the Mughal Empire, took the Timurid style to Kabul and India, where it met local Hindu art. By the late 16th century, Mughal architecture evolved into its own elegant characteristics, with few colours, pure lines and fine polished surfaces. In Kabul, the mosque in Babur's Gardens, built by his great grandson Jahangir, is a beautiful example that was visited by his son, the fifth emperor Shah Jahan, who later commissioned the Taj Mahal. The Mughal emperors inherited their love of gardens from Babur. The Nimla Gardens (page 156) are another rare survivor in Afghanistan, while lush Paghman (page 140) outside Kabul was one of their favourite retreats.

Nuristani architecture Long cut off from the rest of Afghanistan, the Nuristani built unique houses of timber and stone, often piled high on slopes so steep that one house's roof is another house's terrace. Many of the older homes and mosques, especially in the more remote valleys, are decorated with elaborate carved wooden doorways, pillars, beams and façades that are one of the joys of visiting this remote region.

Kabul architecture In the 1920s, King Amanullah, determined to make Kabul a modern, Western-style capital, built monumental public buildings in pastel colours in a style described as **Afghan Baroque**: the Darulaman and Tajbeg palaces and the **Shah e Do Shamshira** (Mosque of the King of Two Swords) are fine examples. There are also hints of this style in Amanullah's tomb in Jalalabad.

Traditional houses in the historic centre of Kabul were made of wood and brick. The houses on Kabul's hillsides, mostly built irregularly on government land, are made of mud brick adobe, designed to be warm in winter and cool in summer (at one point during the Islamic Republic there was a programme to jolly them up in bright colours, a few of which survive). People often made do with what they had: it's common to see shipping containers turned into shops.

Then there are Kabul's so-called **poppy palaces**, mansions resembling over-decorated wedding cakes built with profits from the drug trade. 'Narcotecture' combines ancient Greek with Mexican, Pakistani and everything else in between. Some have 60 rooms, all in marble and concrete, with garages for 50 cars. One belonging to General Dostum (page 232) had a massive interior greenhouse, aquariums and gardens; another was the 'safe house' where al-Qaeda leader Aiman al-Zawahri was staying when he was killed by US drone attack in 2022. Recently, as many were built on state land, the government has begun to expropriate these 'poppy palaces'.

Art today Visual arts in Afghanistan are now largely shaped by religious and cultural constraints. Under current regulations, the depiction of living beings is discouraged, so figurative painting and sculpture have virtually disappeared from public life. In their place, calligraphy, geometric design and architectural embellishment have taken prominence. Religious themes dominate, with Quranic verses and Arabic calligraphy adorning everything from wall hangings to carved wooden panels as artists and artisans draw on Afghanistan's rich Islamic artistic heritage.

Art workshops and small exhibitions still take place quietly, especially in places like Herat, which has a longstanding tradition of miniature painting and calligraphy. Some of these spaces now focus on craft-based arts such as tile work, embroidery and bookbinding. They offer a creative outlet that fits within current expectations while preserving traditional important skills. Perhaps the best-known Afghan craft, and one that is economically important for many communities, hasn't had to adjust to politics at all: carpet making (page 60).

LITERATURE Whether in Dari or Pashto, Afghans love **poetry**. Past rulers often patronised scores of poets, while wandering troubadours called *mutrib or sazinda* entertained everyone else with their songs and poems. The Persian poet Ferdowsi's massive epic, the *Shahnameh* ('The Book of Kings'; late 10th–early 11th century) written in couplets – and three times longer than the *Iliad* – was and is much loved in Afghanistan (part of the Persian Empire when the epic was written), where some of the most exciting action involving his great hero Rostam takes place (pages 229 and 240). He also wrote the first positive Persian tales of Alexander the Great.

1 | BACKGROUND INFORMATION

Most poems are composed either in rhyming couplets *(mathnavi)* or quatrains *(ruba'i* or 'Rubaiyat Quatrain', from Edward FitzGerald's translation of the *Rubaiyat of Omar Khayyam)*. A *qasida* is an ode, while the much-loved *ghazal* was beautifully defined by Cheryl Benard in *Moghul Buffet* (1998):

> The ghazal sings of that second of eternity when the eyes meet of the hunter and the prey. Petrified with fright, the gazelle is not able to flee; overcome with its grace, the hunter is not able to shoot. They each lose themselves in the sight of the other, but both knowing the moment is not designed to last; when it comes to an end, it is inescapable that the grace will be finished, and turned into carrion. All the energy of the ghazal hangs on the idea that this fatal moment is, in every respect, an analogy of love.

Afghanistan has produced a long stream of poets since the early Middle Ages, many of whom belonged to a Sufi order. In the 10th century, Balkh gave the world Rabi'a Balkhi, the first woman to write in Persian (page 246), and Molana Jalal ad-Din Muhammad, knows as Rumi (page 53), as his family fled west before Genghis Khan and he settled in Konya, Türkiye (or Rum, aka Rome, the Turkic name for Anatolia in the Middle Ages).

Herat's 11th-century poet Abdullah Ansari was the first of many from the city, which reached its zenith under the great Timurid Sufi poet Nur al-Din Abd al-Rahman or Jami (1414–92), who was inspired by the lyrical mystical love poetry and ghazals of the great Persian poet Hafez. Here too was Mir Ali Shir Nava'i who preferred to write in Chagatai (an eastern Turkic language), saying it was better for poetry, which later influenced Babur to write his own memoirs, *The Baburnama* (page 136), in the same language.

The warrior poet Khushal Khan Khattak (1613–89) first served in the Mughal army, then led the Pashtun independence movement, trying to rally the tribes against the Mughals. His output was extraordinary: he wrote more than 45,000 poems, among the first to appear in Pashto, on all subjects including falconry, while fathering 57 sons and 30 daughters. Another Pashtun poet, much loved on both sides of the border, was Sufi mystic Abdul Rahman Momand, better known as Rahman Baba (c1632–1706), although his gentle syncretism and humanism is considered un-Islamic by the Taliban, who bombed his shrine in his native Peshawar in 2009.

In the 20th century, Khalilullah Khalili (1907–87) was the poet laureate of Afghanistan, a Sufi whose works in Persian were also widely read in Iran. His mother was a Pashtun, his father a Tajik who served as finance minister under King Habidullah, but was then executed by the king's son Amanullah. Khalili's reputation as a poet saw him appointed Minister of Culture in the 1950s; he was a good friend of King Zahir Shah, and after Daoud's coup went into exile in the United States, where he did much of his writing. His best-known work is the *Hero of Khorasan* about the brief rule of Habibullah Kalakani (page 30), who was born in the same village. His English-speaking son was one of Ahmad Shah Massoud's right-hand men (page 145).

Pashtun women have a strong tradition of producing couplets called *landays*, many of which reflect their everyday life. Since most don't read or write, their poetry is oral, and generally only shared with other women – marriage, politics and sex are all fair game.

Poetry continues to hold a central place in Afghan society. It is not only a literary form but also a communal activity. Poetry recitals *(mushairas)* still take place – sometimes in private homes, cultural centres or in bookshops in larger cities like Kabul, Herat and particularly Jalalabad. These gatherings often involve the reading of classical Persian and Pashto poets such as Rumi, Khushal Khan Khattak and Hafez, as well as contemporary voices. Themes of love, faith, exile, war and longing are explored, offering a subtle but powerful form of emotional expression and intellectual engagement.

MUSIC Since the return of the Taliban to power in 2021, music has been effectively banned in Afghanistan. Music is no longer played on television or radio, concerts are not held, and music schools and academies have been closed or forced underground. However, as with many things in Afghanistan, music has

FILMING IN AFGHANISTAN

Benjamin Gilmour (w benjamingilmour.com)

Making a film in wartime may seem like a ludicrous idea. But in many ways the shooting environment brought a tension to our film *Jirga* that the audience responded to. *Jirga* – an Afghan word meaning a 'tribal court of elders' – is about an Australian soldier who returns to Afghanistan as a tourist in order to apologise to the family of a civilian he killed by mistake.

The film feels authentic because it *is* authentic. The story may have been fiction at the time it was written, but the setting was real and most of the actors played themselves. Apart from Australian Sam Smith who played the soldier, the rest were Afghan villagers and our Taliban kidnappers were ex-Taliban foot soldiers. No set-builds were required, no fake dust or spray-on sweat. We continuously dodged the risk of attack by insurgents and 'friendly fire' from British and American drones. Smith suffered a mental breakdown due to these ever-present risks, which added to the authenticity of the unhinged character he was playing. While taxing on us all, it was an unforgettable adventure that allowed us to experience the spectacular beauty of provinces such as Bamiyan and Nangarhar. The lakes at Band e Amir have a star role in *Jirga*, of course. They are an untouched natural wonder like none I have ever seen in my life.

That was 2016. But I've been back several times since, working on my next feature film, *Angel of the Taliban*. Shooting under the watchful eye of Taliban 2.0 has actually been much easier and safer than my experience on *Jirga* was. Officials of the Islamic Emirate of Afghanistan (IEA) in Kabul have been very helpful and accommodating. Moreover, the mujahideen who have taken over security in the streets and rural areas are incredibly friendly and courteous. Even travelling through very conservative provinces like Uruzgan and Zabul in the south, where some of the fiercest battles of the last 20-year war were fought, has been surprisingly easy. The Pashtun hospitality in these places remains as alive as ever, which is remarkable given the pain and suffering many Afghans in these areas experienced at the hands of foreign forces. The level of forgiveness and willingness to move forward to a new relationship with foreigners has been deeply touching. I hope this is also the experience of other Westerners now visiting this truly beautiful country which has, for the most part, fiercely preserved its traditional way of life.

Ben is the writer/director of the award-winning drama Jirga. *He is also a psychotherapist and guides former soldiers with PTSD back to Afghanistan for healing.*

1 | BACKGROUND INFORMATION

not disappeared entirely – it survives in private homes, family gatherings and on mobile phones. Many people listen privately – whether in the safety of their homes or quietly in their cars. Drivers often keep the volume low, and it's not unusual to hear soft strains of Afghan pop or traditional melodies on long taxi rides.

Still, Afghan music survives among the diaspora, in recordings and online, reflecting its rich ethnic and regional diversity. Traditional music includes the classical forms of ghazal and *rāg*, as well as regional folk styles associated with the Pashtun, Hazara, Tajik, Uzbek and Turkmen communities. Music is often deeply poetic, drawing from centuries of verse and oral tradition. The ***rubab***, considered the national instrument of Afghanistan, is a short-necked lute with a deep, warm tone. Other traditional instruments include the ***dambura*** (a long-necked lute popular with the Hazara community and in the north), the ***tabla*** (hand drums), and the ***harmonium*** (a keyboard instrument played with bellows).

In more recent decades, Afghanistan developed a vibrant pop music scene, especially during the 1970s and again in the 1990s and 2000s, often by musicians in exile. Afghan pop blends traditional melodies with modern rhythms and instruments, and it remains popular, especially among the diaspora. Notable Afghan musicians include **Ahmad Zahir**, often called the 'Elvis of Afghanistan', whose soulful voice and fusion of Western and Afghan styles made him a cultural icon. Other well-known singers include **Farhad Darya**, **Nashenas**, and **Aryana Sayeed**, one of Afghanistan's most famous female artists, now living in exile. Female singers, in particular, face heightened restrictions and risk, yet their voices continue to resonate – often shared digitally among fans both inside and outside the country.

CARPETS AND KILIMS The handwoven Afghan carpet is the country's most recognisable and respected textile product, with a history that stretches back centuries and a reputation for both beauty and durability. In 2003, UNESCO declared Afghan rug-making to be a 'Masterpiece of the Oral and Intangible Heritage of Humanity'.

Afghan carpets are characterised by deep reds, earthy browns and strong indigo tones, with intricate repeating geometric patterns and motifs. Turkmen communities are famous for them (page 48), but the Uzbeks, Baloch and Hazara also produce fine rugs, often with distinctive regional variations in style, colour and weave. Most Afghan carpets are still made using **traditional methods**: on horizontal ground looms in villages or on larger standing looms in workshops. The work is time-consuming – sometimes taking weeks or months for a single piece – and typically done by women, often as a form of supplemental income for their families. In the 1920s, King Amanullah commissioned some of the most beautiful and intricate carpets ever made, many of which are now in museums and private collections. In villages across the north, you can still see family weavers at work, although recently production has been moving to co-operative models.

In contrast to pile carpets, **kilims** are flat-woven and lighter, with no pile or knots. Their simpler, bolder patterns and lighter weight make them more portable and more affordable. These pieces are often used as floor coverings, wall hangings or even bed throws, and they come in a wide range of colours – from subtle, natural tones to bright, modern palettes, depending on the weaver and intended market. Baloch kilims and prayer rugs are prized; in dark shades of wine red, blue, grey and brown, they often feature a stylised 'tree of life' pattern.

The rare **Beljik rug** is woven with soft merino wool taken only from the belly of the sheep, then imported from New Zealand to Belgium to Afghanistan; they resemble silk carpets, shiny and colour changing in the light. A **Mauri carpet** (so named because the first weavers came from the Merv Oasis) is actually made with silk.

A more recent development is the **war rug**. Emerging during the Soviet occupation in the 1980s, these rugs incorporate images of tanks, helicopters, grenades, rifles and soldiers – woven into otherwise traditional patterns. Initially made by Afghan refugee weavers in Pakistan and Iran, they were a form of expression or protest, documenting the realities of war through the medium of craft. Over time, they became a niche collectible item; and they are still made today, sometimes as satire, sometimes as social commentary, sometimes purely for the foreign market. While not to everyone's taste, war rugs reflect Afghanistan's recent history and resilience in a striking and sometimes unsettling way.

OTHER TEXTILES While Afghan carpets are the best known, the country's women produce a wide range of other traditional textiles that reflect the country's rich cultural diversity. One notable tradition is the **Hazara needlework** of central Afghanistan, particularly in Bamiyan. Typically embroidered on to dark cloth with bright, geometric designs, this style of needlework is precise, symmetrical and full of character. It is often used for cushions, bags or small panels.

In the north, particularly in the Uzbek and Turkmen areas around Mazar e Sharif, Sheberghan and Andkhoy, you may come across *suzani*-style embroideries. These large, decorative cloths – usually made for dowries or household decoration – feature flowing floral and vine motifs stitched in bold colours on to a white or cream background. While more commonly associated with central Asia, Afghan-made suzanis are often beautifully executed and make excellent wall hangings or bed covers.

Also in the north, particularly near Andkhoy and among the Uzbek communities, you might find examples of *ikat* fabric, known locally as *abrbandi*. This is a resist-dyed textile that produces slightly blurred, vibrant patterns, usually on silk or cotton. Though not widely produced today, older or imported examples do appear in bazaars, often used for scarves, turbans or clothing. The Kuchi nomads of eastern and southern Afghanistan specialise in **mirrorwork** and **appliqué**. These pieces are often bright, bold and densely decorated, used for dresses, bags or household decoration.

Incidentally, the English word 'afghan' for a crocheted blanket goes back at least to the early 19th century when the British associated Afghanistan with colourful textiles, carpets and karakul wool; the first written reference was in 1831, when Thomas Carlyle mentioned 'Afghan shawls' in his *Sartor Resartus*.

CLOTHING The **chapan** is perhaps the most iconic outer garment in Afghanistan, famously worn by former President Hamid Karzai (which led at one point to him being designated 'the world's best-dressed man'). It is a long, padded coat, often in deep colours with striped patterns, traditionally worn over other clothing during the winter months. Predominantly an Uzbek or Turkmen outfit, chapans are lined with cotton and stitched in bold vertical or diagonal lines and provide warmth without being overly bulky.

The **pathu** (sometimes called a *patou* or *patwa*) is another traditional item – a large woollen cloak or shawl used by men across Afghanistan's highland areas. Typically draped over the shoulders or wrapped around the upper body for warmth, the pathu is especially common in Bamiyan, Ghazni and parts of the Central Highlands. They are often found in earthy tones – brown, grey or cream – and made from locally produced wool. These garments are not only practical for the cold, dry winters but also highly symbolic of rural and tribal Afghan dress.

1 | BACKGROUND INFORMATION

AFGHAN COATS

John Lennon helped popularise a craze in the 1960s and 70s when he wore an Afghan coat (fur inside and suede outside, covered with embroidered flowers) on the album cover of *Sgt Pepper's Lonely Hearts Club Band*. Since 2000, they have also been known as 'Penny Lane coats' – after the rock groupie Penny Lane played by Kate Hudson in the film *Almost Famous* – and come in three lengths: *pustinchas* (sleeveless or short-sleeved hip-length jackets – favoured by Jimi Hendrix); *pustakis* (knee-length, long-sleeved coats); and *pustins* (ankle-length, either as coats or cloaks). Originally nearly all were made in Ghazni, where men would cure the skins (sometimes bear, fox or goat, but usually karakul sheep), tan them with pomegranate rinds, then cut and sew them together, while women and girls embroidered them with red or yellow geometric and floral designs. In 1966, the coats were exported to London and beyond, becoming so popular that workshops also opened in Kabul and employed hundreds of people. Today they're back in style, although most of the ones worn by fashionistas are made outside of Afghanistan with fake fur.

The ***pakol*** is a soft, round-topped woollen cap, said to be a descendant of the *kausia* worn by Alexander the Great, usually in muted colours like grey, brown or black. Originating in Nuristan and worn widely across eastern and northern Afghanistan, it is commonly associated with the mujahideen fighters of the 1980s and has become something of a cultural emblem. The rolled rim of the pakol can be adjusted for warmth and fit, and the hat is prized for its comfort in the cold.

For something more exclusive, the **Karakol hat** – made from the pelt of newborn Karakul lambs – is a high-end piece of Afghan attire. These hats (also known as *astrakhan*) are traditionally worn by elders, tribal leaders, and high ranking officials, and are considered symbols of prestige and authority. Handmade versions can cost several thousand US dollars, particularly those made from high-quality pelts and finished with precision. Their signature texture – soft, glossy curls – gives them a unique and recognisable look. While less commonly worn by everyday people, they are still made and sold in specialist shops, particularly in Kabul and Mazar.

In the south, particularly in Kandahar, you'll come across the **Kandahari cap** – a flat-topped hat intricately embroidered with colourful geometric designs. These caps are worn with pride by men and boys and are often handmade in local workshops. The quality of the embroidery can vary, but the best examples are exquisite pieces of craftsmanship. Afghan men often wear turbans (*lungis*) in a dozen shapes and forms that can quickly unravel to protect the face from sand and dust storms.

Men's scarves, often in neutral shades or simple patterns, are worn wrapped around the neck or shoulders and serve both practical and stylistic purposes. Women's scarves, by contrast, range from everyday cotton hijabs to luxurious silk shawls with hand embroidery or embellishment, often worn loosely or wrapped more traditionally depending on the setting.

SPORT Sport for women is banned by the Taliban, but Olympic sports as well as traditional Afghan sports for men are allowed, which helps the Afghan Olympic Committee get their funding. As the Taliban government remains unrecognised around the world, the country is represented by the Republic of Afghanistan flag in international sports. Six athletes, three men and three women all residing outside the country, represented Afghanistan at the 2024 Paris Olympics in athletics, cycling, judo and swimming (the Taliban officially recognised only the men). Break dancer Manizha Talash, however, was disqualified for wearing a cape with the slogan 'Free Afghan Women'.

In 2025, the Taliban leadership added chess to the list of banned sports, claiming it promotes gambling.

Traditional sports

✳ **Buzkashi** Said to have been inspired by Genghis Khan's hordes, galloping pell-mell into villages and making off with the women and livestock, buzkashi – literally 'get the goat' – is Afghanistan's national sport. It is best described as rugby on horseback but with a 25kg dead goat instead of a ball. It is played with great skill, as well as copious amounts of violence. Rules and team numbers vary, but the simple object of the game is for one team to get the goat into a circle marked on the ground. Beyond that, anything goes. Fists and whips are frequently used by opposing players to try to persuade the man with the goat to drop it.

The players, known as *chapandaz*, are local heroes and earn a good enough wage not to have to work beyond the few days each winter during the buzkashi season. The best buzkashi horses can cost up to US$250,000 and have their own security teams. The goat itself is headless and has the organs removed before the carcass is soaked in salt to toughen the flesh. These days, though, you're more likely to see fake rubber goats.

You can often find matches between mid-November and mid-March in northern cities and towns, as well as Herat. However, the spiritual home of buzkashi in Afghanistan is Mazar e Sharif. If you are in Afghanistan in winter, it is well worth checking out a game.

Cock fighting Bird fighting, actually fought between partridges and sometimes quail, remains a popular traditional pastime in parts of Afghanistan, especially on Fridays and during public holidays. These events are typically held in winter, in open spaces or courtyards, drawing crowds of men who gather to watch, bet and cheer. Though officially discouraged and frowned upon by the authorities, fights continue in many areas, particularly in cities such as Kabul, Mazar and Jalalabad. The atmosphere is loud and competitive, with the birds specially trained. Unlike in many countries where cock fighting is part of the culture, the birds do not wear spurs and fights are not to the death. Dog fights and even camel fights also take place in Afghanistan.

Ghorsai The Taliban approve of this traditional Afghan hopping sport, and in fact in 2022 they started a proper league and standardised the rules, which are quite simple: teams of four hop around on one leg and try to knock over the other team. It is also played informally by children and young men across Afghanistan.

Kaftar bazi Keeping pigeons is a beloved pastime in Afghanistan, particularly in Kabul. *Kaftar bazi* ('pigeon playing') enthusiasts train their flocks to fly in elegant, co-ordinated patterns, often competing to lure rival pigeons from neighbouring rooftops. The practice is especially popular in the early mornings and evenings, when the sky fills with circling birds.

✳ **Kite flying** Made famous by Khaled Hosseini's novel *The Kite Runner* (2003), and the film of the same name, making kites from coloured tissue paper and bamboo sticks is a traditional, joyful part of Afghan culture played by boys who would try to knock their opponents' kites out of the sky in aerial battles using razor sharp string coated in powdered glass and flour. It has been banned by the Taliban, but you may still see kites flitting over Kabul.

Tent pegging Riding a galloping horse while leaning over with a sabre or lance to extract tent pegs or other items on the ground is an ancient equestrian sport that once formed part of cavalry training. Despite its name, which suggests riders storming into a camp at dawn and upping pegs to make tents collapse on their enemies, the sport is believed to have begun in India as a way to deal with war elephants – stabbing them between their toes would make them rear up and throw their riders. Afghanistan is one of 28 countries that compete in the International Tent Pegging Federation.

Tokham Jangi In this game, which translates as 'egg war', players tap a hard-boiled egg against their opponent's egg until one egg cracks without cracking their own – the losing cracked egg goes to the winner. Tokham Jangi used to be celebrated during Nau Ruz (page 238) but is now officially banned, though you may still see kids playing in Bamiyan.

Zourkhaneh/Pahlevani A *zourkhaneh*, or 'house of strength', is a special round, domed gymnasium, which is also the general name for the mix of martial arts, calisthenics, strength training and wrestling that happens here, inside a sunken octagon called the *gowd*. Around the gowd are seats for spectators (men only), with raised seats for the drummer and for the man who chants the Persian poetry that accompanies the sessions. First mentioned in the Safavid era, the training is believed to have roots in Zoroastrianism (page 239), with its belief that physical and mental strength could be used to enhance spirituality; a strong man can also be kind and humble. Over time Sufi and Shi'a ethics were added. Zourkhaneh nearly died out in Persian-speaking lands, until 1934, when the millenary celebration of Ferdowsi's birth encouraged a revival.

A *miandar* stands in the centre of the gowd and conducts proceedings, which start with the *varzesh-e bastani*: participants do warm-up exercises, with the option of going off to one side, lying down and lifting heavy wooden boards with each arm. As the drum beats, the men do push-ups and swing heavy Indian clubs, one in each hand. Afterwards they take turns whirling around rapidly in the centre, swinging an iron bow with heavy rings on a metal string over their head. The wrestling that follows, *koshti pahlevani*, is divided into three weight classes.

Afghanistan has a national zourkhaneh team which competes against other countries (there are 72 in the International Zurkhaneh Sport Federation, IZSF).

Cricket Especially popular among Pashtuns, cricket is played informally in all Pashtun areas. Grounds in Kabul, Kandahar, Khost and Jalalabad host matches between provincial teams. Tournaments are held in the winter. When the national team, the Blue Tigers, coached by former English cricketeer Jonathan Trott, reached the semi-final in the T20 Cricket World Cup in 2024, the country celebrated with banned music and dancing in the street (except in the Taliban stronghold of Kandahar). The Blue Tigers' home matches are currently played in the UAE. Members of the Afghan women's cricket team who escaped are currently in Australia.

Football Along with cricket, football is the most popular sport in the country. Kabul-based Mahmoudiyeh FC, founded in 1934, is the country's oldest team.

Along with a national men's team, Afghanistan also fields a national under-17 team and a national futsal (indoor football) team. The women's national team is based in Australia.

Marathon of Afghanistan First run for men and women in 2015 amid the beautiful scenery of Bamiyan, the marathon attracted runners from across the country and abroad. For security reasons the date and route were not put in the public domain in advance and it was informally known as the 'Secret Marathon'. Women trained discreetly with the Free to Run (w freetorun.org) programme, and a film called *The Secret Marathon* (w thesecretmarathon.com), based on the story of famous Canadian marathon runner Martin Parnell who ran in the race, was made in 2019. The addition of a mini 10km marathon and children's run made it more popular, but since 2020 it has been paused because of the current political situation. For more information, see page 186 and w marathonofafghanistan.com.

Snooker In these austere times in Afghanistan it is a surprise to see that snooker is allowed by the Taliban. More than two dozen snooker clubs have sprung up in Kabul and in the other cities and it is becoming increasingly popular. The national team plays in tournaments and has done well in recent years.

Taekwondo This is the only Olympic sport that has won medals for Afghans. Rohullah Nikpa won bronze in 2008 and 2012 and is currently coaching New Zealand's national team. In 2024, when Paralympian Zakia Khudadadi, an Afghan Hazara woman who fled the country in 2021, won a bronze, it was the first time the Refugee team medalled in the Paralympics, or any other major competition. Khudadadi, who trains in France, dedicated her win to all women in Afghanistan and refugees.

Volleyball Volleyball is a popular sport and commonly seen being played in Afghanistan. There's a national men's team, as well as a women's team which competes abroad, made up of players from the diaspora.

2

Practical Information

WHEN TO VISIT

Afghanistan's climate varies dramatically depending on location and season. Much of the country experiences harsh winters, with heavy snowfall in the mountains making some routes impassable. The road from Kabul to Bamiyan and even the Salang Pass can be blocked by snow in winter. Summers, on the other hand, can be scorching, with cities like Herat, Mazar e Sharif and Kandahar experiencing temperatures regularly exceeding 40°C. Spring and autumn generally offer the most comfortable conditions for travellers. As one of the world's most conservative Muslim-majority countries, Ramadan and religious holidays (page 101) are strictly observed. As such these dates are usually best avoided.

FEBRUARY–MAY Spring arrives at different times across the country depending on altitude and latitude. In Kandahar, temperatures start rising as early as February or March, while in the mountains of Badakhshan, winter lingers well into May. Travel in spring offers a balance – mild temperatures at lower elevations and manageable cold in places like Bamiyan. It's also ideal for photographers, as winter rains clear the air of dust, creating excellent visibility. Spring was traditionally marked by the Nau Roz festival, though at the time of writing, celebrations are no longer held.

JUNE–AUGUST Summers are brutally hot in most cities, but this is the best – and often the only – time to explore the high-altitude regions of the Wakhan Corridor and the Afghan Pamir. The milder summer temperatures in Nuristan and Bamiyan also make these areas particularly pleasant for travel.

SEPTEMBER–NOVEMBER Autumn is arguably the best time to visit. The weather is stable and comfortable, the snow has melted from the high passes and it's harvest season, meaning Afghanistan's finest fruits – world-class melons, enormous bunches of grapes and other seasonal produce – are sold cheaply by the roadside.

DECEMBER–FEBRUARY Winter in Afghanistan can be harsh, with plummeting temperatures and barren landscapes making travel challenging. However, this season also offers unique experiences. Seeing the country under a blanket of snow provides insight into the resilience of the Afghan people. This is also the best time to visit the remote desert forts of Nimruz. For those seeking adventure, Bamiyan offers ski rentals, allowing visitors to explore the Hindu Kush on skis. Additionally, winter is the season for **buzkashi**, Afghanistan's dramatic equestrian sport (page 63).

HIGHLIGHTS

For many, the highlight of Afghanistan is simply being in Afghanistan. It can feel like being transported to another time and place when sitting in a *chaikhana* with a plate of kebabs and a steaming pot of green tea watching a stream of customers go about their business. Yet Afghanistan's location and history means it has a wealth of geographical and architectural wonders to enjoy.

BAMIYAN Although the giant Buddhas are no more, the enormous niches left in cliffs pocked with monks' cells are fascinating to explore, and the ruins of the cities of Shahr e Gholghola and Shahr e Zohak destroyed by Genghis Khan are unforgettable. Many visitors combine a visit to the Buddha Niches with the Dragon Valley, Band-e Amir National Park and walks through some of Afghanistan's most dramatic Silk Road landscapes.

BAND E AMIR LAKES Nestled high in the Hindu Kush mountains, these lakes in Afghanistan's first national park are one of the country's most spectacular natural wonders. Band e Amir refers to a series of six interlocking, deep, blue lakes surrounded by rugged cliffs, like a mini flooded Grand Canyon. The lakes are a vivid lapis lazuli which, after days of arid mountainous landscapes, looks completely surreal.

HERAT Herat is widely regarded as the country's cultural capital. Unlike many other Afghan cities, much of Herat's historic core remains intact, with its mosques, shrines and caravanserais not only offering glimpses into its illustrious past but also serving as a vital part of the city's present-day life. Once the capital of the Timurid Empire, Herat was a centre of art, learning and architectural brilliance. The Friday Mosque, the remains of the Musallah Complex and Gazar Gah each bear witness to the city's former splendour. Despite the passage of time, Herat retains an air of elegance, with tree-lined avenues, domed mausoleums and bustling bazaars that reflect its rich history. Beyond its architectural and cultural heritage, Herat also offers a more refined dining scene than other Afghan cities. During the summer months, the city comes alive in the evenings, with locals enjoying its vibrant atmosphere well into the night.

KABUL Afghanistan's sprawling capital enjoys a spectacular setting in the Hindu Kush, and in the past decades the city has grown to sweep up and around the surrounding slopes. Along with the city's celebrated sights – the Old City and its bazaars, Chicken Street, Sakhi Shrine, the Mughal Emperor Babur's Gardens and the National Museum – you'll find Afghanistan's most varied dining options. Kabul also makes a great base for day trips to the pottery village of Istalif, lush Paghman, Panjshir Valley or ancient Buddhist stupas.

MAZAR E SHARIF With its mix of Uzbek, Tajik, Hazara and Pashtun inhabitants, the largest city in the north has a multi-cultural vibe, an exquisite centrepiece in its Shrine of Hazrat Ali and a chance to take in a thrilling buzkashi match in its spiritual home in Afghanistan. From here it's easy to visit the vast, eerie walled ruins of Balkh, the 'Mother of Cities' with its Shrine of Khoja Abu Nasr Parsa and the exquisite remains of the country's oldest mosque, No Gombad.

MINARET OF JAM Afghanistan's first recognised **UNESCO World Heritage Site** is the world's second tallest medieval minaret, standing in an isolated valley deep in

TREKKING IN THE WAKHAN CORRIDOR AND THE AFGHAN PAMIR Wedged between Tajikistan, Pakistan and China, this strip of land, at times only 16km wide, offers some of the most spectacular high-altitude trekking on earth. The vast open valleys and dramatic snow-capped peaks of the Hindu Kush and the Pamir mountains are home to centuries-old Kyrgyz nomadic culture and a diverse range of wildlife including Marco Polo sheep and snow leopards.

SUGGESTED ITINERARIES

Afghanistan does not lend itself to tight schedules. Roads through the mountains can be closed (especially the Salang Pass), flights can be delayed and the need to register at the ministry in each city before visiting sites can be tedious. In addition, any drive away from the main roads becomes slow and eats up time.

TWO DAYS With 48 hours at your disposal, you should base yourself in Kabul and visit the city and its surroundings. First, head to either the National Museum or maybe the Omar landmine museum, depending on your taste. Then head to Babur's Gardens to pay your respect to the first Mughal emperor, and a quick trip to the nearby blue-tiled Sakhi Shrine is great for people-watching. After a quick lunch in a chaikhana, head to the Old City for a stroll through Afghanistan's largest bazaar, not missing Ko Faroshi, the bird market. Shopping for lapis lazuli trinkets and drinking tea with carpet salesmen in Chicken Street is a must before heading to Teppe Maranjan to see dusk fall over Kabul and maybe join in an impromptu cricket match. On the second day, take a day trip to the Panjshir Valley to get a sense of rural life in Afghanistan. Visit the tomb of Ahmed Shah Massoud, the great mujahideen leader, stopping for local fish at a riverside restaurant.

ONE WEEK With a week you could visit Kabul, Bamiyan and Mazar e Sharif. Bamiyan is famous for the giant Buddha Niches and is the jumping-off point for the stunning lakes at Band e Amir. Then drive back to Kabul and fly to Mazar e Sharif. Visit ancient Balkh where Alexander married Roxana and stand awestruck in front of the polychrome tile work of the Shrine of Hazrat Ali in Mazar e Sharif. Finally take the long, hard road trip from Mazar to Kabul, stopping at the Buddhist stupa of Samangan and crossing the 3,800m Salang Pass back to Kabul.

TWO WEEKS With two weeks you could visit Mazar e Sharif and Bamiyan, then attempt the central route across Afghanistan from Bamiyan to Herat via the Minaret of Jam: a rough but rewarding journey. After resting in Herat, Afghanistan's city of culture, return to Kabul along the southern road through the Pashtun heartland of Helmand, Kandahar and Ghazni. This wild 2,000km road trip will take in all the main cities and sights of the country.

ONE MONTH If you are planning to spend a month in Afghanistan it suggests an adventurous soul. What is more adventurous than obtaining your Afghan visa at the great border city of Peshawar in Pakistan and entering Afghanistan via the legendary Khyber Pass? After a night in Jalalabad, visit the mountainous pine forests of Nuristan, inspiration for *The Man Who Would Be King*. After this Kiplingesque entry to the country, follow the two-week itinerary listed opposite. Finally head into the high mountains of Badakhshan and drive to Lake Chaqmaqtin at the end of the Wakhan Corridor before skipping out of Afghanistan into Tajikistan. A truly epic traverse of Afghanistan.

ROADS LESS TRAVELLED Afghanistan is certainly not short of roads less travelled. However, if you are looking for parts of the country that are rewarding but rarely see visitors, here are some of the most intriguing and off-the-beaten-path journeys.

Farah and Nimruz provinces The far southwest of Afghanistan, bordering Pakistan and Iran, is an area seldom explored and brutally hot in the summer. However, those with a spare day or two will be rewarded with a striking desert landscape, complete with dried-up riverbeds, ancient forts and Zoroastrian ruins. The drive from Farah to Zaranj skirts the Iranian border and crosses the now-arid lake bed of Hamun e Helmand. Once a vast inland sea, it is now a desolate dust bowl, with abandoned boats scattered along its former shoreline – a haunting reminder of the region's changing environment.

Drive between Mazar e Sharif and Herat Follow in the footsteps of Robert Byron through the backwaters of Oxiana, from Mazar e Sharif to Herat. This journey takes you through desert Turkmen towns, remote villages and vast plains, with the rugged foothills of the Hindu Kush forming a backdrop. The roads are rough, and settlements sparse, but this is a part of Afghanistan that has remained largely unchanged for centuries. The journey offers an authentic glimpse into a way of life lost to modernity elsewhere in central Asia.

Cross the Anjoman Pass from Panjshir to Badakhshan For lovers of big mountains and epic journeys, entering Badakhshan via the 4,300m-high Anjoman Pass is something you'll never forget. The route, once an essential link for traders and travellers, is now an extremely rough track winding through dramatic high-altitude terrain. Towering peaks, deep river valleys and remote villages dot the way, making this one of the most stunning yet challenging road trips in Afghanistan.

Nuristan Tucked away in the northeast, Nuristan is unlike any other region in Afghanistan. Its lush pine forests, steep-sided valleys and intricately carved wooden mosques give it a distinct character, more reminiscent of the alpine landscapes of Kashmir than the arid deserts often associated with Afghanistan. Historically isolated and fiercely independent, Nuristan was the last region of Afghanistan to be converted to Islam in the late 19th century. Today, its unique culture, traditional wooden villages and sports make it a fascinating yet rarely visited destination. Those venturing here will find a land of pristine rivers, hidden mountain trails and communities that have preserved their ancient way of life.

Loya Paktia The provinces of Paktia, Paktika, Logar and Khost are unlikely to feature on the typical highlights list of Afghanistan, but for those interested in Afghanistan's Pashtun borderland, this is a region that has rarely seen outside visitors. Loya Paktia has long played a role in Afghanistan's turbulent history, making it a fascinating, if challenging, area to explore. In the summer months, thousands visit Aryob Zazi on the border of Pakistan to picnic and escape the heat.

2 | PRACTICAL INFORMATION

TOUR OPERATORS

Independent travel in Afghanistan is possible, but it's not for the faint-hearted and navigating the country can present significant challenges: English is rarely spoken by government officials or security forces; road signs are almost non-existent, and online maps are often inaccurate, making travel difficult without local knowledge; obtaining the necessary permissions in Kabul (page 122) and in each province can be complicated without a strong command of Dari or Pashto; at checkpoints, without the ability to communicate effectively, misunderstandings can arise, sometimes leading to detention; Afghan laws and customs are not always clearly communicated by the authorities, meaning that even small cultural missteps can result in unexpected complications – all of this before even considering the security risks posed by anti-government groups. Photography is another sensitive issue – many government and military buildings are unmarked, and taking photos in the wrong place can quickly lead to trouble.

While hiring a guide is not mandatory, travelling with one minimises the difficulties you might encounter.

Since the Taliban's return to power, the number of tour operators in Afghanistan has increased. Below is a list of the most experienced companies currently operating in the country. A reputable tour operator should be able to demonstrate a thorough risk-assessment process and a strong track record of guiding and working in Afghanistan.

IN THE UK

Lupine w lupinetravel.co.uk. Offers 9-day tours in winter of Kabul, Bamiyan & Mazar, including a buzkashi match.

Safarat w safarat.co. Offers a range of group & private tours from a long weekend based around Kabul to 2-week journeys 'From the Timurids to the Taliban'.

Untamed Borders w untamedborders.com. Untamed Borders has been guiding in Afghanistan since 2007 & arranges private & group trips including cultural trips, as well as ski, trekking & horseriding trips. The company also organises a virtual tour run by a female Afghan guide.

IN AFGHANISTAN

Afghan Logistics Hse #11, St #01 Ansari Sq, Shar e Naw, Kabul; +93 (0) 786 44 33 11; w afghan-logistics.com. Long-time & experienced local tour operator for Afghanistan. Now tends to be more involved in vehicle hire & logistics for NGOs. However, well worth contacting.

Let's Be Friends Azizi Plaza, Mazar e Sharif; +93 (0)729 216 144; w letsbefriendsafghanistan.com.af. Mazar-based company in business since 2015 offering a wide variety of group & private tours from 2 weeks across Afghanistan to the Wakhan Corridor.

ELSEWHERE

A2A Journey (New Zealand) e a2ajourney24@gmail.com; w a2ajourney.co.nz. 2 weeks of hiking & camping in the Wakhan & Pamirs.

YPT (China) e tours@youngpioneertours.com; w youngpioneertours.com. Highlights of Afghanistan & special women's tours.

RED TAPE

Afghanistan is famed for its warm hospitality, but when it comes to travel, visitors often find themselves navigating a maze of bureaucracy. It is very much a case of rolling up the red carpet and rolling out the red tape. Obtaining a visa and securing the necessary permissions to move around the country can be a complex process. Since the Taliban took power in 2021, procedures have changed multiple times and are likely to continue evolving during the lifetime of this guidebook.

The website of the Afghan Ministry of Foreign Affairs (w mfa.gov.af), which should provide all the information you need, isn't consistently updated. This lack of a reliable central resource makes planning challenging, particularly for independent travellers. For those venturing beyond Kabul, additional permission is required, and rules vary from province to province. It is advisable to check with local contacts or tour operators before travelling, as regulations can shift with little notice. Navigating Afghanistan's red tape requires patience, persistence, and a flexible approach.

VISAS A visa is required for all nationalities visiting Afghanistan. However, obtaining a valid visa can be challenging due to the limited number of Afghan embassies and consulates that issue them (for the current list and their contact details, see w mfa.gov.af). This is because the Taliban, who took power in August 2021, have only staffed embassies in certain countries. At the time of writing, only Russia (in July 2025) has officially recognised the Taliban as Afghanistan's government. Despite these challenges, Afghanistan has been strengthening bilateral relations, leading to the appointment of Taliban representatives in more embassies worldwide. Currently, most travellers obtain their visas on their way to Afghanistan in Dubai, Istanbul, Islamabad or Peshawar.

Be aware that visas issued by non-Taliban embassy staff from the former government, the Islamic 'Republic' rather than the 'Emirate', are invalid due to the lack of diplomatic recognition, even though their websites may claim to offer visas. Do check the latest embassy arrangements before making any travel plans.

Current visa process Before visiting an Afghan embassy or consulate, you must first obtain pre-approval from the Afghan government by completing a Visa Application Form. To begin the process, applicants must register on the official e-consulate website: w econsulate.mfa.gov.af. However, the platform is known to be unreliable, so it is advisable to complete this step well in advance of your embassy visit. At the interview you may be asked about your contacts in Afghanistan (the phone number of the guide or the hotels you have booked) and your plans, to show your flight tickets and any other visas (eg: for Pakistan). They may also ask which other countries you have visited. The main concern is that you are adequately prepared.

At the time of writing, the documents required are:

- **Letter of Invitation** – Some embassies and consulates require a letter from a tour operator. If you don't have one, try uploading a copy of your passport or you won't be able to send in the form.
- **Payment** – Visa fees vary by nationality and location but generally range between US$80 and US$150.
- **Passport copy and photos** – A copy of your passport's photo page and two identical passport-sized biometric photos are typically required. You must have at least six months' validity remaining on your passport and several blank pages.

As requirements may change, it is always best to confirm with the specific embassy or consulate before applying, and arrive early. Generally, tourist visas are valid for three months, allowing you 30 days' travel in Afghanistan starting on the day you arrive; however, **visa extensions** are possible and can be obtained through the tourism office of the Ministry of Information and Culture in Kabul (page 122).

Listed on page 72 are, at the time of writing, the most frequently used Afghan embassies and consulates.

2 | PRACTICAL INFORMATION

Dubai Villa 23 29B St, Al Jaffiliya, Dubai, UAE; +971 4 398 8229; e dubai@afghanconsulate.ae; w afghanconsulate.ae; ⏱ 08.30–14.00 Mon–Wed, 09.30–noon Fri
Islamabad Hse No. 56, Main Nazimudin Rd, Islamabad Capital Territory, Pakistan; +92 51 282 4505/6; e afghanembassyisb@gmail.com; w islamabad.mfa.gov.af; ⏱ 09.00–16.00 Mon–Thu
Istanbul 1. Levent mah., Levent Cd. No: 28, 34330 Beşiktaş/İstanbul, Türkiye; +90 212 343 87 22; e info@afghancounsulate.org.tr; w mfa.gov.af/en/page/31773; ⏱ 09.00–15.00 Mon–Fri
Mumbai 115 Walkeshwar Rd, Walkeshwar, Malabar Hill, Mumbai, India; +91 22 2363 3777; w mumbai.mfa.gov.af; ⏱ 09.30–14.00 & 15.00–17.00 Mon–Fri
Peshawar 10 Mall Rd, Peshawar Cantonment, Peshawar, Pakistan; +92 91 5285962; e cgap@brain.net.pk; w no website; ⏱ 09.00–15.00 Mon–Fri

REGISTRATION AND PERMISSIONS Every visitor to Afghanistan must register with the government in Kabul (or if arriving by land at the nearest major city). The registration process can be time consuming and frustrating. On arrival in Kabul, you must visit the Ministry of Information and Culture's **Afghan Tour Department** (opposite the Macroyan District; page 122; ⏱ 08.00–16.00 Sat–Wed, 08.00–14.00 Thu) and state which provinces you wish to visit in Afghanistan (if you're travelling with the assistance of a tour operator or travel agency, your guides may be able to arrange permission in advance without the need for this visit). The ministry will then issue a letter showing that permission is granted to visit the listed provinces. A fee – at time of writing 1,000AFN – is to be paid for each province requested. Note that only provinces in which you are planning to stay the night and/or visiting places of interest need to be listed. If you are merely passing through a province, you don't need to add it to the list. At the time of writing, the Afghan government was proposing that travellers could visit only if accompanied by a guide; do check before travel.

Once you arrive in each province, you must visit the Department of Information and Culture in the provincial capital and show the letter. This letter will then be authorised and possibly a short interview will take place. Once that is completed, then you can travel freely within that province. You may need to show the authorised letter at checkpoints and places of interest. Note that the process varies greatly from province to province. In some, such as Bamiyan, your guide may be able to send your documents to the department and avoid the interview. In others, such as Kandahar, you will need to visit the department in person for permission before being allowed to visit any sights. If you don't speak Dari or Pashto, this can be quite a difficult process. Since these ministries all keep the same office hours (⏱ 08.00–16.00 Sat–Wed, 08.00–14.00 Thu, closed Fri), figuring out which days to be in which cities is crucial when planning a trip.

In addition, you may need to register on arrival on domestic flights into Mazar e Sharif, Herat and Kandahar (see arrival information in the relevant chapters).

Even with all the correct documentation, you may not be permitted to visit certain areas if the provincial department does not want you to or the provincial intelligence or security services tell you not to. Finally, in some provinces the intelligence services can be extremely thorough. They may ask you in for questioning and to see your documentation at any time during the day or night. A few hours' delay at a police station or a late-night visit to your hotel room are not unheard of. It is not always clear what is wanted by these visits or detentions.

Additional permits Each government ministry is responsible for issuing permission to visit places that fall under their specific responsibility. For places of geographical and cultural importance, this is the Ministry of Information and Culture.

Should you wish to visit, for example, a school or a mine or a hospital, then you would need to seek permission from the Ministry of Education, of Mines or of Health, respectively. Generally speaking, people arriving as tourists will not be given this permission without the support of an organisation within Afghanistan which works in that sector. This mean that places such as the lapis lazuli mines at Sar e Sang in Badakhshan or the Buddhist remains at the copper mine at Mes Aynak in Logar Province are for all intents and purposes not possible to visit for a tourist. Also note the Wakhan region of Badakhshan has its own permit system (page 270).

GETTING THERE AND AWAY

Upon arrival in Afghanistan, you will need to complete an ID card. These are available at a small booth by the luggage collection carrousel at Kabul Airport. You will need two passport-sized photos. Do not throw this away as you will be asked for it when you leave. These ID cards are not always available at land borders so you might not have one to hand in if you arrive in Afghanistan overland but depart by plane. However, in such cases simply show your entry stamp indicating that entry to the country was at the land border rather than Kabul and the security staff will understand.

In certain situations, particularly at airports or when passing through checkpoints, security staff may ask you to 'prove' that your camera is indeed a camera by switching it on and demonstrating that it works. For this reason, film cameras can raise more suspicion than digital ones, as they cannot easily be 'turned on' or shown to function on the spot. If you are carrying a film camera, be prepared to explain it clearly and carry a digital backup if possible to avoid delays or misunderstandings.

BY AIR Most visitors arrive in Afghanistan at Kabul Airport. It has good links with Dubai, Istanbul and Pakistan, which is where most people obtain their visas (page 71). There are occasional international flights from Mazar e Sharif, Herat and Kandahar. However, these are less reliable.

FlyDubai (**w** flydubai.com), Turkish Airlines (**w** turkishairlines.com) and Air Arabia (**w** airarabia.com) are currently the major international airlines serving Afghanistan from Dubai, Istanbul and Sharjah in the UAE respectively.

Afghanistan has two airlines. Internationally, the government-owned Ariana Afghan Airlines (**w** flyariana.com) has links to Dubai, Jeddah, Ankara, Istanbul and Delhi, and there's a long-standing weekly flight to Moscow. Ariana used to have a particularly poor reputation for punctuality and reliability; however, in recent years this reputation is less deserved. Privately owned Kam Air (**w** kamair.com) flies to destinations in Pakistan, the Gulf States, Saudi Arabia, Uzbekistan, Türkiye and India, and bizarrely offers direct flights from Dubai direct to the new airport in Khost. Its business model has focused on leasing aircraft at low cost from airlines facing financial difficulties, often due to reduced flight schedules caused by conflict; hence the use of planes previously used in countries like Venezuela and Ukraine. There are also flights to Tehran with Iranian airlines such as Mahan Air, Kish Air and Yazd Airways, although these are often not seen on flight comparison sites due to Western economic sanctions on Iran. For Iranian airlines, we suggest visiting a travel agent in Kabul – due to the financial sanctions between most nations and Iran, it is not easy to book flights from outside Iran or Afghanistan.

OVERLAND Travelling overland into Afghanistan is always a thrill but border crossings can be chaotic and regulations can and do change. Before setting out,

2 | PRACTICAL INFORMATION

you will require a visa and sometimes additional permits for the neighbouring countries. If you are driving your own vehicle, you will also need a road permit (US$100 at the time of writing), available when you pick up your visa. Afghanistan's relations with its neighbours often change and as such borders can close without warning. Up-to-date information is also hard to obtain; one possible resource is iOverlander (w ioverlander.com), which features recent travellers' reports.

There is currently no road, let alone a border post between China and Afghanistan. However, at the time of writing, a road linking the two nations is being built over the Wakhjir Pass. Whether the route is one that travellers can use remains to be seen.

From Pakistan The most exciting entry point into Afghanistan is through the **Torkham** crossing from Pakistan. The route from Peshawar in Pakistan to the border winds its way through the legendary Khyber Pass (page 157). The border itself is chaotic and occasionally closes due to armed conflict between the Afghan and Pakistani military. The Pakistani customs officials will confiscate any cash over US$1,000. The Afghan health ministry may well insist that you take a polio vaccination on arrival so your first mouthful of food in Afghanistan is likely to be a sugar cube if entering from here. The other crossing available for international travellers from Pakistan is at **Spin Boldak**, south of Kandahar. This crossing links Afghanistan to the province of Balochistan, although it is a restricted area and permissions are required to enter Balochistan.

In 2005 and 2006 there was a special permission system that, with advanced planning and the correct paperwork, allowed groups to cross from the Wakhan Corridor in Afghanistan to Pakistan via the Irshad Pass. However, this permission was short-lived and it seems unlikely in the current climate that it will be restored.

From Tajikistan There are many crossings between Tajikistan and Afghanistan, but at the time of writing, entry from Tajikistan is currently only available at the **Sher Khan Bandar** border. It is the only land border in Afghanistan that issues visas on arrival. In fact, they do not accept any visas issued in advance from embassies or consulates and will insist on issuing a new visa. This may change as the Afghan government becomes more standardised. The border is busy with freight transport but not particularly so with passenger traffic.

The other border crossings between Tajikistan and Afghanistan are at remote stops on the Tajik Pamir Highway and are not busy at all. Historically, you could cross from **Khorog** and **Ishkishim** into Afghanistan. At the time of writing these are not open to international travellers; however, this is likely to change as the Ishkishim crossing is particularly handy for linking trips between Tajikistan's Pamir region to Afghanistan's Wakhan Corridor.

From Uzbekistan There is one crossing into Afghanistan at the **Termez-Hayratan border**. This is both a road and rail link albeit the rail link is for freight only. The crossing takes you over the Amu Darya River via the 'Friendship Bridge' used by the Soviet Union to invade Afghanistan in 1979.

From Turkmenistan There are two open borders between Afghanistan and Turkmenistan. The most reliable is at **Torghundi** north of Herat. There is also a very remote crossing through the desert east of Andkhoy at **Imam Nazar**. Turkmenistan is a country where you need to travel with a guide and at times additional permissions have been needed to visit areas close to the Afghan border.

From Iran The main crossing from Afghanistan to Iran is at **Islam Qala**. This is an extremely busy trading and transport link. There is another crossing that should be open at **Zaranj**. Note that the deserts around Zaranj in Nimruz Province are widely used for people, drugs and goods smuggling so expect Iranian authorities to be interested in you should you cross here.

HEALTH with Dr Daniel Campion

With sensible precautions, including appropriate immunisations, the risk of experiencing anything more than traveller's diarrhoea during your visit to Afghanistan is minimal. Ensuring you are up to date with routine vaccines and consulting a travel health professional for region-specific recommendations can significantly reduce health risks.

Travellers should be aware that emergency medical services in Afghanistan are limited and response times can be prolonged. Pharmacies may not stock a full range of medications, and counterfeit drugs are a concern. It is advisable to bring an ample supply of any necessary prescription medications and a well-equipped first-aid kit. In the event of a serious medical issue, evacuation to a facility in a neighbouring country with more advanced health-care capabilities may be necessary.

BEFORE YOU GO

Travel insurance When planning a trip to Afghanistan, securing comprehensive travel insurance is essential owing to the country's unique challenges and potential risks. However, travellers should be aware that many standard insurance policies exclude coverage for destinations where government bodies, such as the UK's Foreign, Commonwealth and Development Office (FCDO), advise against all travel. The FCDO currently advises against all travel to Afghanistan, citing security concerns and the heightened risk of detention of British nationals. Given these advisories, obtaining appropriate coverage requires selecting specialised insurance providers that offer policies for high-risk areas. Notable companies include:

Battleface w battleface.com. This insurer provides customisable travel insurance plans that cover destinations under government travel advisories, including Afghanistan. Its policies cater to adventure travellers & those visiting unconventional or remote locations, & offer benefits such as emergency medical assistance & evacuation.

High Risk Voyager w highriskvoyager.com. Specialising in medical & travel insurance for high-risk destinations, High Risk Voyager offers coverage for individuals travelling to areas where the FCDO advises against all travel. Its policies include emergency medical evacuation & repatriation, addressing the unique needs of travellers to Afghanistan.

Immunisations It is advisable to be up to date with all primary vaccinations including **tetanus**, **diphtheria** and **polio** – a three-in-one vaccine protects for ten years. Afghanistan is one of the few countries in the world where polio is endemic. Travellers visiting Afghanistan for four weeks or more should be aware that a certificate of polio vaccination given four weeks to 12 months before departure from Afghanistan may be required on exit. Similar restrictions may apply when entering from Pakistan. If you do not have a certificate, you may be asked to take a live oral polio vaccination at the border. Those for whom live vaccines are unsuitable (eg: travellers with a weakened immune system) should ensure they get a dose of the injected polio vaccine before travel. There is no risk of yellow fever, so no need to carry a yellow fever certificate. It is also important to be protected against **hepatitis**

A and **typhoid**. The hepatitis A vaccine comprises two injections given about a year apart. The course may be available on the NHS; it protects for 25 years and can be administered even close to the time of departure.

A **hepatitis B** vaccination should be considered for longer stays or for those working with children or in situations where contact with blood is likely. Three injections are needed for the best protection and can be given over a three-week period (if time is short) for those aged 16 years or over. Longer schedules give more sustained protection and are therefore preferred if time allows. Combined vaccines against hepatitis A and B are also available.

Injectable polysaccharide typhoid vaccines last for three years and are about 55% effective. Oral capsules (Vivotif) may also be available for those aged six years and over. A course of three capsules over five days similarly prevents around half of typhoid cases during the first three years after vaccination.

Pre-exposure vaccination against **rabies** should be considered by all visitors to Afghanistan, but is particularly important for travellers visiting more remote areas, especially if they will be more than 24 hours away from medical help and definitely if working with animals. For more information, see page 79.

Visit your doctor or a recognised travel clinic (see below), ideally around eight weeks before you leave.

Deep vein thrombosis Prolonged immobility on long-haul flights can result in deep-vein thrombosis (DVT), which can be dangerous if the clot travels to the lungs to cause pulmonary embolus. The risk increases with age, and is higher in obese or pregnant travellers, heavy smokers, those taller than 6ft/1.8m and anybody with a history of clots, recent major operation or varicose veins surgery, cancer, a stroke or heart disease. If any of these criteria apply, consult a doctor before you travel.

TRAVEL CLINICS AND HEALTH INFORMATION A list of current travel clinic websites worldwide is available on w istm.org. For other journey preparation information, consult w travelhealthpro.org.uk (UK) or w wwwnc.cdc.gov/travel (USA). All advice found online should be used in conjunction with expert advice received prior to or during travel.

IN AFGHANISTAN Afghanistan's **health-care infrastructure** faces significant challenges. The health-care system relies heavily on international aid, and the withdrawal of major funding following the Taliban's takeover in August 2021 has severely impacted the availability and quality of medical services. Many health facilities lack essential supplies and adequately trained staff, particularly in rural areas. Consequently, for major medical procedures, Afghans often seek treatment abroad, in countries such as India, Iran or Pakistan. The situation is further complicated by recent restrictions on women's participation in health-care education and employment. In December 2024, the Taliban banned women from attending nursing and midwifery courses, exacerbating the shortage of female health-care professionals.

If you need **treatment**, hotels in the main cities will have the number of a doctor and the details of the local hospital; otherwise, your guide or any business contact or friend will be able to recommend a doctor or dentist. However, even in Kabul facilities are basic and in rural areas almost non-existent. Due to the economic sanctions, any payments must be made by cash as credit cards are not accepted.

PERSONAL FIRST-AID KIT

As on any trip a small **medical kit** is useful. Consider some or all of the following:

- A good drying antiseptic, eg: iodine or potassium permanganate (don't take antiseptic cream)
- A few small dressings (plasters)
- Suncream
- Insect repellent; anti-malarial tablets; impregnated bednet or permethrin spray
- Paracetamol or ibuprofen
- Antifungal cream (eg: Canesten or clotrimazole)
- Loperamide and rehydration salts for diarrhoea
- Antibiotics may be prescribed for self-treatment of severe diarrhoea in those at high medical risk
- Antibiotic eye drops, for conjunctivitis
- A pair of fine-pointed tweezers (to remove caterpillar hairs, thorns, splinters, etc)
- Alcohol-based hand rub or bar of soap in plastic box
- Condoms or femidoms
- If going to remote areas, consider taking a travel thermometer

Should you need any assistance when in Afghanistan, contact a local pharmacy, although be aware that many sell 'counterfeit' medicines. Ideally, anticipate what you might need and bring it from home; otherwise, be sure to visit a pharmacy that has a good reputation with your guide or accommodation.

Potential medical concerns

Malaria There is a low risk of malaria in areas below 2,000m from May to November and there is a very low risk of malaria during the rest of the year. For most travellers, malaria tablets are not recommended and measures to prevent insect bites are advised. However, a minority of travellers will be advised to take tablets if they are travelling to risk areas. This would include longer-term travellers visiting friends and relatives, the immune suppressed, those aged 70 or over, pregnant women or those who have complex medical conditions. Options include atovaquone/proguanil, doxycycline or mefloquine and you should take advice from a travel clinic about which tablets are suitable for you. It is imperative to complete the prescribed course unless you have been advised by someone suitably qualified to stop.

Insect repellents and cover-up clothing can help ward off voracious mosquitoes. These should be used both day and night when mosquitoes are around. Products containing 50% DEET are considered effective and are safe for use in pregnancy and on children from two months upwards. For those who prefer a more natural approach, repellents containing eucalyptus citriodora oil can be used instead but this is less potent than DEET and must be applied every 1–2 hours. Another effective alternative is 20% icaridin. Mosquito coils can be purchased everywhere. Regarding other insects, avoid low-quality hotels and very cheap local buses; saving a few dollars can result in great discomfort.

Dengue fever and chikungunya Cases of **dengue fever** have only been detected in Afghanistan since 2019 and the few cases have been restricted to the seven border provinces of Kandahar, Khost, Kunar, Laghman, Nangarhar, Paktia and Paktika. Dengue fever is transmitted by aggressive day-biting *Aedes* mosquitoes and it is therefore important to avoid mosquito bites by covering up with trousers and a long-sleeved shirt, and applying insect repellent (page 77). Symptoms of dengue include strong headaches, rashes, excruciating joint and muscle pains, and high fever. The illness lasts only for a week or so and is not usually fatal. Complete rest and paracetamol are the usual treatments; plenty of fluids also help. It is especially important to protect yourself and consider vaccination if you have had dengue fever before: a second infection with a different strain can result in the potentially fatal dengue haemorrhagic fever. A dengue vaccine is now available in the UK and Europe, although it is used mainly in those who have had dengue once already, to prevent a severe second infection.

Chikungunya is a virus carried by the same *Aedes* mosquitoes. It occurs in periodic outbreaks and the symptoms overlap with dengue, although joint pain is predominant and some patients may develop ongoing and sometimes disabling joint inflammation. Two vaccines against chikungunya have recently been licensed, and may be recommended for long-stay or high-risk travellers.

Tick-borne diseases Tick-borne relapsing fever, caused by infection with spirochaetes of the genus *Borrelia*, is endemic in Afghanistan. Infections typically occur during the summer months in rural and mountainous areas in both the north and the south of the country. Tick-borne relapsing fever is treatable with antibiotics. To avoid this unpleasant disease and other dangerous infections transmitted by ticks, it is wise when walking in forested areas to cover up by wearing trousers tucked into socks and boots, and consider wearing a hat if there are overhanging branches. Always check for ticks at the end of any walk and follow the advice given below.

Leishmaniasis Although uncommon in travellers, a parasitic skin disease called cutaneous leishmaniasis is endemic in parts of Afghanistan. (A more dangerous 'visceral' form of the disease is far less common.) It is transmitted by tiny, blood-sucking, low-flying sandflies. Again, insect bite prevention with repellents and an

> **TICK REMOVAL**
>
> Ticks should ideally be removed intact, and as soon as possible, to reduce the chance of infection. You can use special tick tweezers, which can be bought in good travel shops; or failing this, with your fingernails, grasp the tick as close to your body as possible, and pull it away steadily and firmly at right angles to your skin without jerking or twisting. Applying irritants (eg: Olbas oil) or lit cigarettes is to be discouraged as a means of removal since they can cause the ticks to regurgitate and therefore increase the risk of disease. Once the tick is removed, if possible douse the wound with alcohol (any spirit will do), soap and water, or iodine. If you are travelling with small children, remember to check their heads, and particularly behind the ears, for ticks. Spreading redness around the bite and/or fever and/or aching joints after a tick bite imply that you have an infection that requires antibiotic treatment. In this case seek medical advice.

impregnated mosquito net at night are key to preventing infection. Consult your doctor if you notice a persistent skin lesion or an open sore in the weeks or months after travel.

Rabies Afghanistan is classified as a high-risk rabies country. Few dogs in Afghanistan are kept as pets, but beware of sheepdogs as they are trained to see off unwelcome guests. Stand still and if necessary, make as if you are throwing a stone in their direction, shouting angrily. If you intend to spend a long time travelling or are staying in rural areas, consider having a course of rabies shots before departure. Ideally three doses of vaccine should be given over at least 21 days.

Rabies is passed on to humans through a bite or scratch (or even a lick to an open wound) from any warm-blooded mammal. You must always assume any animal is rabid, and seek medical help as soon as possible. Meanwhile, scrub the wound with soap under a running tap or while pouring water from a jug for a good 15 minutes. Then pour on a strong iodine or alcohol solution. This helps stop the rabies virus entering the body and will guard against wound infections, including tetanus.

If you think you have been exposed to rabies, seek medical help as soon as possible to obtain the relevant post-exposure prophylaxis – your travel insurance helpline can advise you where to go. Those who have not been immunised will probably need a blood product called rabies immunoglobulin (RIG) injected around the wound and four doses of rabies vaccine given over 21 days. RIG is expensive (around US$800) and is very hard to come by – another reason why pre-exposure vaccination should be encouraged. If you have had the full pre-exposure vaccination you will not need RIG and should only need two further doses of vaccine given three days apart following the exposure.

Death from rabies is probably one of the worst ways to go, and once you show symptoms it is too late to do anything – the mortality rate is virtually 100%.

Travellers' diarrhoea Many visitors to unfamiliar destinations suffer a dose of travellers' diarrhoea, usually as a result of consuming contaminated food or water. Rule one in avoiding diarrhoea and other sanitation-related diseases is arguably to wash your hands regularly, particularly before snacks and meals. As for what food you can safely eat, a useful maxim is: PEEL IT, BOIL IT, COOK IT OR FORGET IT. This means that fruit you have washed and peeled yourself should be safe, as should hot cooked foods. However, raw foods, cold cooked foods, salads, fruit salads prepared by others, ice cream and ice are all risky. Drinking water can also be contaminated with bacteria, so stick to bottled water or take your own filter bottle.

If you suffer a bout of diarrhoea, it is dehydration that makes you feel awful, so drink lots of water and other clear fluids. These can be infused with sachets of oral rehydration salts, though any dilute mixture of sugar and salt in water will be beneficial, for instance a bottled soda with a pinch of salt. If diarrhoea persists beyond a couple of days, it is possible it is a symptom of a more serious gastrointestinal illness (typhoid, cholera, dysentery, worms, etc), so see a doctor. If the diarrhoea is greasy and bulky, and is accompanied by sulphurous (eggy) burps, one likely cause is the parasite *Giardia*. Again, seek medical advice if you suspect this.

Cholera Cholera is a bacterial infection that can cause severe diarrhoea and dehydration, spreading through contaminated water and food. Afghanistan experiences periodic cholera outbreaks, particularly during the summer months and after heavy rainfall, when poor sanitation and limited access to clean drinking water increase the risk of contamination. The disease is most prevalent in rural areas and refugee camps, where access to medical care and sanitation infrastructure is limited.

To minimise the risk of contracting cholera in Afghanistan, it is important to take basic food and water hygiene precautions as listed on page 79. If cholera is contracted, symptoms such as severe watery diarrhoea, vomiting, and rapid dehydration can develop quickly. Immediate rehydration is essential, either by drinking oral rehydration salts or by preparing a homemade solution with one litre of water, six teaspoons of sugar, and half a teaspoon of salt. Seeking medical help as soon as possible is crucial, as untreated cholera can be fatal. In severe cases, antibiotics may be prescribed by a health-care professional to shorten the duration of the illness. Most travellers are at low risk, but oral cholera vaccines are available for those heading to known outbreak areas or who are undertaking high-risk activities such as humanitarian aid work.

Heat illness and dehydration The sun can be very harsh in Afghanistan, in particular in the mountains. Heatstroke and dehydration are serious risks. Wearing a hat, long loose sleeves and suncream will help avoid sunburn. Prolonged unprotected exposure can result in heatstroke, which is potentially fatal. Try to stay out of the sun between noon and 15.00 when the rays are at their strongest. In the heat you sweat more, so dehydration is likely. Don't rely on feeling thirsty to tell you to drink – if your urine is anything other than colourless and odourless then you aren't drinking enough. Carry bottled water with you at all times and make sure you stop to drink it. For advice on rehydration, see page 79.

Tetanus Tetanus is caused by the *Clostridium tetani* bacterium. This can be found in soil, dust and manure and is commonly associated with rusty objects such as nails. Cutting yourself or otherwise puncturing the skin brings the bacteria inside the body, where they will thrive. Clean any cuts thoroughly with a strong antiseptic.

Immunisation against tetanus gives good protection for ten years, and it is standard care practice in many places to give a booster injection to any patient with a puncture wound. Symptoms of tetanus may include lockjaw, spasms in any part of the body, excessive sweating, drooling and incontinence, and the disease results in death if left untreated.

Mild cases of tetanus will be treated with the antibiotic metronidazole and tetanus immunoglobulin, while more severe cases will require admission to intensive care.

Snakes and scorpions Snakes are very secretive and bites are a genuine rarity. However, Afghanistan is home to a variety of species including cobras and vipers (page 11). Certain spiders and scorpions can also deliver venomous bites and stings. In all cases, the risk is minimised by wearing closed shoes and trousers when walking in the bush, and watching where you put your hands and feet, especially in rocky areas. If you are entering a ruined building from broad sunlight, make a noise to alert snakes to retreat. Shake out boots before putting them on to ensure no creatures have taken up residence.

Many 'traditional' first-aid techniques such as cutting into the wound or applying a tourniquet are dangerous and ineffective. The only effective treatments for a venomous bite are antivenom and supportive medical care. In case of a bite that you fear may have been from a venomous snake:

- Try to keep calm – it is likely that mild venom or no venom (a dry bite) has been dispensed

ALTITUDE SICKNESS

Acute mountain sickness (AMS or altitude sickness) can occur at any altitude above 2,500m, so travellers to (among others) the Hindu Kush, Safed Koh or Pamir mountain ranges are at risk. People with existing medical problems should seek advice from their GP or specialist before high-altitude travel. Further information on AMS is available from the Academic Unit of Respiratory Medicine (w altitude.org), the British Mountaineering Council (w thebmc.co.uk) and Medex (w medex.org.uk).

SYMPTOMS OF AMS If you spend more than 6 hours at an altitude of 2,500m or more, you may start to experience headaches, nausea and vomiting, loss of appetite, fatigue, breathlessness and inability to sleep.

PREVENTION OF AMS The single most important piece of advice is to take time to acclimatise. If you are travelling by land, increase your sleeping altitude steadily, ideally by less than 500m per day once over 3,000m. If you are flying straight to a high-altitude destination, spend at least two to three days acclimatising there before going any higher. Get lots of rest, drink plenty of fluids (but avoid alcohol), eat lightly and do only gentle exercise while you are acclimatising. If gradual ascent is not possible, consider taking acetazolamide (Diamox), which can be prescribed by your GP or at a travel clinic.

TREATMENT OF AMS If you are suffering the early symptoms of AMS, stop and do not go any higher. Always seek advice. You may be advised to rest for 24 hours, drink plenty of fluids and to take ibuprofen or paracetamol to treat your headaches to see if your symptoms improve. You may also be advised to descend 500m straight away.

HACE AND HAPE Left untreated, AMS can develop into the far more serious high-altitude cerebral oedema (HACE) causing swelling of the brain, or high-altitude pulmonary oedema (HAPE) when fluid builds up in the lungs. Both of these conditions are medical emergencies and can be fatal if not treated quickly. Casualties would need to be rapidly evacuated to lower altitude by stretcher or helicopter, as continued physical exertion would worsen their condition.

- Remove any jewellery or tight-fitting clothes from the bitten limb (most dangerous snakebites cause severe swelling)
- Immobilise the bitten limb by applying a splint
- Evacuate to a hospital, ideally on a stretcher to limit movement

And remember:

- Never give aspirin or other non-steroidal anti-inflammatory drugs like ibuprofen, which may exacerbate bleeding. Paracetamol is safe
- Never cut or suck the wound
- Do not apply ice packs or electric current
- Never apply a tourniquet
- Do not try to capture or kill the snake, as this may result in further bites

Scorpion stings are intensely painful and may cause generalised toxic effects. Pain relief is essential and hospital treatment may be needed. Specific antivenom against some species of scorpion may be available.

SAFETY

> May God keep you away from the venom of the cobra, the teeth of the tiger, and the revenge of the Afghans.
>
> Alexander the Great

Afghanistan has long been regarded as one of the most challenging and unpredictable travel destinations in the world. For much of the last 50 years, conflict, political instability and armed opposition groups have kept the country in a near-constant state of turmoil. Today, official travel advisories from the UK Foreign, Commonwealth and Development Office (FCDO) and the US State Department remain unwavering in their stance: do not travel. The risks include armed insurgencies, kidnappings, arbitrary arrests and detentions, and should an emergency occur, no consular support is available to foreign nationals.

However, despite its reputation for danger, Afghanistan is also home to some of the most hospitable and welcoming people in the world. For those who choose to visit, understanding the risks and taking proactive measures can significantly reduce the likelihood of encountering serious issues. Careful planning, the use of reputable local guides, and strict adherence to cultural norms and security protocols all contribute to a safer experience. Travel routes and accommodations should be selected with security in mind, avoiding areas with known instability. Additionally, blending in as much as possible by dressing conservatively and adopting local customs can help minimise unwanted attention.

Given the complexities of travelling in Afghanistan, taking a Hostile Environment and First Aid Training (HEFAT) course is advisable. These courses provide essential knowledge on situational awareness, conflict avoidance, emergency response and first aid, equipping travellers with the skills needed to navigate high-risk environments. While no amount of preparation can eliminate all risks, those who approach travel in Afghanistan with caution, cultural awareness and strategic planning stand a far greater chance of having a rewarding and trouble-free experience.

MAJOR RISKS

Armed anti-government groups Before the Taliban took power in the summer of 2021, the threat from anti-government groups was severe, with frequent attacks across the country. Since then, the overall risk has decreased, largely because the Taliban – formerly the largest insurgent group – now governs Afghanistan. However, armed opposition groups continue to operate. The most prominent of these, IS-K (Islamic State Khorasan Province), seeks to impose an even more extreme form of Islamist rule and foment sectarian conflict. Their attacks primarily target Taliban government officials, security forces and Afghanistan's Shi'a population, particularly in western Kabul.

In 2024, IS-K claimed responsibility for an attack in Bamiyan that killed three Afghan tourism workers and three Spanish tourists, highlighting their continued threat to both locals and foreigners. Other resistance groups, such as the Afghanistan Freedom Front, are composed of former government officials, military commanders and warlords who were part of the US-backed administration from

2001 to 2021. Their attacks are mostly aimed at Taliban government targets rather than civilians.

While the current risk of travelling between cities is relatively low, the security situation can change rapidly. A solid understanding of areas where these groups are active and staying informed of any developments is essential for safe travel.

Detention by the government Afghanistan is governed by a strict interpretation of Islamic law, and for visitors unfamiliar with local customs, it is not always clear what is and isn't permitted. Actions that might seem ordinary elsewhere can be considered serious offences in Afghanistan, sometimes leading to arrest and detention.

Since the Taliban took power in 2021, several foreign visitors have been arrested and held, often for reasons that may not be immediately apparent. Afghanistan does not have formal diplomatic relations with most countries, meaning there is no consular support if you find yourself in trouble. The best way to minimise risk and significantly reduce the chance of misunderstandings with authorities is to travel with a trusted, knowledgeable Afghan guide who understands local laws, customs and security protocols. An experienced guide can help navigate potential issues, avoid missteps and act as a crucial intermediary with authorities should any problems arise.

The following is a non-exhaustive list of actions that could result in detention:

- Anything perceived as proselytising, including discussing religion with the local population
- Photographing women, military installations, government buildings, military personnel or checkpoints (even if they appear scenic). Anything that could be construed as security-related is strictly prohibited and can lead to serious consequences. If in doubt, don't take the shot.
- Entering a mosque without permission
- Speaking to or even looking at women (if you are a man)
- Women travelling without a *mahram* (male guardian)
- Wearing military-style clothing or boots, as they may be considered government property
- Carrying or using drones and satellite phones
- Being out after dark, as curfews are enforced inconsistently
- Spending time in residential areas rather than established tourist spots
- Camping in remote areas without prior approval

Road accidents Statistically, road accidents pose a greater threat to personal safety than insurgent attacks in Afghanistan. Over 6,000 people die on the country's roads annually, equating to about one death every hour, far outstripping fatalities caused by insurgency attacks by six to one. The high incidence of traffic accidents is attributed to poor road conditions, inadequate vehicle maintenance and reckless driving practices. Travellers should ensure they travel in well-maintained vehicles with working seatbelts and consider hiring experienced local drivers familiar with the challenging terrain and traffic conditions. Making sure drivers have adequate rests is also important.

Mines and UXO Afghanistan remains one of the most heavily mined countries in the world, with decades of conflict leaving a deadly legacy of landmines and unexploded ordnance (UXO) scattered across the landscape. Mines were first laid during the Soviet–Afghan War (1979–89) and later by various factions during the civil wars

2 | PRACTICAL INFORMATION

> **LANDMINES**
>
> All sides fighting in Afghanistan since 1978 used antipersonnel mines, particularly Soviet forces and the Afghan government between 1979 and 1992. Despite pledging not to (Mullah Omar described the use of landmines as an 'un-Islamic and anti-human act'), the Taliban made liberal use of improvised explosive devices (IEDs) against coalition forces, as does the IS-K.
>
> The Mine Action Programme of Afghanistan (MAPA) was established in 1989, and in 2002, the Afghan government signed the Mine Ban Treaty of 1997 and oversaw the destruction of 525,504 stockpiled antipersonnel mines between 2003 and 2007. Over 18 million were removed by the UN Mine Action Service (UNMAS) between 1989 and 2021. According to the International Campaign to Ban Landmines, even in 2024 landmines killed and maimed more people in Afghanistan than anywhere except Myanmar, Syria and Ukraine. Explosive hazards block hundreds of square kilometres of agricultural land, grazing areas and irrigation canals. Since the return of the Taliban, MAPA has been severely underfunded. In 2011, MAPA employed nearly 14,900 people; at the time of writing, only 3,047 operatives are working towards eliminating these deadly leftovers of war.

of the 1990s and the NATO intervention (2001–21). Significant progress has been made in clearing contaminated areas. You may see large writing on walls in small towns which designates that the area has been cleared of mines. However, large parts of the country – particularly rural and mountainous regions – remain dangerous.

The greatest risk comes when travelling off-road, hiking in remote areas or exploring abandoned buildings and military installations. Many minefields are unmarked, and shifting terrain due to floods or erosion means that even previously cleared areas can become hazardous again. The safest way to avoid landmines and UXO is to stay on well-used roads and paths, follow the guidance of local experts, and never touch or disturb any suspicious objects. If travelling in areas with a known mine risk, hiring an experienced guide is essential.

Two museums in Afghanistan provide insight into the country's long history with landmines and the efforts to remove them: the OMAR Landmine Museum in Kabul (page 134), run by the Organization for Mine Clearance and Afghan Rehabilitation (OMAR), and the Jihad Museum in Herat (page 219).

If you suspect you have entered a mined area, stop immediately and retrace your steps exactly. Alert authorities or mine-clearance organisations about any suspicious devices.

Theft and robbery The risk in Afghanistan is relatively low compared with many other countries. Street crime, such as bag-snatching, is uncommon, and violent robberies targeting foreigners are rare. The strong cultural values of hospitality and community oversight deter petty crime, particularly in rural areas. However, that does not mean theft is non-existent. Opportunistic crime such as pickpocketing can still occur, especially in crowded markets in larger cities like Kabul and Herat. To minimise risk, keep valuables out of sight, avoid displaying large amounts of cash and store passports and important documents securely. Using a money belt or concealed pouch can help. When travelling, keep bags within reach and avoid walking alone at night. Staying in reputable guesthouses and following local advice on safe areas further reduces the risk of you being in the wrong place at the wrong time.

Other risks In rural Afghanistan, particularly in farming communities, large mastiffs are often used as guard dogs to protect livestock, especially sheep, from predators such as wolves. These dogs are typically fiercely protective and can be aggressive towards strangers who approach their territory. They are trained to be territorial and will often patrol the area, keeping an eye out for any potential threats to the flock. These mastiffs are known for their strength and size, with some even having their ears docked as part of a traditional practice to prevent injuries from animal attacks. While these dogs are loyal to their owners and are vital for the safety of livestock, they can pose a danger to travellers who may inadvertently wander too close to their territory or flocks. The dogs are not accustomed to outsiders and may view any unfamiliar person as a threat. It's crucial to be cautious around such dogs. Avoid making sudden movements or attempting to interact with them.

WOMEN TRAVELLERS

Afghanistan is a deeply conservative country, and the rights and freedoms of movement of women are heavily restricted by its governance. However, despite these challenges, Afghanistan can be relatively safe for female travellers, although 'safe' and 'easy' are far from synonymous. Travelling as a woman in Afghanistan comes with a range of unique challenges, limitations and cultural expectations.

SHARIA LAW

The Islamic Emirate of Afghanistan is the world's most conservative example of a theocracy, with political authority centralised in the hands of a supreme leader, Hibatullah Akhundzada, known as the Amir al-Mu'minin, and his close circle of clerical advisors. This ruling body, collectively referred to as the Leadership, wields absolute power over the state's affairs. Major policy decisions are made behind closed doors, without public transparency or participation, and are subsequently implemented by the country's civil service, judiciary and security apparatus.

As a Muslim-majority state, Afghanistan's governance is rooted in Sharia law, which serves as the foundation for its legal and political framework. Alongside Sharia, Pashtunwali – the traditional tribal code of the Pashtun people (page 44) – also influences many aspects of governance, particularly in social norms and dispute resolution. Laws governing dress codes, gender roles and public morality are rigidly upheld, with religious police and local authorities ensuring compliance.

In practice this means that beyond holy scripture and edicts from the Leadership there is no code of laws. If someone is deemed to have broken the law, then they are taken to the nearest town and questioned. They are either warned or imprisoned for a short period. There are no fines or misdemeanours. If it is a severe transgression then the accused goes to Kandahar to be judged by members of the Leadership. Punishment is prison and, in extreme cases, capital punishment. Capital punishment is usually by hanging within the prison but occasionally there have been public executions by firing squad. Under the current Taliban regime, there have been no instances yet of governmental approved public stonings. There is no due process and there are no lawyers.

> **TRAVELLING AS A WOMAN IN AFGHANISTAN** *Jane Eagleson*
>
> As a woman I have never felt unsafe travelling in Afghanistan, where female foreign travellers are treated almost as a separate species. We are not held to the standards of local women but also not treated the same as men. On my last trip, some checkpoints just waved us through after seeing a woman in the vehicle. My guide said that sometimes the Taliban found that easier to do than to work out how to engage with a foreign woman.
>
> I ate with my guides and driver and sometimes with their friends. Some restaurants have a family section that foreign women will be encouraged to use, but I never found much difficulty when I refused to be shut in with the women and children.
>
> The response of local people will be better and you will be treated with more respect if you wear culturally appropriate clothing. You will never blend in, but an *abaya* is comfortable and you can wear as much or as little clothing under it as you want. The head cover can be loose in the city but should be more concealing in remote areas.
>
> Unfortunately, it is difficult to meet local women, especially if accompanied by a male guide. Even sophisticated urban women are very careful about speaking when there is a man present. It is even more difficult to engage women outside of cities as most don't speak any English and are seldom outside the home. It's more relaxed in the Wakhan area and parts of Badakhshan, where it is possible to meet and speak with women, for instance, within a guesthouse-owning family. Guesthouse owners may also take you to local family homes to see the inside of the house and possibly speak with family members including women. It is possible to remove your head covering in some guesthouses.
>
> Foreigners are not supposed to visit private homes, but it is possible in cities if you can make contact. In my experience the male guide could not accompany

A key requirement for women travelling in Afghanistan is the necessity of a male chaperone, known as a *mahram*. This means that women must either travel with a male companion or hire a male guide. While it is not uncommon to see women in some urban areas walking alone or with other women, this is typically accepted only in the neighbourhoods where they live, close to their homes. In addition, many restaurants have men-only sections and also 'family' sections for mixed groups. In theory all women should eat in the 'family' sections although for non-Afghan women this is usually overlooked.

Additionally, there are locations where women are sometimes not allowed to visit, which has included the lakes at Band e Amir and the shrine complex of Hazrat Ali in Mazar e Sharif.

On public transportation or flights, women are not permitted to sit next to a man who is not their family or a mahram. If you do find your ticket places you next to a man you do not know then people around you will typically help arrange seating accordingly.

For advice on the dress code for women, see page 110.

TRAVELLING WITH A DISABILITY

Because of the wars, Afghanistan has one of the largest populations per capita of persons living with disabilities in the world, but there has been little progress in me, so there needs to be some language in common. Once inside, women take off their outer covering clothes, although older women may retain some sort of headscarf. Your hostess will check if you accept meeting any male members of the family. I visited a home where the younger brother and uncle joined us for a meal but otherwise only the women of the family socialised with me.

Take a gift if you are invited into a home. My guide suggested fruit. The woman who invited me gave me a scarf and some turquoise jewellery as gifts in return.

Women are not allowed to work for NGOs or the government except in specialised roles such as security personnel who examine women at airports, but there is no rule against women working in private companies, although they can't work with men who are not closely related. In Kabul, I visited a female-owned company, and in Herat a carpet-weaving workshop that employed ex-high school girls and a small complex of cultural workshops started by ex-university students.

I took photos of women in the family and two women-operated enterprises that I visited but did not post any to social media where girls or women could be identified. I took photos of men outside, usually after having my guide ask permission. They mostly agreed, even Taliban which seemed to surprise my guide. Taliban usually wanted to be photographed as a group rather than as individuals.

City girls with friends from school or university communicate by WhatsApp but can't meet up because they aren't allowed in a house with unrelated males such as a friend's father or brother, nor can they go out without a male guardian. In rural areas literacy is low so it doesn't seem likely that girls would communicate much outside the family if at all. The exception to this is Nuristan, where women do all of the agricultural field work and are outside together.

addressing their needs, much less those of visitors. You will not find modified or accessible transportation systems, or ramps or wheelchair-accessible toilets (most are squat). Lifts are rare.

The UK's gov.uk website (**w** gov.uk/government/publications/disabled-travellers/disability-and-travel-abroad) has a downloadable guide giving general advice and practical information for travellers with a disability (and their companions) preparing for overseas travel. The Society for Accessible Travel and Hospitality (**w** sath.org) also provides some general information.

LGBTQIA+ TRAVELLERS

In a deeply conservative society such as Afghanistan, where public displays of affection even between heterosexual couples cause offence, it's essential to conform to expectations and be extremely discreet at all times. Be aware that same-sex sexual activity is criminalised and can lead to long prison terms.

TRAVELLING WITH KIDS

Afghanistan is a very family-orientated place but, although Afghans love children and kids are warmly welcomed wherever they go, the rigours of travel in the country do not make it a suitable destination for younger children – generally those under

2 | PRACTICAL INFORMATION

the age of ten. Long road journeys, basic facilities, security procedures and limited medical infrastructure can make travel challenging, even for adults.

WHAT TO TAKE

When travelling to Afghanistan, it's important to be well prepared. You should consider packing the following:

- **Passport-sized photos and printed copies of your passport and visa.** The Taliban bureaucracy can change frequently, and sometimes additional documentation may be required, particularly in remote provinces where resources like power, photo shops and print shops can be scarce. We recommend bringing at least three passport-sized photos for the consulate or embassy, and two for arrival at Kabul Airport.
- **Plug adaptors.** Afghanistan uses Type C and F plugs (continental European style). Electrical goods in Afghanistan come from various countries, and plug/socket mismatches are common. Many hotels provide adaptors, and they can be purchased cheaply across the country. The voltage is 220V.
- **Footwear** including shoes or sandals that you can easily slip off and on when entering homes or ministries. Pack flip-flops for indoor accommodation or to wear in less-than-ideal bathrooms; sturdy shoes or boots are essential for rural areas or mountainous regions where the terrain can be rough. If you plan to travel into remote areas or hike, waterproof boots are a good choice.
- **Sunglasses.** The sun is intense, especially in summer. Quality sunglasses will protect your eyes from UV rays, which can be very strong in Afghanistan, especially in higher altitudes and in the afternoon.
- A **torch** is also important, as most areas, including city streets, are unlit at night. Pavements may hide dangers, such as uncovered manholes, and power cuts are common.
- **Power banks** are useful, as electricity can be unreliable, particularly in rural areas. Having extra power for your phone and camera is essential. In the colder mountain regions, battery performance drops rapidly. Batteries deplete much faster in freezing temperatures, so it's wise to carry spares and keep them close to your body to preserve charge. Rotating them throughout the day can help avoid being caught out.
- **A lens cloth or blower brush.** Afghanistan is a dusty country. Fine dust is ever-present, particularly in the warmer, drier months, and it can be hard on camera equipment. Keep your gear in a sealed bag when not in use, and try to avoid changing lenses in open, dusty areas.
- **Back-up memory cards** and some way to store your images, whether that's a portable drive or cloud access. Afghanistan's internet can be unreliable, so plan to work offline where needed.
- **Water purification tablets** if you will be travelling in rural areas such as Badakhshan, where bottled water is less available.
- **Mosquito repellent**, especially in the summer.
- A **sheet sleeping bag** can help ensure a more comfortable stay in basic accommodation.
- **Warm clothing** for winter travel or trips to the mountains, including jackets, scarves and thermals. Temperatures can drop sharply, especially at higher elevations, and it is essential to stay warm with insulated clothing, gloves, and a woollen hat.

- A **wide-brimmed hat** offers protection from the harsh sunlight, particularly during the hot summer months. Consider picking up an Afghan pakol (soft woollen hat), a practical item for both men and women, particularly useful in the cooler mountain regions or when travelling in the sun. In cities like Kabul, it's common to see people wearing **pakols**.
- **Wet wipes**
- **Tissues for the bathroom**
- **Hand sanitiser gel**
- Lastly, **small gifts** related to your home country make great presents for hosts. Consider bringing chocolates, photographs or souvenir items like tea towels or postcards, which are often well received.

MONEY AND BUDGETING

MONEY The local currency is the Afghan Afghani (AFN), with banknotes available in denominations of 5,000, 1,000, 500, 100, 50, 20 and 10 Afghani. Coins are now rare and are typically only found in souvenir shops. For smaller purchases, it's a good idea to carry lower-value notes, as change may not always be available. In some cases, shopkeepers may offer sweets or chewing gum instead of change if they lack the correct amount.

Due to economic sanctions, credit and debit cards do not work in Afghanistan, so it is essential to bring all the cash you will need for your trip. To exchange money, you can visit exchange shops (*sarrafi*) or street moneychangers, both of which are common in major cities. Street changers, who generally offer fair rates, are easily identifiable by their small glass boxes containing cash, a calculator, and phone credit cards (except in Herat, where they all seem to wear cowboy hats for some reason). US dollars, euros and sterling typically get the best exchange rates, with US dollar notes printed after 2013 being preferred. For less common currencies, exchange services are only available in Kabul.

In border cities like Herat, Jalalabad and Mazar e Sharif, currencies from neighbouring countries such as Iranian rials, Pakistani rupees and Uzbek som are easily exchanged. Many larger hotels and travel agencies will accept foreign currencies like US dollars or euros for payment.

When entering Afghanistan, you can bring up to US$10,000. However, if crossing the land border from Pakistan, any amount over US$1,000 may be confiscated by authorities. Money transfer services such as Moneygram, Western Union and Ria operate in Afghanistan should you need additional funds.

BUDGETING Afghanistan is an inexpensive country for many items including food and public transportation, although accommodation is usually more expensive and of a lower quality than in neighbouring lands. If travelling with a tour company, you can expect to be charged US$200–350 a day including private transportation, guiding, permissions and accommodation.

Travelling independently, you could get by on US$30 a day per person, but this involves sharing a cheap hotel room and travelling by bus and public transport between cities. Below is a list of rough price guidelines for some common purchases (as of 2025):

Water (1½-litre bottle)	US$0.60	Local naan bread	US$0.20
Meal at a chaikhana	US$2.50		
Cheap hotel room	US$25		

2 | PRACTICAL INFORMATION

GETTING AROUND

Az to harakat, az Khoda barakat
(In movement there is blessing)
                    Persian proverb

Travelling in Afghanistan is an adventure in itself, requiring flexibility, patience, and a willingness to embrace the unexpected. The country's transportation network is largely informal, with little reliable information available online, and what does exist is usually in Dari or Pashto. Scheduled transport is rare outside of the limited internal flights between major cities, and even these may not run on time. There are no ride-hailing services like Uber, but then again, Afghanistan lacks formal addresses, making traditional taxi apps impractical.

The condition of the roads varies widely. While some major highways, such as the one connecting Kabul to Mazar e Sharif, are in reasonable shape, many others, particularly in remote or mountainous regions, can be in poor condition. Dirt tracks, washed-out roads, and even seasonal river crossings can make travel slow and unpredictable. However, despite these challenges, Afghans are highly mobile, and there is no shortage of cars and drivers willing to take you almost anywhere – often at a moment's notice. Shared taxis, private hires and even long-haul buses exist, though they often require some negotiation and local knowledge to arrange.

The upside of all this? The journey is rarely dull. Afghanistan's landscapes are breathtaking, and with no generic motorways to speed through, every trip is filled with fascinating sights. Whether winding through dramatic mountain passes, passing nomadic camps on open plains, or navigating the chaotic streets of a city, there is always something to see. While getting around may be challenging, the experience of travelling through Afghanistan is one of the most rewarding aspects of visiting the country.

FINDING LOCATIONS Finding places in Afghanistan can be challenging. Afghan addresses rarely have house numbers, and street signs are almost non-existent, although some roads and streets do have names. These names, however, can change depending on the government, meaning some locals may refer to streets by their old names, while others use newer ones. While apps like Google Maps and Maps.me can be helpful, they can also be inaccurate, with many false listings of places that don't exist. Maps.me is generally more reliable in this regard. Additionally, many locals may not be familiar with places that are of interest to tourists, and some may struggle to read maps.

That said, the Afghan people are known for their kindness and hospitality. Directions are often given by referring to the district, well-known major roads (Jada or Serac), junctions (Chowk or Charahi), or notable landmarks. As you get closer to your destination, ask more people along the way. Security guards and shopkeepers are often good sources of directions since they are familiar with the area.

In this book, addresses have been given where possible although they may not be the best method of finding every location. The maps will be more accurate but if in doubt, ask.

BY AIR There are no trains in Afghanistan, leaving flying as the only option if you want to avoid extra days on the road. The major cities – Herat, Kandahar and Mazar e Sharif – are connected to Kabul by air, with domestic flights operated by **Kam**

GETTING AROUND

Air (Chowk Haji Yaqoob, Shah e Nau, Kabul; +93799 974422; w kamair.com) and **Ariana Afghan Airlines** (Shahid Rd, Shah e Nau, Kabul; +93 7900 71 333; w flyariana.com). While both airlines maintain reasonably up-to-date schedules on their websites, tickets must be purchased through a travel agency or directly from the airlines' main offices; online booking is not reliably available at the time of writing. Between Kam Air and Ariana, Kam Air is generally the preferred option for its greater reliability and better service.

Kam Air often displays a message claiming that only five seats remain on a given flight, likely as a marketing tactic to encourage quick bookings. Some travel agents may also state that a particular airline is 'sold out' simply because their credit with the airline has been exhausted, so checking with multiple agencies can be helpful. **Tolo Travels** (House no 119, St No. 12, Wazir Akbar Khan Main Rd; m 7996 70000; w toloaviation.com) in Shah e Nau, Kabul is a well-established and reliable agency for booking flights.

Additionally, there are two humanitarian airlines – **UNHAS (United Nations Humanitarian Air Service)** and **Pactec** – which operate flights to more remote airports. However, these services are restricted to registered development workers, so they are not available to tourists. You may spot their aircraft at airports during your travels.

INTERCITY TRANSPORT Travel between cities and major towns in Afghanistan relies on shared transport, with several options available. The most common are **shared taxis** (usually Toyota Corollas), **smaller minivans** (such as TownAce 7-seaters), **larger minivans** (HiAce or Flying Coach 16-seaters) and full-sized **buses** – often still displaying their original German or Polish branding. Pricing is based per seat, so if you want a shared taxi all to yourself, you want to have more space or you want the vehicle to leave quickly, then you simply pay for the extra seats.

Air conditioning is rare, and in the summer large buses often drive with doors and sunroofs open for ventilation, which can make journeys on unpaved roads extremely dusty. Drivers – especially those of larger coaches – are known for their fast and sometimes reckless driving.

For larger buses, tickets are sometimes sold in advance, but generally, the system is informal: passengers simply show up at the **bus station** (called *istga* in Dari and *hada* in Pashto), and vehicles depart once full. For some routes vehicles usually depart at certain times of day, which are specified in each chapter. These stations may be official terminals or informal roadside gathering points.

In recent years, many *istgas* have moved to larger, more organised coach parks on the outskirts of cities, but shared taxis often still leave from central locations in the early morning. The names of transport hubs can vary depending on language and local usage. For example, in Kabul, the area for transport to Mazar e Sharif may be referred to as *Khai Khana* (the neighbourhood name), *Terminal* (the modern bus station), *Sarai Shomali* (the old transport hub), or *Lewa Baba Jan* (the nearby landmark). For simplicity, we list these transport areas as '*Istga e*' plus the destination in Dari, or '*Hada e*' plus the destination in Pashto – using these terms will generally get you the right directions.

BY PRIVATE CAR Travelling by hired car in Afghanistan is a common and often the only way to get around, particularly for visiting remote sites. You can arrange this through a reputable tour operator, your accommodation, or by negotiating directly with drivers at the istga, the bus and shared transport station.

2 | PRACTICAL INFORMATION

For travel within a city, a reasonable daily rate for a car and driver is around 3,000AFN. However, for longer journeys on rough roads, costs can be significantly higher, with prices starting at 8,000AFN for a standard car and US$250 (17,000AFN) for a 4x4 for a full day's journey. While hiring a car for excursions is a common practice among Afghan families, language barriers and different expectations between local travellers and tourists can make the process challenging.

There are no formal **car rental** services in Afghanistan. While it may be possible to negotiate renting a car or motorbike for self-driving, this is not recommended. In the event of an accident or legal issue, resolving the situation could be extremely difficult. In the Wakhan Corridor, vehicle hire operates with fixed rates from Ishkishim (page 273).

WITHIN CITIES There are no metro or train services in Afghanistan, so travel within Afghan cities relies entirely on road transport, and it can be a challenge, as public transport systems are informal and not always easy for visitors to navigate. Larger cities such as Kabul, Herat, Mazar e Sharif and Kandahar do have basic transit networks, primarily consisting of **minivans** that follow set routes. These vans operate with a conductor who calls out destinations while passengers hop on and off, paying small fares. While efficient for locals, these systems can be difficult for outsiders to use without assistance. Some useful routes are listed in the Kabul chapter on page 120.

The most common and practical way to get around is by **taxi**. There are no official taxi ranks, but taxis are easy to spot, painted yellow or blue depending on the city. Since there are no meters, fares must be negotiated before the journey begins. In addition to taxis, **autorickshaws** (tuk-tuks) are common in cities such as Herat, Jalalabad and Kandahar. Herat's tuk-tuks, in particular, are known for their colourful decorations, often featuring musical motifs. Despite the Taliban's ban on music, many of these designs have remained.

CHECKPOINTS These are a fact of life in Afghanistan, especially when travelling between towns and provinces. At present, most are passed through quickly as long as your documentation is in order. However, under no circumstances should you take photos. The Taliban security personnel are focused on identifying anti-government groups, not foreign visitors. As one observer put it, 'They are not looking for foreigners, they are looking for people that look like them.'

Checkpoints are usually located at the edges of towns and cities, on mountain passes, at provincial borders, and near military bases – much as they were under the previous government. The style and set-up of checkpoints varies widely across the country. Around Mazar e Sharif, they are formal structures – large, decorated archways with uniformed soldiers stationed beneath them. In rural areas, they can be far more makeshift, using whatever materials are available. In some places, old tank tracks have been repurposed as speed bumps, while in Nimruz, a checkpoint was constructed from an old shell casing. In Badghis, a wrecked US Humvee formed part of the barrier. In Khost, plastic flowers decorated some of the structures, while in Nuristan, plants and flowers grew from the Hesco barriers.

Taliban fighters manning these checkpoints can appear in a range of attire. In cities and areas where they want to project authority, they often wear matching military fatigues and carry modern weapons like M16s. In more remote regions, their clothing is mismatched, and they tend to carry older wooden-handled AK-47s. Despite these variations, one thing remains consistent – the 'Taliban uniform' of a long beard, shoulder-length hair, and kohl-rimmed eyes.

ACCOMMODATION

Accommodation options in Afghanistan are generally functional rather than inspiring. In larger towns and smaller cities, you may find mid-range hotels with basic amenities such as air conditioning, attached Western-style bathrooms, and Wi-Fi. While these hotels are rarely luxurious, they are often made homely by the attentive staff, who may bring tea to your room in the afternoon as part of the service. Soap and towels are usually provided, but you may need to ask for them. Outside of these cities the accommodation options drop dramatically with basic *mussafarkhanas* and *chaikhanas* providing basic rooms with blankets and cushions to sleep on.

Reservations can be made by phone one or two days before, but outside of larger hotels in Kabul, they are not always honoured. Fortunately, rooms are usually available even without a prior booking.

Personal space is less of a concern in Afghanistan than in many other countries, and hotel staff – especially in places that see fewer tourists – may enter your room unannounced to deliver tea, clean, or if you are needed for something. If privacy is important, it is worth locking the door from the inside. For female travellers, cultural norms should be considered when meeting male visitors in accommodation. If inviting a man to your room, it is best to leave the door open for propriety's sake. A better option would be to meet in the lobby or a communal area.

AFGHAN TOILET ESSENTIALS

In mid-range hotels in major cities such as Kabul, Herat or Mazar e Sharif, you'll usually find Western-style toilets, often in en-suite bathrooms. However, even in some hotels, toilet paper may not be provided, so it's wise to carry your own supply of tissues or toilet paper at all times. Outside the cities and in rural areas, squat toilets are the norm. These are simple ceramic or concrete fixtures set into the floor, and they often require some balance and flexibility to use. They do not come with toilet paper, as the traditional method of cleaning in Afghanistan is with water, usually from a plastic jug or small hose located nearby. It's also a good idea to carry hand sanitiser, as soap is not always available.

Using squat toilets can be more challenging when wearing traditional loose-fitting Afghan clothing such as a shalwar kameez. The extra fabric can get in the way and requires some care to keep clean and dry. It helps to hold garments out of the way with one hand, which can be tricky while managing a water jug or other items at the same time.

When driving between towns or on longer road trips, the most common place to find a toilet is at a roadside chaikhana. These places are essential rest stops where travellers eat, stretch their legs, and use the facilities. However, the toilets at chaikhanas tend to be very basic squat types – functional but far from clean by most standards. Be prepared for a lack of running water or flushing systems, and bring your own supplies.

In Afghan cities, there are no public toilets as such, so your best option is to ask to use the facilities in a restaurant, café or guesthouse. In bazaars and marketplaces, toilet access is more informal. Often, a group of shopkeepers will share a locked communal toilet, and if you ask politely and with patience, they might allow you to use it.

2 | PRACTICAL INFORMATION

There are few hotels with real character in Afghanistan, although the Intercontinental in Kabul (page 122) and the Spinghar in Jalalabad (page 152) hark back to an age before all the troubles of the last 50 years, when travel to Afghanistan seemed only as outlandish as travel to Nepal.

HOTELS Hotels only exist in Afghanistan's larger cities, and even then, they vary widely in quality. The only hotel that could be described as anything beyond three-star standard is the Kabul Grand Hotel (page 122), a high-end establishment that was once part of the Serena chain but has since been nationalised by the Taliban government.

Other hotels in Kabul, Herat, Mazar e Sharif and Kandahar range from modern, semi-luxurious options with some security features to more basic accommodations aimed at business travellers. Options in smaller towns may label themselves as 'hotels' but offer no more than mussafarkhana-level service. Note that many of the mobile numbers listed are also on WhatsApp, making it relatively easy (and cheap) to book a room.

GUESTHOUSES A common type of accommodation in Afghanistan, a guesthouse is a large mansion-style house with between eight and 30 rooms of varying sizes. These were originally built as private residences but were repurposed for NGO staff, journalists and long-term travellers. Some still cater to that crowd, offering services such as laundry, tea and coffee, and occasionally meeting rooms. Security is often a key feature, with high walls, guards, and controlled entry. Although they are often called 'hotels', guesthouses have a more informal and homely feel. Many were constructed in the early to mid 20th century in the traditional Kabuli style, though newer ones – sometimes referred to as poppy palaces (page 57) – are grander, built with money from Afghanistan's opium boom.

MUSSAFARKHANAS Literally meaning 'traveller's place', mussafarkhanas are found in bazaars across Afghanistan and are often the cheapest lodging option. In smaller provincial capitals, they may be the only available accommodation. These are very basic and cater mainly to traders, truck drivers and pilgrims rather than tourists. Rooms are usually available, although often with a shared bathroom; communal sleeping in the restaurant area is also often an option albeit owners are unlikely to want international guests to sleep outside of a room. Instead of beds, mussafarkhanas often provide *pakhta* – cotton-filled mattresses – placed directly on the floor. These can be surprisingly comfortable and often better than the low-cost Chinese-made mattresses that are used when beds are available.

CHAIKHANAS (TEAHOUSES) A step down from mussafarkhanas, chaikhanas are roadside teahouses where travellers can sometimes sleep overnight. They are even more basic, usually consisting of a raised wooden or mud platform where guests can lay out a blanket and sleep. These are most common in rural areas and along highways.

HOMESTAYS In remote areas homestays (sometimes known as *mehmankhanas*) are an option, particularly in the Wakhan Corridor (page 266) where community-based tourism projects allow travellers to stay with local families. The legality of homestays is uncertain. On one hand, Afghan authorities – particularly the National Directorate of Security (NDS) – may question or restrict foreign visitors staying in private homes. On the other, hospitality is a core principle of Pashtunwali

> **ACCOMMODATION PRICE CODES**
>
> The following rates are based on a single room:
>
> | | | |
> |---|---|---|
> | Upmarket | $$$$ | US$100+ (6,850AFN+) |
> | Mid-range | $$$ | US$50–100 (3,425–6,850AFN) |
> | Inexpensive | $$ | US$20–50 (1,370–3,425AFN) |
> | Shoestring | $ | less than US$20 (1,370AFN) |

(page 44), making it instinctively acceptable to the Taliban. However, for the safety of the host, it is best to avoid homestays unless they are officially sanctioned.

CAMPING Camping is only practical in Afghanistan's remote regions, such as the Wakhan Corridor, by the Minaret of Jam, and some parts of Bamiyan Province. It is essential to check with the authorities at the ministry to get permission before you do. If permission is granted, then wild camping is possible, but you'll need to be self-sufficient, as there are no designated campsites.

EATING AND DRINKING

Located at the crossroads of the Silk Road, linking the Middle East, Iran and central Asia to the Indian subcontinent and the Far East, Afghanistan has always been in the centre of a great cultural exchange, not least of all in its kitchen. At its finest, Afghan cuisine is a mix of sweet, salty, smoky, sour and spicy, often blending unexpected together to create something new.

It features a wide range of rice dishes, kebabs, curry-like stews, fresh herbs and chutneys. As expected for a landlocked country, there are not many seafood options, although trout and carp are caught in the nation's rivers. Some Afghan dishes are found in almost every restaurant in Afghanistan while others are solely the preserve of home-cooked family meals.

Each region has a different flavour, depending on its neighbours. Pashto areas in the south such as Jalalabad and Kandahar are influenced by the spice and heat of the subcontinent. Heratis often take their kebabs with white rice rather than bread, like their Persian neighbours in Iran. While in Mazar e Sharif, the bread resembles the small, thick breads of Uzbekistan. Urban Afghans enjoy dishes from their neighbours and further afield. Restaurants serving Pakistani and Chinese food are common, and pizza, burgers and fried chicken are as popular in big cities in Afghanistan as anywhere else.

AFGHAN CUISINE Afghans love their spices. Saffron has been cultivated around Herat for centuries, while *siah jeera* (green cumin) is grown in the mountains of Badakhshan. Meat dishes may be flavoured with *gard-e-ghooreh* (a powder made from sour grapes) or sumac. Other common spices include turmeric, cardamom, coriander, cinnamon and black pepper, combined in a mix called *char masala*.

Naan bread, baked in a tandoori oven and occasionally brushed with oil or butter, is served with almost every traditional meal. The size and shape of the naan varies from large skateboard sized in Herat to small thicker breads in Mazar e Sharif. *Roghani* is a softer, puffier kind of naan, often topped with sesame and nigella seeds.

Meals in people's homes often start with a plate of naan and *badenjan-burani*, a dip made with fried or roast aubergines, garlic and yoghurt, or perhaps a plate of *osh pyozee*, onions stuffed with ground lamb or chickpeas, prunes, cheese and spices.

Dairy A key ingredient in Afghan cuisine, yoghurt (*mast*) is especially eaten in the high mountain regions where fresh produce can be hard to come by. You will often find it served as an optional side dish in restaurants. Some home-cooked dishes are served alongside or atop a layer of *chakkah* (strained Greek-style yoghurt with garlic and mint). If you want to avoid it, say '*ne chakkah, lutfan*' (no chakkah, please).

Unique to Afghanistan is *quroot*, sour balls made from strained, salted and dried yoghurt that can be reconstituted or eaten as they come. If you are travelling during Eid, you might find *sheer khurma*, a thick soup made with whole milk, almonds, dates, sugar, saffron and vermicelli served either for breakfast or dessert. *Qymaq* is a thick cream, sometimes served at breakfast. Afghan cheese, *panir*, is similar to the Indian version; in springtime, Afghans eat it with raisins (*kishmish panir*).

Rice dishes Rice (*pulao*), one of Afghanistan's main crops, is the staple, served with nearly every meal along with *chai* (tea) and naan. The national dish, and the test of any Afghan cook, is *kabuli pulao*. Originally made by the chefs working for the elite in Kabul, it became better known as *qabili palao* ('excellent rice') in Dari as it spread across the country. Basmati rice, fried onions, caramelised carrots (which originally come from Afghanistan) and raisins, are slowly cooked and steamed in spices and broth with chunks of beef or mutton, then garnished with slivered pistachios and almonds. It's a dish commonly found in all Afghan restaurants, cooked in the morning in a large pot.

A pulao can also be made with thin noodles (*rehta pulao*). Other variations include *maash pulao* (with mung beans, spices, onions, tomatoes, chillis and often dried fruit), *yahkoot pulao* (with tomatoes) and *zamarod pulao* ('emerald rice'), a striking green dish traditionally served at Nau Ruz (page 238), made by slowly cooking the rice with spinach and beef. On other special occasions you might see *narinj pulao*, rice made with candied orange zest and flavoured with saffron, cumin and cardamom.

Like Iranians, Afghans make *tahdig* ('the bottom of the pan'): rice cooked in saffron, turmeric, butter, yoghurt and eggs, and cooked over a flame (or baked) so the bottom of the pot forms a crispy golden crust when it's turned out upside down. Then there's *zereshk pulao*, a creamy sweet and sour risotto made with caramelised barberries (or beberis, similar to cranberries), butter, saffron, turmeric, lemon juice and chicken thighs.

Chalau is plain white rice, while *bata* is short-grained, sticky rice; either are served with *qorma* (stew, similar to a mild curry). A popular version is *qorma sabzi*, made with spinach, and often beans and beef. Bata is notably used in *shola*, a dish that means comfort food to many Afghans: rice, mung beans and chickpeas are cooked with garlic, onion and spices, then often topped with *gheymeh* (tomato and chickpea sauce), then baked and served with chakkah.

Meat dishes Lamb is the most popular meat in Afghanistan, but you'll also find goat, beef and chicken, most often served as kebabs at restaurants or *dukan-e-kebabi* (kebab stands). There are spicy minced beef kebabs called *koobideh*, and Pashtun shepherd-style *chopan kebab*, lamb chunks interspersed with fat (*dumba*) from the tail of the fat-tailed sheep to keep them moist, seasoned with sumac and threaded on skewers grilled over an open fire. *Kebab-e-Jigar* (liver kebabs) are best found early in the day when the organs are still fresh from the butchers. If you like it spicy hot, try the deep-fried sandal-shaped *chapli kebab* (literally 'shoe kebab') from Jalalabad. In bigger cities, you'll also find *shoarma* – doner kebab, made up of thin slices of meat (lamb or chicken) pressed into a cone and cooked on a spit.

Mantu (steamed meat and onion-filled dumplings) are a big favourite, especially in the north, served with chakkah and topped with a tomato sauce that often includes mung beans or split peas. *Ashak* are dumplings filled with green onions, spinach or leeks, usually topped with a lamb or beef sauce and chakkah. *Chai nakhi* is a stew similar to Iranian *dizi* but cooked in a teapot, with bread to mop up the sauce; Heratis have a special method of eating it where they mash it all up to a paste. *Rosh* is a slow-cooked lamb shank, which is also called *maicha* if served with rice.

Meatballs cooked in a rich tomato sauce served with rice is *kofta chalau*. *Aush-e-asli* is a dish of noodles and meatballs. *Karahi* is a popular chicken dish named after the pan it's cooked in, usually with tomatoes, onions and garlic. In winter you may find hearty *pacha*, cow's foot in a gelatinous chickpea broth, or *mastawa*, made with *lahndi* (dried salted slices of lamb), chickpeas and rice, finished with orange zest, chillis and *quroot*. *Haleem*, also popular in Pakistan, is a slow-cooked stew of wheat, lentils and beef, flavoured with cloves, cinnamon, cardamom, cumin, coriander, nutmeg and other spices.

Fish You will find fish on the menu in major cities, but it will not be from Afghanistan. River and sea fish are imported frozen from Pakistan and usually deep fried. The place to try Afghan fish are the restaurants in the Panjshir that serve fish from the Panjshir River, deep-fried, bones, head and all. It's certainly a change from kebabs and rice.

Vegetarian dishes As rice and legumes (lentils, chickpeas, mung beans) are an important part of the Afghan diet, vegetarians should do quite well, although the reality is that most restaurant patrons consider vegetable dishes to be best served at home and so vegetarian dishes can be hard to come across when eating out. Vegans may also struggle with all the yoghurt. In small towns where vegetarians are not catered for, a **tip** is to visit the restaurants early and ask what the staff are eating. Often the owner provides a frugal, traditional, and often delicious, vegetarian meal before their shift, and can make some extra for you.

Among the vegetarian dishes to look for are *borani banyan*, aubergines fried until they melt in the mouth and combined with tomatoes, onions and garlic and served on a layer of chakkah; *borani kadoo* is pumpkin or squash, similarly braised with tomatoes, onions, garlics, spices and sometimes a chilli pepper; *golpi* is a spicy tomato and cauliflower curry.

Dishes are often served with a side of *salata* (chopped cucumbers, tomatoes and red onion in lime juice). *Aush* (noodle soups) are often meatless, served with tomatoes, garlic, mint and often beans (and chakkah). Mushroom lovers should look out for *samaroq*: mixed mushrooms cooked in a sauce with tomatoes, garlic, onions and chillis. One of the best-known egg dishes is *tokhme banjanromi*, an omelette cooked with onions, garlic, tomatoes and hot peppers, then topped with fresh coriander. *Daal*, lentil dishes, are often found in restaurants that serve Pakistani cuisine.

Bamiyan in central Afghanistan is famous for *katchaloo*, potatoes. Nuristan is the place to look for wild mushrooms, especially morels.

Fruit Afghanistan's fruit is legendary, and with good reason. The country's high-altitude valleys, fertile soil and hot, dry summers create the perfect conditions for producing some of the world's most flavourful and naturally sweet fruit; Marco Polo and Babur left rapturous descriptions of its luscious deliciousness. Unlike mass-produced fruit found in supermarkets, Afghan farmers use traditional agricultural methods, letting the fruit ripen on the tree or vine rather than harvesting crops early for transport. The result? Explosively juicy melons, melt-in-the-mouth figs, and pomegranates so rich in flavour they feel almost otherworldly.

Afghanistan is especially famous for **melons**. In the late summer, market stalls overflow with different varieties, from the long, pale **Tarbuza** melons of Kunduz (they can weigh up to 30kg!) to the smaller, intensely fragrant **Zamindar** melons of Kandahar.

Fruit follows the rhythm of the seasons. In spring, markets are filled with fresh fruit including **mulberries**, cherries and apricots. If travelling in spring, also look out for rhubarb, eaten raw dipped in salt and great for car journeys. By summer, plums, peaches and *kharbuza* (watermelons) dominate. Autumn brings the famed *anaar* (pomegranates), most famously from Kandahar, *angur* (grapes) from the Shomali plains north of Kabul, *sib* (apples) from Bamiyan, and figs and walnuts from Nuristan. Winter is the season of dried fruits and nuts – essential to Afghan hospitality.

For a more sour, tangy alternative to pomegranate, try *zirishk* (also known as *chakar* or **barberry**). These tiny, bright-red berries are packed with tart flavour and are often used in Afghan cooking, particularly in rice dishes like *zirishk pulao*.

Street food and snacks Afghan cities have a thriving street food culture, thanks to the *tabang wala* (street vendors). Be sure to try *bolani*, a flatbread filled with a savoury mix that might include mashed potatoes, spinach, spring onions, pumpkin, lentils or *gandana*, a unique variety of Afghan leek, served with chakkah and coriander chutney. Another favourite is *shor nakhod*, potato and chickpea salad in a tangy coriander chutney and chilli sauce. *Chips burger* is a chip butty using naan bread found in Bamiyan and central areas where potatoes are harvested. You'll also find pakoras and samosas, and during Eid, *kulcha shor*, a savoury biscuit made with butter, sesame and nigella seeds.

Popular snacks include walnuts, pistachios, cashews, hazelnuts or almonds, often roasted to bring out their flavour, as well as dried fruits – including mulberries, raisins, apricots and dates.

Sweets and desserts Afghan meals are often followed by fresh fruit such as melons or grapes. *Sheer birinj* is a creamy rice pudding made with rice, butter, rose water, milk, cardamom and cinnamon; another rice pudding is *daygcha*, flavoured with rose water and cardamom. *Firnee*, another pudding, is made with milk and sugar, thickened with corn starch or rice powder, and flavoured with cardamom, rose water and saffron, and topped with chopped pistachios and dried or fresh fruit.

Special occasions such as Eid or Ramadan call for *sheer pira*, a candy made with milk, cardamom, nuts and hot sugar syrup, then cut into squares, and *khetayee*, pistachio cookies. Pashtun communities make a dessert called *malida*, made of fine breadcrumbs combined with ghee, sugar, cardamom and nuts.

Popular pastries include baklava, *jalebi* (gram flour rings coated in a thick sugar syrup), and *gosh e-fil* ('elephants' ears'), crispy lightly fried dough covered with powdered cardamom, icing sugar and crushed pistachios.

Afghan ice cream (*sheer yakh*, 'frozen milk') is a popular treat on summer evenings. Handmade in vats of ice, with cream, vanilla, *salep* (wild orchid powder) and rose water, it's usually topped with chopped pistachios and thick cream. Mazar e Sharif is famous for it, and you might find other flavours such as mango, pistachio, strawberry, etc.

EATING AND DRINKING

DRINKS Green tea (*chai sabz*) is the national drink, served with meals, when meeting people, when making a deal for a carpet in the bazaar, and in chaikhanas (teahouses) – an institution that grew up with the Silk Road, offering meals and basic accommodation for caravans and travellers; even the smallest village will have at least one chaikhana. The tea is made from constantly boiling samovars sometimes flavoured with cardamom (don't expect any milk) and may be accompanied by a handful of *nuqal* (sugared almonds) or sometimes candy. Typically, Afghans drink very little water and tea is the major source of hydration; as such, the tea is served quite weak.

Chai siaa (black tea) is also drunk but less commonly. *Sheer chai* ('milk tea', black tea with milk) is drunk in the mornings in Kandahar and Jalalabad, an introduction from the subcontinent. Saffron tea is well worth a try in upmarket restaurants especially in Herat. Coffee is not a traditional drink in Afghanistan, and outside one or two new hipster coffee shops in the cities it is better for coffee drinkers to bring their own if they want anything more than instant coffee.

For non-tea drinkers, Afghanistan restaurants offer freshly squeezed juices in season. Pomegranate (*anaar*) flavoured with salt is a favourite when in season. Look out for mango and watermelon, too. Most shops and restaurants have a selection of carbonated soft drinks, including international brands, as well as the Iranian 'super cola' and Afghan Alokozay brand.

A classic summer thirst quencher, *doogh* is made with fermented milk or yoghurt, water, mint and salt, and sometimes cucumber, served cold and delicious with grilled meats, bread or rice. It is most commonly served in Herat both as a packaged bottled drink and homemade *doogh watana*.

Alcohol is illegal and unavailable, although you may find Iranian 'malt beer'. There is a wide selection of international and locally made energy drinks, which seem very popular with Afghan youth. The Taliban have banned *chillams* (hubble-bubble pipes) which used to be available in many restaurants, and they don't approve of cigarettes. Although they aren't banned, few Afghans smoke; they may light up in a chaikhana or similar, but never in a proper restaurant.

EATING OUT Eating out in Afghanistan is a unique experience, and the dining culture can vary widely depending on the region, type of establishment, and time of year. Most restaurants do not take reservations. The restaurant scene is informal, with the concept of a 'menu' more of an aspiration than a strict list of available items. Kabul is the only city where there's something resembling a restaurant 'scene', with a range of local and international options, albeit with a few quirks.

Chaikhanas The backbone of Afghan dining, the chaikhana (page 94) can range from basic to slightly fancier but share a similar set-up. In the centre, a steaming samovar provides hot water for tea, while diners sit cross-legged at low tables or on the floor, often accompanied by a TV showing the news. Boys often take orders, serve pots of green tea, bring fresh naan from local bakers, and sometimes run to the market for additional supplies. Outside, chefs cook fresh kebabs to order, and in the back kitchen, large pots of pulao and dishes like yakhni or qorma simmer on the stove. The atmosphere is relaxed, with the owner usually watching over the proceedings at a counter near the door and taking payment from the customers as they leave.

The variety of food at these simple restaurants depends on the time of day and the location. Kebabs and pulao are staples, though there might also be other dishes, especially in more populated areas. The further you are from major cities, the fewer

2 | PRACTICAL INFORMATION

> **RESTAURANT PRICE CODES**
>
> Average price of a main course.
>
> | | | |
> |---|---|---|
> | Expensive | $$$ | US$8+ (550AFN+) |
> | Moderate | $$ | US$3–8 (200–550AFN) |
> | Inexpensive | $ | US$1–3 (70–200AFN) |

options you'll find. These restaurants are affordable and generally not suited to vegetarians due to the heavy focus on meat dishes.

Herati-style restaurants In Herat, dining tends to be a bit more sophisticated, with a wider variety of kebabs and Persian dishes like *sabzi korma*. These restaurants often serve food with rice instead of naan, and you can expect a larger menu that reflects the regional Persian influence. Herati-style restaurants can be found in other cities as well.

Turkmen restaurants Often run by Uzbeks, Turkmen restaurants serve Turkmen pulao, which is made with sesame oil. They typically offer a wider menu than what is on offer at a chaikhana including dishes such as mantu (dumplings). These are great places to experience a fusion of Afghan, Turkmen and Uzbek flavours.

Shinwari restaurants These are easy to identify by the sheep carcasses hanging in the window. Shinwari restaurants focus on barbecue-style cooking, where meat is ordered by the kilo and grilled over coals or else cooked with tomato and chilli in a karahi (skillet). This style of cooking is especially popular among the Pashtuns, but you'll find Shinwari restaurants in most major cities.

Fast-food outlets Though the name might suggest a focus on Western fast food, some fast-food outlets in Afghanistan, particularly in cities like Herat, Mazar e Sharif and Kandahar, serve a variety of excellent Afghan and regional cuisine, including Herati, Afghan, Turkmen and Pakistani dishes such as *handi* and *biryani*. While burgers, pizzas, and fried chicken are also available, the Afghan options are usually more authentic and varied, making these spots a popular choice.

Picnic spots Afghans love to picnic, especially in summer. In fine weather, areas around Band e Amir, Herat and Paghman see large numbers of families, as well as groups of young men, eating outdoors. Some traditional meals include *kholokhi*, a method of cooking in which food – usually potatoes, and sometimes chicken – is wrapped in foil and placed in a mud oven, then covered and left to cook for 30–40 minutes. The food is dug up and eaten afterwards, offering a communal and rustic experience.

DINING ETIQUETTE Meals are typically served on a communal basis, where diners eat from large dishes, always with their right hand. In more formal settings, you may find a tablecloth, but in many places, the seating is informal, and plastic or wipe-down surfaces are common. In traditional restaurants, you won't find many chairs, as eating is traditionally done sitting on the floor with crossed legs. If you're invited to a local meal, keep in mind that sharing is key, and most people will eat directly from the communal dishes.

PUBLIC HOLIDAYS AND FESTIVALS

Some Afghan public holidays run on the Gregorian calendar and some run on the Islamic calendar. Since the Taliban government took power, some holidays have been phased out and new ones have been introduced. As such, for practical purposes, we have included some that have been phased out as they might come back; but also to enable you to see if they are being observed as a statement of defiance if you are travelling during that period. The number of victory and liberation days reflects Afghanistan's tumultuous history.

The Islamic calendar holidays change by around ten days each year as the Islamic calendar is lunar. Note that both Eid holidays officially begin when the new moon is sighted. As such, should it be cloudy, the holidays can start a day later than expected.

Public holidays are a time when families get together and often go to places of natural beauty for picnics. Official leisure destinations, places such as Band e Amir in Bamiyan Province, as well as Paghman and Lake Qargha on the outskirts of Kabul, have been designated 'men only' by the Taliban authorities. As such, families tend to drive to other rural areas.

GREGORIAN CALENDAR PUBLIC HOLIDAYS

15 February	Liberation Day (when Soviet forces left Afghanistan in 1989)
28 April	Mujahideen Victory Day (when the mujahideen defeated the communist government in 1992)
1 May	International Workers Day
15 August	Afghan Jihad Victory Day (when the Taliban entered Kabul in 2021)
19 August	Independence Day (when Afghanistan gained full independence from the British in 1919)
31 August	American Withdrawal Day (when the international forces finally left Afghanistan in 2021)
9 September	Massoud Day/Martyrs Day (when Ahmad Shah Massoud, page 144, was killed in 2001; currently not a holiday)

ISLAMIC CALENDAR HOLIDAYS

Ramadan	17 February–19 March 2026, 7 February–8 March 2027, 27 January–26 February 2028, 15 January–14 February 2029
Eid Al-Fitr	(the feast marking the end of Ramadan) 20 March 2026, 9 March 2027, 26 February 2028, 14 February 2029
Eid Al-Adha	(honouring Ibrahim's willingness to obey God and sacrifice his son) 27 May 2026, 16 May 2027, 5 May 2028, 24 April 2029
Ashura	(this is a Shi'a day of mourning and while not officially a holiday will be observed in Shi'a areas such as Bamiyan) 25 June 2026, 15 June 2027, 3 June 2028, 23 May 2029
Prophet Muhammad's birthday	25 September 2026, 15 September 2027, 3 September 2028, 24 August 2029

FESTIVALS Outside of religious dates and liberation days, the Taliban do not really approve of festivals. Those that are still permitted have no music or dancing and as such may not appeal to the casual observer.

Baloch Day (2 March) If you find yourself in Nimruz at the beginning of March, then look out for Baloch cultural celebrations. Traditionally this would have included music and dance but under the Taliban government, there will be craft shows and recitals.

Nau Ruz (21 March) Nau Ruz falls on the Spring Equinox, the day when the night and day have equal length. It is a celebration that pre-dates Islam and as such is not seen as Islamic in the eyes of the Taliban leadership. However, especially in Shi'a areas, you may find shops shut, cows' horns painted and people in new clothing going for picnics.

Naranj Gul Jalalabad 'Orange Blossom' poetry festival (Mid-April) The Naranj Gul Poetry Festival is a cultural event known throughout Afghanistan, held each spring when Jalalabad's orange blossoms are in full bloom. Poetry has long been a revered art form in Afghanistan, and this festival brings together poets from across the country to share their work in both **Pashto and Dari**. Historically, themes of **love, nature and national identity** dominated the recitations, but since the Taliban's return to power, poetry at the festival has shifted towards **more religious and moral themes**, reflecting the new cultural landscape. Despite this change, the festival remains an important platform for poets and literary figures to express themselves and celebrate Afghanistan's rich poetic tradition.

SHOPPING

Shopping in Afghanistan is centred around the **main bazaar**, usually found at the heart of the town or city. Meat, fruit, vegetables, clothing and other goods are typically bought from stalls or small shops, and whether or not you intend to purchase anything, these bazaars are excellent places for people-watching. Generally, the bazaar begins to wake up around dawn, and at this hour you should be able to find hot bread. There are **general stores** in most cities that sell water, cold drinks, tissues, tea, batteries, and other basic necessities. Kabul has a few larger supermarkets, although these would be considered normal-sized grocery stores by international standards.

Shopping in Afghanistan offers not only rich pickings for those wanting a souvenir but a great opportunity to explore the country's cultural heritage through its variety of textiles, gemstones, handicrafts and local specialities. With Buddhist beads, British rifles and Russian medals you can even combine retail therapy with a history lesson. Markets and bazaars in the cities of Herat, Mazar e Sharif and Kandahar are home to an array of goods that reflect Afghanistan's traditions, craftsmanship and diverse regional influences. However, **Kabul's Chicken Street** remains the best place for variety and convenience, with shops offering examples of handicrafts from all over the country. Bargaining is expected, and carpet sellers will usually bring out tea and roll out dozens of rugs for inspection with good humour and hospitality.

CARPETS AND KILIMS Purchasing one of the country's famous carpets (pages 48 and 60) is near the top of many visitors' wish lists. Some vocabulary: kilims are reversible flat-woven tapestry rugs, a *purdah* is a rug used to hang as doors in yurts or tents, with a four-quarter design; a *jallar* is a long, narrow bag, often with a fringe, traditionally used by nomads to transport their belongings; a *khurjin* is a camel saddlebag.

Be aware that prices vary greatly depending on size, age, condition and provenance of the item. In Mazar e Sharif or Andkhoy, you may be able to negotiate a cheaper price from one of the wholesale markets. The bazaar in Herat is also a good place to look. If you're investing in a more expensive piece, always ask for a **receipt**, especially if you plan to take it through customs. Export restrictions can exist on older or 'antique' pieces, so it's wise to confirm what's allowed before purchase. Reputable dealers can also assist with shipping rugs abroad if you don't want to carry them.

OTHER TEXTILES AND CLOTHING Travellers interested in embroidery, fabric arts and decorative pieces will find a wealth of options, many of which are lighter and easier to pack than carpets. Ikat, Kuchi mirrorwork and appliqué textiles can sometimes be found in Kabul or Jalalabad markets. In addition, hand-stitched wall hangings, often with patchwork or symbolic motifs, are common throughout the country.

Afghan traditional clothing (page 61) such as the chapan, pathu or pakol, and other various regional hats are popular with visitors. Scarves and shawls, widely worn across Afghanistan by both men and women, are readily available in the bazaars. Their unique styles make great souvenirs but they are also quite practical for use in colder climates. Many of these items are made from wool or cotton, often hand-stitched or embroidered, and can be found in bazaars and markets across the country.

JEWELLERY Afghanistan is famous for a wide array of gemstones (page 42) and if you like your jewellery on the chunky side, there's plenty on offer. Large semi-precious stones set in oxidised silver as necklaces or bracelets are often described as 'Kuchi' jewellery, although other ethnic groups produce them as well.

HANDICRAFTS AND WOODWORK Afghanistan's markets are filled with beautiful, handcrafted items, many of which are made of local materials like wood, metal and stone. Nuristani wood carvings are particularly well known, with skilled artisans creating intricate furniture, bowls and decorative objects from walnut and other hardwoods. These hand-carved pieces showcase the artistry of Afghan craftsmen and make for excellent souvenirs.

The country also has a long history of weapon crafting, and *jazails* – traditional Afghan muskets – are often beautifully adorned with mother-of-pearl inlays. Although not used in Afghanistan today, these weapons are highly collectible, especially for those interested in Afghan military history. While these items are often sold in markets, it's important to check local regulations regarding the sale and export of weapons.

Another speciality is blue glassware from Herat. This vibrant, hand-blown glass comes in various shades of blue and is used to create both decorative and functional items such as vases, cups and pitchers.

ANTIQUES Afghanistan's long and rich history is reflected in the antiques found in some markets. However, buyers should exercise caution when purchasing these items, as some may be illegal to export without the proper permits. Antique coins, beads and artefacts are sometimes available, but it's important to request a receipt and ensure the items are sourced legally.

Be wary of shops offering items that may appear to be looted or from uncertain origins, particularly in conflict-affected regions. Purchasing such items could lead to legal complications, so it's always a good idea to choose reputable shops or markets

2 | PRACTICAL INFORMATION

> ### TRADITIONAL AFGHAN CRAFTS   *Shoshana Stewart*
>
> Afghanistan's rich cultural heritage is beautifully expressed in the traditional crafts practised by its many skilled artisans (page 102). Best known for carpet making and high-quality wool from provinces like Ghazni, the country also produces fine woodwork, calligraphy, miniature painting and ceramics, and an incredible wealth of gems provide important work for gem cutters and jewellers.
>
> After decades of war, many of Afghanistan's master artisans had stopped working. They had no students, no customers, no opportunities to pass on their skills to the next generation. But with the support of organisations like Turquoise Mountain (and many others, which I won't name here simply so as not to exclude anyone), they are leading a revival.
>
> Crafts also play a key role in Afghanistan's economy. Textiles are a major export industry, and there are more than a million skilled weavers and other artisans working in textile manufacturing, 90% of whom are women. Today, with the support of organisations like Turquoise Mountain, Afghan artisans are working with international designers and retailers like Christopher Farr and Oliver Laws to create products for international markets, generating livelihoods for families all over the country.
>
> But ultimately, traditional crafts are so much more. For the artisans that practise them, they are a source of great pride, a bridge to the past, and a contemporary celebration of the beauty of Afghan culture. Visitors who seek out opportunities to meet with artisans, visit their workshops and learn about their crafts will get a window into Afghan heritage but also the joy and pride connected to these traditions. Buying beautiful, handmade products is an excellent way to support them and take a piece of Afghanistan home.
>
> *Shoshana Stewart is President of Turquoise Mountain (w turquoisemountain. org), a non-profit organisation supporting artisans and communities to protect and revitalise their cultural heritage.*

that have a long-established presence. If you are keen on collecting antiques, make sure to verify their authenticity and legality before making a purchase.

OTHER GOOD BUYS Afghan saffron, particularly from the Herat region, is considered some of the finest in the world and it is often sold in small packets or jars, making it an easy and useful souvenir for those interested in Afghan cuisine or the spice trade. There are other culinary delights to consider, such as pistachios and olive oil from the Nangarhar region or dried fruit like apricots, raisins and figs, which are commonly found in Afghan markets.

Whether you intend to buy or not, when in Afghan souvenir shops, keep an eye out for old stamps, Tsarist Russian banknotes, Taliban 1.0-era banknotes, buzkashi whips, British Lee Enfield rifles, Russian samovars and medals from various nations. Afghan souvenir shopping is a genuine history and culture lesson.

ARTS AND ENTERTAINMENT

Cinema and live concerts are currently banned in Afghanistan, but you may find a poetry recital, or *mushaira*, in cultural centres, or in bookshops in larger cities like Kabul, Herat and particularly Jalalabad. Although figurative art is discouraged, art workshops and small exhibitions still take place quietly, concentrating on calligraphy and geometric art.

ACTIVITIES

While tourism in Afghanistan is still in its early stages, the country offers a wealth of opportunities for adventurous travellers drawn to its unique landscapes and rich cultural heritage. Although there are few outfits currently offering organised activities, Afghanistan remains an untapped playground for those willing to explore with local guidance and a spirit of adventure. With a bit of planning and flexibility, visitors can access incredible outdoor experiences that few others have had.

CLIMBING Mountainous Afghanistan boasts countless climbing opportunities, from alpine ascents to technical rock routes. The Wakhan Corridor was popular with international expeditions in the 1970s, with many teams attempting peaks including Noshaq, Afghanistan's highest mountain. More recently, Noshaq was climbed by Afghans in Louis Meunier's documentary *Afghans to the Top*. The dramatic peak Mir Samir in the Panjshir Valley was famously attempted in Eric Newby's classic *A Short Walk in the Hindu Kush*. The Koh-i-Baba range also offers numerous climbing prospects. That said, climbing in Afghanistan is not for the faint-hearted and should only be attempted by very experienced, self-sufficient and well-prepared climbers with suitable safety measures in place, as rescue services are virtually non-existent.

HORSERIDING Horses are still commonly used in rural Afghanistan for personal transport and as pack animals. While organised horse treks are not yet widespread, converting a hiking trip into a riding journey is certainly possible with the right local support. However, don't expect a canter across open fields – horses are typically used to carry loads, and your ride may be more functional than fast-paced.

KAYAKING Afghanistan's rivers are largely untouched by the kayaking world, but there have been exploratory trips, including one on the Panjshir River. The Kochar River is also said to offer great paddling sections. While whitewater kayaking remains rare, there is a growing interest. In Bamiyan, the Bamiyan Alpine Ski Club has a few kayaks and stand-up paddleboards available for rent, allowing visitors to explore the calm stretches of water of Band e Amir during the warmer months.

SKIING Afghanistan's only established ski scene is in Bamiyan, where a surprisingly active community exists (page 180). There are no ski lifts, but the Bamiyan Alpine Ski Club (page 178) offers ski touring and backcountry equipment for rent, along with local knowledge and informal guiding. Supported by international partners, the club has a small but well-equipped ski shop. For the truly adventurous, the vast Hindu Kush range presents limitless opportunities for ski mountaineering and touring in the winter months.

TREKKING Afghanistan has the potential to become a world-class trekking destination. The Wakhan Corridor (page 266) is the primary hub for trekking, where experienced Wakhi guides from Ishkashim lead treks to high-altitude lakes and the remote passes of the Afghan Pamir. In Bamiyan Province (page 171), the Koh-i-Baba Mountains and Band e Amir National Park offer both day hikes and multi-day trekking routes, with stunning views of lakes, alpine valleys and dramatic cliffs. Nuristan (page 158) is another province with huge, largely untapped potential for trekking, although logistics and access can be challenging.

OPENING TIMES

Shops in Afghanistan start opening from around 08.00, and things usually begin winding down around 18.00 or at dusk, whichever comes earlier. On Fridays, most shops and stalls in central bazaars are closed. Official buildings such as banks, embassies and provincial offices of the **Department/Ministry of Information and Culture**, where you'll need to register on arrival, all keep the same hours (⊕ 08.00–16.00 Sat–Wed, 08.00–14.00 Thu). Afghanistan's few museums and ticketed tourist sites usually follow the same opening times as these, though the days of the week can vary as they are often open on Friday. **Restaurants** generally open around 11.00 or noon and stay open until between 21.00 and midnight, though this can fluctuate depending on the season and location. Larger, hotter cities tend to have later openings, and summer too often sees restaurants open later than in winter. Most are open daily, even on Fridays.

MEDIA AND COMMUNICATIONS

The media landscape in Afghanistan has changed dramatically since the return of the Taliban to power in August 2021. What was once one of the region's most dynamic and diverse media sectors has now become more restricted, with many independent outlets shutting down, operating in exile, or shifting to less politically sensitive content. Despite this, Afghans remain deeply engaged with news, and access to information – though increasingly limited – is still a vital part of daily life.

TELEVISION AND RADIO Television remains one of the most popular forms of media in Afghanistan, especially in cities. Channels such as TOLOnews, which was once known for its open reporting and critical analysis, continue to operate but with a significantly more cautious editorial tone. The national broadcaster, RTA (Radio Television Afghanistan), now largely serves as a state media channel, reflecting the official positions of the Taliban government. Other domestic broadcasters such as Shamshad TV continue to air, generally sticking to topics such as religious programming, news bulletins and cultural content. In October 2024, the leadership in Kandahar sent out a directive banning photography and broadcasting images of living beings. There is resistance, notably among the Taliban in Kabul and the Haqqani Network, which produces much of Afghanistan's propaganda, and at the time of writing the ban has yet to be widely enforced.

In rural areas, **radio** remains the dominant medium. Its accessibility, low cost, and wide reach make it especially important in regions with limited access to electricity or internet. The BBC's Pashto and Dari services are still widely listened to. Local stations such as Arman FM have scaled back operations or changed programming formats to comply with new media regulations. Radio news that strays into politically sensitive territory is increasingly rare.

NEWS AND OTHER MEDIA **Print media**, once an important part of Afghanistan's public discourse, has been hit hardest. Many formerly respected publications, such as *8AM Daily* and *Etilaatroz*, have relocated abroad, and those that remain inside the country tend to avoid controversial topics. The collapse of the economy and a sharp decline in advertising have further undermined print journalism, making newspapers a far less visible presence in daily life.

A number of Afghan **media outlets** now operate in exile, broadcasting or publishing online from abroad. Afghan International TV and TV1 are prominent examples. Both broadcast via satellite from outside the country and are notable for their more critical stance on the current government. Their coverage offers perspectives that are often absent in domestic Afghan media and, as a result, they are followed closely by viewers both within Afghanistan and in the diaspora. Their popularity is helped by the fact that many Afghan households – despite Taliban restrictions – have satellite dishes. These are technically illegal but remain widespread, especially in urban areas, allowing people to access a wider variety of international and exile-based content.

The appetite for **news** and information remains strong. Many Afghans turn to social media, messaging apps, and YouTube channels for updates and alternative viewpoints, though access to these platforms is occasionally restricted.

The official government news website (in excellent English) is w alemarahenglish.af. There are a range of English-language sources, namely: Afghan News International (w afintl.com/en), written by journalists in and outside of the country, as is Future Afghanistan (w future-afghanistan.com); the AAN (Afghanistan Analysts Network; w afghanistan-analysts.org); 8am media (w 8am.media); Kabul Now (w kabulnow.com); BS Afghan Witness (w afghanwitness.org); and The Afghan Times (w theafghantimes.com). The women-led Zan Times (w zantimes.com) covers human rights violations in Afghanistan while Tolonews (w tolonews.com) is more circumspect regarding any criticism of Afghanistan.

INTERNET Access in Afghanistan has improved in recent years, particularly in urban centres like Kabul, Herat and Mazar e Sharif, where mobile data and Wi-Fi networks are commonly available. However, internet speeds and reliability can be inconsistent depending on the location. In October 2025 the government cut the internet to the entire country for 48 hours, and total communication blackouts are possible. In larger cities, internet access is relatively decent, with mobile data speeds of 2–4 Mbps, depending on the provider and network traffic. In rural and more remote areas, internet access can be extremely limited or non-existent, and connection speeds tend to be slower. While 4G is available in some urban centres, the majority of mobile internet users still rely on 3G, especially in less populated areas.

Public Wi-Fi networks are found in many cafés, restaurants, and hotels in urban areas, but these can be slow and unreliable. Security is also a concern when using public Wi-Fi, and it is strongly recommended to use a VPN (Virtual Private Network) to protect your personal data. You may also experience occasional censorship, as certain websites – especially those related to social media or political content – may be blocked. However, for general browsing, messaging apps and light streaming, the internet in major cities is usually sufficient.

MOBILE PHONES These are the lifeblood of communication in Afghanistan, where they serve as the primary means of staying in touch with friends, family and colleagues. The country has an extensive mobile network, but the infrastructure is not as advanced as in some other countries. Although mobile coverage is generally available in cities and major towns, it can be more limited in rural and remote areas, especially in the mountainous regions.

2 | PRACTICAL INFORMATION

PHONE NUMBERS AND DIALLING CODES

In Afghanistan, **mobile numbers** typically begin with 7, which is the most common prefix. Using a mobile is often the cheapest way to make calls within the country, especially as many people (notably hotels) use WhatsApp. **Fixed-line numbers** in cities such as Kabul and Herat are relatively rare, but you will still find them in some older hotels or large establishments.

If you don't have an Afghan SIM card, dial +93 before the numbers in the text. If you do, add a 0 in front of the number.

In case of an emergency, the **emergency services number** is generally 102. In Kabul, Herat and the Salang Pass this should get you through to a 24/7 ambulance service although it's unclear how reliable or responsive the service may be. In practice, many Afghans will turn to mobile phones for more immediate needs, like calling a taxi or local contacts for help.

SIM cards, roaming and mobile data When travelling in Afghanistan, purchasing a local SIM card is the most convenient and affordable way to access mobile data and make calls. The country has several mobile network providers, including Roshan (w roshan.af), ATOMA (w atoma.com.af) and Afghan Wireless (w afghan-wireless.com). These companies offer 4G coverage in most urban areas, and even some rural areas, though speeds and availability may vary.

To get a SIM card, visit the shop of one of the local telecom companies, which are easily found in cities. You will need to provide your passport for registration, as this is required by Afghan law. SIM cards are inexpensive, and you can choose from a variety of prepaid plans, which are ideal for short-term visitors. Once you have a SIM card, you can activate a data plan that suits your needs, whether you need just a few megabytes for light browsing or a larger data package for more intensive use.

While **eSIMs** are becoming more common globally, they do not work reliably in Afghanistan, and most people still rely on traditional physical SIM cards. Be aware that **international roaming** might not always work well in Afghanistan, so it's best to check with your mobile provider before you travel.

POST Afghan Post (w afghanpost.gov.af/en) is the national postal service, although in practice it is unknown and unused by the vast majority of the country. In Afghanistan, sending mail can be a challenge due to the lack of standardised addresses, particularly in rural areas. While the capital, Kabul, has some postal services, the system can be slow and inconsistent. However, under the Taliban, Afghan Post has been working to improve its operations and expand services.

Afghan Post is primarily used for sending or receiving international items (making it a fun way to send postcards) and for official documents. It's particularly used for handling correspondence with government ministries, and many people rely on it for passport applications, which are now processed through post offices located in regional centres. In addition, the post office in Kabul offers stamps that celebrate Afghan achievements, such as the first Afghan-made sports car, a symbol of the country's growth and modernisation. For larger or more valuable parcels, choose an international private shipping company, as they provide more reliable and secure services. These companies are a better option for anything beyond postcards or small documents.

Domestically, many Afghans rely on the shared taxi and minivan services to send mail or small packages. This informal yet popular method involves handing documents or parcels to a driver, who then transports them to the destination city. For a fee, the recipient meets the driver at the other end to collect the item. This system is quicker, more direct and for the time being more reliable than the official postal service.

CULTURAL ETIQUETTE

When visiting Afghanistan, it is essential to be aware of the cultural etiquette and respect local traditions. Understanding these customs helps build positive relationships with the local people and ensures that interactions are conducted respectfully.

TEA DRINKING One of the most common customs in Afghan culture is the offer of tea. Tea is a central part of Afghan hospitality, and it is often offered to guests as a gesture of respect and warmth. However, the offer of tea can occasionally be more of a polite formality, much like the *tarouf* in Iran. When offered tea, it is generally polite to accept, but keep in mind that sometimes the offer may be simply to show courtesy rather than a genuine invitation. For example, when the Taliban offer tea at checkpoints, they might not always mean it, though at times, they might indeed offer you tea with sincerity. It's important to read the situation carefully. If you're unsure, politely rejecting the offer is typically a safe choice.

COMMUNICATING When greeting others, men in Afghanistan often touch their hearts as a sincere gesture of respect, particularly when they are meeting someone of importance or older than them. It's important to note that women typically do not shake hands with men, especially in public (Afghan people do understand that a handshake is an international gesture, though it's not traditional, even between men). If you are meeting a woman, a smile and a nod are usually sufficient to show respect, and it is better not to initiate physical contact unless it is with a close family member.

Afghans are sensitive to bodily functions in public. It is important not to break wind or blow your nose in public as these actions are considered impolite and disrespectful. If necessary, it is best to do so discreetly and away from others. This extends to other forms of communication as well: verbal and non-verbal communication is highly nuanced, and being aware of the context is crucial. When communicating with someone older or of the opposite gender, the conversation tends to be more indirect and deferential. People show respect by using polite language and softer tones. For those of the same age or gender, conversation can be more direct, but it is always courteous and mindful of the other person's comfort. Afghans admire articulate speakers, and communication is seen as an art.

Eye contact in Afghanistan is also culturally significant. Afghans generally avoid sustained eye contact with members of the opposite sex, as well as with elders, out of respect for their status. This is a sign of modesty and reverence for social hierarchies. However, direct eye contact is common and expected when speaking with someone of the same age, gender, or status. In these instances, making eye contact is a sign of attentiveness and engagement.

TOUCHING Physical contact between men and women is highly restricted in public. It is inappropriate to show affection to someone of the opposite sex unless you are in a private setting. There might be an initial handshake with a guide, but then after that no further physical contact should occur. However, men often show affection in public by walking arm in arm or holding hands, which is completely acceptable in Afghan culture. Women are expected to refrain from any form of physical affection in public, with such actions reserved for private spaces with family or close friends.

Personal space in Afghanistan is also different from Western norms. People of the same sex often stand or sit very close to one another, sometimes closer than what Westerners might be used to. This is not meant to be intrusive, but rather a sign of camaraderie and closeness. However, when it comes to the opposite sex, personal space is respected, and an arm's length is typically maintained.

GESTURING Gesturing should also be approached with care. For instance, the thumbs-up gesture is considered rude, equivalent to raising one's middle finger in Western cultures. The 'OK' hand sign, forming a circle with the index finger and thumb, can also be offensive, as it may symbolise the evil eye or something more lewd. On the other hand, hooking your index fingers together is a sign of agreement, and stroking one's beard or pounding a fist into one's hand may signify anger or a desire for revenge.

In Afghanistan, the use of the right hand holds cultural significance. Islamic principles dictate that the left hand is reserved for hygiene purposes. Therefore, it is important to use your right hand when eating, offering items or gesturing. Offering something with the left hand, such as food or a gift, can be seen as disrespectful. Similarly, it is best to avoid using the left hand for gestures or touching people.

Feet and foot gestures are another area where cultural sensitivity is important. Pointing your feet towards someone, or showing the bottom of your feet while sitting, is considered extremely disrespectful and can be perceived as a serious insult. It is always best to sit with your feet tucked underneath or facing the ground to avoid causing offence.

Lastly, winking at a member of the opposite sex is considered highly inappropriate and can be seen as a form of flirtation or disrespect. A man would be deeply offended if he saw his female relative being winked at, and this should be avoided at all costs.

CLOTHING When travelling in Afghanistan, it is important to dress modestly and respectfully to fit in with the local culture, which is generally conservative especially in rural areas. The way you dress will also influence how you are perceived.

For **men**, it is highly recommended to wear traditional Afghan clothing particularly in more rural or conservative areas. The **pirhan tumban** or **shalwar kameez** (long tunic shirt and long baggy trousers) are the most common and comfortable clothing choices for men. These garments are not only practical for Afghanistan's climate, but they also help visitors blend in with the local population. Wearing a pirhan tumban or shalwar kameez will avoid attracting unnecessary attention and show respect for Afghan customs. In urban areas like Kabul, you may see men in Western-style clothing, but even in these places, it's still considered more respectful for visitors to wear traditional attire. Shorts and tight-fitting clothing must be avoided. When swimming, men must wear shorts that give coverage from the waist to the knee.

Women are expected to dress very modestly and cover their body outside of private spaces, though the expectations can vary by region. Although the burqa (a full-body covering, nicknamed the 'shuttlecock' by the women who wear it) is not mandatory for Afghan women under the current government, many still wear it in rural areas. In southern Afghanistan and when travelling outside major cities or in rural areas, it is advisable to wear an *abaya* (long, loose black robes which leave only the face visible) plus a **headscarf** or shawl to cover your hair. In cities like Kabul and Bamiyan, a shalwar kameez, along with a headscarf, is generally acceptable providing both comfort and modesty. A *chador* (large scarf or shawl) is commonly used by women to cover their head and shoulders in colder conditions.

PHOTOGRAPHY Photography in Afghanistan requires a respectful and cautious approach, especially when photographing people. Always ask first, particularly in rural areas. Do not photograph women unless you have clear and enthusiastic permission, which is rare. Even asking can be inappropriate in many situations and may cause discomfort or offence. Most men are happy – or at least willing – to be photographed if you ask politely. A friendly nod to your camera followed by a smile often goes a long way. However, always respect a refusal and never push it.

Using a small, unobtrusive camera or phone can make people feel more at ease and may attract less attention. In conservative or tightly controlled areas, being discreet helps you avoid unwanted scrutiny.

Always be courteous and it's a good idea, if asked, to show people the photos you've taken of them. This often builds trust and can open the door to further opportunities. If someone asks you not to take a photo or to delete one, it's important to comply without argument.

TRAVELLING POSITIVELY

Travelling in Afghanistan is a privilege, and with that comes the responsibility to do so thoughtfully and respectfully. Afghanistan is a conservative society with deeply rooted traditions, and visitors should always aim to minimise their impact and be aware of local customs. Dress modestly and be respectful of religious practices. It's important not to photograph military personnel, checkpoints, or government buildings. The country also struggles with waste management infrastructure, so managing your own trash and carrying re-usable items – like water bottles or bags – is essential. Taking your litter with you when hiking or refusing plastic bags at shops are small acts that can make a real difference.

Be conscious of how you portray Afghanistan online. While it's tempting to share striking images or stories, try to avoid reinforcing stereotypes. Highlight the country's complexity and resilience – not just its hardship or contrasts. When it comes to giving, you'll see people begging in cities and at roadside stops. Whether or not to give is personal, but handing out money can sometimes fuel dependency or organised begging. A more helpful option is to ask a restaurant to pack up your leftover food and give it to someone in need – this is a culturally appropriate and appreciated gesture.

In traffic jams or in restaurants, you may see boys waving smoking bundles of *spandi* (a mix of grass and wild rue seeds) to ward off bad luck or evil. A small tip is customary and offers these boys a modest but important income. If you'd like to support verified initiatives, you can also consider donating to organisations that help Afghan communities more sustainably. One such group is **Street Child Afghanistan** (w street-child.org), which works with children living or working on the street by providing them with education and support.

Listed below are a number of reputable organisations working in Afghanistan that welcome donations to continue their work:

Afghanaid w afghanaid.org.uk. Longstanding development NGO working on education, livelihoods & emergency response throughout Afghanistan.

Afghan Peaks w afghanpeaks.org. Working directly with the Bamiyan Alpine Ski Club (page 178) to develop skiing & mountaineering in the Central Highlands.

Afghan Sports Trust w afghansportstrust.org. Supporting a wide range of grassroots sports initiatives, including education & equipment provision.

Free to Run w freetorun.org. An NGO using sports to empower Afghan women & girls, currently operating underground or in exile.

Médecins Sans Frontières MSF; w msf.org. Delivering vital medical care across the country in challenging conditions.

Turquoise Mountain w turquoisemountain.org. A non-profit supporting artisans and communities to protect and revitalise their cultural heritage. See also page 131.

World Food Programme WFP; w wfp.org. Wakhan-specific projects focus on food security in remote, mountainous communities.

TAJIKISTAN & AFGHANISTAN

The Pamir Highway, Wakhan Corridor, Kabul, Bamiyan and Mazar-I-Sharif.

Discover the hidden gems and rich cultural tapestry of these two countries in small groups!

Guaranteed departures at budget-friendly prices!

WWW.PENGUINTRAVEL.COM

quote Bradt for 5% discount

Part Two

THE GUIDE

3

Kabul and Around

Home to more than 7 million people and counting, Afghanistan's lofty capital is currently the world's 75th largest city. Since 2012, Kabul is also one of the five fastest growing in the world, a 'primate city', twice as large and important as any other city in the country. Founded on the Kabul River, a tributary of the Indus, the setting is spectacular. One of the world's highest capitals at 1,790m, Kabul occupies a triangular valley in the Hindu Kush at the southern end of the Shomali Plains; the buildings appear from the air like a sea sloshing against the mountains that surround and divide it.

It has also been described as an 'amnesiac city' like Baghdad, where it's impossible to measure the beauty and human knowledge that has been lost over the centuries. Old hippies would hardly recognise the place: Soviet occupation, civil war and modern reconstruction have changed the city dramatically in the last 50 years. There's a lot more traffic, and in one way it feels more like a capital, thanks to the cosmopolitan variety of people now living there from all corners of Afghanistan.

This chapter goes beyond the city to include several important Buddhist sites around Kabul, the Panjshir Valley, Paghman, the 'garden capital of Afghanistan', the hill village of Istalif, and the Salang Pass.

HISTORY

Archaeologists in Kabul have found artefacts going back to the 3rd century BCE – although a settlement may well be much older; the Kabul River is mentioned in the Rig Veda (as 'Kubah') in the 2nd millennium BCE. Afghans have come up with several far-fetched stories to explain its name: one tells how it was founded by two sons of Noah named Cakool and Habool, who split their names to form 'Kabul'.

In ancient times, Bagram (page 141) to the north was the important city along the favoured trade routes between the Khyber Pass and central Asia. After forming part of the Greek-Bactrian and Indo-Greek kingdoms, Kabul was ruled after 560CE by the Buddhist Turkishahi tribe, a time when Chinese travellers mentioned 'a million' monasteries and stupas in the environs. Several attempts to conquer and convert it to Islam succeeded only when Sabuktigin took it for the Ghaznavid Empire in the late 10th century.

Even the earliest surviving accounts of Kabul remarked on its delightful climate: 'one of the choicest and most pleasant towns' wrote the 12th-century geographer al-Idrisi, who marvelled at its saffron and indigo crops, its fortress and the iron mines – before Genghis Khan destroyed all in 1221. In 1333, the Moroccan scholar ibn Battuta paid a call. 'We travelled on to Kabul, formerly a vast town, the site of which is now occupied by a village inhabited by a tribe of Persians called Afghans. They hold mountains and defiles and possess considerable strength, and are mostly highwaymen.'

HISTORY

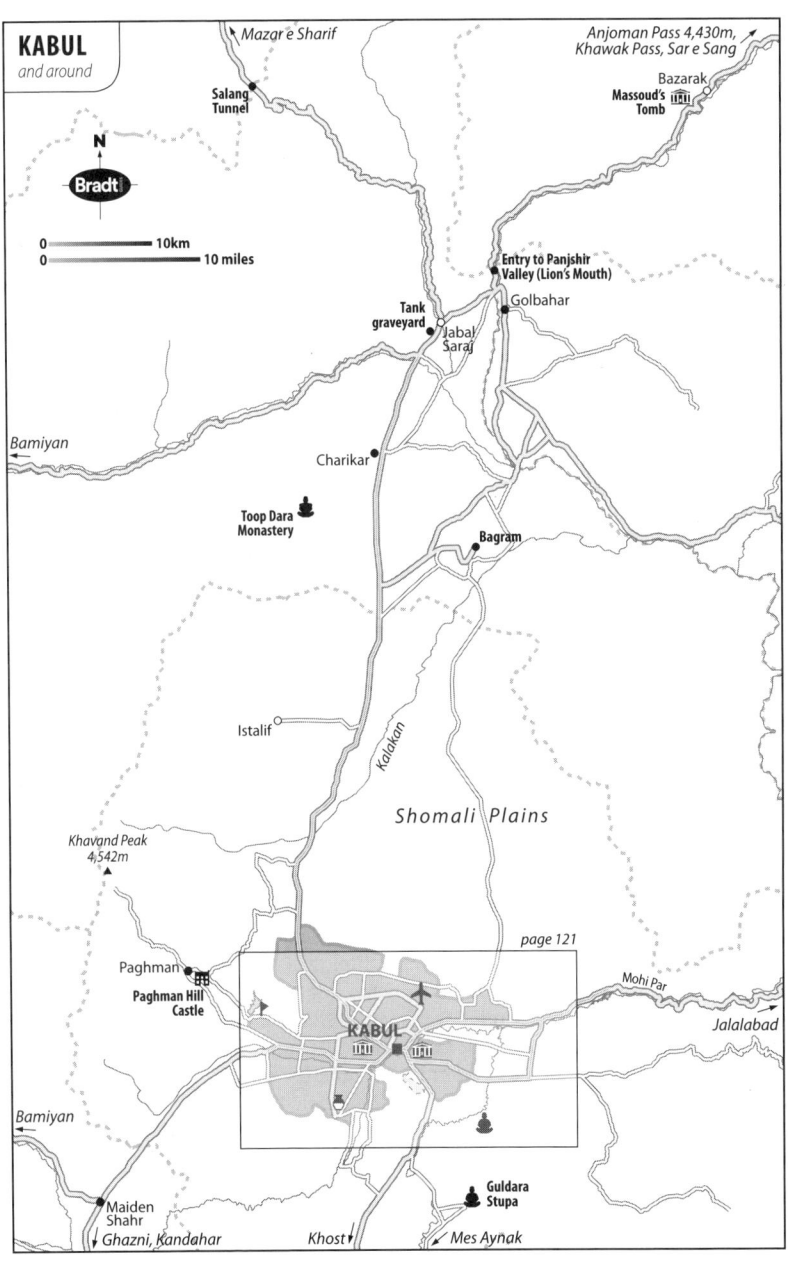

Timur conquered Kabul in 1325, as did his descendant, Babur, in 1504, taking it from the Arghuns and installing himself in the Bala Hissar as king of Kabul and Ghazni. Under his rule, Kabul became a great trading hub. 'In Kabul can be had products of Khursan, Rum (Istanbul), Iraq and China, while it is Hindustan's own market,' he wrote. Even after his later conquests in India, when he founded the Mughal Empire, Kabul remained close to his heart (page 135).

Later Mughal emperors made Kabul their summer resort. Babur's grandson Akbar, later to be one of the greatest emperors, was raised in Kabul. But later Mughal lords neglected it, and by the early 18th century Kabul's population had dwindled to around 10,000, making it an easy prey for the Turkmen adventurer Nader Shah, who took it in 1739 on his way to India. While the next ruler of Afghanistan, Ahmad Shah Durrani, made Kandahar his capital, his son Timur Shah moved the capital to Kabul shortly after acceding to the throne in 1772. It has remained ever since.

Timur Shah and Zamen Shah encouraged educated people to move there; more Westerners came to visit. It became a city of splendid bazaars (the restored Double Column Serai in Murad Khani is a survivor). Visitors were impressed by its friendliness, hospitality and its tolerance of the city's Jewish and Armenian Christian minorities, although all this was severely put to the test when Kabul became the base of the British cantonments during the Anglo–Afghan wars (page 28). It was a dark time; Kabul saw massacres and the loss of its great bazaar and the Bala Hissar, both destroyed in retribution by the British Army.

KABUL IN THE 20TH CENTURY Kabul began to noticeably expand into Shahre Nau (New Town) on the north bank of its river in the 1900s. The Arg (royal/presidential palace) was built to replace the Bala Hissar. The population grew rapidly as Tajiks, Uzbeks and Turkmen fled Soviet rule of their homelands. So many Muslim refugees poured in from India that King Amanullah Khan had to ban any more from coming.

In the 1920s, Amanullah, inspired by Hausmann's Paris, dreamed of creating a planned modern capital, and hired German engineers to build boulevards, bridges and buildings. This included a new region southwest of Kabul which he called Darulaman ('Abode of Peace'); he also founded numerous schools, including the Franco-Afghan Lycée Esteqlal attended by Ahmad Shah Massoud. His successor, Nadir Shah, established Kabul University before he was assassinated and replaced by his son, Zahir Shah, who would live long enough to return to Afghanistan in 2002, aged 87.

In 1948, when the city's population had yet to reach 170,000, the first elected mayor began to obliterate the old street plan to make room for cars and expand the city. Hotels catering to Westerners sprouted up, and as the Soviets courted Afghanistan, they erected prefabricated concrete apartment complexes called *macroyans*, designed to nudge Kabulis into thinking communism was the future.

As the West too began to court Afghanistan, Marks and Spencer chose Kabul to open their first branch in central Asia. Cinemas showed the latest from Hollywood and Bollywood. The Kabul Zoo opened in 1967. 'It' couple Louis Dupree and Nancy Hatch Dupree ran an open bar from their home (page 118). Young people from around the world converged on Kabul on the hippie trail, where they camped out and bought hashish on Chicken Street for less than 10 cents a day. The Kabulis didn't quite know what to do with them as they ran out of money and started to beg. Worried parents wrote to embassies wondering where their children were. Most eventually asked their parents to pay for a ticket back home as winter set in.

It all began to go wrong with the assassination of President Daoud and family in the Arg, in April 1978. The Saur Revolution that followed nationalised businesses and began to clamp down on Kabul's liberal ways. And then came the Soviet invasion in December 1979. More macroyans went up around Kabul, although many were inhabited by Soviet bureaucrats. Local resistance was so fierce that the city was put under a nightly curfew that lasted for seven years. At the same time, Kabul's population exploded as up to 1.5 million from around the embattled countryside sought safety in the city.

Once the Soviets withdrew and President Najibullah was overthrown, all hell broke loose when Hekmatyar refused to join the other mujahideen in signing the Peshawar Accords and started rocket bombing Kabul (page 34) from the surrounding slopes. This started a civil war that would leave 80% of Kabul in ruins, without electricity and water. Kabulis fled to the countryside to survive. In 1996, just as the mujahideen agreed to a power-sharing agreement, the Taliban began their assault and took over what remained of the broken city in 1998.

KABUL IN THE 21ST CENTURY In spite of the destruction, Greater Kabul's population stood at around 2.4 million as NATO took over Kabul after the Taliban abandoned the city in November 2001. Kabulis who had fled returned; expatriate Afghans flooded back. These were boom times as the city became a magnet for construction and office workers, students and NGOs as its infrastructure, monuments and palaces were restored. Entire new neighbourhoods, shiny skyscrapers, shopping centres and Western-style residential complexes (*shahraks*) went up, their apartments often selling out long before the buildings were finished.

'Poppy palaces' (page 57) sprouted up around the city, notably in Sherpur, built over the 19th-century British army cantonment on land handed out to cronies during the Karzai years. Many were rented out to news organisations, security firms and NGOs. Large garish neon-bedecked wedding halls became some of the most prominent buildings in Kabul, able to seat thousands, catering for weddings of the wealthy and serving as locations for political rallies. The working class made do with squatters' slums. In 2004, the World Bank wrote that informal settlements, built outside of Kabul's master plan and mostly on state-claimed land, accounted for 70% of the housing, home to 80% of the population.

Almost from the beginning, however, security was an issue, and there were attacks, mainly by the Taliban and Haqqani Network. A Green Zone in the centre was protected by a 'Ring of Steel' (25 Afghan National Police checkpoints) and blast walls. In spite of these precautions, a truck bomb exploded near the German embassy on 21 May 2017 at rush hour, killing over 150 and injuring over 400 (Afghan intelligence pointed to the Haqqani Network). On 8 May 2021, IS-K killed 90 school-age girls and wounded hundreds of others in a horrific car bombing in the Hazara-majority Dashte Barchi district.

As coalition forces withdrew from Afghanistan and the Taliban approached, the price of burqas soared. Security forces fled abroad in panic; President Ghani fled in a helicopter (15 August), 11 days before the IS-K suicide bomber killed hundreds of Afghans and US personnel at the airport. The last plane left just before midnight, on 30 August 2021, leaving behind some 1,000 US citizens and thousands of Afghans, translators, security guards and others who had worked with the coalition, who went into hiding and tried to get over the border in any way possible. Many sold their houses for whatever they could get; for Kabulis who remained behind, the cost of buying or renting became much easier.

KABUL TODAY The change of governments happened so quickly that Kabul suffered little damage. The affordable rents, however, are now a distant memory, as people from around the country have flooded into the capital. The lack of work in the provinces and climate change in rural areas have seen a surge of families moving to the city in search of jobs, competing with nearly 1 million recent returnees from Pakistan. Afghans living abroad with second passports have been buying up property, along with Taliban authorities, many of whom have three or four wives and want to buy a house for each. As one estate agent dealing in high-end properties

3 | KABUL AND AROUND

> **THE GRANDMOTHER OF AFGHANISTAN** *James Willcox*
>
> Fondly known as the 'Grandmother of Afghanistan', Nancy Hatch Dupree devoted decades of her remarkable life to the country. Born in New York in 1927 to a father who worked in the state department, she spent her childhood in India and Mexico, then studied art and Chinese art at Barnard College. There she met her first husband, CIA agent Alan Wolfe, and lived with him in Iraq, Pakistan and Afghanistan. When the Afghan Tourist Organisation asked her to write a guide to Bamiyan, she was sent to meet archaeologist Louis Dupree, to ask him to check over her text. Instead, they fell in love, and in 1962 divorced their partners so they could marry (the divorced partners then married each other, so everyone was happy).
>
> During the hippie trail days of the 1960s and early 70s, Nancy and Louis invited anyone who was anyone to their after-work 'five o'clock follies'. The only open bar in Kabul, it allowed foreign diplomats, journalists, Afghan government officials, professors and communists to get to know one another informally.
>
> Nancy finished her 491-page *An Historical Guide to Afghanistan* (page 287) in 1979, just as the Soviets invaded. Louis was briefly imprisoned under the hard-line Taraki regime before the couple escaped to Peshawar. Louis travelled back and forth with the mujahideen while Nancy stayed in Pakistan, helping thousands of Afghan refugees. They were involved in discussions with the US government to move the Kyrgyz nomads of the Afghan Pamir to Alaska (page 269) before they went back to the US, where Louis became a professor at Duke University.
>
> Nancy was heartbroken when Louis died in 1989 and brought his ashes to Bagh e Bala in Kabul, where they had married. Eventually she returned to Peshawar,

told US News and World Report (3 December 2024), 'People think this country has no jobs and no economy. But Afghans have made their money, illegally or legally, over the years. You wouldn't believe it.'

The government has embarked on a major urban redevelopment scheme, building new wider streets and housing, and bulldozing slums built on 'government' land, giving residents little warning and very little if any compensation. They have revised the 2006 plans for Kabul New City (w kabulnewcity.com) northeast of Kabul, designed to be built over 30 years and house 3 million people; in August 2023 the first phase was finally inaugurated.

The city today feels less under siege than it has in decades, although blast walls around government buildings decorated with religious, civic and anti-US messaging and the odd checkpoint do not let you forget that Kabul is the capital of a heavily militarised nation. The years of conflict, rebuilding and increasing population have left a poorly planned city with few civic places, lots of dusty concrete and gridlocked traffic. Even so, Kabul remains a low-rise, human-scale city – and when looking down from one of the hills, you can see a suprisingly green city. The courtyards and internal gardens of homes are a refuge from the urban bustle, reminding one that, while Afghanistan can appear rough on the outside, beauty is never far away.

GETTING THERE AND AWAY

BY AIR Kabul has one airport, Kabul International Airport (formerly Khwaja Rawash and Hamid Karzai International Airport) located 3–4km from Shahre Nau and most of the city's hotels. It has two terminals. Afghan and foreign airlines (page compiling and protecting the Afghan archives which would become her project for the next 30 years. In 1992, hearing that her beloved National Museum in Kabul had been damaged, she made the dangerous trip to the capital to help the staff preserve what the rockets and looters had left and establish the Society for the Preservation of Afghanistan's Cultural Heritage (SPACH). Realising how little young Afghans knew about their country's history, she organised the Mobile Museum Outreach Project: buses went around the country with 3D copies of artefacts from the museum.

After 2001, she worked to make the Afghanistan Centre at Kabul University (ACKU) the permanent home for the archives, documenting and storing images and documents of national interest to its website, where I met her in the early 2010s. She would have been about 85 and, tiny and frail as she was, she was a force of nature and the other staff acted on her every command. We went out for kebabs at a nondescript restaurant close to the university rather than any of the typical expat haunts. I think she liked me and what I did in Afghanistan because, like her, it came from a genuine love of being in Afghanistan rather than being in Afghanistan because it was broken and needed fixing. Two things she mentioned that seemed prescient: first that, compared with ISIS, the Taliban did not seem so bad; and, second, she was a friend of Ashraf Ghani, former chancellor of the university. She questioned why he was getting himself involved in politics and warned that it would only end badly.

Nancy died in 2017 in North Carolina in the United States, and her friends hope someday to bring her ashes back to lie with her two loves: Louis and Afghanistan.

---

73) arrive at the international terminal; upon arrival on an international flight, you will need to complete a registration card (page 73) available from a booth in the luggage reclaim area. Domestic flights arrive at the second terminal, 200m away. As there are no direct flights between Afghanistan's other cities, you may well visit Kabul Airport several times.

Airport facilities are basic, limited to moneychangers, drinks and snacks, although the international departure area has a small gift shop. The layout of the area outside the terminals has changed multiple times over the last 15–20 years, mainly to restrict non-ticket holders from coming too close to the terminal buildings.

When departing Afghanistan or taking a domestic flight, give yourself plenty of time. There are currently six security checks of varying thoroughness between arriving at the airport and boarding the plane, in addition to delays caused by Kabul's badly congested traffic.

Getting to/from the city Upon leaving the airport, you must cross an empty car park to a secondary car park, where taxis will take you into town for around 500AFN, though there is no set fee. This is one place in Afghanistan where you will need to negotiate a little on price; most drivers will speak little English. Make sure you leave plenty of time to travel to the airport when departing. Afghanistan's terrible traffic and security delays mean that even a short journey can take longer than expected.

BY ROAD Kabul has three large coach stations on the north, west and east edges of the city. Shared taxis and minivans also use smaller locations closer to the centre. The government is on a constant drive to move all shared transport to the large coach stations with varying degrees of success. Below are the main locations used at the time of writing.

Transport serving destinations **north of Kabul** arrive and depart from two main areas, both in northwest Kabul, on or just off the main road leading to the north. Large coaches depart from **Khai Khana** or **Terminal**. Shared taxis can also be found here but also closer to the centre at an intersection known as **Serai Shomali**. Large 30–40-seater coaches serving Mazar e Sharif and Kunduz (600–1,000AFN; 12hrs) or Fayzabad (1,200AFN; 15hrs) primarily depart in the early morning, while shared minivans and taxis travel more regularly between Kabul and Mazar e Sharif (1,200–1,500AFN; 12hrs) and Fayzabad (1,500–1,800AFN; 15hrs), and less regularly Panjshir (200–300AFN; 3hrs).

For destinations **southwest and west of Kabul** there are two main stations. Shared taxis and minivans from/to Bamiyan (350–500AFN; 4hrs), Ghazni (300AFN; 3hrs) and destinations in Daykundi use **Istga e Bamiyan** on the far west side of Kabul. Large coaches, minivans and shared taxis arrive/depart from the area called **Istga e Kandahar** (also known as Company or Hada e Kandahar) to Kandahar (900–1,500AFN; 7–9hrs) and Herat (1,900–3,200AFN; 17–20hrs). Shared taxis to Qargha Lake and Paghman also leave from Company, as well as from the major roundabout close to the Intercontinental Hotel.

For destinations **east of Kabul** the best bet are shared taxis (for instance to/from Jalalabad; 500AFN; 3–5hrs) arriving and departing near the Eid Gah Mosque. Cheaper minivans and coaches from/to Jalalabad (350–400AFN; 3–5hrs) can be found at two istgas/adas 10km and 12km out of the centre of Kabul on the Jalalabad road. Note that travel times to Jalalabad can vary dramatically due to traffic at Mohi Par (page 143). This route is usually quieter in the mornings.

Minivans and shared taxis serving destinations **south of Kabul** (Gardez (350–400AFN; 2½–3hrs) and Khost (600–750AFN; 5hrs) use an area 2km south of the Bala Hissar called **Beni Hesar** or **Hada e Khost**.

GETTING AROUND

Navigating Kabul can be a challenge. Traffic rules are unclear, unfollowed and for the large part unenforced. There are very few street signs and the city is not designed for the volume of traffic that moves through it. This is exasperated by the hills that divide west Kabul from the rest of the city and the fact that the administrative centre is closed to traffic. This causes pinch points especially around Zarnegar Park with its complex one-way system. There are plenty of traffic police in Kabul, although they restrict their duties to managing busy crossroads and monitoring double parking – which is often enforced by slashing tyres.

If distances are not far, **walking** is the best option. However, after dark street lighting is not universal and there are open drainage ditches between many streets and pavements, so be careful. Otherwise, the most convenient way of getting around is by **taxi**. Pale blue (they were yellow, but the Taliban changed the colour) taxis are ubiquitous. Although other cars may also offer rides, they are not legitimate and best avoided. A typical fare is around 400AFN from the Old City to Darulaman Palace.

There are shared taxis and **minibuses** from the city centre to other districts. These are unmarked but can be identified by the conductor calling out destinations and cramming as many people as possible inside. The routes of these can be hard to fathom as there are multiple names for the same places (for instance, Shahre Nau might be called out as Charahi; the main junction in the Old City can be called Shahr, Firoz Koh or Murad Khani). Costs are usually 30–50AFN depending on the

GETTING AROUND

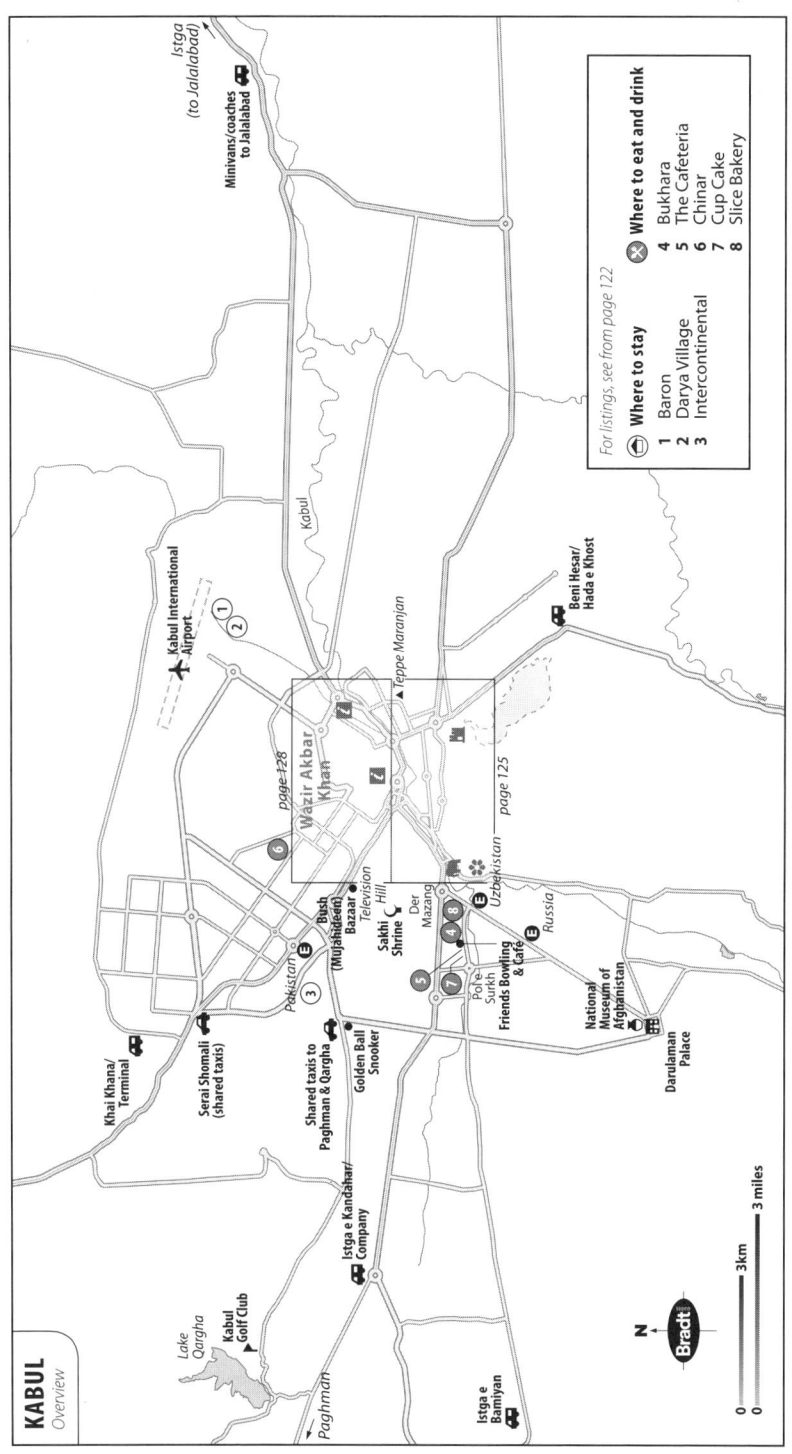

distance. One easy navigable route is between Der Mazang junction and Darulaman; thanks to King Amanullah, it's one long straight road with the Darulaman Palace as a handy landmark for the nearby Kabul Museum.

TOURIST INFORMATION AND REGISTRATION

All tourists must visit a branch office of the **Ministry of Information and Culture** [128 C4] (page 72). The main ministerial department (Wazir Akbar Khan Rd, behind Gulbahar business centre) currently outsources the permit process to the **Afghan Tour Department** [128 F2] (opposite the Macroyan District; both ⊕ 08.00–16.00 Sat–Wed, 08.00–14.00 Thu). Beyond issuing permissions, they offer basic tourist brochures and information and can arrange guiding and transport on request.

ORIENTATION

Despite Kabul's sprawl, most places of interest are in and around the Old City. Northwest of the Old City is the Shahre Nau district, where most visitors stay. East of this is the Wazir Akbar Khan district. The northern part of Wazir Akbar Khan is open to the public but the southern part, containing the old US Embassy [128 F2], the Arg, and other governmental and embassy buildings, is off-limits to visitors.

The Old City, located south of Shahre Nau and Wazir Akbar Khan, between the Kabul River and the hills of Sher Darawaza and Asamayi (or 'Television Hill' for all the antennae and masts on its summit), covers an area of just over 3km by 3km. Between walking and taxis it is easy enough to get to, though heavy traffic can mean even short trips can take a relatively long time. On the west slopes of Sher Darawaza and Asamayi are Sakhi Shrine, Babur's Garden, Kabul Zoo and the road towards Darulaman Palace and the museum.

 ## WHERE TO STAY

> If there is a paradise on earth, it is this, and it is this, and it is this!

These lines, inscribed on the tombstone of Babur (page 135), were written about his beloved Kabul, but they also apply to the feeling of sleeping and dining in Kabul compared with the rest of Afghanistan. The majority of the best mid-range hotels are in the Shahre Nau district, where you'll also find a good number of eating and shopping options, making the area a handy base. Note that some of the budget options may not accept international guests.

UPMARKET

Kabul Grand Hotel [125 D1] (Formerly Serena Hotel) Froshgah St; m 7996 54000; w kabulgrandhotel.com. Robert Byron (page 285) once wrote that the King David Hotel in Jerusalem is 'the only good hotel in Asia this side of Shanghai'. 100 years later he would as likely describe the Kabul Grand as the only good hotel between Tehran & Peshawar. Originally part of the Serena chain, the government nationalised it in early 2025 & appointed a German-based management company to run the services. Beautifully designed using traditional motifs, it is a real 5-star with lovely rooms, attentive staff, sauna & the coffee shop has possibly the best pastries in central Asia. Security is tight. At the time of writing, high standards are still being maintained. **$$$$**

MID-RANGE

Intercontinental [map, page 121] Bagh e Bala, 4th district; \2025 62767; m 7663 88220; w intercontinentalkabul.com. Built in 1969 on a small hill in west Kabul, the Intercontinental was Afghanistan's 1st 5-star hotel & with 200 rooms

WHERE TO STAY

it's the largest in the country. The rooms are clean, functional & all have balconies with views of the city. The hotel boasts a gym & a pool (photos of bikini-clad bathers can be found online from the early 1970s in the hotel's heyday). However, the whole place is a little tired & elsewhere would probably be classed as a 3-star. The hotel is owned & run by the government, which is why it has Taliban as well as private security. It is not affiliated to the Intercontinental hotel chain. AC, Western-style toilet. **$$$**

Kabul Star Hotel [128 C3] Zanbak Sq, Ankara St; 2023 13131; m 7288 83305; w kabulstarhotel.af. Large well-equipped hotel & a favourite for those wanting comfort but not keen to splash out on the Kabul Grand. It has a gym, sauna & pool. The rooms, en suite with Western-style toilets, are spacious, each with a balcony overlooking either the city or the giant flag on Bibi Mahru hill. Heavy security, AC; b/fast inc. **$$$**

INEXPENSIVE

Baron Hotel [map, page 121] m 7900 13878; w kabul.thebaronhotels.com. At the time of writing the Baron, along with Darya Village (opposite), are the last 2 functioning hotels from a clutch of 4 extremely high-security options attached to the airport. They really only welcome long-term visitors & staff are not comfortable with people who pop by looking for a room. The Baron was used as the processing centre by the British government in August 2021 during the airlift after the Taliban took control of the country. Many guests staying in these hotels never see the city & simply stay here while they conduct their work. The rooms are functional rather than luxurious. Mealtimes in the restaurants are extremely regimented; the well-equipped gym has a sauna. If you want to get a taste of the life of a security contractor or development consultant, then these are the places for you. Reservations are essential. AC, Western bathroom, extremely tight security; b/fast inc. **$$**

Cedar House [128 B3] 7 Yaftali St, behind Kabul City Centre mall, near Chowk Ansari; m 7002 24757; e cedarhouse@gmail.com. Lebanese-inspired & -run guesthouse. Rooms are based around a pleasant courtyard & the restaurant offers Lebanese dishes. Security, AC, Western-style toilets, b/fast inc. **$$**

Darya Village [map, page 121] Near the airport; m 7292 02287; w daryavillage.af. See Baron Hotel (opposite) for details. **$$**

Golden Star Hotel [128 B2] Haji Yaqoob Chowk; m 7913 33777. The Golden Star is now 15 years old & sometimes shows its age. However, it is in a good location with large rooms & the upper floors can have decent views. They have VIP rooms with better fittings, though they're the same size as the regular rooms. No security but they have a blast door, AC & Western-style toilets; b/fast inc. **$$**

Khyber Hotel [128 B3] Near Chowk Ansari, Shahre Nau; m 7988 88141; e khyberhotel622@gmail.com. Large clean rooms with amenities such as kettles, tea & coffee. A solid option & great for people with their own vehicles as it has underground parking. AC, Western-style toilets, b/fast inc. **$$**

Park Star Hotel [128 B3] Behind Kabul City Centre mall, Chowk Ansari, Shahre Nau; 2022 13331; m 7772 20221; w parkstarhotel.af. Comfortable, clean rooms set around a courtyard with a fountain. Good security, AC, Western-style toilets, b/fast inc. **$$**

Safi Landmark [128 B2] Chowk Ansari; 2022 03131; w safilandmarkhotelandsuites.com. The Safi Landmark is in the Kabul City Centre shopping mall, which boasted Afghanistan's first set of escalators. It's a well-known landmark so you will always be able to get directions to the hotel. The shopping mall now stands empty, giving the hotel a slightly eerie feeling. Small but comfortable rooms where things like Wi-Fi, AC & hot water work pretty much all the time. If you want mod cons like a kettle, they will bring you one. Security, Western-style toilets, b/fast inc. **$$**

Spinzar Hotel [125 C1] Aasmayi Wat; m 7080 35001; e kabul_hotel@spinzar.gov.af. Built in 1964 as part of a government initiative to increase tourist infrastructure and managed by various governments ever since, it's a stalwart of Afghan tourism. The rooms are faded & the whole hotel has a lacklustre air. The location, however, is fabulous & right in the thick of the action of the Old City. No AC, Western-style toilets, low-level security; b/fast inc. **$$**

SHOESTRING

Baba Wali [125 D2] Jada e Maiwand, next to Chowk Maiwand; 2021 08934; m 7829 00012,

7725 53654. For a real feel of old Kabul this simple mussafarkhana offers the best budget option in Afghanistan. The long, narrow two-floored inner atrium gives it the feel of a prison but rooms at the front have views overlooking the traffic jams & general chaos of Jada e Maiwand. No AC, no attached bathroom or Western-style toilets, no security. They may not accept non-Afghans. **$**
Baheristan Aria Guesthouse [128 B3] Opposite the AIB bank, Zargona Rd; m 2022 01546. Situated above a small restaurant, this slightly eccentrically furnished guesthouse is the best of the budget options in Shahre Nau, & is in the thick of the action. Check out a few rooms as the number of beds, functionality of the bathroom, & décor vary widely, & some rooms can smell a bit musty. Some rooms have bathrooms & some have Western-style toilets; AC, basic security & b/fast inc. **$**
Naikzad Guesthouse [125 C1] Andarabi Rd, near Spinzar Hotel; m 7901 05252, 7000 58686;

e naikzad.hotal@gmail.com. Another super budget option in the Old City. This 4-storey block on one of the busiest thoroughfares in Kabul is noisy. Even if you do not stay here, a meal in the restaurant watching the world go by is an experience. Very basic rooms with bed & fan. Squat toilet, non-attached bathroom, no security. **$**
Park Hotel [125 C1] Asamayi Wat; m 2021 03355. Tiny box-like rooms opposite the Spinzar Hotel at the edge of the Old City. It is grubby, noisy, but cheap. No Western-style toilets, no AC, no attached bathroom, no security. They may not accept non-Afghans. **$**
Shahr Guesthouse [128 B3] Zargona Rd; m 7750 06374. On the same strip as the Baheristan, the Shahr (formerly Salsal) has small, simple sgl, dbl & trpl rooms. It had a refurbishment at the time of writing & looks in decent condition. Rooms have shared bathrooms, squat toilets, generator, hot water, Wi-Fi & b/fast. **$**

WHERE TO EAT AND DRINK

You are never far away from somewhere to eat and drink in Kabul. Every district has its traditional restaurants servings pulao and kebabs. Vendors sell snacks and juices at major junctions and retail areas. It is hard to go hungry, although note that traditional restaurants open for breakfast then close around dusk. Often, they close even earlier in winter.

Kabul has by far the greatest number and variety of restaurants, coffee shops (where you can drink real coffee, rare elsewhere in the country) and bakeries in Afghanistan. If you have spent time in smaller towns, this is your chance to get a little bit of something different, or to grab a coffee or a tea and hang out.

Shahre Nau has the greatest choice of restaurants and is the only area that feels busy once night falls. Many establishments also do a roaring take-away trade and your hotel can usually assist if you want to dine in. Some of the mid-range hotels also have decent restaurants or they will have an association with a nearby restaurant. **Taimani and Qala e Fathullah** northwest of Shahre Nau used to have the best selection of upmarket restaurants and late-night venues catering for the NGO and expat crowd, although many have shut permanently or temporarily due to lack of trade.

SHAHRE NAU Along with the places listed below and on page 126, there's a strip of restaurants & fresh **juice stands** on the north side of Shahre Nau Park. If you're after street food, check out the **bolani stands** selling savoury-filled Afghan crepes on the south side of the park (both [128 B2]; **$**).

Barg Continental [128 B2] Next to Qasre Bakhtawar, opposite Shahre Nau Park; m 7921 71000. This busy, cavernous restaurant is hard to miss, set on the corner of the park. The garish décor & fast-food vibe should not hide the fact that this is a solid option. **$$**
Bukhara Restaurant [128 A3] Qowai Markaz, beside Malalay Hospital; m 7894 44222. One of the best places to eat in Kabul. The refined Afghan & Pakistani dishes are some of the best in Afghanistan & include a smattering of vegetarian offerings. The menu also features a few familiar Western dishes such as pizzas & fried chicken, as

WHERE TO EAT AND DRINK

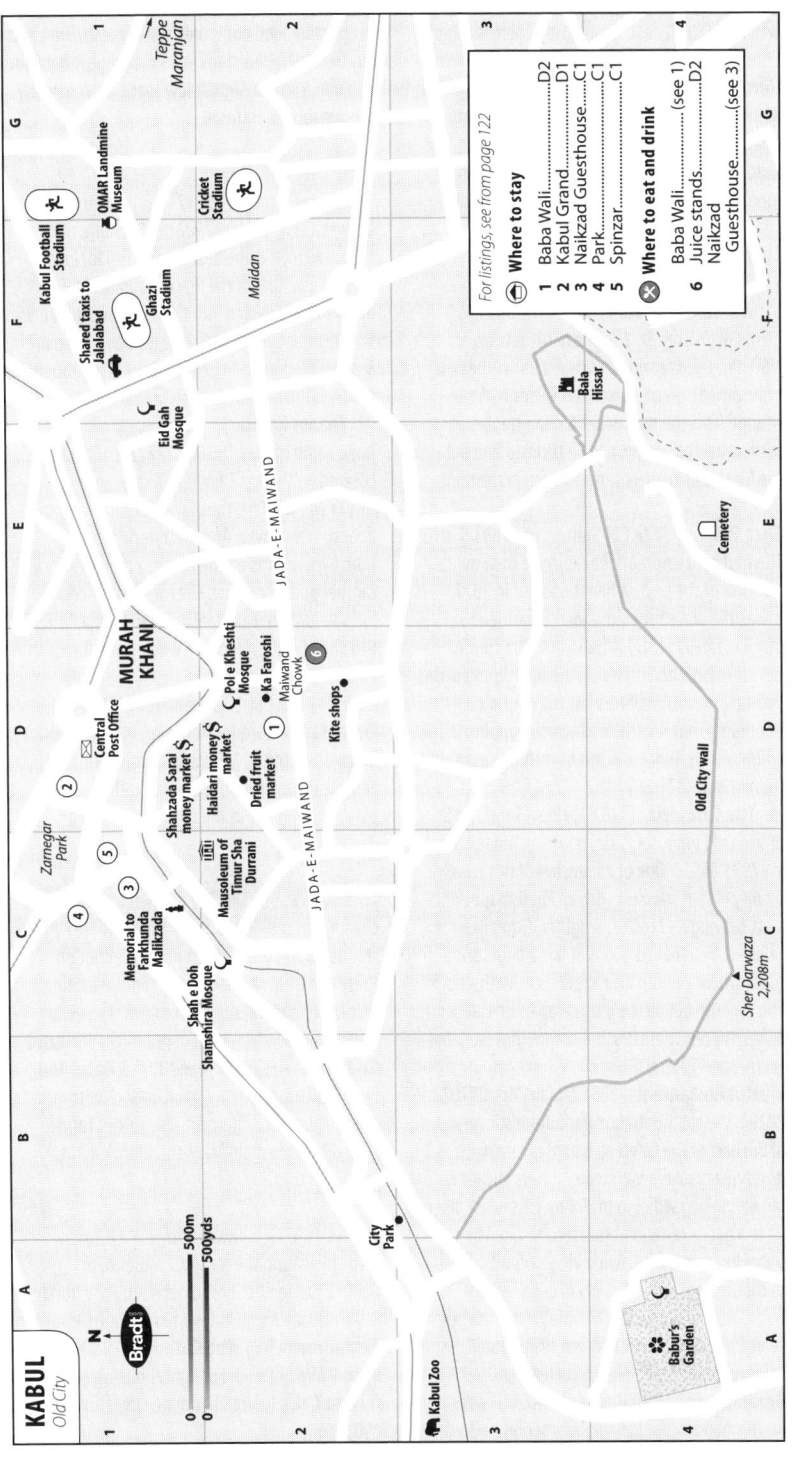

well as salads & daal. Great juices. There is a 2nd branch in west Kabul [map, page 121]. $$
Herati Restaurant [128 B2] Sulh Rd; m 7002 94977. A popular place in Shahre Nau offering a selection of Afghan dishes & fresh fruit juices. The shady garden at the back, populated by a small menagerie of birds including peacocks, is a nice spot to sit on warmer days. $$
Le Bistro [128 B3] Near Chicken St; m 7971 25130. This Afghan French café with a comfy garden is a great place to escape the hustle & bustle of Chicken St, & is one of the few expat/NGO hang-outs that has survived under the new government. Soups, pastries & salads make a change from the traditional Afghan staples. Serves real coffee, too. Can be tricky to find but the local shopkeepers can point you in the right direction. $$
Slice Bakery [128 C2] Sulh Rd; m 7863 57070. The first contemporary bakery/café in Kabul & still one of the best. When it opened in 2017, it was *the* place for young men & women to buy a coffee & pastry & hang out. The current government's ban on mixed-gender dining & the opening of similar places has rather cooled its popularity, but it's still well worth popping in for a light lunch. There is a 2nd branch in west Kabul [map, page 121]. $$
✻ **The Cafeteria** [128 B2] Noor Plaza, 2nd St, in front of Computer Plaza, near Haji Yaqoub Sq; m 7995 85856. One of 2 branches of this relaxed, quality café-restaurant with an English-speaking staff, serving real coffee, & lighter dishes like salads & fresh baked goods. It has 2 floors & is a place where you can lose a few hours with a book. You can also get all the usual Afghan specialities & fresh juices. There is a 2nd branch in west Kabul [map, page 121]. $$
Ziyafat Restaurant [128 C2] Sulh Rd; m 7702 00200. The glitzy entrance of this futuristic version of Bukhara or The Cafeteria is hard to miss, with its retinue of take-away scooter drivers outside & families taking selfies in the lobby. Lifts whisk diners up to a gaudy restaurant that feels inspired by a Dubai Instagram feed, where they swipe iPad menus to choose from a great variety of good-quality Pakistani, Afghan, Turkish & some Western dishes, served by the helpful & attentive waiting staff. It's wildly popular. Great selection of teas, too. $$
Derakhshan Kebab House [128 C3] Flower St. This nondescript kebab house serves perfectly serviceable food but is only worth mentioning as it sits below Afghanistan's last synagogue & home of Zabolan, the last Afghan Jew (page 54). Currently the synagogue is closed. $

TAIMANI AND QALA E FATHULLAH

✻ **Chinar** [map, page 121] Qala e Fathullah, between sts 5 & 6; m 7902 08080. Authentic Lebanese food & the best *fatoosh* (salad) in the Hindu Kush. One of the few restaurants in this district that survived into the new government & still popular with expats. Nice garden for summer & a real fire for winter. Worth the walk or cab to Qala e Fathullah. AC. Real coffee. $$
✻ **Shaam Kabul** [128 A3] Qwaye e Markaz Najib Zarab Market; ☏ 2022 27722; m 7312 27722. Located on the top 2 floors of a caravanserai of carpet wholesalers, the place is decorated from floor to ceiling with Afghan cultural artefacts, from Kyrgyz yurts on the roof to a green 1960s VW camper parked outside. The excellent offerings include Afghan, Pakistani & international dishes. Call ahead & they'll roast a whole lamb for 10,000AFN. $$
Sufi [128 B1] St 1, Taimani; m 7491 00101. Elegant restaurant located in an old Shahre Nau house from the 1920s. Serves Afghan dishes, as well as pastries, soups & real coffee. A lovely place to hang out in the garden on a warm day. $$

OLD CITY

The Old City is full of traditional chaikhanas selling kebabs & pulao, where hygiene standards can be less than perfect, although these can be great places for people-watching. Just look for plumes of smoke from the kebab chefs or follow the aroma of pulao. The **Naikzad Guesthouse** [125 C1] (page 124) & **Baba Wali** [125 D2] (page 123) are good options with views over busy streets. There are also **juice stands** [125 D2] at the main Maiwand Chowk in the middle of the Old City.

WEST KABUL *Map, page 121*

If you're visiting the National Museum or Babur's Gardens, the road between Pol e Surkh & Darulaman Rd includes a branch of **Bukhara Restaurant** ($$), **The Cafeteria** ($$) & **Slice Bakery** ($$). For lighter bites & coffee, try **Cup Cake** (Carte Char main street; m 7994 09030; $).

ENTERTAINMENT AND NIGHTLIFE

With music and shisha bars banned, nightlife in Kabul is limited. In winter there tend to be few people on the streets after 18.00 and in the summer after 21.00 or 22.00. Beyond dining out there is little to do – outside of snooker halls. Older Kabulis seem to think that they are full of ne'er-do-wells, but the young men running them all seemed extremely friendly. **Friends Bowling and Café** [map, page 121] (Karte e Char, next to Bukhara Restaurant; m 7909 99919; f; ⏱ 10.00–22.00 daily; 200AFN/hr) offers bowling, as well as snooker. The **Golden Ball Snooker Centre** [map, page 121] (Karte Mamureen, in the basement of the restaurant on the southeast corner; m 7887 88113; ⏱ 08.00–01.00 daily; 200AFN/hr), near the Intercontinental, is a well-kept and friendly snooker club with six full-size tables.

SHOPPING

There are small convenience stores all over town selling water, snacks, drinks and basic goods. For a slightly wider range of goods, try the **Finest Supermarket** [128 B2] or **ABC Supermarket** [128 B1] in Shahre Nau or **Spinneys** [128 C2] in Wazir Akbar Khan.

The most famous place for souvenir shopping is **Chicken Street** [128 B3]. Once the epicentre of Kabul's 1970s hippie trail (page 116), Chicken Street earned its name from the live poultry once sold here – long gone now. Many of the original low-slung buildings have been replaced with modern blocks and shopping centres, but the street still holds on to its legacy as the heart of Kabul's tourist trade. While a few shops sell tackier souvenirs – think fridge magnets, mugs and generic trinkets – Chicken Street remains a hub for wholesale handicrafts and antiques, with a diverse range of goods: stamps, coins (real and fake), semi-precious stones, textiles and old Buddhist beads. You'll also find traditional clothing, Afghan coats (page 62), animal skins, rugs – including the infamous 'war rugs' (page 61) – buzkashi whips, and all manner of tribal hats, from pakols to karakuls. For those into weaponry, there are decorative jezails and Khyber knives, though of course exporting such items is often a grey area.

Prices are rarely fixed, and **bargaining** is expected. Shop around before committing, as prices and quality can vary, but in general, most goods represent excellent value. Even if you're not planning to buy, the shops offer a chance to try on traditional outfits or browse through relics of Afghanistan's past. North of Chicken Street is **Flower Street** [128 C3], which still retains its eponymous florists.

Just beyond Chicken Street, the **Shah M Book Co** [128 B4] (Etihad Market, Charahi Sadarat; \2021 01569; m +47 462 61323 (WhatsApp, Norwegian number), 7002 76909; e info@shahmbookco.com) was founded by Shah Muhammad Rais, who rescued and sold banned books and rose to international prominence after being portrayed in *The Bookseller of Kabul* by Norwegian journalist Åsne Seierstad. Shortly after the fall of the Taliban, Seierstad had lived with Rais and his family to document daily life in post-war Afghanistan. The agreement was she would write a factual account, although names were to be changed for privacy. The resulting book, published in 2002, was a global success, praised for its intimate look into Afghan family life and the complexities of tradition, gender roles, and post-conflict society. However, Rais was deeply unhappy with how he and his family were portrayed. He claimed the book misrepresented him, violated the family's privacy, and put them at risk. In response, he wrote his own version of events titled *Once Upon a Time There Was a Bookseller in Kabul*. In 2010, Rais's

3 | KABUL AND AROUND

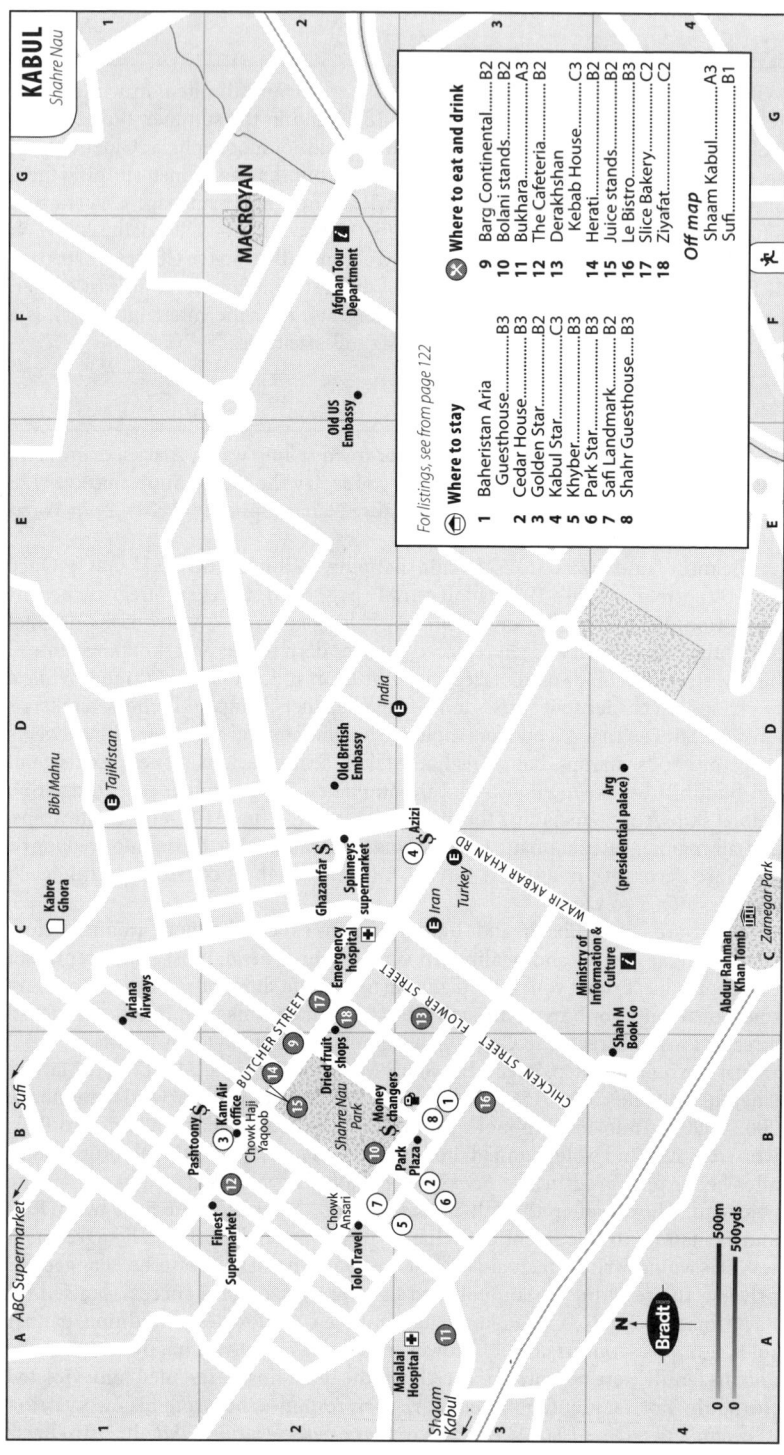

wife sued Seierstad in Norway for defamation and invasion of privacy. Initially, a lower court ruled partially in her favour, awarding damages, but the decision was later overturned on appeal. The case sparked international debate about the ethics of immersion journalism and the responsibilities of foreign correspondents working in fragile societies. Despite the controversy, this remains one of the most well-known and respected bookshops in Afghanistan. It reopened under the new regime who have banned certain books…one title they do *not* stock is Åsne's.

The **Bush Bazaar** (⊕ 08.00–dusk, most shops close on Fri) is officially now known as the Mujahideen Bazaar, but everyone still calls it the Bush Bazaar. (During Soviet times it was known as the Brezhnev Bazaar.) Here shops and stalls sell food, clothing and other items once pilfered from Russian and then American army bases. These days most of the wares are Chinese-made replica clothing, boots and protein powders, but if you search hard enough you can probably still find US army-issue tents, food, energy bars, ID holders and out-of-date MRE ('meals, ready-to-eat') ration packs.

SPORTS AND ACTIVITIES

City Park [125 B3] Near the zoo; ⊕ 08.00–16.00 (later on Fri & hols); 100AFN for foreigners. Situated on the strip of land between Shah e Do Shamshira Mosque & the zoo, City Park is Kabul's best-known theme park. Rides are very popular… but for men only.

Football & cricket These sports are both widely followed. While Afghanistan plays all of its international matches abroad, the national league games are almost all played in Kabul. The schedules are hard to find & people seem to find out about fixtures only days before via social media. If you are keen, your best bet is to pop down to the stadiums, both close to each other between the Old City & the hills of Teppe Maranjan & see if there is a game on.

Kabul Golf Club [map, page 121] Near Qargha Lake; m 7888 08068 (WhatsApp: Zabiullah). Founded in 1967 by King Zahir Khan, the Kabul Golf Club has, like the city itself, been through a lot in its lifetime. Currently it's in a sorry state of repair. The course is now used as a general recreation area with a swimming pool & a swinging pirate ship on the 7th green; on holidays, cricket matches take over the fairways. However, on other days you can hire some clubs & have a round with the local players. Best to call ahead. Caps & T-shirts available in the club shop.

Kite fighting Kite fighting may be officially banned, but people do still fly & fight kites. Fri is the best day but any evening you can usually find people at Teppe Maranjan or the hills of Bibi Mahru. Just follow the kites; you can't miss them.

OTHER PRACTICALITIES

At the time of writing only certain neighbouring countries, including Pakistan, Iran, Russia, India, China, Tajikistan, Uzbekistan and Türkiye, have **embassies** in Kabul, although this may change during the lifetime of this guide; for an up-to-date list, see w embassypages.com/afghanistan. There is an EU Mission, but its location and contact details are not in the public domain. Should you need urgent consular support, we suggest contacting the Information and Culture Ministry (page 122) to obtain the details.

MEDICAL
Emergency Hospital [128 C2] Suhl Rd; m 7486 14351; w emergencyuk.org; ⊕ 24hrs. The best place for emergency care.

MONEY The main **money markets** are in the Old City at Shahzada Sarai & Haidari market [125 D2] (⊕ 08.00–16.00 Sat–Thu), but if you are staying in Shahre Nau you can use the moneychangers on the south side of Shahre Nau Park [128 B2] (⊕ dawn–dusk daily). They are easy to spot as they sit behind glass boxes containing SIM cards & bundles of various currencies. The ones in the Old City might be useful if you have less common currencies to change. Rates should not differ too much, though they might be slightly better at the central markets. **Azizi Bank** [128 C3], next door to the Kabul Star Hotel, **Pashtoony Bank** [128 B1] near Chowk Haji Yaqoob & **Ghazanfar Bank** [128 C2] off Wazir Akbar Khan Rd are the most useful for money transfers. The Central Post Office also has a Western Union counter.

POST AND COMMUNICATIONS Closed after the Taliban government took power, the **Central Post Office** [125 D1] (Pashtoonistan Sq; m 7002 87393; w afghanpost.gov.af; 08.00–16.00 Sat–Wed, 08.00–14.00 Thu) reopened in 2024. It sells stamps & can send postcards internationally. There's also a **DHL office** in Park Plaza [128 B3], Zargona Road, opposite the petrol station. **SIM cards** for data & calls can be obtained at the relevant carrier's offices. Roshan, ATOMA & Afghan Wireless (AWCC) also all have offices at Park Plaza.

WHAT TO SEE AND DO

THE OLD CITY Medieval Kabul was bounded by the Sher Darwaza mountains (page 122), Kabul River and the central Maidan. Today, this area still functions as Kabul's traditional shopping district, a labyrinthine bazaar network that remains the largest in the country. Unlike Herat or parts of Kandahar, little of Kabul's medieval architecture survives. The original covered bazaar – once a defining feature – was destroyed by the British in 1842 in retribution for the murder of their envoy during the First Anglo–Afghan War. In the 1920s, King Amanullah's urban improvement programme altered the layout further, introducing European-inspired civic planning. And in the 1990s, intense shelling during the civil war between rival mujahideen factions damaged the area even more. What remains today is a vibrant mishmash of early 20th-century structures, mid-century shopfronts and newer concrete blocks – but the narrow alleys, bustling stalls and buzzing street life still feel timeless.

A good place to begin exploring is the striking **Shah e Do Shamshira Mosque** [125 C2], the 'Mosque of the King of Two Swords'. Built during Amanullah Khan's reign in the early 20th century, this two-storey lemon-yellow Baroque building is unlike any other mosque in Afghanistan. Its Viennese-style architecture – with arched balconies and corniced windows – recalls Amanullah's ambitions to modernise Kabul with European influences; the Darulaman Palace (page 137) is the biggest example.

Just east of the mosque, along the Kabul River, lies a solemn and deeply symbolic site – the **Memorial to Farkhunda Malikzada** [125 C1], a woman falsely accused of burning a Quran in the Shah e Do Shamshira Mosque and brutally murdered by a mob in 2015. The incident shocked the nation and sparked a reckoning over violence against women. The memorial marks the place of her death and is a rare civic monument to a victim of gender-based violence.

Directly across the river stands the **Mausoleum of Timur Shah Durrani** [125 C2] (09.00–16.00 daily), son of Ahmad Shah Durrani. It was King Timur Shah who moved the Afghan capital from Kandahar to Kabul. The domed mausoleum, built in the 18th century, has recently been restored. Its elegant red-brick façade and peaceful courtyard are quite a contrast with the hectic traffic just outside.

The two-storey pastel buildings with metal roofs on the banks of the Kabul River at this point are from the 1920s. From here, head toward **Pol e Kheshti Mosque** [125 D2], a local landmark. The surrounding bridges, streets and alleys are busy with street vendors selling rings, knives, scarves, perfume and prayer beads.

Wandering the narrow lanes between the Kabul River and Jada-e-Maiwand, you'll find some of the best street-level experiences in the city. Don't miss the **dried fruit market** [125 D2], where traders shout prices for apricots, mulberries, pistachios and raisins. A little further on is **Ka Faroshi** [125 D2], the bird market, a tight, twisting lane where not even motorbikes can enter, where it feels like stepping back in time to another, more ancient Kabul. The birds on sale include *kowk*, fighting partridge, usually displayed in traditional wicker domed cages; *bundana*, tiny fighting larks; as well as singing canaries and finches.

Wide **Jada-e-Maiwand** was bulldozed through the Old City during Amanullah Khan's 1920s urban redesign, in stark contrast to the maze-like alleyways nearby. Along this street heading south from **Maiwand Chowk**, look for **kite shops** [125 D2], where children (and adults) buy kites and the glass-coated string used in the competitive Afghan sport of kite fighting, especially popular during holidays and on breezy Friday afternoons.

At the eastern end of the Old City stands the **Eid Gah Mosque** [125 F1], one of the largest mosques in Kabul. Although it's not generally open to tourists or used for daily prayers, it becomes a major site of worship during the Eid festivals, when thousands gather in the open-air courtyard for communal prayers. Opposite the Eid Gah Mosque is the **Maidan** [125 F2], just beyond where the Old City walls would have stood, and where the king would display his troops and festivals would be held. It is now a dilapidated park used for football and cricket.

On the northern banks of the Kabul River lies the **Murad Khani** [125 D1], a historic quarter once gifted by Timur Shah to the Qizilbash community, a Shi'a minority of Turkic origin. Long neglected, the area was beautifully restored by Turquoise Mountain, a British–Afghan NGO (see below). Here you'll find mud-brick buildings, and artisan workshops producing calligraphy, jewellery, woodwork and ceramics. The narrow lanes here feel like a walk back in time – they are some of the most atmospheric in Kabul.

Bala Hissar and the City Walls [125 F1] Rising above the southern edge of Kabul's Old City, the Bala Hissar (High Fortress) is where the fate of rulers, empires and revolts has played out for centuries. Strategically perched on a rocky outcrop, its imposing ramparts offer commanding views of Kabul's sprawl and the surrounding mountains.

TURQUOISE MOUNTAIN

Founded in Kabul in 2006 by His Majesty King Charles III (then Prince of Wales), Turquoise Mountain began in Kabul's historic Old City neighbourhood of Murad Khani, which was over 40% destroyed. Using wheelbarrows and shovels, the organisation cleared over 30,000m^3 of rubble and earth, employing 4,000 builders to restore more than 150 historic buildings.

In the centre of Murad Khani, it established the Turquoise Mountain Institute for Afghan Arts and Architecture, which trains the next generation in traditional crafts, alongside a family health clinic which has seen over 250,000 patients. In Bamiyan and the north, they support weaving communities who make traditional hand-knotted carpets, and they are restoring a historic caravanserai. In Afghanistan, Turquoise Mountain has created over 20,000 jobs by connecting artisans to international markets. Building on its work in Afghanistan, Turquoise Mountain now also works in Myanmar, Saudi Arabia and the Levant.

To support the Afghan craft industry, you can donate to Turquoise Mountain (page 112).

The earliest fortifications may date back more than 1,500 years, but much of what stands today reflects its Mughal and later British-era history. The Mughal emperor Babur extended the fortress during his reign, using it as both a military base and a royal residence. In the centuries that followed, it served as the seat of Afghan kings – until it was heavily damaged in the aftermath of the British invasion during the Second Anglo–Afghan War in 1879. That year, Afghan forces fired on the British Residency from the Bala Hissar, prompting brutal retaliation. Much of the upper citadel, once the royal stronghold, was destroyed, but lower sections of the complex have remained in military use up to the present day.

Long off-limits to the public, the Bala Hissar is now undergoing restoration. Efforts led by the Aga Khan Trust for Culture, in collaboration with the Afghan government and supported by archaeologists and historians, aim to stabilise the crumbling structure and uncover the many layers of history buried within. Although entry to the interior is still restricted, visitors can walk around parts of the exterior. Be cautious when taking photographs, as it remains an active military site.

One rewarding walk begins at the cemetery on the western side of the fortress and follows the ridgeline up along the walls to the top of Sher Darwaza, then descends towards Babur's Gardens. The route passes a flat platform above the gardens – once the firing site for a noonday cannon. The walk takes about 2 hours, and while the path is visible, the footing can be uneven.

Important note: At the time of writing, this route is officially closed to the public. It is essential to seek permission from the Afghan Tour Department before attempting it, to avoid possible detention. Walking this ridge has long been forbidden. Should you find yourself questioned, know that you're in good company – historian William Dalrymple is among those whose 'short walk in the Hindu Kush' was memorably interrupted by Afghan police.

Abdur Rahman Khan Tomb [128 C4] (Zarnegar Park; ⊕ currently not accessible)

The tomb of Abdur Rahman Khan – Afghanistan's powerful and often controversial 'Iron Amir' – sits in Zarnegar Park just north of the Old City. Built in 1901, the tomb reflects the Indo-Islamic architectural influences of the time, with a central dome and red-brick construction. It's a monument to the man who unified Afghanistan through a mix of military strength and authoritarian rule, shaping the borders and political structure of the modern Afghan state. The tomb stands in a public park that was, until recent years, open to visitors. However, at the time of writing, access to the park is restricted, although the tomb can be viewed from the road on the north side of the park.

Kabre Ghora [128 C1] (British or Foreigners Cemetery; St 13, Wazir Akbar Khan; ⊕ 08.00–16.00 daily, though sometimes no-one is there; free, but tips appreciated)

Tucked away behind a quiet compound wall, the Kabre Ghora in Kabul is an evocative, reflective spot. Despite its name, the cemetery is not solely British. Originally created in 1879 by the British army for casualties of the Second Anglo–Afghan War, it serves as the final resting place for foreign nationals who died in Afghanistan over the past century, including aid workers, diplomats, soldiers and journalists. Some were casualties of war, others of illness or accident, but all were drawn to Afghanistan in some way – through duty, curiosity or compassion.

There are about 150 graves, mostly from the years before the wars. Members of the British diplomatic community, aid workers, hippies and journalists are all buried here. Many gravestones bear moving epitaphs in multiple languages – a quiet international mosaic of service and loss.

Among the notable figures buried here is Sir Aurel Stein, the famed Hungarian British archaeologist, explorer and scholar of central Asia. He was obsessed with Afghanistan but was only given permission to visit, aged 82, in 1943. He died in Kabul within weeks of his arrival. His grave, modest and easily missed, is a pilgrimage spot for lovers of Silk Road history and archaeology.

Among the headstones from earlier periods are fragments of 19th-century memorials from the Second Anglo–Afghan War mounted respectfully on the walls. They are joined by 21st-century memorial plaques from various ISAF contingents including British, US, Canadian, New Zealand and Australian.

One of the cemetery's most remarkable tales involves its old *chowkidar* (watchman). During the first Taliban, the chowkidar received a small stipend from the British Council to maintain the graves. He tells of an encounter when Mullah Omar himself paid a visit and asked the chowkidar why he still did this job. In an extraordinary, bold act of diplomacy, he suggested to the Taliban leader that the dire economic situation meant this was the only job he could get and if he let the place go to ruin then he would be jobless. As such, he kept his role. His son now follows in his footsteps as chowkidar.

Bibi Mahru and Teppe Maranjan Defining the north and east boundaries of central Kabul, the hills of Bibi Mahru and Teppe Maranjan offer some of the most atmospheric and panoramic viewpoints over the city. They are also layered with history and the lively chaos of daily Kabul life.

From Bibi Mahru in the north, visitors are treated to commanding views over the now off-limits embassy district and government buildings. Atop the hill flies Afghanistan's largest flag, visible from much of the city, while on its eastern edge lies the **grave of Burhanuddin Rabbani,** the former president and prominent mujahideen figure. Just below the ridgeline is the now-derelict swimming pool, a grim site where the Taliban during their first regime carried out public executions. The government has complemented this eclectic mix of structures with a **replica of Jerusalem's Al Aqsa Mosque**. For those with a keen interest in the First Anglo–Afghan War, the lone red-and-white smokestack visible to the east marks the site of the British Cantonment of 1841; it is likely the Afghan fighters fired at it from Bibi Mahru. The hill is also a place where Kabulis come to relax and take in the view.

To the southeast, **Teppe Maranjan** [125 G1] is the raucous brother of Bibi Mahru and comes alive particularly in the late afternoon and early evening, when the open hilltop becomes a sprawling, loosely organised arena of urban recreation. Here, cricket games, football matches and kite battles all unfold simultaneously, with scant regard for boundaries. Horses are available for hire, and learners practise driving cars – resulting in a chaotic but joyous overlap of whirling dust, soaring kites with glass-coated strings, galloping hooves and flying cricket balls. The atmosphere at dusk can be especially magical: the golden haze of Kabul's dusty sunset casts a soft, cinematic glow over the entire scene, creating a surreal yet deeply local sense of place. The far side of Teppe Maranjan is a cemetery, site of the **tomb of King Nadir Shah**, assassinated in 1933 and easily spotted by its metal roof and high marble walls. More photogenic is the final resting place of Nadir Shah's great-great-grandfather, the run-down **Sultan Mohammed Khan Telai Mausoleum** on the south side of the hill.

It's important to note that Television Hill, Kabul's other prominent hill, is strictly off-limits to visitors and under military control – photography or attempts to climb it are not advised.

OMAR Landmine Museum [125 F1] (Near Ghazi Stadium; ☏ 2023 13700; ⊕ 08.00–16.00 Sun–Thu; 100AFN, camera fee 100AFN) Tucked away in an unsignposted compound, this offers one of the most unusual and sobering museum experiences in Afghanistan. Established by the Organization for Mine Clearance and Afghan Rehabilitation (OMAR), the museum serves as both an educational resource and a stark reminder of the long-lasting impact of war.

What makes this museum so distinctive is its vast collection of deactivated landmines, unexploded ordnance and improvised explosive devices (IEDs), deadly remnants from decades of conflict: Soviet anti-personnel mines, American cluster bombs, disguised explosive devices like pen bombs, Molotov cocktails, and even booby-trapped toys. You will find explosives manufactured in a multitude of countries and yet, despite all the destruction, only one device made in Afghanistan – a homemade pressure-cooker bomb, an example of an IED. This crude yet effective device underscores the tragic resourcefulness born of war and desperation.

The museum doesn't shy away from the grotesque ingenuity of modern warfare. Visitors will find examples of a cluster bomb, designed to scatter smaller explosives over wide areas, many of which remain unexploded and lethal long after a conflict ends (page 83). There are anti-tank mines big enough to destroy a truck, and anti-personnel mines so small and discreet they could easily be mistaken for stones.

Although the exhibits are inert, the museum grounds are fortified and supervised. Each weapon on display is carefully labelled, often with information about where it was found and who used it. The goal is as much about education and prevention as it is about documentation – many school groups visit the museum as part of landmine awareness efforts.

WEST KABUL

Sakhi Shrine (Karte Sakhi District; ⊕ dawn–dusk daily; free) Standing in the shadow of Asamayi (Television) Hill, the Sakhi Shrine is one of Afghanistan's most revered religious sites. It holds profound significance for Shi'a Muslims, particularly the Hazara community. According to tradition, during the 18th century, the group transporting the Prophet Muhammad's cloak from Badakhshan to Kandahar paused in Kabul. Here they reportedly experienced visions of Imam Ali praying at the site. Interpreting these visions as a divine sign, a shrine was established to commemorate the event.

Architecturally, the Sakhi Shrine is renowned for its intricate, neo-Safavid Persian-style blue tilework and calligraphy. Of the shrine's multiple domes, the original was constructed during the reign of Ahmad Shah Durrani (page 26), while a second dome was commissioned by Queen Hayat Begum, mother of King Amanullah Khan, in 1919; others were added in the early 20th century.

The shrine is always busy but visitors are respectful, so it has a serene atmosphere and is a great place to escape the city noise and people watch. It was a focal point for the annual Nau Ruz celebrations (Persian New Year; page 238), when a large flag would be raised in honour of Imam Ali. These festivities are banned under the current government.

Sakhi Shrine has faced a number of tragic events in recent years. Notably, on 21 March 2018, a suicide bombing during Nau Ruz celebrations resulted in more than 30 fatalities and numerous injuries. The attack was claimed by the IS-K group, which has continued to attack Shi'a communities in Kabul ever since.

The shrine stands in a large cemetery, reached by a road lined with vendors selling food, drinks and religious items. A small road running over a ridge behind the shrine towards Shahre Nau offers great views of the shrine and cemetery. This ridge is also a dividing line between Hazara and Tajik communities and during the civil war saw a lot of hostility.

Babur's Gardens (Bagh e Babur) [125 A4] (⏱ 08.00–16.00 daily; 100AFN, camera fee 250AFN) Located on the southern slopes of the Sher Darwaza hills, Bagh e Babur is one of the most serene and historic places in the Afghan capital. Laid out in the early 16th century by the first Mughal emperor, the gardens were intended as his final resting place. Although he conquered much of northern India, Babur loved the cooler climate and mountains of his homeland.

The layout reflects his central Asian sensibilities: a traditional *charbagh* (four-part garden) design, flowing water channels, and a harmonious blend of architecture and nature. In his memoirs, *The Baburnama*, Babur wrote of his fondness for the village of Istalif (page 140), where he straightened the river to resemble a charbagh. He later modelled Bagh e Babur after Istalif, choosing a site that commands expansive views over the Kabul River plain. Though he died in Agra, his body was returned and buried here in accordance with his wishes. His simple tomb remains the spiritual heart of the garden.

Visitors enter the gardens through a restored caravanserai, originally built to receive and accommodate travellers. The grounds are arranged in gentle terraces bisected by a central water channel that runs (often dry) from an octagonal pool at the top of the garden. This pool is an original feature, though in the early 20th century it was briefly replaced with a European-style fountain. Babur's tomb, modest and elegant, is at the far end of the garden. Its style echoes the aesthetic of his Timurid ancestors, though the surface bears the scars of 20th-century conflict, pockmarked with bullet holes. In the 17th century, Babur's great-grandson Shah Jahan visited the site and commissioned a small marble mosque – one of the few surviving Mughal buildings in Afghanistan – and an enclosure around the grave. The current enclosure, added in the early 21st century, was built using Agra marble and Indian craftsmanship as a nod to the original.

The gardens fell into decline in the 1700s but in the late 19th century were revived by Amir Abdur Rahman Khan, who built both the pavilion at the upper end for royal guests and a *haramserai* in the southeast corner to accommodate royal women and travellers. Bagh e Babur then became a social hub. During World War I, King Habibullah Khan received Austrian envoys Oskar von Niedermayer and Werner Otto von Hentig here, as they attempted to convince him to attack British India and accept that Kaiser Wilhelm was, in fact, a Muslim. During the reign of King Zahir Shah, a public swimming pool was added and the gardens were opened to ordinary citizens. During the civil war of the 1990s, Bagh e Babur suffered extensive damage but was painstakingly restored in the early 2000s. In the 21st century, the caravanserai became a cultural venue, hosting classical concerts and Shakespeare plays.

Thanks to ongoing restoration efforts led by the Aga Khan Trust for Culture since 2002, the gardens have regained much of their former splendour. Many of the plants have been chosen based on Babur's own descriptions in *The Baburnama*, and the flowerbeds, shaded walkways and carefully maintained terraces once again offer a peaceful refuge from Kabul's bustle.

Although once a place for leisure – where couples strolled, families picnicked and city dwellers came to relax – the garden's character has changed. Local women are now largely absent due to social restrictions, and visitors tend to be men and the occasional foreign woman.

BABUR, THE FIRST MUGHAL EMPEROR

Born in 1483, Zahir-ud-Din Muhammad was the eldest son of Umar Shaikh Mirza II, a grandson of Timur and governor of Fergana in modern Uzbekistan, while his mother Qutlugh Nigar Khanum was a descendant of Genghis Khan. As his name was difficult for his Turkic-speaking followers to pronounce, he was better known by his nickname Babur ('Tiger').

We know more about Babur than any other Asian ruler of the period, thanks to his lively, tell-all memoir, *The Baburnama*. In the introduction to the recent English translation of *The Baburnama* (page 286), Salman Rushdie wrote: 'Who, then, was Babur – scholar or barbarian, nature-loving poet or terror-inspiring warlord? The answer is to be found in *The Baburnama* and it's an uncomfortable one: He was both.'

Babur became governor of Fergana at the age of 12 after his father tumbled to his death over a cliff while feeding pigeons. Babur's warlord side got off to a promising start at age 15 when after a seven-month siege he captured Samarkand, but central Asia at the time was like *Game of Thrones*, with too many relatives and not enough thrones. He held it for three months before a younger brother took Fergana; Babur tried to take it back, but lost Samarkand to another in his absence. After another failed attempt, he gave up in 1502 and wandered into Afghanistan with a band of followers. His chance to gain a fief of his own occurred when his uncle Ulugh Beg II, ruler of Kabul, died leaving only an infant as heir.

Babur would spend time with his cousins in Herat, where the gardens inspired him and the drinking and dancing repelled him, although he later changed his mind after taking his first drink at age 30. It was in Herat, too, that he was inspired to write his memoirs, when he encountered the poetry of Mir Ali Shir Nava'i (page 58).

In January 1506, when Babur heard that Kabul was threatened, he crossed Afghanistan (in 2002, Rory Stewart re-traced his steps, also in winter, in his book *The Places in Between*). Afterwards, he teamed up with Ismail I, the Safavid Shah of Persia, to retake the ancestral Timurid territories; in 1513 Babur captured

Kabul Zoo [125 A3] (Asmayi Rd; m 7806 69577; f; ⊕ 08.00–16.30 daily; 100AFN) Tucked along the Kabul River near the foot of the hills leading up to Bagh e Babur, **Kabul Zoo** is a popular spot for Kabul residents. Established in 1967, it has long served as a rare green space and family outing spot, despite decades of conflict. The zoo is perhaps best remembered for Marjan, a lion gifted by Germany in the 1970s. In 1993, Marjan survived a grenade attack that left him blind and disfigured. His story became emblematic of Kabul's endurance. After his death in 2002, a **statue of Marjan** was placed outside the zoo as a tribute to his resilience, and he remains a symbol of Afghan survival through war and hardship.

Although the zoo has seen better days, it continues to operate, housing a modest collection of animals – deer, monkeys, birds, wolves and, at one point, a pair of pigs, which caused a certain amount of fascination and amusement among the locals, given pigs are never seen in predominantly Muslim Afghanistan. However, for most visitors, the reason to visit is simply to people watch.

Directly east of the zoo, between it and the City Park amusement park, stands a lesser-known but curious relic of King Amanullah Khan's 1920s' modernisation efforts: the Minar-e-Elm-wa-Jahil or **Monument to Knowledge and Ignorance**. Built during his brief but ambitious reign, this squat obelisk was at the centre of

WHAT TO SEE AND DO

Samarkand and Bokhara before the Uzbeks kicked him out for the third time (although today he is regarded in Uzbekistan as a national hero). He wrote, 'In the presence of such power and potency, we had to think of some place for ourselves', so he turned his attention to India. He made good use of artillery supplied by the Ottomans and Safavids to scare the war elephants, won great battles and founded the Mughal Empire, creating a dynasty that ruled for a unified India for the first time since Ashoka in 300BCE.

Along with his honest accounts of his actions and his lively observations of the people around him, Babur's sense of irony and good-humoured lack of self-regard are unique for an Asian writer of his time. He wrote of gardening and nature, flora and fauna; he also wrote beautiful poetry and ghazals; he loved to get sloshed and chew opium. 'The new year, the spring, the wine and the beloved are joyful. Babur make merry, for the world will not be there for you a second time.'

In 1530, when Babur heard that his eldest son, Humayum, was dying, he was told by a courtier that God would sometimes spare a person if a friend made an offering of his most precious possession. Babur replied his own life was the most precious thing to Humayum and vice versa. The courtier was horrified and said he should offer the Koh-i-noor diamond instead (which Babur had received in tribute in 1526 after his victory at Panipat). Babur refused and prayed, and as Humayum recovered, he sickened and eventually died on 26 December 1530. His wife moved his remains to his beloved gardens in Kabul, where he asked to be interred, uncovered, so the sun and rain would fall on him and a wildflower might grow. In the white marble mosque that stands nearby, his great-grandson left the beautiful inscription translated by Peter Levi:

> Only this mosque of beauty, this temple of nobility, constructed for the prayers of saints and the epiphany of the cherubs, was fit to stand in so venerable a sanctuary as this highway of archangels, this theatre of heaven, the light garden of the godforgiven Angel King who rest is in the garden of heaven, Zahirudden Muhammad Babur the Conqueror.

the fighting during the civil war in the 1990s and is left damaged, unrestored and seemingly uncared for. Perhaps symbolic of Afghanistan?

Darulaman Palace (Darulaman Rd) Rising from the dry hills southwest of Kabul, this iconic Neoclassical structure tells the story of Afghanistan's modernist ambitions and turbulent history. Commissioned by King Amanullah Khan in the 1920s, the palace was intended to be the centrepiece of his new administrative capital – Darulaman, or 'Abode of Peace'. German and French architects were enlisted to design a palace that blended European grandeur with Afghan symbolism. Its symmetrical design, arched windows and columned façade echo the style of European state buildings of the time.

Darulaman was never used as a royal residence; instead, it housed government ministries and later served as a military base. Over the decades, it was repeatedly damaged – first by fire in the 1960s and then by shelling during the civil war, leaving it a burned-out husk surrounded by landmines and bullet holes. The ruin became a landmark in its own right with urban explorers, tourists, music video location managers, journalists and graffiti artists all using it for their own ends.

In 2019, Darulaman was brought back to life after an extensive restoration, with support from the Afghan government and international donors. The reconstruction aimed to preserve the original architecture while updating the structure to serve once more as a public building. It now houses exhibitions and has become a venue for official events, though public access remains limited.

The palace stands at the end of a ceremonial avenue and is flanked by other 20th-century landmarks, including the National Museum of Afghanistan and the copper-domed old Parliament building, reinforcing Amanullah's dream of a modern capital.

National Museum of Afghanistan (Opposite Darulaman Palace; ⏱ 08.00–16.00 Sat–Wed, 08.00–14.00 Thu; 200AFN, camera fee 100AFN) The only real museum of note in Afghanistan, this may be smaller than many national museums, but it houses a collection that speaks volumes about the country's unique role as a crossroads of civilisations. Founded in 1919, the museum once housed over 100,000 objects spanning several millennia – from prehistoric artefacts to Islamic manuscripts. But during the brutal civil war of the 1990s, the building was shelled repeatedly, its roof collapsed, and looters stripped its galleries of priceless artefacts. More than 70% of the collection was lost or stolen. Since then, the museum has

> **BACTRIAN GOLD**
>
> One of Afghanistan's most dazzling archaeological discoveries, the Bactrian Gold, is a glittering reminder of the region's ancient wealth, craftsmanship and cultural crossroads. Discovered in 1978 by Soviet archaeologist Viktor Sarianidi at the site of Tillya Tepe ('Hill of Gold'; page 248) in northern Afghanistan, this extraordinary hoard came from the burial mounds of six nomadic elites – five women and one man – believed to be from the 1st century BCE, during the Kushan period.
>
> The treasure consists of more than 20,000 pieces of gold, turquoise, lapis lazuli and ivory, such as intricately worked jewellery, coins, weapons and ornaments, including remarkable 'flat pack'-style gold crowns, which could be disassembled and transported – perfect for the semi-nomadic aristocracy who once ruled these lands. The pieces reflect a stunning fusion of artistic traditions: Greek, Persian, Indian and Chinese, testament to Afghanistan's place at the heart of ancient Silk Road trade and culture.
>
> When civil war broke out in the 1990s, the fate of the Bactrian Gold was unknown. Many feared it had been looted or lost forever. In fact, a handful of brave National Museum staff, along with officials from the Central Bank, had secretly locked the collection away in an underground vault. There it remained for over a decade – untouched, undocumented, and sealed under layers of secrecy.
>
> In 2003, after the fall of the first Taliban regime, the vault was finally opened. The moment was captured on film: as safes were cracked and crates opened, the glitter of ancient gold re-emerged into the light, intact and awe-inspiring.
>
> After its rediscovery, the Bactrian Gold has become a travelling ambassador for Afghan heritage, exhibited at major institutions around the world – from the British Museum in London to New York's Metropolitan Museum of Art. The treasure was returned to Afghanistan and since the Taliban government came to power, its whereabouts are once again unknown.

slowly been rebuilt, with help from international partners. Some artefacts that had been hidden or stolen were returned. It now features a small but well-curated set of exhibitions that offers a fascinating insight into Afghan history.

Some of the museum's key exhibits are not on display at the time of writing. The Bagram Ivories (page 141) are outside Afghanistan; since the Taliban came to power, exhibits that feature human imagery such as carved wooden Nuristani idols in the ethnographical room and some of the larger Graeco-Buddhist stone bodhisattvas have been removed; and the location of the Bactrian Gold (see opposite), hidden for years to avoid being looted, is currently unknown.

One of the standout objects that remarkably stayed in the same place throughout is the colossal stone **'Buddha bowl'**, an enormous ritual vessel from the Buddhist period (note the lotus carvings on its base), repurposed during the Islamic period as a bowl for ablutions. As an Islamic artefact weighing over a tonne, it could not be destroyed or stolen. It sits in the centre of the main hall, quietly defiant. It is flanked in the entrance hall by a large tablet of Greek inscriptions from Ai-Kanoum (page 255) and the **Rabatak Tablet**, discovered in 1993 near Pol e Khomri (page 251) and written in a script that has yet to be deciphered.

Another highlight are the **bodhisattva sculptures** – serene, elegant figures in grey schist and stucco, unearthed at Hadda and Tapa Sardar among others, showcasing the syncretic Graeco-Buddhist art that flourished in Afghanistan during the Kushan era. Recent additions from this era include artefacts unearthed from **Mes Aynak** (page 142) less than ten years ago. The Mes Aynak finds – statues, frescoes and architectural fragments – underscore how much still lies beneath Afghanistan's soil, waiting to be rediscovered.

Outside, there is a small selection of royal and presidential vehicles of the last 150 years including a horse-drawn coach, bullet-proof limousines and Afghanistan's first ever train locomotive.

AROUND KABUL

> In one day a man may travel from Kabul to a place where the snow never falls, on another to a place where the snow never melts.
>
> Babur

Many visitors leave the capital after two or three days, drawn to the famous sights of Bamiyan, Herat or Mazar e Sharif. Which is a shame, because there are fascinating places easily reached in full- or half-day trips from Kabul. To the north, the Shomali Plains extend into a patchwork of vineyards, orchards and smallholdings. In autumn, roadside stalls sell plastic bags filled with decadently delicious grapes. On warm Friday evenings, be prepared for heavy traffic heading back into the city, as locals return from countryside picnics.

While Ghazni (page 203) and Jalalabad (page 149) are also possible day trips from Kabul, they are covered in their own dedicated sections.

QARGHA LAKE Just a 40-minute drive west of Kabul, Qargha Lake is a popular weekend escape for Kabulis seeking a breath of fresh air and a bit of leisure. Shimmering amid gentle hills, the lake was formed by a dam in the 1950s and has since become one of the capital's most beloved recreational spots. On weekends and holidays – especially Fridays – Qargha used to come alive with families picnicking, children running between stalls, and the smell of grilled meat drifting from the lakeside restaurants. However, at the time of writing, Afghan women are prohibited from visiting so the lake is far less busy. You'll find a mix of casual eateries and teahouses lining the shore, serving kebabs, karahi and fried fish, best enjoyed under a shaded pergola or sprawled on rugs beside the water.

You can hire pedalos to explore the calm waters – these brightly coloured swan-shaped boats are particularly popular with children. Horseback rides along the shore are another common sight, with locals offering short rides for a few Afghanis. In recent years, a small funfair has popped up on busy days, with swings, dodgems and carnival-style games. While facilities are basic and cleanliness can vary, the lake offers a slice of normality and fun in a city often marked by tension and concrete.

ISTALIF (47km northwest of Kabul) High in the foothills of the Hindu Kush, the picturesque village of Istalif enjoys sweeping views over the Shomali Plains. Known for its pottery, cool, green Istalif is a popular weekend getaway for Kabul residents, especially on Fridays when families arrive in droves for picnics beside the river.

The village is predominantly Tajik, with storied history that includes a mention by the Emperor Babur, who recorded in his *Baburnama* that the river running through the valley was straightened under his orders, a piece of hydrological engineering that defines Istalif's layout today. Water still flows briskly through this channelled stream, its banks shaded by tall trees and flanked by terraces.

Istalif's greatest fame, however, lies in its distinctive ceramics which have been produced here for over 500 years, glazed with signature turquoise blue and green hues; shops in the bazaar display an array of plates, bowls, teapots and jugs crafted by generations of potters. Visitors are welcome to wander among the small workshops where local artisans shape and fire their wares using traditional techniques passed down over centuries. Turquoise Mountain (page 131) has been instrumental in ensuring these pottery techniques do not die out.

The Shomali Plains were badly damaged in 1999 when the Taliban subdued the primarily Tajik population, and Istalif was no exception. Since then, the village has been steadily rebuilt and retains much of its former charm. Narrow lanes wind through clusters of mud-brick homes and grape vines, with the ever-present mountains rising behind. There are a few basic tea shops and restaurants serving simple Afghan food, and the peaceful atmosphere – especially outside the Friday rush – makes it an enjoyable half-day trip from Kabul. Minibuses from Serai Shomali (page 120) for Istalif run sporadically albeit you are likely to find more on Friday mornings (150AFN; 90mins).

PAGHMAN (20km west of Kabul) Paghman is the closest thing Kabul has to a subcontinental hill station. Built by King Amanullah as part of his European-inspired modernisation drive, it was renowned for its lush gardens and cool mountain air. Once dubbed the 'garden capital of Afghanistan', Paghman remains a favoured retreat for Kabulis seeking respite from the summer heat.

The town's landmark is the white marble **Taq e Zafar** (Arch of Victory), a Neoclassical triumphal arch constructed in 1928. Designed by a Turkish architect and inspired by the Arc de Triomphe in Paris, it commemorates Afghanistan's independence following the Third Anglo–Afghan War and features intricate calligraphy. In the 1980s, when Paghman was used as a base for the mujahideen leader Abdul Rasul Sayyaf for attacks against the communist government in Kabul, the arch was heavily damaged. It was meticulously restored in 2005 and now stands as a symbol of national pride and resilience. It features on banknotes and on the old Afghan flag.

Beyond the arch, the Paghman River winds down the mountains past gardens with day beds for lazy picnics. For the very active, trails run up to **Khavand Peak** (4,542m) commanding fabulous views across the Shomali Plains and Hindu Kush.

Recently, Paghman has seen renewed development, including the construction of the **Paghman Hill Castle** (⊕ 08.00–16.00 daily; free) in 2014 as a venue for festivals. It's just north of the main road as you enter Paghman from Kabul. A buzkashi field just to the south of it doesn't look very used at the time of writing.

Minibuses (100AFN; 1hr) run to Paghman from Company (page 120). With your own transport, you can visit Paghman on the same day as Qargha Lake.

BAGRAM (60km north of Kabul) Here Afghanistan's layers of history sit starkly beside one another. In antiquity Bagram was known as Kapisa and it flourished from the 1st to 3rd centuries CE under the Kushans, when it stood at the major crossroads of trade and culture – linking central Asia, the Indian subcontinent, and the Mediterranean. The extraordinary Bagram Hoard, unearthed in the 1930s, included Roman glassware, Chinese lacquer boxes and Indian ivory carvings (known altogether as the Bagram Ivories; see below), clear evidence of its status as a cosmopolitan hub on the Silk Road.

Fast forward nearly two millennia, and Bagram again found itself at the heart of global power dynamics – this time as Bagram Airfield, the largest American military base in Afghanistan. Built by the USSR in the 1980s and expanded significantly by the US after 2001, the base became the operational and logistical hub for coalition forces during the war, a self-contained city with hospitals, shops, fast-food outlets and even a prison. When US troops withdrew in 2021, the handover of Bagram was symbolic of the end of an era.

Today, the Taliban use it as a military base. The fate of its vast infrastructure is still evolving, but echoes of its foreign occupation remain – runways stripped of aircraft, hangars standing empty, and barriers rusting along miles of perimeter fencing. At the time of writing, you won't get permission to visit, but future visitors may get to go there and understand more of Afghanistan's ancient and recent history.

> **THE BAGRAM IVORIES**
>
> Among the most exquisite finds from ancient Kapisa are the delicate, intricately carved Bagram Ivories, dating back to the 1st or 2nd century CE and believed to have been crafted in India and imported to Afghanistan along early trade routes. Used to adorn furniture or luxury items, the plaques depict floral motifs, animals and human figures with remarkable artistry, offering a glimpse into the cosmopolitan tastes of the Kushan elite. Ivory is an organic material, yet the dry air of Afghanistan meant they were preserved for 2,000 years until they were uncovered by French archaeologists in the 1930s.
>
> Once proudly displayed at the National Museum in Kabul, they were stolen during the chaos of the Afghan civil war in the 1990s. For years, they were feared lost to the black market. However, in a remarkable turn of events, dozens of pieces resurfaced in the UK and were recovered by British authorities. After negotiations and restoration work, they were repatriated to the Afghanistan government in the early 2010s. When the Taliban returned to power in 2021, the ivories were sent abroad, and it is unclear where these remarkable objects will turn up next.

BUDDHIST SITES Between the 1st and 4th centuries CE, Afghanistan was a key link on the Silk Road, connecting the Indian subcontinent with central Asia, China and the Mediterranean world. This period marked the height of the Kushan Empire, when Buddhism flourished and spread. While the Buddha Niches at Bamiyan (page 179) and the stupa at Samangan (page 251) are the iconic Buddhist monuments in Afghanistan, the area around Kabul actually contains a far greater number of lesser-known yet significant Buddhist sites. These were first recorded in detail between 1833 and 1835 by British explorer and antiquarian Charles Masson (see opposite), who documented more than 100 Buddhist locations around Kabul and Jalalabad. However, he is also remembered as one of the first recorded individuals to loot these ancient sites – breaking into stupas and removing more than 30,000 coins, many of which bore the names of Kushan kings. While these coins helped historians date the structures, his actions also began a long legacy of looting that unfortunately continues today.

Shewaki Stupa (10km south of Kabul) The closest Buddhist site to Kabul, hilltop Shewaki Stupa is thought to date from the 3rd to 4th century CE. It was restored in 2022 and offers grand views of the surrounding countryside and Kabul itself on a clear day. There are additional unrestored stupas and remains scattered throughout the hills nearby.

To get there, take the Gardez road south, then turn east at the village of Yakhdara and ask for Shewaki. The final stretch is unpaved but can be driven with a regular vehicle.

Guldara Stupa (25km south of Kabul) Located in a secluded valley, Guldara Stupa is believed to date from the 2nd century CE. Unrestored, it remains as it would have been seen by the light-fingered Charles Masson, as one of the best-preserved stupas in the country. The square base, collapsed dome and fragments of decorative elements, including remnants of Greek-style Corinthian columns, are still visible. According to local commanders, the valley around the stupa was used as a Taliban hideout during the conflict of the early 21st century.

To get Guldara Stupa, follow the Gardez road south for around 15km, then turn east to Mowsawi village and ask for Guldara. The road beyond the village is rough; you'll need to walk around 15 minutes after the end of the track. A 4x4 vehicle is recommended.

Toop Dara Monastery (70km north of Kabul) The Toop Dara site is among the largest stupas in the country. Restored in 2019, the central stupa is notable for its band of 56 sculpted niches that once held statues. Before restoration, much of the site was buried under 10m of earth. The complex includes not just the stupa but also remnants of a monastery, with evidence of multiple building phases.

To reach the monastery, drive north along the main highway to Charikar, then take local roads northwest towards the village of Toop Dara. The turn-off is easy to miss; a guide or local help is recommended.

Mes Aynak The grandest and most historically significant of all the Buddhist sites near Kabul, Mes Aynak is located in Logar Province, about 40km southeast of the capital. This vast archaeological complex sits atop one of the world's largest untapped copper deposits. Mes Aynak was a major Buddhist city from the 1st to 7th century CE, where monasteries, stupas, statues, manuscripts and residential structures offer an incredible insight into the fusion of Buddhist, Hellenistic and central Asian art and culture.

CHARLES MASSON

> If any fool this high samootch explore,
> Know Charles Masson has been here before.
>
> Inscription in a cave above the taller Buddha Niche at Bamiyan

In the first half of the 19th century, no Briton spent more time in Afghanistan than Charles Masson (1800–53), the pseudonym of James Lewis. He enlisted in the British East India Company's Bengal Artillery regiment in July as a soldier, but deserted from Agra in 1827, joined up with Josiah Harlan (page 146) before falling out, and setting off exploring, living off his wits as he wandered, joining caravans when he could. He was often ill, frequently robbed and once falsely imprisoned, but more was often treated with respect and kindness.

When he came in contact with the East India Company again, he claimed to be an American from Kentucky to cover up his deserter past. In 1833, the company began to fund his archaeological explorations around Kabul and Jalalabad. He travelled with his books, a stout stick, dervish drinking cup, compass, map, astrolabe and a camera lucida which enabled him to accurately sketch the sites. He bought up ancient coins and antiquities in the bazaars of Kabul; he identified the ruins at Bagram as ancient Alexandria in the Caucasus. In 1835, after his ex-friend Harlan blew his cover, Masson was compelled to become a spy in return for an official pardon for his desertion. It was a role he hated, feeling that he was betraying his Afghan friends. He duly warned his superiors that British machinations in the Great Game would lead to disaster, but his accurate warnings went unheeded, and he resigned in disgust after the First Anglo–Afghan War. When he returned to Britain in 1842 it was with a trove of 7,417 coins and 1,970 other relics for the East India Company Museum, most of which is now in the British Museum. He married, had two children, and until his death carried on writing about his finds, always dreaming of returning to Afghanistan. Masson's methods of cataloguing antiquities were ahead of his time. They preserve a unique record of Afghanistan's archaeological sites and early history, especially as so much has since been lost to wars and looters.

However, Mes Aynak is currently under the control of the Ministry of Mines owing to the planned copper extraction by a Chinese consortium. As such, it is not possible to visit the site, as permissions are not issued to the general public. Access is strictly controlled. Conservation efforts have been underway to salvage key finds before full-scale mining begins (page 16), but the long-term future of the site remains uncertain.

MOHI PAR Afghanistan is not short of epic drives, but the Mohi Par stretch of the Kabul–Jalalabad highway is one for lovers of impressive engineering feats. The name roughly translates to 'fish falls' or 'where the fish fly' – a nod to the sheer cliffs and serpentine curves that define this narrow mountain pass. Cut into the rugged precipices above the Kabul River gorge, about 25km east of Kabul, the road clings to the rock face, with vertical drops to one side and overhanging rock on the other. It's a heart-in-mouth stretch, especially when convoys of lorries or buses attempt to overtake each other on the hairpin turns. Landslides and traffic jams are common.

Despite the hazards, the views are stunning: steep canyon walls, cascading mountain streams, and occasional glimpses of the blue-green river below. Mohi Par has long had a reputation among Afghan drivers as one of the most dangerous roads in the country, but also one of the most breathtaking. Patience, a good vehicle and a steady driver are essential.

PANJSHIR VALLEY

Deep in the rugged embrace of the Hindu Kush, the Panjshir Valley cuts a dramatic swathe through the mountains, just 150km northeast of Kabul. Named after the 'Five Lions' who, according to legend, built a dam here in the 10th century, the valley is both breathtakingly beautiful and rich in symbolism. A ribbon of emerald-green fields and orchards follows the Panjshir River, flanked by steep, often snow-dusted peaks. The valley also serves as a vital route north when the Salang Pass is closed – its high-altitude defiles have been used by traders, armies and refugees for centuries.

Travellers have long admired the valley's dramatic landscape. British author Eric Newby attempted to climb Mir Samir, the Panjshir's highest peak – an adventure recounted in his classic travelogue *A Short Walk in the Hindu Kush*. Even Alexander the Great is said to have passed through here (page 146).

The people of Panjshir are predominantly ethnic Tajiks, known for their pride, resilience, and fierce independence. Villages cling to steep hillsides surrounded

THE LION OF PANJSHIR: AHMAD SHAH MASSOUD

With his piercing gaze, sparse beard and pakol hat, the charismatic Ahmad Shah Massoud was the face of Afghan resistance to the Soviet occupation. An ethnic Tajik, born in 1953 into a liberal-minded military family in the Panjshir Valley and named after Ahmad Shah Durrani (page 26), he studied at the Franco-Afghan Lycée Esteqlal in Kabul and was fluent in French (his enemies would mock him as 'the Parisian', but French journalists loved him). He took courses in engineering at the Polytechnic School, although in 1975 he left after an argument with one of his Russian professors. He went to Pakistan where he adopted 'Massoud' as his *nom de guerre* and trained with Pakistani intelligence (ISI) alongside Gulbuddin Hekmatyar (page 254).

Massoud studied the works of Che Guevara, Mao, Sun Tzu's *Art of War*, and Régis Debray, who wrote a guide to guerrilla tactics after studying the Cuban revolution. Visitors often remarked on his thousands of books in several languages. Victor Hugo was his favourite. He believed the best hope for Afghanistan, with its diverse peoples and languages, was a Swiss model of government, emphasising the importance of decentralisation and de-concentration of power. He was only 22 when his former classmate Hekmatyar, realising Massoud was a serious rival, tried to kill him.

Massoud became the most effective of all the mujahideen commanders, fighting with courage and imagination and making good use of Western intelligence to repulse the Soviets in the Panjshir Valley. MI6 helped to train his mujahideen, while by the late 1980s the CIA was handing him a weekly stipend worth half a million dollars in today's money.

After the Soviets left, Massoud's stint as defence minister in Kabul was doomed from the start because of Hekmatyar's intransigence and rockets, leading to the by orchards of mulberries and apricots. In summer, the area buzzes of roadside restaurants serving fresh river trout, popular with families escaping Kabul's heat.

Rukha is the main administrative town, where **permissions** for visiting the Panjshir Valley need to be confirmed at the governor's office, located just beyond the main road's only roundabout. The Panjshir was the last region of Afghanistan to submit to the Taliban and there is often talk of a possible future Panjshiri resistance movement. As such security is tight and movement beyond the main valley can be restricted.

GETTING THERE AND AWAY Minibuses from Terminal or Serai Shomali (page 120) in Kabul leave for Bazarak (118km; 200–300AFN; 3hrs), though you may have to change at Jabal Saraj at the bottom of the Salang Pass. If the Salang Pass is closed for maintenance or another reason, traffic between Kabul and Mazar e Sharif is diverted through the Panjshir Valley via the Khowak Pass.

It is possible to travel the length of the Panjshir and cross into Badakhshan Province via the 4,430m Anjoman Pass. There is no public transport and the route from Bazarak to Sar e Sang (8hrs) is rough. Currently, the paved road ends at Parian, although work was done to improve the Anjoman Pass road in the summer of 2024. At the time of writing, it's unpaved but graded, and it's unclear if it will eventually be paved.

For trekking routes within Panjshir or into Nuristan, check with the local government officials in Rukha.

---

disastrous war between mujahideen factions. In 1995, he went to talk to a Taliban leader, hoping to involve them in a peace process. The leader declined – only to be killed by the Taliban for not killing Massoud when he had the chance. By 1996, Massoud and fellow Islamist moderate President Rabbani were at the point of creating a power-sharing government, with Hekmatyar as prime minister. But instead, the Taliban took Kabul, and Massoud retreated to Panjshir to avoid any more bloodshed.

The Taliban swore they would kill the Lion of Panjshir with the Quran. But he held on in the north, creating democratic institutions, fighting the Taliban with limited funds. He managed once again to bring the different Afghan ethnic groups together at a loya jirga. His success provoked al-Qaeda, which tried to assassinate him in early 2000.

His aide and English translator, Masoud Khalili, was with him in Takhar Province on 9 September. Khalili said Massoud was restless, unable to sleep, and they sat up until 03.30 planning their next moves and reading poetry. Massoud opened his volume of Hafez (page 58) and Khalili read the stanza: 'Take out from your heart all the siblings of enmity, plant the tree and seed of love – Tonight you two are together. Valuate, many nights go, many days disappear. You two will not be able to see each other again.'

A few hours later Massoud would be dead; this time, bin Laden's men, disguised as journalists, detonated a bomb they had hidden in their camera. Khalili was badly wounded; only the passport in his shirt pocket kept the shrapnel from hitting his heart. Massoud's funeral, in spite of its remote location in the Panjshir, attracted hundreds of thousands of mourners in person, and millions in spirit around Afghanistan.

JOSIAH HARLAN, THE MAN WHO WOULD BE KING

Of all the extraordinary stories about 19th-century adventurers in Afghanistan, few can match those of Josiah Harlan (1799–1871), a Quaker and Freemason from Pennsylvania who was fascinated by Alexander the Great, and who in 1822 sailed to Asia after being jilted by his fiancée. Equipped with supreme confidence, a gift for languages and a convincing line of chat, he was hired as a surgeon by the East India Company even though he had no medical training.

In 1827, Harlan met the deposed king of Afghanistan, the appendage-removing Shuja Shah (page 27) who promised to make him vizier if he led an army of Muslims, Hindus and Sikhs to overthrow the current amir, Dost Mohammed. He found a tailor to sew an American flag, and marched towards Kabul. Charles Masson briefly joined (much to his regret; page 143), before deserting like the rest of Harlan's army when faced with the Pashtuns. Afraid for his life, Harlan disguised himself as a dervish and arrived in Afghanistan.

In Kabul he was welcomed at the Bala Hissar by Dost Mohammad, who treated him as a guest, and was very interested in Harlan's stories of the United States and its government. Harlan loved Kabul; there he survived a cholera epidemic thanks to 'hard drinking and smoking intoxicating drugs', then fell in with a humbug maulvi (scholar) alchemist, before he was accused of plotting to assassinate Dost Mohammad. He escaped to Lahore to the court of Ranjit Singh, the maharajah of Punjab and Dost Mohammad's sworn enemy.

Harlan convinced Ranjit Singh to appoint him governor of Gujrat, where he ruled for 15 years (once startling a passing British missionary who heard him singing 'Yankee Doodle' while smoking a hookah). During his rule he was a one-man precursor to the Great Game, involving himself in the plots, betrayals and battles between arch-rivals Ranjit Singh, Dost Mohammad and his half-brother – including the taking of Peshawar, former summer capital of the Afghan kings, by Ranjit Singh in 1834.

When the latter accused him of counterfeiting money, Harlan fled back to Afghanistan and took service under Dost Mohammed, with apparently no hard feelings, who put in charge of training his son's army. In 1838, fancying himself the new Alexander the Great, Harlan led a successful expedition into the Hindu Kush against the Uzbek Murad Beg who had been enslaving hundreds of Hazara. Murad Beg then recognised Dost Mohammed as Afghanistan's rightful ruler. Harlan, who believed in equality of the sexes, much admired the Hazara at the time; they admired him back and made him Prince of Ghor.

His suzerainty would be short-lived as the real Great Game between Britain and Russia was kicking off. As Dost Mohammed's agent, he tried negotiating with the British, but they still invaded Kabul to re-install the unpleasant Shuja Shah on the throne. Soon after, Harlan was expelled by the British and forced to return to the US, where he wrote his book (page 286) and was feted as a hero. But he always yearned to return to Afghanistan. He talked the US Army into importing camels so he could go to Afghanistan to make the arrangement, although they ended up getting them from Africa. At age 62 he briefly and unsuccessfully led Harlan's Light Cavalry in the American Civil War, before returning to medicine and dying all but forgotten in San Francisco.

PANJSHIR VALLEY

WHERE TO STAY AND EAT There are no real hotels in Panjshir, but, if staying the night, the **Khorshed Hotel and Restaurant ($$)** in the centre of Bazarak is probably the best bet, with its simple restaurant, and very basic rooms upstairs. In summer, feast on freshly caught fish at the riverside restaurants.

WHAT TO SEE AND DO Isolated yet strategically vital, the Panjshir has long played an outsized role in Afghan history. Entry to the valley is via a very narrow gorge called the Lion's Mouth, the road pinned between the pounding Panjshir River and a sheer wall of rock. It is easy to see why the Panjshir was such a hard place to conquer.

It rose to international prominence in the 1980s for its fierce resistance to Soviet forces. In terrain they knew intimately, Panjshiri fighters equipped with little more than rifles and basic explosives repelled six major Soviet offensives in just the first three years of the war. The valley remains littered with the rusting hulks of Soviet tanks and armoured personnel carriers, haunting reminders of the struggle. If you're driving or in a taxi to Panjshir, look out for a compound at the north end of the Shomali Plains, containing a **'tank graveyard'** of Russian tanks and APCs. The compound is adjacent to a military camp so it is not possible to enter, and photography should be done with caution. If in doubt, ask the Taliban at the entry checkpoint to the compound if you can take photos.

The resistance to the Soviets was led by Ahmad Shah Massoud (page 144), who became a national hero and a symbol of Afghan resilience. Stories of his tactical genius became legend – on one occasion, he evacuated the entire valley, leaving Soviet forces to spend the summer inspecting every side valley, only to find no-one. In another story, a seam of emeralds was revealed after a Russian bombardment, allowing Panjshiri forces to sell the gems and buy more weapons. **Massoud's Tomb**, once a humble whitewashed tomb with a green dome, now stands as a large striking marble monument on an outcrop near the village of **Bazarak**. It is by some margin the tallest structure in the Panjshir and a pilgrimage site for many Afghans.

Today, beyond paying your respects to Massoud or enjoying a plate of fried fish, there may not be much 'to do' in Panjshir by traditional tourist standards. But the views are unforgettable – especially the Lion's Mouth, where towering cliffs close in to just a few dozen metres apart, visually reinforcing why this defiant region was able to hold off one of the world's superpowers for a decade.

The Salang Pass One of Afghanistan's most dramatic and vital routes, the Salang Pass slices through the Hindu Kush, linking Kabul to the north. Towering at over 3,400m, the pass was long a lifeline between central and south Asia. Yet the treacherous zigzagging route over the pass was often blocked by snow for months at a time. In the 1950s, the Soviet Union constructed the **Salang Tunnel**, an engineering marvel that cuts beneath the mountains for over 2.6km. Completed in 1964, it radically shortened travel time between Kabul and Mazar e Sharif, Kunduz and the Tajikistan and Uzbekistan borders. It remains in use today, the country's most important road corridor, although often in poor repair and subject to closures during winter storms or maintenance.

Driving through the Salang is not for the faint-hearted. The ascent from the south winds past rocky cliffs and plunging valleys, with dramatic views over snow-covered ridges and alpine villages clinging to steep slopes. The tunnel itself is unlit and often choked with exhaust fumes, but emerging on the other side into the northern provinces feels like stepping into another world – greener, lusher, and often warmer depending on the season.

ALEXANDER THE GREAT AND THE KHAWAK PASS

> Nothing put him off. Starvation, the freezing cold, nothing – he just kept coming on and on. And in the end his enemies were struck with fear and amazement.
>
> Arrian, *The Anabasis of Alexander*

In the winter of 329BCE, hot on the trail of Persian regicide Bessus (page 17), Alexander was resting his frostbitten, exhausted troops in the Kabul River valley after their high-altitude march from Kandahar. But now Alexander was faced with a predicament. His scouts informed him that Bessus, having taken refuge in Balkh, had laid waste to the lands under the passes he expected Alexander to take over the Hindu Kush. If he took those routes, Alexander knew his army would starve, so in April he decided to take an unexpected route over the easternmost pass: the 3,848m snowbound Khawak Pass in the Panjshir Valley.

As he moved north, he founded the fortress city of Alexandria in the Caucasus at Bagram, near or on the same site as Kapisa, and left thousands of Macedonian veterans, Greek mercenaries and natives to man it. Then he led his army and its hangers-on, a massive column 25km along, up the Panjshir Valley. It took 16 days. Midway they ran out of food. They slaughtered their pack animals but there was no wood to make a fire to cook the meat, so they ate it raw with the juice of a plant that Arrian calls *silphium* (believed to be asafoetida, which grows in the Khawak Valley) which kept them from becoming ill.

As soon as the army had recovered in Kunduz, Alexander moved quickly towards Balkh. When Bessus heard to his horror that Alexander was near, he fled over the Amu Darya and burned all the boats, thinking he was safe at last. Only he wasn't; Alexander just kept coming on and on.

In summer, the pass is fringed by herders grazing sheep and goats in high pastures, and you may spot children selling boiled eggs, tea or even chunks of mountain ice by the roadside. In winter, the route can transform into an icy gauntlet, where convoys of trucks move cautiously over snow-packed roads with the ever-present risk of avalanches. Icicles hang from the ceiling of the tunnel and snow drifts into the avalanche galleries. The same entrepreneurial boys selling boiled eggs now also sell snow chains to unprepared motorists. Look out for the numerous car-wash stations on the roads between the Salang Pass and Kabul; no-one, it seems, likes to enter the city with a dirty car after this exhaustive journey.

4

The East: Jalalabad, Nuristan and Loya Paktia

Eastern Afghanistan is a patchwork of mountains and high plains, where jagged ridgelines rise sharply along the border with Pakistan. Blessed by the outer edges of the Indian monsoon, its valleys are greener, more humid, and more fertile than the arid expanses of the central plateau or the sun-baked deserts of the south. Conifers fill lush Nuristan and olive and citrus trees flourish in Jalalabad's relative warmth.

Along with southern Afghanistan, the east is part of the Pashtun heartland. However, unlike Kandahar and Helmand, these are the borderlands, divided by the controversial Durand Line (page 165), the colonial-era boundary which cuts across tribal areas with little regard for ethnic or geographic logic. To the east lies Pakistan's former Federally Administered Tribal Areas (FATA) – a region as wild and politically sensitive as the Afghan side of the border. Cross-border ties are deep: linguistically and often culturally, the Pashtuns living here have more in common with their neighbours in Pakistan than with Pashtuns in Kandahar, and loyalties often blur the notion of nationhood.

Jalalabad, by far the largest city in the east, lies between Kabul and the **Khyber Pass** – the traditional entry point into Afghanistan from south Asia. Further south lies the little-visited region of **Loya Paktia,** a wild region whose tribes have been independent for millennia. North of Jalalabad is **Nuristan,** a land of steep valleys, remote villages and home to a unique Indo-Iranian culture and people who only converted to Islam in the late 19th century. Its isolation, linguistic diversity and dense forests set it apart even within this already distinctive region. Though rarely visited by outsiders, eastern Afghanistan offers a raw, strikingly beautiful look at Afghan life – at once timeless and in constant flux.

Note that IS-K/ISIS/Daesh historically have had their largest influence in Nangarhar and Kunar provinces and conflict between the Taliban and IS-K is fierce. Do check with the Department of Information and Culture in Jalalabad (page 151) to see if any areas should be avoided.

JALALABAD

Set on the banks of the Kabul River, with the snowy Spin Ghar Mountains forming a majestic backdrop to the south, Jalalabad is a friendly, lively city that serves as a natural crossroads between Afghanistan and Pakistan. While it may lack the grand historical monuments of Herat, Kabul or Kandahar, it's an excellent place to pause – either when entering Afghanistan via the Khyber Pass, en route to Nuristan,

4 | THE EAST: JALALABAD, NURISTAN AND LOYA PAKTIA

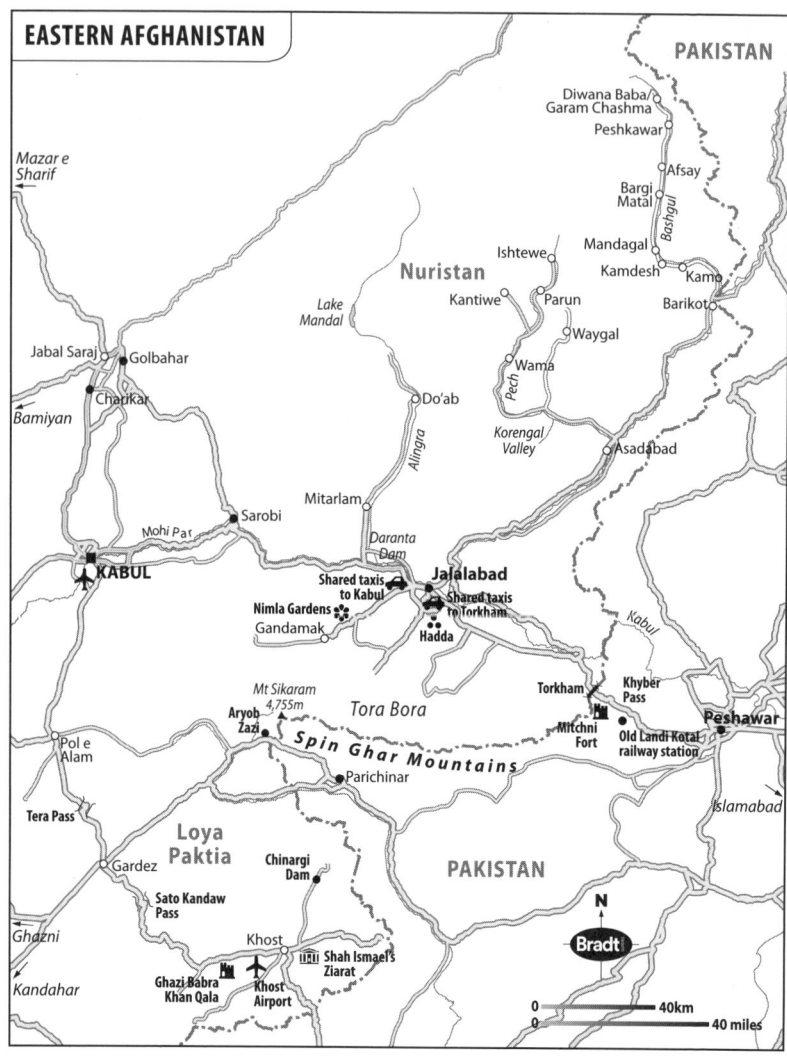

or simply as a day or overnight trip from Kabul to experience the rhythms of a bustling Pashtun city.

Approaching from Kabul, the landscape suddenly softens as you near Jalalabad's wide fertile plain. Lush fields, palm trees and citrus fruit orchards line the road. Coming from steamy subcontinental Peshawar, however, it feels arid and barren. This contrast makes Jalalabad feel like a hinge between two cultural worlds: Afghanistan's highlands and south Asia's plains.

You can at once sense the kinship with Peshawar. Jalalabad's rickshaws, colourful and noisy, look and sound just like their Pakistani cousins. The air smells of spices and frying chapli kebabs. Omnipresent shinwari barbecue joints serve sizzling mutton karahi and grilled lamb with fresh naan, washed down with sugarcane juice. Especially on Fridays, every scrap of land in and around Jalalabad seems to be used by cricket-playing children.

As remote and mysterious as it is exquisite, the Minaret of Jam is a challenging 14-hour journey from the nearest paved road PAGE 190 (JW/D)

above (JP/S) A rare relic of the 12th-century Ghorid dynasty: Chesht e Sharif is the birthplace of the Cheshti Sufi order PAGE 190

below (TP/S) For over 2,000 years, Herat Citadel has dominated the city centre PAGE 218

Carved to replicate the interior of a Buddhist stupa, this cave is part of the Samangan Buddhist cave and stupa complex PAGE 251
above (UB)

The two surviving 12th-century minarets in Ghazni are made entirely of mud-baked bricks PAGE 205
right (JW/D)

With more than 70 towers, Farah Fort is one of the most remarkable citadels in Afghanistan, but today it stands empty PAGE 225
below (JW)

above left & right (SU) — One of Herat's ancient crafts, tile making is still going strong; many of the traditional painted designs go back centuries PAGE 207

below (SS) — Istalif has been famous for over 500 years for its handmade glazed clay pottery PAGE 140

Carpet shop hospitality on Kabul's Chicken Street PAGE 127   above left (UB)

Informal dining in an outdoor restaurant in Kandahar Province PAGE 99   above right (JW)

Shoppers at the vegetable bazaar in Bamiyan town PAGE 178   below (UB)

above (JD/S) High-altitude hiking in the Wakhan Corridor PAGE 272

below (SS) The split in the spine of the 'dragon' in Dragon Valley PAGE 184

Descending into the arid lakebed of Hamun e Helmand PAGE 226 — above (JW)

The Khyber Pass, the legendary gateway through the Hindu Kush into Afghanistan PAGE 157 — right (SS)

A Russian tank at Tora Bora, a centre of mujahideen resistance during the Soviet–Afghan War and Osama bin Laden's cave network PAGE 156 — below (JW)

above (JW) Badakhshan's capital, Fayzabad, is the starting point for adventures in the Wakhan Corridor and Afghan Pamir PAGE 258

below (UB) Fishing at 4,000m altitude; Wakhi horsemen stop to net fish at Lake Chaqmaqtin in the Afghan Pamir PAGE 275

JALALABAD

Once the winter capital of the Afghan kings, Jalalabad has long been a seasonal retreat on account of its mild winters and bountiful orchards. The Mughal emperors loved it for the same reasons, making it their summer capital to escape the heat of the subcontinental plains. Today, that legacy lives on each spring when the city hosts an orange blossom poetry festival, a celebration of fragrance and verse that draws poets and performers from across Afghanistan.

HISTORY The Nangarhar plains were an important trading hub for over 2,000 years. Early on, it flourished as a centre of learning and spiritual life. The nearby ruins at Hadda – once home to monasteries, stupas and exquisite Graeco-Buddhist sculpture – stand as a powerful reminder of the city's ancient past and its role in the spread of Buddhism along the Silk Road. Later, Jalalabad was redeveloped under the great Mughal emperor Jalaluddin Akbar, from whom the city takes its name. Besides a seasonal capital, it became a garrison town. Its strategic location near the Khyber Pass made it the key for controlling eastern Afghanistan, from the Mughals and Durranis to British colonial forces and, more recently, the Soviets and Taliban.

In 1989, Jalalabad was the focus of the first major mujahideen offensive following the Soviet withdrawal. With the Afghan communist government still in power, mujahideen forces launched a large-scale assault. Although this was a change from their traditional guerrilla tactics, they expected the city to fall quickly. Instead, it held out in a brutal siege, withstanding sustained attacks. The failure to take Jalalabad shocked many and demonstrated the resilience of the Najibullah regime. It also signalled that the end of Soviet influence would not mean an immediate transition to peace, but rather the beginning of Afghanistan's descent into civil war.

GETTING THERE AND AWAY At the time of writing, Jalalabad Airport is closed.

By road Shared taxi and bus stations are dotted all along the Jalalabad Bypass Road south of Jalalabad. Transport to/from **Kabul** uses the junction of the main Kabul–Jalalabad road and west end of the bypass; shared taxis (500AFN; 3–5hrs) fill up quickly. Ask for **Kabul hada**. Note that travel times to Jalalabad can vary dramatically due to traffic at Mohi Par (page 143). This route is usually quieter in the mornings.

For the **Torkham border**, shared taxis leave from the junction of the main Jalalabad road and east end of the bypass. Shared taxis (500AFN; 3hrs) ply this route regularly.

For **Kunar and Nuristan**, shared taxis and pick-ups use the first junction north of the Behsud bridge next to Abdul Haq Park. They leave regularly for Asadabad (150AFN; 2hrs). Pick-ups to Parun (900AFN; 9hrs) and further afield are occasionally found here but you may be better off travelling to Asadabad and changing there.

TOURIST INFORMATION AND REGISTRATION If just passing through Jalalabad or visiting briefly on a day trip, there is no need to register. But if staying the night and especially if you wish to go to Tora Bora or Gandamak, a visit to the **Department of Information and Culture** (Qasabi Rd, east of the Seraj al Emirat Gardens) is essential.

ORIENTATION The centre of Jalalabad is quite compact and based around the Seraj al Emirat, the old royal gardens and palaces. The central bazaar is to the south and east, with Talashi Chowk, Malang Jan Chowk and Mokheberat Chowk major junctions. Administrative buildings and accommodation options are concentrated west of the gardens. Most places of interest and hotels are within walking distance of each other. The embankment of the Kabul River to the north of Abdul Haq Park is a nice spot for a walk once the heat has gone out of the day. In summer people fish or swim at Daranta Dam west of town.

WHERE TO STAY *Map, opposite*

The accommodation falls into two categories: large, modern mansions converted into small hotels aimed squarely at NGO staff (the exception is the Spinghar); or mussafarkhanas in the bazaar area, which will probably not accept foreign visitors.

Afghan Shahee Hotel Opposite Nangarhar Business Centre; m 7820 02530; e af.shaheehotel@gmail.com. A 3-storey mansion with attached restaurant. Large rooms all have AC & Western-style toilets. Security; b/fast inc. $$

Spinghar Hotel At the west end of the Seraj al Emirat Gardens; m 7786 00005; bookable on Booking.com. Built in 1934 by King Zahir Shah for his guests, including the French archaeologists who excavated Hadda (page 155), Spinghar is by far the most characterful hotel in Jalalabad, possibly in Afghanistan. Set next to the Seraj al Emirat in large well-kept grounds with 90-year-old date trees & a lovely rose garden, the building has beautiful Art Deco details; squint & you could imagine yourself in Palm Springs. The interior is very tired, however, & the whole place could do with a renovation. All rooms have AC & Western-style toilets. The VIP rooms are huge. Security; free tea & coffee; b/fast inc. $$

Spogmai Hotel Near Pohanton Hospital; ✆ 6020 00999; m 7751 51511; w spogmaihotel.com. This mansion is aimed squarely at NGO bookings but will take international tourists. It has a pleasant garden, & large rooms all with AC & Western-style toilets. Security; coffee & b/fast inc. $$

Sultan Hotel On the Kabul–Jalalabad road; m 7800 03334. A medium-sized hotel with a nice garden & fruit trees & on-site restaurant. The rooms are large & well kept, all with AC & Western-style toilets. Security. B/fast inc. $$

White House Hotel Behind University Hospital; m 7861 64762; e whitehouse.hotel2015@yahoo.com. An imposing white 5-storey hotel complete with kitsch cupola inspired, as the property's name suggests, by the residence of the President of the USA. The whole edifice is garishly lit at night. The rooms themselves are large, functional but a little dingy, all with AC & Western-style toilets. Attached restaurant with garden; security; coffee & b/fast inc. $$

Kabul Hotel & Guesthouse m 7006 14510. One of the cheap, noisy mussafarkhanas of dubious cleanliness in the central bazaar. No attached bathroom, different prices for different size rooms, & very basic. May refuse international guests. $

WHERE TO EAT AND DRINK *Map, opposite*

You'll find traditional Afghan restaurants, and **fruit juice and ice cream sellers** in the main bazaar and snack sellers at the Seraj al Emirat Gardens. Beyond these, there is a string of higher-end Afghan restaurants between Abdul Haq Park and the Kabul River with rooftop seating for views over the river and to catch the breeze coming down the valley. Most hotels serve Afghan, Pakistani and Chinese food, as well as fried chicken and burgers. The **White House** is probably the pick of the bunch, as the restaurant has a pleasant garden and offers the chance to bask in the glow of its kitschy illuminations. **Sultan** and **Afghan Shahee hotels** both have less attractive gardens and air-conditioned areas.

The speciality of Jalalabad is the chapli kebab, essentially a spicy deep-fried lamb burger. *Chapli* means 'shoe' in Pashto.

Green Hut Pizza On the Kabul–Jalalabad road; m 7888 86263. Come here for pizzas & good Afghan food in a pleasant garden; also AC indoors. $$

Mahtarlam Baba By the Daranta Dam; m 7820 87408, 7006 04975. The pick among many restaurants along here serving Afghan dishes & fried fish. $$

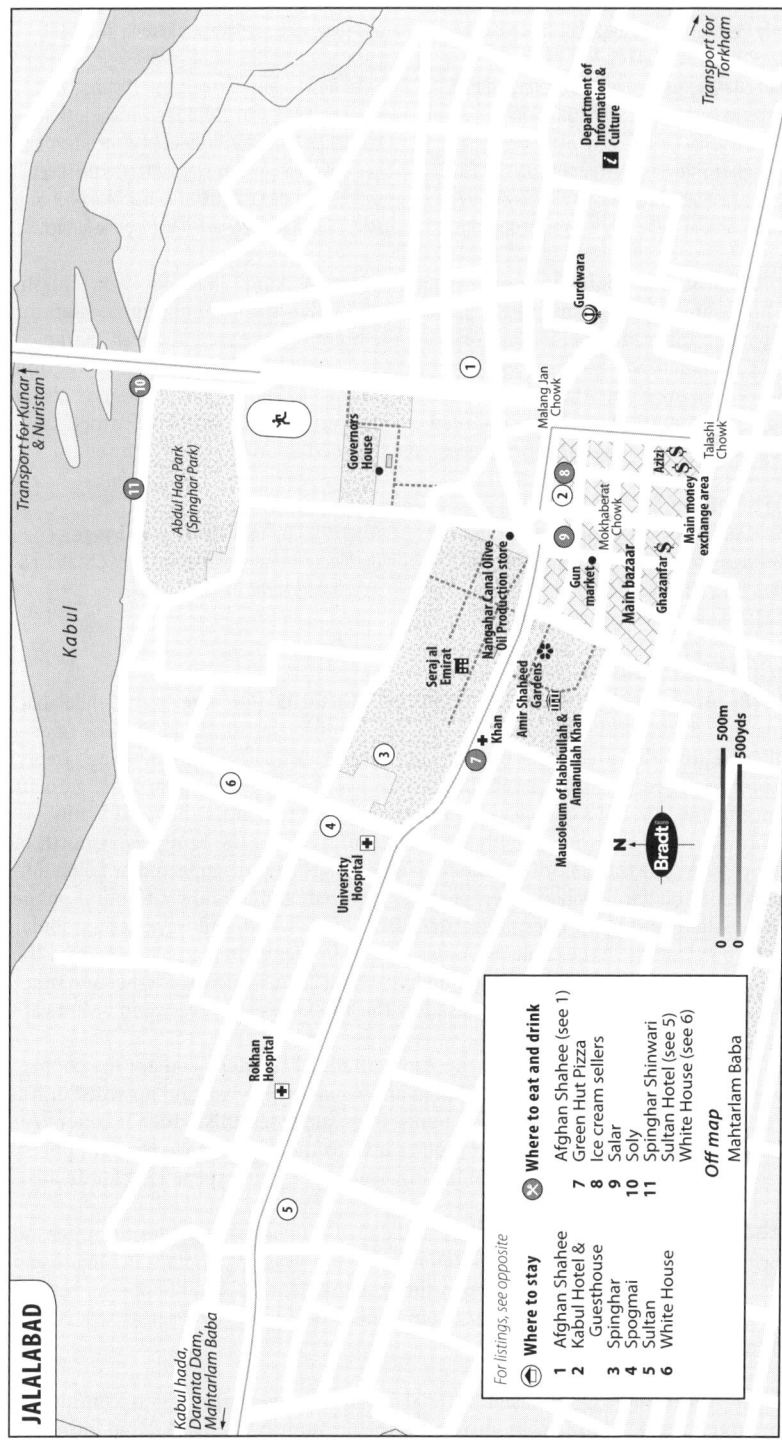

Soly Restaurant By the Kabul River near Abdul Haq Park; m 7994 24245, 7994 24150. One of the better riverside restaurants offering karahi & barbecue food, as well as Afghan cuisine & fried fish. It also has the best views of the river. $$

Spinghar Shinwari Restaurant By the Kabul River near Abdul Haq Park; m 7877 77878, 7771 81386. Similar to the Soly in terms of offerings and style, with a terrace overlooking the cricket pitch. $$

Salar Restaurant On the Kabul–Jalalabad road; m 7742 48220, 7801 06070. People come to this very simple restaurant, in the heart of the action, for its chapli kebab, fried by 3 men sitting by the street with 1.5m-wide karahis filled with smoking-hot oil. If spicy lamb burgers are your thing, look no further. $

SHOPPING The **main bazaar** is located between Amir Shaheed Park, Talashi Chowk and Malang Jan Chowk. Jalalabad is known throughout Afghanistan for olive oil. It is traditionally used for skin care but has more recently been marketed for cooking, too. A good place to buy some is **Nangarhar Canal Olive Production Store** (on the Kabul–Jalalabad road; m 7802 57734, 7881 75080). There is also a small **gun market**; traditionally men in Pashtun regions would be armed on a regular basis although this practice is now frowned upon by the government.

OTHER PRACTICALITIES

Medical **Rokhan Hospital** (on the Kabul–Jalalabad road; 6020 00800) offers the best emergency care. **Khan** (also on the Kabul–Jalalabad road) is the best centrally located pharmacy.

Money The main **currency exchange** is in the block northwest of Talashi Chowk. Ghazanfar & Azizi **banks** are on the same street.

WHAT TO SEE AND DO

Seraj al Emirat and Amir Shaheed gardens (On the Kabul–Jalalabad road; dawn–dusk daily; free) In the centre of Jalalabad, these gardens offer a glimpse into the city's royal past and a peaceful escape from its bustling streets. Commissioned by Amir Habibullah Khan in the early 20th century, the gardens once formed part of a complex intended as a winter retreat for the royal family.

The **Seraj al Emirat**, roughly translating to 'Light of the Emirates', is north of the road. While the majority of the palace buildings have disappeared or fallen into disrepair, the gardens have been partially restored, and are now a tranquil public space filled with palm trees, flowering plants and shaded walkways. It's a popular spot, particularly in the cooler evenings, when families gather to picnic or enjoy the relative calm, disturbed only by vendors hawking corn, samosas, sherbet and other snacks. One building is currently used by the Taliban as a madrasa and visitors are not permitted.

Opposite the Seraj al Emirat, the **Amir Shaheed Gardens** contain the copper-domed mausoleum of Habibullah Khan and Amanullah Khan and his wife Soraya. All loved the winter capital. Full of orange trees and roses, this garden is better kept than its neighbour and in spring it plays host to the city's orange blossom poetry festival. Ask at the Department of Information and Culture (page 151) for details.

Abdul Haq Park and Kabul River (Jalalabad–Kunar road, south side of Behsud Bridge) The park and river embankment make for pleasant people-watching to end the day, especially in summer when the embankment catches the breeze. Named after Abdul Haq, the local military commander during the 1980s, the park is now officially called Spinghar Park.

Sikh Jalalabad (Off Behsud Rd) Jalalabad has the largest Sikh community in Afghanistan, a nod to its proximity to the Punjab plains. A large gurdwara (currently closed to visitors) sits behind imposing blast walls at the heart of a small Sikh bazaar selling herbal medical products. Seeing men in Sikh-style turbans and colourful Sikh imagery comes as a surprise in Afghanistan and a reminder that the subcontinent is half a day's drive away. However, since the Taliban took power, the community is not as visible.

AROUND JALALABAD

Hadda (10km southeast of the centre of Jalalabad, just off the Jalalabad Bypass Road) Hadda is a sobering example of Afghanistan's lost cultural heritage. From the 1st to the 4th century CE, this was a major Graeco-Buddhist complex, with multiple monasteries and dozens of stupas. Excavations from the 1930s and 1970s recovered more than 20,000 Graeco-Buddhist statues. The intervening years have not been kind to the site, which has been looted to the point that there is very little to see. One surviving stupa, now little more than a mound of bricks and mud pocked with holes left by treasure hunters, sits behind a protective wall and you'll need to find the chowkidar (who grows wheat inside the complex) and show him your documentation from the Department of Information and Culture for the key. Kuchi nomads camp within the complex.

Gandamak

It is easy to enter Afghanistan, the problem is getting out again.

Arthur Wellesley, 1st Duke of Wellington

For students of Victorian British history, few places have more resonance. In 1841, Gandamak was the scene of the final stand of a convoy of 16,000 British soldiers

THE FIRST ANGLO–AFGHAN WAR AND THE RETREAT FROM KABUL

The First Anglo–Afghan War (1838–42) is best remembered not for the British army's invasion and occupation of Afghanistan, but for its catastrophic retreat.

After occupying Kabul in 1839 to install Shuja Shah Durrani as a pro-British ruler, British forces quickly found themselves in a city simmering with resentment. When local uprisings flared in late 1841, including the killing of the British envoy Sir William Hay Macnaghten, the occupying army negotiated a truce to withdraw to Jalalabad, 145km away.

In January 1842, around 16,000 men, women and children – a mix of British soldiers, Indian sepoys and camp followers – set out through the snowbound passes, poorly supplied and under constant attack by Ghilzai tribesmen. The route taken in 1842 is different from the modern road, but anyone driving between Kabul and Jalalabad can see what difficult terrain it is. What followed was a massacre. The army made its last stand at Gandamak Hill, where the final survivors – some 20 officers and 45 sepoys – were surrounded and killed. Only one European, Dr William Brydon, half-dead and on a dying horse, reached Jalalabad, the sole survivor of the most infamous retreat in British history, immortalised in the dramatic Victorian painting *Remnants of an Army* by Elizabeth Butler.

Although a British punitive force later returned to Kabul and razed parts of the city, they soon withdrew, and the former king, Dost Mohammad Khan, was reinstated. These events fixed the image of the Afghan highlands as a graveyard of empires, an image that remains to this day.

4 | THE EAST: JALALABAD, NURISTAN AND LOYA PAKTIA

and camp followers travelling from Kabul to Jalalabad (page 155). For generations this tiny village was synonymous with British military ineptitude but also Afghan military tenacity and tactical superiority in Afghanistan's tough terrain.

When the British returned to Afghanistan 40 years later for the Second Afghan War, the peace accord was signed here. The Treaty of Gandamak, ending the first phase of the Second Anglo–Afghan War, was signed under a tree on 26 May 1879, by the Afghan Amir Muhammad Yaqub Khan and Sir Louis Cavagnari, representing the British Government of India. The treaty ceded various frontier areas to British control and granted the British the right to control Afghan foreign affairs. It remained in the mind of later writers including Rudyard Kipling, and later George McDonald Fraser's Flashman books; his eponymous hero resides in Gandamak Lodge.

In 1841, Gandamak was on the main Kabul–Jalalabad route, but these days it's a tiny village at the end of a bumpy 2-hour drive from Jalalabad. The road takes you past smallholdings and typical large compounds in which multiple generations of Pashtun family members live together. The hill where the last stand took place is directly northwest of Gandamak and the villagers will show you a large tree under which they claim the treaty was signed.

The road also takes you past the Mughal-era **Nimla Gardens** (site of another springtime poetry festival; enquire at the Department of Information and Culture). These well-maintained gardens with their citrus trees were perhaps the Bagh e Wafa (Garden of Fidelity), mentioned by the first Mughal emperor Babur in *The Baburnama*: 'There oranges, citrons and pomegranates grow in abundance… I had plantains brought and planted there; they did very well. The year before I had had sugar cane planted there; it also did well.'

Tora Bora Tora Bora (meaning 'black cave') is a rugged mountain region in Nangarhar Province, near the border with Pakistan. Part of the Spin Ghar range, its steep ridges and deep limestone caves have made it both a natural fortress and a legendary stronghold for fighters over the centuries.

Tora Bora hit the headlines around the world in 2001, during the early stages of the US-led invasion of Afghanistan. It was here that Osama bin Laden was believed to have taken refuge after the fall of the Taliban regime. In December of that year, American and allied Afghan forces launched a massive assault on Tora Bora. Despite intense bombing and a ground offensive, bin Laden famously escaped, likely crossing the porous border into Pakistan – a moment that would shape years of further conflict.

Due to its inaccessibility and proximity to Pakistan's tribal areas, the area had been used as a base by mujahideen during the Soviet–Afghan War, then later by insurgent groups. Its cave systems, some naturally formed and others manmade and expanded over decades, served as arms depots, hideouts and command centres. Internationally, Tora Bora remains synonymous with Afghanistan's complex terrain and history – where geography has repeatedly shaped the fate of empires, militias and global conflicts. Locally it is just another name in a long litany of places shaped by conflict.

There is no public transport and it's a 2-hour drive each way on increasingly poor roads. A 4x4 would be useful but not essential. The caves have gone, completely destroyed by the attacks of 2001, but what remains are hillsides marked with white paint, to show the area has been cleared of mines and UXO. You'll see a few burnt-out Russian tanks and sangars (temporary fortified positions), as well as an 'Arab' cemetery, where the bodies of al-Qaeda soldiers were buried. It is worth having a

THE MOTHER OF ALL BOMBS

Its real name is the GBU-43/B Massive Ordnance Air Blast (MOAB). It's just over 9m long, weighs 9,850kg and has the blast power of 11 tonnes of TNT, and when it was made in 2003, during the Iraq War, it was America's most powerful non-nuclear bomb, a GPS-guided 'smart bomb'. It was invented on the hop by the US Air Force, designed to use against underground tunnels in difficult terrain; but mostly the US$16 million bomb was designed to intimidate Saddam Hussein, as a warning during his 'mother of all battles'. The film of its test in 2003 creating a giant mushroom cloud was widely seen.

A MOAB explodes in the air just before reaching the ground, blasting fuel into the air that instantly atomises. A secondary explosion ignites the atomised fuel, creating a blast wave of overpressure that sends a destructive wave for a mile in every direction. As Edward Priest, a former Air Force Special Operations combat controller, explained: 'That type of bomb wouldn't work well, for example, to destroy tanks, although the overpressure would kill the people in them. You'd overpressure the people hiding in the caves there. You'd never find them – it just blows your lungs out of your mouth. It kind of turns you inside out.'

Which is why it was never used…until 13 April 2017, when the United States dropped it on an IS-K tunnel complex in the Achin district in southern Nangarhar Province. The Afghan army claimed it killed 94 IS-K members and four commanders. A BBC reporter who went to the site shortly after said it was something of a damp squib, at least on the surface – although there were a few trees and buildings that had been flattened, only 35m away there were healthy green trees still standing. No-one really knows how many were killed. And the locals told the reporter that there were hundreds of nearby caves filled with IS-K fighters, and there were always more, and at the end of the day it didn't change things really at all.

---

chat with the local inhabitants; older people will talk of the days when the 'sheikh' (bin Laden) would visit and the damage caused by the assault. From Tora Bora it is 'a day and a night' to walk to Pakistan albeit this is not a legal entry point. It predominantly seems to be used to import sheep and cows into Afghanistan.

At the time of writing a restaurant was being built next to a Russian tank overlooking the hillside where the caves used to be. Until this is finished, visitors will need to bring their own food; the nearest restaurant is in the village of Chaprahar where they serve chapli kebabs to go.

Khyber Pass Though it lies within Pakistan's borders, the Khyber Pass has long been synonymous with Afghanistan. For millennia, this rugged mountain corridor has been a key route for traders, pilgrims and invading armies flowing in and out of Afghanistan. From Alexander the Great to the Mughals, from British troops to US convoys and beyond, the pass has served as the principal gateway between central Asia and the Indian subcontinent.

The pass begins at Torkham, the chaotic and heavily guarded border crossing between Pakistan and Afghanistan. From there, the road climbs steeply through a dry, dramatic landscape to Landi Kotal, which sits at the crest of the pass. Historically a strategic military post, Landi Kotal was also the terminus of the Khyber Railway, one of the engineering marvels of British India. The old railway line runs parallel to the modern road, snaking through tunnels and bridges carved into the rock between Landi Kotal and Jamrud Fort. The Landi Kotal Railway Station can still be seen from the road, and was the terminus of the Khyber Steam Safari, which operated a steam train ride between 1996 and 2006. It's hoped that with relative stability in the region it can be restored once again.

Mitchni Fort offers the classic vantage point looking into Afghanistan, seeing the road snake back down towards Torkham. Once on the eastern side of the pass, on the outskirts of Landi Kotal lies the Sphola Stupa, a 2,000-year-old Buddhist relic, a reminder of the area's place on the ancient Silk Road and in the wider Buddhist world. As the road descends towards Peshawar, it passes vast compounds owned by local warlords and tribal chiefs, and numerous forts. The land becomes greener and the air more humid until Jamrud Fort is reached, historically the sentinel guarding the mouth of the pass. Nearby stands the Khyber Gate, a symbolic arch that marks the eastern end of the Khyber Pass. This iconic structure even appears on the Pakistani 10-rupee note, underlining its national significance.

The Khyber Pass cuts through the heart of the Khyber Tribal Agency, part of Pakistan's former Federally Administered Tribal Areas (FATA), now merged with Khyber Pakhtunkhwa Province. This remains a highly sensitive security zone, with frequent checkpoints and military convoys. The region has seen multiple armed conflicts, not just from insurgent groups, but also intermittent skirmishes between Afghan and Pakistani troops near the Torkham border, making travel here potentially volatile and subject to rapid changes in the security situation.

NURISTAN

Afghanistan's least populous province, with only around 167,000 inhabitants, Nuristan is tucked deep within the Hindu Kush, where the ridgelines meet the northwesternmost edge of the monsoon. It's a province of spectacular natural beauty – dense pine and cedar forests and dramatic river valleys, with a biodiversity unmatched anywhere else in the country; rhesus monkeys, markhors and black bears all call it home. Three rivers drain it, the Bashgul to the east, the Pech in the centre and the Alingra in the west. There are no roads to link these three rivers and the villages that dot their banks, so access to each valley is only possible by hiking (which can take hours, and even days) or multi-day drives via neighbouring provinces.

Villages cling to the sides of steep gorges. Traditional houses, made of wood, mud and stone, are stacked one on top of another, often perched on rocky ledges to conserve arable land. Some of these homes are centuries old and feature central hearths and elaborately carved beams. Terraced fields – sometimes no wider than a metre – rise above rushing rivers, where children swim in summer and women tend to grapes, walnuts, *jalghoza* (a prized black pine nut found only in Nuristan and Kunar) and corn.

In 2020, Nuristan was officially declared a national park, and there's even a dedicated website (w nuristani.com) promoting its heritage and local products – gemstones, morel mushrooms, saffron, rugs, carved wooden furniture, jewellery, pakol hats and leather goods. The Taliban appear to administer it with a light touch, leaving a surprising degree of autonomy in local hands. Many Nuristanis follow traditional tribal codes similar to the Pashtunwali (page 44), and it's understood that some old festivals still quietly take place in the high pastures, out of sight. There are still Taliban checkpoints and illegal logging is reportedly down compared with previous years.

Nuristan remains deeply rural and agricultural, with life revolving around the seasons. In summer, sheep are herded into the alpine pastures while crops are planted and harvested. In winter, the land grows quiet and daily life slows. Women shoulder much of the labour indoors and out, while men traditionally play roles centred around protection, honour and, historically, conflict. There's a visible cultural vibrancy in Nuristan. Local sports like archery and wrestling-style games are still played – some competitively, others just for fun. Ask around and you might find yourself watching or partaking in an impromptu match or being invited to a village festival.

One quirky tradition is *akhwat* or 'brothery' – a mischievous game played between villages. Under the cover of night, young men from one village sneak into another and play a prank on it: knocking over an outhouse, stealing livestock, or – as one Nuristani proudly claimed – hoisting a donkey on to a roof. If they succeed without being caught, the pranked village must host a festival in their honour. If they're caught, they must do the hosting instead. This tradition is thought to date back to Nuristan's pre-Islamic past, when inter-village raiding was part of the local culture.

However, life is changing. Traditional wooden homes are being replaced by ones built of cheaper and sturdier modern materials. The wooden mosques complete with carvings and wooden ablution bowls are often the first to be upgraded under the Taliban's mosque-building mission. Domestic tourism is also slowly changing the face of Nuristan; during Eid festivities, the area becomes particularly busy with visitors from other provinces.

HISTORY The people of Nuristan were perhaps first mentioned by the ancient Greeks, who wrote that Alexander the Great encountered a people who made their own wine and instead of burying their dead, they were left excarnated in wooden coffins above ground – traditions that the people of Nuristan still carried out into the late 1800s.

Once Afghanistan had converted to Islam, the inhabitants of this remote corner resisted, preferring to remain the last *kafirs* or 'pagans'; hence for centuries this was called just that, Kafiristan or 'Land of Unbelievers'. Mahmud of Ghazni (page 204) who subjugated the Hindu and Buddhist populations of Afghanistan, Pakistan and northern India and forced many to convert to Islam, raided Kafiristan in 1014 but failed to convert anyone. Even the great Timur (Tamerlane) failed miserably and wrote in his memoirs that he and his horses got stuck and had to be lowered from a cliff in a basket.

The infidels were incredibly fierce fighters and great archers – the various Nuristani tribes kept in shape by practising on each other in bitter feuds. Fiercely independent, each village had its leaders (the cattle and goat owners) and craftsmen (the Bari, who were enslaved by the cattle owners, and made everything they needed, from houses down to bowls). They also raided nearby Muslim towns and murdered; a Kafir boy wasn't properly a man unless he killed a Muslim.

In 1895, when Amir Abdur Rahman signed the treaty with the British that established the Durand Line, he decided it was time to put his foot down, partly as he feared the Russians might grab Kafiristan. When diplomacy failed, he ordered the army in, ordering them to take the Kafirs alive, which often proved impossible; one group, the Siah Posh, burned their houses down around them rather than submit and convert. Others did, and in 1896 Abdur Rahman changed the name to Nuristan, the 'Land of Light'.

The legend of Nuristan/Kafiristan was lit by Kipling in his novella *The Man Who Would Be King* (1888), based on the premise that the Nuristani were either descendants of the Greek armies of Alexander or a lost tribe from earlier times.

WHO ARE THE NURISTANI?

The Nuristani (page 50) have been described as 'a treasure for historians, linguists, archaeologists and anthropologists'. For decades they have intrigued outsiders. Why are they so different from other Afghans? They often have red or blond hair and blue eyes. They use tables and chairs, unlike most Afghans, who sit on the floor. Until the 20th century the Nuristani buried their dead above ground in open four-legged cedar coffins, then after a year, interred them and erected distinct wooden effigies, usually on horseback, over the graves.

Once divided between the Safed Posh (white dress) and Siah Posh (black dress), Nuristan's valleys are each inhabited by one of 15 tribes who speak their own variations of Nuristani, a Dardic language – which are so different from each other they are considered separate languages. Their old polytheistic religion seemed to have combined ancient Greek and primitive Hindu rites, as described by British agent George Scott Robertson, who lived in Kafiristan in 1890, and was the first (and last) Westerner to do so before it became Nuristan (his *Kafirs of the Hindu Kush* is available on Internet Archive, w archive.org/details/in.ernet.dli.2015.24815/mode/2up).

Some Nuristani believe they are the descendants of the 10,000 or so men Alexander left behind to settle in his new cities in Afghanistan. Others believe they were pushed back into this remote corner over the centuries because they resisted Islamisation. Thousands from the Waygal Valley who didn't convert are the Kalash, who escaped into the remote mountain valleys above Chitral in Pakistan, where they still worship their pagan gods, drink wine, sing and dance their dances to drums and pipes.

DNA tests showed that some 60% of the Nuristani belong to the Y-DNA Haplogroup R1a, a marker of the Indo-Iranian migrations, and suggest they may be pretty much the same as the Indo-Aryans who created the Bactria–Margiana Archaeological Complex (page 16). Richard F Strand has dedicated his career to researching the Nuristani and especially their language: see his excellent website w nuristan.info.

Their reputation only grew due to their inaccessibility. One of the funniest scenes (of many) in *A Short Walk in the Hindu Kush* comes at the very end when Eric Newby by chance runs into the famous explorer Wilfred Thesiger in remotest Nuristan – where Thesiger mocks them for having inflatable beds.

The Nuristani have been good Muslims ever since, and in fact were the first to rise up against the Saur Revolution (page 32). What followed were decades of instability as Nuristan, which shares a frontier with Pakistan, became the theatre of intense guerrilla warfare, first against the Soviets followed by NATO forces fighting the Taliban, a fight so brutal that General McChrystal, in an unprecedented move, withdrew all troops from Nuristan. It remained one of the most dangerous parts of the country until the Taliban took over in 2021.

Following some early friction, the Nuristanis seem to be content with the current administration, and an area that has seen few visitors since the time of Alexander is eminently possible to visit.

GETTING THERE AND AROUND Getting into Nuristan itself is no easy feat; although it lies only 100km from Kabul as the crow flies, the journey by public transport can take up to two full days. But those who make the effort are richly rewarded. In Nuristan, shared pick-ups are the main form of public transport. A lucky few passengers get a seat in the cab, but the rest usually stand in the back, the journey on unpaved roads being too uncomfortable to sit on a metal floor. Southbound they run from Parun's bazaar between Wama (200AFN; 2hrs) Asadabad (700AFN; 7hrs) and Jalalabad (900AFN; 9hrs). Northbound there are occasionally links with Ishtewe (150AFN; 1½hrs).

TOURIST INFORMATION AND REGISTRATION You must register with the authorities in Parun (located on the north side of the village on the opposite side of the river to the main road) before travelling to any other part of Nuristan. Even visitors wishing to go to Kamdesh will need to take a 14-hour detour to Parun for permission. You will more than likely be assigned an official guide from the Department of Information and Culture during your stay, too.

ORIENTATION The eight districts of Nuristan can be divided into three areas along the three main rivers. The **Central** districts, drained by the Pech River, include Parun, Wama and Waygal. This is the most commonly visited part of Nuristan as all visitors must register with the ministry in Parun. You can reach Parun by taking a road west from Asadabad in Kunar Province (page 164). The **Eastern** districts are drained by the Bashgul River that abut the Pakistan border, including Kamdesh and Bargi Matal. These are the second most-visited districts, and can also be visited from Asadabad. The **Western** districts are drained by the Alingra River. These include the Nurgaram, Do'ab and Mandol districts, which are accessible from Laghman Province.

CENTRAL NURISTAN
Parun Parun serves as the provincial capital of Nuristan. Unlike the steep, narrow gorges that define much of the province, Parun sits in a wide valley, where the landscape opens up to reveal a small but growing town surrounded by lush smallholdings and terraced fields.

Where to stay
National Park Hotel 100m north of the bridge in Parun; m 7050 15013, 7901 02076; e milliparkrestaurant@gmail.com. This small, basic, but clean hotel was built during the current Taliban regime. Some rooms have AC & attached squat toilets. B/fast inc. **$$**

Spogmai Hotel Next to bridge, Parun; m 7047 73677, 7047 73567. Before the National Park Hotel was built, this used to be the best place to stay. It's a basic chaikhana with small unclean rooms, with no beds or attached bathroom. The one saving grace is that you can hear the sound of the river as you drift off to sleep. **$**

Festivals The two main festivals are Orba aw in the spring and Jesht in the autumn after the harvest. Typically they include traditional dancing, music and sporting contests such as archery. However, their exact make-up under the new government is uncertain.

What to see and do Parun makes for a good base for exploring the surrounding valleys and villages. Despite its status as a provincial capital, the town remains quiet and undeveloped, with a modest bazaar selling essentials and a handful of administrative buildings. The craftsmanship of Nuristani carpenters is renowned – traditional furniture workshops dot the lanes, and you may find a few pieces for sale.

4 | THE EAST: JALALABAD, NURISTAN AND LOYA PAKTIA

At the north end of town, open spaces serve as informal gathering areas where locals engage in traditional pastimes. Archery is particularly popular, as is a stone-throwing game reminiscent of pétanque. Recently, cricket has gained popularity, with impromptu matches often taking place on flat stretches of land. Also north, just outside Parun, there's a small lake that forms where the river widens, where visitors can rent pedalos in the summer.

Around Parun You will pass the village of **Wama** on the way to Parun. The valley is particularly steep, dotted with typical Nuristani villages where houses appear stacked one on top of another. A very precipitous hike or hour's drive from Wama leads to Wama Qadim (Old Wama), where ancient, now empty, 'wine storage vats' are still visible, harking back to the days when the Nuristanis were boozy kafirs. Some 2 hours south of Parun, a turn-off leads northwest up the **Kantiwe Valley** – offering another great scenic drive.

A 1–2-hour hike starting from the main bridge in Parun leads up the steep valley to **Shot**. Here the valley opens on to a small pasture where Parun's youth sometimes play cricket. It offers great views over the Parun Valley.

Ishtewe, situated a 1½–2-hour drive north of Parun, is the final village in the main valley. The road passes many villages, some with attractive wood-carved decoration and riverside restaurants that get busy with Afghan tourists during the Eid holidays. After Ishtewe, a trail crosses over a high pass into the Kamdesh district (see opposite). This would be a long full day hike on an unmarked route, so speak to the Department of Information and Culture office in Parun for a guide to escort you.

Korengal Valley Although the Korengal Valley is in Kunar Province, it's best visited as a side trip on the drive to or from Parun. The Korengal Valley is infamous in modern Afghan history. A narrow, steep valley covered in a dense pine forest, it became a focal point of US military operations in the late 2000s due to its strategic location and fierce local resistance, seeing near-constant combat between American forces and insurgents for over five years.

Restrepo (2010; page 287), an award-winning documentary by journalists Sebastian Junger and Tim Hetherington, brought the valley to the attention of the world. The film chronicles the deployment of a US platoon to Outpost Restrepo, named after a fallen medic, and captures the psychological toll of war, the relentless firefights and isolation experienced by soldiers. Despite massive efforts, the US withdrew in 2010, conceding that the high cost in lives and resources was failing to yield any lasting strategic benefit.

Today Korengal is a sleepy valley of attractive wood and stone buildings and peach and cherry orchards. You can visit the gutted US base, an hour's drive from the main Parun–Asadabad road. Outpost Restrepo is another 45 minutes further on. Most villagers are happy to discuss the history of the valley. If you plan to visit, you should get permission from Asadabad's Department of Information and Culture (page 164).

EASTERN NURISTAN Tucked into the far northeast of Nuristan, Kamdesh and Bargi Matal are among Afghanistan's most remote districts – historically, culturally and geographically closer to Chitral across the border in Pakistan than to Kabul. These high valleys are home to Dardic-speaking Nuristani, who retain some unique traditions. Traditional wooden architecture is more common here than in Parun.

Visits by outsiders have had mixed fortunes. Afghanistan's last king, Zahir Shah, built a summer retreat here, attracted by its cool climate and isolation. A few kilometres further up the valley, Kamdesh gained global attention during the Battle of Kamdesh in 2009, when US troops at remote **Combat Outpost Keating** were surrounded and attacked in one of the deadliest engagements of the war.

The following places are listed in order if driving from Kunar.

Getting there and away Pick-ups are less frequent the further up the valley you travel. Transport between Kamdesh and Asadabad (600AFN; 6hrs) or Bargi Matal (250AFN; 2hrs) is more common than between Bargi Matal and Afsay (150AFN; 1½hrs), Peshawerak (250AFN; 2hrs) or Diwana Baba (400AFN; 3hrs).

Kamdesh When coming from Kunar, **Kamo** is the second village you'll find after entering Nuristan. Located on the south side of the valley, it was here that King Zahir Shah built his residence. It's on the east side of a bridge; ask locally as it is well known.

The heart of this district is a cluster of four small villages, **Najjarha**, **Barkali**, **Beprestan** and **Payenda** (collectively also called Kamdesh), which stretch upwards towards a high meadow. Get there by driving up a serpentine road that starts 2km east of the villages or by hiking (1½–2hrs) from the district administration building at **Ormol** on the main road. The hike to Najjarha passes through all four villages and by some wonderful examples of wood-carved mosques and homes. One particular house in Najjarha claims to be the oldest in Nuristan, with thick, ornately carved walnut pillars. The meadow (*chaman*) at the top has stunning views and is used for cricket and archery on holidays.

The largest village in the Kamdesh district, **Mandagal** occupies a steep section of the valley, where houses teeter high over the rushing river. With a small local bazaar, it is a good place to stop or base yourself. You can eat or stay at the basic **Bahadurkhel Hotel and Restaurant** (m 7022 01005 – ask for Hashim Khan or his son Quaid e Rehman; $). There are three rooms and one bathroom.

Bargi Matal district The road from Mandagal to Bargi Matal runs through a long narrow gorge with only a few small villages. The village of **Bargi Matal** is one of the first in the district and has the only real accommodation and food: **Mama Mazar Restaurant** (m 77081 00207; $), a very basic mussafarkhana.

Both **Afsay** and **Peshawerak** are attractive villages, where some old homes have traditional wood carvings.

The uppermost village of the valley, which opens up to the largest arable area in eastern Nuristan, **Diwana Baba** is also famed for a natural hot spring called Garm Chashma, reputed to cure muscle and bone pain. You may find people travelling from as far as Jalalabad for its healing properties. Further north tower the high peaks of Badakhshan Province.

WESTERN NURISTAN Western Nuristan is the least-visited region and was not researched as part of this book. Highlights include Mandal Lake and the chance to follow in the footsteps of Eric Newby and cross between Panjshir and Nuristan.

To reach Western Nuristan you would pass through Mitarlam in Laghman Province, where the **Kaka Jan Hotel** (m 7303 58310; $) has clean rooms but no beds. Once in Western Nuristan, the villages of Do'ab and Mandol have restaurants that will let you stay the night. You may also be able to negotiate homestays.

KUNAR PROVINCE

This small narrow province follows the length of the Kunar River which flows out of the Pakistani district of Chitral before emptying into the Kabul River. There are very few reasons to visit Kunar unless passing through en route to Nuristan or visiting Korengal (page 162) and needing to obtain permission. You may also need to spend the night or change vehicles if using public transport. Kunar was seriously affected by the earthquakes in 2025; this included reducing access to many parts of Nuristan. The Afghan Tour Department in Kabul will let you know its current status.

Asadabad is the provincial capital, where the **Department of Information and Culture** is by the Kunar River south of the main bazaar. It is notable for the Russian tanks piled on top of each other at the entrance to the compound. **Barikot** is on the border, separated from the Pakistani town of Arundu by the Chitral River. While crossing is not permitted, it's a good place to stop for a break when heading from Jalalabad or Asadabad to Kamdesh and Bargi Matal.

GETTING THERE AND AWAY The main transport base in Asadabad is north of the road, on the east side of the Pesh River bridge in the main bazaar. Shared taxis run to/from Jalalabad (150AFN; 2hrs). Shared pick-ups run to/from Barikot (250AFN; 2hrs), Parun (700AFN; 7hrs), Kamdesh (600AFN; 6hrs) and occasionally Bargi Matal (850AFN; 8hrs). Sometimes you will need to change at Barikot, which has shared pick-ups to Kamdesh (400AFN; 4hrs).

WHERE TO STAY AND EAT

Spogmai Hotel & Restaurant Asadabad; m 7776 20710, 7045 39468; e naqeebsafi1370@gmail.com. Small, simple rooms – some with attached bathrooms – in a friendly 2nd-floor mussafarkhana overlooking the bazaar. This is also a good place to break a journey & eat typical Afghan food. AC, squat toilets, no security; b/fast inc. $–$$

Nuristan Hotel & Restaurant Chaman Toot Barikot; m 7029 38122. Basic, located at the north end of town just before the bridge. Squat toilets, no security; b/fast inc. $

SOUTHEAST AFGHANISTAN: LOYA PAKTIA

Loya Paktia ('Greater Paktia') traditionally refers to the southeastern provinces of Paktia, Paktika and Khost. A mountainous and forested area along the Pakistan border, this is one of the historic and cultural heartlands of the Pashtun people, particularly the Zadran, Mangal, Tani and Jaji tribes. It's known for its fiercely independent tribal structures, deep adherence to the Pashtunwali (the Pashtun code of honour; page 44), and a long history of resistance to central authority – whether British, Soviet or Afghan. These characteristics have made Loya Paktia strategically significant but also politically complex.

This independence is ingrained. Centuries ago, Babur described this region as unmanageable. His main complaint centred on his inability to get them to pay their taxes by handing over their sheep, let alone to stop attacking his armies. In the early 20th century, King Amanullah struggled to exert control over Loya Paktia, and even today, governance often hinges on agreements with tribal elders rather than formal institutions. It was also one of the key centres of mujahideen resistance during the Soviet occupation, and in recent decades, parts have hosted insurgent groups, including the Haqqani network (page 169).

Despite its turbulent reputation, Loya Paktia is known for its scenic beauty, with pine-covered hills and alpine valleys. This region is rarely visited by

THE DURAND LINE

After the Second Anglo–Afghan War, the British assumed control over Afghanistan's foreign affairs and, together with Russia, helped define the country's northern boundaries. The next step was to establish where British India ended and Afghanistan began. This led to the creation of the Durand Line in 1893 – a 2,640km (1,640-mile) border drawn by Sir Mortimer Durand, a British colonial official, under an agreement with Abdur Rahman Khan, the amir of Afghanistan. The goal was to form two buffer zones: tribal areas under British control to the east, and Afghan-administered territory to the west, which would help protect British India from Russian encroachment.

Importantly, the Durand Line was never meant to be a permanent international border. It cut directly through Pashtun tribal lands, dividing one of the region's largest ethnic groups and leaving millions of Pashtuns on the British side – what would later become Pakistan. Afghanistan has never formally accepted the Durand Line as a legitimate boundary, viewing it as a colonial imposition.

The legacy of the Durand Line continues to generate political friction, particularly between Kabul and Islamabad, with airstrikes by Pakistan and border skirmishes between troops all along the border becoming more commonplace. The line slices through communities, severing longstanding social, economic and familial connections. For many Pashtuns, it is not just a geopolitical issue, but a symbol of historical injustice and a fractured identity. To this day, the Durand Line remains one of the most disputed and porous borders in the world, shaping regional tensions and affecting daily life for those who live along its path.

foreigners due to security concerns, but its role in Afghan politics, history and identity is disproportionately large – a place where the old ways still shape the present.

PAKTIA

Gardez The capital of Paktia sits in the centre of a 2,300m high plain which is often snow covered in winter. The Bala Hissar, a fort dating from the 4th–5th century CE, dominates the town, although currently it is occupied by the military and was off-limits at the time of writing. The main bazaar occupies the streets west of the Gardez–Kabul highway opposite the Bala Hissar, where you will find moneychangers, restaurants and other shops. The **Department of Information and Culture** is hidden away at the far north end of town, 6km from the centre behind the governor's office 'Darftar e Wali' among a bleak set of government buildings. You will need to visit if staying the night, trying to get permission to visit the Bala Hissar or planning a trip to Aryob Zazi.

Getting there and away Shared taxis between Gardez and Kabul (350AFN; 2½–3hrs) leave from an area on the main Kabu–Gardez road by the entrance to the airport (the airport has no commercial flights). As you cross the Tera Pass between Kabul and Gardez, look out for the attractive new central Asian-style mosque on the Gardez side of the pass. Shared taxis from/to Khost (350AFN; 2½hrs) use an area south of the bridge on the main highway.

Where to stay

Shahi Restaurant & Guesthouse Near Rahim Garfdezi Chowk, Gardez (head west from the main chowk & take the 3rd left); m 7901 11122, 7925 55205; e gardizihotel@yahoo.com. Occupying a 6-storey building, Shahi is the best bet in Gardez. With very large apartment-style rooms with multiple beds & kitchens, it's aimed at families passing through; some rooms have views of the Bala Hissar. Clean, AC, squat toilets, fridge, free tea; b/fast inc. No Wi-Fi. **$$**

Naseeb Hotel South of river on the west side of main road in Gardez. If you are on a real budget or the Shahi is full, this is a back-up option. Basic rooms, no AC, no beds, squat toilets down the hall. **$**

Aryob Zazi For Afghans, there is only one place to visit in Paktia, so if you want to party like a Pashtun then an overnight trip to Aryob Zazi is a must. Aryob Zazi is a lush green plain 2,500m up, tucked against the Pakistan border on the Gardez–Parichinar road, with the highest peak of the Spin Ghar Mountains, Mount Sikaram (4,755m), looming over the whole spectacle. In summer, especially on Fridays, the roads are very busy with friends and families camping, walking and barbecuing. There is no fixed accommodation, but tents can be rented for 1,000AFN and can fit six (at a squeeze). It gets extremely busy on holidays and in good weather.

For decades this stretch of road between Gardez and Parichinar in Pakistan would have had CIA agents twitching.

Another, closer, picnic spot is the **Sato Kandaw Pass** near the border with Khost.

From Gardez, transport to Aryob Zazi (400AFN; 2½–3hrs) runs from a spot opposite the entrance to the Bala Hissar.

KHOST Set in a bowl of hills at 1,225m, Khost is the biggest city in Loya Paktia, on the border of Pakistan's tribal areas. Known for its cloudier skies and subtropical climate, it occasionally catches the edge of the south Asian monsoon, giving it a greener and more humid feel than much of the country. Khost is very much a Pashtun city, and its streets offer a chance to observe various regional styles. Men stroll the market lanes in distinctive tribal garb: with curled shoulder-length hair, and wearing wide and/or ribbed pakols (favoured by the Gurbaz and Timi tribal groups) or wound turbans with one end jutting up and the other trailing down, in Loya Paktia style.

Always a hotbed of rebellion, people from Khost are proud of their position as 'kingmakers' of Afghanistan (page 169). During the Soviet–Afghan War, the city was one of the most isolated garrisons held by Soviet and Afghan government troops, besieged by mujahideen forces for years. Supplies were only possible via air. The isolation of this stronghold became a symbolic flashpoint in the conflict.

Khost has a more recent tradition of sending its young men to work in construction in Dubai and this influence is rubbing off on newer civic constructions. The **Khost Minar** (a brightly lit minaret sitting on a roundabout) at the entry to Khost and the illuminated archway of LEDs that light the road from the Minar to the main city are regularly featured in Afghan Instagram reels, although in person 'Afghanistan's Dubai' is rather underwhelming. You'll find a city defined by low-slung mountains, roadside bazaars and generic new four-storey shopping centres.

Getting there and away

By air The new airport is 8km west of the city. At the time of writing there were no domestic flights but there is talk of further international flights from Dubai on Kam Air (w kamair.com; three times a week; 2hrs 45mins). The old airport is 1km east of the town and is home to governmental 'special forces'.

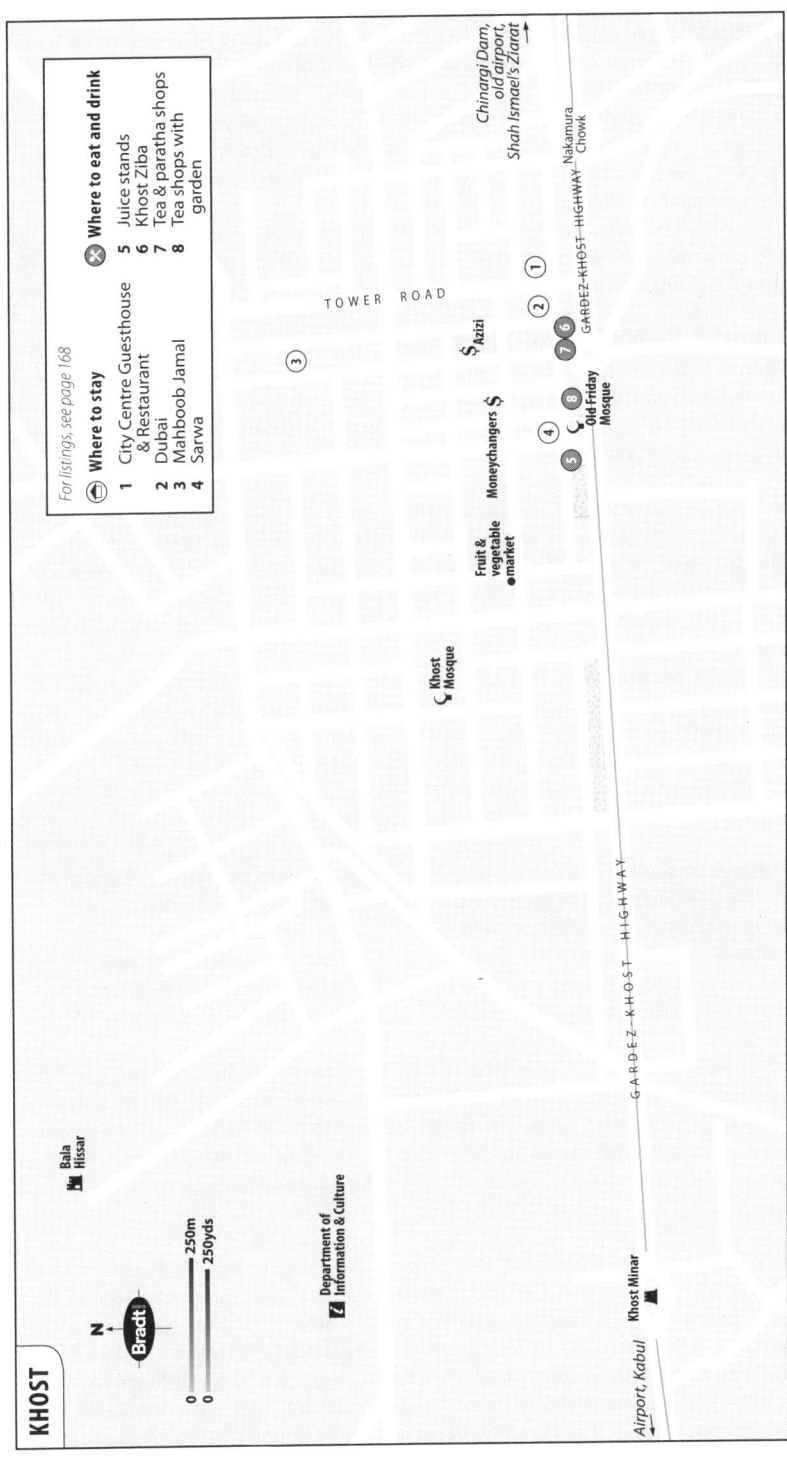

By road Shared transport from/to Kabul and Khost (600–750AFN; 5hrs) is based at the Khost Minar on the main Kabul road west of town. Shared transport to the **Pakistan border** leaves from Nakamura Chowk (named after Tetsi Nakamura, a Japanese development worker who for 30 years helped to improve agricultural and medical facilities in the region before he was killed in Nangarhar Province in 2019) on the main road east of the centre. Currently the border is closed to international crossings.

The road between Gardez and Khost is very scenic. Coming from Gardez (page 165), it crosses the **Sato Kandaw** pass before descending through a narrow defile into the plains of Khost.

Tourist information and registration The Department of Information and Culture (University Rd) is in a compound about 1km west of the Central Mosque. It is essential you register here no matter how long you plan to stay or what you plan to do in Khost. Tourists are an unknown quantity in Khost and there will be genuine interest in why you have come.

Where to stay and eat *Map, page 167*

In the bazaar, the street that runs parallel to the north of the main highway has a clutch of basic mussafarkhanas from the mid 20th century which call themselves hotel-restaurants, their crumbling balconies and curved façades offering more faded charm than comfort inside. These include the **Dubai Hotel ($)** and **Sarwa Hotel ($)**.

Khost's proximity to Pakistan means milk tea and parathas are a common breakfast option. Shops and restaurants, as well as juice stands, sell these. In the blocks between the main highway and the bazaar, restaurants with gardens provide a pleasant break from the hustle and bustle. These include **Khost Ziba** ('beautiful Khost'; **$**), and the always busy fruit and vegetable market is located two blocks further west. The hotels listed here also offer meals.

Mahboob Jamal Hotel 1 road west of Tower Rd; m 7744 44588. The most modern hotel in Khost occupies the upper floors of a 10-storey building. It has aspirations; the lifts play 'Careless Whisper' by George Michael on repeat, there's a real coffee shop & possibly the only Western-style toilets in Loya Paktia. The rooms are large & aimed at large self-catering families. AC, Wi-Fi, hot water, security, b/fast inc. **$$$**

City Centre Guesthouse & Restaurant m 7714 60037. Simple rooms with beds & non-attached squat toilets. AC, fridge, Wi-Fi. **$$**

Shopping and other practicalities The **bazaar** stretches between the Great Mosque, Tower Road and the main Gardez–Khost highway, where shops sell everything from solar panels and mobile phones to tribal daggers and embroidered turbans. **Banks** and moneychangers can be found on or just off New Medicine Street in the main bazaar. The small **old Friday Mosque** is also located in this part of town.

What to see and do **Khost Museum** consists of one room at the Department of Information and Culture. The majority of items would not get a second look in a poorly stocked shop on Kabul's Chicken Street, but they have a couple of lovely small Kushan-era (5th–7th century CE) statues. Northwest of the city, the **Bala Hissar** – a squat fort constructed during the reign of Nadir Shah – sits atop a hill affording great views of the city and surrounding plains and is notable for its white tower. The fort is currently occupied by the Taliban but the Department of

SOUTHEAST AFGHANISTAN: LOYA PAKTIA

THE HAQQANIS

The Haqqanis are part of the long tradition of Loya Paktia kingmakers. The family's journey – from US-funded allies to a central force in Afghanistan's new regime via being among the most wanted men in the world – illustrates the complex and often contradictory nature of Afghan geopolitics over the past four decades.

The family patriarch, **Jalaluddin Haqqani**, rose to prominence during the Soviet–Afghan War. A charismatic and ruthless commander from Khost, Haqqani was a favourite of both the CIA and Pakistan's ISI, receiving substantial funding, weapons and praise from American officials as a 'freedom fighter'. He was known for his skill in guerrilla warfare and for maintaining strong ties across the tribal areas of Afghanistan and Pakistan.

After the Soviet withdrawal, Jalaluddin allied with the Taliban in the 1990s but maintained a degree of independence. Following the 2001 US invasion, the fighters he led, now known as the **Haqqani Network**, transformed into a powerful insurgent group, launching high-profile attacks – including suicide bombings in Kabul and assaults on foreign embassies – while operating from safe havens in Pakistan's North Waziristan. Their operations were marked by brutal tactics, international kidnappings and close ties with al-Qaeda.

After Jalaluddin's death, leadership passed to his son **Sirajuddin Haqqani**, who became deputy leader of the Taliban, and following the Taliban's return to power in 2021 was appointed as Afghanistan's Minister of the Interior. Privately, he has invested heavily in many projects, including the country's major cricket tournament, the Afghan Premier League. Sirajuddin now holds a key portfolio in the Taliban government, overseeing internal security and policing. His brother Khalil Rahman Haqqani also serves as a minister for refugees.

Sirajuddin was one of the FBI's most wanted men, with a US$10 million bounty on his head – until early 2025, when the Trump administration lifted the bounties on him, his brother and brother-in-law, though at the time of writing the US still considers them 'Specially Designated Global Terrorists'.

Information and Culture may give you permission to visit. Visitors are so rare that anyone wishing to visit is a novelty.

The most notable and largest building in the city is the **Khost Mosque**, capable of holding 2,000 worshippers, its façade covered with pointy arcades. One of the few major buildings constructed during the first Taliban reign, it was built by Jalaluddin Haqqani (see above) with money sent from the Gulf. Non-Muslims are not allowed to enter but photography is permitted and there are a number of street food sellers in the area.

AROUND KHOST

Ghazi Babrak Khan Zadran Qala This 160-year-old fort is located just south of the usually dry Kurram River at the west end of the Khost plains, just before you enter the narrow Rokian defile that runs to the border of Paktia. It is the ancestral home of Ghazi Babrak Khan (page 170) and was used as the family residence up until the 1980s, when the family moved to Pakistan for over two decades due to the conflict. It is currently in a poor state of repair. If you ask at the Department of Information and Culture, they may send someone with you to visit, and the family

GHAZI BABRAK KHAN

Ghazi Babrak Khan Zadran was a prominent leader from the Zadran tribe of eastern Afghanistan, active during the early 20th century. A fierce Pashtun chieftain, he is best remembered for his role in resisting British and later central Afghan government encroachment into the tribal territories along the frontier. The most famous image of him shows him in formidable form, barefoot with a bandolier of ammunition across his chest.

During the Third Anglo–Afghan War in 1919, Babrak Khan earned the title 'Ghazi' – meaning warrior of the faith – for his participation in the fight against British forces. His base in the Khost and Paktia regions placed him at the heart of the borderlands near the Durand Line, where loyalty was owed more to tribe and Islam than to any central authority.

Following the war, Babrak Khan emerged as a key player in the tribal uprisings of the 1920s, particularly those opposing King Amanullah Khan's attempts to modernise and centralise Afghanistan. His defiance helped galvanise opposition among conservative factions who viewed Amanullah's reforms – such as unveiling women and introducing Western-style education – as a direct threat to Islamic and tribal tradition.

His sons continued his defiance. Mazrak Khan was a major force in revolts of the 1940s and Said Akbar killed Pakistan's first prime minister, Liaquat Ali Khan, in 1951.

Today, Babrak Khan remains a folk hero in the Zadran heartland, seen by many as a symbol of resistance against both foreign domination and unwelcome changes imposed by Kabul.

who still live in the surrounding buildings may show you around. The grandson of Ghazi Babrak Khan was living in the area at the time of research and has a wealth of information. The grave of Ghazi Babrak Khan is just south of the fort.

Shah Ismael's Ziarat (10km east of Khost, on the western outskirts of the village of Ghoda Khera) The small, elegant brick-built Shah Ismael's Ziarat dates from the 18th century. The legend states that, when Ahmad Shah Durrani passed here on his way to India as part of the Persian army, a holy man prayed for his success. Upon becoming king of Afghanistan, Ahmed Shah Durrani came in search of the holy man and, finding he had passed away, commissioned this tomb. On the way you'll pass through **Faram Bagh**, a royal garden built by King Zahir's siblings. Currently men play volleyball in the shade, especially on Fridays.

Chinargi Dam (30km northeast of Khost) The reservoir of the Chinargi Dam is around 100m long and in spring the water tumbles over the 4m-high weir. It's pleasant and a good excuse to drive closer to the Pakistan border and see rural life in Khost.

5

Bamiyan and Central Afghanistan

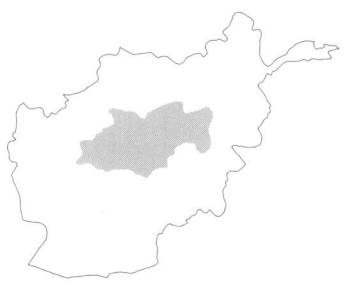

Central Afghanistan is a knot of peaks, highlands and scattered mountain communities. To the east lies the Hazarajat – the heartland of the Hazara people (page 174), dominated by the rugged Koh-i-Baba range and one of the country's most visually striking and culturally rich regions. To the west, the highlands of Ghor stretch out, mysterious and remote, gradually losing altitude towards the city of Herat. Tucked among these dramatic landscapes are some of Afghanistan's most important landmarks: the towering Buddha Niches of Bamiyan, once vibrant monuments of Silk Road Buddhism; and the Minaret of Jam, a towering 12th-century Ghorid masterpiece hidden deep in the valleys of Ghor and recognised as a UNESCO World Heritage Site. The jewel of the region, Band e Amir National Park, features a string of cobalt-blue lakes rimmed by natural travertine dams – as breathtaking as they are rare.

Yet the greatest reward for travellers may lie not in these sights, but in the quiet rhythm of rural Afghan life, where time slows, hospitality runs deep, and the mountain scenery unfolds in cinematic grandeur.

In winter, snow often cuts off access and plunges these highlands into deep freeze, although this offers the exhilarating chance to go ski touring. From spring through autumn, Central Afghanistan opens up, offering unforgettable journeys by 4x4 or on foot. Still, in these warmer months, this is Afghanistan at its most timeless – a place to explore and experience the heart of the country, a place where you may linger longer than expected.

BAMIYAN TOWN

Bamiyan is the capital of Bamiyan Province and the commercial and cultural heart of Central Afghanistan. Set at 2,550m above sea level, at a crossroads where two valleys meet and ringed by the snow-streaked Koh-i-Baba – the 'Old Man Mountains' – its highland setting is both dramatic and lush, with pastures, poplar groves, and jagged peaks framing every view. Around 100,000 people live in and around the main valley, spread across villages tucked into countless side valleys.

The town was once famous for its two towering Buddha statues, but their empty niches now loom solemnly over the town, in cliffs honeycombed with more than a thousand ancient monastic caves, a powerful reminder that Bamiyan was once one of the great Buddhist centres of Asia.

Today, Bamiyan offers more than just a monumental past. It's a peaceful and welcoming base for exploring the jewel-blue lakes of Band e Amir National Park;

5 | BAMIYAN AND CENTRAL AFGHANISTAN

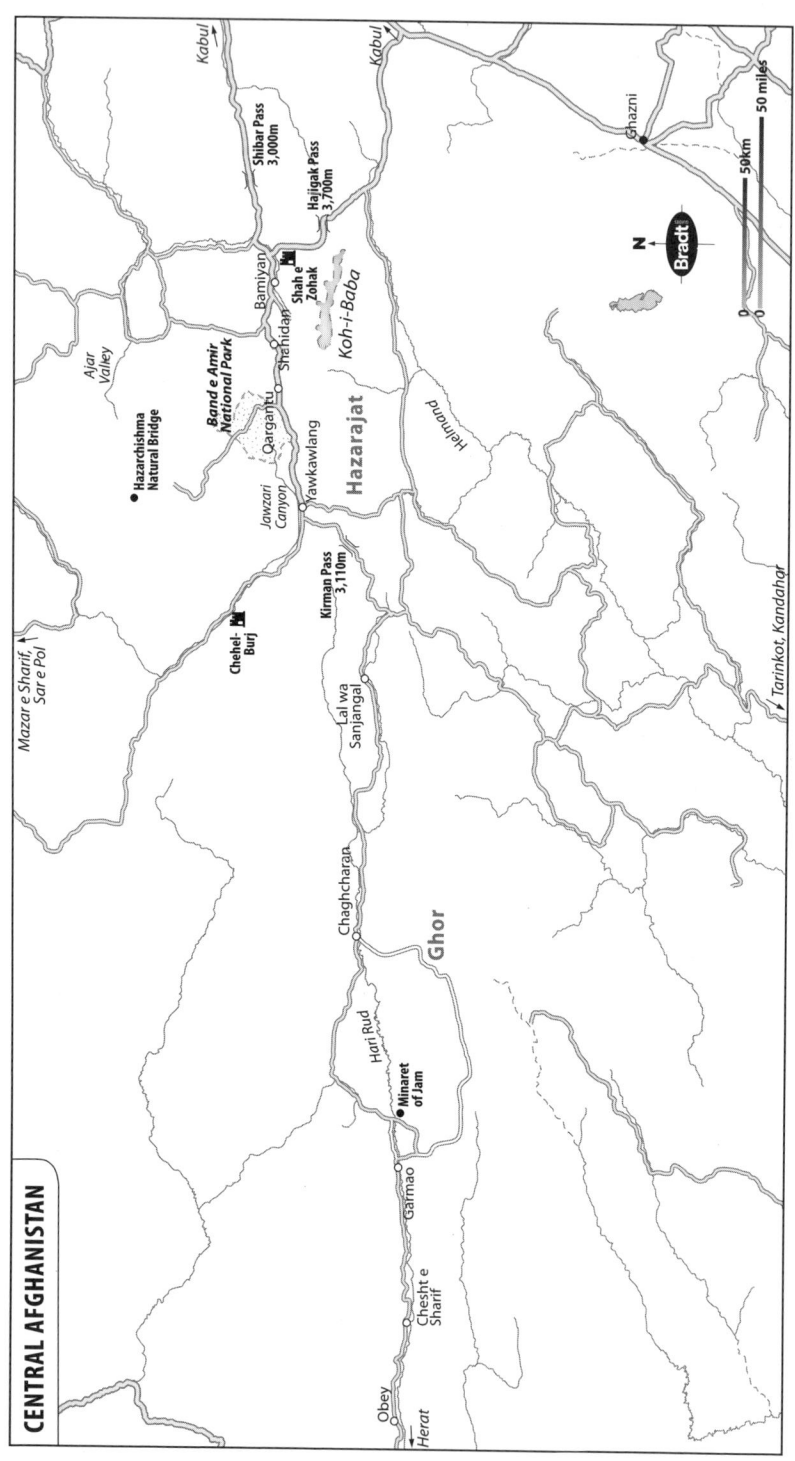

the ruined citadel of Shahr e Gholghola, the 'City of Screams'; Darya e Ajdahar, the Dragon Valley; and Chehel Burj, the fabled 'Forty Towers'. The surrounding mountains and valleys also offer superb trekking – and even skiing. In 2011, Bamiyan hosted Afghanistan's first national ski championships (page 180), and the annual Marathon of Afghanistan (page 186) took place here each summer, with both men and women competing freely – until the Taliban's return in 2021.

Bamiyan lies at the heart of the Hazarajat, homeland of the Hazara people, most of whom live from the land. The province is Afghanistan's potato capital, producing 60% of the national crop, alongside wheat, barley, cucumbers, broad beans and fruits.

Strategically located just below the Shibar Pass – the first westerly pass in the Hindu Kush under 3,000m – Bamiyan's broad, sheltered valley made it a critical node on ancient trade routes for millennia. Traders, pilgrims and armies funnelled through its defile, protected by natural barriers and the fortresses at Shahr e Zohak and Shahr e Gholghola.

In the 7th century CE, the Chinese monk Xuanzang (page 182) passed through Bamiyan and described a thriving, multi-cultural city where thousands of monks lived in richly decorated monasteries, where music, trade and ideas flourished. Buddhism flowed from India to China through these mountains. It was a time when Bamiyan was perhaps the Dubai or Hong Kong of its day, a cosmopolitan gateway between East and West, instead of one of the most isolated and least developed provinces in the poorest country in Asia. Even after the conversion to Islam, it prospered as a strategic hub on the Silk Road until the valley was devastated under Genghis Khan. It took centuries to recover.

Following the forced Sunnisation campaigns of Abdur Rahman Khan in the late 19th century, Bamiyan town became a market hub dominated by Tajik and Pashtun traders, while the Hazaras were pushed into the surrounding hills. After 2001, many Pashtuns left and Hazaras returned in strength, reclaiming political and commercial control. Since 2021 the local administration has reverted to Tajik and Pashtun control.

Even today, infrastructure remains basic. In 2001, not a single paved road existed in the province; even today only the main highways are paved. Bamiyan is still not connected to the national electricity grid and medical facilities are limited. Despite these challenges, the region has seen real progress: guesthouses have opened, road links to Kabul and Band e Amir have improved, and Bamiyan remains one of the safest and friendliest parts of the country to visit. The town itself, thanks to its human, pre-industrial scale, single strip bazaar and slow pace of life, offers a rare window into both the quiet dignity of rural Afghanistan and the fading echoes of a once world-famous city.

GETTING THERE AND AWAY Bamiyan Airport is closed and unlikely to reopen due to the relative proximity to Kabul. It used to have commercial flights that NGO staff took to avoid the insecure roads. However, under the Taliban government that is less of an issue.

The **istga**, located in the middle of the bazaar, has minivans and shared taxis to/from Kabul (350–500AFN; 4hrs), Yawkawlang (150–200AFN; 1hr 30mins) and Chaghcharan (800–1,200AFN; 8hrs). The quickest Kabul–Bamiyan route crosses the 3,700m Hajigak Pass, although in winter you may be taken via the 3,000m Shibar Pass route; both are breathtakingly beautiful drives.

You can rent cars or minivans with drivers in Bamiyan from the istga or, at a higher rate, from your accommodation.

5 | BAMIYAN AND CENTRAL AFGHANISTAN

> **THE HAZARA PEOPLE**
>
> A popular legend claims that the Hazara are descendants of the Mongol armies of Genghis Khan, and it's true that many Hazara have strikingly east Asian features. However, genetic studies reveal a more complex ancestry – a blend of Mongolian, Turkic and Iranian DNA, similar to many other central Asian populations. This cultural fusion is reflected in their language, Hazaragi, a dialect of Persian enriched with Turkic and Mongolic vocabularies. The Hazara converted to Shi'a Islam in the early 18th century, when the region was under the control of the Persian Safavid Empire.
>
> By the 19th century, the Hazara made up a far larger proportion of Afghanistan's population than they do today. Living semi-autonomously under tribal leaders, they remained desperately poor, and their lands were increasingly expropriated by the central government in Kabul, often in favour of more powerful Pashtun groups. In 1834, British officer Alexander Burnes wrote: 'The Hazaras are a race of good disposition, but are oppressed by all the neighbouring nations, whom they serve as hewers of wood and drawers of water. Many of them are sold into slavery.' In cities, they formed a distinct underclass, perceived to be more sympathetic to the British, which only deepened their marginalisation.
>
> The situation worsened in 1888, when the 'Iron Amir' Abdur Rahman Khan appointed Sardar Abd al-Quddus Khan, a hard-line Sunni Pashtun nationalist, as governor of the Hazarajat. His campaign was brutal: Hazara leaders were executed or imprisoned, the population was disarmed, women were seized, and Sunni religious practices were forcibly imposed. The Hazara rebelled, sparking a three-year war. In response, Abdur Rahman declared a jihad against all Shi'a and Ismaili communities, promising Ghilzai Pashtun tribes the Hazara lands and flocks as spoils. The result was one of the worst massacres in Afghan history.
>
> More than half the Hazara population is thought to have been killed. Thousands fled to Iran and what is now Pakistan. In Quetta and Baluchistan, many Hazara became camel drivers. When the British needed camels for railway construction across the Australian deserts in the early 20th century, the Hazara came too – today, the Ghan Railway (Ghan being an Aussie abbreviation of Afghanistan), which runs

TOURIST INFORMATION AND REGISTRATION The **Department of Information and Culture** is located amid other governmental buildings in the new town south of the airport. In addition, there are three, yes three, other tourist information centres. Next to the large Buddha Niche is a small tourist office selling tickets for the Buddha Niches, Shahr e Gholghola and Shahr e Zohak. Just to the west of this office and up a small rise is a second visitor centre, built in 2015 when Bamiyan was the SAARC City of Culture. In the lifetime of this book, it will be eclipsed by the UNESCO- and Korean-funded Argentinian-designed Bamiyan Culture Centre – set on the plateau opposite the Buddha Niches with a majestic view of the same across the valley.

ORIENTATION Bamiyan's layout is shaped by the scarcity of arable land in the Central Highlands. The valley floor, where the Bamiyan River runs, is tightly conserved for agriculture. Any flat, irrigable land near the river is used for crops, so most settlements cluster inside valleys and on higher plateaus.

The bazaar originally stood beneath the Buddhas. However, due to a mixture of political tensions, land disputes and UXOs, it was relocated. The current bazaar is a 2km-long strip, flanked on both sides by cultivated fields. The giant mound of from Adelaide to Darwin, owes its name to these early Afghan cameleers, many of whom were Hazara.

Those who remained in Afghanistan were subjected to punitive taxes such as the *jizya* (a head tax traditionally levied on non-Muslims). Public celebrations of Shi'a holidays were outlawed – restrictions that remained in place until the communist takeover in 1978. Under the Democratic Republic, the Hazara, like many other minorities, were courted politically and began to receive opportunities they had long been denied.

During the Soviet–Afghan War, the Hazarajat saw less direct fighting than other parts of the country, but Hazara resistance factions were deeply divided. Abdul Ali Mazari, head of Hezb e Wahdat, believed (like Ahmad Shah Massoud) that Afghanistan's diversity required a federal political system. Although Hazara factions were disunited during the 1980s, they united under the Northern Alliance against the Taliban in the late 1990s.

The Taliban were particularly brutal in their treatment of the Hazara. After a failed Hazara uprising in Mazar e Sharif in 1997, Taliban forces carried out mass killings in Bamiyan and other Hazara strongholds. Aid was cut off, and during the drought of 1998–2001, thousands more were forced to migrate to Iran and Pakistan.

Despite their history, the Hazara have demonstrated extraordinary resilience. Under the Islamic Republic, many Hazara seized opportunities to gain higher education and enter public service. Hazara women, who traditionally had more freedoms than women in conservative Pashtun communities, made significant strides. In 2005, Habiba Sarabi became the first female provincial governor in Afghanistan, appointed in Bamiyan. Azra Jafari – editor of a cultural magazine and a school director for refugee children in Iran – became the country's first female mayor, although threats from the Taliban forced her into exile in the United States in 2014.

In recent years, as IS-K established a presence in Afghanistan, the Hazara have again found themselves targeted. Bombings at schools, mosques and maternity wards in Kabul and elsewhere have been aimed explicitly at Hazara civilians, part of a chilling pattern of sectarian violence.

Shahr e Gholghola sits in the middle of the valley southwest of the bazaar. South of the bazaar, a winding road climbs to a plateau that hosts key infrastructure: the airport, government buildings and administrative centres. From this elevated vantage point, visitors can enjoy sweeping views of the Buddha Niches in the northern cliffs. Scattered around the area are remnants of past conflicts, including Soviet-era tanks and armoured personnel carriers, rusting silently on a square just uphill from the bazaar. One of these has been painted red with white spots as an art project to resemble a giant ladybird.

To the southwest lies the Foladi Valley, delving deeper into the Koh-i-Baba mountains, which act as both a dramatic backdrop and geographical barrier; beyond them lies the province of Wardak.

WHERE TO STAY *Map, page 177*

In the mid 2010s, Bamiyan had a bit of a hotel boom in the hopes of attracting tourists. This means that, despite its size, the town offers the best accommodation for tourists outside of Kabul and Herat. Many have rooms with wonderful views of the Buddha Niches. Bear in mind that Bamiyan is not linked to the national

5 | BAMIYAN AND CENTRAL AFGHANISTAN

electricity grid and so, with all the hotels listed, not all the facilities will be working all the time.

Bamyan Royal Hotel On a dusty road near Shahr e Golghola; m 7752 28090; w bamyanroyalhotel.com. The Bamyan Royal Hotel was built by Mohamed Mohaqiq, an ex-mujahideen leader & second deputy of the chief executive of Afghanistan for 6 years, and a political rival to Karim Khalili (see right). The Bamyan Royal was, until the advent of the Golghola, the best hotel in Bamiyan. When Mohaqiq held political rallies here, the unpaved road between the hotel & the airport would be watered to reduce dust. It's a well-kept hotel with small but comfortable & clean rooms, some facing the Buddha Niches. En-suite rooms, Western-style toilets, Wi-Fi, security, b/fast inc. **$$$**

Golghola Hotel Foladi Rd, Bamiyan; m 7953 66666; f. This large marble edifice is the smartest-looking hotel outside of Kabul. It was built & owned by Karim Khalili, ex-mujahideen leader &

THE SILK ROAD

The term 'Silk Road' was first coined in the 19th century by German geographer Ferdinand von Richthofen to describe the ancient network of overland trade routes that linked China with the Mediterranean world. While today 'Silk Road' is just as often used to market trips to Uzbekistan as it's used in historical texts, the truth behind the name is compelling: for over two and a half millennia, going back to the ancient Persians and Alexander the Great, these routes (for there were many 'Silk Roads') facilitated not only the movement of goods, but the exchange of ideas, cultures, religions and people across continents.

Afghanistan, at the crossroads of central and south Asia, was one of the Silk Road's most vital arteries. The country formed a natural bridge between China and the Indian subcontinent, and between Persia and central Asia. Unlike the impassable glaciated heights of the Himalayas or the thick jungles of Burma, Afghanistan's high mountain passes and sweeping valleys – though formidable – were traversable, making them essential corridors for merchants, monks and empires.

From east to west and north to south, countless caravans moved through the region, stopping in Balkh, Bamiyan, Herat and Kandahar. Silk, paper, porcelain and lacquerware from China passed through Afghan cities en route to Persia, Arabia and the Roman Empire. From India came spices, gems, cotton and exotic animals. From the West flowed glass, wine, silver and wool. Afghanistan was not just a transit zone – it was a marketplace, a melting pot, and a cultural hub.

But it wasn't just commodities that journeyed along these routes. The Silk Road also carried the great ideas of the ancient world. One of the most transformative was Buddhism, which spread from India northwards through Afghanistan into central Asia and China. The Buddha statues of Bamiyan – once the largest standing Buddhas in the world – were physical testaments to this era of spiritual exchange.

The decline of the Silk Road happened gradually. As maritime technology improved, especially with the adoption of the Chinese-invented magnetic compass in Europe in the 15th century, trade began to shift to sea routes. The Portuguese and other European powers could transport goods – especially spices – from Asia to Europe more efficiently and at lower cost by ship. This development marked the beginning of the end for the overland routes of central Asia, and the bustling trade cities of Afghanistan slowly faded into obscurity.

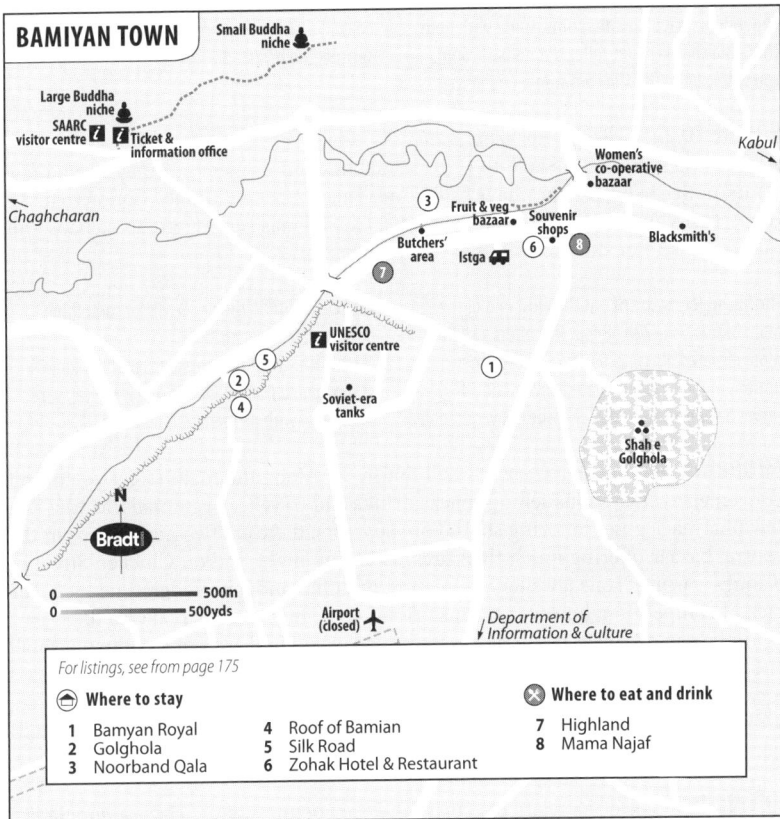

second vice president of Afghanistan for 10 years. The building also served as a centre for political meetings & governmental conferences. The 2-storey high foyer, lifts, sauna & gym are luxuries that had never been seen before in Bamiyan. However, this is still Bamiyan & not everything works; the hot water is very temperamental & the cavernous dining area is freezing in winter. It does have wonderful views from the rooms facing the Buddha Niches & from the roof. At the time of writing the restaurant was not serving food except for b/fast. En-suite rooms, Western-style toilets, Wi-Fi, security, b/fast with real filter coffee inc. **$$$**

Silk Road Hotel Foladi Road, Bamiyan; m 7984 05486; w silkroadbamiyan.com. The third best place in town. A charming low-rise hotel run by a Japanese journalist & her Hazara husband, it used to be as famous for its tempura dinners as its facilities; and if you book ahead, they will still do Japanese food (probably your best/only option in Afghanistan). Its dozen or so rooms are tastefully decorated, & it has great views of the Buddha Niches from the roof. At the time of writing, it was only open during summer months. En-suite rooms, Western-style toilets, Wi-Fi, security, b/fast inc. **$$$**

Noorband Qala Hotel Next to the football pitch, Bazaar Rd; m 7710 71854. This cute low-rise accommodation close to the bazaar is a good-value option. In winter the rooms are heated by *bukharis* (traditional wood or coal burning stoves). En-suite rooms, Western-style toilets, Wi-Fi, security, b/fast inc. **$$**

Roof of Bamian Hotel East of the football pitch; m 7775 50758. This small 2-storey hotel, perched on the plateau overlooking the valley with fabulous views of the Buddha Niches, has been operating since its hippy trail heyday. On a recent visit it was run-down with very basic rooms & yurts on the roof. No en-suite rooms, some Western-style toilets, no Wi-Fi, no security, no b/fast. **$$**

Zohak Hotel & Restaurant In the bazaar, this is the town's best chaikhana/mussafarkhana. The upper floors have private rooms, some with beds. There is a shared squat toilet but no bathroom. You will have to use the communal one in the bazaar, a fun experience in itself. No Wi-Fi, no security, no b/fast. **$**

✘ WHERE TO EAT AND DRINK Map, page 177

All the hotels should be able to provide lunches and dinners but may need a few hours' notice to ensure they have fresh food. This does allow you the option to make requests if you have dietary requirements. Chaikhanas serving pulao, kebabs and other Afghan fare dot the length of the main bazaar.

Highland Restaurant At the west end of the main bazaar; m 7778 88448. This offers a slightly more elevated dining experience to the other options in the bazaar. Situated downstairs, it serves a wide array of Afghan dishes, & vegetarians can pop in during the day & ask for something to be cooked for later on. **$$**

Mama Najaf At the crossroads in the middle of the main bazaar road. This one is typical, very traditional with no menu & no seating. **$**

SHOPPING Bamiyan's bazaar is small but lively. Along the main street you'll find convenience-style shops selling snacks drinks and travellers' essentials, as well as a few pharmacies and tailoring stalls. For souvenirs, there are two main shops in the central bazaar offering much the same items you might find on Chicken Street in Kabul – carpets, lapis jewellery, miniature Buddhas and embroidered textiles. The lack of competition, however, means prices can be higher, so bargain hard.

In the narrow alleys north of the main road, you'll find around eight to ten small shops run by women's cooperatives. These stalls sell handmade crafts produced locally, including textiles, jewellery and embroidered clothing. If you're tempted, look out for distinctly Hazara crafts such as knitted wool socks, colourful felt wall-hangings and traditional needlework.

ACTIVITIES Bamiyan's relative security and the openness of the Hazara population during the 2000s and 2010s meant that it became something of a mountain playground for the trickle of expats and tourists visiting from Kabul. For six years it hosted the Marathon of Afghanistan (page 186), the country's only mixed-gender sporting event, and it still offers the most accessible range of activities in Afghanistan. **The Bamiyan Alpine Ski Club** (BASC; ◼ bamyanalpineskiclub) is the hub, where visitors can hire guides and rent equipment such as **kayaks** and **stand-up paddleboards** (to take to Band e Amir) and **mountain bikes** in various conditions, left behind by former sporting enterprises.

Hiking The Koh-i-Baba mountains offer many options for day hikes as well as multi-day treks. The valleys south of Bamiyan town are the most accessible. Further afield, there's the Band e Amir National Park and the Ajar Valley (a 6hr drive north of Bamiyan town). Ask at your accommodation, the Department of Information and Culture or at the BASC about guides. Equipment is scarce but basic pop-up tents can be found in the bazaar and the BASC has some equipment it might be willing to rent.

✳ Skiing If you are in Bamiyan in winter, then you will have the chance to meet and participate with one of the world's most unlikely ski communities (page 180). The BASC offers ski touring in the Koh-i-Baba mountains; they also organise ski races and make wooden skis for local communities. The club also assists with training young Afghans to ski safely and understand avalanche risks. The main ski race is usually held on the first Friday in March, but check with the club to confirm. Even if you don't ski, check to see if there are any races or training you can observe.

OTHER PRACTICALITIES There's a Kabul Exchange/Western Union office in the bazaar. The **provincial hospital** (w agakhanhospitals.org) is 5km to the west of the centre of Bamiyan. Built by the Aga Khan Foundation, it is the best hospital in central Afghanistan.

WHAT TO SEE AND DO
✱ The Buddha Niches (600m walk north of town; ⊕ 08.00–16.00 daily; 300AFN – tickets valid for 3 days & include entry to Shahr e Gholghola (page 181) & Shahr e Zohak (page 183); ticket office near the larger Buddha niche) Even without their giant statues, this pair of towering, shadow-filled hollows remain an iconic landmark of Afghanistan. Etched into cliffs that rise abruptly from the valley floor, surrounded by hundreds of caves like the cells of a giant beehive, the niches dominate the view from all sides.

The setting was no accident. Just off the Silk Road route that linked the Indian subcontinent to China, Bamiyan lay in a sheltered, easily defensible valley. The cliffs are made from a soft, compacted conglomerate – the Buddhas were carved directly into the rock, then coated in layers of straw-mixed plaster and painted in vivid colours. How the upper *samooches* (monastic cells) that surround them in the vertical faces were carved and reached by their inhabitants remains uncertain, although parallels with sites such as Dunhuang in China suggest the use of ropes or wooden ladders. The cells were decorated with elaborate frescoes that count as some of the oldest oil-based paintings in the world. The dry climate has helped preserve them, for over 1,400 years.

The Buddhas were sculpted under the Hephthalites, who left no written history of their own, so what we know of the Buddhas in their prime comes from the 7th-century Chinese pilgrim Xuanzang (page 182), when the surrounding cliffs were alive with monks, music and colour, and Bamiyan was one of the greatest Buddhist centres in Asia.

The giant statues were defaced over time. Their faces were removed in earlier centuries. Curiously Babur, the usually observant founder of the Mughal Empire (who would famously lose his army in a blizzard on the plateau above), made no mention of them when he passed through the valley in 1507. When Alexander Burnes sketched the Buddhas in 1834, they still had most of their forearms, extended outwards. Around the same time, British East India Company explorer Charles Masson left his mark in a pencilled couplet above one of the caves (page 143).

Abdul Rahman Khan is said to have blasted off the lower legs. The final destruction came in March 2001, when the Taliban spent several weeks methodically blowing up both Buddhas. While often cited as an act of iconoclasm, Mullah Omar later claimed he ordered their destruction in protest after the international community offered funds to restore the Buddhas but refused to send humanitarian aid during a deadly drought.

What remains are two vast, echoing voids – silent and powerful. Fragments of the Buddhas, some weighing tonnes, lie at the bases, catalogued but unrestored. Discussions about reconstruction continue, though UNESCO protection imposes strict limits. One partial effort has recreated the feet of Shah Mama. A short-lived sound and light show projected holograms into the niches, but in a town still unconnected to the national grid, such efforts feel out of place.

Allow 2 hours to visit the niches.

HISTORY OF SKIING IN AFGHANISTAN

Every February in the Koh-i-Baba mountains of Bamiyan, groups of young men and boys gather in the Khushkak Valley for a ski touring race like no other. The event, held every year since 2011, sees participants equipped with wildly different gear – some using modern ski touring equipment, often with mismatched decades-old skis and boots, while others use homemade wooden skis crafted from scrap timber and tin. It's one of the most enduring legacies of the international community after their two-decade presence in Afghanistan.

Skiing may seem an unlikely sport in one of the world's poorest and most war-torn countries, but sliding on snow is nothing new here. Across the mountains of Afghanistan, the mention of '*yakh molak*' – sledding on metal trays or planks – brings fond memories. Snow is celebrated each winter not just for fun, but as a vital lifeline. It replenishes water reserves essential for the spring and summer crops. In this rugged land, snow means survival.

Though skiing was introduced formally only in the 1960s, the roots go deep. German diplomat Mr Dauer helped establish the country's first ski tow in 1967, near Kabul. Afghan youth like the Kargar family embraced the sport with such enthusiasm that by the 1970s they were organising races. Political unrest in the 1980s and Taliban rule in the 1990s, however, brought this golden age of Afghan skiing to an end.

After 2001, with the fall of the Taliban, skiing was reborn. Aid workers and journalists formed the Salang Ski Club, skiing in the Salang Pass and beyond. Yet it was **Bamiyan**, in between 2008 and 2011, where the New Zealand government funded an ecotourism programme through the Aga Khan Foundation. Most of Bamiyan's tourism potential is seasonal – spring to autumn – but a press officer from the Salang Ski Club suggested winter ski tourism to create a year-round draw. With no ski lifts, **ski touring** was the only option. Special bindings and climbing skins allow skiers to ascend the mountains before skiing down. A ski guide training programme was launched, and a new chapter of Afghan skiing began.

In 2010, a Swiss journalist stranded in Bamiyan during a snowstorm vowed to return with skis. In 2011, he did – bringing equipment, giving lessons and organising a ski race. That same year, the British company Untamed Borders brought international tourists to ski in Bamiyan. These efforts coalesced into the **Afghan Ski Challenge**, a classic ski touring race where locals quickly outpaced

Salsal The larger Buddha, known locally as Salsal ('the light that shines through the universe'), stood 57m tall – roughly the height of a 20-storey building – and is dated to around 618CE. The feet of this Buddha are still intact, and the buildings directly in front of the niche house large fragments of the Buddha itself. You can access a cave high up above where the head would have been by taking a winding path to the west of the niche, past a Soviet-era gun emplacement. You will need to bring someone from the ticket office as the entrance to this samooch is via a locked door. This route around the back also passes lesser-visited caves with fine views of the Bamiyan Valley.

Shah Mama From the foot of Salsal, it's about a 1km walk east to the niche that held the smaller Buddha, Shah Mama (so named by locals who believed the figure was female). Shah Mama was completed around 570CE and stood 38m tall; you'll find it easier to make out its original shape in the niche than that of the seasoned international skiers thanks to their altitude-hardened lungs and stamina. No foreigner has ever won.

What began as a novelty soon grew into a craze. Young villagers ditched sleds and demanded skis. A cottage industry of homemade wooden skis sprang up, with boys racing each other on cobbled-together bindings and improvised snowboards. A new race category emerged: the wooden ski race.

The **Bamiyan Ski Club** became the hub of this growing community. They managed donated equipment, organised races, and provided avalanche and mountain safety training. In partnership with Swiss supporters and the Volkl ski brand, two skiers – Sayed Alishah Farhang and Sajjad Husseini – trained in Europe, eventually representing Afghanistan at the FIS World Championships. Their journey was chronicled in the film *Where the Light Shines* (page 288).

In 2015, in the same year as the first mixed-gender Marathon of Afghanistan, the club broke new ground by training female skiers and hosting the first **Afghan Women's Ski Challenge**. International donations, including containers of gear from the Slovenian army and a German NGO called HELP, allowed more locals to graduate from wooden skis to proper gear. The sport took root not just in Bamiyan town but in the surrounding valleys, becoming a source of local pride and purpose.

But this progress was halted in 2021 with the return of the Taliban. The club's core members – advocates for women's sports and public figures – were forced to flee. Under the Taliban's ban on women in sport, and with international support cut off, the Bamiyan Ski Club ceased activities. Their story is captured in the documentary *Champions of the Golden Valley* (page 288).

Yet skiing in Bamiyan didn't die. The enthusiasm was too deeply embedded. The villagers, the boys and the new generation of skiers refused to stop. From the ashes of the old club rose the Bamiyan Alpine Ski Club (BASC), which launched its own annual race – the Afghan Peaks Race – and in a poetic nod to the past, the prizes at the latest race were presented by a member of the Kargar family, the pioneers of Afghan skiing in the 1970s.

Today, Afghanistan has no ski lifts, no luxury resorts, and no formal infrastructure. But in Bamiyan, where snow still falls, the spirit of skiing lives on. As long as winter comes, young Afghans will find ways to glide down their mountains – on carbon fibre or wood, racing with joy and pride. Long live yakh molak!

larger Buddha. Sections of smooth plaster remain in situ. The samooches flanking this niche offer the best-preserved mural fragments, including vivid images of Bodhisattvas, royal donors in double-lapelled kaftans, and delicate floral motifs. Be sure to go with one of the site guards who carry the keys – some of the most beautiful samooches are locked and not otherwise accessible.

Further caves Today many cave complexes to the east and west of the main archaeological zone are occupied by families of internally displaced people (IDPs) from other provinces who moved to Bamiyan due to the conflict. Other uninhabited but less impressive Buddhist caves are at the entrance to the Kakrak and Foladi valleys.

Shahr e Gholghola (No ticket office here, but visit included in your ticket for the Buddha Niches; page 179) Just a 20-minute walk from the Bamiyan bazaar, through peaceful fields and past crumbling mud-brick homes, stands the haunting hilltop

5 | BAMIYAN AND CENTRAL AFGHANISTAN

XUANZANG AND BAMIYAN'S GOLDEN AGE

One of the most remarkable figures to travel through what is now Afghanistan was Xuanzang, the 7th-century CE Buddhist monk, scholar and pilgrim. A native of Xi'an in China, Xuanzang grew weary of Buddhist teachings and felt that if he could travel to where Buddha was born, lived and taught, he might find greater meaning. On his epic journey from China to India in search of original Buddhist scriptures, Xuanzang crossed the heart of central Asia and left behind detailed, vivid accounts of the lands he passed through – including some of the earliest surviving eyewitness descriptions we have of Afghanistan, notably of Bamiyan and the Wakhan Corridor.

What sets Xuanzang apart from later travellers like Marco Polo is the remarkable accuracy of his accounts. Whereas Polo often recounted second-hand stories or tales embellished with hearsay, Xuanzang's meticulous observations have been corroborated by modern archaeology, making his writings a vital source for reconstructing the Buddhist history of the region.

Xuanzang arrived in Bamiyan in the 630s CE on his way to India, and described a thriving Buddhist kingdom 'situated in the midst of the Snowy Mountain…These people are remarkable, among all their neighbours, for a love of religion…there are ten convents and around 1,000 priests.' He described the two standing Buddhas, adorned in gilded robes and encrusted with gems that 'dazzled the eyes'. Nancy Hatch Dupree in *An Historical Guide to Afghanistan* evoked what Xuanzang saw:

> In the niches of the colossal Buddhas, the smaller stood resplendent in a blue cloak, the larger in red, their faces and hands shining with gilt unrivalled by the glitter of countless ornaments festooned upon them. At the foot of the cliffs tall pennants fluttered above monasteries filled with myriads of yellow-robed monks, and pilgrims dressed in exotic costumes of far-off lands roamed about the entire complex.

Xuanzang also reported a third Buddha, an incredible reclining one stretching 300m in length, which was said to represent the Buddha at the moment of entering nirvana. While no sign of this once mighty figure has been definitively identified, archaeologists continue to search for traces.

citadel of Shahr e Gholghola – the 'City of Screams', a name that stems from the blood-soaked legend surrounding its fall to the Mongols in the 13th century, when the fortress was the last stronghold of resistance in Bamiyan.

According to tradition, it was here that Jalaluddin, son of the Khwarezmian ruler, made a final stand against the invading Mongol army led by Genghis Khan. But in a devastating twist, the city's downfall came from within: Jalaluddin's own daughter, in a moment of betrayal – whether by political calculation, coercion or desperation – revealed a weakness in the city's defences. The Mongols poured in, and what followed was a massacre so brutal that the city's name has echoed through history ever since.

Today, Shahr e Gholghola is a silent ruin scattered across the steep hill. At the base, there's a small checkpoint where you show your ticket before you begin the ascent. Restoration work in the lower sections was carried out in the 2010s by an Italian-led archaeology team, while the upper areas, including the central tower, were partly stabilised by a 1960s archaeology mission, although in the 1980s it was repurposed by Soviet-backed military forces as a strategic lookout.

You will need to show your ticket again to visit the upper city and you may well be accompanied by a watchful Taliban soldier. Climbing to the top takes around 15–20 minutes, but the views over the Bamiyan Valley are nothing short of spectacular – particularly in the golden hour, when the setting sun sets the cliffs and fields aglow. From here, you can see the outlines of the Buddha Niches, the Band e Amir plateau in the distance, and the full sweep of this high mountain valley that has been home to empires, monks and warriors.

AROUND BAMIYAN

Shahr e Zohak (The Red Fort; 19km east of Bamiyan town (hire a car & driver for the day from your hotel or the istga); visit included in your ticket for the Buddha Niches – page 179) You'll need to show your entry ticket at a small military checkpoint at the end of the valley where the road splits for the Shibar and Hajigak passes; the fort sits just off the Hajigak Pass road. When driving between Bamiyan and Shahr e Zohak, keep an eye out for the large caravanserai south of the road, 1,500m or so before the checkpoint.

Once controlling the southeastern approach to the Bamiyan Valley, Shahr e Zohak, the 'Red City', is another of Afghanistan's dramatic and storied ruins. Named for the surrounding iron-rich hills, Shahr e Zohak is visible from afar – especially at sunrise or sunset, when the cliffs glow crimson. With its blood-red hue, commanding views and tragic past, the fort offers a spectacular vantage point over the Silk Road routes that once threaded through these mountains.

The foundations of the fort go back to the 6th century CE and the Hephthalites, but most of the surviving ruins were built under the Ghorid dynasty (12th–13th centuries), a time of prosperity and fortified expansion in Bamiyan. That came to a brutal end in 1221, when Genghis Khan's favourite grandson, Mutugen, was killed here. In retaliation, Genghis ordered the Mongols to raze the fort and massacre the population – exacting especially harsh revenge at Shahr e Gholghola (page 181), where they killed every living thing.

The ruins sprawl over two main levels. The lower level, easily reached by a dirt path, holds the majority of the original buildings: crumbling bastions, long curtain walls and barracks. From here, a steep and rougher trail climbs 150m to the upper

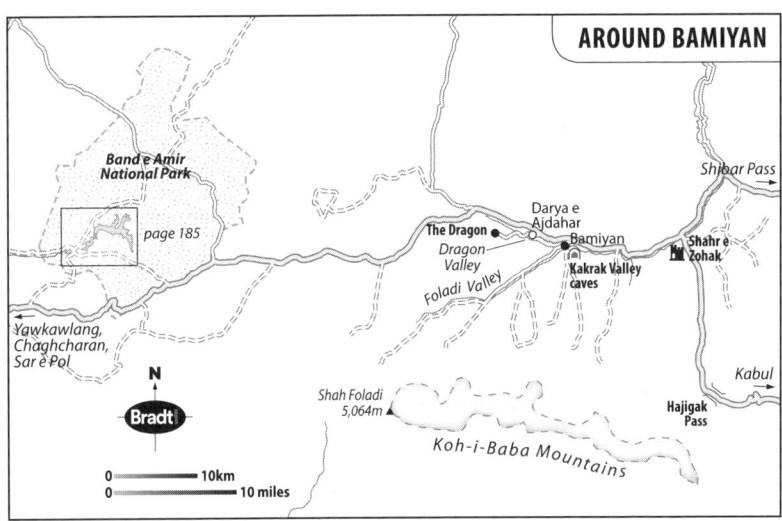

level, where footing can be slippery. At the very top stands another Soviet-era gun emplacement, offering panoramic views of the Hajigak Pass to the north and the Bamiyan Valley to the west.

Though the buildings are ruins, wandering among them gives a sense of the fort's scale and importance. There are no signs or safety barriers, so come prepared with water, proper shoes and, ideally, a guide. The windswept upper ramparts, with their Soviet relics and commanding views of the coloured landscape, make for a great half-day excursion from Bamiyan.

Dragon Valley (Darya e Ajdahar; 7km west of Bamiyan town) Folklore tells of a fearsome dragon that once terrorised the region, demanding fuel, livestock and even virgins until Hazrat Ali, the Prophet's revered son-in-law, slayed the beast, wielding his mighty sword Zulfiqar to split its backbone. Whether Ali slew the dragon before or after he created the dams at Band e Amir (see below) is unclear. However, in this valley the dragon lies to this day moaning, bleeding and crying.

Geologists would argue that the dragon's scaly back and horns are rock formations formed from sedimentary molasse, and the split spine was caused by an earthquake. They would argue that the horns are calcium carbonate deposits and the 'dragon's tears' are two springs; that the blood is formed from iron ore deposits and the moaning is simply the sound of the water moving under this formation. Whether you believe the legend or the geologists, from certain angles you can imagine the shape of a massive beast.

There is a further twist to Dragon Valley. Xuanzang (page 182) mentioned a 300m-long reclining Buddha that was never found and stated it was about 7–8km west of the standing Buddhas. Could the Dragon be the Buddha? It does not look much like a Buddha, but then again it does not look all that much like a dragon, either.

Shared taxis from the bazaar for around 30AFN will drop you off at the Hazara village of Ajdahar, built by the UN in a waterless valley (which is why it never had people living there before) as a village for Hazara refugees from Pakistan, which is why it is a bit soulless, although it does have the new provincial hospital. Dragon Valley is an easy walk from there. Try to go in early morning or late afternoon, when the dusty light softens the valley. Wear sturdy shoes: the paths are rocky and uneven.

✱ BAND E AMIR NATIONAL PARK

(75km west of Bamiyan town; ⊕ always) With its unique geology and fragile ecosystem, Band e Amir was declared Afghanistan's first national park in 2009. Its six **lakes** are the greatest natural wonder in Afghanistan. Even the drive to Band e Amir from Bamiyan is unforgettable, passing through spectacular terrain: a narrow canyon guarded by a lone stone tower, followed by two expansive plains. The road passes two villages; the westernmost, **Qargantu**, is known for the production of krut, a dried yoghurt delicacy. Near **Shahidan**, you'll see a small hilltop fort overlooking the route.

Spread across a valley in a harsh, high-altitude plateau of dusty dun hills and barren ridges, the breathtakingly blue waters of Zulfiqar, Haibat, Panir, Pudina, Gholaman and Qambar seem like a surreal mirage as you descend into the park. Their intense colour comes from their high mineral content (primarily limestone and calcium carbonate), which reflects light in dazzling hues of sapphire, cobalt and turquoise. But these are no ordinary lakes: they are travertine lakes, created by mineral-rich water that has slowly formed natural stone dams over thousands of years. The most famous of these formations is **Band e Haibat**, the 'Lake of Awe'. Its calm surface hides a dramatic fact – this immense body of water is held back by

BAND E AMIR NATIONAL PARK

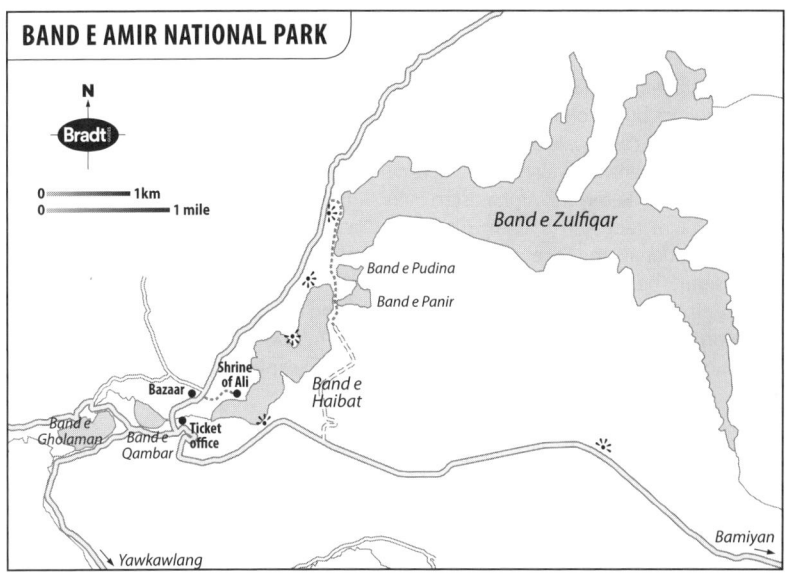

a 12m-tall curtain wall of solid travertine, broken in a few places where waterfalls spill over its edge, a geological marvel that seems almost too perfect to be natural. Like all of Band e Amir's lakes, it is crystal clear and astonishingly deep.

According to legend, the area was once threatened by a catastrophic flood. The people, desperate to stop the water, tried throwing in everything they had, including cheese (*panir*) and mint (*pudina*), lending their names to Band e Panir and Band e Pudina. Nothing worked until Ali, the cousin and son-in-law of the Prophet Muhammad, struck the ground with his mighty sword Zulfiqar, causing the water to halt and travertine barriers to rise out of the earth. The lakes are named in his honour, including Band e Zulfiqar, and a **shrine** dedicated to Ali at Band e Haibat remains an important pilgrimage site.

Near the shrine, you can rent pedalos and boats and swim, though swimming is culturally sensitive. Traditionally, women were occasionally thrown into the water near the shrine by relatives as a form of spiritual healing for mental illness, although this practice has been banned by the current government. Be cautious about where and whether to swim, and female visitors should always ask about gender access before approaching the shrine.

In high summer especially on Fridays, the lakeside can be very busy, so you may enjoy the experience more by moving away from the southern shore of Band e Haibat. The western heights above the lakes offer great viewpoints and there is a wonderful trail that drops down between Band e Zulfiqar and Band e Haibat and passing next to Band-e Panir and Band e Pudina. To circumnavigate Band e Haibat lake completely, you would need to factor in 2–3 hours; however, it is possible to drive to the start of the trail down across the smaller lakes and be collected on the other side.

You can circumnavigate all the lakes, a route of 42km which formed the basis of the Marathon of Afghanistan (page 186), on horseback or by foot, although it is a strenuous all-day affair. You can also explore the park on multi-day treks which include trips far up in the **Jawzari Canyon** to the **Hazarchishma Natural Bridge**, the 12th largest natural arch in the world, hidden in a remote tributary gorge. The route is long and difficult, so a guide is essential – ask at your hotel or the BASC.

THE MARATHON OF AFGHANISTAN
Zeinab Rezaie and James Willcox

Participation, equality and inclusion are core democratic principles – not only in politics but also in sport. From 2015 to 2020, the Marathon of Afghanistan embodied these values, becoming the country's largest-ever mixed-gender sporting event and a rare space where democracy could be practised in motion.

Held in Bamiyan, Afghanistan's first official marathon offered both a full 42km race and a 10km run. It was launched by three founders, two international and one Afghan, combining global experience with local insight. Their goal was simple but powerful: to create an inclusive event open to all, promoting national unity and challenging deep divisions – particularly along gender and ethnic lines. In a society where women's participation in public life was limited, the race aimed to offer a rare platform for them to take part safely and visibly.

Starting with just one Afghan woman completing the marathon in 2015, participation rapidly grew. By 2019, more than 770 runners took part, with women making up half the field – and most of them were Afghan. Their involvement was initially supported by local sports clubs and international organisations, notably a US-based group promoting running for women. But increasingly, Afghan women began to train and participate independently, and it was no longer unusual to see groups of women running together in Bamiyan. Many travelled from cities like Kabul in mixed-gender group outings, determined to participate in spite of the considerable cultural, financial and security challenges. Their visibility helped shift local perceptions and inspired other women to see sport as a right rather than a privilege.

Organisational control also began to shift locally. In 2020, due to the Covid-19 pandemic, only one international organiser could participate. Yet the race went ahead successfully, managed by an Afghan-led team of three men and one woman. This evolution – from international initiative to a locally driven, gender-inclusive event – was a crucial step towards sustainability and local ownership.

The Marathon of Afghanistan became much more than a race. It was one of the few outdoor public events where Afghan women could feel safe asserting their right to sport and visibility. For many, it was a deeply personal act – about being seen not as victims, but as strong, resilient individuals telling their own stories. Through the marathon, they could connect with international runners and show the world what Afghan women are capable of when given the opportunity.

Sadly, following the change in government in 2021 and the Taliban's restrictions on women, the race came to an end. Women are no longer allowed to participate in or even practise sports publicly. Though short-lived, the Marathon of Afghanistan was a powerful example of how community-based sporting events can promote democratic values, gender equality and unity. It served as a microcosm of what inclusive, people-driven initiatives can achieve – even in the most challenging environments – and a hopeful template for the future.

This is an excerpt of a longer article on w sportanddev.org by Zeinab Rezaie, the first Afghan woman to complete an ironman, and James Willcox, co-founder of the Marathon of Afghanistan (and co-author of this guide).

Getting there In high summer, minivans run from the Bamiyan istga on Friday mornings (150AFN; 1hr 30mins); on other days you can get a seat in a shared minivan between Bamiyan and Yawkawlang (200AFN; 2hrs) and get off at the entrance to the park, where it's a 15km walk to the lakes. A private hired car from Bamiyan would cost around 3,000AFN for the day; there's an additional 100AFN fee for vehicles to enter the park, to be paid at a ticket office below the Dam of Band e Haibat.

Practicalities **Women** have been banned from visiting the park since 2023; however, international women are sometimes allowed entry.

What **facilities** the park possesses are based near the road entrance below Band e Haibat, where you'll find trinket stalls, hats for sale, horses for hire and simple chaikhanas selling kebabs, albeit hygiene is poor at these establishments and it's best to bring your own snacks. Most families set up daybeds, rent tents and cook meals by the lakeside. A driver with a pressure cooker can prepare a proper lunch while you explore.

Chehel Burj (144km west of Bamiyan town) If you have time, the long day trip to Chehel Burj, the best preserved of all the fortifications in Bamiyan Province, is well worth it. Chehel Burj means 'forty towers' and this Ghorid-era citadel controlled the northern approach into the region in the same way Shahr e Zohak guarded the eastern approach. The fortification with its towers, which do number about 40, sits on a conical hill overlooking the valley, and it is hard to imagine that this remote location was once so important it required such a mighty citadel to guard it. Look out too for the main drum of a Buddhist stupa about 30 minutes before you arrive at Chehel Burj.

To get there, head to Yawkawlang from Bamiyan (1hr), then north on the road to Sar e Pol for another 45km (2–3hrs). A private hire car with driver would cost in the region of 5,000AFN for the day. Bring food and water; although you will pass rural smallholdings after Yawkawlang, this is a remote area with no amenities.

THE CENTRAL ROUTE FROM BAMIYAN TO HERAT

For those seeking the raw, untamed soul of Afghanistan, the central route – riding along the country's mountainous spine from Bamiyan to Herat – offers one of the most adventurous overland journeys in Asia. Equal parts challenge and reward, this three-day odyssey takes you into narrow valleys, over barren passes, and through remote villages where time has stood still for generations. It is not for the faint-hearted: rough roads, minimal infrastructure and long driving hours make this an excursion for seasoned and self-reliant travellers only. But those who make the journey are rewarded with a unique insight into Afghan life off the grid, and one of the greatest and most mysterious monuments in the world – the Minaret of Jam.

The route should be tackled only between April and October, when the passes are clear of snow. Be prepared for very basic accommodation, otherwise bring camping gear. Food is not abundant and phone connections are limited, although you can pick up data in Chaghcharan. Fuel is only available in the larger towns; the section between Yawkawlang and Chaghcharan is particularly remote.

GETTING THERE AND AROUND Although minibuses do run sporadically between Bamiyan and Chaghcharan (800–1,200AFN; 8hrs) you can't rely on public transport if you're on a tight schedule; you may have to travel to Yawkawlang and wait there for onward transportation. Chaghcharan to Herat (2,000–3,000AFN; 20hrs) is a better-connected route, with daily shared taxis or minivans leaving desperately early in the morning. Outside of these options, you will need to find private hires.

Access to the Minaret of Jam is either from Chaghcharan via a rough northern road (about 6hrs each way), or from the west by turning off the Herat–Chaghcharan road at Garmao. Both routes are in poor condition and lead to the opposite bank of the river. Vehicles can usually ford the river, but during spring floods, access is by a zip wire strung across the water.

TOURIST INFORMATION AND REGISTRATION In Chaghcharan, stopping at the **Department of Information and Culture** (200m west of Jam Sq, south side) is essential for visiting the Minaret of Jam and paying the 1,000AFN entrance fee. If you're prepared and wish to camp at the minaret, tell them in Chaghcharan so they note it on the documents. If coming from Herat, you should mention this to the Information and Culture office in Herat and there pay the fee for Jam as well.

At the time of writing, a basic hotel was under construction at Jam. On arrival, the Taliban will check your paperwork and, if you stay overnight, expect to be watched for your own protection.

BAMIYAN TO CHAGHCHARAN From **Bamiyan**, the road climbs west across the high plain containing the lakes of Band e Amir National Park before descending into the **Yawkawlang valley**, a landscape of wind-cut cliffs and patchwork fields hemmed in by the Hindu Kush. **Yawkawlang** offers simple accommodation, but its easy proximity to Bamiyan thanks to the new paved road means there is no reason to linger.

Beyond Yawlawkang, the new paved road becomes a rough track and visitors are welcomed to life in Afghanistan before the international community arrived. The road crosses the 3,110m **Kirman Pass** before dropping down into **Lal wa sarjangal** (or **Lal** as everyone calls it). The pass marks the boundary between Bamiyan and Ghor provinces and the watershed between Bamiyan's rivers which drain into the Helmand River system and the rivers of Ghor which form the Hari Rud. Lal also marks the edge of Hazarajat and the beginning of an area populated by the Aimaq, a small minority group of Persian-speaking semi-nomadic people (page 48).

The road continues to Chaghcharan, the capital of Ghor (sometimes known as Firozkoh, named after the Turquoise Mountain, the city razed by the Mongols). Chaghcharan is paved and reasonably well stocked for food and necessities. You can overnight at **Firuzkuh Palace Guest House** (450m south on the Hari Rud bridge road; m 7920 00963, 7760 16700; **$$**) or the **Wasim Hotel** (north bank of the Hari Rud, west of the bridge; m 7894 44400; **$$**). Both are simple places but have shared showers and private rooms. They are the best accommodation options in Ghor Province.

CHAGHCHARAN TO HERAT This road largely follows the course of the Hari Rud River as it drops down through the Hindu Kush from Chaghcharan (2,230m above sea level) to Herat at 920m. You will notice the increase in warmth as you descend. The main road is unpaved but graded in many sections, making for rough but manageable driving conditions.

Shortly after leaving Chaghcharan, the Hari Rud enters a complex series of narrow gorges. At this point, the main road veers south on a long detour – taking 5–6 hours – before rejoining the river at a small village called **Garmao**. From

THE GHORID EMPIRE

Located between Bamiyan and Herat, the mountainous province of Ghor was populated in the Middle Ages by eastern Iranian Tajiks. They were initially Buddhists or pagans, but went on to become Sunni allies of the Abbasid Caliphs, starting with the famous Harun al-Rachid. They later became vassals of the vast Ghaznavid Empire (page 204).

In 1149, the ruler of Ghazni, Bahram Shah, poisoned the Ghorid leader, then followed up by crucifying his brother. It was a fatal act of brutality that brought down the wrath of a third brother, Ala al-Din Husayn, who would soon earn the nickname the 'World Burner' as he destroyed Ghazni to build a new capital called Firozkoh, also known as the Turquoise Mountain – after the colour of its tilework (page 190).

Between 1175 and 1206 another member of the family, Muhammad of Ghor, would conquer an empire that stretched across much of modern Afghanistan and northern India, which he divided into sultanates ruled not by his kin, but by trusted Mamluks (Turkic enslaved warrior knights). One of these Ghorid sultanates, at Delhi, would last until 1526, when Babur founded the Mughal Empire.

The western part of the Ghorid Empire was ruled by Muhammad's younger brother Sultan Ghiyath al-Din, a great patron of architecture, metal and tilework and calligraphy, who left a few but exquisite surviving Ghorid buildings, which include the Minaret of Jam, the *gumbads* of Chesht e Sharif and the old section of the Friday Mosque in Herat.

Bamiyan and Herat were key Ghorid centres, and in between was their summer capital, Firozkoh, once a highly anticipated stop on the Silk Road. Contemporary accounts describe a multi-cultural, tolerant city, which, while having a Muslim majority, had active Zoroastrian, Buddhist, Nestorian Christian, Jewish and Manichaeist communities. Rory Stewart in *The Places in Between* suggests the Ghorids constructed their capital in such a remote spot to emphasise the fact that they came from the mountains and were not nomads, although the location wasn't enough to protect Firozkoh from Genghis Khan when he razed the city in 1223, so completely that no-one knows for certain where this glittering mountain stronghold once stood; no other Ghorid structures have survived near the Minaret of Jam.

---

there, the road and river run side by side, heading due west for about 12 more hours until reaching Herat. It's a remote and sparsely populated region until you approach **Obey**, where occasional villages begin to appear, some with basic shops and electricity.

This main road, however, bypasses the Minaret of Jam. To visit the minaret, you must take a separate road at Chaghcharan, heading northwest before turning sharply south down a narrow gorge to reach the site on the banks of the Hari Rud. This detour takes roughly 6 hours and is considered the most difficult section of the central route. From Jam, you can carry on westwards along another rugged track along the river which eventually connects back to the main road at Garmao, from where you can continue to Herat.

The full journey from Chaghcharan to Herat – over 20 hours of driving – can be broken up with overnight stops at Jam (where a basic hotel is currently being constructed and due to open in spring 2026) or at Chesht e Sharif.

5 | BAMIYAN AND CENTRAL AFGHANISTAN

✵ Minaret of Jam (See page 188 for admission) The Minaret of Jam is truly one of Asia's most breathtaking sights, an otherworldly vision rising 65m over a remote gorge – reward indeed after 14 hours' travelling on unpaved road from either Bamiyan or Herat. It is the second highest medieval minaret ever built, after the Qutb Minar in Delhi – although the settings could not be more different. Built in 1194 during the reign of the Ghorid Sultan Ghiyath al-Din Muhammad, the minaret was little known outside of Afghanistan until the late 1950s, when it was studied as part of a French archaeology survey. It stands as a remarkable testament to the artistic and engineering brilliance of the Ghorids some 830 years ago, and has delighted and continues to delight the few hardy souls that make this journey.

Constructed entirely of brick, intricate geometric patterns, Kufic calligraphy and Quranic verses spiral up its cylindrical form. Although most of the turquoise-glazed tiles that once adorned the surface have vanished, the remaining fragments and the elaborate brickwork are still strikingly well preserved. Unlike most minarets, Jam is not attached to a mosque, leading scholars to believe it may have served as a victory tower or could possibly be the only surviving remnant of Firozkoh, the lost Turquoise Mountain capital of the Ghorid Empire (page 189) – although it is hard to envisage a city in such a narrow gorge. Its ambiguous origins only add to its mystique.

The minaret's isolated setting, at the confluence of the Hari Rud and Jam Rud rivers surrounded by steep mountains, is as spectacular as the monument itself and has helped shield it from human interference, although erosion and seasonal flooding continue to pose serious threats. Listed as a UNESCO World Heritage Site in Danger and by the Islamic World Educational, Scientific and Cultural Organization (Afghanistan's first entry), the minaret has undergone limited conservation, including reinforcement of the riverbank platform to keep it from collapsing into the water below. The internal staircase, once used by the muezzin to ascend the tower, has been bricked up.

Chesht e Sharif Chesht e Sharif marks the beginning of the end of the Hindu Kush; from here on the towering peaks give way to rolling hills as they yield to the plains and deserts that stretch towards Iran. The architecture changes too, adapting to the warmer, drier climate. Mud-brick compounds with rooftop wind-catchers become increasingly common.

Today Chesht e Sharif is a small town, but during the Ghorid period it was an important religious centre, closely associated with the Chishti Order of Sufi mystics, which began here in around 930CE; one of its founders, Maudood Chishti, is buried in a large 20th-century mausoleum. The Chishti Order grew to become one of the most widely followed Sufi movements across central Asia and the Indian subcontinent, with followers in Ajmer, Rajasthan and in Nizamuddin West, Delhi. It is a striking reminder of the vast influence of the medieval Ghorid kingdom – an influence hard to imagine when standing in Ghor today.

For most visitors, the two ancient domes (*gumbads*), built by Ghiyath al-Din Muhammad, are the star attraction. These crumbling structures – one of which features on the original 2004 cover of Rory Stewart's book *The Places in Between* – can be seen from the road in the centre of town.

There is a basic chaikhana **$$** on the south side of the main road, about 100m east of the domes, which has four rooms without beds.

6

Kandahar and Southern Afghanistan

In southern Afghanistan you have the arid deserts of Registan and Dasht e Margo (the 'desert of death') and the southern slopes of the Hindu Kush, bisected by a ribbon of arable land where people live in the provinces of Kandahar, Helmand, Zabul and Ghazni. This is the heartland of the Pashtuns, who have ruled Afghanistan for the past 300 years. Historically, southern Afghanistan was a key artery of commerce, linking Persia, India and central Asia. As early as 1000BCE, its plains boasted flourishing cities, sustained by sophisticated *qanat* (underground irrigation) systems that channelled meltwater from the Hindu Kush into fertile farmland. But in the 13th century, Genghis Khan's Mongol armies swept through the region, destroying cities and their canal and qanat networks. Vast areas, especially in Zabul and Helmand, never fully recovered.

The south is where the modern unified country of Afghanistan was born in 1747, when Ahmad Shah Durrani chose Kandahar as his capital. That decision gave Kandahar – and by extension, the south – historical weight and lasting influence in Afghan politics. In the 1990s, it took centre stage as the Taliban rose out of the religious schools of Kandahar, capitalising on the chaos and corruption of the mujahideen civil war. Former president Hamid Karzai was chief of the Popalzai Durrani tribe of Kandahar.

The climate and landscape are harsh. In the scorching summers, temperatures often soar above 45°C. Water is scarce, with life dependent on the dwindling streams descending from the Hindu Kush. The cities and towns of the south – Kandahar, Lashkar Gah and Ghazni – rarely feature on tourist itineraries today, but the minarets of Ghazni, the ruins of Bost, and the Old City of Kandahar each offer glimpses into a less-known but fascinating side of Afghanistan. Accommodation and infrastructure are limited, but for those who do venture south, the cultural rewards are undeniable.

The south remains deeply traditional. Burqas, tribal turban styles and gender segregation are, along with the Pashtun-dominated east, more commonly observed here than elsewhere in Afghanistan. Look out for more varied colours of burqas: along with the more common blue, you'll see pale brown, green and white.

Southern Afghanistan witnessed some of the fiercest fighting between the Taliban and the internationally backed government between 2001 and 2021, when Helmand and Kandahar became practically synonymous with the war itself. Partly as a legacy of conflict, you may find that the security forces are a little more inquisitive about your movements, and you may be asked for your documentation more regularly than in other parts of the country.

6 | KANDAHAR AND SOUTHERN AFGHANISTAN

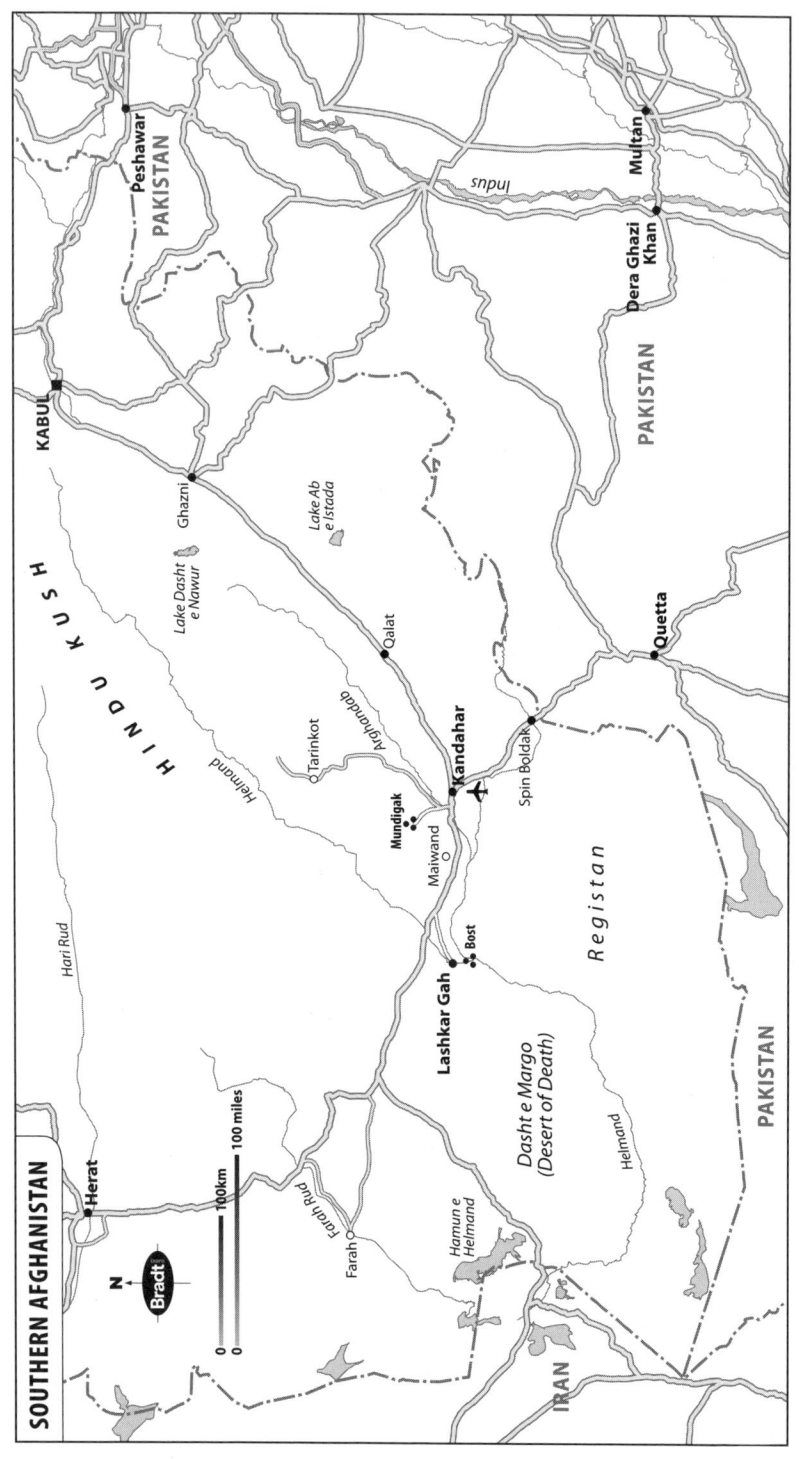

KANDAHAR

Afghanistan's second city, Kandahar (population c580,000) is by far the largest in the arid south. It grew up along the trade routes between Persia and India in the Arghandab Valley, where the river disappears into the sands of the Registan Desert. A fortified city stood here by the 2nd millennium BCE; by the 6th century BCE it was absorbed into the Achaemenid empire.

Kandahar's name is derived either from 'Iskander', the Persian form of Alexander the Great, who founded Alexandria Arachosia here in the 4th century BCE, or from 'Gandhara', the Achaemenid name for the region. It was shaped by a succession of empires, including the Mauryans, Kushans, Sassanids and Ghaznavids, before it was destroyed by Nader Shah Afshar in 1738 (page 25).

Kandahar took on its current appearance after 1747, when Ahmad Shah Durrani (fondly known as 'Baba', or father) made it the capital of Afghanistan. He laid out the Old City, Zorr Shaar, himself, with its tight layout and covered bazaar. But Kandahar's heyday was short-lived; Ahmad Shah Baba's son, Timur Shah, moved the capital to Kabul. Kandahar has been Afghanistan's second city ever since, playing a role in nearly every chapter of Afghan history. During the Second Anglo–Afghan War, it was from Kandahar that the British rode out only to be defeated at the Battle of Maiwand (page 201). As a centre of mujahideen resistance during the Soviet occupation, the city saw such fierce fighting that the Russians carpet bombed the city. Thousands were killed, or fled; the population dropped from 200,000 to 25,000. The subsequent battle for control of the city by the warlords was even worse, leading to the creation of the Taliban (page 195).

Since then, Kandahar has been called the de facto capital of Afghanistan, during the first Taliban rule and again since 2021, an epicentre of power, and source of major legal rulings and edicts. Religious leaders tend to remain behind the scenes, but their influence is deeply felt. The birthplace of modern Afghanistan continues to be the spiritual and political heartland of the Pashtun people. Kandahar's motto says it all: 'The City of Power'.

GETTING THERE AND AWAY

By air Ahmad Shah Baba Airport lies 15km southeast of Kandahar and is linked with Kabul by flights operated by Kam Air and Ariana. The terminal is a set of low-rise buildings resembling the barrel-vaulted ceilings of the covered bazaar designed by the airport's namesake. As usual at Afghan airports, security is heavy so arrive in plenty of time before your flight. On departure you may be asked to leave your luggage in a room which is then discreetly screened by a curtain (so passengers do not observe sniffer dogs investigating their bags).

The Kam Air sales office and other travel agents are located north of Sardar Madad Khan Watt. Others are near the Fowara awal in Aino Maina.

Getting to/from the airport There is no public transport linking the airport with the city centre, so take a taxi (700AFN; 30mins). They can be found a short walk from the terminal building.

By road Transport for **directions east** arrive/leave from the Kabul hada, a large transport station north of the large roundabout along the road to the airport. Large buses (900AFN; 7–9hrs) and shared taxis (1,500AFN; 7–9hrs) leave for Kabul, as well as to the Pakistan border at Spin Boldak (300AFN; 2hrs).

For **directions west**, you need the Herat hada set back on the south side of the main road, 1km west of the Shrine of Mirwais Hotak. Shared taxis (1,700AFN; 9–10hrs) and large buses (1000AFN; 9–10hrs) for Herat ply this road regularly.

For **directions north**, shared taxis (500AFN; 4hrs) and big buses (350AFN; 4hrs) leave from the Tarinkot hada to Tarinkot, the capital of Oruzgan Province. This could be the first leg of an exciting multi-day through Oruzgan and Daykundi Province towards Bamiyan. It is on the northern side of the city. Just south of the hada is a scrap of ground where dozens of Millie buses (the state-run bus company of the 1980s and 90s) are stacked on top of each other.

GETTING AROUND There is no public transport to speak of in Kandahar, although rickshaws and taxis are easy to find. A taxi from the Old City (Zorr Shaar) to Aino Maina will cost around 250AFN.

Kandahar has no traffic lights, relying instead on uniformed traffic police to direct the flow. While Zorr Shaar is relatively compact, you'll need to hire a car and driver to visit places such as Mirwais Hotak, Chilzina and the shrine of Baba Wali.

TOURIST INFORMATION AND REGISTRATION It is essential to visit the **Department of Information and Culture**, where you will be invited for a short interview by the minister himself. Without their documentation, you will be unable to visit the Ahmad Shah Durrani Mausoleum, Chilzina, or the shrines of Mirwais Hotak and Baba Wali.

ORIENTATION Kandahar is split into several distinct zones. **Zorr Shaar**, laid out by Ahmad Shah Durrani, is centred around the **Charsu intersection**, site of the traditional covered bazaar and historic quarters. At its western end, the **Shaheedan Chowk** (Martyrs Square) was once a gathering spot for hippies in the 1970s and

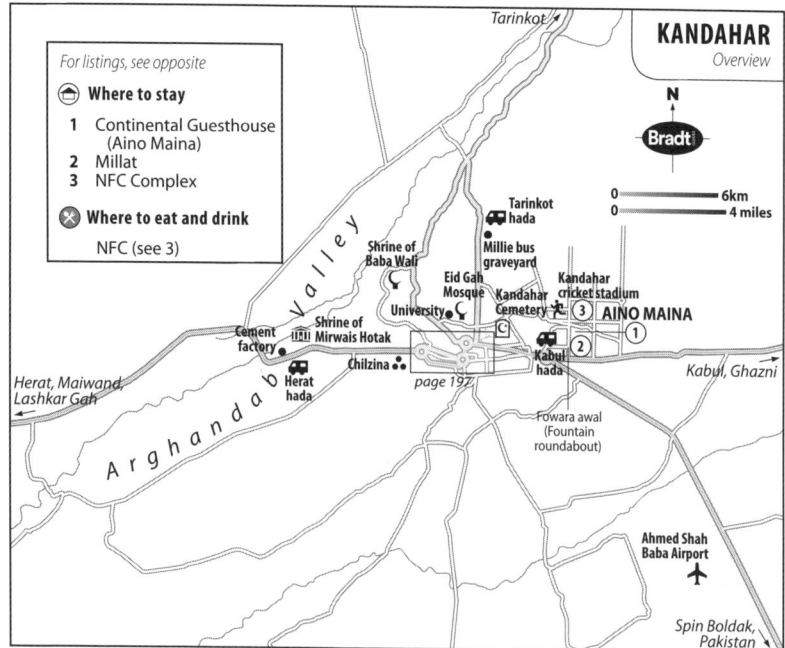

MULLAH OMAR AND THE RISE OF THE TALIBAN

By the early 1990s, Afghanistan was a country broken by war. After the withdrawal of Soviet forces in 1989 and the collapse of the Moscow-backed regime in 1992, power fragmented among rival mujahideen factions, many of whom had once fought together against the Soviets. The leaders, now turned warlords, carved up the country into fiefdoms. Thousands of civilians were killed, and basic services collapsed.

Checkpoints sprang up on roads across the country, manned by gunmen demanding bribes, looting and sometimes abducting travellers. The road between Kandahar and the Pakistan border at Spin Boldak was a notorious gauntlet with a dozen checkpoints manned by local commanders often operating with total impunity. Civilians suffered robbery, extortion, rape, and lived in constant fear, without a functioning justice system to turn to.

It was in this climate of desperation that the Taliban emerged. In 1994, a former mujahideen fighter and village cleric named Mullah Mohammad Omar gathered a group of students (*taliban*) from local religious schools in Kandahar. According to one popular account, the movement's birth was sparked by an incident in which a local warlord had kidnapped and raped two girls. Omar and his students hanged the man and restored the girls to their families. Whether apocryphal or not, the story symbolised the Taliban's appeal: a promise of justice, order and moral clarity after years of lawless chaos.

Their message – rooted in religion, anti-corruption and strict order – spread quickly. With Pakistani support and popular backing from Pashtun communities tired of warlord abuses, the Taliban swept through southern Afghanistan, capturing Kandahar in late 1994. In the spring of 1996, holding up the cloak of the Prophet Muhammad (page 199), Mullah Omar addressed a crowd in Kandahar and declared himself Amir al-Mu'minin (Commander of the Faithful). Later that year they took Kabul, driving out the last remnants of the mujahideen.

Mullah Omar, a soft-spoken but austere figure, rarely appeared in public. Only one known photograph of him exists. He led the Taliban both in government and as a guerrilla anti-government force until he died of natural causes in Pakistan in 2013, although this was only confirmed in 2015.

---

still buzzes with local energy, although the backpacker vibe is long gone and the area is overshadowed by the imposing new mosque to the south. To the west is **Shahre Nau** (New City), the administrative hub with government buildings and more modern services.

East of the centre, the new suburb of **Aino Maina** was clearly influenced by Islamabad's layout in neighbouring Pakistan. With its wide boulevards, occasional fountains, and reliable electricity, it offers Kandahar's best accommodation and dining options, although it lacks some of the character of the older parts of the city. **Fowara awal**, the first fountain roundabout, has what passes for its commercial area.

WHERE TO STAY *Map, opposite, unless otherwise stated*

Hotels and guesthouses that accept international guests (all with between 20 and 30 rooms) are concentrated in the Shahre Nau and Aino Maina districts. While Pashtun hospitality is felt in all of them, options are limited and none offers great value for money. The cheaper mussafarkhanas around Shaheedan Chowk would not take foreigners at the time of writing. The reason given varied slightly from hotelier to hotelier, but it is clear that the authorities would prefer that visitors stayed in the handful of authorised accommodation options, and this seems unlikely to change soon.

Continental Guesthouse (Aino Maina) 2 blocks northeast of Fowara awal; m 7003 07495. Located in the quiet backstreets of Aino Maina, the buildings occupy some lovely grounds, but the rooms are tired & only some have Western-style bathrooms. No restaurant, but staff can order in from places nearby. AC, some Western toilets, good security, b/fast inc. **$$$**

Continental Guesthouse (Shahre Nau) [map, opposite] Opposite the Clinic Shahidan Instruction, Herat Darwaza; m 7003 02613, 7003 16159; e info@kdrcgh.com. The original Continental Guesthouse (not to be confused with the new one in Aino Maina – they are not affiliated) has a great location in Shahre Nau, a short walk from the Old City. The reception area & first set of rooms are in a part of the building constructed in the 1950s with barrel-vaulted ceilings & skylights reminiscent of the covered bazaar at Charsu, giving it a nice guesthouse vibe. But it is expensive for what is on offer. AC, Western-style toilets. Laundry, b/fast, tea, coffee & cold drinks all inc. **$$$**

Millat Hotel Near Fowara awal in Aino Maina; m 7002 81000. Smaller hotel with the same owner as the Continental Guesthouse in Aino Maina. It's closer to the small commercial centre of Aino Maina than NFC Complex or the Continental. Some Western-style toilets, AC, no security; b/fast inc. **$$**

NFC Complex Between 27 & 28 Second Phase, Aino Maina; m 7003 45803; w kandaharnfc.com. NFC stands for New York Fried Chicken, but don't be put off by the name; this is probably the best-value accommodation in Kandahar. It also functions as a sports & leisure venue complete with a big attached restaurant, football pitch, swimming pool & sauna. Small but well-functioning rooms & friendly staff; do check that your room has AC as this is essential in the summer months. Attached bathroom, Western-style toilets; b/fast inc. **$$**

Mirwais Hotel & Restaurants [map, opposite] Main St, west of Shaheedan Chowk; m 7003 05806. An old stalwart of the hippie trail, this basic hotel has been standing for 75 years & has a great location right between Zorr Shaar & Shahre Nau. Currently not accepting international guests. No AC; some rooms have attached bathroom; squat toilets; no security. Some rooms have beds. **$**

✴ WHERE TO EAT AND DRINK *Map, opposite, unless otherwise stated*

Dining options in Kandahar are heavy on traditional Afghan dishes. There are restaurants everywhere in the city, especially around Shaheedan Chowk. Kandaharis will tell you that their pulao comes with more meat than that served elsewhere in Afghanistan, which they traditionally wash down with *shurumbey*, a watered-down doogh (page 99), made from yoghurt, cucumber and water, served plentifully from large containers. There is a Pakistani influence, too: paratha (fried chapati) and milk tea are common breakfast staples, while biryani is becoming a common alternative to pulao, especially among younger Kandaharis. This Pakistani influence is a boon for vegetarians as daal and chana are more common here than in other parts of the country. For street food (pakora, chips, burgers and, at lunchtime, biryani), try Charsu in Zorr Shaar. Juice and ice cream shops dot the main drag between Aino Maina and Zorr Shaar.

Anar Chowk Anar. *Anar* means pomegranate, which Kandahar is famous for throughout Afghanistan; there's even a pomegranate on top of the building. The square this restaurant sits on used to have a statue of a pomegranate but the current government has removed it. Anar is the best of the many restaurants in this area. It has AC & all the usual Pakistani & Afghan dishes, plus pizzas & juices. **$$**

NFC [map, page 194] See NFC Complex (see above). The chef here claims to have worked for the Americans at Camp Leatherneck & is able to

KANDAHAR

KANDAHAR *Centre*

For listings, see from page 195

Where to stay
1. Continental Guesthouse (Shahre Nau)
2. Mirwais
3. Noor Jahan

Where to eat and drink
4. Anar
5. Shandar Biryani
6. Turkman Andkhoi

Aino Maina, Airport, Kabul hada, Kabul →

Bird market
Covered bazaar
Jami'Mui Mobarak
Charsu
Governor's office
Mosque of the Cloak
Ahmed Shah Durrani Mausoleum
Travel agents
Kam Air
Moneychangers
Dried fruit bazaar
Rock
OLD CITY (ZORR SHAAR)
Ghazanfar
Islamic Bank of Afghanistan
Department of Information & Culture
Shaheedan Chowk (Martyr's Square)
New Mosque
SHAHRE NAU
Red Mosque
Mohmand Hospital
Kandahar football stadium

← Herat hada, shrine of Mirwais Hotak

0   500m
0   500yds

cook 'anything'. Salads, handi, karahi, biryani, fried chicken, pizza, burgers, fish & soups are all of a high standard. It's always busy despite being a long way from anywhere. $$
Turkman Andkhoi Restaurant Pol e hawayi; m 7028 38701. For a change from Kandahari kebab & pulao, this Turkmen restaurant offers mantu and Turkmen pulao, as well as the usual Afghan specialities. $$
Shandar Biryani On a street of busy biryani restaurants, Shandar is the pick of the bunch. $

SHOPPING There are a few souvenir and traditional jewellery shops on the main road between Charsu and the bird market in the bazaar in Zorr Shaar (⊕ 08.00–dusk, mostly closed on Fri). They also sell the specialities of Kandahar: plain, colourful or intricately beaded Kandahari caps, waistcoats and embroidered shalwar kameez.

SPORTS AND ACTIVITIES Cricket is less popular in Kandahar than in other Pashtun areas in the east, albeit you might be able to catch a match at the city stadium. However, if you want to spend time with large Pashtun men: the green areas at the north end of Aino Maina see traditional **pahlevani** (Afghan wrestling) matches on Fridays after lunchtime prayers. Ask around as locations change.

Swimming pool & sauna In the basement of the NFC complex (page 196); men only; 500AFN, free for hotel guests. All swimmers are issued with identical blue calf-length shorts & there is a friendly atmosphere, though the lifeguards have a very relaxed attitude to patrons throwing their friends in the pool.

OTHER PRACTICALITIES
Medical
Mohmand Hospital see map; m 7080 00740; w mohmandhospital.com
Rock Pharmacy Nawi Sarak St, Shahre Nau; m 7052 31387

Money There are **banks and moneychangers** on the road north of Shaheedan Chowk between the Old City & Shahre Nau. In Aino Maina there are moneychangers next to the Millat Hotel.

WHAT TO SEE AND DO
Zorr Shaar Ahmad Shah Durrani's early 18th-century town plan centred on the four-way crossroads still known as Charsu today, in the heart of a warren of covered bazaars, caravanserais and public buildings. Civic improvements in the intervening years, especially the road expansions carried out in the 1970s and 80s under President Daoud and Dr Najibullah, resulted in much of it being demolished. There is, however, a portion of the covered bazaar in good condition on the northeast corner of Charsu encompassing the 19th-century **Jami Mui Mobarak** (Mosque of the Hair of the Beard of the Prophet) built to house the relic; men only can enter the courtyard and Muslims only may enter the mosque.

In the bazaar to the northwest of Charsu, shops selling dried goods, spices and tea are still housed in some of the original 18th-century buildings, although the layout of the complex can be hard to discern at ground level; go up the steps for a better idea of what the trading areas were originally like.

The bazaar branches out in all directions from Charsu, notably to the east to the jewellery, textiles and bird market. You can easily spend an hour or two getting lost in the alleyways of this resolutely Pashtun city.

Ahmad Shah Durrani Mausoleum (North end of Zorr Shaar; ⊕ 08.00–dusk; you will need to show the police your papers; entry inside permitted on Fri only, although this is a recent rule so might change during the life of this book) This octagonal grand mausoleum, covered in blue and turquoise tiles, is the final resting place of the founder of modern Afghanistan, surrounded by the graves of Abdali/Durrani family members. For such a revered figure there are rarely many people here, making it a quiet place of reflection. A mullah attached to the Taliban detachment that manages the mosque security is often seen teaching children Quranic lessons in front of the tomb.

To the northeast is a concrete replica of the mausoleum, designed for General Razzaq who led the Afghan National Army's flight against the Taliban in the 2010s. It is not permitted to visit and is in line for demolition.

Mosque of the Cloak (Kherqa Mubarak) (Opposite the tomb of Ahmad Shah Durrani; non-Muslims are not allowed to enter the shrine, and its interior remains off-limits to most visitors) This is one of the holiest sites in Afghanistan. Constructed from striking green marble, the shrine houses a cloak believed to have been worn by the Prophet Muhammad when he undertook the Night Journey and ascended to heaven in 621 CE.

The cloak's journey to Kandahar is steeped in legend and political symbolism. Originally brought from Iraq to central Asia during the campaigns of Timur, it was kept in Bukhara. In 1768, Ahmad Shah Durrani acquired the cloak from the Emir of Bukhara as a token of their agreement over Afghanistan's northern border. Another, more popular story goes that Ahmad Shah swore to the keepers of the cloak in Bukhara that if they would let him hold the cloak, he would not move the sacred relic from beside a large stone stele in the courtyard. He kept his word – but only by transporting the stele itself along with the cloak to Kandahar. That same stele now sits in the northern courtyard of the shrine.

Before arriving in Kandahar, the cloak spent around eight months in Kabul, at the Sakhi Shrine (page 134). Once installed in Kandahar, it was placed under tight protection. Access to the cloak itself is strictly limited – it has only been displayed publicly a handful of times in history, most famously in 1996 when Mullah Omar held it aloft while addressing a crowd, symbolically linking the Taliban's religious authority to that of the Prophet and of the founder of Afghanistan.

Chilzina Perched on a rocky cliff above Kandahar and the Arghandab Valley, overlooking western approaches to the city, Chilzina (Forty Steps) is one of Kandahar's most atmospheric and historic landmarks. Accessed via a modern path from the north side, through a recently landscaped public park, the site is reached by climbing a steep flight of some 40 stone rock-hewn steps. A modern handrail has been installed, making the ascent more manageable for visitors. At the top a **rock-cut chamber**, flanked by two worn lion figures, offers panoramic views of the surrounding plains. Inside, an **inscription** attributed to Babur, the 16th-century founder of the Mughal Empire, is carved into the wall in Persian, reflecting his admiration for the region's strategic and natural beauty. The hill on which Chilzina is located was once the location of the main Kandahar citadel, which was destroyed by the Persians in the early 18th century. Chilzina's origins, however, pre-date Babur by many centuries.

Near the base of the cliff are a famous series of **Ashokan rock edicts**, inscribed during the reign of Emperor Ashoka of the Mauryan Empire in the 3rd century BCE (page 20). Written in Greek and Aramaic, the edicts affirm that living beings, human or animal, cannot be killed in Ashoka's realm. A second inscription, in Greek, was discovered in 1963, 1.5km south in the long-gone ruins of Old Kandahar (Alexandria Arachosia) – here Ashoka describes his remorse over his blood-stained past and conversion. They are among the westernmost evidence of Ashoka's Buddhist influence, promoting moral and ethical governance. However, at the time of writing these edicts were not possible to visit and may have been removed.

The panoramic view is something that seems to concern the local authorities, and to climb the stairs additional permission is often required from the District 7 police station (opposite the Mirwais Hotak shrine on the main Herat–Kandahar road).

Shrine of Mirwais Hotak Ahmad Shah Durrani may be the founding father of Afghanistan, but he was not the first Pashtun from Kandahar to throw off the shackles of a neighbouring empire in the 18th century. Mirwais Khan Hotak, also known as Mirwais Neeka (Grandfather Mirwais), was a powerful Pashtun tribal leader from the Ghilzai confederacy, who in 1709 successfully led a revolt against Safavid Persian rule (page 25). He then declared independence and founded the Hotak dynasty, briefly establishing Kandahar as the capital of an independent Afghan state. The Hotak dynasty was eventually crushed by the Persians, and the Kandahar of Mirwais Hotak was levelled; but his rebellion is widely viewed as a precursor to the later unification of Afghanistan by Ahmad Shah Durrani.

The shrine itself is of a similar design to the mausoleum of Ahmad Shah Durrani, an octagonal domed structure surrounded by quiet courtyards shaded by trees. However, it is constructed of simple brick and is not tiled – yet it is elegant and provides another peaceful sanctuary away from the chaos of Kandahar.

Red Mosque Of limited architectural interest and usually only sparsely attended, the Red Mosque was constructed in the 1950s as the Shahre Nau expanded. It was well known as the mosque in which Mullah Omar and the original Taliban leadership used to pray and preach. As such it has huge importance historically and spiritually to the nation.

Eid Gah Mosque Located east of the university, this huge mosque holds prayers at major religious dates. These are the only occasions that Mullah Hibatullah Akhundzada, the current leader of the Islamic Emirate, is ever heard in public, albeit he is never seen.

Kandahar Cemetery North of the city, the many cemeteries of Kandahar include a section for foreign fighters killed while fighting for the Taliban, recognisable by green or black flags marking the graves. People often come to this graveyard for good luck. There's also a memorial to those who died in the Dasht e Laila massacre (page 233).

AROUND KANDAHAR

Arghandab Valley This fertile valley, 10km northwest of Kandahar, is known for its orchards and lush greenery. The river provides life to the region's famous pomegranates, which are some of the best in the world. A visit to the valley offers a peaceful escape from the city's hustle and bustle; though the whole valley is thick with picnicking Kandaharis on Fridays and holidays.

Shrine of Baba Wali (9km north of Kandahar; ⊕ 08.00–dusk; free) This shrine is dedicated to the 16th-century Sufi Baba Wali, a contemporary of Guru Nanak, the founder of Sikhism. Guru Nanak undertook various journeys, including one to Kandahar where he met Baba Wali. The shrine sits inside a new marble-and-glass building created in the early 2000s and has great views over the Arghandab River valley; for better views climb the steps to the south of the shrine. It's a popular place to visit and there are vendors selling ice cream, snacks and juices nearby.

The drive from the centre of Kandahar takes you through and over a pass across the hills, at the top of which is a checkpoint where you will need to show your documents. Mullah Omar's expansive old compound is on the south side of the pass, to the north of the road. On 7 October 2001, it was the first place in history to be hit by a drone-fired missile in combat, although the drone missed its target: Omar had secretly fled a few hours before and was rarely seen after.

Maiwand (68km west, north of the Lashkar Gah road; turn north on the west side of the bridge at the village of Maiwand, sometimes called Hotal; it's remote, infrequently visited, the roads are poor and it's likely your driver will need to ask for directions, as there are no signs; the round trip takes about 90mins) The name Maiwand holds deep national significance to Afghanistan's identity. It was here, on 27 July 1880, that one of the most famous battles of the Second Anglo–Afghan War took place – a rare and stunning victory over the mighty British Empire by the Afghan army, under the leadership of Ayub Khan.

At the heart of the legend of the battle is **Malalai of Maiwand**, the 'Afghan Joan of Arc'. A young Pashtun woman from a nearby village, Malalai is said to have rallied retreating Afghan fighters by seizing a fallen banner and reciting a couplet urging them not to flee:

> 'Young love, if you do not fall in the battle of Maiwand,
> By God, someone is saving you as a symbol of shame!'

Her words shouted through the dust and chaos of battle, reignited the soldiers' courage and inspired a fierce counterattack, turning the tide of the battle. Malalai was later killed, reportedly by a British bullet, but her bravery has become immortalised in poetry, popular memory, and national pride. Whether Malalai existed or not, the British officer, Lieutenant Hensman, who witnessed the battle, wrote: 'Never before in all my experience have I seen such a gallant charge as the one made by the Ghazis at Maiwand. It was a sight to stir the blood of every man.' Heavy casualties were suffered on both sides. The British were forced into a retreat, with hundreds of men killed, and the morale of the empire deeply shaken.

Today, the battlefield of Maiwand lies in a broad, dusty plain framed to the north by a crescent of low hills. Two monuments remain. To the north of the battlefield, a tall, phallic pillar marks the **graves of the Martyrs of Maiwand**, commemorating the Afghan warriors who fell. Southeast of the battlefield lies the **tomb of Malalai**, a simple yet powerful site of remembrance for one of Afghanistan's most iconic folk heroines.

HELMAND PROVINCE

Helmand Province in recent years has been shaped by war, water and opium. It was not always like this. During the Ghaznavid Empire (page 204), its capital Bost sat at the centre of a vast and prosperous irrigation network which was destroyed by Genghis Khan's and Timur's armies, from which it arguably has never recovered. In the mid 20th century, Helmand became a focal point of US Cold War development efforts, with massive investment in canals and agriculture. Today, those same canals feed the region's most notorious crop – opium poppy – which helped to make Helmand one of the world's largest producers.

In recent decades, Helmand witnessed some of the fiercest fighting in the country. During the US and British military campaigns, small districts such as Sangin north of the Herat–Kandahar highway became notorious in UK news reports, as a byword for attritional combat. Roads are still littered with checkpoints, many now destroyed; nearly every culvert became a potential bomb site, often rigged with homemade devices fashioned from pressure cookers, samovars, and water boilers. The British established their main base at Camp Bastion, which was later joined by the USA's Camp Leatherneck, to form NATO's largest military installations in the country. Helmand later saw ferocious combat in 2021 when the Taliban came back to power (see the film *Retrograde*; page 288).

Today, Helmand is at peace, as the new government has removed both the conflict and the poppy production. Yet the infrastructure and the people have been battered and it is taking time to recover. Compared with other areas of Afghanistan, Helmand is a province where the Pashtun hospitality, while felt deeply, comes with a slice of wariness, understandable after decades of conflict.

LASHKAR GAH Lashkar Gah, the provincial capital, lies at the conflux of the Arghandab and Helmand rivers about 40km from the Herat–Kandahar highway. The city has little to keep the visitor except the incredible Bost arch.

The **Department of Information and Culture** (⊕ 08.00–16.00 Sat–Wed, 08.00–14.00 Thu) is south of the stadium, just west of Cinema Chowk. Even if you aren't spending a night, stop here for permission to visit Bost, as the ruins lie within a Taliban military compound. Once at the Bost compound, you will be issued with a Taliban soldier or two to escort you on your visit.

Getting there and away There's an airport, but no flights. All transport arrives/leaves from the **Kandahar hada** at the east end of the town near the new mosque: you'll find shared taxis for Kandahar (400AFN; 3hrs), Herat (1,000AFN; 7hrs) and Kabul (1,500AFN; 12hrs).

Where to stay and eat Shah Jahan ($$) and Ameri ($$) are among the best of the restaurants clustered north of Cinema Chowk. Alternatively, further south is **Simni** (or Samimee) **Restaurant** ($$) near Minar Chowk. All offer the usual Afghan dishes.

Helmand Star Hotel Near Qumandani Chowk, opposite the cemetery; m 7037 56616. The only place authorities will let visitors stay in Lashkar Gah is the worst-value accommodation in Afghanistan. The staff are friendly & welcoming, but the basic cell-like rooms give off the vibe of a borstal. Pack mosquito spray as the little bloodsuckers love this place. Squat toilet, no AC, attached bathroom, security; b/fast inc. **$$$**

Other practicalities The best medical facility is the Italian-run **emergency hospital** (w en.emergency.it) southwest of the governor's office and the stadium. **Pharmacies** can be found in an area opposite the Al Fataha Jami Mosque.

BOST (Roughly 10km south of Lashkar Gah on a bumpy road past the old airport; ⊕ 08.00–16.00; free – see above for permission to visit) Located at a commanding position at the confluence of the Helmand and Arghandab rivers, Bost was once one of southern Afghanistan's most powerful cities. Today it is a partially excavated and atmospheric ruin, but during the Ghaznavid (page 204) and Ghorid (page 189) empires, it was a capital and cultural centre, influenced by Persia, India and central Asia. Its wealth stemmed from its junction at two great rivers and the fertile agricultural lands and once-famous gardens that surrounded it.

The highlight is the **Bost Arch** – a colossal and remarkably well-preserved pointed arch that once marked the entrance to a royal palace or mosque. Its intricate brickwork and sheer scale make it one of Afghanistan's architectural wonders, one so iconic that it appears on the 100 Afghani banknote. In recent years, the arch has been bricked up at the base – part conservation, part security measure – but it remains an awe-inspiring sight, rising starkly from the scrubby desert landscape. Behind the arch lies a fascinating, if crumbling, complex of ruins. In one corner, you can descend through four levels of chambers into what was likely a storage or administrative area. These underground vaults – pitch dark, dank, dripping with moisture, and thick with the soft fluttering wings of bats – are filled with an eerie, unforgettable atmosphere.

A taxi there and back including an hour to look around should cost around 1,000AFN (ask for Qala e Bost – the fortress of Bost).

GHAZNI

Ghazni's name comes from the Persian *ganj* (treasure) and even now, a millennia after its heyday, it still offers riches for the visitor. Located along the road between Kandahar and Kabul, Ghazni in the 10th and 11th centuries was the pre-eminent city in the south and outshone its two neighbours. As the capital of the Ghaznavid Empire (page 204), it ruled over an area that stretched from the Himalaya to the Caspian Sea, the largest empire ever ruled by a people based in what is now Afghanistan.

Its golden age extended from 998CE to 1030 when Sultan Mahmud Ghaznawi (or Mahmud of Ghazni) created an empire over 17 major campaigns across the subcontinent and central Asia, bringing untold wealth and prestige to Ghazni. After Mahmud's death the empire slowly declined, and in 1151 Ghazni was captured by the Ghorids, who moved its wealth, artisans, bricks and tilework en masse to their capital in Ghor (page 189), although they did leave a few outstanding monuments behind.

Even as Ghazni declined, its position as a gateway to Kabul lent it strategic importance. At one time the great fort of Ghazni was deemed impregnable, although a British expeditionary force successfully stormed it in the summer of 1839 on their way to the doomed occupation of Afghanistan during the First Anglo–Afghan War.

Ghazni's historical importance was recognised when it was named the SAARC (South Asian Association for Regional Cooperation) City of Culture in 2013. It's well worth a day trip from Kabul or a stop between Kandahar and Kabul.

Getting there and away The **Kandahar hada**, 2km south of the citadel on the main highway, has shared taxis (800AFN; 6hrs) to/from Kandahar while the **Kabul hada**, 2km north of the citadel just before the Gardez turn-off, has shared taxis (400AFN; 3hrs) to/from Kabul and Gardez.

Tourist information and registration The **Department of Information and Culture** (⏱ 08.00–16.00 Sat–Wed, 08.00–14.00 Thu) is located within the group of ministry buildings 750m due south of the fort. Permission is required if you wish to visit the minarets, fort or tomb. The energetic historian from the department may insist on accompanying you.

6 | KANDAHAR AND SOUTHERN AFGHANISTAN

THE GHAZNAVIDS

Afghanistan may be nicknamed the 'Graveyard of Empires', but not a few empires were homegrown, producing dynasties that reigned far and wide for a couple of hundred years before another came to kick them off the top of the hill. The Ghaznavids rose to be one of the greatest, and were among the hardest to fall.

In the 10th century, Ghazni like much of Afghanistan was under the Samanid Empire based in far-off Bukhara. There was constant pressure from the Saffarids to the west, and so the Samanids decided to bring in mamluks to reinforce their army. Mamluks (Turkic 'slave soldiers') were first used by the Abbasid caliphs in the 830s CE, but they rose to become powerful military dynasties of their own.

In a power vacuum in Bukhara, created by the death of ruler Abd al-Milik in 961CE, mamluk commander Alp-Tegin made a play for the throne, lost, then captured Ghazni. It changed hands a couple of times before Alp-Tegin's son-in-law, the mamluk Sabuktigin, took over, and the Ghaznavid Empire was on its way. Sabuktigin took Kabul from its last Indian ruler in 988CE and imposed Islam. His son Mahmud conquered Herat and much of the rest of Khurasan, then went to the caliph in Baghdad to confirm his legitimacy as ruler; Caliph Al-Kadir Billah granted him a robe of honour and the title Yamin-ad-Dawla, the 'Right Arm of the State'.

Mahmud the Great, who ruled from 998 to 1030, actually preferred to be known as the 'Shadow of God on Earth'. He had a cavalry of Arabian horses and used it to take eastern Persia and the rest of the Samanid Empire, eventually extending his own realm from the border of Azerbaijan to Rajasthan. The Shadow of God led his army into northern India 17 times, introducing Islam, ravaging Mathura (then the richest city in India), and pillaging temple treasures, and earning himself the sobriquet the 'Idol-Breaker'. He became the first Muslim ruler to use war elephants.

He became immensely wealthy along the way, making Ghazni into the brilliant culture capital of its day, a Persian-speaking rival of Baghdad, building splendid mosques, palaces, caravanserais and founding universities of mathematics, religion, the humanities and medicine. He transported entire libraries to Ghazni and attracted the best and brightest scholars and poets, among them Ferdowsi (page 286) and the brilliant al-Biruni (973–1050CE), historian, scholar, linguist, scientist and the 'Father of Comparative Religions'.

His twin sons quarrelled over the throne, blinded and imprisoned one another, and were defeated by the Seljuks, who took much of the western half of the Ghaznavid Empire. Under the rule of Mahmud's calligrapher grandson Ibrahim, Ghazni enjoyed a second period of peace at home while continuing to plunder India; Mas'ud III followed, without causing much notice, and was followed by the last Ghaznavid Sultan Bahram Shah, a cruel and obnoxious coward, who in 1151 brought about Ghazni's destruction at the hands of his Ghorid vassal, Ala al-Din Husayn (page 189), although Bahram escaped to Lahore. There was more to and fro between the Ghaznavids and Ghorids as Ghazni was rebuilt. Briefly, the Khwarezmian Empire took charge, before the city was destroyed (again) by Ögedei Khan, son of Genghis.

When the future Mughal Emperor Babur passed through Ghazni in 1504, he was unimpressed and wondered what all the fuss had been about.

Where to stay and eat

Uranus Guesthouse Near the police station, Bazazi Rd; m 7772 31901. The pick in Ghazni. This very simple place has friendly staff & simple rooms with attached bathrooms. Downstairs is a lively chaikhana serving the usual Afghan staples. Good central location; no security, squat toilets, AC. B/fast inc. **$$**

Qambar Bargah Near Chowk Yadgah, Bazazi Rd; m 7928 68282. The best of a clutch of restaurants on the same street, Qambar Bargah offers a wider selection of the usual Afghan fare you'll find in the chaikhanas, plus passable pizzas. They have a wide range of 'mojitos' & fresh juices. The mojitos are non-alcoholic, of course, but come in a glass with a salted rim. **$$**

What to see and do

Ghazni Fort (City centre; ⊕ always; free) It's been said 'those who have Ghazni have Kabul', and it's impossible to miss this fort looming 45m tall over the city. It was there during the city's heyday, and rebuilt in the 13th century, but now gets by minus most of its original 32 towers (one collapsed in a rainstorm in 2019). People still live within the fort, but visitors are free to come and wander around albeit being respectful of the people living there. The walls offer great views of the valley from the upper reaches, a nice spot when the light is soft at the end of the day.

Minarets (1km north of the fort, ask for *minar*; ⊕ always) These two 12th-century minarets, among the very few remnants of the once-great Ghaznavid Empire, are the highlight of a visit to Ghazni. Known as the Mas'ud III Minaret and the Bahram Shah Minaret, they are named after the kings who commissioned them and were once part of a much larger complex of religious buildings and palaces. They now sit on a plain dotted with graves and the odd burnt-out Russian tank. The minarets used to be much taller, but their top halves crumbled in an earthquake in 1902. The now 20m towers are built from mud-fired bricks and decorated with intricate geometric patterns. Preservation has been minimal.

Tomb of Mahmud of Ghazni (3km from the fort on the main road to Kabul, on the left-hand side – signposted at time of writing; ⊕ during daylight hours; free) This tranquil spot is the last resting place of the great 11th-century Ghaznavid ruler and a great place to escape the hustle of the city. The wonderfully intricate doors of the tomb are over 150 years old but are not original. The originals were reputedly taken in 1026 by Mahmud as spoil from the temple of Somnath in Gujarat. Over 800 years later when the British and Indian troops took Ghazni, the doors were taken and 'returned' to Agra in India, where they remain to this day.

7

Herat and Western Afghanistan

Western Afghanistan stretches from the edge of the Hindu Kush to the Iranian border, a landscape shaped by the great rivers that flow down from the mountains – most notably the Hari Rud, the Farah Rud and the Helmand. In the past, this was part of the eastern Persian region known as Khorasan, the 'land of the rising sun'. Even today, it retains a distinct identity, with strong Persian influence in its language, culture and architecture.

This is a land of domed houses, with ingenious windcatchers designed to temper the fierce summer heat, and of the legendary 'wind of 120 days' – Sadobist Roozeh – which sweeps across its deserts in the summer. The verdant farmland irrigated by the Hari Rud and Farah Rud contrasts starkly with the parched landscapes of the surrounding deserts.

Herat, Afghanistan's cultural capital, is the heart of western Afghanistan. A jewel of the Timurid Empire, once nicknamed the 'Pearl of Khorasan', Herat is the country's most architecturally complete city, boasting some of the finest monuments of Islamic art and architecture anywhere in central Asia. Beyond Herat lie the provinces of Farah and Nimruz, where traces of the old Sistan kingdom linger in rarely visited deserts, caravanserais and ruined forts. The once populous Sistan Basin is now mostly empty, a casualty of water shortages and environmental change. These southern expanses remain some of Afghanistan's least explored areas. With Iran and Turkmenistan just a few hours' drive from Herat, western Afghanistan is also a natural entry or exit point for travellers on Silk Road adventures.

HERAT

> If anyone asks thee which is the pleasantest of cities, thou mayest answer him aright that it is Herat. For the world is like the sea, and the province of Khurasan like a pearl-oyster therein, the city of Herat being as the pearl in the middle of the oyster.
>
> Rumi

Set on the fertile plain of the Hari Rud River, Herat is Afghanistan's third largest city (population 580,000) and one that for 2,000 years played a key role in central Asian and Persian history, where its strategic location and mild climate made it a prize for every ambitious ruler. In the 15th century, the descendants of Timur (Tamerlane) made it the Renaissance Florence of the Muslim world, patronising the greatest architects, poets and artists of the day. It's the one Afghan city that still has the power to evoke the Silk Road of old, so much so that Herat is on UNESCO's World Heritage Tentative List.

It is a well-ordered city of pine-shaded avenues and gardens, where people dine late into the evening. Restaurants often serve meals in courtyards or open-air pavilions,

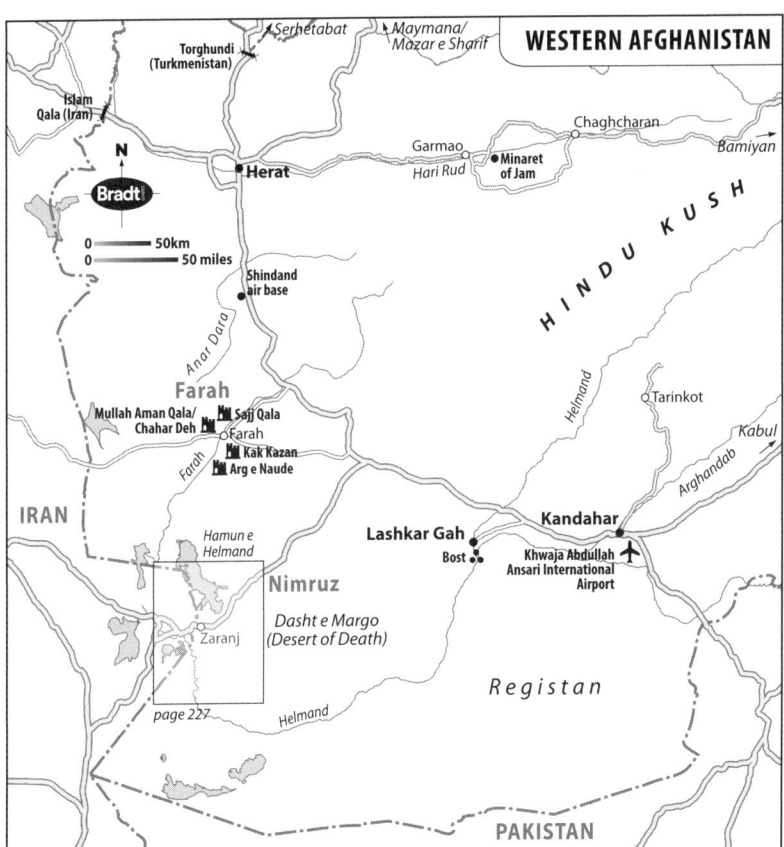

offering a level of refinement rare elsewhere in the country. Iranian influence is immediately visible. Women are more likely to wear a chador rather than a burqa, Iranian-branded goods fill the markets, and saffron – cultivated in fields outside the city – is a proud local speciality and rivals Iran's own. Food here is subtly different too, drawing on Persian flavours and traditions that echo Herat's long-standing ties across the border.

Herat has long been famous for its craftmanship including handmade tiles, still produced in a workshop by the Friday Mosque, and for its silk – in the old days, they say there were at least two weavers in every household. The lush groves of mulberry trees around the city provide food for the silkworms; raising them is often the work of women, although today their craft is threatened by cheap imports from Pakistan and China, which charge a fraction of the price of a handwoven silk scarf from Herat.

Herat's extensive array of world-class monuments, crafts and Persian culture make for a heady mix. This is a city to savour; lingering an extra day, wandering the alleyways of the old city and discovering hidden caravanserais will be a highlight of your travels in Afghanistan.

HISTORY
Persians, Greeks and early Muslim dynasties Herat was first mentioned as 'Haraewa' in the *Avesta* (page 240), but it was better known as Aria or Ariana (the

name of Afghanistan's national airline) recalling the Indo-Aryans who came through around 1500BCE. By the 6th century BCE Ariana was a wealthy satrapy of the Persian Achaemenid Empire, equipped with a sophisticated underground irrigation system; Herodotus called it the 'breadbasket of central Asia'. When Alexander the Great showed up in 330BCE, Herat's governor Satibarzanes submitted to save the city, then massacred the small garrison Alexander left behind. Furious, Alexander sent troops to put down the insurrection under his oldest commander, Erigyius. When the battle that followed reached a stalemate, Satibarzanes threw aside his helmet and challenged the Greeks to a one-on-one combat. Erigyius accepted, threw off his helmet to reveal a shock of white hair, and drove his lance through Satibarzanes' throat.

Herat's location, linked in the west to Persia and the Mediterranean, north to Merv and Bukhara, southeast to India via Kandahar, and east to Balkh, Samarkand and China, made it a key trading hub. It prospered under the Seleucids, who built the first citadel, followed by the Parthians and Hephthalites. A Christian bishop was noted in the 5th century CE. It briefly, in 659–61CE, marked the westernmost extent of China, under the Tang dynasty. Muslim and Arab tribes fought for it, but Herat would resort to its Zoroastrianism once they were out of sight, until 870CE when it was definitely claimed for Islam under the Saffarids of Sistan. Even so, travellers noted a church and Zoroastrian fire temple a century later.

Herat came under the Samanids of Bukhara, then in 998CE the Ghaznavids took Herat, a time when the city produced Abdullah Ansari, the 'Sage of Herat' (1006–88), one of the first Sufi scholar-poets to write in Persian and Arabic. He was famous for loving cats, and left behind two classics, *Munajat Namah* (Dialogues with God) and *Kashf al-Asrar* (The Unveiling of Secrets). His shrine, Gazar Gah, remains one of Herat's most popular sights (page 221).

In 1040, the Ghaznavids were replaced by Seljuk Turks. Herat especially prospered under the next dynasty, the Ghorids (page 189); in 1175, the Persian historian Hamdallah Mustawfi counted 359 colleges, 12,000 shops, 6,000 bath-houses, caravanserais, mills, a dervish convent and a fire temple. The Ghorids built the Friday Mosque and the Pol e Malan bridge. Herat was renowned for metalwork and textiles, grapes and wine.

Under the Mongols Herat then came briefly under the Khwarazmian shahs, former vassals of the Seljuks. And then in 1219 came Tolui Khan, son of Genghis. Tolui liked Herat and offered it a chance to surrender, but the Khwarazmian shah sultan replied by killing Tolui's messenger. After the siege that followed, the Mongols slayed 10,000 of the sultan's soldiers and supporters, but when the surviving Herati submitted, Tolui installed a Mongol governor and left the city in peace. But afterwards, the Khwarazmian Shahs made the same mistake as Satibarzanes: they killed the Mongol governor.

Genghis scolded his son for his leniency and ordered his army to leave no-one alive. Herat held out for six months before the great massacre of more than 1,600,000. The Mongols went back a few months later to see if anyone had survived and killed another 3,000. But Herat soon recovered, rebuilt by Shams-uddin Mohammed, a member of the Kartid dynasty, who took over most of Khorasan as vassals of the Mongol emperor (although the emperor didn't really trust him and slipped him a poisoned watermelon in the bath).

Timurids By 1381, when Timur passed through on his way to conquer Persia, Herat had regained much of its former splendour. This time the ruler surrendered, but Timur sacked the city anyway, took all the treasure and pulled down the walls

– only to realise he might have been a bit hasty. He ordered his eldest son Miran Shah to rebuild Herat's walls, then in 1396 sent his fourth son, Shah Rukh, from Samarkand to govern it.

Shah Rukh was seduced by the city's charms and decided to stay put, making Herat the centre of an empire that stretched from the Tigris to China. Keen to repair the damage caused by his father, Shah Rukh promoted stability and diplomatic relations. He and his wife, Gowhar Shad (page 211), were the power couple of their day, the Medici of Herat, patronising a remarkable 15th-century flowering of the arts. They sent their eldest son, Ulugh Beg, then only 16 but already a mathematical prodigy, to govern Samarkand, where he built his famous observatory and became one of the most important astronomers of the Middle Ages. Their younger son Baysanghor remained in Herat where he founded the Kitabkhana, an academy of 200 artists and calligraphers who produced the beautiful illuminated books his father loved, culminating in the stupendous 700-page Baysanghor's *Shahnameh* (1430), now in Tehran's Golestan Palace Museum.

A succession battle followed, leaving Abu Said Mirza, son of the third son of Timur, in charge of Herat and Khorasan until 1469, although he spent most of his time fighting off rivals and was noted for his exceptional cruelty to anyone who crossed him. He divided his lands between four of his many sons; but eventually,

7 | HERAT AND WESTERN AFGHANISTAN

and fortunately for Herat, another great grandson of Timur, Sultan Husayn Bayqara (1468–1506), fought his way to the top. Husayn Bayqara was a poet, who oversaw the apogee of the fusion of Turko-Mongol and Persian cultures. His vizier, the humanist poet Mir Ali-Shir Nava'i (page 58), was a great builder and patron of the arts, a magnet to the brightest stars of the age, including the great Sufi poet scholar Nur ad-Din Abd ar-Rahman Jami (1414–92), 'the foremost authority of the age in all of the sciences and as a poet of such renown that the mere mention of his name is a source of blessing' according to Babur. Herat's Kitabkhana reached new heights under the greatest Persian miniaturist of them all, Kamal al-Din Bihzad (c1455–1535).

After being forced from Samarkand, Babur (page 136) arrived in Herat in 1505 hoping to encourage Husayn Bayqara to go to war with him against his Uzbek enemy Shaybani, but he soon died, and all his sons wanted to do was drink (their father had banned wine during his reign). Babur stayed with his cousins for two months, absorbing the art, poetry and beauty of the gardens of Islam's culture capital.

After the Timurids In 1507, the Uzbeks occupied Herat, but Shah Isma'il, founder of the Persian Safavid dynasty, slew Shaybani and took over in 1510. The Safavids considered Herat the greatest of their provincial cities. In 1716, the Abdali confederation of Pashtun tribes (soon to become the Durrani) revolted, creating the Sadozai Sultanate of Herat. The Persians took it back in 1732 until Ahmad Shah Durrani seized it in 1747, only for it to become an independent city-state.

Qajar Iran briefly captured Herat in 1816, withdrew, then besieged the city again in 1837 with the backing of Russia; Eldred Pottinger, a young Bombay Army officer who happened to be undercover in Herat at the time, helped the defenders hold out for a year and became famous in Britain as the 'Hero of Herat'. The city definitively became part of Afghanistan in 1863 when Dost Mohammed conquered it just before his death.

20th–21st centuries Although the US built Herat's airport in the 1960s, there were always more Russians in the city during the Cold War, and they were widely despised. When the hard-line Khalq communists took over Afghanistan, the army in Herat mutinied on 29 March 1979. Hundreds of locals joined the soldiers, killing government officials and Soviet advisors and their families. The Taraki government blamed the Iranians, who had thrown out the shah the month before, and asked Moscow for aid; Moscow airlifted armour and heavy weapons into nearby Shindand air base and bombed Herat from the air, leaving anywhere between 3,000 to 25,000 dead in less than a week. No-one knows for sure. It was the worst violence in Afghanistan in 50 years, but a preview of coming events.

One mutineer, Captain Ismail Khan, a Tajik from Herat, escaped into the hills and rallied the mujahideen, joining the Northern Alliance. In 1992, Khan, now nicknamed the 'Lion of Herat', finally captured the city and became governor of the province. He defended it against the Taliban until September 1995, when he fled to Iran.

After Kabul, Herat is the most liberal city in Afghanistan, and Taliban rule didn't go down well. In early November 2001, Khan with his 5,000-strong militia co-ordinated with the US, UK and Iranian Special Forces to stage an uprising against the Taliban; just as Khan predicted, once the undercover Iranian commandos started a protest, the Heratis quickly joined as the US bombed Taliban targets around the city. Karzai appointed Khan governor, and he ran Herat as his own fief, keeping the lucrative customs fees on goods from Iran to pay workers and restore

GOWHAR SHAD

Daughter of a high-ranking member of Timur's court, Gowhar Shad ('Shining Jewel') was born in the 1370s into a society still influenced by Mongol tradition, where a woman could ride horseback beside men and go into battle. One of her father's ancestors had saved the life of Genghis Khan, who granted the family their title 'Tarkhan', which meant they never had to pay tax. She became the favourite wife of Shah Rukh, and actively patronised the best architect of the day, Qavam al Din Shirazi, and had him build a mosque in Mashad (Iran) and the spectacular Musallah madrasa in Herat.

Robert Byron wrote that, when he visited Herat in 1933, people were still telling stories about her. A famous one has it that when the Musallah was completed, Gowhar Shad asked all the students to exit one day so she and 200 maidens of her court could tour the building; one student, however, had fallen asleep and stayed behind, and when he realised what was occurring, he peeped through a small window, long enough for a lady 'with ruby lips' to fall in love with him and slip into his room. When Gowhar Shad found out, rather than condemn the couple, she married all her ladies to the students and gave all the newlyweds gifts, on the condition that they only met one night a week, so the students could keep up their studies.

Gowhar Shad's son Baysanghor, the great art patron, died from the family vice, drink, leaving several sons; she openly favoured one, Ala al-Dawla, over her other grandson, Ulugh Beg's son Abd-al-Latif – who was Shah Rukh's favourite. When Abd-al-Latif went off in a huff to Samarkand, it broke her husband's heart, and Gowhar Shad, in spite of her age, rode to Samarkand in the winter to bring him back to Herat.

Leaving Ala al-Dawla in charge of Herat, Abd-al-Latif accompanied Shah Rukh and Gowhar Shad to Ray, Persia where Shah Rukh died in 1447. Abd-al-Latif brought his grandfather's body back to Herat but, still angry at his grandmother made her walk the whole way back to Herat. In the messy decade that followed, Abd-al-Latif defeated his father Ulugh Beg in a battle, then had a servant kill him. He in turn was killed by Ulugh Beg's servant.

Another son of Baysanghor, Abul-Qasim Babur Mirza, ruled Herat until he died of alcoholism. Gowhar Shad then favoured Ala al-Dawla's son Ibrahim. When Abu Said, a great-grandson of Timur, came to take Herat, Ibrahim held out in the citadel, and Abu Said, suspecting Gowhar Shad (who was then over 80) of intrigue, had her executed.

---

public services rather than passing them on to Kabul. When Karzai dismissed him in 2004, it led to widespread protests. Khan later served as Minister of Energy and again took refuge in Iran when the Taliban returned in 2021.

But history was not finished with Herat: four earthquakes in October 2023 shook the province, leaving 1,500 dead, flattening villages and damaging the Timurid-era buildings. The last 24 tilemakers by the Friday Mosque are slowly replacing tiles lost in the quake.

GETTING THERE AND AWAY

By air Khwaja Abdullah Ansari International Airport lies 8km south of Herat and is linked with Kabul by both Kam Air and Ariana. On arrival you will be asked to register at a counter. As at all Afghan airports security is tight, so arrive in plenty of time for a departing flight. The Kam Air office and other travel agents are located north of Farhang Park.

There is no public transport to or from the airport – take a taxi (500AFN; 20mins).

By road Transport for **directions south** arrive/leave from the Kabul istga on the northern edge of Herat. Large coaches, minivans and shared taxis arrive/depart from here to Kandahar (1,000–1,700AFN; 9–10hrs) and Kabul (1,900–3,200AFN; 17–20hrs). You may need to buy a ticket in advance from one of the offices for the coaches. This is also the station used by minivans and shared taxis for/from Farah (500–800AFN; 5hrs) and Lashkar Gah (900AFN; 7–8hrs).

For **directions west to the Iranian border**, ask for the Islam Qala istga, a collection of shared taxis at Jami Square, the main junction 1km north of the Musallah Complex. Shared taxis (300AFN; 2hrs) will take you to the border. For **directions north to the Turkmenistan border**, ask for the Torghundi istga, a small area of shared taxis 100m northwest of the Kabul istga. Shared taxis (500AFN; 3hrs) will take you to the border. For **directions north and east** towards Maymana, Mazar e Sharif and Chaghcharan, shared taxis depart less frequently from an area east of the city. They usually leave early in the morning.

A **taxi from the old city** to the istgas for directions south and west would be around 150AFN, for directions west and north around 200AFN.

GETTING AROUND Most of Herat's sights around the old city are walkable. For further distances, take an autorickshaw or a taxi. Traditional Herati **autorickshaws** have an extra-large raised front wheel (apparently for extra manoeuvrability), and are often adorned with pictures of musical instruments and riffs on *Afghan Star* – Afghanistan's 'pop idol' type TV show which was widely popular and first won by a Herati – though they are becoming less visible due to cheaper Chinese imports and the government's ban on music. A rickshaw from the Friday Mosque to the restaurants at Taraqi Park should cost around 50AFN. There is **public transport** but the routes are hard to understand, although the buses that run from the Pol e Malan to Kandahar Chowk might be handy; expect to pay 20AFN one way.

Taxis are turquoise; it costs around 200AFN to Gazar Gah from the Friday Mosque.

TOURIST INFORMATION AND REGISTRATION You'll need to visit the **Department of Information and Culture** (Khaja Ali Movafaq Rd) before taking in the main sights. Your documentation will be checked at the citadel, the Friday Mosque, Gazar Gah and the Musallah Complex. If you plan to visit the Minaret of Jam (page 190) from Herat, then you will need to notify the department here, too.

ORIENTATION Herat is set on a wide plain watered by the increasingly feeble Hari Rud River, which runs through the southern suburbs. The old city occupies the alleyways around the Char Su crossroads with the Friday Mosque to the east and the citadel, the Qala Ikhtiyaruddin, to the north. North of the citadel rise the minarets of Musallah Complex and the hills, with the large parks and the Jihad Museum on their lower slopes. These hills mark the edge of the Persian world and the start of central Asia.

East and north of the old city is Shahre Nau, the new town which sprang up during the early 20th century, containing administrative buildings and some hotels. Further east is Taraqi Park, shaded by pine trees introduced from America in the 1950s. This area is filled with restaurants and is regularly the scene of Afghanistan's liveliest nightlife. Taraqi Park is also the location of the Park Hotel (currently closed), the original Herat hotel frequented by Robert Byron in the 1930s. If tourism returns to Afghanistan, we hope it will reopen.

WHERE TO STAY After Kabul, Herat has the best hotels in Afghanistan. None matches Kabul's Grand Hotel, but if you have driven to Herat from any direction you can expect a big step up in comfort. It also offers the best value, with decent rooms costing what you might pay for a spartan box in a remote provincial capital. Air conditioning is a must in the summer and most hotels come with a fridge and include bottles of water.

Arg Hotel [map, page 209] Bagh e Azadi St, opposite Herat University; m 7992 30000; w arghotel.af. Owned by the same people as the Tejarat, Arg has the feel of a real hotel, the VIP rooms furnished with nice sofas. There's also a gym & a sauna (times split for men & women). Big security; AC; Western-style toilets; b/fast inc. **$$$**

Nazary International Hotel [217 D2] Walayat St, opposite the Department of Information & Culture; m 7993 51899; w nazaryhotel.com. This large, though slightly soulless, 5-storey hotel in the centre of Shahre Nau offers comfortable en-suite rooms. AC; security; b/fast inc. **$$$**

Tejarat International Hotel [217 C2] Chowk e Golha, Imam Moslim St 4; ✆ 4022 22314; m 7994 25555; w tejarathotel.af. A real hotel where almost everything works all of the time in a great location just outside the old city. Large, comfortable rooms with mod cons like kettles & hairdryers. Security; sauna; AC; b/fast inc. **$$$**

Apple and Asil hotels [217 C2] Near Chowk e Golha, down an alleyway in front of Fahim Supermarket; m 7811 44000, 7905 50006; f asilhotel1. These 2 simple little hotels, owned by the same people, sit side by side down a small alley north of the old city. The Asil is newer, but Apple has the more recognisable logo – lifted straight from the tech company, it seems, intellectual property rights not being a huge concern in Herat. Mixture of rooms, some with sofas, some with Western-style toilets; AC; b/fast inc. **$$**

Kakh Hotel [217 A2] Shahre Nau, Jada e Id Gah, south of Shirkat e Asia Farma; m 7998 28245, 7806 31010; e kakhhotel@yahoo.com, telegram@ kakhhotel. Mini apartments only, with sofas & kitchens. A good option for families or groups of 3 or 4. AC; Western- & local-style toilets. **$$**

Mowafaq Hotel [217 C2] Chowk e Golha; m 7956 16957; e mowafaq@yahoo.com. Long-standing Herat hotel in a great location in need of some TLC. Hard beds, no AC & bathrooms that look like they were last renovated under Dr Najibullah's rule. However, some rooms have balconies overlooking the street, great for people-watching. It's noisy during the day, but Herat is not New York so it is quiet at night. Some Western-style toilets. **$$**

WHERE TO EAT AND DRINK Herat offers the widest selection of places outside of Kabul and the Persian influence is strong. In most of Afghanistan the choice of kebab might be simply meat or chicken; Herati restaurants offer a multitude of cuts and styles including *shashlik*, *shami*, *kofta*, *juju* and *kobida*, and they are likely to be served with rice rather than bread. Look out for platters with a variety of dishes (a good-value way for a group to share), *dogh watana* (homemade dogh) and Herati rice with *zereshk* (barberries) and saffron. Waiters often bring soups, salads, desserts and cans of soft drink without you ordering them. Some are complimentary and some not, but if you don't want them just send them back.

There is a wide selection of places to eat around Taraqi Park which are often open as late as 23.00 in summer. Options in the old city are usually simple affairs selling **kebabs** [214 B4] which close at dusk when the shops do, with the exception of a new **simple restaurant in an old restored water cistern** ($) [217 B6] just south of Char Su. There are also **fruit stands** [214 C3] that open late on the main road south of most of the hotels.

7 | HERAT AND WESTERN AFGHANISTAN

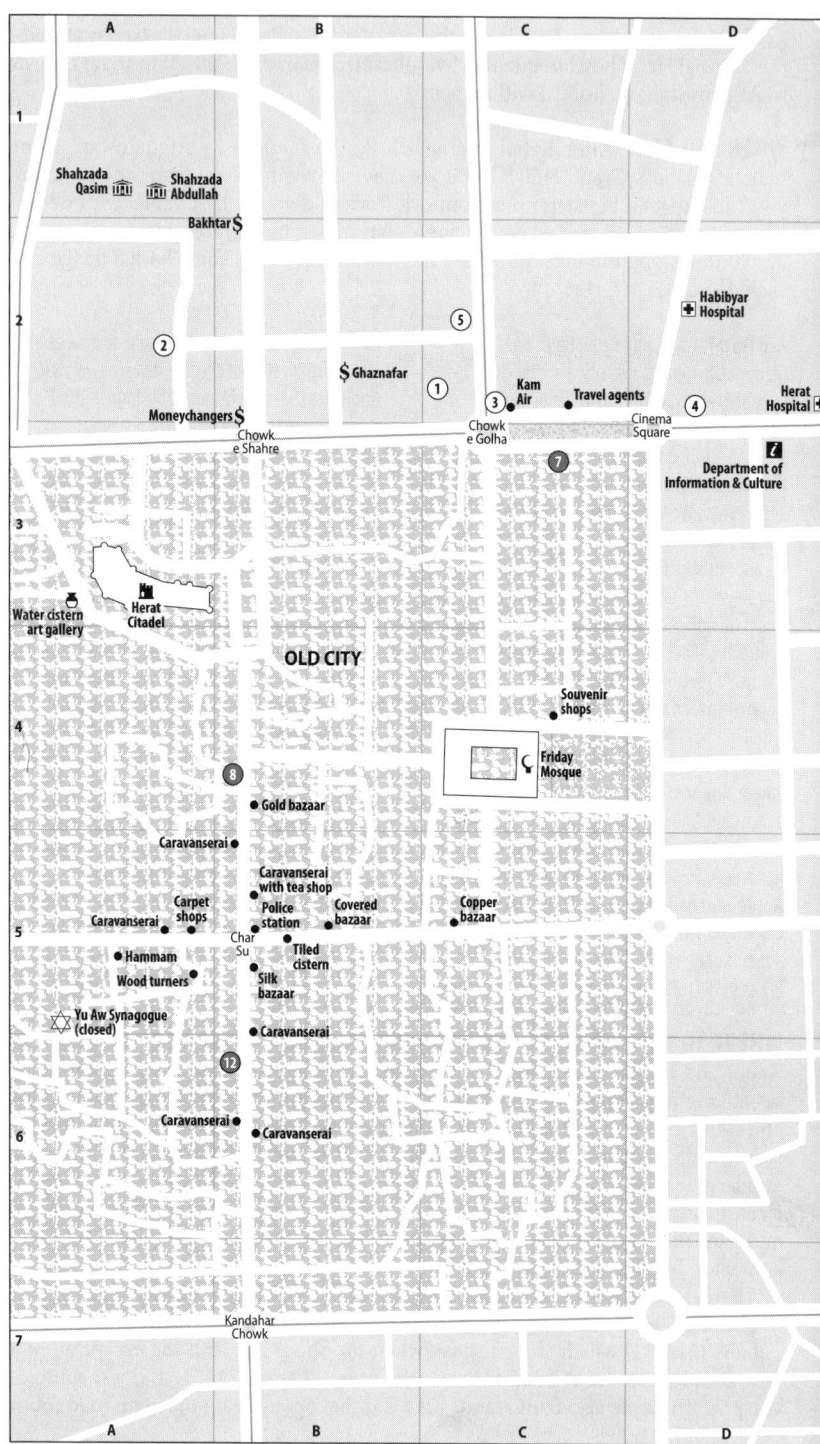

HERAT

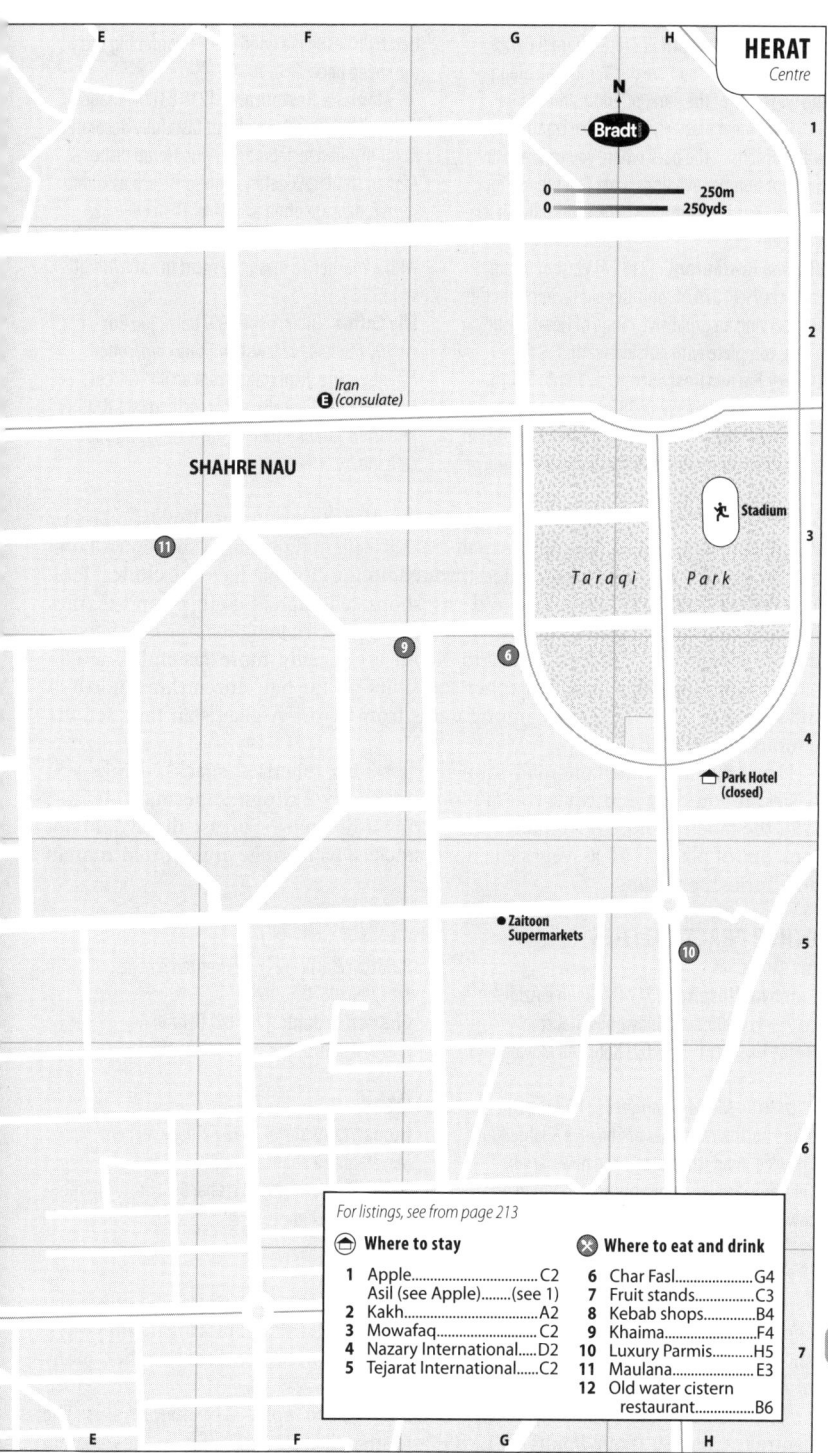

Char Fasl Restaurant [218 G4] Taraqi Park; m 7988 11414. There are restaurants all along the west side of the park, offering similar fare including meat platters, juices & ice cream, most with gardens at the back where you can relax in the cool summer evenings. Char Fasl means 'four seasons' & is an institution here, especially for its ice cream. $$

Khaima Restaurant [218 F4] West of Taraqi Park; m 7994 97474. Another old favourite in the area serving an expansive range of Herati dishes & juices, complete with outside seating. $$

Luxury Parmis Restaurant [218 H5] South of Taraqi Park; m 7992 08282. Very popular restaurant with indoor seating & private booths in the garden for reclining. It has a good selection of Herati dishes so is a good place to order big – try the sheep neck. $$

✳ **Maulana Restaurant** [218 E3] Mokhaberat Rd; m 7996 98560. Small but tastefully decorated Rumi-inspired restaurant serving Herati dishes & Afghan staples; vegetarian options such as *korma sabzi* & daal are often available. Their *chainaki* (stew served in a tea pot) is delicious & served with a 'masher' to mash the meat to eat it 'Herati style'. $$

Elly Coffee [map, page 209] Danshjoo Rd; m 7907 84444; w jawshangroup.com/coffee; elly_caffe. Real coffee from an Illy-coffee-inspired café. They also sell French presses & other imported paraphernalia if you are missing your caffeine fix. $

SHOPPING Herat is famous for its aromatic saffron, sold in small plastic jars or metal tins (usually 1, 2, 5 or 10g) which make excellent lightweight souvenirs. Look out for specific saffron shops located throughout the city that have the clinical look and feel of a perfume shop. The old city shops sell Afghan clothing and textiles including burkhas, pakols, pathu shawls and carpets. The gold bazaar is extensive, though designs in Chicken Street in Kabul are usually more tasteful. The silk bazaar is well worth a look. For other souvenirs try the half-dozen shops north of the Friday Mosque [217 C4]; among items from across Afghanistan they sell the famous Herati blue glass.

Herat has a number of small mini-marts selling toiletries, snacks, drinks and basics. If you can't find what you are looking for, try **Zaitoon Supermarkets** [218 G5], the fanciest shop in Afghanistan, starring a sweeping staircase that would not look out of place in a Las Vegas casino. It stocks a wide range of imported Iranian and Turkish products.

OTHER PRACTICALITIES
Medical
Habibyar Hospital [217 D2] Bagh e Azidi Av; m 7994 04000; w habibyarhospital.com
Herat Hospital [217 D2] Kahja Ali Movafaq Rd

Money
Moneychangers [217 B2] gather at the northwest corner of Chowk e Shahre Nau/Chowk e Jihad (the latter is the new name). They are easily recognisable as all seem to wear cowboy hats.

Bakhtar Bank [217 B2] Behzad Av; m 7709 20870
Ghazanfar Bank [217 B2] Behzad Av; m 7978 60070

Other
Iranian Consulate [218 F2] Jade Ali ben Movafagh; w en.mfa.gov.ir
Police station [217 B5] Char Su. Located in the centre of the old city.

WHAT TO SEE AND DO
The old city Herat's kilometre-square old city is the best-preserved medieval centre in Afghanistan, and it's well worth spending half a day exploring its alleyways, shops and caravanserais. Note that it's far less busy and fun on Fridays when many of the shops are closed.

The walls and gates that once surrounded it have been replaced by major roads. The centre is **Char Su** (Four Points) [217 B5] and main streets lead off it in the cardinal directions. Originally the old city was divided into three areas: an administrative centre by the citadel, the religious centre by the Friday Mosque and the commercial heart around Char Su and to the south. Herat used to store water in large **cisterns**, which are no longer used but three still exist. One is now an art gallery [217 A3] (⏱ 08.00–16.00 daily; free) near the citadel entrance; and two lie close to Char Su – one, to the east, is delicately tiled [217 B5] and the other is now a restaurant.

Behind the shops on the main roads are smaller **covered bazaars** and **caravanserais** – places that acted as storage and inns for merchants who travelled to Herat to sell their wares. Beyond these is the maze of alleyways where old traditional Herati families still live. The joy of Herat is getting lost in these serais and narrow lanes, discovering hammams, traditional craftsmen, barbers, tiny community mosques and tea shops. North of Char Su you'll find the **gold bazaar** [217 B4], as well as two caravanserais; the one on the east side of the road has a large entrance (high enough for a camel to enter) with a tea shop [217 B5]. Directly east of Char Su there's a covered bazaar on the north side and the covered **silk bazaar** [217 B5] to the south, while further along the road east is the **copper bazaar** [217 C5].

South of Char Su are a number of well-preserved caravanserais on the east and west sides of the road, and the aforementioned (and wonderful) **restaurant** (page 213) in a restored cistern. At the end of the road is **Kandahar Chowk** [217 B7], complete with a Russian tank in the middle of the roundabout. The tank used to have metal figures of mujahideen fighting the Russians, looking very similar to the diorama at the Jihad Museum (page 219); nowadays they have been replaced by flesh-and-blood young men looking at their phones. West of Char Su are **carpet shops** [217 A5] and another caravanserai. In the alleys southwest of Char Su you'll find wood turners and a local hammam. Further into the alleyways is the **Yu Aw Synagogue** [217 A5] (closed at time of writing) which years ago served Herat's Jewish population.

Friday Mosque [217 C4] (East of the old city; ⏱ dawn–dusk; but not accessible during Friday prayers; free) The main entrance is through the gardens on the east side, but these gates are often locked. Entry is usually via a narrow passageway on the north side, where guards may ask to see your documentation and request you to remove your shoes. It is a wonderful introduction to the mosque as the dark corridor opens into the light of the interior. As you enter, a 13th-century cauldron, once used to store water for ablutions, sits to your left. Photography is generally not an issue.

The Friday Mosque of Herat is one of Afghanistan's finest surviving examples of Islamic architecture and a landmark that reflects the layered history of the city itself. Construction began in the late 12th century under the Ghorids, who established Herat as one of the cultural and religious centres of their empire. Although much of the mosque has been rebuilt and renovated over the centuries, it still retains traces of its earliest Ghorid brickwork, offering a rare glimpse of its original appearance.

The mosque took on much of its current appearance in the 15th century, when Gowhar Shad had it extensively rebuilt and embellished, with the four soaring iwans that surround the courtyard, expanded prayer halls and the intricate tilework that covers its façades. Gowhar Shad's renovations transformed the Friday Mosque into a statement of the Timurid wealth and artistic brilliance that placed Herat at the centre of the Islamic world.

The mosque's design follows the classic four-iwan plan, with vaulted halls opening on to a spacious courtyard. The façades dazzle with polychrome tiles, their deep blues, turquoises and whites catching the changing light throughout the day.

Early morning and dusk are the best times to see the tiles at their most vivid – and to photograph them without the glare of the midday sun.

A unique feature of the mosque is the **tile workshop** (⊕ closed Fri), accessed through a door to the left when facing the mosque from the east gardens. Here, craftsmen continue the centuries-old practice of creating tiles by hand: mixing pigments, sketching designs, painting, and firing in traditional kilns. The tile makers are usually happy to show you their work and even sell you a tile or two as a souvenir. In the courtyard where you enter the workshop, sections of the original Ghorid glazed brickwork survive.

The Friday Mosque remains the centre of worship and spirituality for the city. On Friday at midnight, zikr – an act of Sufi devotion involving rhythmic recitation and movement – is performed in the northwest corner of the mosque, though it is unclear if foreign visitors are permitted to attend. Avoid visiting during midday prayers when the mosque is crowded and access may be restricted

Herat Citadel [217 A3] (Qala Ikhtiyaruddin; north of the old city; ⊕ 08.00–16.00 daily; 500AFN, plus an additional 500AFN to enter the museum) Herat's mighty fortress is sometimes referred to as the 'Citadel of Alexander': local tradition holds that the site was first fortified by Alexander the Great after he captured Herat in 330BCE. While no structures from that period remain, the location's strategic importance ensured that successive empires continued to build upon and expand the citadel over the following two millennia. Although the Ghorids, Khwarazmians and Mongols each left their mark, what survives today largely dates from the Timurids. In later centuries, it remained a stronghold under the Safavids, Mughals and, eventually, the modern Afghan rulers. Its walls have witnessed sieges, conquests and the rise and fall of dynasties. It would have been a familiar sight to Genghis Khan, Tamerlane and Shah Rukh.

The complex consists of two main enclosures: the outer fort, consisting of massive brick walls and 18 towers, some of which rise over 20m tall (note the tower in the northwest corner, which still has Timurid tile work); and the inner fort, a citadel within the citadel which served as a royal palace and administrative heart. By the 20th century, much of the citadel had fallen into ruin after its use as an army barracks and prison. Restoration efforts began in the 1970s, but were interrupted by decades of conflict. Between 2006 and 2011, a major conservation programme was carried out by UNESCO, the Aga Khan Trust for Culture, and the Afghan authorities, stabilising the structure and opening it to visitors. The citadel was slightly damaged by the earthquakes of 2023, although it remains accessible. The restoration work, while preventing deterioration, does leave the citadel looking a little like a reconstruction rather than a restoration. In addition, it was restored in a way that, for security reasons, does not allow for easy access to its vantage points. Views over the old city and surrounding mountains are limited.

Inside the complex, a small well-labelled museum houses archaeological finds from Herat and beyond, including ceramics, coins and textiles. The Department of Culture and Information has also moved a number of artisans into workshops under the south wall of the fortress including a camel-powered mill for grinding sesame seeds into oil and a glass-blowing workshop.

The Musallah Complex (North of the citadel; ⊕ 08.00–16.00 daily; free; at the time of writing, the area is an ongoing archaeological site, so the exact extent of official access is unclear) The Musallah Complex was the grandest of all the projects commissioned in the early 15th century by Queen Gowhar Shad and is one of the most magnificent ensembles of Islamic architecture anywhere in central Asia. Contemporary writers waxed lyrical about its scale and beauty, remarking that it rivalled – if not surpassed – the Registan in Samarkand. At its peak, the complex contained a mosque, madrasas, minarets, caravanserais, and Gowhar Shad's mausoleum, all executed with the finest craftsmanship of the Timurid era. The polychrome tilework, Kufic inscriptions and soaring minarets dazzled visitors.

Tragically, that glory is only a memory. After the fall of the Timurids, the complex fell into disrepair. Then in 1885, during the Panjdeh Incident the Russians, who already conquered much of Turkmenistan, took the fort at Panjdeh (Serhetabat), just over the modern Turkmenistan border, leading to a conflict. The British, fearing Herat would be next, deliberately dynamited the Musallah to give their artillery clear lines of fire, reducing most of it to rubble – not long before the two sides settled the incident diplomatically by agreeing on Afghanistan's northern border. Earthquakes compounded the damage. Travel accounts from the early 20th century by Aurel Stein, Oskar von Niedermayer and Robert Byron recorded the fading remains.

Originally the Musallah boasted around 20 minarets, arranged in pairs flanking the mosque and madrasas. Over the years, one by one they collapsed – in 1932, two fell in an earthquake; two others fell in the mid 20th century. Today only five remain, their slender shafts rising like immense chimneys above the city. From a distance, they may appear like smokestacks, but closer inspection reveals hundreds of intact glazed turquoise and lapis tiles, still gleaming in the sun.

Tomb of Gowhar Shad (In a small enclosed park, where a chowkidar (caretaker) staffs the gate and will unlock the tomb; a small tip is appreciated for this service) The mausoleum has had some restoration work and is in good condition. Its domed ribbed roof once glittered with intricate mosaics and tilework, of which fragments remain, and the interior still displays fine paintwork. Gowhar Shad lies here, along with her son Baysanghor and several other Timurids. Shah Rukh was originally buried here but his body was moved by his son Ulugh Beg to Samarkand, where it lies today. The gardens also contain the tomb of Mir Ali Shir Nava'i, the prime minister of Sultan Husayn Bayqara. One of the five surviving minarets of the Musallah Complex is here too, leaning at an alarming angle. The four other minarets are in a locked compound just north of the mausoleum, and the chowkidar should let you in for a closer inspection – depending on the archaeologists.

Bagh e Mellat and Takht e Safar (Both ⊕ sunrise–sunset daily; free) These two pleasure parks occupy the hills on the north edge of Herat. Takht e Safar was originally a pleasure garden for Sultan Bayqara and was restored under the rule of Ismail Khan for Heratis to picnic and enjoy a small theme park. It is less lively now owing to the ban on women entering the park but the views from the top over Herat are impressive.

Jihad Museum (In Bagh e Mellat; ⊕ 08.00–16.00 Sat–Wed, 08.00–14.00 Thu; 500AFN) The Jihad Museum occupies a striking circular building clad in white and turquoise tiles, inscribed with the names of thousands of martyrs from Herat Province who died in the struggle against Soviet occupation. Outside, the shady gardens are dotted with relics of war: tanks, artillery pieces and armoured personnel carriers (APCs), all reminders of Herat's central role in Afghanistan's resistance. In this respect it is similar to Kabul's Omar Museum (page 134).

Inside are more reminders of the conflict including guns, mines and rockets. The highlight is the vast diorama inside the main hall. This immersive display traces the trajectory of the uprising against Soviet influence, from the first stirrings of resistance in the late 1970s to the battles of the 1980s. Miniature figures of fighters crouching behind sandbags, children with catapults and women in burkhas throwing stones are set in tiny villages set ablaze. Painted backdrops evoke both the brutality of the war and the pride of defiance. It is part theatre, part memorial, and remains one of the most unusual exhibits in the country.

The narrative presented today, however, is carefully managed. While the Taliban celebrate the expulsion of Soviet forces as a national triumph, many of the resistance commanders later became their rivals. Displays that glorify these commanders have been downplayed, and some sections of the museum may be inaccessible. Photography is often restricted and can vary depending on the mood of the staff on duty.

For years, the most remarkable member of staff was a man with an unusual story: a former Russian soldier captured during the 1980s. Given the choice between execution and conversion, he embraced Islam and remained in Herat, eventually working at the Jihad Museum where he guided visitors with surprising candour about his past. His presence embodied the tangled human stories of that war. He has since passed away, but his grave is situated in the grounds of the museum.

Pol e Malan (Malan Bridge) Spanning the wide Hari Rud River just outside Herat, the Pol e Malan is a rare surviving example of Afghanistan's medieval engineering. Its 22 stone arches bear a striking resemblance to the famous bridges of Isfahan in Iran, such as the Si-o-se Pol. But the Pol e Malan is over twice as old. Legends claim it was first built around 900CE by two sisters who mixed eggshells into the mortar to strengthen the clay. The existing structure dates mostly from the early 12th-century Ghorid period. Since then it has withstood centuries of floods and seasonal surges.

Until the 1960s, Pol e Malan was the only reliable crossing over the Hari Rud in this part of western Afghanistan. Today, while modern roads and bridges have taken over much of its function, Pol e Malan remains a powerful symbol of Herat's historical significance and resilience. You can stop to admire the bridge from either bank, especially around sunset, when the arches cast dramatic reflections in the water below. The setting is peaceful, with the views of distant hills offering a glimpse of rural Afghan life little changed for centuries.

Buzkashi Buzkashi is played most Fridays between November and mid-March. The 'new' buzkashi ground is south of the road heading northeast out of the city towards Gazar Gah (see opposite). The entrance is not clear but, if buzkashi is being played, follow the crowd or the noise. The 'old' buzkashi ground, near the banks of the Hari Rud, is often used for training, and on days other than Friday the chapandaz can be seen working out their horses. Keep an eye out if visiting the Pol e Malan bridge.

Herat's shrines

> Stretch a leg in Herat and you will poke a poet in the ass.
>
> Babur

Herat's reputation as the cultural capital of Afghanistan is partly due to its long history as a centre of Sufi mystics, poets and scholars. These roles are never separate but intertwined. As such, the city's most atmospheric, ancient and loved buildings are shrines to these revered men. The casual visitor might run a risk of shrine fatigue, however; if you visit any, choose Gazar Gah and the delicately beautiful shrines known as Shahzada Abdullah and Shahzada Qasim, or the **Shahzadagan Tombs**.

✱ *Gazar Gah* (Northeast edge of Herat; ⏰ sunrise–sunset daily; free) This is one of Afghanistan's most beloved shrines and among the most atmospheric places in the entire country. At its heart lies the tomb of Abdullah Ansari (1006–88), the great Sufi 'Sage of Herat'. Ansari's writings and teachings stressed humility, devotion and divine love, and his influence spread widely across the Islamic world. For centuries pilgrims have travelled to Gazar Gah to pay their respects, and that sense of reverence is still palpable today. An inscription on his shrine reads 'The tombstone of his sepulchre is a beautiful cypress which, by its excessive beauty, has so moved the angels that they exclaim and cry like turtle doves.'

The shrine complex you see today was developed under the Timurids, when the indefatigable Gowhar Shad commissioned an impressive courtyard complex with monumental gates, tiled iwans, and shaded arcades around the tomb. The artistry of this period – delicate tilework in blue, turquoise and white – can still be glimpsed in places. Look up to see the hand-painted pomegranates on the ceiling at the entrance to the compound. Upon entering the shrine, you will take off your shoes and pass security guards and the Sufis who live at the shrine. Men and women must then split up and walk along separate sides to the glass-covered tomb of Abdullah Ansari in the shade of an ilex tree. Prayers are often made at the tomb. Pilgrims will often turn to face Mecca and pray again. It is common for women to write prayers on rags and tie them to the tree and lattice work around the tomb. The atmosphere is heavy with devotion: pilgrims murmur prayers and recite verses. Many Afghans consider it the most sacred place in Herat.

Several other notable figures are buried within the complex, including Dost Mohammad Khan, the Amir of Afghanistan (1826–63), who rests here beside poets, saints and scholars. This layering of history – from medieval Sufi mystics to modern rulers – underscores Gazar Gah's dual role as a spiritual centre and site of national memory.

Southwest of the shrine is a garden containing the **Namakdan pavilion** (so named in Dari because it resembles a salt cellar), built under the reign of Bayqara. When his vizier Mir Ali Shah Nava'i retired, he took up a post as custodian of the shrine and received guests here.

Shahzadagan tombs: Shahzada Abdullah and Shahzada Qasim [217 A1]
(Between the Musalla Complex & the old city; ⏰ sunrise–sunset daily; free) These two 15th-century tombs contain the remains of two princes, Abdullah and Qasim, who died in the 8th century CE. Although built of unremarkable brickwork, the interiors are delicately decorated with 500-year-old paintings and tilework, offering the best example of decorations from that era. Despite being so close to the hustle and bustle of central Herat, the tombs are set in a very peaceful graveyard. Each has a Sufi who tends and lives at the tomb and appreciates a small donation.

Jami's Shrine
(3km north of the old city; ⏰ sunrise–sunset daily; free) Mawlana Nur ad-Din Abd ar-Rahman Jami was the greatest poet in a city of poets and one of the greatest Persian poets ever. A regular at the court of Husayn Bayqara and mentor to Mir Ali Shir Nava'i, he was a titan of mystical Sufism whose writings are still studied today. Nevertheless, his tomb shaded by a pistachio tree is simple compared with the Shahzada tombs or Gazar Gah.

AFGHANISTAN'S FIRST FEMALE TOUR GUIDE
Fatima Haidari

My passion for travelling began in childhood. I was just seven years old when, as a shepherd, I would take my animals into the hills near our village in Afghanistan. It was hard work, but I loved wandering the mountains. There I felt a deep connection to the wild, to nature, and to the freedom of movement.

In 2020, I officially became a tour guide working with Untamed Borders. But guiding, for me, has never just been a job – it is a passion, a purpose, and a way of life. It is about learning and teaching, sharing stories and connecting with people from all kinds of backgrounds. Through guiding, I have found freedom and courage. It gives me the opportunity to show the beauty of places, share their histories and bring to life stories that are often overlooked. The first time I guided someone around Herat, I realised the power of this work. Helping others see a place from a new perspective, witnessing their curiosity and exchanging knowledge filled me with surprise. I had found a platform to break stereotypes, educate others and inspire change – it was like building bridges between cultures.

As a girl in Afghanistan, however, growing up was never easy. From an early age, I was constantly reminded of my limitations. Society had firm ideas about what a girl could and couldn't do. Boys were given freedom, opportunities and encouragement; while girls were expected to be silent, obedient and dependent. These disparities were chains that I needed to break. But I never regret being born a girl in Afghanistan: it helped me truly understand the meaning of freedom. If I had never lived without it, I might never have come to value it so deeply. The restrictions shaped my resilience and taught me to fight for my rights and for the rights of others.

Becoming a female tour guide was difficult too. People stared at me, whispered behind my back and insulted me. Guiding was seen as a man's profession, and my

---

Near Jami's tomb is that of **Khawaja Ghaltan**. Khawaja Ghaltan was a Sufi saint famous for his mischief, and at the tomb they say if you lie on the ground and close your eyes, you will be pushed and start to roll. It is not unusual to see men rolling around on the ground with their hands in front of their faces in front of the shrine. This shrine was unusual in the fact that it also had a female Sufi attendant.

Jewish cemetery (South of the old city; not accessible at the time of writing) Herat was once home to Afghanistan's largest Jewish community. In recent years their cemetery has been walled off for protection and it is understood that international money is being used to protect and restore some of the tombs. Just to the north, the **tomb of Sultan Agha** was the centre for Herat's Nau Ruz celebrations although under the current government these are banned.

SOUTHWEST AFGHANISTAN

The provinces of Farah and Nimruz in Afghanistan's southwest offer a journey into the least visited parts of the country. It's a region of vast open plains populated by Persian, Pashto and Baloch communities struggling to survive as the rivers that support them, the Farah Rud and Helmand, carry less and less water as the years pass by. It was not always like this. Nimruz in particular was part of Sistan, a prosperous community centred around the great lakes in the desert formed by the Helmand River. A visit today can include crossing these now arid lakes and exploring the old mud-brick forts in various states of repair from those times.

presence was considered shameful by many. But I refused to let their beliefs define me. I kept going because I believed in myself and what I enjoyed doing. I wanted to prove, to myself and to other women, that we can pursue our dreams, no matter the obstacles. My dream is to one day create my own tour company in Afghanistan. I want to show the world the true face of my country – not the one shaped by conflict, but one rich in culture, history, beauty and untold stories. Afghanistan is so much more than what headlines portray. I want people to experience that forgotten beauty.

Although I currently live in Italy, my passion continues through virtual tours (w untamedborders.com/itinerary/virtual-tours-with-fatima-afghanistan). Being far from home hasn't stopped me. I've found a way to keep telling Afghanistan's story to those who cannot visit. These tours are more than just a substitute – they are a bridge between worlds, keeping the spirit of my homeland alive in people's hearts. More importantly, I still have my job. In the meantime, I want to travel the world, learn from new cultures and continue my journey as a free spirit. It keeps me alive, grounded, dreaming.

I have fought hard for my independence and freedom, and I will never allow anyone to take these away. No matter where life takes me, I will keep fighting – for my dreams, for the rights of women and for a brighter future for the girls of Afghanistan. Alongside my tours, I founded an association in Italy to support girls' education in Afghanistan, called Alefba. Education is the most powerful tool we have to change lives. Through my organisation, I am working to provide resources, support and hope to those girls who are denied their right to learn by the Taliban. My dream is to one day open schools for them – safe places where they can grow, dream and build their futures.

The journey between Herat and Kandahar can be extended to three days to visit these areas, and if you have more time you can follow the Helmand River all the way to Lashkar Gah (page 202) as it passes between Afghanistan's two great deserts, the Registan and the Dasht e Margo (Desert of Death).

FARAH The road south from Herat to Farah is a barren drive through the desert and rolling foothills of the Hindu Kush broken only by occasional camps of Kuchi nomads and the vast Shindand air base. After 200km you meet the Farah Rud River and the turn-off to Farah.

Long an important trading town linking Sistan (page 226) with the Herat–Kandahar trade route, Farah was either founded as, or renamed, Alexandria Prophthasia ('Anticipation') by Alexander the Great. It was destroyed by the Mongols in the 13th century and, like much of southern Afghanistan, arguably never fully recovered. Between the 16th and 19th centuries, Uzbeks, Persians and Timurids fought over it, then Persians and Mughals, then Persians and Afghans, then finally rival Afghan rulers, reducing the once great city to a shadow of its former self, so that there were 'no more than sixty houses in the interior of the place, which would easily contain four thousand five hundred' (J P Ferrier, *Caravan Journeys and Wanderings in Persia, Afghanistan, Turkistan, and Beloochistan*; page 285). Finally, when the new road was built between Herat and Kandahar in the 1930s, it missed Farah altogether.

The mid 20th century saw a new town built outside the walls of old Farah. If you wander south of the bazaar, you will find remnants of the old brick-and-mud buildings that were constructed when people first relocated, although they are gradually being replaced.

Set among the final jagged teeth peaks of the Hindu Kush, today's low-rise Farah is dominated by the vast fort and the once great Farah Rud River that only a generation ago used to flow all year round, but which now has no water at all; its fields use water pumped from increasingly deep wells. It's a friendly town but one where you can't help feel a sense of impending environmental doom. The odd palm tree leads an air of exoticism, but, overall, this region feels arid and lifeless compared with the central, northern and eastern provinces.

Historically a Tajik town, Farah feels very much like a crossroads between Persian Herat and the Pashtun provinces further south. You'll see both Tajik and Pashtun clothing, women wearing both chadors and burkhas, and hear both Dari and Pashto in the bazaar.

Getting there and away Buses from/to Herat (500–800AFN; 5hrs) and Kandahar (900–1,500 AFN; 8hrs) are based at the istga 4km north of the Fruit Bowl Chowk on the road towards the Herat–Kandahar highway. Shared taxis to Zaranj (750AFN; 5hrs) via the desert road arrive/leave from an istga 1km west of the main bazaar.

Tourist information and registration Visit the **Department of Information and Culture** (Jada e farhang, 2nd district, 1 block northwest of the Fruit Bowl Chowk) if you wish to visit Farah Fort. The staff rarely see visitors and they may join you on your tour of the city, and are keen to give information on other places of interest in the deserts around Farah.

Orientation Modern Farah lies south of the ancient fort. The main street of the bazaar runs east–west, parallel to the fort's south wall. The Da Wulayat Maqam Salor Lare Roundabout, or Fruit Bowl Chowk (with a large statue of a fruit bowl in the centre) marks where the main road into town intersects with the main road of the bazaar. This road leads from the Fruit Bowl Chowk (given the Taliban's penchant for changing roundabout designs, this may change) in the east for three blocks west and one or two blocks south. This area of the city has uniform, two-storey buildings with solar panels (Farah is not linked to the national grid), a legacy of the international community days. Most administrative buildings are southwest of this road, except for the Department of Information and Culture (see above).

 Where to stay and eat The Department of Information and Culture can supply details of **private overnight accommodation** for 1,500–2,000AFN per room, which can be more comfortable and secure than the Khorma Hotel. If you're not staying this is a good place for dinner, though (**$**). There are kebab stands in the bazaar, but for more variety head a couple of blocks south of the main street for Onab Restaurant.

Khorma Hotel Minar Chowk, in the middle of the bazaar; m 7240 83244. This hotel is dirty & very basic (no beds or attached loos), but the owner is friendly & will provide blankets. Eggs & fresh bread for b/fast not inc. **$**

Onab Restaurant Jada Kami Sary, in front of Bilal Masjid; m 7083 24090. As well as the usual Afghan offerings of kebabs & pulao, there is karahi & pizza. Vegetarians should try asking for *solar*, the vegetable side dish served with pulao. They might be rewarded with some chickpea chana or a vegetable stew. **$**

What to see and do

Farah Fort (Entrance on the north side; ⊕ dawn–dusk; free) Dominating northwest Farah, this remains one of the most imposing strongholds in Afghanistan. Measuring 400m by 400m, with more than 70 defensive towers, these walls encompassed a major city for over 2,000 years, filled with homes, workshops, granaries, cisterns and garrisons. It now stands empty, surrounded by a dry moat.

The foundations date back to antiquity, possibly to the Achaemenid or Sassanian periods when Farah defended the frontier of the Persian empires. It was strengthened during the Islamic era, especially under the Ghorids and Timurids, who understood its value on the caravan routes that linked Herat with Sistan, Kandahar and beyond to Persia and India. Because of its sheer size and towering mud-brick ramparts, it was almost certainly the great fort mentioned in the *Shahnameh*, where Rostam (page 229) fought the local king.

Old Farah's importance continued into the 19th century, when both the British and Persian armies considered it a key stronghold on Afghanistan's western frontier. Although deserted by the local population, in the 1980s, it was pressed into service as a military fort during the Soviet–Afghan War, with Russian troops garrisoned inside. Today it is a grand yet solemn reminder of what Farah was and how far it has fallen. The walls are in very good condition but the interior is empty bar one or two rusting Russian tanks and APCs. In the northeast corner you can explore the citadel. The southwest corner once housed a hotel, complete with palm trees and an Arabian Nights vibe. It was gutted by fire during a Taliban assault on Farah in 2018, when they nearly took control of the town. If department staff accompany you, they will probably let you have a look around it. It is possible to climb the ramparts here to look into the fort and over the town.

Around Farah The Department of Information and Culture, and people in Farah, may well recommend a visit to Anar Dara, 65km northwest of Farah. It is a narrow, verdant river valley regarded as the most beautiful place in the province, where they often go for recreation, but for international visitors there is little of interest, unlike the desert forts listed below.

Kak Kazan (20km southeast of Farah, past the airport, main hospital & university; ⊕ dawn–dusk) If you are going to spend any time in Farah, a visit to Kak Kazan is a must. Sometimes called the Kafir Qala (foreigners' fort), set on an 80m rocky outcrop above the desert, this remarkably positioned fortress overlooked the trade route between Helmand and Kandahar. It is a fairly steep climb on loose ground to reach the walls halfway up the rock, and a very steep climb to reach the top of the outcrop. However, the views of the desert with the occasional rocky peak of the Hindu Kush jutting above are fabulous. Also visible from here, looking due north, is the huge compound for wealthy Arabs who come here to hunt houbara with their falcons (page 11).

A taxi to Kak Kazan and back should cost around 1,500–2,000AFN.

Other forts If Farah Fort and Kak Kazan are not enough to sate your appetite for desert forts, then three others wait north of Farah on the west bank of the Farah River. A car and driver to visit them should cost in the region of 3,000–4,000AFN. The most impressive and in best condition is **Sajj Qala**, 20km north of Farah. Closer are **Mullah Aman Qala** and **Chahar Deh**, both 5km northwest of Farah. All are on unpaved roads. **Arg e Naude** (15km south on the desert road to Zaranj) is a fort in the small village of Naude, which the department will recommend but this

7 | HERAT AND WESTERN AFGHANISTAN

> **SISTAN: LAND OF THE HAMUNS**
>
> The region of Sistan, straddling today's Afghanistan–Iran border, was for millennia a centre of civilisation in an otherwise arid landscape. Fed by the Helmand River, the waters spread out across the desert into a series of vast inland lakes and marshes known collectively as the Hamuns. Chief among these was the Hamun e Helmand, the 'sea of Sistan', which at times extended to hundreds of square kilometres, sustaining rich fisheries, reed beds, birdlife and fertile farmland along its banks.
>
> Ancient texts and traditions speak of Sistan as the homeland of Rostam (page 225), the great hero of the *Shahnameh*. Once a satrapy of the Achaemenid Empire, it later became a frontier zone for the Parthians, Sassanians, Arabs, Ghaznavids and Timurids, its fortunes tied to the ebb and flow of the Helmand's waters. The Hamuns were the lifeblood of the region, supporting not only agriculture but also bustling towns and fortresses along the lakeshores.
>
> In recent decades, however, this landscape has undergone dramatic change. Upstream damming, irrigation projects and shifting rainfall patterns have drastically reduced the Helmand's flow. By the early 21st century, the Hamun e Helmand and its sister lakes had almost completely dried up. The opening of the Kamal Khan Dam in southern Nimruz in 2021 has meant the river's last kilometres no longer hold water. What was once a shimmering inland sea is now cracked desert floor, scattered with the ruins of fishing villages and abandoned boats. Dust storms whipped up from the exposed lake beds now plague the region, driving many families to leave, making Sistan Afghanistan's most visible victim of environmental collapse.

seems more to do with the fact it can be reached by paved road than any particular importance of the fort.

Farah to Nimruz Province This 4–5-hour drive is a journey through the most visible casualty of Afghanistan's environmental struggles, passing through what was the kingdom of Sistan and driving along the dry bed of the Hamun e Helmand (see above). It is worth negotiating a private car (3,500–4,500AFN) from the istga in Farah for this route to allow you to stop and take photos. Bring plenty of water in case of a breakdown and beware that this route skirts the Iranian border and is a favourite area of smugglers.

The road begins along the Farah Rud southwest from Farah. At 15km you will pass the Arg e Naude fort (page 225); after another 35km, the paved road crosses a bridge and the drive continues on unpaved and unclear roads. Soon the farmland disappears completely. After another 15km there is an unremarkable hot spring before the road continues south, dropping in altitude to the dry lake bed of Hamun e Helmand. After 10km on the lake bed, 30m-high cliffs appear on the east edge, marking the spot of the last lake before it disappeared completely. Fishing boats lie forlornly in the desert, miles from any water.

For another 20km, the drive is on the unmarked white lake bed. The route is used by trucks, cars and Baloch camel herders either passing from Farah to Zaranj or crossing the border away from prying eyes. These convoys shimmer in the heat, and in a mirage appear to float above the landscape. At this point you are only about 5km from the unmarked Iranian border. The road finally rises out of the seabed on the eastern side of the Hamun e Helmand, passing the Qala e Ibrahim Khan (page 229) and two radio antennae before joining the main Zaranj–Deralam road 30km northeast of Zaranj.

ZARANJ

The word Zaranj comes from the ancient Persian word *zaranka* (waterland); originally the town stood on the banks of the Hamun e Helmand, 3km north. Its name is now grimly ironic as Zaranj now exists in a desert. However, despite the lack of water, it exists, as it has always done, to facilitate border trade (both legal and illegal) between Iran and Afghanistan. Zaranj's business is often visible, through groups of young men waiting to enter or having been evicted from Iran. The streets south of the main highway are full of warehouses stocking Iranian goods bound for Kandahar or Kabul. You'll also notice the lack of number plates here – this is

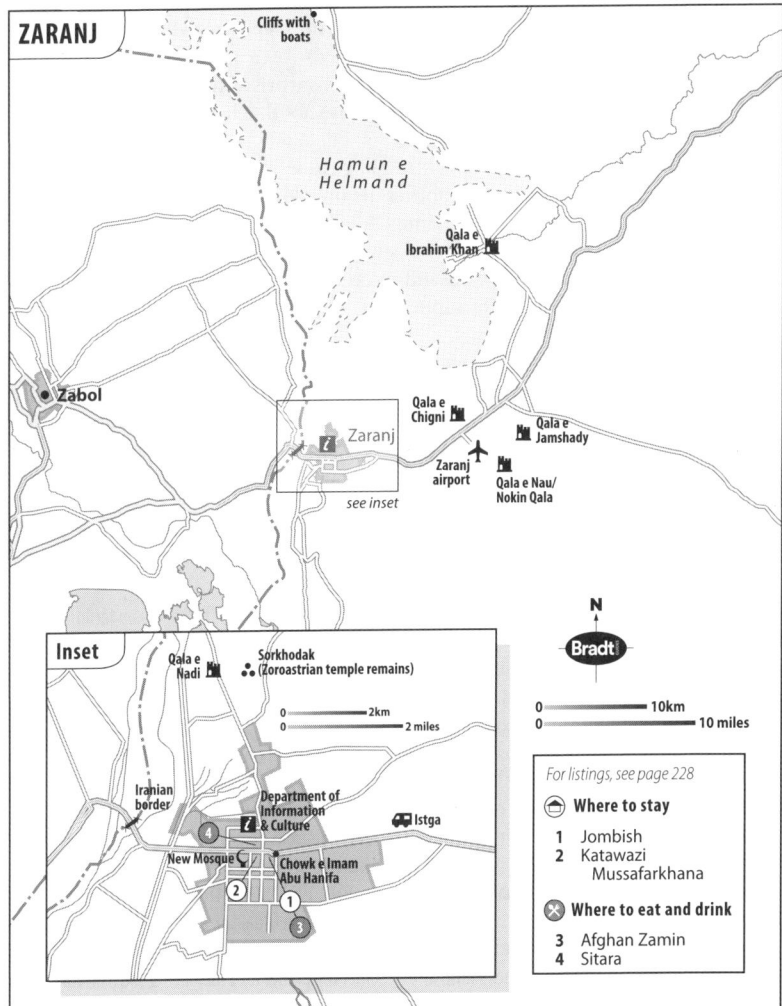

For listings, see page 228

Where to stay
1 Jombish
2 Katawazi Mussafarkhana

Where to eat and drink
3 Afghan Zamin
4 Sitara

7 | HERAT AND WESTERN AFGHANISTAN

a tax-free zone for cars, so no-one bothers to register them if they do not plan to leave Zaranj.

Nearly 50% of the inhabitants are Baloch (page 50). Zaranj is one of the few places where you might see them, although it's hard to distinguish Baloch from Pashtuns in their daily dress and there are no Baloch restaurants. Zaranj, a border town synonymous with drugs and people-smuggling, may be a hard place to love, but it is laid-back and everybody is very friendly. It gets incredibly hot in the summer.

GETTING THERE AND AWAY The istga for all Afghan destinations is on the east edge of town, 3km from the Chowk e Imam Abu Hanifa, with buses and shared taxis from/to Farah (500–800AFN; 5hrs), Herat (900–1,500; 8hrs) and Kandahar (900–1,500; 8hrs). A taxi to the **Iranian border** costs 80–100AFN. Hiring a car and driver for the day to visit the forts around Zaranj should cost around 3,000–4,000AFN.

TOURIST INFORMATION AND REGISTRATION The **Department of Information and Culture** is six blocks north of the highway – turn north opposite the new mosque with two giant minarets. They are usually surprised to see visitors and have some basic information about places to see but are not that helpful for locating sites.

ORIENTATION The main drag is the straight east–west Zaranj–Deleram highway that runs all the way to the Iranian border. Its only kink is the roundabout known as Chowk e Imam Abu Hanifa (old name Chowk e Naqsha). The bazaar is situated south of the highway and runs ten blocks west of Chowk e Imam Hanifa. As well as the usual wares including bolani and juice stands, here you'll find wholesalers loading and unloading goods from Iran.

 WHERE TO STAY AND EAT *Map, page 227*
Zaranj is not short on accommodation options, but it is very much a case of quantity over quality. All are catering to Afghans travelling into and out of Iran with low cost being the prerequisite feature. There are mussafarkhanas **$** around main chowk; but the many mussafarkhanas around the istga are best avoided as they are grim even by Zaranj standards.

There are kebab sellers around Chowk e Imam Hanifa but the larger, better restaurants are on the road running west of there.

Jombish Hotel 3 blocks west of Chowk e Imam Abu Hanifa on the main road through Zaranj. This 4-storey glass building with red trim is easy to spot, but the unmarked entrance is hidden on the southwest corner next to a row of travel agencies. Go up the steps into the building; the reception is on the right side. The interior looks like a derelict shopping centre & the dirty rooms do not change this perception. However, this hotel does have AC which is worth its weight in gold in the summer. Squat toilets that might work; no b/fast. **$$**

Katawazi Mussafarkhana Opposite the entrance to the Jombish & a little further south. In a 2-storey block, this mussafarkhana offers no bed, no AC & no bathroom. The hammam facilities are extra if you want a wash. **$**

Afghan Zamin Zaranj-Deleram Rd, 1 block west of Chowk e Imam Hanifa. A solid option with large Afghan meals & sharing platters. Comes with juice bar & ice cream counter, complete with a nice display of 0.0% Iranian malt beer drinks. There is an in-house money exchange man for those returning from Iran. **$$**

Sitara Restaurant Chahraki di Afghanistan Bank; m 7943 19000, 7041 41080. On the main drag, this offers the usual fare albeit on raised day beds. The sharing platters are huge – if there are 4 of you, order the platter for 2 for lunch & you'll be able to get them to pack enough for dinner as well. **$$**

OTHER PRACTICALITIES Moneychangers are on the north side of Chowk e Imam Hanifa; if coming from Iran, Iranian rials are accepted and can also be changed in most restaurants and shops. There is also a hammam in the area, useful given the lack of facilities in most mussafarkhanas.

WHAT TO SEE AND DO Zaranj does not have any real sights but the surrounding flat deserts are dotted with abandoned but atmospheric forts that recall Sistan's former importance. The Department of Information and Culture lists 44 forts, but some are little more than mounds; the following are the most impressive. Be aware that on Fridays young men often drive out into the flat deserts east of Zaranj and race their cars for fun.

Once in the centre of old Zaranj on the edge of the Hamun e Helmand, **Qala e Nadi** (4km north of Zaranj) is one of the less remarkable of Zaranj's forts, but you can see Iran from the top – the border is 1,500m away. The residential area en route to Qala e Nadi was where fishermen and reed cutters used to live, although their boats are now used for sitting rather than fishing. **Sorkhodak**, 500m east of Qala e Nadi, is (according to the Department of Information and Culture) the remains of a Zoroastrian temple.

Qala e Chigni (15km east of Zaranj, opposite the entrance to the airport) was part of a much larger settlement. One section of the fort has been recently reconstructed, with the rest left to be eaten away by the wind and sand, returning it to the desert. The large **Qala e Jamshady** (1km after Qala e Chigni, then 3km southeast of the road) is in fabulous condition, rising out of the desert like a mirage. People visit the shrine attached to it to pray. **Qala e Nau/Nokin Qala** (2km south of Qala e Jamshady) is another large fortress in good condition.

The exceptional **Qala e Ibrahim Khan** (40km north of Zaranj on the desert road to Farah) consists of outer walls and a high inner citadel, unusual in that it sits directly in the middle of the walls rather than, like the others, attached to one side. There are scatterings of blue tiles on the ground and signs that treasure hunters have been busy here.

> **ROSTAM, THE HERO FROM SISTAN**
>
> Rostam, the legendary warrior from Ferdowsi's *Shahnameh* (Book of Kings), is one of the great figures of Persian mythology. His name often crops up in Afghanistan, not least because his mother was a Kabuli and he was born in the Sistan region, back when it was a well-watered wetland.
>
> Central to Rostam's fame are his *Haft Khan* – the Seven Labours. In this cycle, Rostam overcomes monstrous beasts, deserts, demons and sorcerers to rescue King Kay Kavus of Persia. Each trial tested his endurance and bravery, from slaying a raging lion barehanded to defeating the White Demon in his mountain lair. These stories became symbols of the eternal struggle between order and chaos, light and darkness.
>
> In Afghanistan, several Buddhist stupas, including the one in Samangan (page 251), are called Takht e Rostam ('Throne of Rostam'), tying his legend to pre-Islamic sacred places. Both Farah's Fort and the nearby ruined fort of Kak Kazan are both named locally as locations where Rostam battled the king of Sistan. These echoes of his story reflect how myth and geography became entwined, embedding the hero into the cultural memory of the region. For Afghans, Rostam is a reminder that their land lies not on the fringes of Asia but at the heart of one of the world's greatest storytelling traditions.

8 | MAZAR E SHARIF AND NORTHERN AFGHANISTAN

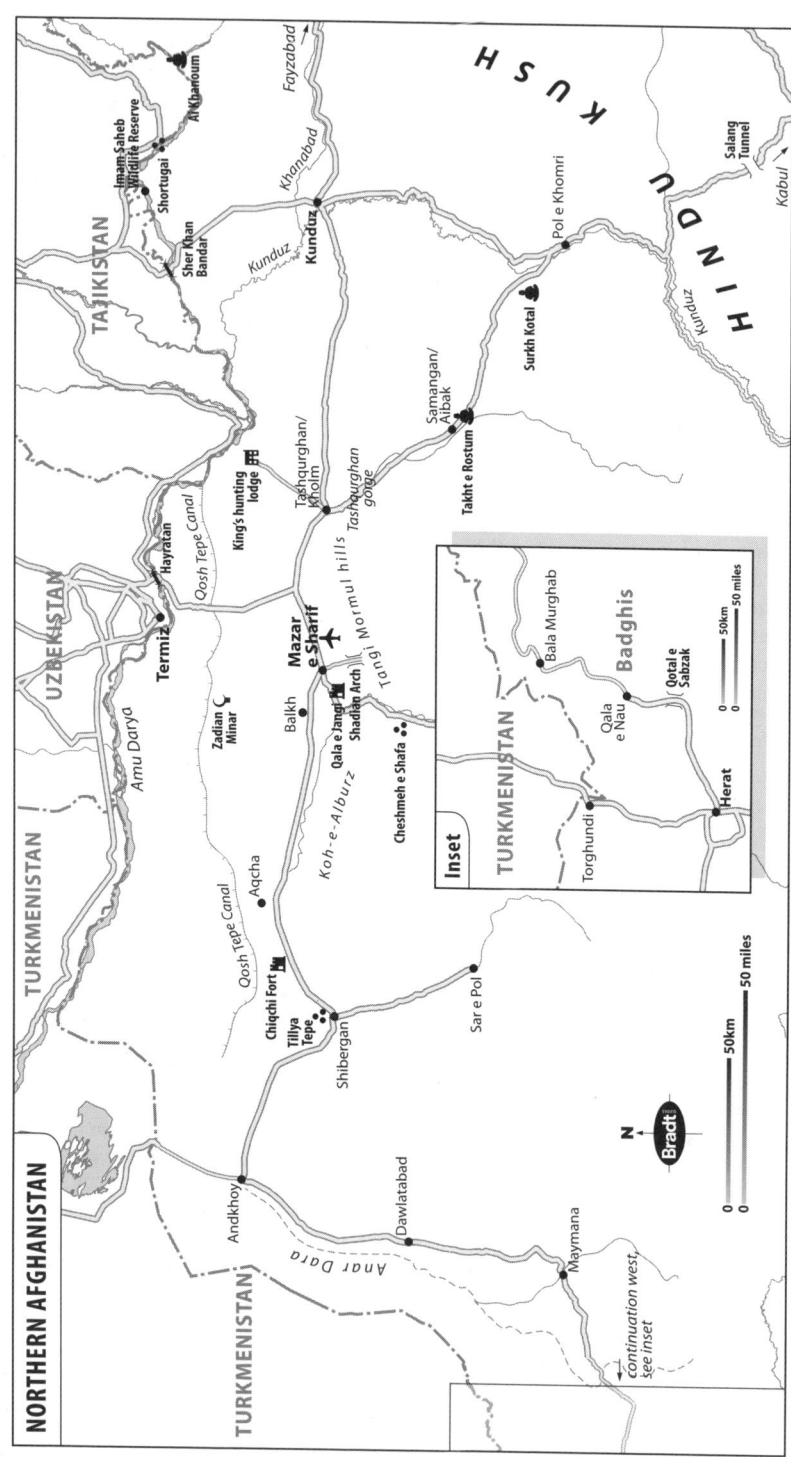

8

Mazar e Sharif and Northern Afghanistan

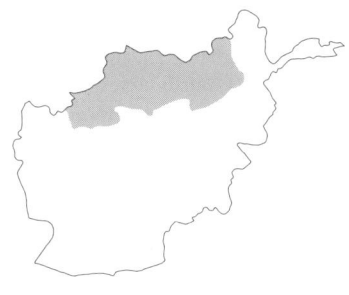

Northern Afghanistan is where the mountains end and the central Asian steppe begins. Bounded by the Hindu Kush to the south and the Amu Darya River to the north, this fertile, flat region is not a modern construct but has been home to empires since the dawn of civilisation. It has been named many things. Bactria to the Greeks, Oxiana and, in more recent times, Afghan Turkestan.

Northern Afghanistan has always had its own flavour compared with the rest of the country. This region has historically looked north towards the central Asian plains and the city states of Bukhara and Samarkand. It only became part of modern Afghanistan in the mid 19th century and it was only in the 1960s that it was linked by road to the rest of the country when the Russians built the Salang tunnel.

The north is the most ethnically diverse in the country. It is the region where Turkmen, Uzbeks and Tajiks live in greatest numbers, visible in the faces, clothes and food of the region. Look out for chapans (page 236) often worn by older men, and central Asian-style bread.

Highlights include the blue-tiled Shrine of Hazrat Ali in Mazar e Sharif and the remains of the once great city of Balkh. It is possible to visit both in a day. The Buddhist stupa at Samangan is another exceptional day trip from Mazar e Sharif. For the adventurous, the two-day road trip from Mazar e Sharif to Herat is a glimpse into central Asia's past through small trading towns and the odd Bactrian camel caravan. Horsemanship is much prized on the flat plains and the north of Afghanistan is the spiritual home of the traditional sport of buzkashi. If travelling to this region in winter, then catching a game is a must.

MAZAR E SHARIF

Biyaki burim ba Mazar,
Saili Gul i Lala zar

Let's go to Mazar,
and see the wild Tulips
   Mullah Mohamed Jan (traditional Afghan song lyric)

Mazar e Sharif exists because of a dream. Legend has it that in the 12th century a group of mullahs simultaneously dreamed that the body of Hazrat Ali, the son-in-law and nephew of the Prophet Muhammad, was buried in the area that is now Mazar e Sharif. A shrine was built over the grave and eventually a town grew up around it. Mazar e Sharif ('Shrine of the Saint') is now the pre-eminent city in northern Afghanistan, and with a population of just over half a million it's currently the country's fourth largest metropolis.

The shrine is still the focal point of the city. Set in a large park in the centre, it was the hub of Nau Ruz (new year) celebrations each spring (page 238) until it was banned in the 1990s by the Taliban and again in 2021. Otherwise, Mazar does not have many sights, but it's a useful base for day trips to Balkh and Samangan. It underwent a major renovation in the 1960s, so compared with other large cities in Afghanistan, Mazar has no 'old city'. This does mean it is well ordered in a grid system spreading out from the shrine and park.

It is also one of Afghanistan's most multi-cultural and progressive cities, with a fairly even mix of Tajik, Hazara, Pashtun and Uzbek people, wearing everything from long, striped silk Uzbek chapans to Hazara caps. Home to Balkh University, the country's third largest, it is relatively liberal (for Taliban-controlled Afghanistan) and women are often seen on the streets, wearing sometimes headscarves or chadors, as well as burkhas.

HISTORY The original shrine of Ali was in a different, now lost, location ever since the 13th century when Genghis Khan, hearing rumours of a treasure buried underneath its pillars, destroyed it in a futile search. The grave remained unmarked until the Timurid era (15th century) when a second dream-revelation occurred, Ali's remains were rediscovered and a new shrine was commissioned at the current location. A settlement soon grew around it and, over the centuries, Mazar e Sharif

ABDUL RASHID DOSTUM

The story of the last 40 years of northern Afghanistan cannot be told without the story of Abdul Rashid Dostum. An ethnic Uzbek born in 1954 in Jowzjan Province, he commanded an Uzbek militia that carried great weight in the geopolitics of Afghanistan. His militia fought with the Russian-backed government throughout the 1980s to great effect and he was decorated for his efforts. Then in 1992, he defected and joined the mujahideen.

The combination of his Uzbek militia and Ahmad Shah Massoud's troops helped bring a quick end to Afghanistan's communist government in 1992. Yet he was very much at the heart of the problems that brought about the civil war between 1992 and 1996, having been allied to both Massoud and Hekmatyar at different points during the period. This was perhaps the peak of his power. During the chaos of the civil war, his proto state in northern Afghanistan functioned well. He ruled the north as if it were his own kingdom, printing his own currency and even founding his own airline, Balkh Air. The peace and stability Dostum brought about during this period saw many Afghans move to northern Afghanistan for safety.

The rise of the Taliban saw him leave Afghanistan in 1997, then return at the head of the international forces in 2001. He never regained the influence and power he had in the 1990s, but during the time of the international community he held senior positions in the Afghan government, including Joint Chief of Staff and Vice President under Ashraf Ghani.

Loved by the Uzbek and Turkmen communities yet seen as a war-crime-perpetrating warlord by many other ethnic groups, Dostum now resides in Türkiye.

outgrew and absorbed much of the population of neighbouring Balkh (page 239). In 1869, it became the capital of Afghan Turkestan.

Mazar was vital to the Russian-backed communist government during the 1980s. With the border to the Soviet Union less than 100km away, the city became a major hub of trade between the Soviet Union and Afghanistan. It was easily defended as it sits on a flat plain with few places for any mujahideen forces to hide.

With the withdrawal of Russian forces in 1989, the city was left in the hands of Uzbek militias commanded by General Abdul Rashid Dostum (see opposite). When the Soviet Union collapsed, Dostum broke from the government and much of northern Afghanistan fell under his rule, precipitating the final collapse of the communist government in Kabul in 1992. The mid 1990s saw Dostum build up a personal fiefdom, financed by northern Afghanistan's gas reserves, with easy trade access to newly independent Uzbekistan.

Mazar e Sharif was nicknamed a 'glittering jewel in Afghanistan's battered crown' and by and large managed to escape the worst of the conflicts that plagued the country in the late 20th century – until 1997, when the Taliban took the city. Dostum fled, but a day later there was a local uprising led by Hazara militias, forcing the Taliban fighters to leave. This was a short respite; later that year the Taliban were back. This time they wanted revenge: between 2,000 and 8,000 Hazaras were summarily executed. Corpses were left in the street for dogs to eat.

In 2001, Dostum and his Uzbek militia (as part of the Northern Alliance) were back, this time with the US army and the international community behind them. Mazar was the first city to be captured in a battle that included a cavalry charge on horseback led by Dostum. The retaking of the city was not without controversy. After a Taliban prisoner revolt at Qala e Jangi (page 238), Dostum's forces packed prisoners into shipping containers, where they suffocated or were shot in the Dasht e Laila desert (page 200). About 3,000 people are believed to have died.

While Dostum remained important on a national stage, his influence in Mazar faded under the government supported by the West. A rival commander, the Tajik Atta Mohamed Noor, became the governor of Balkh Province and the most powerful leader in Mazar. The city escaped the worst of the violence during the period of international occupation and in 2021, with the Taliban advancing, both Dostum and Ata Mohammed pledged to defend the city, but they eventually fled to Uzbekistan. The city has been under Taliban rule ever since.

GETTING THERE AND AWAY Afghanistan's only rail track runs between Mazar e Sharif and the Uzbekistan border at Hayratan. At the time of writing the route is for freight only.

By air Mazar e Sharif's airport, officially **Mawlana Jalaluddin Mohammad Balkhi International Airport** (the full name of the poet Rumi), is 8km east of the city. **Kam Air** (page 73) has flights from and to Kabul (daily), Herat (weekly, Fri) and Istanbul (weekly, Tue). Tickets can be bought from travel agents in town. A taxi between Mazar city centre and the airport costs about 500AFN.

Note that, when flying into the airport, you will be asked to show your letter from the Afghan Tour Department (page 122) and register at a counter. There is no public transport connecting the airport to the city, but taxis leave from a car park 200m north of the arrivals terminal.

By road The base for transport from and to points north, south and east of Mazar is the **Istga e Kabul,** located 5km east of the shrine in a large car park set back from

8 | MAZAR E SHARIF AND NORTHERN AFGHANISTAN

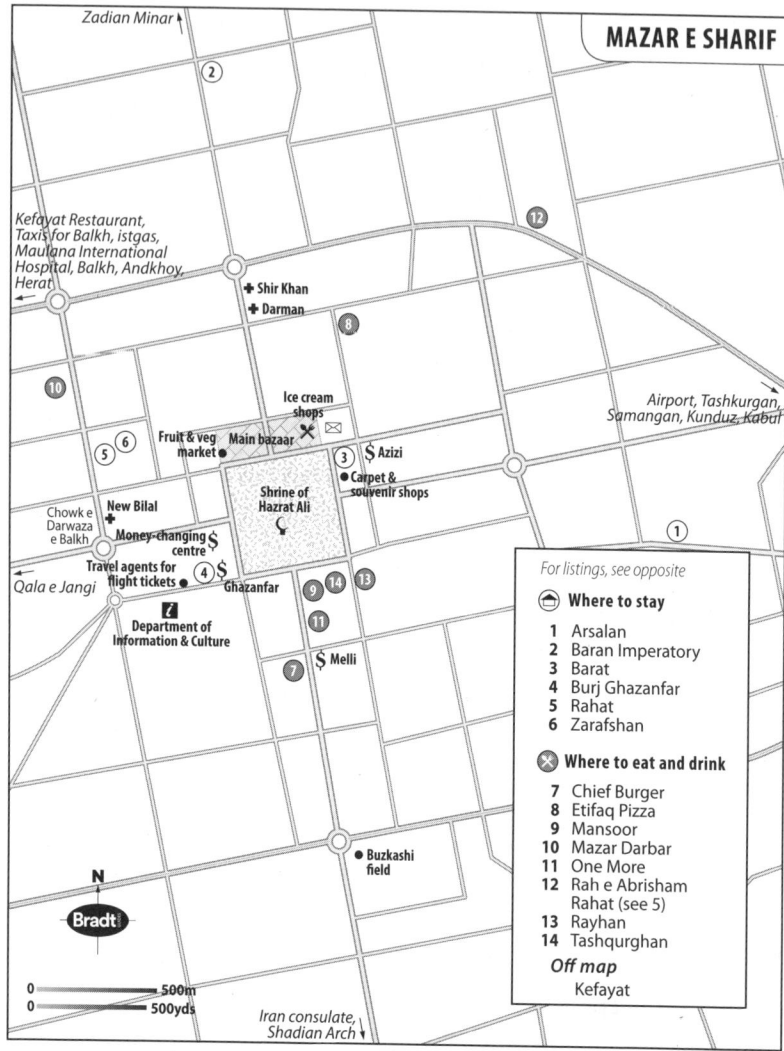

the south side of the main road. From or for Kabul, large 30–40-seater coaches (600–1,000AFN; 12hrs) travel more frequently at night (during the hours 22.00–04.00), while shared minivans and taxis (1,200–1,500AFN; 12hrs) run throughout the day, albeit more frequently at night. Shared minivans and taxis also link up to Kunduz (400–500AFN; 4hrs) and the Uzbekistan border at Hayratan (300AFN; 2hrs). Note that the route to Hayratan may be closed for periods on windy days when sand dunes block the road. A taxi to the Istga e Kabul from the centre will cost in the region of 500AFN.

Transport for points west of Mazar arrive and depart from the **Istga e Maymana** east of the centre, 4km from the shrine. Located in a car park on the north side of the road, it is hard to spot from the road, but the entrance is opposite a Ziayee petrol station. It is the base for cars or minivans from/to Aqcha (250AFN; 1hr), Andkhoi (500AFN; 3hrs) and Maymana (600–700AFN; 5hrs). Travelling to Herat, you will need to stop at Maymana and switch to vehicles that can handle the rough road of Badghis. However, once the road (page 247) is repaired it is likely that direct services to Herat will operate.

GETTING AROUND If your destination isn't within walking distance, taxis are the best form of transport around Mazar. For instance, a taxi from the shrine to the buzkashi area would cost 200–300AFN.

TOURIST INFORMATION AND REGISTRATION The **Department of Information and Culture** is west of the shrine on Baihaqi Street. You will need to register here to visit the Shrine of Hazrat Ali or the town of Balkh.

ORIENTATION Almost everything of interest in Mazar e Sharif, including hotels and restaurants, is within walking distance of the shrine. Thanks to its grid layout, the city is easy to navigate, with traffic lights and even directional road signs – both things almost never seen elsewhere in Afghanistan. The main bazaar is north of the shrine.

The city used to be famous for its roundabouts, each featuring giant statues depicting different aspects of Afghanistan and the city. However, the more evocative ones, such as the scene depicting a buzkashi match, have been replaced by the Taliban government with religious imagery.

WHERE TO STAY *Map, opposite*
For such a large city drawing thousands of pilgrims, Mazar e Sharif is not graced with a huge variety of accommodation options. Functional rather than inspirational, most are located within a short walk of the shrine.

Burj Ghazanfar Baihaqi St, in the southwest corner of the main square, entry via the security door on south side of the building; m 7906 92828; e burj.reception@ghazanfargroup.com; burjghazanfar. This 9-storey hotel overshadows its neighbours. The best hotel in Mazar, it boasts a gym, a snooker table & views of the shrine from the 9th-floor terrace. The rooms are a small step up from others in the city. All have AC & Western-style toilets; the VIP rooms are huge. Security, & free tea & coffee; b/fast inc. **$$$$**

Arsalan Balwar e Massoudi Shaheed, behind the University of Balkh; m 7020 20844; . This is the best place outside of the Burj Ghazanfar although it is starting to look a bit tired. Most rooms have Western-style loos. Security & AC; b/fast inc. **$$$**

Baran Imperatory Hotel North of Alkozai roundabout, Hakim Naser Khesrow Av, opposite Balkh Province Military Hospital; m 7965 66000; e info@baranhotels.com, baranhotels@gmail.com. A big hotel with grand aspirations, & a large foyer, albeit one with a ceiling so low some might bang their head on the chandelier. If the hotel is using its solar back-up power, it can have a gloomy feel; it also means the lifts will be out of order. Clean if small rooms. Security, AC; b/fast inc. **$$$**

Barat Northeast corner of the main square; m 7740 03121. This small hotel is an old staple in a great location above the carpet shops & across from the shrine. Refurbished in 2012, but now in need of a new makeover. Passable rooms, both sgls & dbls, with threadbare carpets, bits of peeling paint & damp. No b/fast. **$$**

Rahat North of Chowk e Darwaza e Balkh; m 76711 1100. Small hotel with clean rooms (some have Western-style bathrooms) & cheap furniture. The friendly staff offer free tea. There's no communal area, but there is a restaurant attached. No security, but they have a blast door, which is closed at night. AC; b/fast inc. **$$**

Zarafshan North of Chowk e Darwaza e Balkh; m 7990 13800. Opposite the Rahat in a large mansion with a dozen rooms, the Zarafshan has more of a guesthouse vibe than that of a hotel. Rooms vary in size, shape & number of beds; some have Western-style toilets. It has been recently refurbished with fresh paint & new carpets. **$$**

8 | MAZAR E SHARIF AND NORTHERN AFGHANISTAN

✖ WHERE TO EAT AND DRINK Map, page 234

Located near the borders of Uzbekistan and Turkmenistan, Mazar's cuisine has abundant Turkic influences. Look out for Uzbek bread (similar to a large holeless bagel), mantu (ravioli covered in yoghurt and tomatoes) and ashak (mantu for vegetarians). There is a good selection of restaurants on the road leading south from the main square, serving kebab, pulao and other Afghan staples. All restaurants remain open from morning until around 21.00 (sometimes later in the summer).

For **snacks, ice cream and juices** visit the bazaar to the north of the square. Even if you don't like ice cream or worry about its effect on digestion in a country with limited electricity, it's well worth coming to watch Mazar's famous ice-cream makers in action: men with huge forearms churning vats of cream set in even larger vats of ice. Aim for **Tashqurghan** ✳ (m 7985 91060) for a chance to try something other than *sher yakh* (the default 'ice cream flavour'). This Mazar e Sharif institution is run by a family who have been making ice cream for over 60 years. Among the many flavours on offer, their pistachio is highly recommended.

Kefayat Restaurant The grandest restaurant in Mazar is 1km west of the shrine, just north of the Maulana Hospital, & serves Turkish & Afghan food in grand style. Specialities include *pide*, shoarma & Turkish-style liver. $$–$$$

Chief Burger Shadian Rd; m 7773 58000. Using the same branding as but not affiliated to the Pakistani Chief Burger chain, this place is good for south Asian dishes such as biryani & handi. The 'fast food' options such as burgers & pizzas are of lower quality. $$

Etifaq Pizza Shar Shara St; m 7995 16363; w ettefaqpizza.com. If you are missing real coffee, this is the place to visit. They also serve pizzas. It's opposite one of General Dostum's many residences, currently lying empty. $$

Mansoor 1 street south of the main square. Good, clean restaurant serving the usual Afghan dishes; a great place to try mantu. $$

Mazar Darbar Northwest of the main square. If you are based in the west side of town, this is the best of the Afghan restaurants, offering Afghan staples & pizzas. They had good mantu when we visited. Some staff speak English. $$

One More Restaurant South of the main square; m 7000 06100. The most aspirational of the restaurants with an upmarket décor. The menu features Afghan classics (exceptional kabuli pulao), as well as pizza. $$

Rah e Abrisham Restaurant Chahraki Saeedabad, next to Hamsafar wedding hall; m 7772 99995. Nicely appointed restaurant with Uzbek-style floor seating & raised tables serving Afghan foods, as well as subcontinental dishes such as daal & handi. $$

Rahat Restaurant In the Rahat hotel; page 235. No kabuli or kebab here: come for the pizza, fried chicken, juice & ice cream. $$

Rayhan Restaurant South of the main square; m 7282 62033. An upscale dining option, with a great selection of Afghan dishes. Platters are great value for groups. Good place to try mantu. $$

SHOPPING

Northern Afghanistan is the country's carpet and kilim production centre, making Mazar a good place to shop, and prices are usually a little cheaper than in Kabul. There is a row of **carpet and souvenir shops** on the east side of the shrine. Also look out for men on the pavement selling old and sometimes ancient bits and bobs dug up by farmers. Some of the beads they offer will be extremely old.

For more contemporary Afghan **clothing** such as chapans (Uzbek striped overcoats, made famous by former president Hamid Karzai), pakols (woollen flat caps) and scarves, try the bazaar on the north side of the shrine.

The **fruit and veg market**, located on the northwest corner of the main square, is the place to go for seasonal fruit: the melons from the north and pomegranates from Tashqurghan are excellent when in season.

OTHER PRACTICALITIES
Medical
Maulana International Hospital (west of the main square, off the AH76; m 7284 94949) is the best option for emergency care. For medicines, try the **New Bilal Pharmacy** (4 streets west of the main square; m 7804 03774).

Money
The main money-changing centre is southwest of the main square near **Ghazanfar Bank**; **Azizi Bank** is northeast of the square in Zainat Plaza; & **Melli Bank** is 3 streets south of the square.

Post and communications
There is a **post office** (m 7372 76087; ⊕ 08.00–16.00 Sat–Thu) just off the northeast corner of the main square.

WHAT TO SEE AND DO
✻ Shrine of Hazrat Ali (The shrine is the centrepiece of a complex that sits inside a large park. To enter one of the park gates, you must bring your paperwork from the Tourism Office signed by the Department of Information and Culture in Mazar e Sharif, page 235; ⊕ dawn–dusk daily; free) Mazar e Sharif does not boast many sights – it's a bit of a one-trick pony, but what a trick! The stunning blue-tiled Shrine of Hazrat Ali (sometimes mistakenly called the Blue Mosque) is Afghanistan's most important pilgrimage site. People travel from all over the country to pay their respects. Although only Muslim men can enter the shrine itself, male visitors can tour the surrounding complex.

The shrine is said to contain the remains of Hazrat Ali, the son-in-law and nephew of the Prophet. Ali was assassinated in 661BCE. Historians and the vast majority of the Muslim world believe that Ali was killed and buried in Najaf, in modern day Iraq. However, in the 12th century it was revealed in a mass dream that his body had been exhumed by his followers and tied to a white camel, which wandered the earth until it died, and that was the spot where Ali was buried.

His grave was duly found and a shrine built by the Seljuk Sultan Sanjar in 1136, only to be destroyed in 1220 by Genghis Khan. However, when the Timurid Empire was at its peak, it was decided to revive the story and build a new shrine at the current location. The shimmering tiles we see today are not the originals. In the 1860s, the shrine was untiled and painted white, but when Mazar e Sharif was incorporated back into Afghanistan and made the capital of Afghan Turkestan by King Sher Ali Khan, the king restored it to its original Timurid glory. In a sense, this is a neo-Timurid shrine, in the same way the Houses of Parliament or Tower Bridge in London are neo-Gothic. Sher Ali Khan, as well as Wazir Akbar Khan (page 28), are buried in the grounds.

Within the park you'll find many people selling bird seed to feed the large flock of white pigeons that live around the shrine. Legend has it that any pigeon that arrives at the shrine and stays for 40 days will turn white. It is true that almost all the pigeons are white; if they aren't, the story goes it's because they have yet to pass the 40-day mark.

You can enter the courtyard of the shrine from the north, east and south through blue tiled gates. Shoes must be removed and left in the care of the shoe minders within the gates. A small tip for the custodian is appreciated but not obligatory. The west side of the courtyard is the mosque where people gather five times a day to face west to pray. You may be asked to leave the courtyard at this point, especially ahead of the Friday noon prayers. Recently, a small **museum** was installed in the shrine, containing early editions of the Quran, coins, ceramics, historic weapons, and a Taliban motorbike bomb.

> **NAU RUZ**
>
> Nau Ruz is the Persian New Year – a 3,000-year-old tradition rooted in Zoroastrianism. It literally means 'New Day' and falls at the spring equinox. Traditionally there would be a three-day holiday, when people would have new clothes made and go walking in the mountains (known as *sabza laghat*, putting your feet in the grass) or the city centres for picnics or entertainment – such as games of buzkashi. Mazar e Sharif used to be the heart of Afghanistan's Nau Ruz celebrations, when around 100,000 people would descend on the city and the shrine, where a large religious banner would be unfurled. To touch it would bring good luck.
>
> As it's a Persian and non-religious festival, Nau Ruz was not celebrated by the Pashtun population and is considered un-Islamic by the Taliban. As such, it is officially banned, so there are no longer any mass gatherings in Mazar e Sharif. However, at the spring equinox you may well see people in new clothes and visiting the hills and mountains for picnics, where the odd cow might have painted horns. Nau Ruz lives on in people's hearts.

In pre-Taliban days, you would see quite a few families here from across Afghanistan and beyond; but visitor numbers at the shrine have dropped since women have been banned. It still has a lovely atmosphere. The park and courtyard are great for people-watching and making new acquaintances. There are usually kids playing football, and traditionally a Zikr on Thursday evenings. Non-Muslims may be asked to leave the courtyard at prayer times, especially ahead of Friday noon prayers, but you can watch from the park area.

The shrine is well worth two visits. Dawn is the quietest time, when the light is clearer and tiles seem exceptionally blue, and you'll have the place to yourself. At dusk, the rich light allows the shrine to show off its polychrome details.

Be aware that the park and surrounding areas are frequented by people begging and others who are sick asking for alms.

Buzkashi matches (Chowk e Sham; ⊕ mid-Nov–mid-Mar Fri mornings; free) Mazar e Sharif is probably the best place in the world to watch buzkashi (page 63), although you have to come in the winter to take in a match. The buzkashi field is 1km south of the shrine. If travelling by taxi, ask for 'Chowk e Sham' or 'buzkashi'.

AROUND MAZAR

Zadian Minar (Zadian village, a 60km/90min drive north of Mazar on mainly unpaved roads; ⊕ dawn–dusk; free) This 25m-tall, 12th-century Seljuk minaret built of baked clay bricks arranged in geometric patterns is one of the few structures in Afghanistan that escaped the ravages of Genghis Khan. You may encounter Afghans visiting a nearby shrine to a saint who, it is said, can cure skin diseases.

Qala e Jangi (Fort of War) (13km west of Mazar; entry not permitted) The notorious Battle of Qala e Jangi took place here in a fortress used by General Dostum's forces. When they overthrew the Taliban in 2001, it was used to house prisoners. The prisoners revolted and a six-day conflict ensued, one of the bloodiest of the 2001 war. The first US casualty of the conflict died, as did all but 86 of the prisoners. One survivor, John Walker Lindh, was a US citizen who had joined the

Taliban before the conflict. You can find the interview Lindh gave at the end of the battle online.

Shadian Arch and the hills of Tangi Mormul (15km south of Mazar; ⊕ dawn–dusk; free) Tangi Mormul are the hills south of Mazar where people travel to picnic and see the wild tulips in the spring, especially around Nau Ruz (see opposite). En route you will pass the Samanid-era (10th century) Shadian Arch dramatically spanning a very narrow gorge.

BALKH

Few places in Afghanistan give a sense of history like Balkh. 'The Mother of all Cities', as it has been known for centuries, was pre-eminent in the region since the dawn of civilisation. Rumi, Zarathustra, Alexander the Great, Marco Polo, Genghis Khan and Ibn Battuta are just some of the people who passed through its legendary gates. Yet today Balkh is a small market town, so small that it barely reaches its ancient city walls. Much was lost when Genghis Khan swept through, but there is more than enough left to see. The town is only 20km from Mazar e Sharif and makes a great day trip.

Balkh was also a centre of hashish production. Before 2021, you would often find groups of men smoking water pipes in the Bala Hissar and marijuana growing freely. Under the current government smoking is prohibited, and it is much less likely that you will see production or consumption.

HISTORY One of central Asia's fabled cities, Balkh (or Bactra) was the capital of ancient Bactria, which in its heyday encompassed northern Afghanistan and large swathes of central Asia. Located on a fertile, alluvial plain between the Amu Darya (which in antiquity flowed much closer to the city) and the Koh-e-Alburz – the northernmost ridge of the Hindu Kush – Balkh was likely the first capital of the ancient Iranian Indo-European speakers once they crossed the Amu Darya (page 17); archaeologists so far have discovered artefacts in the Bala Hissar which date back to the Early Iron Age (1500BCE).

Balkh occupied a key junction of trade routes along the Silk Road, an oasis city watered by the Balkh River, renowned for its locally grown oranges, grapes and sugarcane. The warehouses of its many caravanserais bulged with silks, furs, spices, gems, ivory, gold and silver vessels. But it wasn't only the luxury goods of India, China, central Asia and points west that travelled along these routes: ideas did too.

There was something very special about Balkh that makes you wish you could travel back in time and see what it was all about. Some say it had a Bactrian temple of the sun (Shams-i-Balkh) which was the origin of the spiritual kingdom of Shambhala in Tibetan Buddhism. In Zoroastrian myth, Balkh was founded by the first human, Keyumars (or Gayomart, the 'King of the Mountain'), who in Ferdowsi's *Shahnameh*, the Persian national epic, was the first shah of the world.

Zarathustra His dates are notoriously elusive, but most scholars believe Zarathustra (or Zoroaster as he was called by the Greeks) was born sometime around the year 1000BCE to a noble family. His dualistic vision of the Wise Lord, Ahura Mazda – the force of good and light standing against Ahriman or Angra Minya, the spirit of darkness and destruction – inspired him to prophesise an early monotheistic religion, Zoroastrianism.

According to the *Oxford Dictionary of Philosophy*, Zarathustra was the world's first philosopher. He invented the concepts of free will and ethics, and heaven and hell. 'Good thoughts, good words and good deeds' was the aim, but everyone was free to choose their own path. His ideas would influence Judaism during the 6th-century BCE Babylonian captivity. Zoroastrian priests, the Magi, were the Three Wise Men in the New Testament.

It was all too radical for his tribe, and for a decade Zarathustra wandered in exile, until King Vishaspa of Balkh welcomed him, according to Ferdowsi (others place him in Persia). Ferdowsi wrote that Zarathustra spent the rest of his life in Balkh, which he called the 'land of high-lifted banners' and died there aged 77. If not its birthplace, Balkh was the central seat of Zoroastrianism. It was the first place to celebrate Nau Ruz (page 238).

Much of Zoroastrianism's original scripture, the *Avesta*, written in an ancient language related to Sanskrit, was burned by Alexander the Great in 333BCE when he conquered Persia; as the self-proclaimed son of Zeus, Alexander had little truck with Zoroastrianism. What have survived are the 17 *Gathas*, stanzas written by Zarathustra himself, along with the *Yashts* (hymns of praise to various intermediate spirits, or angels, adapted from early Iranian mythology), plus sections added in Middle Persian in Sasanian times.

Although Zarathustra recommends praying in the presence of *atar*, or fire (the sun or hearth) to better concentrate on the divine revelation, the great fire temples open to the sky were a later development. One was at Cheshmeh e Shafa (locally known as the 'City of Infidels'), 30km south of Balkh, excavated in 2008 by French and Afghan archaeologists, although today little remains to be seen.

Some identify the Koh-e-Alburz as Zarathustra's Hara Berezaiti, the 'High Watch post', the first mountain created by Ahura Mazda and source of all the other mountains in the world, around which the stars and planets revolve. It was the home of the Simurgh, the benevolent giant bird of Persian mythology, who rescued the abandoned infant Zal and brought him up. Zal was the father of Rostam, the great warrior and hero of the *Shahnameh*, who would fight his

SEMIRAMIS

Another story, first popularised by the Greek Sicilian historian Diodorus Siculus, involves Semiramis. The real Semiramis began as the 9th-century BCE Assyrian queen Shammuramat, who conquered much of the Middle East and left such an impression that her name was used in a dozen later tales. Diodorus's version has it that her husband Onnes was a general in the Assyrian army besieging Balkh without success. Onnes missed his beautiful, clever wife and when he asked her to join him, she invented Persian trousers to wear so no-one on the journey could tell if she were a man or a woman. Once at Balkh, she devised a way to breach the walls and capture the city. In the meantime, Ninus the Assyrian king fell in love with her, demanded her from Onnes, who refused and then in a frenzy killed himself, and Semiramis married Ninus and ruled Balkh as its queen.

Later stories made her a goddess, a builder of great earthworks along the Euphrates, and a founder of cities. Christian writers turned her into a woman of ill repute, or even the Whore of Babylon, whom Dante condemned to the Inferno for lust – while other writers have been more complimentary, often describing women in power as 'another Semiramis'.

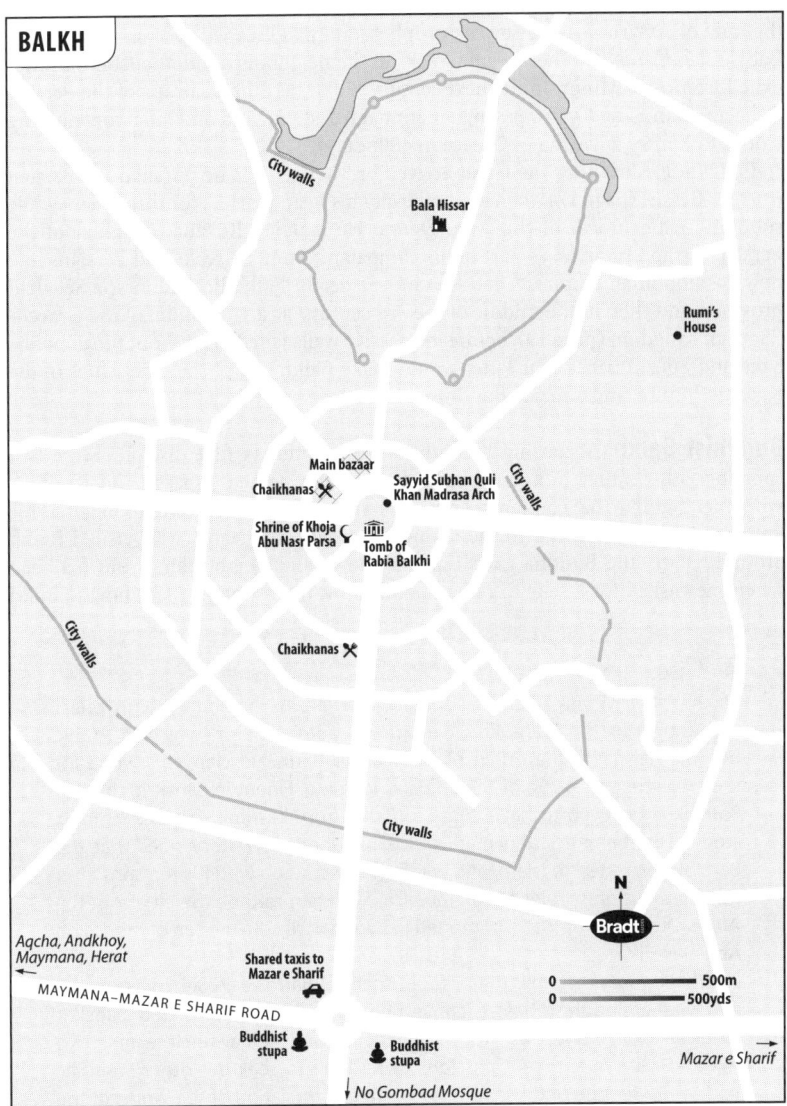

climactic battle against his son Sohrab on the banks of the Amu Darya, a tale retold by Matthew Arnold's narrative poem *Sohrab and Rustum* (1853), which fired the imagination of so many Victorian adventurers, inspiring them to seek 'the far-distant Oxus'.

A handful of Zoroastrians are said to live in Kabul, but most now live in India, Iran and North America. One born to an Indian family in Zanzibar was Freddie Mercury, whose funeral in London in 1991 was conducted by a Zoroastrian priest.

The capital of Bactria Along with its Zoroastrians, Balkh is believed to have had a temple or shrine to Anahita, the Persian goddess of water and the Oxus River. The city had a Jewish population from the 7th century BCE, exiled there by the king of Assyria – some say the prophet Jeremiah escaped to Balkh during the Babylonian Captivity. There were Greeks in the neighbourhood, too, communities exiled from Asia Minor. In the next century Balkh became a satrapy of the Persian Achaemenian King Cyrus, paying an annual tribute in gold and later contributing troops to Xerxes' invasion of Greece in 480BCE.

In 329BCE Alexander the Great arrived on the scene as he pursued the Persian usurper Bessus (page 17), then made the city his headquarters for three years while subduing tribes north of the Amu Darya. He married Roxana, daughter of the Persian satrap Oxyartes, as part of his campaign to unite Greeks and Persians in a new cosmopolitan empire. After Alexander's death, Balkh became first a Seleucid province, and then in the middle of the 3rd century BCE, the capital of the Graeco-Bactrian Kingdom (page 19), before its massive walls failed to keep out the nomadic Saka and Yuezhi tribes. The latter would make Balkh one of the chief cities of the Kushan Empire, and a major Buddhist centre.

Buddhist Balkh According to tradition, the Buddha's first disciples were two (possibly 5th-century BCE) merchants from Balkh named Tapassu and Bhallika, who met Siddhartha Gautama and were the first to offer him food after his enlightenment. According to the Chinese traveller Xuanzang, who visited Balkh around 630CE, the Buddha gave Tapassu and Bhallika eight hairs from his head when they asked for a relic to remember him by, then showed them how to build

BARMAKIDS: FROM BUDDHIST PRIESTS TO THE ARABIAN NIGHTS

Balkh's Nava Vihara had a fascinating afterlife. Its hereditary high priest was known as the Pramukha, Sanskrit for 'administrator', which in Arabic became Barmak – the origin of the famous Barmakid clan, renowned for their wealth, patronage of the arts and learning. Fluent in Sanskrit, the first Barmak is believed to have come to Balkh from Kashmir; family members studied mathematics and medical treatise there. The story goes that the Barmak converted to Islam, and was beheaded along with his ten sons after the city's Buddhist ruler Nazak (or Nizak) Tarkhan re-took the city from the Arabs. Others say he was summoned to Baghdad to cure the son of the Caliph Abd al-Malik.

What is more certain is that his son, Khalid al-Barmaki (705–82CE), survived and was a Buddhist before converting to Islam. He translated Sanskrit medical texts, served as vizier of al-Saffah and al-Mansur, the first two Abbasid caliphs, and sent missions to Kashmir to seek out other scientific texts. In 773CE one of these returned with a compilation of the works of the great Indian mathematicians Brahmagupta and Aryabhata (with their system of numbers which we call Arabic numerals) to Baghdad's great library, the House of Wisdom.

His son Yahya al-Khalid, vizier to Caliph al-Mahdi, was entrusted with educating Harun al-Rashid while patronising the great physicians of the day. Yahya's son, the eloquent Jafar, served as Harun's vizier in *The Thousand and One Nights* (and was made into a villain in Disney's *Aladdin*). In real life he introduced, among other innovations, the Chinese secret of making paper, leading to the opening of the first paper mill in Baghdad. Then Harun, for reasons unknown, had Jafar beheaded, and that was the end of the Barmakids.

a stupa by folding his robes and topping it with his bowl. They took other relics (a tooth, a basin and brush) back to Balkh and enshrined them in the two stupas by the gate, and introduced Buddhism to the Zoroastrian West.

An important Buddhist monastic complex was founded at Nava Vihara (or Nawbahar, 'New Temple') near the fire temple of Chashma-i-Shafa along the Koh-e-Alburz ridge, 31km south of Balkh. In 630CE, Xuanzang wrote that he found around a hundred *viharas* (monasteries) in Balkh and 30,000 monks at Nava Vihara. It became synonymous with beauty in Persian poetry ('A heart-rendering Bahar was in Balkh/Whose beauty surpassed the red tulips…,' wrote Nezami). Its lofty green flags were visible for miles around, showing the way to pilgrims who admired Nava Vihara's innumerable statues draped in silk robes and jewels, and an enormous statue of the Buddha.

The Arabs first attacked Balkh in 654CE, but their hold would be tenuous until 715CE when Qutayba captured central Asia for Islam under the Umayyad caliphs. Some chroniclers say Nava Vihara was destroyed then and its treasures destroyed. Yet 10th-century writer Umar ibn al-Azraq al-Kermani visited and wrote that its most important temple boasted a Kaaba-like stone cube in the centre, covered in a cloth, as if it had become a miniature Mecca. Other writers say Nava Vihara was destroyed after its protector, Jafar al-Barmaki, was executed.

Balkh and Islam Balkh's mighty walls failed to keep out a merry-go-round of Islamic and Turkic armies and rulers, yet all the while it continued to thrive as a multi-cultural hub under the Samanid Empire in the late 9th century, where Zoroastrians, Buddhists, Hindus, Christians, Jews and Muslims lived in harmony. The Arab geographers Ya'qubi (d897CE) and Moqaddasi (d991CE) described a prosperous city stretching for 3 square miles, the capital of Tokharistan (as Bactria was known in the Middle Ages). Many of the greatest medieval poets writing in Persian would hail from Balkh. It became a hub for Sufism, birthplace of the beloved female poet Rabi'a Balkhi (page 246), and scholarship: the father of Islam's greatest philosopher-physician Ibn Sina or Avicenna (d1037) came from Balkh.

Then in 1220 Genghis Khan destroyed it all, putting the inhabitants to the sword. An estimated 200,000 inhabitants had already fled Balkh on the rumour of the Mongols' coming, including the family of 12-year-old Mawlana Jalaluddin Balkhi, son of a famous Sufi teacher, who would later be better known as Rumi, one of the greatest of all Sufi poets.

Marco Polo showed up some 50 years later and described Balkh as a 'noble and great city, though it was much greater in former days. But that Tartars and other nations have greatly ravaged and destroyed it.'

Timur passed through and levelled the Bala Hissar, but the Timurids, especially Shah Rukh and his wife Gowhar Shad, restored the city to some of its former glory. Balkh, as capital of Afghan Turkestan, would later ping pong between various rulers and was often ruled by Bukhara until 1751, when Ahmad Shah Durrani added it to Afghanistan – though as it was located a two-week journey from Kabul (before the building of the Salang Tunnel), it was de facto ruled by the Uzbek Qataghan dynasty from their capital in Tashqurghan. The whole region south of Amu Darya (Afghan Turkestan) became more firmly part of Afghanistan after the conquests of Dost Mohammad Khan in the 1850s and Abdur Rahman Khan in 1888.

Balkh was in a dire state in the early 20th century; outbreaks of malaria caused the administrative capital to move to Mazar e Sharif. Robert Byron, who visited in 1933, evoked it at the time:

the colour of the landscape changed from lead to aluminium, pallid and deathly, as if the sun had been sucking away its gaiety for thousands and thousands of years: for this was now the plain of Balkh...first on the north and then on the south of the road, rose the worn grey-white shapes of a bygone architecture, mounds, furrowed and bleached by the rain and sun, wearier than any human works I ever saw...suddenly a line of bony dilapidated walls jumped out of the ground and occupied the horizon. Passing inside them, we found ourselves in a vast metropolis of ruins stretching away to the north: while on the south of the road, the shining greens of mulberries, poplars and stately isolated planes were balm to eyes bruised by the monstrous antiquity of the preceding landscape. We stood in Balkh herself, the Mother of cities.

Not long after Byron's visit, new streets were laid out, radiating from the central square. Today Balkh is the eighth largest city in Afghanistan, with a majority Uzbek population, a trading centre for cotton, almonds, melons and karakul sheep skins.

GETTING THERE AND AROUND Balkh is north of the main Mazar e Sharif–Maymana road. The junction is flanked by two great mounds – the remains of two 5th-century CE Buddhist stupas, said to contain the relics of Tapassu and Bhallika. The circular street plan radiates from the main square.

Shared taxis run to and from Mazar e Sharif from the turn-off from the Mazar–Maymana road. You can also often find them close to the main square (100AFN; 30mins).

Renting a car and driver from Mazar e Sharif for half a day would cost in the region of 1,500–2,000AFN.

TOURIST INFORMATION AND REGISTRATION You will need to register at the Department of Information and Culture in Mazar e Sharif (page 235) before coming to Balkh. The police will check your documents at a checkpoint as you enter the town from the Mazar e Sharif–Maymana road. The authorities in Balkh are very strict about this.

 WHERE TO STAY AND EAT There is no accommodation in Balkh, and with Mazar e Sharif so close there is no need to stay. Chaikhanas north of the main square and along the street from the Mazar–Maymana road to the square offer simple Afghan staples. Fruit is also available in the bazaar located north of the square.

WHAT TO SEE AND DO
Shrine of Khoja Abu Nasr Parsa (⊕ dawn–dusk daily; free) Known simply as Khoja Parsa, or the Green Mosque, this imposing Timurid shrine dominates the main square. Standing at nearly 30m, it is one of the most impressive Timurid buildings in Afghanistan. The ribbed 'pumpkin' dome, ribbed columns and Kufic script are reminiscent of buildings in Samarkand and Bukhara.

Khoja Parsa was an Islamic teacher and mystic of the Naqshbandi Sufi order. Built in the 1460s, his shrine is the only surviving monument in Balkh from the glory days of the Timurid Empire when the city was still a regional power, before its gradual decline. The shrine was carefully restored in the 2010s. There is a madrasa next door which the caretaker might be persuaded to open for you.

On the opposite side of the park, shrouded by trees, is a monumental **arch**, all that remains of the 17th-century Sayyid Subhan Quli Khan Madrasa.

Tomb of Rabi'a Balkhi
(⊕ dawn–dusk daily; free) The turquoise-tiled tomb of Rabi'a Balkhi is situated across from Khoja Parsa in the centre of the main square, housed in a low building with four arches built over the dungeon where she died, discovered in 1964. It is common to see young women at the tomb. Rabi'a Balkhi is without doubt the most famous female Persian poet and her name is known by everyone in Afghanistan. Many girls' schools across Afghanistan are named after her.

Bala Hissar and the city walls
(⊕ dawn–dusk daily; free) Located on the north side of Balkh, the vast sun-bleached walls of the Bala Hissar date from the 15th-century Timurid era, although a citadel has stood here since antiquity. In 327BCE Alexander the Great married Roxana, 'the most beautiful woman in Asia', on this site. A walk up on to the Bala Hissar's walls affords great views of the town and surrounding countryside, where the old city walls snake through the fields on the edge of the current town. The ground is littered with shards of blue glazed pottery, hinting at the people and lives from centuries long past.

You will see pits and holes in the Bala Hissar and around the city walls where people have decided they want to do more than imagine what lies under the earth. Looting is very common in and around Balkh.

For those wishing to circumnavigate the city walls, still standing 25m tall and 100m thick in places, they stretch for 12km albeit some sections have collapsed or been removed over time. The section near the road into town is in good condition and is easiest to access for photos.

Rumi's House
(200m east of the Bala Hissar; ⊕ dawn–dusk daily; free) On the edge of town lie the remains of a 13th-century madrasa. It is in poor condition, but walls and half a domed roof remain of what was a larger building. It is easily found as it has a protective metal roof to protect its mud walls from the elements. Everybody in Balkh will tell you this was the childhood home of one of the world's most famous Islamic mystics, Rumi. While Rumi did live in Balkh as a child and left due to the imminent attack by Genghis Khan, there is no real evidence to suggest that this was his home. However, it is well worth a stop if you're taking a walk around the city walls.

No Gombad Mosque
(1.5km southwest of the junction for Balkh off the Mazar e Sharif–Maymana road – you can see the metal canopy from some distance away; ⊕ dawn–dusk daily; free; currently there is a small Taliban presence managing the site & you will have to show your documentation to enter) The No Gombad ('Nine Domes') Mosque, is probably the oldest in Afghanistan. It is believed to have been built over a Buddhist monastery in the 9th century CE, possibly under Samanid rule.

The mosque is a masterpiece of early Islamic architecture in central Asia. As its name suggests, it originally featured nine domes supported by 12 columns, following a layout typical of early mosque designs. It collapsed in an earthquake not long after it was built, and only remnants of the domes and columns remain, but the intricate stucco carvings on these columns and the mihrab (prayer niche) showcase a high level of artistic skill, with patterns and motifs including floral patterns, Kufic inscriptions and geometric shapes that blend Persian and early Islamic styles.

The area around the mosque has been subject to various archaeological efforts aimed at preservation and restoration. The whole structure sits under a metal canopy constructed under the Daoud government in the 1970s. Efforts by UNESCO and the Aga Khan Trust for Culture in the 2010s have further stabilised the remains.

RABI'A BALKHI

> ...although she was a woman, was superior to men in accomplishments. She possessed great intelligence and sharp temperament. She used to continuously play the game of love and admired beautiful youths.
>
> Muhammad 'Awfi, in the 13th-century *Lubab ul-Albab* ('The Essence of Essences')

Believed to be a Persianised Arab during the time of the Samanid Empire, perhaps the daughter of Ka'b, the Emir of Balkh, Rabi'a Balkhi belonged to the educated elite of one of the cultural centres of Islam. She was the first woman to write in New Persian or Parsi-ye Dari ('Persian of the Court'), innovating and contributing to the literary canon.

Beyond that her story is wrapped in legend and romance, thanks to the Sufi writers who made her life into a tale of mystic love that has reverberated to this day. Rabi'a, they say, was as beautiful as the moon. After spotting her brother Haris's beautiful Turkish slave Baktash, she fell metaphorically in love and secretly dedicated all her poems to him.

Baktash was also a great warrior, and when Balkh was attacked Haris sent him out to save the day. But when Haris went to Bukhara for a poetry festival, the great poet Rudaki recited one of Rabi'a's poems and spoke of her love for the slave. Furious, Haris returned to Balkh and imprisoned Rabi'a and threw Baktash in a well. Rabi'a slit her wrists, and before dying, she wrote a final love poem for Baktash on its walls in her blood:

> I wish my body was aware of my heart
> I wish my heart was aware of my body
> I wish I could escape from you in peace
> Where can I go regretfully

Baktash was rescued from the well and, finding his dead love, killed himself at her side.

Rabi'a's story is especially popular among Afghan women. She is depicted in several ways – as a martyr for her mystic love of God, symbolised by Baktash, or as a victim of honour within a patriarchal order, a symbol of the price Afghan women pay for any kind of freedom. Perhaps most of all these days Rabi'a is a feminist icon, symbolising a spirit of defiance against the extremely unjust constraints imposed upon her sex.

By the north wall is the green pyramid Tomb of Haji Piyadah, 'the walking pilgrim' who walked all the way to Mecca from Balkh and back in the 15th century.

THE DRIVE FROM MAZAR E SHARIF TO HERAT

The road between Mazar e Sharif and Herat was once part of a major trading route between Persia and central Asia. Now it is a forgotten corner of Asia and very much a road less travelled. Skirting the northwest flank of the Hindu Kush, it follows a string of long-forgotten trading and administrative towns, but it was not always so. At the time of the Mongol invasion, Merv, now in modern Turkmenistan, was probably the largest city in the world and these towns were important satellite cities. Occasionally it feels like things have not changed since those times.

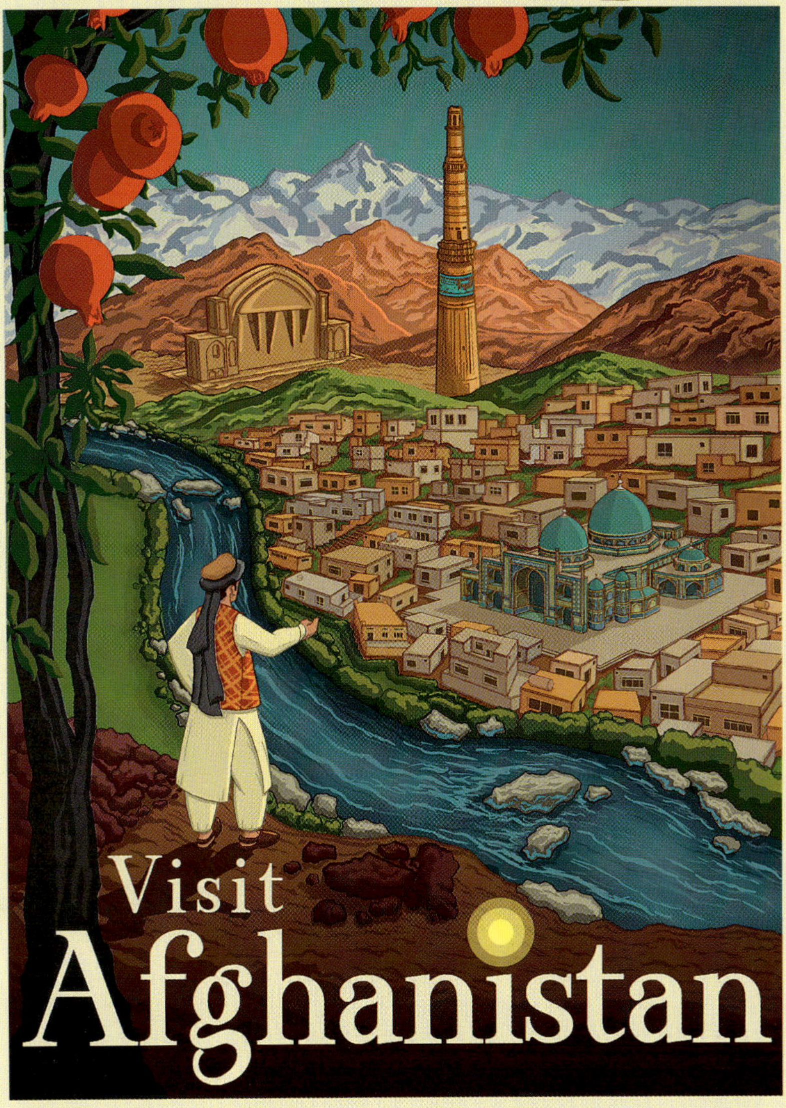

Visit Afghanistan

Safarāt Travel was founded by journalists Joe Sheffer and Qudratullah Noory to tell Afghanistan's story in a deeper, more human way. We are passionate about this wild and complex country, its beauty, its struggles, and everything in between.

We have worked here since 2012 and we open up our networks to give travelers meaningful access. Whether you want a short private tour of Bamyan's sights, immersive homestays in Helmand, or treks across the Hindu Kush, we use our decade of experience to make it possible. We look forward to welcoming you to Kabul.

+44 7458611911
www.safarat.co

Safarat

TRAVEL TAKEN SERIOUSLY...

bradtguides.com/shop

@bradtguides

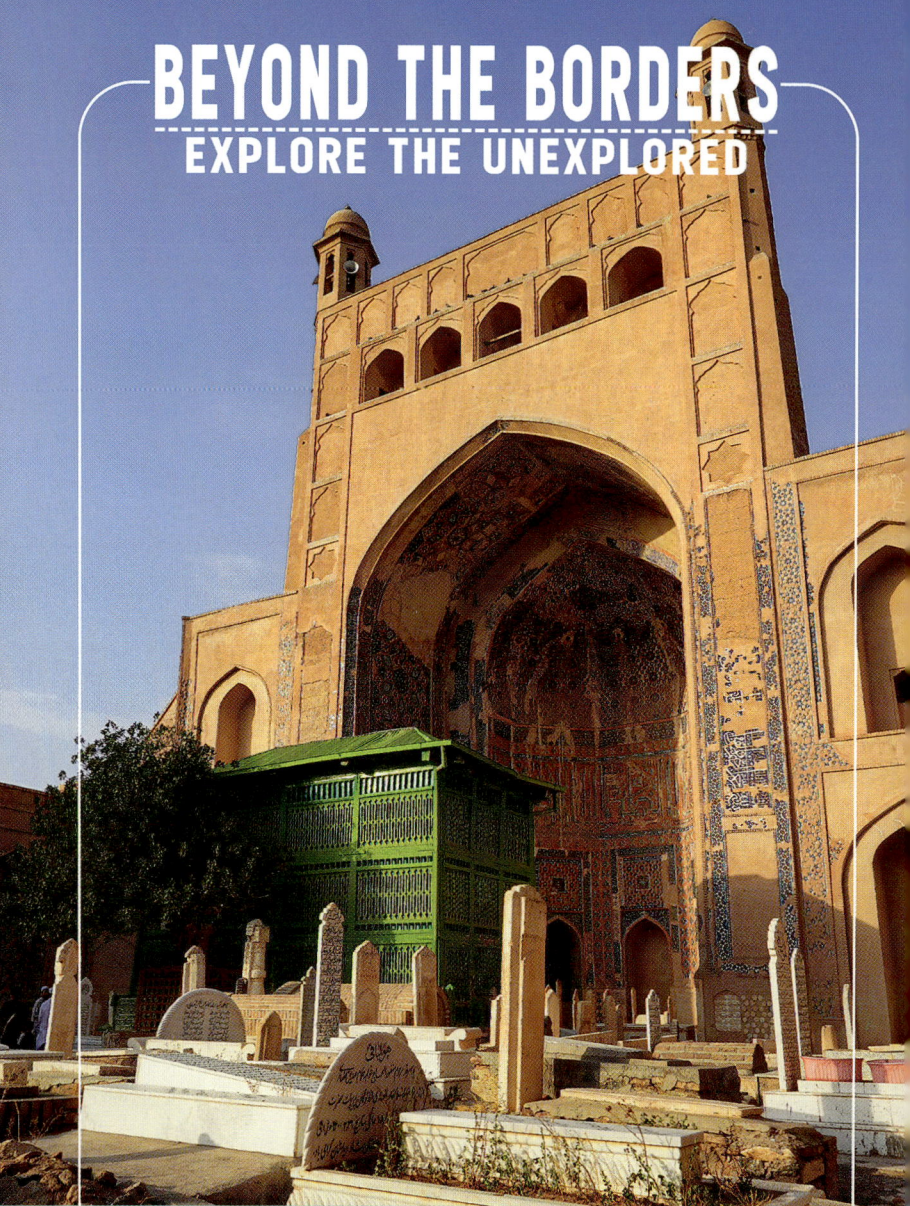

THE DRIVE FROM MAZAR E SHARIF TO HERAT

It is a land of cotton fields, sheep and Afghanistan's only gas reserves. It is rapidly changing, but the bi-weekly Uzbek and Turkmen markets in Aqcha and Andkhoy or a night in a basic chaikhana in Bala Murghab allow a glimpse into a life that has disappeared in other parts of the world. Even if your time is limited, you can get a great feel for it by making a day trip from Mazar to Aqcha.

This route was travelled in the opposite direction by Robert Byron in his groundbreaking 1937 travelogue *The Road to Oxiana*, a book often seen as the travel writers' travel book (Bruce Chatwin said he never travelled without a copy).

At the time of writing the journey takes two days, with an overnight at Maymana or a basic chaikhana in Bala Murghab. The road is being improved (currently there is no paved road in Badghis Province and speeds are reduced to a crawl at times), so in the future this could become a long single day's travel.

AQCHA (100km west of Mazar e Sharif; take a car or minivan from Mazar e Sharif – 250AFN, 1hr) The drive to Aqcha is flat and largely featureless (though you'll be accompanied all the way by a gas pipeline connecting Afghanistan's gas fields near Shibergan to Mazar e Sharif), but this small Turkmen town is well worth a visit on market days (Mondays and Thursdays) and can be combined with a day trip to Balkh from Mazar e Sharif. It is a great place for people-watching and photography. On market days the town buzzes with people from the surrounding smallholdings shopping and trading. Older Turkmen and Uzbek men with wispy beards, turbans and wearing thickly padded chapans look as if they were taken straight from central casting. It is easy to spend half a day enjoying the whole spectacle. If the tuk-tuks were removed it really would feel like stepping back in time. On non-market days the town is very quiet.

Don't miss the people selling animal skins including karakul sheep pelts. You may notice what looks like a pair of testicles being sold with the skins. These are the animal's sebaceous glands and are used during the processing of the pelts. You can also buy carpets, but the trade is wholesale so you will need to ask around; it is unlikely you will see piles of carpets for sale in the bazaar.

Some 2km north of the main bazaar are remains of the old city of Aqcha, dating from the time when it was one of a string of fortified towns skirting the Hindu Kush. There is a large fort to the west and a walled caravanserai to the east. Both are in poor condition. As at Balkh, the area is littered with pottery fragments hinting at what lies beneath. Indeed, treasure hunters have dug in the area.

Local restaurants in the bazaar sell Uzbeki pulao and kebabs. There is no real need to stay in Aqcha as Mazar e Sharif is so close.

SHIBERGAN About 20km before Shibergan, you'll see **Chiqchi Fort** on the north side of the road. The fort would have been a safe place for caravans to overnight between Shibergan and Aqcha – essential even into the 19th century, along with heavily armed escorts when Turkmen raiders could come thundering on horseback out of nowhere.

Shibergan itself is the largest ethnically Uzbek city in Afghanistan and was the home town of Rashid Dostum (page 232). Owing to the patronage of Dostum and income from the nearby Khowaja Gogerak gas fields, Shibergan has always felt more prosperous than its neighbouring towns. The Uzbek people and Shibergan in particular have strong links with Türkiye, evidenced by the signs for Turkish NGOs and its central landmark, a grand Turkish-style mosque.

Close to Shibergan is **Tillya Tepe** ('hill of gold'), which in 1978 proved to be one of Afghanistan's most remarkable archaeological finds: a huge nomad burial

THE CONTROVERSIAL QOSH TEPA CANAL

The largest infrastructure project undertaken by the Taliban government, the Qosh Tepa Canal stretches 285km from the Amu Darya due north of Mazar e Sharif, designed to turn 550,000ha of desert into farmland in Balkh, Jowzjan and Faryab provinces. It runs parallel to the main road from Mazar e Sharif to Maymana. The canal project features on the 50AFN stamp.

Climate change and an increasing population are putting a huge strain on Afghanistan's capacity to feed itself and the Afghan government sees the canal as an essential part of its economic commitment. However, the project has many critics. The canal will put extra pressure on the Amu Darya. Already the river disappears before reaching its former terminus in the Aral Sea. Cotton-growing Uzbekistan in particular is unhappy that it has not been consulted. However, as Afghanistan was never previously consulted about water usage, it is understandable that the country also wants a share of the precious resource.

mound complete with a hoard of more than 2,000 gold ornaments known as the Bactrian Gold (page 138).

Buzkashi is played on a Friday.

ANDKHOY Like Aqcha, Andkhoy is a Turkmen and Uzbek trading town, famous as the centre of Afghanistan's carpet production. In fact, most traditional Afghan carpets are woven by Turkmen and Uzbek women (page 48). Andkhoy's central roundabout sports a newly built replica of the mosque at Medina in Saudi Arabia, part of the Taliban's civic improvement programme. From here, the town extends out along main cardinal streets linked by circular streets. The main bazaar is northwest of the main roundabout. As in Aqcha, Andkhoy is a great place for people-watching, where you'll spot faces that look as if they've come straight out of a 19th-century photograph. Tuesday and Thursday are market days, when the town is at its best. Buzkashi is played on Fridays in the winter.

Wander down Andkhoy's side streets to find carpet wholesalers – ask for Serai Qalim Watani or Qalim Watani. There is also a lovely caravanserai full of wholesalers 100m west of the Medina Mosque roundabout on the south side of the street.

Accommodation is currently limited to the **Restaurant wa Shir Yakhi dae** ('Restaurant we invite you for ice cream'; southwest of the square; m 7817 52150; $), which means a room with no beds, a shared toilet, and no shower. However, larger, less charming buildings are being constructed east of the main roundabout, so better lodgings may be found in the future.

There are many chaikhanas for kebabs and Uzbek pulao, cooked with sesame oil. Try the **Turkestan restaurant** ($), south of the Medina Mosque roundabout on the east side of the street; the sign is in English.

The Turkmenistan border at Aqina is near here as well, but only open for local truck traffic at the time of writing, although you can take a taxi to Turkmenistan (1,000AFN; 1hr).

MAYMANA The road from Aqcha to Maymana takes you out of arid Jowzjan Province, home of Uzbeks and Turkmen, and into the rolling hills of Faryab Province. These hills are remarkably fertile due to the winds from the central

Asia steppe carrying a fine dust of topsoil called loess. In summer they are parched, but in winter they turn a rich velvety green unlike anywhere else in Afghanistan.

The largest town between Mazar e Sharif and Herat, Maymana was once an important Samanid-era cultural centre. The Mongols made sure that very little of it remains in spite of all its history; the old fortifications now occupy a park in the centre. The bazaar runs along the main road northeast of the park.

Maymana is linked to Mazar e Sharif via shared minivans and taxis (500–700AFN; 5hrs), while shared 4x4s or high-wheeled minivans go to and from Herat (1,500–1,800AFN; 10–12hrs).

Maymana is the best place to break the journey between Mazar e Sharif and Herat, although the options are still very limited. The best options are the **Baharistan Hotel** (Turbat Jan Baba St, behind the Aria Market; m 7955 85838; **$$**) which has attached bathrooms and no hot water; and **Mussafarkhana Aka e Abdulhaq** (Jada e Turbat Jan Baba Bukhul Bazaar Sq; m 7970 67818; **$**) with no attached bathroom.

These hotels have **restaurants**; in addition, there are restaurants found on the roads heading northeast of the central park.

BADGHIS PROVINCE

> Pastel pinks dominate this vast panorama of hidden valleys, purple shadows and lofty peaks…sprinkled with gnarled, dark-green pistachio and juniper which the high winds have whipped into exotic shapes.
> Nancy Hatch Dupree on Qotal e Zabrak, in *An Historical Guide to Afghanistan*

This is Afghanistan's poorest province, a throwback to an Afghanistan from the noughties. The roads are very rough – the 200km from the Badghis–Faryab border to Qala e Nau will take around 9 hours; and very little traffic exists beyond Russian Kamez trucks, land cruisers and the odd motorbike. You'll see far fewer signs of modernity or development here than in Jowzjan and Faryab provinces. Until the Taliban took power, Badghis was a byword for lawlessness. Illegal roadblocks were commonplace. Signs from these bad old days, including bullet-strewn buildings and war-torn checkpoints, are rife.

Predominantly Pashtun, Badghis is ethnically different as well. Families moved here in the 19th century during King Abdul Rahman Khan's demographic repopulating plan. Today the province acts like a Pashtun parenthesis between central Asia and Persia. No-one plays buzkashi. 'That is an Uzbek game,' I was simply told. Taliban flags appear in much greater numbers than in neighbouring provinces. In Herat or Jowzjan you'll see them only on government buildings; in Badghis, many shops and homes fly the flag.

The first settlement of any size, **Bala Murghab** lies only 20km from the Turkmenistan border. In the 10th century it was so beautiful and prosperous that it was described by geographers as a 'mini Merv' – until Timur destroyed it in the 14th century. In another world it would still be a thriving border town; only this border has not been open for decades, and despite Afghanistan getting much of its electricity from Turkmenistan, Bala Murghab is not yet connected to the grid. For a really wonderful genuine Afghan experience, stop for the night at one of the chaikhanas (**$**) by the main square.

The road to Qala e Nau passes villages with distinctly Herati-style houses, built of brick with domed rooms and windcatchers. Along this stretch in winter, you can frequently spot Kuchi nomads, with their colourful patchwork tents and flocks of fat-tailed sheep.

Qala e Nau is the capital of Badghis, where you'll pick up the paved road again. Only 3 hours from Herat there is no need to stay, but, if you get stuck, the **Daria Safar ($)** or **Mofaqiat mussafarkhana ($)** both on the road west of the bazaar offer simple accommodation and food.

Between Qala e Nau and Herat, the road hairpins up to a 2,400m pass and watershed at the **Qotal e Zabrak**, where you'll leave central Asia and enter the Persian-influenced area. Families from Herat come up here, especially on Fridays either to escape the summer heat or to play in the snow in winter. There are majestic views looking back into Badghis.

EAST OF MAZAR E SHARIF

TASHQURGHAN/KHOLM A small trading town 60km east of Mazar e Sharif, Tashqurghan (its frequently used Uzbeki name, meaning 'stone fort') marks the point where the road to Kabul leaves the central Asian steppe and enters the Hindu Kush. The change in geography is marked by the **Tangi Tashqurghan** (Tashqurghan Gorge), a narrow 12m-wide defile with cliffs over 300m tall. The road winding through it has many stalls selling pomegranates, large speciality breads with poppy and sesame seeds and excellent figs when in season; all that Tashqurghan produces is famed across Afghanistan. Coming from Kabul, the gorge marks the end of the mountains as you are spat out on to the central Asian plains which stretch almost unbroken to the Urals.

Like Balkh, Kholm was an important trading centre on the Silk Road until Genghis Khan destroyed it so thoroughly that the site (11km north of Tashqurghan) was left as a desolate mound. Under the Timurids it was rebuilt, only to be destroyed again, this time by Ahmad Shah Durrani who re-founded the town as Tashqurghan at its current more defensible location and built the now-ruined Bala Hissar fort overlooking town. Afghanistan lost the town to various rival khanates until Dost Mohammed recaptured it and restored its ancient name in the early 20th century. As Mazar and Kunduz had bridges over the Amu Darya, they took over the international trade and Tashqurghan's importance dwindled. This is as far as Robert Byron got in his quest to see the Oxus River in *The Road to Oxiana*. It was once famous for its old-fashioned covered bazaar, one of the last of its kind in central Asia, but sadly it was destroyed during the conflict in the 1980s.

Beyond a brief pause in the gorge, the reason to stop is the old **King's hunting lodge**, or Bagh e Jahan Nama (just outside town on the south side of the road towards Mazar e Sharif; ⊕ dawn–dusk daily; free). Easy to spot on account of the Russian tanks and APCs rusting outside its long mud walls (the Russians used it as a base after 1979), this lodge, or rather palace, was built in 1892 by the 'Iron Emir', Abdur Rahman Khan, in the central Asian style with a dome in the centre and large rooms for parties; in 1853, when he was only 13, Khan was appointed governor of Tashqurghan by his father – until he cancelled all taxes, which his appalled father had to spend months un-cancelling.

The arcaded façade overlooks pleasant gardens and a reflecting pool that is hugely popular with local children in the hot summer months. The lodge was restored with funds from the Netherlands in the 2010s and used to show art and historical photographs. Now it remains empty, but makes a striking sight with the bare mountain peaks rising in the background. Taliban soldiers are happy to allow visitors to have a look around; ask to visit the roof for the splendid views. The big mound visible to the north was ancient Kholm.

SAMANGAN/AIBAK AND TAKHT E ROSTAM A further 70km south of Tashqurghan lies the town of Samangan, sometimes called Aibak. In the 4th or 5th century CE the town was an important Kushan Buddhist trading town, and its most famous sight is from this era. **Takht e Rostum** (Throne of Rostum; ⏲ dawn–dusk daily; 250AFN) refers to a Buddhist stupa and monastery cave complex 3km south of the main town. You may be met by the caretaker-curator who will issue tickets and give you a guided tour.

Many Buddhist stupas in Afghanistan are named after the hero of Ferdowsi's epic *Shahnameh*. What makes Takht e Rostum in Samangan so different from all other stupas in Afghanistan is that, rather than being built of bricks, it is carved out of the bedrock, rather like the churches of Lalibela in Ethiopia (although there is no connection, and the stupa is not as ornate). Standing 8m tall it is an impressive sight, quite unlike anything else in Afghanistan, and, since the destruction of the Bamiyan Buddhas, arguably the country's most impressive pre-Islamic site. The rough caves are still topped by the harmika (the square enclosure symbolising heaven, the abode of god, which once contained relics of Buddha). Legend has it that Rostum celebrated his marriage to Tahmina, daughter of the king of Samangan, here by building his 'throne' in half a day and drinking wine from the basin on top.

A short walk down the hill and to the north wait five **monastic caves**. Their interiors have designs similar to those at Bamiyan (page 171). From left to right: the first cave, the largest, contains a carving of a lotus flower that covers the entire ceiling. It is covered with soot from fires so is not easy to make out. The second cave is a thin corridor with smaller rooms. The caretaker will tell you this is the bazaar (possibly due to its likeness to the old covered bazaar in Tashqurghan), but it is likely these were meditation cells or simply large alcoves for statues. The third cave opens into a well-proportioned square room with a domed roof, squinches in each corner and a niche in each wall for a Buddha or bodhisattva statue. Note the Doric columns over each niche, an example of the Greek influence on Buddhism in the region. The fourth and fifth caves are smaller and seem to have been converted at a later date to a hammam and toilet block.

Surkh Kotal (18km from Pol e Khomri, 1km west of the Pol e Khomri–Mazar e Sharif road) One of Afghanistan's most important archaeological sites, Surkh Kotal ('Red Pass') was a temple built by the Kushan king Kanishka sometime around 130CE, with five massive flights of stairs leading to the summit. It yielded numerous artefacts, now in the National Museum in Kabul, including the famous Surkh Kotal inscription in Bactrian Greek script. It was so extensively looted during the conflicts of the 1990s that today there is little to see.

If you do wish to visit, you can rent a car for the day (1,500–2,000AFN) from Pol e Khomri, but be warned the last kilometre of the road is unpaved.

Pol e Khomri Pol e Khomri is the largest town between Kabul and Mazar e Sharif. Stretching along the banks of the Kunduz River, its most notable building is the large Russian-built cement factory silo on the south side of town. The town also marks the intersection of the Kunduz–Kabul and Mazar e Sharif–Kabul roads, so you may need to change at Pol e Khomri or stop here if you want to visit nearby Surkh Kotal.

There is no real reason to stop overnight, but the air-conditioned **Payman Guesthouse** (off Shaheed Rasul Mohseni St, near the governor's office; m 7485 43515; **$$**) offers a more comfortable option than the chaikhanas and mussafarkhanas in the bazaar.

8 | MAZAR E SHARIF AND NORTHERN AFGHANISTAN

KUNDUZ

Afghanistan's sixth largest city sits at the centre of a wide, well-irrigated plain where the Kunduz and Khanabad rivers meet as they flow out of the Hindu Kush. In spring the hills are emerald green. Kunduz is famous for its cotton, fruit and vegetables, as well as rice and perhaps the country's best kebabs. The locally grown rice is so highly prized that it fetches prices two or three times higher than imported rice. The Spinzar (Pashto for 'white gold') Cotton Company, founded here in 1936, made Kunduz one of the most prosperous cities in the country, employing some 5,000 workers before 1979; now owned by the state, it is back in business as of 2024.

During the 18th and 19th centuries Kunduz was the capital of an Uzbek Khanate that ruled over a region stretching from Balkh to Badakhshan. This Khanate reached its zenith under the rule of Murad Beg until he was defeated in 1839 by the Afghan King Dost Mohammad and all of what is now northern Afghanistan was absorbed into Afghanistan.

Kunduz with its majority Pashtun population is an anomaly in the north. In the late 19th century, King Abdur Rahman Khan gave lands to rival Pashtun tribes as 'rewards' for assisting him. The land was welcome, but it also put rival tribes on the far side of the mountains from Kabul where they would find it harder to oppose him. One infamous Pashtun son of Kunduz is Gulbuddin Hekmatyar (page 254).

This large Pashtun population explains in part why the city was the last to fall to the Northern Alliance and their Western allies in 2001. It was also the first provincial capital to be captured by the Taliban in 2015. The Taliban occupied

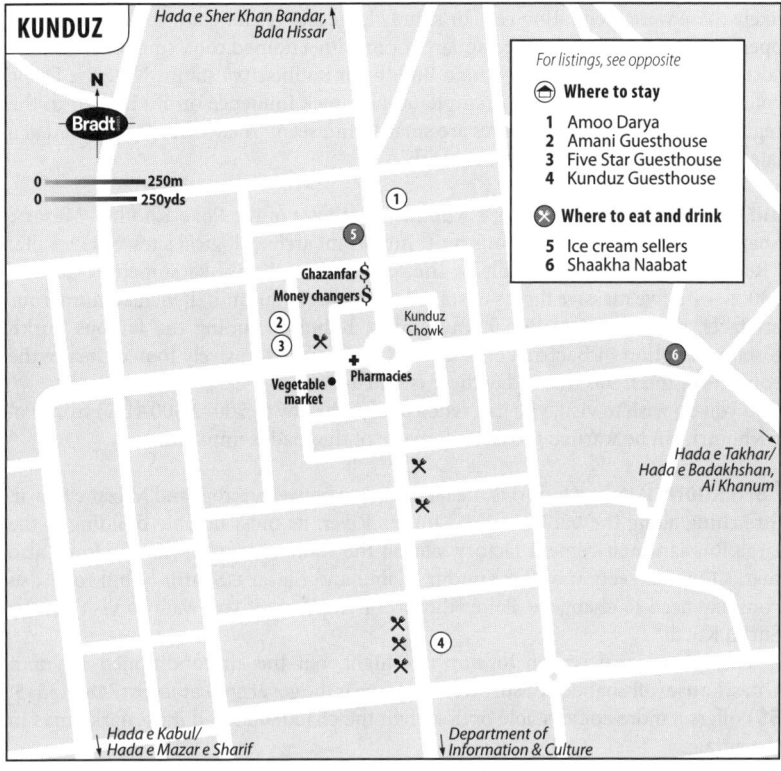

Kunduz for only three days before they retreated, but the attack was a warning of their growing power. It was during this time that the US bombed the new Médecins Sans Frontières trauma hospital, tragically killing 42 patients and staff.

Provincial Kunduz is not a destination in its own right but a handy place to stop if travelling to Badakhshan, visiting the ruins at Ai Khanoum or entering or departing Afghanistan via Tajikistan. Almost all services can be found close to Kunduz Chowk – the main intersection in the city centre. Make sure you pack mosquito spray as the city and surrounding areas have a history of malaria (see page 77 for advice).

GETTING THERE AND AWAY The base for transport for points west of Kunduz is the **Hada e Kabul/Hada e Mazar**, located 2–3km south of Kunduz Chowk on the west side of the main road to Kabul. Travelling from or to Kabul, large 30–40-seater coaches (600–1,000AFN; 12hrs) leave more frequently at night (22.00–04.00), while shared minivans and taxis (1,200–1,500AFN; 12hrs) depart throughout the day, albeit more frequently at night. Shared minivans and taxis also link Mazar e Sharif (400–500AFN; 4hrs) to Kunduz. A taxi to the Hada e Kabul from the centre will cost in the region of 250AFN.

Cars or minivans from or to Fayzabad (700AFN; 4hrs) and other points east of Kunduz depart from the **Hada e Takhar/Hada e Badakhshan** east of the centre, 2km from Kunduz Chowk on the south side of the road.

A small collection of cars go to and from the Tajikistan border over the bridge at Sher Khan Bandar based at **Hada e Sher Khan Bandar**, 500m north of the Bala Hissar on the left side of the road (200AFN; 1hr).

There is no public transport between Kunduz and Ai Khanoum. A car or a 4x4 (US$100/200; 4hrs each way) can be rented for the day from Kunduz. The last section of road is unpaved.

TOURIST INFORMATION AND REGISTRATION If you are coming from Tajikistan you will need to register at the Department of Information and Culture in Kunduz, 1.5km south of Kunduz Chowk. Otherwise, there is little reason to visit.

WHERE TO STAY *Map, opposite*

There is nothing really to keep you in Kunduz and the accommodation options are functional rather than inspiring. You may need to stay overnight if visiting Ai Khanoum or travelling to or from Tajikistan. In addition to the guesthouses listed below, there are a number of mussafarkhanas west and north of Kunduz Chowk. Try **Amoo Darya ($)**, where they may let you sleep in the communal room.

Five Star Guesthouse 200m west of Kunduz Chowk; m 7988 06680. This hotel & wedding hall is always a hive of activity, although with the Taliban ban on music any weddings are unlikely to be overly disturbing. Once away from the wedding area, the rooms are large, clean & functional. AC, squat toilet attached, b/fast inc. **$$**

Kunduz Guesthouse (Formerly Shah Wali guesthouse) Jada e walayat St, an 11min walk south of Kunduz Chowk; m 7995 48989. This small 2-storey government-run guesthouse situated in its own grounds also has a wedding hall attached. Clean albeit it feels a bit tired. Blast door & high security; AC, attached Western-style toilet; b/fast inc. **$$**

Amani Guesthouse Next to Five Star Guesthouse (see left); m 7908 40401. This simple but clean guesthouse is a quieter, cheaper option than its neighbour. The rooms are small but the staff friendly. No security. AC; non-attached squat toilet, no b/fast. **$–$$**

GULBUDDIN HEKMATYAR

None of the mujahideen were angels, but only one was called 'the Butcher of Kabul'. Born in 1949, Gulbuddin Hekmatyar studied engineering at Kabul University and was always known as 'Engineer Hekmatyar' by his followers. While in university, he joined Burhanuddin Rabbani's Jamiat-i-Islami (Islamic Society), along with Ahmad Shah Massoud (page 144), though their goals diverged from the beginning. Hekmatyar was in favour of radical change and founded Afghanistan's first Islamist party, the Hezb e Islami. Massoud believed in Rabbani's more moderate, inclusive goals. Even in 1975, when Massoud was only 22, Hekmatyar sensed he was a dangerous rival and tried to assassinate him.

Partly because he spoke perfect English, Hekmatyar and his Hezb e Islami mujahideen received the lion's share of funds (at least US$600 million) from the CIA and the Saudis to fight the Soviets, funnelled to him by Pakistan's ISI, who were grooming him to be their man in Afghanistan. Even though, as Peter Bergen wrote in *Holy War, Inc*, 'his party had the dubious distinction of never winning a significant battle during the war, training a variety of militant Islamists from around the world, killing significant numbers of mujahideen from other parties, and taking a virulently anti-Western line.'

In the late 1980s, Hekmatyar began diverting funds from the CIA into opium and manufacturing heroin, becoming one of the world's top drug dealers. During the civil war that followed, he refused to join the other mujahideen in the Peshawar Accords, even though, as a leading Pashtun, he was repeatedly offered the top post as prime minister in a provisional government. Even Osama

WHERE TO EAT AND DRINK *Map, page 252*

Everything is based around Kunduz Chowk, where there are many Afghan restaurants. For more variety, take a walk on the road south of here. Don't miss Kunduz's famous watermelons in season. For **ice cream**, head a couple of streets north of Kunduz Chowk.

Shaakha Naabat Main road, 500m east of Kunduz Chowk; m 7054 68478. Restaurant, bakery & reasonably well-stocked convenience store all in one. The AC restaurant serves good Afghan dishes, as well as pizza & fried chicken. The décor would not look out of place in Kabul's restaurant 'scene'. Smaller Shaakha Naabat bakeries are found in other parts of Kunduz city but this is the main one. $$

OTHER PRACTICALITIES Ghazanfar Bank (m 7978 60075) is one block north of Kunduz Chowk; in the same area you'll also find moneychangers. There are several **pharmacies** around Kunduz Chowk.

WHAT TO SEE AND DO

Bala Hissar Kunduz's only historical building, this was once the seat of power of Murad Beg, who controlled all of northern Afghanistan. Today it sits a little forlornly on the northern edge of town and is currently used as a Taliban military base. Not as impressive or complete as the citadels in Balkh or Farah, it has fine views of the city from the battlements and a charming 19th-century bridge that crosses a river to a high citadel on the western side of the complex. Inside the walls, containers and rusting Russian military hardware lie scattered about while kids play cricket in the dried moat. You will need permission from the **Department of**

bin Laden advised him to 'join his brothers'. Instead, he wanted total control, and bombed Kabul, released 10,000 dangerous criminals from prison, cut off the city's water and electricity, and shifted alliances with other warlords whenever it suited.

Hekmatyar's brutality made him unpopular even among the Pashtuns. It was only when the advancing Taliban forced him to flee that he belatedly agreed to serve as prime minister in Rabbani's power-sharing government. But by then Pakistan had new favourites: the Taliban. As the Taliban moved into Kabul in 1996, many of Hekmatyar's Hezb troops went over to their side. Hekmatyar took refuge in the Panjshir. Despite the bad blood between them, Massoud helped him escape to Iran.

He came out against the US invasion of Afghanistan in 2001, urging the Taliban to re-form. Iran expelled him and he lived in different locations on the Pakistan border. Accused of ordering bombings and attacks on coalition forces, Hekmatyar was labelled a war criminal in Afghanistan and a Global Terrorist by the US.

In 2016, after two decades in exile, Engineer Hekmatyar and members of his Hezb e Islami were pardoned by President Ghani, in spite of the protests by human rights organisations. In May 2017, the Engineer was back in Kabul, running for president in the 2019 election (and finishing third). He has since remained in Kabul, the last of the major mujahideen commanders still living in Afghanistan, writing books and supporting the Taliban, although in 2024 they banned him from giving weekly sermons on the radio.

Information and Culture in Kunduz (located 3km south of Kunduz Chowk) to visit and the bored Taliban soldiers will happily show you around.

Ai Khanoum (131km northeast of Kunduz) Ai Khanoum, meaning 'Lady Moon' in Uzbek, was one of the most significant Hellenistic cities founded by the Greeks in ancient Bactria. Situated on a high plateau, overlooking the point where the Kochka River empties into the Amu Darya with the hills of Tajikistan as a backdrop, the founders of Ai Khanoum picked a truly splendid spot for this far outpost of Hellenic culture (page 18). Founded by one of Alexander the Great's generals or possibly by Alexander himself during his eastern campaigns, most historians believe it was originally named (or renamed) Eucratideia, the capital of King Eucratides I, who conquered northern India.

Ancient Greek geographers described it as a city of great wealth straddling the Oxus, and in its heyday it played a key role as a cultural and economic hub. Proof of its riches was one of the coins discovered nearby which was nothing less than the largest gold coin minted in antiquity, the 169.2g 20-stater coin of Eucratides I (now in the Cabinet des Médailles in Paris). Another unique find was the silver-and-gold Ai Khanoum plaque in the National Museum in Kabul, 'the most important work [of] the Graeco-Oriental style' showing the Greek goddess of victory Nike and Cybele, the Asian mother goddess, arriving in a lion-drawn chariot at a sacrifice to the sun god Helios, next to a sun and crescent moon.

Ai Khanoum's decline likely came in the 2nd century BCE, as the Graeco-Bactrian Kingdom weakened under pressure from nomadic invasions, particularly by the Saka, Yuezhi and later the Kushans. Ai Khanoum was eventually abandoned and fell into ruin.

These days the site is so remote it was only rediscovered by accident in 1961 by King Zahir Shah while on a hunting trip. Excavations in the 1960s and 1970s by French archaeologists revealed extensive remains that provided insight into Bactria's multi-cultural character, showcasing Hellenistic civilisation's influence deep in central Asia. The city had a classic Greek urban layout, including a central agora, gymnasium, theatre, mint and temples – all designed in the Hellenistic style.

Today there is little to see of this ancient city: foundations of buildings and Doric and Corinthian columns surrounded by hundreds of smaller holes where looters have searched for treasure. But the setting of Ai Khanoum is a wonder.

9

Badakhshan and the Wakhan Corridor

The topographical map of Afghanistan resembles a giant fan, with its ribs – mountain ranges and valleys – radiating southwest from a single point in the far northeast. This point is the Pamir Knot, where five of Asia's great mountain ranges converge: the Hindu Kush, the Pamirs, the Tien Shan, the Kunlun, and the Karakoram. Nicknamed the 'Roof of the World', part of this vast, high-altitude region lies within Afghanistan's remote Badakhshan Province.

Historically, Badakhshan was nearly always autonomous, loosely tied to a nearby power, notably Bukhara or Kunduz under Murad Beg. Its modern division came in the late 19th century, when Great Game players Britain and Russia redrew Afghanistan's northern frontier, slicing Badakhshan in two and splitting families and communities. Yet cultural and familial ties remain between the Afghan and Tajik sides – closer than any other region bordering the former Soviet central Asian states.

Badakhshan is the centre of a mountainous flywheel, with towering ridges and deep valleys spinning out in all directions to shape the geography of central and south Asia. Remote even by Afghan standards, here travel is slow, difficult and often adventurous – but deeply rewarding. Best known today for the Wakhan Corridor, a narrow finger of land that reaches deep into the Pamirs, the province offers some of

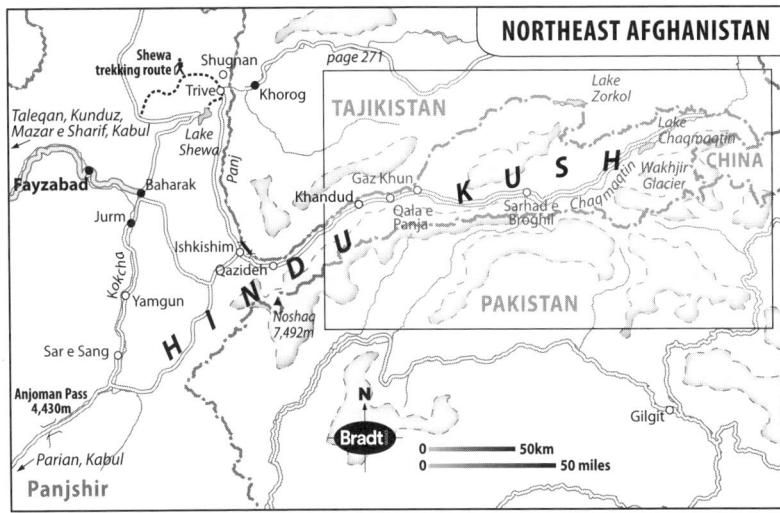

> ### THE ROYAL RUBY OF BADAKHSHAN
>
> In the texts left to us by the great empires of the Middle Ages, Badakhshan is rarely mentioned. But when it is, it usually has to do with the fabulous rubies mined there, famous for their 'pigeon blood red' colour coveted by kings and emirs from Bukhara to Delhi.
>
> One of the largest ruby spinels (or balas rubies) ever found in Badakhshan – a great 170-carat red gem – somehow made its way down the Silk Road to Spain, where it was owned by the Muslim king of Granada in the 14th century. He was killed by Pedro the Cruel who stripped the jewel from his body; the ruby then passed to King Pedro's brother Henry of Trastamara, who gave it to the Black Prince, Edward of Woodstock, in 1366 in return for some help on the battlefield.
>
> The Black Prince took the gem to England, where it was embedded in the helmet of Henry V. It then made a brief foray to France at the Battle of Agincourt and may even have helped to save the king's helmet and head when he was struck by a battleaxe. They say Richard III wore it, with rather less luck, at Bosworth. It disappeared under Cromwell, only to reappear in 1661 when the Crown purchased it for £400. The ruby took pride of place in Victoria's coronation crown, and is currently embedded, front and centre, in the Imperial State Crown.

Afghanistan's most spectacular trekking, alongside the unique Wakhi and Kyrgyz communities who call it home.

For millennia, Badakhshan has also been prized for its mineral wealth, particularly its lapis lazuli and rubies (see above). Today, this isolated region may once again be on the verge of change. A new road linking Afghanistan with China promises to revive ancient trade routes, echoing the journeys of early travellers like Marco Polo (page 268).

FAYZABAD

Strung along the banks of the Kokcha River, surrounded by steep hills and fertile valleys, Fayzabad is the quiet, provincial capital of Badakhshan, the only major settlement and market town for the surrounding rural communities – and a welcome place to rest before venturing into the dramatic highlands. Its isolation, with only one long, winding road connecting it to the rest of the country, gives Fayzabad a peaceful, laid-back charm.

In the 1990s, Fayzabad was an important stronghold for the mujahideen, serving as a centre of resistance first against Soviet occupation and then against the Taliban. It was one of the few towns not to fall into Taliban hands and was often the de facto political centre for anti-Taliban alliances.

For visitors, Fayzabad is the main springboard for adventurous journeys into the Wakhan Corridor, the remote Afghan Pamir or the many rugged mountain districts that make up this remote province. The town has a small but active bazaar, where you can buy basic supplies, and there are a handful of simple hotels catering to travellers. Fayzabad is also known for its natural bounty – pistachios, walnuts and honey are local specialities, particularly in the fertile lowlands downstream towards Keshem. In earlier centuries, Badakhshan's rich deposits of precious stones would also have passed through markets here, destined for traders across central Asia and beyond.

GETTING THERE AND AWAY The **airport** is situated at the far west of town but has no commercial flights. There were commercial flights in the early 2010s, so there is potential for flights to return.

By shared transport For **directions east**, the Istga e Baharak is located 1,500m southeast of Chahari Istiqal and has shared taxis to Baharak (100AFN; 1hr) where travellers can change for vehicles towards Ishkishim (500AFN; 5hrs) and the Wakhan. In the early morning you can also find shared taxis running to Baharak from the main bridge.

For **directions west**, ask for Istga e Kabul or Istga e Kunduz, 5km south of Chahari Istiqal. Shared taxis leave regularly for Kunduz (700AFN; 4hrs). Big buses leave in the afternoon to Kabul (1,200AFN; 15hrs). The ticket offices for the buses are another 500m west.

TOURIST INFORMATION AND REGISTRATION The Department of Information and Culture is on the northwest side of the main bridge. You will need to visit if you plan to travel further into Badakhshan. They can provide guides.

ORIENTATION Dictated by geography, Fayzabad stretches for 7km along the Kokcha River. The older part of the city is centred around Chahari Istiqal (Freedom Sq), with the bazaar to the north, east and west. South of the river is Shahre Nau, the new town. Here you will find government buildings, banks and other more modern facilities. The busiest section is along the main road running north and south of the buzkashi pitch. At the far southern end of this section of the city are the ticket offices for the buses to Kabul and Mazar e Sharif.

WHERE TO STAY Map, page 260

Fayzabad has a few mid-range options overlooking the Kokcha River; the sound of flowing water as you fall asleep, followed by breakfast on a rooftop with views of the river and mountains make a delightful introduction to Badakhshan. At the time of writing, the Pamir Club, set on a high promontory with the river flowing around it on three sides (the best location of any hotel in Afghanistan), only takes bookings from government staff.

Bam e Dunya Hotel Behind the buzkashi field; m 7990 04977. This imposing 5-storey hotel is quite literally the biggest thing on the Fayzabad accommodation scene. It seems to have been built for a golden age of tourism that has yet to arrive & only the 30 rooms of the 4th floor are in use. The views over the Kokcha River, town & buzkashi field are wonderful. The rooms themselves are large, clean & comfortable albeit uninspiring. Attached bathroom with Western-style toilets, security, AC; b/fast inc. **$$$**

MNA Hotel & Restaurant On the Fayzabad–Keshem road, south of the airport; m 7070 48110, 7974 97133, 7064 07622. This 3-storey guesthouse near the airport stands at the far west end of town. It is clean & friendly with dbls, trpls & qdrpls, & has lovely rooftop river views. The interior design is wild; most rooms sport full-length murals. The one on the top floor of the Amalfi coast is particularly garish. No en suites, squat toilet, fan; b/fast inc. **$$**

Sahile Darya Hotel & Restaurant Near the MNA Hotel; m 7089 88943, 7966 10381; e sahildaryahotelandrestaurant@gmail.com. The focus here is on the restaurant (which is the best in town; page 261) rather than the rooms, which are large but have bare concrete floors & no sheets. There's better value elsewhere. AC, Western-style toilet & attached bathroom, security; b/fast inc. **$$**

Awliya Hotel & Restaurant m 7994 83630. Friendly basic chaikhana on the same street as the lapis shops. For 500AFN you can get a bare room but no bed. Squat toilets, non-attached bathroom, no security. **$**

9 | BADAKHSHAN AND THE WAKHAN CORRIDOR

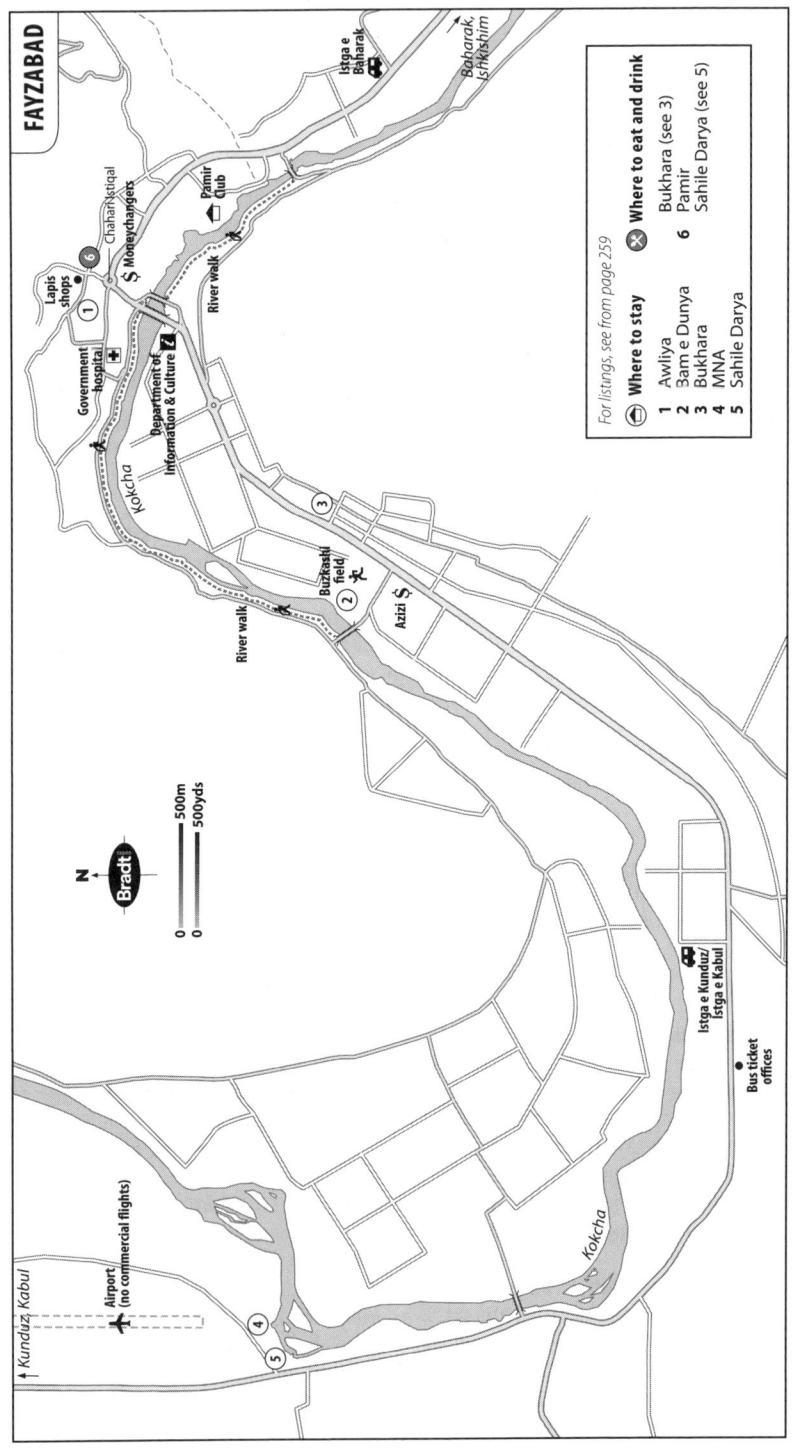

Bukhara Hotel & Restaurant m 7980 04710, 7961 27704. The best of the mussafarkhanas in Shahre Nau. Simple rooms with beds above the restaurant. No en suites, squat toilet, no AC. **$**

WHERE TO EAT AND DRINK *Map, opposite*
All hotels offer food albeit some may need a little advance notification. There are a number of chaikhanas close to Charahi Istaqal: try **Pamir Restaurant** (m 7966 26290; **$**); others are in Shahre Nau on the main north–south road from the buzkashi pitch – **Bukhara Hotel and Restaurant** (m 7980 04710, 7961 27704; **$**) is the local favourite here.

Sahile Darya For contact details, see page 259. Large popular restaurant overlooking the Kokcha River, albeit quite a way out of town. Serves all the Afghan staples but you may find other options such as Pakistani dishes & pizza. **$$**

SHOPPING The road northeast of Chahari Istiqal has a row of shops selling jewellery and worked and raw lapis lazuli. Prices are a little cheaper than in Kabul but the quality of craft in Fayzabad is lower.

OTHER PRACTICALITIES
Medical The government hospital is just west of Chahari Istiqal. Or call the Azim Ullah Osman Clinic (m 7924 58192).

Money Moneychangers are in the bazaar near Chahari Istiqal; banks are south of the buzkashi pitch in Shahre Nau.

WHAT TO SEE AND DO Fayzabad does not have any sights per se, but a **walk** on the less populated side of the Kokcha River is pleasant. Starting at the Bam e Dunya Hotel, cross over the river and walk to the main bridge, cross back to the Shahre Nau side and then walk to the bridge beyond the Pamir Club Hotel.

Buzkashi is a big deal in Fayzabad and due to the cooler mountain environment, the game is played as late as May. Ask at the Ban e Dunya Hotel for details. If you're not staying there, they sell tickets for 50AFN to watch from the 'skybox' of their fourth-floor balcony.

AROUND FAYZABAD
Baharak This small town 39km east of Fayzabad has become the transport hub of Badakhshan now that the paved road from Kabul continues beyond Fayzabad (in fact it actually goes as far as Jurm, another 30mins to the south). The bazaar was widened in 2024 and the buildings on the west side of the main road are all new.

Big buses ply the road to Kunduz, Mazar and Kabul from the bus station on the edge of town on the road to Fayzabad. Most leave for Kabul (1,300AFN; 16hrs) in the early afternoon; buy a ticket from the bus station in advance. There is little shared transportation south of Baharak, so travel to Sar e Sang or Panjshir is best done in your own vehicle.

There is nothing to keep you in Baharak, but if you need to spend the night, try the **Rahnaward Hotel and Restaurant** (north end of the main bazaar; m 7840 88882, 7902 88881; **$**) or the 2024-built **Kabul Pamir Restaurant** (m 7956 95099; **$**), essentially a chaikhana with a couple of rooms in the back.

Lake Shewa At 12km long and over 250m deep, fishhook-shaped Lake Shewa is Afghanistan's largest body of water and a significant source of the Oxus River (page 264). Frozen and inaccessible during the harsh winter months, the area comes to

9 | BADAKHSHAN AND THE WAKHAN CORRIDOR

> **THE ISMAILIS OF NORTHEAST AFGHANISTAN**
>
> The Ismaili people of northeastern Afghanistan are part of a larger group in southern Tajikistan and northern Pakistan, who share a common geography, religion and history divided by modern borders. They follow a distinct branch of Shi'a Islam that split from the main Shi'a tradition in the 8th century over the rightful line of succession. While mainstream Shi'a followed Musa al-Kadhim, the Ismailis recognised his elder brother Ismail as the true imam. From this divergence grew a separate and highly spiritual interpretation of Islam that emphasises inner meaning (*batin*) alongside outward practice (*zahir*). It is sometimes compared to Neoplatonism.
>
> Their faith is led by the Aga Khan, currently Shah Karim al-Husayni, who resides in Monaco and is seen not only as a spiritual guide but as a philanthropist and modernising figure. The Aga Khan Development Network (AKDN) has invested significantly in education, health care and cultural preservation in Ismaili regions of Afghanistan.
>
> Unlike many other Muslim-majority communities in the country, Ismaili women do not traditionally wear the burqa or full face covering, and gender segregation is often more relaxed. Their places of worship are not mosques, but Jamatkhanas – community prayer and gathering spaces that serve both spiritual and social functions.
>
> The Ismailis have no call to prayer, and religious services are typically led by laypeople rather than clerics. Their rituals are less public, and their theology more esoteric than either Sunni or mainstream Shi'a practice. As a result, the Ismailis

life between May and September, when Kuchi nomads and Shughni shepherds move into the pastures with their herds of sheep and goats. Occasionally, you might even see a game of buzkashi being played on the open plains. The Shughni people, while Ismaili like the Wakhi, are culturally distinct although they share some similarities. They graze their animals along the banks of the lake and live in yurts scattered across the meadows. The combination of dramatic scenery, traditional pastoral life, and the high-altitude (3,000m) setting makes this a truly special place.

There are no facilities at the lake, and temperatures can drop sharply, even in summer. It is advisable to take a guide who can help arrange contact with the nomads and shepherds, as well as assist with any necessary permissions or discussions with local communities. For those short on time or looking for an authentic experience of nomadic and semi-nomadic life, Shewa offers an excellent detour either before or after visiting the Wakhan Corridor.

Getting there and away Lake Shewa can be reached by vehicle from Fayzabad in approximately 7 hours, turning off on the western outskirts of Baharak. From Lake Shewa, it's possible to continue by road to Shugnan on the banks of the Panj River and then south to Ishkishim, which would require an additional full day's drive.

Trekking From Shewa you can make a three-day trek northeast to the village of Trive on the Panj River. The trail offers stunning views across the border into Tajikistan and towards Khorog, its regional capital. From Trive, it's possible to extend the trek for another five days, looping westward and eventually rejoining have historically faced suspicion and marginalisation, particularly under more conservative governments.

Yet, how did this isolated region become the only spot in the world with an Ismaili majority? You have to go back to Nasir Khusraw, who was born sometime around 1003 near Balkh. Well educated in Islamic texts as well as in the Greek and Persian classics, Nasir worked as an accountant until he was in his early 40s and had a dream that turned into a full-blown spiritual crisis. He left his job and set out on a seven-year pilgrimage across the Middle East. In Cairo, where the Fatimid Caliphs were Ismaili, Nasir converted and was instructed by the leading scholars, until he was promoted to the ranks of *da'i*, a combination missionary, scholar and guide who took responsibility for the spiritual welfare of his students.

He returned home as a missionary but met so much hostility from Sunnis that he fled to isolated Yamgan in Badakhshan, where he spent the rest of his life, writing the *Safarnama* (Book of Travels) and some of the finest Persian poetry of the era. He soon had a great following among the locals, but also attracted disciples from afar who joined him in Yamgan.

Unlike many mystics, Nasir didn't shun the material world, believing it could be the gateway to wisdom. He has been compared to the poet Ovid, exiled unwillingly to the back of beyond (and like Ovid, Nasir complained about the cold). When he died in 1088, he was honoured as a *pir*, or saint, and his tomb (page 264) is visited to this day.

the road between Shewa and Baharak. The final days of this trek pass near a major gold mine, which provides some employment for locals but can occasionally disrupt the serenity of the trail with dust and truck traffic. These trekking routes pass through rarely visited communities and offer a unique opportunity to explore a remote corner of Badakhshan that few travellers ever reach. Due to the remoteness, a local guide (ask at your accommodation in Fayzabad or Ishkishim) is essential for navigating the area and co-ordinating with communities along the route.

SOUTHERN BADAKHSHAN TO THE ANJOMAN PASS

The road from Baharak in southern Badakhshan to Panjshir via the Anjoman Pass offers one of the most remote and striking road journeys in Afghanistan. Spanning two days, this rugged track cuts through high mountains, scattered settlements, and long-forgotten valleys. It's a route that gives a rare glimpse into rural Afghanistan – untouched, unfiltered and fiercely beautiful. Although seldom travelled, the road is passable in summer months and links the verdant Kokcha Valley with the famed Panjshir Valley to the south. The highlight en route is undoubtedly Sar e Sang of the legendary lapis lazuli mines. Basic accommodation can be found in Yamgan, Sar e Sang, and the village of Anjoman.

BAHARAK TO YAMGAN The journey begins on a paved road heading south to Jurm, a pleasant 30-minute drive. Beyond Jurm, the paved road becomes a narrow, rough dirt track, hugging the Kokcha River, winding through a

9 | BADAKHSHAN AND THE WAKHAN CORRIDOR

remote and sparsely populated region that was once a hub of opium production. After about 4 hours, you'll reach Yamgan, a dusty village with a very basic chaikhana (**$**) on the second floor of a building near the only roundabout. This is the first overnight option if you're breaking up the journey. On the eastern edge of the village lies the **Tomb of Nasir Khusraw**, the Persian poet, philosopher and missionary who introduced Ismaili Islam to the region (page 262).

YAMGAN TO SAR E SANG Another 4 hours on the rough road brings you to Sar e Sang, a stark, arid mining village unlike anywhere else in Afghanistan. With no arable land, Sar e Sang consists of about 200 structures largely built from loose stones – including the occasional block of blue low-grade lapis – each owned by a mining family. The village teeters precariously over a flood-prone riverbed of massive boulders.

The bazaar here is pedestrian-only, narrow and atmospheric – like something from a medieval storybook. Lapis fragments litter the ground. Wholesalers operate out of bare stone rooms filled with raw lapis and green sodalite, preparing shipments for Kabul and beyond.

> ### THE SOURCE OF THE OXUS
>
> The Oxus – as today's Amu Darya was called by the ancient Greeks – is one of central Asia's great rivers. For millennia, it shaped empires, irrigated vast plains, and carved out political boundaries. Rising in the towering highlands of the eastern Wakhan, it flows westwards for over 2,500km, forming much of Afghanistan's northern border with its central Asian neighbours, before eventually draining into what remains of the Aral Sea.
>
> Upstream, before it earns the name Amu Darya, the river is known as the Panj, which forms the natural frontier between Tajikistan and Afghanistan. Yet long before this confluence, the Oxus begins its journey among the glaciers, streams and lakes of the Pamir and Hindu Kush. But where exactly the Oxus begins has been debated for centuries, with no single universally agreed-upon 'source'. Instead, several candidates compete for the title.
>
> Despite the fascination of explorers, geographers, and modern adventurers – many of whom still travel through the Wakhan in search of the 'true source' – this debate means little to the people who live along the river's course. For them, the Oxus is not a mystery to solve, but a vital artery of life: feeding fields, sustaining villages, and providing water in one of the most rugged and remote corners of the world.
>
> **LAKE ZORKOL** British explorer John Wood (1812–71), author of *The Journey to the Source of the River Oxus* (page 286), was one of the first Europeans to explore this remote region, in his 1838 expedition. Initially he believed he was the first to discover Zorkol and patriotically named it Lake Victoria, until he found out it already had a name. However, even he recognised that Zorkol was not the absolute headwater but simply a practical location for a geopolitical divide. In the 19th century, when British and Russian boundary commissions were tasked with defining Afghanistan's northern borders during the 'Great Game', political convenience played a bigger role than geography. The British, largely for mapping and diplomatic clarity, chose Zorkol as the headwater of the Oxus for boundary-drawing purposes.

The historic mine entrances are visible on the slopes above the village, with the nearest defunct mine a short 20-minute walk away. However, all active mines are further up the valley – anywhere from 2 to 6 hours' walk depending on location. While entry to the mining areas is prohibited without Ministry of Mines permission (which is not granted to tourists), it is possible to visit the village itself. There is no official accommodation, but reporting to the local commander will usually result in a place to sleep with one of the mining families. Note: there are no toilets, but the entire northern end of the village is an open bathroom – bring a torch and be prepared for basic conditions.

SAR E SANG TO PANJSHIR From Sar e Sang, it's approximately 6 hours to Anjoman, where the bazaar on the north side of the road has a chaikhana (**$**) with very simple lodging. Beyond Anjoman, the road climbs through stunning scenery towards the Anjoman Pass (4,430m), one of Afghanistan's highest drivable passes (open only in summer due to snow and treacherous conditions). The descent into Panjshir takes a further 4 hours, with the road finally becoming paved again at Parian. You can find accommodation both in Parian, and in Bazarak (page 146), and from there shared minibuses to Kabul.

THE WAKHJIR GLACIER AND CURZON CAVES At the far eastern edge of the Wakhan Corridor, near the Wakhjir Pass on the Chinese border, lies a glacier feeding the Wakhjir River. Within this glacier are ice caves, also known as the Curzon Caves after Lord Curzon (George Nathaniel Curzon, 1859–1925), British Viceroy of India and key figure in the strategic geopolitics of central Asia (see his *Pamirs and the Source of the Oxus*, page 285). Geographically, this is the most distant source from where the Oxus ultimately empties into the Aral Sea, and as such is often cited in atlases as the river's 'true' headwater.

LAKE CHAQMAQTIN Further west lies Lake Chaqmaqtin, which feeds the Chaqmaqtin River. At the point where the Chaqmaqtin and Wakhjir rivers meet near Bozai Gumbaz, the Chaqmaqtin River already carries a larger volume of water. Hydrologically, this gives it a strong claim as the main source of the Panj.

THE UPPER STREAMS ABOVE CHAQMAQTIN Of course, even Lake Chaqmaqtin is fed by multiple upstream tributaries. Depending on how far back one traces these feeder streams, one could argue that the Oxus begins even higher in the mountains. Bill Colegrave, in his *Halfway House to Heaven* (page 285), believes he found the source in 2008, in the stream flowing down the Chelab Valley north of Chaqmaqtin, just over the border in Tajikistan. At the time of writing, an expedition led by the President of the Royal Society of Asian Affairs was investigating which substream of the Chelab Valley might be the source.

THE LAKE SHEWA HEADWATERS Further downstream, the river system fed by the Shewa basin contributes the greatest volume of water before the Panj fully forms above Khorog. Some hydrologists consider this flow the most significant contributor to the Oxus depending on one's definition of a 'source'.

9 | BADAKHSHAN AND THE WAKHAN CORRIDOR

THE LAPIS LAZULI MINES OF SAR E SANG

> a fragment of the starry vault of heaven
>
> Pliny the Elder

Hidden in the mountain-rimmed valleys of the Kokcha River, Sar e Sang is the source of the blue stone that has captivated civilisations for thousands of years. Its world-famous lapis lazuli mines are nothing less than the oldest continuously operated mines on earth, worked since at least 7570BCE – the date of lapis beads found at Mehrgarh, Pakistan.

In ancient times, Sar e Sang's lapis was the only known source of deep blue. Caravans along the Silk Roads transported the stones to faraway kingdoms where they found a place in some of history's most treasured artefacts. In Mesopotamia, lapis adorned the Royal Tombs of Ur as early as 2600BCE. In Egypt, it was carved and inlaid into jewellery and statues and used in the funerary mask of Tutankhamun – the deep blue of his death mask's eyebrows and inlays come from these very mountains. During the European Renaissance, the finest Sar e Sang lapis was ground into the rare and precious pigment called ultramarine, used by Michelangelo to paint the brilliant heavens of the Sistine Chapel ceiling. At times, ultramarine was worth more than gold.

Mining at Sar e Sang has always been an extraordinary feat, carried out in a harsh and remote environment. Traditional techniques included pouring water into cracks in the rock, which would freeze in winter and expand, splitting the marble host rock apart. Later, black powder and simple explosives were introduced to break the stone free. Even today, many miners work by hand in small, precarious tunnels high above the Kokcha Valley, often at altitudes above 3,000m. Access has always been extremely difficult due to both the rugged terrain, ongoing security concerns and governmental restrictions.

THE WAKHAN CORRIDOR AND AFGHAN PAMIR

> To myself the Oxus, the great parent stream of humanity, which has equally impressed the imagination of Greek and Arab, of Chinese and Tartar…has always similarly appealed. Waters, descending from the 'Roof of the World', tell of forgotten peoples and whisper secrets of unknown lands. They are believed to have rocked the cradle of our race.
>
> Lord Curzon

Tucked into Afghanistan's far northeast, the Wakhan Corridor is a narrow finger of land wedged between the towering mountains of the Hindu Kush and the Pamirs. It is one of the most remote and breathtakingly beautiful regions in the world, home to more than a dozen peaks rising over 7,000m, including 7,492m Noshaq – the highest mountain in Afghanistan and the second highest in the Hindu Kush. Life here unfolds slowly and with immense resilience. Scattered along the valley floors and steep hillsides are smallholdings where families grow barley, tend livestock and endure long, harsh winters.

Among the peaks are Kyrgyz tombs and prehistoric petroglyphs carved into the rocks, silent markers of the region's long and layered human presence. Wildlife still roams freely – ibex, snow leopards and Marco Polo sheep.

Ethnically and geographically the region is split into two. The Wakhan, the thin strip of land that runs between Ishkishim and Sarhad e Broghil, is a long, steep-sided valley inhabited by the Wakhi people in small, settled communities. The Wakhi are Ismaili Muslims and speak a language that has the same roots as Persian, albeit distinct.

Beyond Sarhad lie the wide Pamir valleys: the Big Pamir around Lake Zorkol, and the Little Pamir around Lake Chaqmaqtin. They are inhabited by the Kyrgyz nomadic people (page 52), Sunni Muslims who keep their traditional ways of life, living in yurts, herding sheep and using yaks as beasts of burden and only occasionally descending to Fayzabad with huge droves of sheep to sell. Until recently the Pamirs were a two-day drive followed by a four-day hike from the provincial capital Fayzabad.

Since 2020 these nomads' way of life has begun to change dramatically as a road now reaches the Small Pamir. Kyrgyz settlements can be visited without hiking, although by and large their lives have remained the same. However, the Kyrgyz are in a state of flux, and with a new road to China due to open soon, their way of life will probably soon disappear.

The best time to visit is from May to September, but note that passes over 4,000m are often inaccessible until mid-June. In July, snowmelt can cause rivers to swell and occasionally wash out roads and tracks. Even at the height of summer, snowfall is possible in the Afghan Pamir – conditions can be harsh and unpredictable. By late September, snow may again begin to block the high passes, potentially cutting off routes until the following year. Plan carefully and be prepared for rapid changes in weather, especially at higher altitudes.

HISTORY 'Wakhan' comes from Wakhshu, an early name for the Oxus River. Here the two rivers that run through it, the icy cold Wakhan and the Pamir, mingle to create the Panj, the tributary of the Amu Darya that forms the border between Afghanistan and Tajikistan.

Anyone looking at the map may wonder why this thin 350km finger of land, Afghanistan's panhandle (it's only 13km wide at its narrowest), is part of modern Afghanistan. One reason is that the Wakhan Corridor really did serve as a corridor through the Pamir, Hindu Kush and Karakoram mountains, known as the Silk Road's 'Buddhist Route' after it was conquered by the Kushans (c50BCE–250CE). The 7th-century Buddhist pilgrim Xuanzang passed through, as did Genghis Khan and Marco Polo (page 268). The capital Ishkishim (originally Sakashim, after the Saka nomads) was described in a 9th-century Persian geography as a lively, cosmopolitan city, where local Buddhists and the first Muslims lived side by side.

The Wakhan's fortunes, like those of other Silk Road routes, declined with the growth of maritime trade. But history wasn't done with it yet: the second reason the Wakhan is part of Afghanistan goes back to the 19th-century Great Game.

After it was conquered by Ahmad Shah Durrani in 1763, the Wakhan came under the *mirs* of Badakhshan. By the 1860s, after the Russians had gobbled up much of central Asia, they began sending in military explorer-spies into the Pamirs – as did the British, alarmed at their attempts to sneak into the Raj through the back door via Chitral. In 1873, both agreed to make the Panj and Pamir rivers the border between Afghanistan and the Russian Empire, a deal that split the Wakhan in two (the northern bit is now Tajikistan's Gorno-Badakhshan Autonomous Region). Later, the creation of the Durand Line in 1893 (page 165) left a narrow strip of land – the Wakhan Corridor – as a buffer between the two empires which was given to Afghanistan in 1895.

9 | BADAKHSHAN AND THE WAKHAN CORRIDOR

MARCO POLO AND THE WAKHAN

Of all the places Marco Polo (1254–1324) described on his journey to the court of Kublai Khan, Badakhshan is the place that most resembles the sights that Marco described.

After Genghis Khan reopened the Silk Road in the 1220s, Marco's father and uncle, Maffeo and Niccolò Polo, had already met Genghis's grandson, Kublai, on an epic journey that began just before Marco's birth and ended in 1269. One of their prize possessions was a golden tablet from Kublai that acted as a VIP passport, enabling them to travel freely and obtain local assistance wherever they travelled in the Mongol Empire.

Marco first met his father at age 15, and two years later, in 1271, he departed with him and Niccolò to China, only returning to Venice in 1295. Marco learned four languages, served as Kublai's emissary for 17 years and spent time in Badakhshan, recovering from an illness. He noted that all the kings there were descended from Alexander the Great. But he was on much surer ground mentioning the balas (spinel) rubies, lapis lazuli and silver mines in the mountains, 'so the country is a very rich one, but it is also (it must be said) a very cold one'. He admired the Saker falcons, the excellent horses and the fine air that cures all illness. It took him 12 days to ride through the Wakhan Corridor into China.

> And when you leave this little country, you ride three days north east, always among mountains said to be the highest place in the world. And when you have got to this height, you find a great lake (Chaqmaqtin) between two mountains from which flows a very fine river (the Murghab). Here is the best pasturage in the world (the Small Pamir); for a lean beast grows fat in ten days. Here are all kinds of wild beasts; among others wild sheep of great size, whose horns are a good six palms in length. From these horns the shepherds make great bowls to eat from, and they use the horns also to enclose fold for their cattle at night. (Messer Marco was told also that the wolves were numerous, and killed many of those wild sheep. Hence quantities of their horns and bones were found, and these were made into great heads by the wayside, in order to guide travellers when snow was on the ground.)

The sheep he was the first to describe are now named after him (page 7). His *Description of the World* (or *Marco Polo's Travels*) would become one of Europe's most accurate sources of information about the Far East for centuries, and inspire explorers like Columbus to try to find an easier way to get there. Yet no-one would have known about any of it without the Battle of Curzola in 1298, when Marco Polo was taken prisoner by the Genoese for a year, and dictated his travels to his cellmate, Rusticiano da Pisa.

After his adventures, Marco Polo settled down in Venice, married, had three daughters, and confessed on his deathbed: 'I have only told the half of what I saw!'

In 1949, Chairman Mao sealed off the eastern frontier, leaving it a corridor to nowhere. Afterwards, the region was too remote to be seriously involved in the wars that devasted Afghanistan. During the Soviet era, collectivisation policies in Tajikistan and Kyrgyzstan forcibly settled most Kyrgyz communities into collective farms, leaving only those who had fled to Afghanistan to maintain a truly nomadic lifestyle.

Cut off from the modern world and enduring some of the harshest conditions in central Asia, the Afghan Kyrgyz lead extremely tough lives at high altitudes with limited access to health care, education or economic opportunities. Life revolves around herding, seasonal migrations, and survival in an unforgiving environment where winters are long and brutal. Faced with extreme isolation and hardship, the community has long debated its future. In the 1980s, there were serious discussions about relocating the entire population to Alaska or Canada, supported by international aid agencies (with input from Nancy Hatch Dupree; page 118). Eventually, in 1982, around 1,150 Kyrgyz accepted an offer of resettlement in eastern Türkiye, where they were given land and homes on the Anatolian Plateau. The 1,200 or so who remained in Afghanistan continue to live in the Pamirs, still semi-nomadic, but progressively more vulnerable in a changing and uncertain world.

China has been increasingly keen on reopening the Wakhan Corridor and has agreed with the Taliban to finance a new road as part of the Belt and Road Initiative. In 2011, Tajikistan ceded 1,000km^2 in the Pamirs to China, where China is hoping to establish a military base to keep Islamic militants out of its restive Xinjiang Province. Pakistan is interested in the Corridor as well; access to the Wakhan would mean it could trade with central Asia without going through Afghanistan.

GETTING THERE AND AWAY Shared taxis and minivans run to/from Ishkishim to Baharak (500AFN; 5–6hrs) and Fayzabad (600AFN; 6hrs).

There is an international crossing between Tajikistan and Afghanistan at Ishkishim. It crosses the Panj River via two bridges linked to an island in the middle of the river, where a cross-border market is held weekly. The border is 2km from both Afghan Ishkishim (sometimes called Sultan Ishkishim by the Tajiks) and Tajik Ishkishim. For crossing into Tajikistan, note that in addition to a Tajik visa you are required to have a GBAO (Gorno Badakhshan Autonomous Oblast) permit to enter southern Tajikistan. This crossing was open for international visitors until 2021 but at the time of writing is closed.

There are a number of passes linking Afghanistan to Pakistan, but none has been open for visitors for decades. The Pakistani Army monitors these passes and you will be arrested if you attempt to cross.

GETTING AROUND There is no public transport in the Wakhan Corridor, but old 4x4 vehicles can be rented in Ishkishim for a fixed fare per vehicle for the journey. These rates are fixed by the Wakhi community at the start of each year and are usually both higher than you would pay elsewhere in Afghanistan and quoted in US dollars. The road runs from Ishkishim all the way to Chaqmaqtin (US$500; 26hrs) covering a distance of around 250km at a sedate average speed of 10km/h. Flooding during June and July can add additional time to this. The road is in the process of being improved but current journey times per section are:

Ishkishim–Qazideh	2 hours
Qazideh–Khandud	4 hours
Khandud–Qala e Panja	4 hours
Qala e Panja–Gaz Khun	4 hours
Gaz Khun–Sarhad e Broghil	4–5 hours
Sarhad e Broghil–Bozai Gumbaz	5–6 hours
Bozai Gumbaz–Chaqmaqtin	1 hour

TOURIST INFORMATION AND REGISTRATION For such a remote area that often seems ignored by the government, the process of obtaining documentation and declaring this information to the authorities is laborious. As with all visits to Afghanistan, you will have a letter from the Afghan Tour Department in Kabul (page 122). You will need to show this in Fayzabad, where they will present you with new documentation. Make multiple copies of this and your passport while in Fayzabad.

Once in Ishkishim, you will need to present copies of these documents to the **governor's office** (main crossroads; ⊕ 08.00–16.00 Sat–Wed, 08.00–14.00 Thu), where you will be issued with another new document (should the border at Ishkishim reopen, page 269, this process may change). Within the Wakhan Corridor you will need to present all these documents at government offices in Khandud, Qala e Panja and Sarhad e Broghil (⊕ same hours). You will be issued with a handwritten permit in Khandud.

Note that, although Ishkishim is the main town of the Wakhan district, Khandud (by nature of its central location) is the provincial capital. This difference of official and actual importance sometimes leads to friction between the two.

WHERE TO STAY Accommodation along the Wakhan Corridor is basic. Most villages have a small guesthouse/mehmankhanah, often a building adapted to support the limited number of travellers who venture into this remote region. Most options are run by local families and have been established with support from the Aga Khan Foundation, albeit of varying quality. Outside of that you will need to camp.

Guesthouses Most guesthouses consist of one large common room with sleeping mats and blankets where everyone sleeps together in a shared space. Some feature beautiful traditional Pamiri designs, with the classic five-pillar roof structure symbolising the Five Pillars of Islam. Toilet facilities are basic; some guesthouses have a single bathroom. A few may have private rooms, but these are still quite simple and usually share a common bathroom with occasional hot water. The guesthouses where people stay more regularly such as Ishkishim, Qala e Panja and Sarhad e Broghil are kept in better condition. Capacity is generally limited to 10–12 people.

Meals are usually simple, home-cooked food using whatever supplies are available. It is advisable to bring some of your own food to supplement the local meals. Costs are typically around US$30 per night, including dinner and breakfast. Like the transport, these rates quoted in US dollars (which seem high by Afghan standards for services received) are fixed by the community at the start of each year.

Camping In most villages, you are allowed to camp, but a small fee is usually expected. Do ask as you will be shown where you can pitch your tent to avoid disturbing local water sources or farmland. Toilet facilities are not available; practise responsible waste management and avoid polluting streams, which serve as drinking water for the community.

Camping in the mountains In summer pasture areas, Kyrgyz and Wakhi shepherds will usually permit camping nearby for a small fee. Away from villages and pastures, you are generally free to camp anywhere, but do not be surprised if a shepherd stops by to check on you. Be fully self-sufficient for food, fuel and cooking equipment as supplies are not available in the mountains.

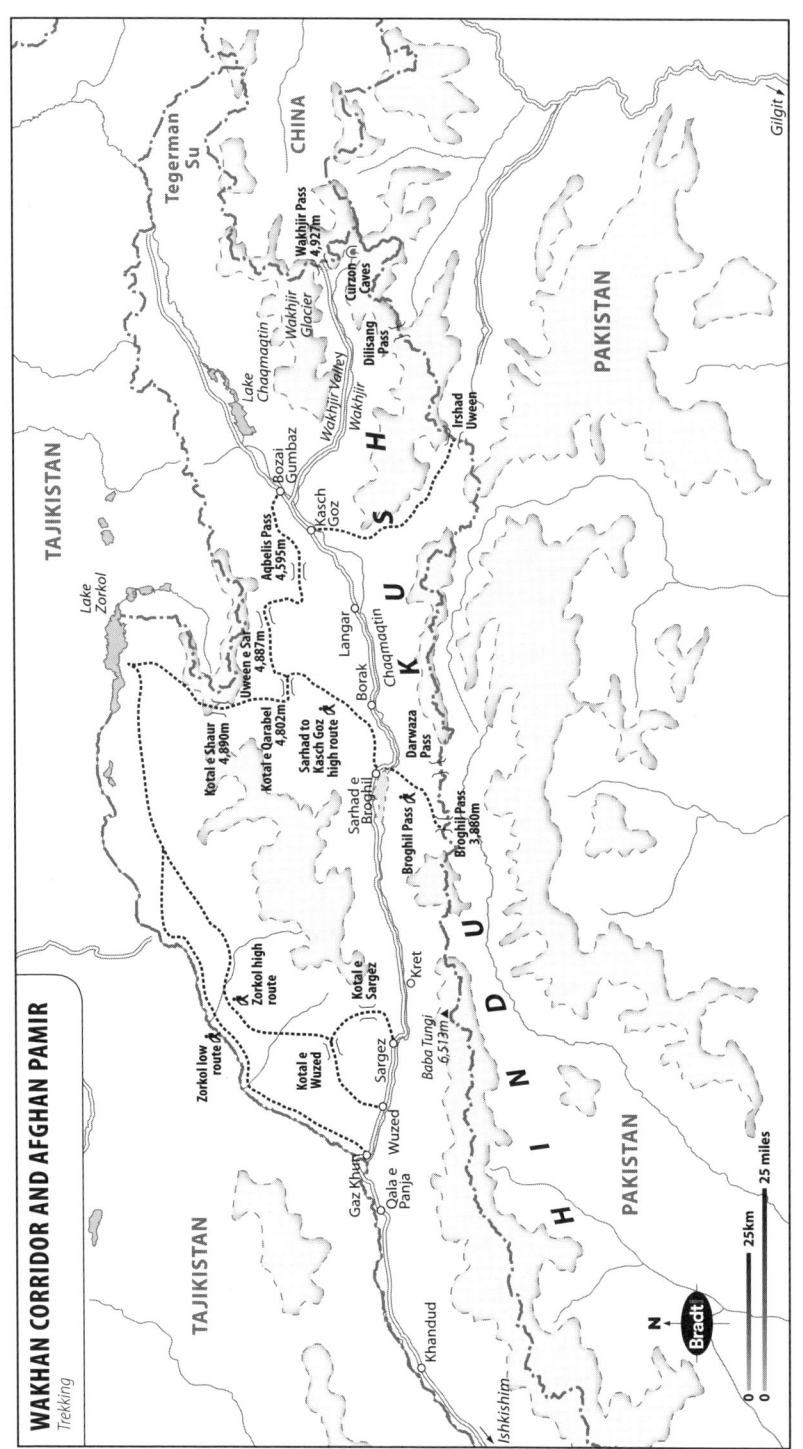

9 | BADAKHSHAN AND THE WAKHAN CORRIDOR

TREKKING IN THE WAKHAN AND AFGHAN PAMIR

WHAT TO BRING Trekking in the Wakhan Corridor offers some of the most spectacular and remote mountain scenery in central Asia, but owing to the region's remoteness and limited infrastructure, careful preparation is essential. Once you pass Ishkishim and head into the Corridor proper, you will need to be largely self-sufficient. There are no real facilities beyond Ishkishim, and resupply options are extremely limited. Essential items are listed below:

- **Clothing** Aim for a layered clothing system – base layers (moisture-wicking), insulated mid-layers (fleece/down), waterproof outer shell (jacket and trousers), warm hat, gloves and good sun protection (hat, sunglasses, suncream) – to deal with rapid temperature changes. Expect strong sun during the day, cold nights, and possible snow even in midsummer at higher altitudes.
- **Cooking equipment** You'll need a portable stove (multi-fuel or gas if you can find supplies locally), fuel, cooking pots, utensils and enough supplies to be self-sufficient for the entire trek.
- **Documentation** Make multiple photocopies of permits as you may be asked for them at police or military checkpoints.
- **First aid and medical** A comprehensive first-aid kit, personal medications, high-altitude medication (if needed) and knowledge of basic wilderness first aid are essential.
- **Food** Bring lightweight, high-energy food. Expect to carry most supplies yourself or arrange pack animals. Fresh meat in the form of a whole sheep is available in most villages.
- **Footwear** Wear sturdy, broken-in trekking boots suitable for rough and rocky terrain, and bring extra socks. Also bring good-fitting sandals for river crossings and perhaps trainers for around camp.
- **Navigation and communication** There is no Afghan mobile signal after Ishkishim, albeit you may pick up a Tajikistan mobile phone signal when opposite Tajik villages on the Afghan side of the Panj, so equip yourself with a satellite phone or GPS messenger for emergencies, as well as detailed maps and a GPS device or mapping app, and a solar-powered recharger or battery packs.
- **Tent and sleeping gear** A high-quality, four-season tent is highly recommended due to cold nights, even in summer. A warm sleeping bag (rated to at least -5°C to -10°C) and an insulated sleeping mat are essential for comfort at altitude.
- **Water purification** Streams are generally abundant, but water safety cannot be guaranteed, so bring reliable water filters or purification tablets.

Hot springs Several villages have natural hot springs which locals will happily direct you to; given the lack of washing facilities in the homestays, these are very welcome. Some have simple bathhouse structures built around them. The best-known springs are in Gaz Khun and Sarhad e Broghil.

Yurt accommodation with the Kyrgyz In the higher sections of the Wakhan, where the Kyrgyz nomads live, you can sometimes rent a yurt for the night; Bozai Gumbaz and the southern shores of Lake Chaqmaqtin are the main locations.

GUIDES AND PORTERS Prices for trekking services, from guiding fees to horse and yak hire, as well as homestay rates are officially fixed. These costs are discussed each winter between the Wakhi and Kyrgyz and are higher than in other parts of Afghanistan compared with the quality of the services. At the time of writing the rates are: **guides** (US$50/day); **cook** (US$40/day); **horses/yaks** (US$20/day including a horseman to guide the horse).

The guides are not professional trekking guides but will get you to your destination, help with shopping, transport, fuel and possibly sourcing equipment. Equipment is transported by pack animals. The Wakhi use horses, but you should switch to the Kyrgyz yaks in Kyrgyz areas. The Kyrgyz are often less keen to stick to the originally agreed rate so some negotiation is needed.

POPULAR TREKS The following are the most popular of many trekking options.

Broghil Pass trek (1–2 days) Starting and finishing at Sarhad e Broghil, this is a great one-day (two if you want to camp near the pass) trek from the main road which you can do on foot or horseback, passing by ancient forts. The broad, green 3,880m Broghil Pass is the lowest pass linking the Wakhi regions of Afghanistan and Pakistan, although crossing here is strictly forbidden.

Lake Zorkol trek (9 days) The lower route from Gaz Khun to the Big Pamir and the 20km-long Lake Zorkol takes four days. You'll be rewarded by majestic views of the Pamir River valley and visits to Wakhi and then Kyrgyz summer camps. The return route takes the high route, crossing three major passes at heights of between 4,300m and 4,500m. It takes five days to reach either Sargez or Wuzed.

Kasch Goz high route (4–5 days) This is a demanding trek crossing three high passes, the Daliz (4,267m), the snow-covered Uween-e-Sar (4,887m) and the Aqbelis (4,595m). En route you will pass Wakhi and Kyrgyz summer camps, as well as ancient petroglyphs at Sang Nevishta.

Kotal e Shaur route (10 days round trip) A very demanding return trek that links the Wakhan River and Lake Zorkol in the Big Pamir. Starting at Sarhad e Broghil it involves crossing the Daliz Pass as well as the mighty Kotal e Qarabel (4,802m) and the glaciated Kotal e Shaur (4,890m) passes. Once at Zorkol, you can return the way you came, continue to Gaz Khun via the Pamir River valley or use part of this trek to link with the Zorkol Lake trek to the Kasch Goz high route. Each option results in a 10- or 11-day trek.

ISHKISHIM Located on the banks of the Panj River, directly across from its Tajik namesake, Ishkishim marks the starting point of the Wakhan Corridor. It is the last place with a bazaar before entering the rugged wilderness and plays a key logistical role for travellers heading east. At the time of writing the village is undergoing a bit of a construction boom with new buildings springing up on a weekly basis.

The town hosts a weekly border market on an island in the middle of the Panj, a rare meeting point for Afghan and Tajik traders; at the time of writing visitors were not able to attend. Though facilities are basic, Ishkishim has a chaikhana or two, and a small but functional bazaar where you can stock up on essentials before heading into more remote territory.

Importantly, Ishkishim has the local administrative office for obtaining **permission** for travel into the Wakhan (page 270). Be sure to stop here early, as paperwork can take time. This is also a hub for trekking guides and drivers – many of whom are from Ishkishim or nearby villages – making it a practical place to arrange logistics, pick up local knowledge, or find someone to join you on your journey.

Most visitors stay at least one night in Ishkishim, where there are several reasonable, simple guesthouses/homestays: **Marco Polo Guest House** (15mins from the bazaar, following the road that crosses the river; m 7963 83422, 7937 02459; **$$**); **Sakis Guest House** (similar area to Marco Polo; m 7977 84331; **$$**); **Wafi Guest House** (last house in the village before you leave Ishkishim to head up the Wakhan Corridor; m 7977 98504; **$$**).

FROM ISHKISHIM TO SARHAD E BROGHIL The first stop is **Qazideh** (20km east of Ishikishim), a village it is possible to visit without a permit. Qazideh is the turn-off for those wishing to climb Afghanistan's highest peak, Noshaq (7,492m). **Malang's Guesthouse** (m 7947 66067; **$$**) is the place to stay. Malang was the first Afghan to summit Noshaq and is featured in the documentary *Afghans to the Top* (page 288).

Khandud is an essential stop as visitors need to show their paperwork to the **governor's office**, located on the north side east of the very basic bazaar and the bridge. There is a basic **nameless guesthouse** (m 7935 27751) near the Ismaili Jamatkhana; however, if having to overnight in this stretch of the Wakhan Corridor it is best to carry on to **Qala e Panja**, where again you'll have to show your permits at the government office (⊕ same hours). The **Qala e Panja/Shae Panja guesthouse** (\ 7987 81358) is the best place to stay when breaking the journey between Ishkishim and Sarhad e Broghil.

The Panj River begins at **Gaz Khun**, fed from the south by the Wakhan River flowing from Sarhad e Broghil and the Small Pamir, and from the north by the Pamir River, which continues to mark the Tajikistan border as far as Lake Zorkol and the Big Pamir. To follow the northern section, you will need to follow the Wakhan River as far as **Wuzet**, where a bridge allows you to cross and return to Gaz Khun, the jumping-off point for treks to Zorkol and the Big Pamir. Accommodation in Gaz Khun can be found at **Wali Jan Guesthouse** (no mobile reception; **$$**), which is kept in pretty good order.

Each village between Ishkishim and **Sarhad e Broghil** sits on the banks of a river flowing from the south, and as you pass there is always a glimpse through the narrow gorge to the high mountains beyond. At **Kret** this mountain is the imposing 6,513m Baba Tungi, framed by the sides of the valley that appears in a thousand photos of the Wakhan. Kret also has one of the few emergency airstrips in the region.

SARHAD E BROGHIL AND BEYOND This village used to be the end of the road and the jumping-off point for treks to the Kyrgyz areas of the Big and Little Pamirs, and it still marks the last Wakhi permanent settlement. There is a final government office (main road) to show your paperwork. Guides and horses can be rented here for treks over the Daliz Pass. There are a number of guesthouses in Sarhad e Broghil, all very similar in standard including **Chaqan Boy Homestay**, **Zareek Homestay** and **Qach Boy Homestay** (all **$$**). None has a phone number as there is no signal in Sarhad e Broghil.

Kasch Goz is the first Kyrgyz settlement; if trekking with pack animals, you may need to exchange your Wakhi horses for Kyrgyz yaks here. The largest Kyrgyz settlement, **Bozai Gumbaz**, occupies the point where the Wakhjir and Wakhan rivers meet. Look out for the conical Kyrgyz tombs in the area. You might be asked to camp in the school compound, but there is also a good flat campsite with running water 10 minutes further up the valley to the east from the school. It is possible to rent a yurt here.

Beyond is long, narrow **Lake Chaqmaqtin**, located on a wide plateau. This acts as a watershed, where the waters from the east of Chaqmaqtin flow into Tajikistan and join the Amu Darya via the Bartang River. There are two Kyrgyz settlements here, one on the north side for winter and one on the south side for summer. There are plenty of camping options, although if you're camping close to the settlement you may be asked to hire a yurt. Remarkably, a small medical clinic has been built in this location funded by the Chinese government.

The new road that will eventually lead to China turns up the **Wakhjir Valley** from here towards the Wakhjir Pass. It was unclear at the time of the writing if permission would be granted to visit the valley, but it would be a 3–4-hour drive or a two- to three-day hike. The road runs north of the river, so trekking would be more pleasant on the south. At the foot of the pass are the famous Curzon ice caves, the most accepted source of the Oxus (page 264).

Tegerman Su, the furthest point of the Wakhan Corridor, is a 2–3-hour trek from Chaqmaqtin. It is unclear how far it is permitted to travel in this direction. The Kotal e Tegerman Su Pass into China is closed.

Appendix 1

LANGUAGE

Some 40 different languages are spoken in Afghanistan, but the two official ones are Dari (Farsi; see below) and Pashto (page 52). Dari is generally used as the lingua franca between people, but you may want to try your hand at Pashto, especially in the south and east of the country.

DARI (FARSI)

	Spoken	Written

Greetings

Hello	Salaam	سلام
Goodbye	Khodaa-haafez (pronounced *ho-da fiz*)	خدا حافظ
Good morning	Sobh-bekheyr	صبح بخیر
Good evening	Sham-bekheyr	شام بخیر
How are you?	Hal-e shomaa chetoreh? (formal)	حال شما چطور ؟
	Chitor?/Chitorasti? (informal)	چطور؟ / چطور استی؟
Fine, thank you	Khoobam, tashakur	خوبم تشکر

Useful words and phrases

It is closed	Bastah ast	بسته است
It is open	Baazeh	باز است
Excuse me! Sorry!	Ma'zerat meekhaaham	معذرت می خواهم
	Bebakhsheed (to get attention/apologise)	ببخشید
Help!	Komak	کمک
A cup of tea, please	Yek chaee, lotfan	یک چایی لطفا
Thank you	Tashakor	متشکرم \ مرسی
You are welcome	Khaahesh meekonam	خواهش می کنم
Yes	Baleh	بله
No	Nakheyr/Na	نخیر \ نه
I	Man	من
I am ill	Mareezam	مریضم
I am English (American/Canadian)	Man engelis hastam (Amrikaa'i/Kaanaadaa'i)	من انگلیسی هستم کانادایی \ امریکایی
I don't speak Farsi	Man faarsee nemeedaanam	من فارسی نمی دانم
I don't understand	Nemeefahmam	نمی فهمم

LANGUAGE

You (polite)	Shomaa	شما
You (informal)	Too	وت
How much is it?	Chand ast?	چند است ؟
Please help me	Bema komak koneed	به من کمک کنید
Where is…?	… kojaast?	کجاست ؟
Where is the toilet?	Dastshuee, kojaast?	دستشویی کجا است
Please show me the way to the…	Raah raa ta beman neshaan bedaheed	بدهید نشان من به ... تا را راه
airport	foroodgaah/maidan hawae	فرودگاه / میدان هوایی
bank	baank	بانک
bus stop/small shared taxi or bus station	eestgaah e milibus	ایستگاه ملی بس
large bus station (intercity)	eestgaah	ایستگاه
guide	ranpannamaye	راهنمای
hospital	beemaarestaan	بیمارستان
hotel/budget hotel	hotel/mussafarkhaaneh	مسافرخانه \ هتل
Ministry of Information and Culture (Kabul only)	Vazart etlaat ve fareang	وزارت اطلاعات و فرهنگ
Department of Information and Culture (other provinces)	Riyasat etlaat ve fareang	ریاست اطلاعات و فرهنگ
mosque	masjed	مسجد
museum	moozeh	موزه
police	polees	پلیس
police station	edareh-e polees	پلیس اداره
post office	edareh-e post	پست اداره
restaurant	restooraan	رستوران
toilet	dastshuee	دستشویی
I need a…	Man ehtiyaj be…daaram	دارم ... به احتیاج من
doctor	doktor	دکتر
dentist	dandaan pezeshk	داندانیزشک
room for 1/2/3 nights	otaaq baraayeh yek/dou/seh shab	شب سه \ دو \ یک برای اتاق
taxi	taaksee	تاکسی

Numbers

1	yek	۱
2	dou	۲
3	se	۳
4	chahaar	۴
5	panj	۵
6	shesh	٦
7	haft	۷
8	hasht	۸
9	noh	۹
10	dah	۱۰
11	yaazdah	۱۱
12	davaazdah	۱۲
20	best	۲۰
30	see	۳۰
40	chehel	۴۰

A1 | APPENDIX 1

50	panja	۵۰
60	shast	۶۰
70	haftad	۷۰
80	Hashtad	۸۰
90	Nawad	۹۰
100	sad	۱۰۰
1,000	hezar	۱۰۰۰

Days of the week

Saturday	shanbeh	شنبه
Sunday	yek shanbeh	شنبه
Monday	dou shanbeh	دوشنبه
Tuesday	se shanbeh	سه‌شنبه
Wednesday	chahaar shanbeh	چهارشنبه
Thursday	panj shanbeh	پنجشنبه
Friday	jom'eh	جمعه

Food and drink

Do you have a menu?	Aya shoma menu darid?	آیا شما منیو دارید؟
Can we eat together? (Assuming you are a group of men and women)	Metawanem baham ghaza bikhorem?	آیا میتوانیم باهم غذا بخوریم؟
I do not eat meat	Man gosht na mekhoram	من گوشت نمی خورم
I'd like…	Man mekhwaham	من میخواهم
Can I have what he is having?	Misheh manom chizi keh on dareh ro dashta bashm?	میشه من هم چیزی که اون داره رو داشته باشم
green tea	chai sabz	چای سبز
black tea	chai siah	چای سیاه
milk tea	sher chai	شیر چای
water	aab	آب
kebabs	kabab ha	کباب ها
Can I pay?	mesha man pardakht konam?	میشه من پرداخت کنم
That was delicious	khoshmaza bod	خوش مزه بود

PASHTO

	Spoken	Written

Greetings

Hello	Salam	سلام
Goodbye	Paa makha mo kha	په مخه مو ښه
Good morning	Sehehar mo pakher	پخیر مو سهار
Good evening	Makham mo pakher	پخیر مو ماښام
How are you?	Taso sanga yai? (formal) Jour yea? (informal)	څنګه تاسو یئ؟ جور یې
Fine, thank you	Kha yum manana	ښه یم مننه

Useful words and phrases

It is closed	Da band di	دا بند دا
It is open	Da khlas di	دا خلاص دا
Excuse me! (to get attention)	Bakhana ghwaram!	بخښنه غوارم!

LANGUAGE

English	Pashto transliteration	Pashto
Excuse me, sorry (to apologise)	Zaa bakhana ghwaram	غوارم بخښنه زه
Help!	Marsta!	!مرسته
A cup of tea, please	Meherbani wakri, yawa pyala chai	چای پیاله یوه ،وکړئ مهرباني
Thank you	Laa taso manana	مننه تاسو له
You are welcome	Taso kha raghlast	راغلاست ښه تاسو
Yes	ho	هو
No	naa	نه
I	Zaa	زه
I am ill	Zaa narogha yam	یم ناروغه زه
I am English	Zaa Angriz yam	یم انګریز زه
American	Amrikaye	کاناډایی
Canadian	Kanadayeein	امریکایی
I don't speak Pashto	Zaa pakhto naa sham welai	ویلای شم نه پښتو زه
I don't understand	Zaa naa poheegam	پوهیږم نه زه
You (formal)	Tasu	تاسو
You (informal)	Taa	ت
How much is it?	Da pa so di?	دا په څو دی
Please help me	Meherbani wakri ma sara marsta wakri	مرسته سره ما وکړئ مهرباني وکړئ
Where is…?	…chirta di?	دی؟ چیري
Where is the toilet	Tashnab chirta di?	دی؟ چیرته تشناب
Please show me the way to the…	Meherbani wakri ma taa lara wakhayast	لاره ته ما وکړئ مهرباني وښایاست
airport	hawaee dagar	ډګر هوایي
bank	bank	بانک
bus stop/small shared taxi or bus station	bas tamzai	بس تمځای
large bus station (intercity)	hada	هډه
guide	lerkhod	لارښود
hospital	roghtun	روغتون
hotel/budget hotel	hotel/Sarae	سرای/ هټل
Ministry of Information and Culture (Kabul only)	Da itlaato ao kaltor wazarat	د اطلاعاتو او کلتور وزارت
Department of Information and Culture (other provinces)	Da itlaato ao kaltor Riyasat	د اطلاعاتو او کلتور ریاست
mosque	jomat	جومات
museum	museum	میوزیم
police	polis	پولیس
police station	da poliso markaz	مرکز پولیسو د
post office	posta	پوسته
restaurant	restaurant	رستورانت
toilet	tashnab	تشناب
I need a…	Zaa yo taa artya larm…	لرم ارتیا ته یو زه
doctor	docter	ډاکټر
dentist	da ghasuno Docter	ډاکټر غاښونو د
room for 1/2/3 nights	da 1/2/3 shpee lapara khuna	خونه لپاره شپې ۱/۲/۳ د
taxi	taxi	ټکسي

A1

Numbers

1	yo	۱
2	dawa	۲
3	dri	۳
4	salor	۴
5	panza	۵
6	shpug	۶
7	awa	۷
8	ata	۸
9	naahha	۹
10	las	۱۰
11	yulas	۱۱
12	dolas	۱۲
20	shal	۲۰
30	dersh	۳۰
40	salwekh	۴۰
50	penzos	۵۰
60	shpeta	۶۰
70	Away	۷۰
80	Atya	۸۰
90	Nawee	۹۰
100	sal	۱۰۰
1,000	zara	۱۰۰۰

Days of the week

Saturday	shamba	شنبه
Sunday	yakshamba	یکشنبه
Monday	doshamba	دوشنبه
Tuesday	saashamba	سه شنبه
Wednesday	cheharshamba	چهارشنبه
Thursday	panjshamba	پنجشنبه
Friday	jama	جمعه

Food and drink

Do you have a menu?	Aya taso meno lari?	آیا تاسو مینیو لری؟
Can we eat together? (Assuming you are a group of men and women)	Aya mog yawzai khorali so?	آیا موږ یوخای خوړلی سو؟
I do not eat meat	Zaa ghokha naa khoram	زه غوښه نه خورم
I'd like…	Zaa ghwaram	زه غواړم
Can I have what he is having?	Aya zaa hagha saa tarlasa koli sham chi hagha ye lari?	آیا زه هغه څه ترلاسه کولی شم چی هغه یی لری؟
green tea	Shen chai	شین چای
black tea	Tor chai	تور چای
milk tea	Da shedo chai	د شیدو چای
water	Oba	اوبه
kebabs	Kabab	کباب
Can I pay?	Aya zaa pesy warkoli sham?	آیا زه پیسی ورکولی شم؟
That was delicious	Hagha khwandawar wo	هغه خوندور وه

Appendix 2

GLOSSARY

Abbasid	based in Baghdad, dynasties of Caliphs (749–1258CE)
Achaemenid	Persian ruling dynasty (550–331BCE)
AFF	Afghanistan Freedom Front, headed by Hazara leader Daoud Naji
Ahura Mazda	'Wise Lord' creator and force for good in Zoroastrianism
Alchon Huns	dynasty that invaded Afghanistan in c370CE
amir	commander, ruler, same as 'emir'; Amir al-Mu'minin, commander of the faithful was a title first adopted by Dost Mohammed in 1826 and is still used by the Taliban leader today
Angra Mainu	the evil, dark opponent of Ahura Mazda in Zoroastrianism
ANSF	Afghan National Security Forces (2004–21)
Ariana	Classical Greek and Roman name for Afghanistan
Avesta	ancient sacred writings and language of Zoroastrianism
Bactria	ancient civilisation south of the River Oxus, named after Bactra (Balkh)
bagh	garden
bala hissar	citadel within a town
band	dam
Barakzai	branch of Durrani tribe, kings of Afghanistan from 1818 to 1973
Basej e Milli	anti-Taliban National Movement party, founded by Amrullah Saleh
Bodhisattva	in Buddhism, a being who forgoes Nirvana to assist others
burj	tower
buzkashi	a game played on horseback somewhat like polo (page 63)
Caliph	Commander of the faithful, successor to the Prophet
chaikhana	teahouse, restaurant, simple inn
charahi	junction, square
chillim	hookah or shisha, banned under the Taliban
chowk	junction, square
Durand Line	British-imposed border established in 1893 between Afghanistan and Pakistan, contested by Afghanistan
Durrani	Pashtun tribe, formerly the Abdali, renamed by Ahmad Shah, first king of Afghanistan
Gandhara	Indo-Aryan civilisation in southeast Afghanistan and northwest Pakistan (5th century BCE–6th century CE), famous for its Hellenistic-Buddhist art

Ghaznavid	empire centred around the city of Ghazni (977–1155CE)
Ghilzai	important Pashtun tribe, based around Herat
Ghorid	empire ruled by a mountain tribe from Ghor (1150–1217)
hada	bus station (Pashto)
hadiths	traditions relating to the Prophet and his companions
Haqqani Network	Islamic fundamentalist group founded by Jalaluddin Haqqani, currently allies with the Taliban
Hephthalites	also known as the White Huns, invaded in c400CE
Hezb e Islami	hardline Islamist Party of Gulbuddin Hekmatyar
Hezb e Islami-Khalis	moderate Islamist Party of Mullah Yunis Khalis, commanded by Abdul Haq
Hezb e Wahdat	Hazara party commanded by Abdul Ali Mazari that fought the Soviets
Hindu Shani	Indian dynasty that ruled Kabul (870–987CE)
IEA	Islamic Emirate of Afghanistan, governed by the Taliban
imam	prayer leader in a mosque; also descendant of the Prophet
ISAF	International Security Assistance Force (UN mandated)
ISI	Inter-Services Intelligence, in Pakistan
IS-K	Islamic State Khorasan
Ismaili	Shi'a sect under the Aga Khan (page 262)
istga	bus station (Dari)
iwan	in Islamic architecture, a rectangular hall, usually vaulted and walled on three sides, with one end entirely open
jada	road (Dari)
Jamiat-i-Islami	moderate Islamist party founded by Burhanuddin Rabbani, commanded by Ahmad Shah Massoud
Jebh-e-Nejat-e Melli	Pro-Islamist National Liberation Front, founded by Sibghatullah Mojaddedi to fight the invading Soviets
jihad	in Islam, a fight on behalf of God, religion or the community
kafir	unbeliever
Khalq/Khalqists	hardline Marxists
khan	nobleman or lord, title of respect
khanaqah	Sufi meeting house
Khorasan	'Land of the Rising Sun'; ancient Persian province that included Herat and Balkh
Khwarazm Shahs	central Asian dynasty that ruled from the mid 1150s to 1220 with the arrival of Genghis Khan
Kidarites	also known as 'Red Huns'; invaded Afghanistan in 335CE
kotal	hill
Kufic	early, ornamental Arabic script
Kurt Maliks	rulers of Herat (1245–1381)
Kushan	c50CE to 4th-century empire of former nomads ruling Afghani
loya jirga	great council, of elders or leaders
madrasa	Islamic religious school
mahram	male chaperone or guardian
mamluks	Turkic enslaved soldiers
Maurya	Indian empire founded by Chandragupta (300BCE)
mazar	tomb or sanctuary
mihrab	prayer niche in a mosque in the direction of Mecca
mir	son of a prince, same as *mirza*

GLOSSARY

Mughal	Indian Muslim Empire extending into southeast Afghanistan, founded by Babur (1526–1857)
mujahideen	guerrilla fighter engaged in *jihad*. Singular *mujahid*
mullah	Muslim cleric or teacher
mussafarkhana	basic inn
Nau Ruz	New Year's Day, 21 March (Shi'a)
Nestorian	Church of the East that held that Christ had distinct human and divine persons
Northern Alliance	mujahideen fighting the Taliban, led by Ahmad Shah Massoud
NRF	National Resistance Front run by Ahmad Massoud
Oxiana	another name for Bactria
Oxus	Classical name of the Amu Darya River
Parchami	communist-nationalists
Pashtunistan	the 'land of the Pashtuns', in south and eastern Afghanistan and northwest Pakistan, divided politically by the Durand Line
Pashtunwali	way of the Pashtuns (page 44)
PDPA	People's Democratic Party of Afghanistan (communist)
pir	Sufi spiritual teacher
qala	fortress
rud	river
Saka	Nomadic tribe that invaded Afghanistan (c150BCE)
Salafism	fundamentalist reform movement, seeking to restore the earliest interpretations of Islam
Samanid	10th-century dynasty ruling Afghanistan, based in Bokhara
Sassanian	Persian dynasty ruling from the 3rd to the 7th century CE
satrap	Ancient Persian governor of a province (satrapy)
Seleucid	descendants of Alexander the Great's general Seleucus
Seljuk	11th-century Turkish dynasty in north and west Afghanistan
shah	king
Shahre Nau	New Town
shaikh	Sufi teacher and guide
Sharia	religious law based on scriptures of Islam, particularly the Quran and hadiths
Shi'a	or Shiite. A Muslim who believes that Ali was the only legitimate successor to the Prophet (page 53)
Soghdia	Persian satrapy north of the Oxus
stupa	mound or domed structure, built to house Buddhist relics
Sunni	largest branch of Islam, believing Muhammad did not appoint a successor, and his companion Abu Bakr was his rightful successor
Timurid	descendants of Timur (Tamerlane); ruled Afghanistan 1364–1530
Tokharistan	another name from Bactria after the 6th century CE
TTP	Tehreek-e-Taliban Pakistan
Turkestan	also Afghan Turkestan; later name for Bactria
Turkishahi	Buddhist dynasty that ruled Kabul before Islam
ulama	Islamic clergy who serve as judges
UXO	unexploded ordnance
wazir	*vizier*; chief government minister
Yuezhi	central Asian tribe that invaded Afghanistan in the 1st century BCE who later became the Kishans

Appendix 3

FURTHER INFORMATION
BOOKS
History and society
Ancient to 1978
Dalrymple, William *Return of a King: The Battle for Afghanistan, a History of the First Afghan War 1839–42* Bloomsbury, 2013. A definitive account.
Doucet, Lyse *The Finest Hotel in Kabul* Hutchinson Heinemann, 2025. Afghanistan from 1969 to the present, as seen through the story of the Kabul InterContinental, by the BBC's chief international correspondent.
Elphinstone, Montstuart *An Account of the Kingdom of Caubul, and Its Dependencies in Persia, Tartary and India, Comprising a View of the Afghan Nation and History of the Dooraunee Monarchy,* 1815. Available online via the Library of Congress: w loc.gov. The first book about Afghanistan by a Westerner since Marco Polo was a bestseller when it came out in its day.
Errington, Elizabeth *Charles Masson and the Buddhist Sites of Afghanistan* The British Museum, 2017. Available online: w britishmuseum.org. Errington has spent her career studying the coins and other relics that Charles Masson collected in Afghanistan.
Errington, Elizabeth *Charles Masson: Collections from Begram and Kabul Bazaar, Afghanistan 1833–1838* British Museum Research Publications, 2021.
Kousser, Rachel *Alexander at the End of the World: The Forgotten Final Years of Alexander the Great* Mariner Books, 2024. A vivid, well-researched page-turning account.
Lee, Jonathan L *Afghanistan: A History from 1260 to the Present* Reaktion Books, 2022. The best history by one of the world's foremost experts on Afghanistan.
Macintyre, Ben *Josiah the Great: The True Story of the Man Who Would Be King* HarperCollins, 2011. The extraordinary deeds of Josiah Harlan, the first American in Afghanistan (page 146).
Macrory, Patrick *Signal Catastrophe: The Story of the Disastrous Retreat from Kabul, 1842* Hodder & Stoughton, 1966. The British Army's biggest catastrophe in the 19th century.

Soviet–Afghan War and first Taliban rule: 1978–2001
Coll, Steve *Ghost Wars: The Secret History of the CIA, Afghanistan and Bin Laden* Penguin, 2005. Superb, Pulitzer-prize winning account covering the years from 1978 to 9/11 in 2001, full of opportunities missed along the way.
Crile, George *My Enemy's Enemy (Charlie Wilson's War)* Atlantic Books, 2003. Page-turner true story of characters behind the CIA's billion dollar a year covert funding of the mujahideen, made into the film starring Tom Hanks and Julia Roberts.
Harnden, Toby *First Casualty: The Untold Story of the CIA Mission to Avenge 9/11* Little Brown, 2021. Award-winning journalist's true account of the CIA's Team Alpha as joint forces with General Dostum in northern Afghanistan on the trail of al-Qaeda.

Coalition years: 2001–21

Anderson, Jon Lee *The Lion's Grave* Atlantic, 2002. Collected essays covering the assassination of Ahmad Shah Massoud and all the betrayals and double dealing around it.

Barker, Kim *The Taliban Shuffle: Strange Days in Afghanistan and Pakistan* Knopf Doubleday, 2013. Witty, insightful, honest account by a reporter for the *Chicago Tribune* in 2004–09, in 2016 made into the film *Whiskey Tango Foxtrot*.

Girardet, Edward *Killing the Cranes: A Reporter's Journey through Three Decades of War in Afghanistan* Chelsea Green Publishing, 2011. In-depth look by a journalist who first reported on the country before the Soviet invasion, and who personally met all the main players, even Osama bin Laden – who wanted to kill him.

Lamb, Christina *The Sewing Circles of Herat* HarperCollins, 2002. As a female journalist, Lamb was able to visit both the home in Rome of King Zahir Shah and the madrasa in Pakistan where the Taliban were trained as boys; as well as women's sewing circles, where they studied Shakespeare and James Joyce under the Taliban.

Mortenson, Greg *Stones into Schools: Promoting Peace through Education in Afghanistan and Pakistan* Penguin Reprint, 2010. Mortenson may have been his own worst enemy, but his ideas are good and the Central Asian Institute that he founded to promote education, especially for girls in rural Afghanistan, has done fine work.

Seierstad, Asne *The Bookseller of Kabul* Time Warner Books, 2004. The controversial bestseller (page 127).

Return of the Taliban: post-2021

Anderson, Jon Lee *To Lose a War: The Fall and the Rise of the Taliban* Penguin, 2025. Anderson, a staff writer with the *New Yorker*, has been visiting and writing about the country since the 1980s.

Massoud, Ahmad *In the Name of My Father: Struggling for Freedom in Afghanistan* Republic Book Publishers, 2024. A personal account of what went wrong under the coalition by Commander Massoud's son and current leader of the National Resistance Front.

Paranda Network of Afghan Women Writers *My Dear Kabul: A Year in the Life of an Afghan Women's Writing Group* Hodder/Coronet, 2024. A compelling diary of the Taliban's return.

Seierstad, Asne *The Afghans: Three Lives through War, Love and Revolt* Little, Brown, 2024. The author returns to Afghanistan to chronicle the lives of a women's rights activist, a member of the Taliban, and a young female law student with the return of Taliban rule.

Whitlock, Craig *The Afghanistan Papers: A Secret History of the War* Simon & Schuster, 2022. A damning indictment of American hubris and how Bush, Obama and Trump let America's longest war hopelessly drift on, by a reporter for the *Washington Post*.

Travel

Byron, Robert *Road to Oxiana* Oxford University Press, 2007. Byron reinvented travel writing when he took off in 1933 through Persia and Afghanistan in search of the origins of Islamic art; now re-issued with a preface by Rory Stewart.

Colegrave, Bill *Halfway House to Heaven* Bene Factum, 2010. Colegrave and companions went to discover the true source of the River Oxus, and believe they have found it.

Curzon, George Nathaniel *Pamirs and the Source of the Oxus* Elibron Classics, 2005. Classic adventure by the rather brilliant and adventurous Viceroy of India, first published in 1895.

Elliot, Jason *An Unexpected Light: Travels in Afghanistan* Picador, 2011. A classic of lyric travel writing, first published in 2000 and covering two trips. Elliot joined the mujahideen in 1979 and returned a decade later with Massoud in Kabul.

Ferrier, J P *Caravan Journeys and Wanderings in Persia, Afghanistan, Turkistan, and Beloochistan* London, 1857; reprinted Westmead, 1971. One of the earliest accounts of Afghanistan.

Harlan, Josiah *A Memoir of India and Avghanistaun* J Dobson, 1842. Available at Internet Archives: w archive.org/details/dli.ministry.04249. Harlan's colourful adventures in his own words.

Ibn Battuta *The Travels of Ibn Battutah* Edited by Tim Macintosh-Smith. Macmillan Collector's Library, 2016. Keen, sometimes X-rated observations by the 14th-century Maghrebi scholar.

Klass, Rosanne *Land of the High Flags: Afghanistan When the Going Was Good* 1964, reissued in 2007 by Odyssey. On the early days of the hippie trail.

Levi, Peter *The Light Garden of the Angel King: Travels in Afghanistan with Bruce Chatwin* 1972, reissued in 2002 by Pallas Athene. Levi, poet and Classics scholar, was in search of signs of Hellenism, but he and Chatwin were curious about everything.

Michaud, Roland and Michaud, Sabrina *Caravans to Tartary* Thames & Hudson, 1999. Stunning photos of a lost world 14 years before the Soviet invasion.

Newby, Eric *A Short Walk in the Hindu Kush* Often reprinted, recently by the Folio Society, 2011. First published in 1958, Newby's delightful account of going from a fashion job in London to Nuristan and almost reaching the summit of 5,809m Mir Samir.

Stark, Freya *Minaret of Djam: An Excursion in Afghanistan* Tauris Parke Paperbacks, 2010. In 1968 one of the world's great travellers at age 75 went to find the remote Minaret of Jam.

Stewart, Rory *The Places in Between* Picador, 2014. Two weeks after the fall of the Taliban, in the middle of winter, perhaps only Rory Stewart would think of walking from Herat to Kabul. Acute observations of people and places woven in with history. Beautifully written.

Wood, John *Journey to the Source of the River Oxus* Kessinger Rare Reprints, 2007. Also available online via Internet Archives: w https://archive.org/details/dli.ministry.15767.

Xuan Zang *The Great Tang Dynasty Record of the Western Regions* Numata Center for Buddhist Translation & Research, 2006. New translation of Buddhist monk Xuan Zang's 7th-century CE travels, written for the Tang Emperor, covering early Buddhism in Afghanistan.

Literature and poetry

Babur *The Baburnama: Memoirs of Babur, Prince and Emperor* New York: Modern Library, 2002. Babur's fascinating autobiography, now available in a sparkling new translation by W M Thackston, Jr, with an introduction by Salmon Rushdie.

Ferdowsi, Abolqasem *Shahnameh: The Persian Book of Kings* Translated by Dick Davis. Penguin Classics, 2016. The national epic of Persia, with many doings set in Afghanistan. Ferdowsi himself spent years in Herat.

Fraser, George MacDonald *Flashman* HarperCollins, 1999. First published in 1969, the first of the Flashman series covers the great antihero's role in the First Anglo–Afghan War.

Hosseini, Khaled *And the Mountains Echo* Penguin, 2014. A tale of love and heartbreak by the Dickens of Afghanistan. Hosseini is probably single-handedly the reason why so many feel an emotional investment in the people of Afghanistan.

Hosseini, Khaled *The Kite Runner* Riverhead Books, 2013. First published in 2003, Hosseini's novel about two boys in Kabul just before the Soviet invasion, on friendship, betrayal and salvation.

Hosseini, Khaled *A Thousand Splendid Suns* Bloomsbury, 2007. A tale of two women during the decades of the Soviet occupation, the horrors of the civil war, and the Taliban's first rule.

Khalili, Khalilullah *An Assembly of Moths* Translated by Whitney Azoy and Masood Khalili. Privately published, 2023. 67 poems by Afghanistan's 20th-century poet laureate.

Khalili, Khalilullah *Khushal Khan Khattak: The Great Warrior/Poet of Afghanistan: Selected Poems* Translated by Paul Smith. CreateSpace, 2012.

Khalili, Khalilullah *A Nobleman from Khorasan* Translated by M F Moonzajer. Privately published 2019. Khalili's best-known novel on the life of the king for a day, Habidullah Kalikani.

Kipling, Rudyard *The Man Who Would Be King* Legare Street Press, 2022. Written in 1888 and inspired by Josiah Harlan, this was made into a film in 1975 starring Michael Caine and Sean Connery.

My Pen Is the Wing of a Bird: New Fiction by Afghan Women MacLehose Press, 2022. An anthology of new fiction by 18 Afghan women, with an introduction by BBC correspondent Lyse Doucet.

Rahman, Baba *The Poetry of Rahman Baba – Poet of the Pashtuns* Translated by Robert Sampson and Momin Khan. Jaja University Book Agency, 2005. The humanist poetry of love, peace and tolerance, by the mystic Sufi. Only the Quran is more beloved by the Pashtuns.

Guidebooks

Ashly, Laurie and Dear, Chad *Ski Afghanistan: A Backcountry Guide to Bamyan and Band e Amir* Aga Khan Foundation 2007. Mountaineering guide to the Hindu Kush; hard to find.

Bakker, Jan *Trekking in Tajikistan: The Northern Ranges, Pamirs and Afghanistan's Wakhan Corridor* Cicerone, 2018. This has a good section on trekking in the Afghan Wakhan Corridor.

Breckle, S W and Rafiqpoor, M D *Field Guide Afghanistan: Flora and Vegetation* 2022. An updated digital version of the rare ground-breaking 2010 guide in English and Dari; the first chapter is available online at: **w** researchgate.net.

Chipchase, Jan, Kellogg, Sam and Simonyi, Gyula *Afghan Pamir Trail Map* Studio Radiodurans, Tokyo, 2026. The latest detailed map of the Wakhan Corridor and the Afghan Pamir.

Dupree, Nancy Hatch *An Historical Guide to Afghanistan* Afghan Tourist Organization, 1977. This excellent first guide to the country is out of print but available online on Internet Archives: **w** archive.org/details/azu_acku_ds351_d87_1977/mode/2up.

Omrani, Bijan and Leeming, Matthew *Afghanistan: A Companion and Guide* Odyssey, 2007. With a foreword by Hamid Karzai and an introduction by Elizabeth Chatwin, this is a richly illustrated guide offering historical and cultural essays.

Pinelli, Carlo Alberto and Predan, Gianni *Peaks of Silver and Jade: An Afghanistan Trekking Guide* Aga Khan Foundation, 2007. A mountaineering guide to the Hindu Kush; hard to find.

FILMS ABOUT AFGHANISTAN The following films are listed in chronological order, as they trace the ups and downs of Afghanistan's recent history.

The Horsemen (1971) John Frankenheimer directed Omar Sharif, Jack Palance and Leigh Taylor-Young in the first Hollywood movie filmed in Afghanistan, about buzkashi.

Osama (2003) Golden Globe winner and the most successful Afghan film, *Osama* tells the story of a girl who disguises herself as a boy to be able to provide for her family under the Taliban.

16 Days in Afghanistan (2007) Documentary on the return of Afghan-American Anwar Hajher to Afghanistan after 25 years, with a whole range of interviews.

The Kite Runner (2007) The Hollywood version of Khaled Hosseini's bestseller (see opposite), banned in Afghanistan for fears it would incite ethnic tensions.

Afghan Star (2009) Prize-winning UK documentary following the lives of four contestants on Tolo TV's music competition.

Restrepo (2010) Photographer Tim Hetherington and journalist Sebastian Junger allow the realities of war to speak for themselves in this unnarrated documentary about a US platoon in Afghanistan (page 162).

The Boxing Girls of Kabul (2012) Canadian documentary directed by Ariel Nasr about Afghanistan's first boxing academy for women, filmed in Ghazi Stadium.

Buzkashi Boys (2012) Directed by Sam French, Oscar-nominated tale of two boys, one a poor orphan and the other a blacksmith's son, who become best friends and dream of becoming buzkashi stars. Filmed entirely in Kabul.

Afghans to the Top (2014) Louis Meunier's award-winning documentary of the first Afghan ascent of 7,492m Mount Noshaq, the highest peak in Afghanistan.

Whiskey Tango Foxtrot (2016) Based on Kim Barker's *Taliban Shuffle* (page 285), starring Tina Fey and Margot Robbie.

Jirga (2018) Benjamin Gilmour's film about an Australian soldier who returns to Afghanistan to apologise (page 59).

Kabullywood (2019) A Franco-Afghan production by Louis Meunier, about a group of artists who restore Kabul's most beautiful cinema after 30 years of war.

The Secret Marathon (2019) Legendary marathon runner Martin Parnell trains director Katie McKenzie to run with the Afghan women in the Afghanistan Marathon in Bamiyan.

Where the Light Shines (2019) Documentary by Daniel Etter on two Afghan skiers who dream of competing in the Olympics.

The Etilaat Roz (2022) As the Taliban closed in on Kabul, the city's newspaper staff member Abbas Rezaie filmed how journalists coped before losing all hope.

Retrograde (2022) Matthew Heineman directed this documentary covering the last nine months of the US War in Afghanistan.

Riverboom (2023) Swiss documentary by Claude Baechtold, who couldn't go home so bought a video camera and filmed his two friends on a road trip in Afghanistan, with plenty of drama and comedy along the way.

Champions of the Golden Valley (2024) Moving documentary directed by Ben Sturgulewski on the Afghan ski challenge in Bamiyan (full disclosure: the author of this guide was an associate producer).

Hollywoodgate (2024) Egyptian filmmaker Ibrahim Nash'at had special permission to film Taliban leaders after the US withdrawal from Afghanistan. Hollywoodgate was the name of the former CIA base.

WEBSITES

w acku.edu.af Archives of the Afghanistan Center founded by Nancy Hatch Dupree at Kabul University.

w afghancultureunveiled.com Afghan-American Humaira Ghilzai's site on Afghan culture and cuisine, with dozens of recipes.

w afghanistan-analysts.org/en Articles on all aspects of Afghanistan.

w bishnaw.com Founded in 2014, this is the website of the Organization for Policy Research and Development Studies (DROPS) dedicated to understanding the situation of women in Afghanistan.

w indoaryanabookco.com Shah Muhammad Rais (the Bookseller of Kabul) now lives in the UK and sells his books through this website.

w mockandoneil.com/wakhan.htm Website of John Mock and Kimberley O'Neil, pioneers in documenting the Wakhan region's geography and people.

Index

Page numbers in **bold** indicate major entries; those in *italic* indicate maps

Abd-al-Latif 211
Abdullah Abdullah (Dr Abdullah) 37
Abdur Rahman Khan 28–9, 46, 51, 132, 135, 159, 165, 173, 174, 250, 252
Abu Said Mirza 209, 211
accommodation 93–5
accommodation price codes 95
Achaemenids 17, 193, 208, 225, 226
addresses, finding locations 90
Afghan Civil War **34–5**, 43, 114, 117, 130, 135, 137, 138, 141, 151, 191, 232, 254
Afghan coats 62
Afsay 163
Aga Khan 135, 218, 245, 177, 180, 262, 270
agriculture 12, 14, **42**, 50, 52, 84, 87, 98, 159, 174, 201
Ahmad Shah Durrani 26, 116, 170, 191, 194, 198–9, 200, 243, 248, 267
Ahura Mazda 239–40
Ai Khanoum 15, 20, 253, **255–6**
Aimaq 46, **48–9**, 188
airlines 73, 90–1
airports 90–1, 118–19, 166, 193, 211–12, 233
Ajar valley 14, 178
Akhundzada, Hibattullah 37, 39–40, 42, 85, 200
Ala al-Din Husayn 'The World Burner' 23, 189, 204
Alchon Huns 15, 21
Alexander the Great 15, **17–19**, 20, 51, 55, 57, 62, 82, 148, 159, 160, 193, 208, 223, 240, 242, 245, 255, 284
al-Qaeda 35
altitude sickness (AMS) 81
Amanullah Khan 9, 14, **30**, 57, 60, 116, 130, 131, **136–8**, 140, 154, 164, 170
Amu Darya *see* rivers
Anar Dara 225
Andkhoy 49, 61, 74, 103, 247, **248**
Anglo-Afghan Wars 116
  First Anglo-Afghan War **27–8**, 130, 133, 143, 155, 203
  Second Anglo-Afghan War **28–9**, 132, 156, 165, 193, 201
  Third Anglo-Afghan War **30**, 140, 170
Anjoman 265
Ansari, Abdullah 58, 208, 221
antiques 103–4
Aqcha 247

archaeology 14–16
art and architecture 55–7
Aryob Zazi 69, 165, **166**
Asadabad 151, 161, 163, **164**
Ashoka 20, 21, 137, 199–200
Babur, Mughal Emperor 25, 56, 115, 122, 135, **136–7**, 140, 156, 164, 179, 189, 199, 204, 210, 220
Baburnama 58, 135, 140, 156, 286
Bactria 17, 18, 19, 20, 22, 45, 239, 241–2
Bactria–Margiana Archaeological Complex (BMAC) 16, 55, 160
Bactrian camel 8
Bactrian gold 20, **138**
Badakhshan 69, 73, 86, 88, 145, 252, 253, **257–75**
Badghis 92, 235, 246, **249–50**
Bagh e Jahan Nama (King's hunting lodge) 250
Bagram (Kapisa) 15, 17, 21 34, **141**, 143, 148
  Ivories 15, 21, 139, **141**
Baharak 259, **261**, 262, 263, 265, 269
Bahram Shah 189, **204**, 205
Bala Murghab 249
Balkh 4, 15, 17, 19, 40, 56, 58, 148, 176, 232, 233, **239–46**, *241*
  Bala Hissar and walls 245
  getting there and around 244
  history 22, 24, 239–44
  No Gombad Mosque 56, 245–6
  Rumi's House 245
  Sayyid Subhan Quli Khan Madrasa 244
  Shrine of Khoja Abu Nasr Parsa 244
  Tomb of Rabi'a Balkhi 245
  tourist information and registration 235
Balochs 50, 60, 102, 222, 226, 228
Bamiyan 5, 7, 8, 14, 15, 21, 22, 24, 35, 38, 42, 46, 56, 61, 64, 65, 66, 67, 72, 82, 97, 98, 105, 131, **171–84**, *177*, *183*
  accommodation 175–8
  activities 178–9
  Bamiyan to Herat (Central route) 187–90
  Buddha Niches 67, 174–5, 179–81
  Dragon Valley 67, 173, **184**
  getting there and away 120, 173, 194
  orientation 174
  restaurants 178

Shahr e Gholghola (City of Screams) 69, 173, 174, 175, 179, **181–3**
Shahr e Zohak (Red City) 69, 173, 174, 179, **183–4**, 187
shopping 178
tourist information and registration 174
Bamiyan Alpine Ski Club 105, 112, 178, 180–1
Band e Amir National Park 5, 13, 59, 67, 68, 86, 100, 101, 105, 171, 178, **184–7**, *185*
banks and moneychangers 40, 89, 106
Bargi Matal 163
Barikot 164
Barkali 163
Barmakids 242–3
Baysanghor 209, 211, 219
Bazarak 145, 147
Beprestan 163
Bihzad, Kamal al-Din 25, 56, 210
bin Laden, Osama 3, 33, 35, 36, 38, 156–7, 254–5
bookshops 58, 104, 129
Bost 191, 201, **202–3**
Bozai Gumbaz 269, 272, 275
Britain, British 9, **26–31**, 45, 75, 116, 123, 130, 132, 133, 135, 141, 143, 155–6, 157, 165, 170, 174, 201, 202, 203, 210, 219, 264–5, 267
Buddhist sites 142
  Buddha Niches *see* Bamiyan
  Guldara Stupa 142
  Hadda 139, 151, **155**
  Mes Aynak 15–16, 43, 73, 139, **142–3**
  Nava Vihara 21, **242–3**
  Shewaki Stupa 16, 142
  Takht e Rostam 15, **251**
  Toop Dara 142
budgeting 89
Burnes, Alexander 27, 28, 174, 179
buses 91
buzkashi 47, **63**, 66, 67, 104, 220, 235, 238, 248, 261, 262, 288
Byron, Robert 69, 122, 211, 213, 243–4, 247, 250, 285

Camp Bastion/Leatherneck 202
camping 95, 270
car hire 92
carpets 57, 48–9, 102–3, 131, 248
cars 91–2
Central Afghanistan 171–90, *172*
Chaghcharan (Firozkoh) 4, 48, 173, 187, **188–9**

289

chaikhanas (tea houses) 94, 99–100
Chalghoza pine 12
Chandragupta Maurya 19, 20
charities 13, 111–12
checkpoints 92
Chehel Burj 173
Chelab Valley 265
Cheshmeh e Shafa 240
Chesht e Sharif 189, 190
chikungunya 78
Chilzina 199–200
Chinargi Dam 170
cholera 79–80
CIA 33, 144, 166, 169, 254, 284, 288
climate 6, 12–13
climbing 105
clothing 61–2, 88–9, 103 *see also* women
Combat Outpost Keating 163
crafts **102–4**, 127, 131, 178, 207, 217
cricket 64, 129, 133, 150, 162, 169, 198, 254
cultural etiquette 109–11
Curzon, Lord George Nathaniel 4, 265, 266, 275

Daoud Khan 31, 32, 58, 116, 245
Dasht e Laila massacre 200, 233
Dasht e Margo (Desert of Death) 189, 223
Daykundi Province 46, 120, 194
deep vein thrombosis 76
dengue fever 78
dentists 76
diarrhoea 79
Diberjin 15
disability, travelling with a 86–7
Diwana Baba 163
Do'ab 161, 163
doctors 76
dogs 8–9, 79, 85
Dost Mohammad 27–8, 155, 221, 243, 252
Dostum, Abdul Rachid 34, 35, 38, 47, 57, **232**, 233, 238, 247
Dowlatabad 49
Dragon Valley (Darya e Ajdahar) 173, **184**
drinks 99
Dubai 71, 73, 166
Dupree, Louis 23, 116, 118
Dupree, Nancy Hatch 116, **118–19**, 182, 249, 269, 287, 288
Durand Line 29, 31, 36, 41, 44, 149, 159, **165**, 170

Eastern Afghanistan 149–70, *150*
eating out 99–100
economy 11, 30, 31, 39, **40–3**, 48, 49, 104, 107
emeralds 42, 51, 147
etiquette 109–11
Eucratides 20, 255

Farah 6, 10, 69, 206, 212, **223–6**, 228, 229
Faryab Province 49, 248, 249
fat-tailed sheep **8**, 48, 96, 249
Fayzabad 120, 253, **258–61**, *260*, 262, 267, 269, 270
Ferdowsi 22, 57, 62, 204, 229, 239, 240, 286
festivals 101–2

films about Afghanistan 59, 65, 162, 287–8
Firozkoh (Turquoise Mountain) 188, 189, 190
first-aid kit 75, 77
flora 11–13
Foladi valley 175, 181
food 95–8
football 64–5, 129, 133
forts
  Arg e Naude 225–6
  Chahar Deh 225
  Chehel Burj 173, 187
  Chiqchi 247
  Farah 224, 225
  Ghazi Babrak Khan Zadran Qala 169–70
  Kak Kazan **225**, 229
  Mullah Aman Qala 225
  Qala e Ibrahim Khan 229
  Qala e Jamshady 229
  Qala e Jangi 233, 238–9
  Qala e Nadi 229
  Qala i Chigni 229
  Sajj Qala 225

Gandamak 28, 151, **155–6**
Gandhara 17, 21, **55**
Gardez 120, 142, **165–6**, 203
Garmao 188
Gaz Khun 269, 273, 274
geography 3–5
geology 5
gesturing 110
getting around 212
getting there and away 73–5
Genghis Khan 3, 14, 16, **23–5**, 33, 46, 48, 51, 52, 56, 58, 63, 67, 114, 136, 173, 174, 182, 183, 189, 191, 201, 204, 211, 219, 232, 237, 238, 239, 243, 245, 250, 268
Ghani, Ashraf 37, 119, 232
Ghazi Babrak Khan 170
Ghaznavids 16, 22, 23, 114, 189, 193, 202, 203, **204**, 205, 208, 226
Ghazni 5, 10, 24, 26, 46, 56, 62, 68, 104, 120, 139, 189, 191, 104, 120, **203–5**
Ghiyath al-Din 189, 190
Ghor 23, 46, 48, 171, 188
Ghorids 23, 56, 68, 183, 187, **189**, 190, 202, 204, 217, 202, 203
Gowhar Shad 25, 56, 209, **211**, 217, 218, 219, 221, 243
Graeco-Bactrian kingdom 19, 20, 242, 255
Graeco-Buddhist art 14, 20, 139, 151, 155
Great Game, The 26–7, 143, 257, 264, 267
Guru Nanak 54, 200

Hanafi School of Islam 45, 49, **53**
Haq, Abdul 33, 35, 154
Haqqani, Abdul Hakim 40
Haqqani, Jalaluddin 33, 169
Haqqani, Khalil Rahman 169
Haqqani, Sirajuddin 38, 169
Haqqani Network 33, 36, 106, 117, 164, **169**
Harlan, Josiah 143, **146**, 284
Hayratan 40, 74, 233, 234
Hazarajat 5, 7, 9, 29, 171, 173, 175

Hazaras 33, 38, 46, 48, 49, 53, 60, 61, 65, 117, 134, 135, **173**, **174–5**, 178, 184, 188, 232, 233
Hazarchishma Natural Bridge 185
Hazrat Ali 86, 184, 231, 235, 237
health 75–82
heat stroke 80
Hekmatyar, Gulbuddin 32, 33, 35, 144–5, 232, **254–5**
Helmand Culture 16
Helmand Province 20, 36, 41, 50, 68, 191, **201–3**
Hephthalites (White Huns) 22, 179, 183, 208
Herat 4, 5, 6, 16, 17, 41, 45, 46, 48, 49, 54, 56, 57, 58, 66, 67, 72, 87, 89, 92, 136, 189, **206–22**, *209*, *214*, 223, 231, **246**, 250
  accommodation 94, 213
  Bagh e Mellat 219
  bazaars and caravanserais 217
  buzkashi 63, 220
  Citadel 218
  eating out 95, 97, 99, 100, 213–16
  Friday Mosque 56, 217–18
  Gazar Gah 208, 221
  getting around 212
  getting there 73, 120, 188, 194, 202, 211–12, 224, 228, 234–5, 249
  history 22, 23, 24, 25, 26, 27, 28, 29, 30, 38, 189, 204, 207–11
  Jami's Shrine 221–2
  Jewish Cemetery 222
  Jihad Museum 84, 219–20
  Musallah Complex 218–19
  Namakdan pavilion 221
  Old City 216–18
  orientation 212–13
  Pol e Malan 220
  Shahzadagan tombs 221
  shopping 102, 103, 104, 105, 216
  Shrine of Khawaja Ghaltan 222
  Takht e Safar 219
  Taraqi Park 212, 213
  tile workshop 207, 218
  Tomb of Gowhar Shad 219
  Tomb of Sultan Agha 222
  tourist information and registration 188, 212
  Yu Aw synagogue 217
hiking *see* trekking
Hindu Kush *see* mountains
Hindus 50, 54
hippies 32, 114, **116**, 118, 127, 132, 194
history of Afghanistan 16–39
holidays 2, 66, 101, 139, 162, 163, 166
homestays 94–5, 163, 274
hospitals 76
Hosseini, Khaled 63, 286, 287
houbara (MacQueen's bustard) 6, 10, 11
Husayn Bayqara 25, 56, 210, 219

Imam Nazar 74
immunisations 75–6
India 8, 16, 18, 19, 20, 22, 23, 26–8, 30, 31, 32, 44, 54, 56, 64, 72, 73, 116, 129, 135, 137, 141, 154, 157, 159, 165, 176, 189, 204, 205, 225, 241

Indus Valley (Harappan) Civilisation 16
insurance 75
internet 88, 106, 107
Iran 34, 35, 38, 39, 42, 46, 50, 53, 68, 73, 75, 129, 174–5, 206, 207, 210, 211, 212, 226
Ishkishim 74, 259, 262, 263, 269, 270, 272, **273–4**
Ishtewe 162
ISI (Inter-Services Intelligence, Pakistan) 33, 36, 38, 144, 169, 254
ISIS Khorasan Province (IS-K) 15, 37, 38, 46, 53, 54, 82, 84, 117, 119, 134, 149, 157, 175
Islam Qala 75
Islamic Emirate *see* Taliban
Islamic Republic 4, 12, 14, **36–7**, 46, 54, 55, 57, 71, 127, 138, 160, 173, 175, 180–1, 191, 202, 210–11, 224, 232, 238, 244, 252, 255
Ismailis 45, 46, 52, 53, 174, **262–3**, 264, 267
Istalif 28, 67, 114, 135, **140**
itineraries 68–9

Jabal Saraj 145
Jalalabad 18, 28, 34, 54, 57, 58, 64, 65, 89, 102, 142, **149–55**, *153*
  Abdul Haq Park 154
  accommodation 151–2
  Amir Shaheed gardens 154
  eating out 95, 97, 99, 152–4
  getting there 120, 151, 161, 164
  Hadda 155
  Seraj al Emirat 154
  shopping 102, 105, 154
  Sikh Jalalabad 154–5
  tourist information and registration 151
Jami (Nur ad-Din Abd ar-Rahman) 25, 58, 210, 221
Jawzari Canyon 185
Jews 54, 116, 217, 222, 241–2, 243
Jowzjan Province 248
Jurm 261, 263

Kabul 3, 6, 8, 12, 39, 40, 41, 45, 46, 47, 53–4, 63, 66, 67, 76, 82, 84, 89, 90–1, 107, 108, 110–11, **114–39**, *115*, *121*, *125*, *128*, 144–5, 147, 149–50, 155, 165, 169, 173, 201, 203, 205, 211–12, 233
  accommodation 92–3, **122–4**
  Afghan Tour Department 70, 71, 72, 122
  around Kabul 15, 139–44
  Bagh e Babur (Babur's Gardens) 15, 56, 135, 137
  Bala Hissar 16, 28, 116, **131–2**
  banks and moneychangers 129–30
  Bibi Mahru 133
  Bush Bazaar 129
  Chicken Street 116, 127, 216
  Darulaman Palace 58, 116, **137–8**
  dried fruit market 130–1
  eating out 96, 98, 99, 124–6
  Eid Gah Mosque 131
  embassies 129
  entertainment and nightlife 129
  getting around 90, 120–2
  getting there 73, **118–20**, 151, 168, 193

history 20, 21, 22, 24, 25, 26, 27, 28, 29, 30, 32, 33, 34, 35, 37, **114–17**
hospital 130
Ka Faroshi (bird market) 131
Kabre Ghora (foreigners' cemetery) 132–3
Kabul airport 37, 73, 88, 116, 117, 118–19
Kabul University 31, 116, 119, 254
Kabul Zoo 116, 136–7
macroyans 72, 122
Maidan 131
Maiwand Chowk (kite shops) 131
Mausoleum of Timur Shah Durrani 130
Memorial to Farkhunda Malikzada 130
Murad Khani 116, 131
National Museum 13, 14, 15, 35, 51, 56, 119, **138–9**, 141, 251, 255
Old City 122, 130–4
OMAR Landmine Museum 134
orientation 122
Pol e Kheshti Mosque 130
post office 108, 130
Sakhi Shrine 68, **134–5**
Shah e Do Shamshira Mosque 57, 130
Shahre Nau 122, 124
Sher Darwaza mountain 122, 130, 132, 135
shopping 62, 102, 103, **127–9**
sports and activities 63, 64, 65, 129
Television Hill (Asamayi) 122, 133, 134
Teppe Maranjan 129, 133
Wazir Akbar Khan district 122, 127, 132
Zarnegar Park 120
Kalakani, Habibullah 30, 58
Kamal Khan Dam 4, 226
Kamdesh 162–4
Kamo 163
Kandahar 5, 6, 17, 20, 25, 26, 29, 35, 38, 39, 41, 50, 62, 64, 66, 68, 72, 74, 78, 85, 92, 115, 149, **191–201**, *194*, *197*, 223, 225
  accommodation 94, 195–6
  Ahmad Shah Durrani Mausoleum 198–9
  Arghandab Valley 200
  Ashokan Rock Edicts 20, 199–200
  Chilzina (Old Kandahar) 199–200
  eating out 95, 98, 99, 100, 196–8
  Eid Gah Mosque 200
  getting there 73, 90, 120, 193, 202, 212
  Jami Mui Mobarak 198
  Kandahar cemetery 200
  Mosque of the Cloak 134, 199
  Red Mosque 200
  shopping 102, 198
  Shrine of Baba Wali 200–1
  Shrine of Mirwais Hotak 200
  tourist information and registration 194
  Zorr Shaar 194, 198–9
Kanishka the Great 21, 251
Kantiwe Valley 162

karakuls 8, 47, 48, 49, 50, 61, 62, 244, 247
Karmal, Babrak 31, 33, 34
Karzai, Hamid 36, 45, 61, 117, 191, 210–11, 236
Kasch Goz 273, 275
kayaking 105, 178
Khalili, Khalilullah 58, 286
Khalili, Masoud 58, 145
Khalqists 32, 210
Khan, Ismail 32, 33, 38, 210–11, 219
Khandud 269, 270, **274**
Kholm *see* Tashqurghan
Khorasan 22, 206, 208, 209
Khorog 74, 262, 263
Khost 3, 4, 8, 9, 69, 73, 78, 120, 164, 165, **166–70**, *167*
Khwarazmians 23, 208, 218
Khyber Pass *see* passes
kids, travelling with 87–8
kite flying 63–4
Koh-i-Noor diamond 26, 137
Korengal Valley 162, 164
Kret 274
Kuchi nomads 9, **47–8**, 61, 103, 155, 223, 249, 262
Kunar Province 7, 8, 12, 13, 38, 42, 50, 53, 78, 149, 151, **162–4**
Kunduz 234, **252–5**, *252*, 257, 259, 261
Kushans 15, 20, 21, 22, 46, 139, 141, 142, 193, 242, 251, 255, 267
Kyrgyz nomads **61**, 68, 118, 258, 266, 267, 268, 269, 270, 272, 273, 274

Laghman Province 7, 13, 50, 78, 161, 163
lakes 5
  Band e Amir *see* Band e Amir National Park
  Chaqmaqtin 69, 265, 267, 269, 272, **275**
  Hamun e Helmand **4**, 10, 69, 226–7, 229
  Mandal 163
  Qargha 101, 120, **139–40**
  Shewa 5, **261–2**
  Zorkul 265, 267, 274
Lal wa sarjangal 188
Lammergeier (bearded vulture) 11
landmines **83–4**, 134, 219–20
language 2, 30, **52–3**, 276–80
lapis lazuli 5, 16, 264–5, **266**
Lashkar Gah 191, **202**, 212
LGBTQIA+ travellers 87
Logar Province 69, 142
Loya Paktia 69, 149, **164–70**

Mahmud the Great (of Ghazni) 22, 203, **204**, 205
Maiwand, Battle of 193, 201
malaria 18, 77, 243, 253
Mandagal 163
Mandol 163
Marathon of Afghanistan 65, 173, 178, **186**, 238
Marco Polo 97, 182, 243, 266, **268**
Marco Polo sheep (Pamir argali) 7, 28, 268
Masson, Charles 15, 142, **143**, 179, 284
Massoud, Ahmad Shah 33, 34, 35–6, 45, **144–7**

Mauryan Empire 19, 20, 193, 199
Maymana 2, 212, 234–5, 247, **248–9**
Mazar e Sharif 35, 46, 47, 56, 61, 62, 63, 66, 67, 68, 69, 73, 86, 89, 93, 102, 107, **231–8**, *234*, 243, 244
  accommodation 94, 235
  buzkashi 238
  drive from Mazar e Sharif to Herat 246–9
  eating out 95, 98, 100, 236
  getting there 90, 120, 145, 147, 210, 233–5, 249, 253, 261
  history 232–3
  orientation 235
  shopping 102, 103, 236
  Shrine of Hazrat Ali 56, 67, 86, 231, 235, 237–8
  tourist information and registration 235
Mazari, Abdul Ali 46, 175
media 39, 106–9
mega-projects 40–2
Mes Aynak *see* Buddhist sites
Minaret of Jam 67–8, 95, 171, 187, 188, 189, **190**, 212
Mir Ali Shir Nava'i 58, 136, 210, 219, 221
Mirwais Hotak 25, 194, 200
Mitarlam 163
MOAB (Mother of all bombs) 157
mobiles 107, 108
Mohi Par 120, **143–4**
Mojaddedi, Sibghatullah 33, 34
money 89
mountains
  Hindu Kush 1, 4, 5, 6, 8, 10, 12, 14, 16, 17, 29, 31, 45, 50, 66, 67, 68, 69, 81, 105, 114, 140, 141, 144, 145, 158, 173, 188, 190, 191, 223, 224, 231, 246, 247, 250, 257, 264, 266
  Karakoram 4, 5, 257, 267
  Koh-e-Alburz 239, 240, 243
  Koh-e-Sulayman 2, 4
  Koh-i-Baba 1, 3, 5, 11, 105, 171, 175, 178, 180
  Mir Samir 1, 105, 142
  Noshaq 3, 105, 266, 274, 288
  Pamir Knot 5, 257
  Pamirs 68, 74, 81, 105, 257, 258, 264, **266–7**, 273, 274
  Paropamisus (Selseleh-ye Safid Kuh) 2, 8
  Spin Ghar (Safed Koh) 1–2, 81, 94
Mughals 16, 25–6, 56, 58, 115–16, 132, 135, 136–7, 151, 156, 218, 233
Muhammad, Prophet 35, 46, 53, 195, 199, 231
Mullah Omar 35, 84, 133, 179, **195**, 199, 200, 201
Mundigak 16
Murad Beg 252, 254, 257
music 59–60
mussafarkhanas 94

Nader Shah Afshar 25–6, 193
Nadir Shah 133, 168
Najibullah, Mohammad (Dr Najib) 34, 35, 47, 117, 151, 198
Najjarha 163
Nangarhar 6, 41, 50, 78, 104, 149, 151, 154, 156, 168

Nasir Khusraw 263, 264
NATO 36, 37, 84, 117, 160, 202
natural history 6–14
Nau Ruz 96, 102, 134, 222, 232, **238**, 239, 240
Newby, Eric 3, 105, 144, 160, 163, 286
newspapers 106–7
Nimla Gardens 156
Nimruz Province 69, 75, 92, 102, 206, 222, **226–9**
Northern Afghanistan *230*, 231–56
Northern Alliance 14, 35, 36, 45, 175, 210, 233, 252
Nurgaram 161
Nuristan 3, 4, 7, 8, 9, 11, 12, 17, 22, 29, 53, 69, 97, 98, 106, **158–63**, 164
Nuristani **50–1**, 57, 103, 158–60

Obey 189
opening times 106
opium 36, **41**, 44, 94, 137, 201, 254, 264
Oxus (Amu Darya), source of 264–5 *see also* rivers

Paghman 56, 67, 100, 101, 114, 120, **140–1**
Pakistan 13, 31, 33, 34, 35, 36, 38, 39, 40–2, 46, 50, 51, 57, 71–2, 75, 117, 129, 144, 149, 174, 89, 149, 156–8, 160, 165–70, 174–5, 193, 195, 196, 254–5, 269
Paktika Province 8, 9, 69, 78
Panjdeh Incident 219
Panjshir Valley 68, 97, **144–6**
Parcham 32, 33, 34
Parian 265
Parun 151, **161–2**, 164
Parwan Province 21, 33, 53
Pashayi **50**, 52
Pashtunistan 31, 45, 283
Pashtuns 16, 25, 26, 28, 29, 30, 35, 36, 39, **44–5**, 46, 47, 48, 50, 58, 64, 68, 69, 96, 98, 100, 149, 150, 154, 156, 164, 165, 166, 170, 173, 174–5, 191, 192, 195, 198, 200, 201, 202, 210, 224, 232, 249, 252, 254–5
Pashtunwali **44**, 85, 94, 158, 164
passes
  Anjoman 69, 145, 263, 265
  Aqbelis 273
  Broghil 273
  Daliz 272, 274
  Hajigak 42, 173, 183, 184
  Khawak 2, 17, **148**
  Khyber 3, 17, 30, 68, 74, 114, 149, **157–8**
  Kirman 188
  Kotal e Qarabel 273
  Kotal e Shaur 273
  Qotal e Zabrak 250
  Salang 3, 31, 68, 108, 144, **147–8**, 180, 213, 243
  Sato Kandaw 166, 168
  Shibar 173, 183
  Uween-e-Sar 273
  Wakhjir 265, 275
passports 71, 84, 88, 108, 270
Payenda 167
PDPA (Afghan communist party) 31, 32, 53

Peshawar 21, 27, 28, 58, 68, 71–2, 74, 118, 150, 158
Peshawar Accords 34, 117, 254
Peshawerak 163
pharmacies 77
photography 73, 83, 88, 111
picnic 100
Pol e Khomri 251
post 108–9

Qala e Nau 250
Qala e Panja 270, 274
Qazideh 269, 274
Qizilbash 49, 131
Qosh Tepa Canal 5, 14, **248**

Rabbani, Burhanuddin 33, 133, 145, 254
Rabi'a Balkhi 58, 243, 245, **246**
rabies 76, **79**
red tape 70
Registan 4, 17, 22, 24, 47, 50, 191, 193, 223
religion 18, 20, 21, 22, 24, 40, 51, **53–5**, 83, 160, 176, 195, 239, 262
responsible travel 111–12
restaurant price codes 100
restaurants 99–100
Restrepo (Outpost Restrepo) 162, 287
rivers 4–5
  Ajar 14, 178
  Alingra 158, 161
  Amu Darya (Oxus) 4, 5, 8, 9, 16, 17, 26, 148, 239, 241, 248, 255, 258, 267, 275
  Arghandab 5, 193, 199, 200
  Balkh 4, 239
  Bashgul 158, 161
  Farah Rud 206, 222, 226
  Hari Rud 5, **188–9**, 190, 206
  Helmand 4, 5, 188, 202, 222, 226
  Kabul 5, 114, 122, 130, 131, 135, 143, 146, 152, 154
  Kokcha 258, 259, 261
  Kunar 5, 164
  Kunduz 251
  Pamir (Wakhsch) 5, 267, 273
  Panj 269, 272, 273, **274**
  Panjshir 41
  Pech 158, 161
  Wakhjir 265, 275
Rostam 57, 225, 229, 240–1, 251
rubies 42, 51, 258, 268
Rumi 53, 58, 59, 206, 239, 245
Russia 26–9, 34, 35, 38, 39, 42, 52, 71, 104, 159, 165, 219, 257, 264, 267

Sabuktigin 22, 114, 204
Safavids 16, 25, 64, 134, 136–7, 138, 174, 200, 210, 218
safety 82–5
Saffarids 22, 208
Safiq, Moosa 32
Saka nomads 4, 20, 242, 255, 267
Salang Tunnel 3, **147**
Saleh, Amrullah 36, 37, 38
Samangan (Aibak) 251
Samanids 22, 204, 208, 239, 243, 245, 246, 249
Sang Nevishta (petroglyphs) 273
Sar e Pol Province 14, 187
Sar e Sang 254–5, 266

Sardar Abd al-Quddus Khan 174
Sarhad e Borghil 269, 270, 273, **274**
Sassanians 21, 22, 225
Satibarzanes 208
Saur Revolution 15, 32, 116
scorpions 80–2
Seleucids 19, 208, 242
Seleucus 18, 19
Seljuks 22, 23, 204, 208, 237, 238
Semiramis 240
Shadian Arch 239
Shah Ismael's Ziarat 170
Shah Rukh 25, 56, 209, 211, 219, 243
Shahnameh (Book of Kings) 239, 240–1, 251, 286
Sharia law 35, 39, 45, **85**
Sher Ali Khan 28, 237
Sher Khan Bandar 74, 253
Shi'a 45, 46, 49, **53**, 82, 101, 102, 131, 134, 174–5, 261–2
Shibergan 247–8
Shindand Air Base 210, 223
Shomali Plains 98, 114, 139, 140, 141, 147
shopping 102–4
Shortugai 16
Shot 162
Shughni **52**, 262
Shuja Shah 26, 27, 28, 154, 155
Sikhs 26, 27, 54, 154–5, 200
Silk Road 8, 15, 20, 21, 23, 24, 47, 95, 99, 131, 138, 141, 142, 151, 158, 171, 173, **176**, 179, 183, 189, 206, 239, 250, 258, 266, 267
SIM cards 108, 130
Sistan 4, **226**, 229
skiing 105, 112, 178–9, 180–1
smoking 99, 239
snakes 11
snake bites 80–1
snow leopards 8, 13, 68, 266
Sorkhodak 229
Southern Afghanistan 191–205, *192*
Soviet Union 5, 12, 14, 30, 31, 32, 33, 40, 46, 116, 129, 156, 147, 210, 223, 268
  Soviet–Afghan War 33–4, 45, 46, 47, 48, 51, 53, 61, 74, 83, 101, 114, 134, 144, 147, 149, 156, 160, 164, 166, 169, 175, 184, 193, 195, 219–20, 225, 254, 258
Spin Boldak 74, 193, 195
sports and activities 62–5, 105–6
Stewart, Rory 136, 189, 190, 285, 286
Sufis 33, 38, 53–4, 56, 58, 64, 190, 200, 208, 218, 220, 221, 222, 243, 244, 246
Sunnis 22, 24, 25, 45, 46, 47, 49, 51, 52, 53, 173, 174, 263
Surkh Kotal 21, **251**

Tajikistan 5, 7, 13, 16, 19, 38, 40, 52, 68, 74, 253, 262, 267, 269, 272

Tajiks 29, 30, 33, **45–6**, 58, 116, 140, 144, 224, 231
Taliban 13, 14, 36–7, 45, 51, 84, 191, 193, 220, 225
  1996–2001 **35–6**, 46, 53, 54, 104, 133, 140, 145, 156, 179, 195, 200, 258
  2021–present 5, 6, 14, **37–43**, 55, 59, 62–3, 64, 70–1, 76, 82, 83, 85–7, 92, 99, 101–2, 106–7, 117, 141, 149, 158–9, 169, 237, 248, 269
Takhar Province 145
Tamerlane *see* Timur
Tangi Mormul 239
Taraki, Nur Mohammad 31, 32, 118, 210
Tarinkot 194
Tashqurghan 250
Tatars 52
taxis 91
tea 99, 109
Tegerman Su 275
Tehreek-e-Taliban Pakistan (TTP) 38
telephones 107–8
television 106–7
tetanus 80
ticks 78
Tillya Tepe (Hill of Gold) 20, 138, 247
Timur (Tamerlane) 24–5, 51, 136, 159, 199, 201, 206, 208–9, 243, 249
Timur Shah Durrani 26, 130, 116, 130, 131, 193, 210
Timurids 25, 56, 68, 115, 135, 206, 208–10, 211, 217, 218, 219, 221, 225, 232, 243, 244
toilet essentials 93
Tokham Jangi (egg war) 64
Tokharistan 22, 243
Tolui Khan 208
Tora Bora 4, 36, 151, **156–7**
Torghundi 74, 212, 247
Torkham 74, 151, **157–8**
tour operators 70
tourism 13, 105, 159, 180
travel clinics 76
travelling positively 111–12
trekking 105–6, 178
  in the Wakhan and Afghan Pamir 68, *271*, **272–3**
Trive 262
tulips, wild 12, 231, 239
Turkestan 28, 52, 231, 233, 237, 243
Turkishahi 22, 114
Turkmenistan 5, 16, 41, 42, 74, 206, 212, 219, 239, 246, 249
Turkmens 25, 30, 47, **48–50**, 52, 60, 61, 100, 231, 232, 247, 248
Turkmen carpets 48–9, 60
Turquoise Mountain (city) 23, 188, 189
Turquoise Mountain (NGO) 104, 112, **131**, 140

Ulugh Beg 25, 136, 209, 211, 219
United States 31, 32, 33, 34, 35, 38, 40, 42, 54, 57, 82, 117, 133, 169, 201
  War in Afghanistan 36–7, 141, 156–7, 162, 163, 202, 210, 233, 238–9, 253
Uruzgan Province 46, 59
Uzbekistan 5, 16, 19, 24, 40, 41, 42, 73, 74, 95, 136–7, 176, 233, 234, 236, 248
Uzbeks 25, 29, 30, 33, 35, 45, **47–8**, 52, 60, 61, 100, 116, 210, 231, 232–3, 243, 244, 247, 248, 250, 252

vegetarian dishes 97
visas 70–2

Wakhan Corridor 4, 5, 7, 10, 13, 29, 52, 66, 69, 70, 73, 74, 86, 92, 94–5, 257–8, 262–3, **266–75**, *271*
Wakhis **52**, 105
Wama 162
Wardak Province 46, 175
Waygal 160, 161
Wazir Akbar Khan 28
weather 66
Western Afghanistan 206–29, *207*
what to take 88–9
when to visit 66
Wi-Fi 107
Wildlife Conservation Society (WCS) 7, 8, 12–13
wolves 7, 9, 85
women 14, 30, 31, 36, 40, 107, 130, 222–3, 262
  education 55
  economy 43, 60, 76, 104, 178, 207
  ethnic groups 45–50, 159, 175
  etiquette 83, 109–11, 185
  poets 58, 245, 246
  sport 62–3, 112, 173, 181, 186
  travelling as a woman 85–6, 86–7
  what to wear 110–11
Wuzet 274

Xuanzang 22, 173, 179, **182**, 184, 242, 243, 267

Yamgan 262, 263–4
Yawkawlang 173, 187, **188**
Yuezhi nomads 20–1, 242, 255

Zabul Province 59, 191
Zadian Minar 238
Zahir Shah 31–2, 54, 58, 116, 152, 163, 256
Zahir-ud-Din Muhammad *see* Barbur
Zaranj 75, 224, 225, **227–9**, *227*
Zarathustra (Zoroaster) 239–41
Zoroastrianism 21, 64, 208, 238, **239–42**

INDEX OF ADVERTISERS

Beyond the Borders 3rd colour section
Let's Be Friends 3rd colour section
Lupine Travel inside front cover

Penguin Travel 112
Rocky Road Travel 3rd colour section
Safarat 3rd colour section

Untamed Borders i
Wanderlust 275
Young Pioneer Tours inside back cover

THE BRADT STORY

In the beginning

It all began in 1974 on an Amazon river barge. During an 18-month trip through South America, two adventurous young backpackers – Hilary Bradt and her then husband, George – decided to write about the hiking trails they had discovered through the Andes. *Backpacking Along Ancient Ways in Peru and Bolivia* included the very first descriptions of the Inca Trail. It was the start of a colourful journey to becoming one of the best-loved travel publishers in the world; you can read the full story on our website (**bradtguides.com/ourstory**).

Getting there first

Hilary quickly gained a reputation for being a true travel pioneer, and in the 1980s she started to focus on guides to places overlooked by other publishers. The Bradt Guides list became a roll call of guidebook 'firsts'. We published the first guide to Madagascar, followed by Mauritius, Czechoslovakia and Vietnam. The 1990s saw the beginning of our extensive coverage of Africa: Tanzania, Uganda, South Africa, and Eritrea. Later, post-conflict guides became a feature: Rwanda, Mozambique, Angola, and Sierra Leone, as well as the first standalone guides to the Baltic States following the fall of the Iron Curtain, and the first post-war guides to Bosnia, Kosovo and Albania.

Comprehensive – and with a conscience

Today, we are the world's largest independently owned travel publisher, with more than 200 titles. However, our ethos remains unchanged. Hilary is still keenly involved, and **we still get there first**: two-thirds of Bradt guides have no direct competition.

But we don't just get there first. Our guides are also known for being **more comprehensive** than any other series. We avoid templates and tick-lists. Each guide is a one-of-a-kind expression of an expert author's interests, knowledge and enthusiasm for telling it how it really is.

And a commitment to wildlife, conservation and respect for local communities has always been at the heart of our books. Bradt Guides was **championing sustainable travel** before any other guidebook publisher. We even have a series dedicated to Slow Travel in the UK, award-winning books that explore the country with a passion and depth you'll find nowhere else.

Thank you!

We can only do what we do because of the support of readers like you – people who value less-obvious experiences, less-visited places and a more thoughtful approach to travel. Those who, like us, take travel seriously.